DATE DUE

DEMCO 38-296

MASTERPLOTS II

AMERICAN FICTION SERIES

MASTERPLOTS II

AMERICAN FICTION SERIES

6

Supplement

Edited by

FRANK N. MAGILL

SALEM PRESS

Pasadena, California   Englewood Cliffs, New Jersey

∞ The paper used in these volumes conforms to the
American National Standard for Permanence of Paper
for Printed Library Materials, Z39.48-1984.

Library of Congress Cataloging-in-Publication Data
Masterplots II: American fiction series. Supplement /
edited by Frank N. Magill.
   p. cm.
   Includes bibliographical references and indexes.
   1. America—Literatures—Stories, plots, etc. 2.
America—Literatures—History and criticism. 3. Fic-
tion—20th century—Stories, plots, etc. 4. Fiction—
20th century—History and criticism. I. Magill, Frank
Northen, 1907-   . II. Title: Masterplots 2. American
fiction series. Supplement. III. Title: Masterplots two.
American fiction series. Supplement.
PN846.M37   1994   94-21511
809.3'0097—dc20   CIP
ISBN 0-89356-719-1 (set)
ISBN 0-89356-721-3 (volume 2)

SECOND PRINTING

PRINTED IN THE UNITED STATES OF AMERICA

LIST OF TITLES IN VOLUME 6

LIST OF TITLES IN VOLUME 6

LINDEN HILLS

Author: Gloria Naylor (1950-   )
Type of plot: Psychological realism
Time of plot: The 1980's
Locale: The fictional community of Linden Hills
First published: 1985

> *Principal characters:*
> LUTHER NEDEED, the descendant and namesake of the founder and owner
> of Linden Hills
> WILLA NEDEED, the wife of Luther, locked in the basement of their house
> with her dead son
> LESTER TILSON, a poet and a resident of Linden Hills who refuses to
> subscribe to its middle-class values
> WILLIE K. MASON, Lester's best friend

The Novel

Linden Hills explores the lives of affluent African Americans who have attained the American Dream of material success, but at the expense of humanistic values. Luther Nedeed is the owner of the Tupelo Realty Company, which holds the mortgages and leases on all the homes in Linden Hills and is the undertaker for the African American community. He lives at the bottom of the hill. The most affluent families live at the bottom of the hill, while the less affluent live at the top.

The novel begins with an introductory chapter and is then divided into sections identified by date, from December 19 to December 24. The first chapter explains the history of the Nedeed family. Luther Nedeed, an ancestor of the current character, bought Linden Hills from its white owners during the antebellum period. It was offered for sale because the white owners considered the hills unsuitable for farming. Realizing that the bottom of the hill bordered the cemetery, Nedeed became an undertaker. He built shacks on the hills and rented them to local black families. He then went to Mississippi and brought back an octoroon wife, Luwana Packerville, who produced a son who grew up to inherit his father's name, looks, and business. To keep the government from taking his land, the second Nedeed sold the land cheaply to the people already living there, on a lease of a thousand years and a day. The lease also provided that they pass their property to their children or sell it only to other black families.

The first chapter also examines the circumstances of the present Luther Nedeed's marriage and the birth of a light-skinned son who does not look like him or his male ancestors. This child causes Luther to suspect his wife, Willa, of adultery and to lock her in the basement, along with the child.

The first dated section, for December 19, chronicles the relationship of Willie K.

Mason and Lester Tilson. It also introduces Ruth, who has rejected residency in Linden Hills. Ruth remains married to Norman despite the fact that he loses his mind once a year with an attack of "the pinks." In this chapter, Willie and Lester first hear the mournful screams of Willa Nedeed.

In the December 20 section, Willa's son dies. She begins to will herself to die until, while looking for a shroud for her son, she discovers the diary of the unhappy Luwana Packerville Nedeed in a basement trunk. Willie and Lester take their first job of the season, as kitchen helpers at the wedding of Winston Alcott. The homosexual relationship of Winston and his friend David is confirmed when David recites a poem at the wedding. Willie and Lester recognize how David has altered the poem to announce his departure from the relationship, which Winston does not have the courage to acknowledge. As a wedding present, Nedeed gives the newlyweds a coveted mortgage on a property on Tupelo Drive, at the bottom of the hill.

The section entitled "December 21st" examines the relationship of Roxanne Tilson and Xavier Donnell. Donnell is upset because he finds himself falling in love. He asks his colleague at General Motors, Maxwell Smyth, for an opinion. Lester and Willie, hired to clean the garage, observe the meeting between Donnell and Smyth. The chapter focuses on the life of the superficial Smyth and the lifestyle he has adopted to rise in his career. Smyth advises Donnell against marriage to Roxanne because of her inferior social standing. Willie and Lester then go to work for Mr. Parker, whose wife, Lycentia, has just died. They are to help prepare Lycentia's bedroom for a new woman on the eve of Lycentia's funeral. Meanwhile, Willa discovers the recipes of the unhappy Evelyn Creton Nedeed.

On December 22, Willa examines the recipes of her predecessor while Lester and Willie work for the Reverend Michael T. Hollis, who is preparing to preside at the funeral of Lycentia Parker. The Reverend Hollis seeks refuge, from both his memories and his cold church, in alcohol. During the Parker funeral, he gives an unusually emotional sermon that causes discomfort among his cold parishioners. Next, Willie and Lester prepare to go to the home of Laurel Dumont. They are rescued from a police patrol by Norman, who has been sent by his wife, Ruth, to check on Mrs. Dumont. Ruth is concerned about Mrs. Dumont's mental health.

On December 23, as Willa discovers fading photographs of Priscilla McGuire Nedeed, it is revealed that Laurel Dumont's husband has left her and Linden Hills, thereby nullifying his lease with Lester Nedeed. After being informed by Nedeed that she must leave her home, Laurel commits suicide by jumping into an empty pool as Nedeed watches secretly. Nedeed hires Willie and Lester to trim his Christmas tree. Before going to the Nedeed house, the young men meet Dr. Daniel Braithwaite, a historian who has collected the history of the Nedeed family and observed the history and lives of the inhabitants of Linden Hills. Willa decides to live and begins to clean the basement that is her prison.

On December 24, Willa Nedeed decides to walk back up the basement stairs. Willie and Lester arrive at the Nedeed house. The door to the basement is accidentally unbolted, and Willa comes up, carrying the corpse of her son. Lester and Willie are terrified and run out of the house. Luther Nedeed enters into a futile struggle with his wife, and the shroud in which she wrapped her son's body is ignited by a candle on the tree. All three Nedeeds are consumed by a raging fire.

The Characters

Luther Nedeed is the villain of the novel. His love for power provides the catalyst for the demise of humanistic values and the triumph of materialism in the lives of the people of Linden Hills. Like the devil he symbolically represents, his delight is in the destruction of lives of the inhabitants of Linden Hills. The first Luther Nedeed lives on in the person of each of the descendants who carry his name; they also carry his personality and his physical appearance. Willa's son, who inherits the recessive genes of his light-skinned grandmothers and does not look like his father, serves as the catalyst for the destruction of the Nedeed dynasty. The modern Luther's inhumanity and selfishness are revealed through his treatment of his wife and son and through his delight in the destruction of the lives of the inhabitants of the lower regions of Linden Hills. Luther is unable to select a wife in the same way that his ancestors did because of changes in the status and expectations of women in contemporary society. Therefore, he waits until his college reunion to pick from the single women uncomfortable with their independent status and desperate enough to consider marriage to him. The purpose of Luther's matrimonial search is simply to find a woman to bear him a son, who must be conceived in a ritual prescribed by his ancestors. Thereafter, he has no sexual contact with his wife.

Willa Prescott Nedeed is the wife of the last Luther Nedeed and the vehicle of his destruction. After being locked in the basement with her son for her supposed adultery, she discovers the plight of her predecessors while looking for a shroud to wrap the body of her son. Willa, however, is unlike the Nedeed wives before her; she is not a weak woman without personality. She has definite tastes and preferences that will not be denied, and she loves her and mourns his useless and unjust death. Through looking at the diaries and pictures of the Nedeed wives, she gains the courage to go up the steps in an attempt to take control of her destiny.

Lester Tilson is half of the team that directs the reader through the enclave of prosperous, well-behaved, and spiritually dead people that is Nedeed's created community. Lester, whose family lives at the top of the hill, has chosen poetry as a way of life instead of joining the race for wealth and career success that his mother and sister value. Lester saw his father die early from working two jobs in order to provide the symbols of prosperity that his wife desired; he vowed never to follow that pattern. As his friend Willie points out, however, Lester is unwilling to leave his home and its comfort.

Willie Mason is Lester's best friend. He dropped out of school and the middle-class race for success. He is the child of an alcoholic father who, unable to provide suitably for his family, abused his wife, Willie's mother. Lester has great insights into the weaknesses and deceits of the people of Linden Hills. As Lester and Willie work their way through the holiday season, they reveal the foibles of the inhabitants.

Themes and Meanings

Naylor's novel examines the negative consequences of achieving the American Dream. The African Americans of Linden Hills attempt to realize this dream at the expense of their souls and their sense of history. The author presents a series of vignettes in the lives of middle-class African Americans who have sacrificed their sense of racial indentity in order to achieve material and career success. The importance of Dante's *Inferno* from *La divina commedia* (c. 1320; *The Divine Comedy*) as a source for the narrative structure of this novel is evident. The topography of Linden Hills resembles Dante's hell, with the evil angel, Luther Nedeed, residing at the bottom, surrounded by a frozen lake.

Naylor constructs the primary narrative line around Willie and Lester's odyssey through the hills, juxtaposing their adventures with the story of Willa Nedeed. The names Willie and Willa are deliberately similar. Willie and Willa's journeys through hell are set in different typefaces to highlight the parallel themes. As Willie passes through Linden Hills, he recognizes and analyzes the moral failures of the lost souls he meets. At the end of Willie and Lester's journey, they have a spiritual awakening, realizing the significance of all they have seen and heard.

Willa also has a spiritual awakening, realized through her discovery of the tragic lives of the previous Nedeed wives. After producing a Nedeed heir, each became a nonentity within her own household. The first Mrs. Nedeed, Luwana Packerville, was bought as a slave and never manumitted, although her husband saw to the legal freedom of her child. She wrote in her Bible in 1837, "There is no God." Likewise, Priscilla McGuire Nedeed's image fades from view as her son's image grows in succeeding years, negating her physically and spiritually into a mere blur on family portraits. Willa's awakening comes when she recognizes her spiritual kinship with these women, which she first denied by labeling them as crazy. At the moment of her awakening, she makes the decision to enter and reclaim her home and her own identity. At this point, the power of the Nedeed men is overcome. Death of the dynasty by fire ensues.

The dating of the chapters is significant to the meaning of the novel. Naylor marks each section by the dates from December 19 to December 24, the time of the winter solstice. As Willie and Lester work on their odd jobs, they encounter the lost souls of Linden Hills. Of all those encountered, the most elaborate caricature is Maxwell Smyth, who has even changed his name from Smith to achieve a complete blending into mainstream society. Smyth attempts to deny any vestige of color in his quest to maintain his "Super Nigger" image. Maxwell's entire life is spent denying not only his racial and ethnic identity but also his natural humanity.

Critical Context

Linden Hills is Naylor's second novel, coming after the extremely successful *The Women of Brewster Place* (1982). *Linden Hills* examines a second panel of twentieth century African American life. *The Women of Brewster Place* reflected the faults, passions, and culture of a poor community. *Linden Hills*, on the other hand, is a representation of the affluent and spiritually dissolute upper class. *Linden Hills* is also a modern version of Dante's *Inferno*; souls are damned here because they have offended human nature and themselves rather than any religious system. Naylor's novel is thus an allegory based on the physical and moral topography of the *Inferno*, covering five days in the life of a twenty-year-old black poet, Willie Mason.

Like Dante, Willie analyzes the lives of the inhabitants of the hills as he works his way from the top to the bottom as a handyman. When he finally escapes from the frozen lake at the bottom of Linden Hills, Willie decides to give up his aimlessness and take charge of his life. Dante's model universalizes the novel and also gives a mythic dimension to what otherwise would have been a narrow subject. Naylor's bow to Dante's work puts her within a long literary tradition. *Linden Hills* is also a part of an explosion of noted works by African American women, including Naylor and her prominent contemporaries Alice Walker, Toni Morrison, and Paule Marshall.

Bibliography

Andrews, Larry R. "Black Sisterhood in Gloria Naylor's Novels." *College Language Association Journal* 33 (September, 1989): 1-25. Andrews examines the female characters in Naylor's novels and shows how African American women form support systems to ensure survival in challenging conditions.

Collins, Grace E. "Narrative Structure in *Linden Hills*." *College Language Association Journal* 34 (March, 1991): 290-301. Collins emphasizes the juxtaposition of the narrative of Willie's physical journey through Linden Hills with Willa's mental journey to self-realization.

Jones, Robert. "A Place in the Suburbs." *Commonweal* 112 (May 3, 1985): 283-285. Places the novel in the context of traditions in American literature, comparing it to classic and contemporary works.

Russell, Sandi. *Render Me My Song: African American Women Writers from Slavery to the Present*. New York: St. Martin's Press, 1990. Russell's work places Naylor's novels in the context of the overall themes presented by African American women writers.

Ward, Catherine C. "Gloria Naylor's *Linden Hills*: A Modern Inferno." *Contemporary Literature* 28 (Spring, 1987): 67-81. Ward, in great detail, compares the plot, setting, and characters of the *Inferno* to *Linden Hills*.

Betty Taylor-Thompson

THE LIVING

Author: Annie Dillard (1945-   )
Type of plot: Historical realism
Time of plot: 1855-1897
Locale: Various sites around Bellingham Bay, Washington
First published: 1992

> *Principal characters:*
> ADA and ROONEY FISHBURN, a couple who set out from Council Bluffs, Missouri, with a wagon train to settle in Whatcom, Washington
> CLARE FISHBURN, their son, who grows up to be a possibly powerful political figure in Whatcom and who is the target of Beal Obenchain's plot
> MINTA and EUSTACE HONER, a couple from prominent Baltimore families who come to Washington to become farmers
> JOHN IRELAND SHARP, the grandson of an early settler, a devotee of philosophy and liberal causes
> BEAL OBENCHAIN, a cruel social outcast, murderer, and wild man

The Novel

Based in part on Annie Dillard's experience of the northern Washington landscape as she lived there from 1975 to 1980, *The Living* recounts the early days of several settlements on Bellingham Bay from 1855 to 1897. The historical epic traces the fortunes and vicissitudes of three fictional families—the Fishburns, the Honers, and the Sharps—through several generations as they negotiate with the landscape, with the native peoples, with Chinese immigrants, with new waves of settlers, and with ever-changing economic fortunes.

The Living is divided into six long sections, each focusing on a major character, family, or event; the book also includes a brief afterword. The stories are told in third-person omniscient narration, with many flashbacks into the thoughts and events of characters' pasts. The epic weaves a tapestry of pattern and variation in the struggles of these early settling families.

The book begins dramatically, with the arrival by boat of Ada and Rooney Fishburn and their two remaining children, Clare and Glee, in Whatcom. The landscape is desolate, wet, and primitive. The heavy evergreen growth seems oppressive; the native inhabitants, primarily of the Lummi tribe, seem strange and exotic. All customary values seem irrelevant in this new land, and Ada obsessively remembers the losses, especially of her small son, Charley, that she had to endure to settle here.

Eventually, the children thrive, and the Fishburns begin to learn the joys of Northwest life. They both respond to the landscape—most notably to towering, snowcapped Mt. Baker—and set out to conquer the land, clearing away with fervor the dense evergreen growth. The native inhabitants become inextricably linked to the daily lives of the Fishburns, participating in sharing their lore and mechanisms for survival with the new settlers. Clare, who is of the first generation of white settlers to be reared here, feels marked for a heroic life. This section ends with Rooney's death by poison gas as he is digging a new well.

Book 2 recounts the formation of the personality of John Ireland Sharp, primarily through his early experiences. As a young man, he participates in a scouting expedition into the Cascade Mountains to seek a route for the Northern Pacific Railroad. During this expedition, the party discovers the evidence of racial hatred and torture: The staked body of a Skagit tribe boy who had been cruelly used by the Thompson tribe. John gets beaten up by Beal Obenchain in a random act of tyranny; ironically, he later is adopted into the Obenchain family when his own family drowns. He witnesses Beal's senseless killing of a newly born calf and the exhilaration it brings the bully. John, who has learned to love socialist causes while working in New York City, in Whatcom witnesses xenophobia in action. He comes to seek the pristine inspiration of the sight of Mt. Baker and prefer it to the cruelty he experiences among humans. The town's economic situation becomes precarious when the train terminus is set for Tacoma rather than Whatcom; there is an immediate financial slump.

In Book 3, Whatcom shrivels in the economic depression. The widow Ada Fishburn moves with her son Clare to Goshen, a neighboring settlement, and there they meet Minta and Eustace Honer. Goshen is a thriving farming community where Clare, now a tall and joyful man, lends a hand with Kulshan Jim, of the Nooksack tribe, to help Eustace with clearing more of the land for farming. Ada remarries, and all goes well until there is an enormous logjam on the Nooksack River. All citizens, native and new settlers alike, set about to clear the jam, but Eustace is drowned in the effort. The vulnerability of life in this hard environment begins to affect young Hugh Honer, especially when his two young siblings die in a house fire after the rest of the family has left briefly to meet the Randalls, Minta's visiting relatives. After the tragedy, Minta's sister June remains in Goshen to be courted by Clare Fishburn, but the other Randalls return to familiar ways in Baltimore.

By the beginning of Book 5, readers feel at home with the Northwest ways and the variety of people the land creates. In another vivid episode, Beal Obenchain performs the senseless and sadistic murder of Lee Chin simply because the victim is Chinese. Whatcom thrives because the Great Northern Railway proposes to have its western terminus there. Clare Fishburn returns and becomes a prosperous land speculator, and everyone believes in progress. Ironically, at the ceremony to honor the Canadians and their railroad, the citizens get involved in a petty water fight and lose the contract.

Beal Obenchain, at loose ends, decides (in the central plot event of the novel) that mere murder of the inferior does nothing to prove his own superiority. He lights upon a plan to humiliate someone: Beal will draw a name from a hat, and he will simply threaten to kill the person, with no intention of actually doing so. Thus, he will gain supreme power over that person's spirit and future, which he will control. The name he draws is that of Clare Fishburn. Clare has a wife, June Randall, whom he adores; he has children; he has a thriving career as a teacher and land speculator and a possible political future. Beal's threat at first pushes him into a kind of poignant despair and fear, yet Clare ultimately resists June's urging that they escape to Portland, Oregon, and begins to undergo a deep interior philosophical investigation about the meaning of life.

Books 5 and 6 show the settlers maturing and vast changes occurring in the political and economic spheres as the land gets civilized. Patterns begin to fulfill themselves: Minta replaces her lost children by adopting some needy Nooksack waifs. She becomes a liberated woman and a highly successful hops farmer, and she votes proudly in 1884, when Washington grants women suffrage. Ada (now Tawes) feels the days getting long and wonders how she can sustain her life after so much living. The novel's events have moved from the primitive burning of trees to clear the land to sophisticated civic festivals such as the launching of a racing sloop built by a new Swedish immigrant. At this festival, Beal Obenchain realizes that his threat has not fazed Clare Fishburn, and he decides to rescind his threat, just to drive Clare mad. At the same time, Johnny Lee sees Obenchain with a handkerchief that is twin to his own; the twin had belonged to Lee's murdered brother.

Meanwhile, in St. Paul, Minnesota, lumber entrepreneur Frederick Weyerhaeuser and railroad magnate James Hill make a mutually beneficial deal to ship immigrants west on trains and to ship lumber in the empty cars coming back. In Whatcom, the land rush is over; once again, the train terminus is set for another locale. Everyone is broke except for the Sharps, who have inherited the Obenchain estate; a stock-market crash is caused by a run on the banks during the debate over the gold standard. The news of the crash comes to Whatcom on the day of the town festival and beach picnic, when everyone feels unified, nostalgic, and full of life.

The final section reveals the ironies that history ushers in with its cycles. Ada Fishburn Tawes dies with the words of her original crossing of the plains on her lips. Clare Fishburn is humiliated that he has lost the fortune of his wife, who had excellent prospects as a senator's daughter yet chose him. Women begin to replant trees in the town that men had spent so many years trying to clear of timber. Minta's son Hugh plans to return to Baltimore to study medicine, a decision that makes the Honers' time in the West seem a detour rather than a commitment. John Ireland Sharp, despite his learning, his social prestige, and his inheritance, feels more and more alienated from his family. As his wife, Pearl, is planning to take over the abandoned grand house that was being built during prosperous times, John wants to retreat to an island in Puget Sound and live simply.

By accident, Johnny Lee's son Walter finds, in the hollowed-out tree that is Beal Obenchain's home, the porcelain dragon that the murdered Lee Chin wore around his neck. Beal has found no comfort in reading the works of Friedrich Wilhelm Nietzsche, and he is filled with despair at the turn his life has taken. Simultaneously, John Sharp seeks Beal to give him his share of the inheritance. Beal is found dead near the spot where Lee Chin's body was found. Whether his death was suicide or revenge remains unclear.

The afterword recounts the continued coping of the remaining characters. In the final scene, Hugh Honer throws himself off a platform in the dark into a pool, venturing into the unknown as his ancestors had.

The Characters

Annie Dillard develops the first half of the book by focusing on the individual sagas of single characters, family groups, or thematically linked pairs of characters. Each subsequent section also moves forward in time in terms of the waves of settlers who come to Bellingham Bay. Each of these introductory sections gives a history of how individuals related to the land upon their arrival, and how their characters and relationships developed as they encountered new hardships in the strange landscape.

Ada Fishburn, who is depicted in the first section, survives until the end of the novel, although the focus will shift to her sons and their generation. She is marked primarily by memories of loss—of her children and husband—and by her progress in accepting the native inhabitants and their ways as familiar. Dillard often presents Ada's character in third-person omniscient narration; sometimes, she shows Ada's emotional response to a scene. Ada is an intrepid pioneer and admirable survivor.

John Ireland Sharp, who is depicted in the second section, has ties to both the East and the West, and he is simultaneously an orphan and a man with historical roots in Whatcom. An educator who is greatly moved by the plight of the Chinese in America, John in his early years devotes himself to liberal social causes. His character is defined primarily by the events that shape him and his response to duties placed on him. Ironically, he becomes hermetic by the end of the novel.

Minta Honer, who loses her husband Eustace after they settle in Goshen, is portrayed as a strong and dedicated frontierswoman with a heart large enough to embrace the destitute and the alienated. She is revealed through the eyes of the omniscient third-person narrator in her response to challenge and tragedy in her life. The daughter of Senator Green Randall of Baltimore, Minta remakes herself entirely in the Western mode and is the model of a woman working toward becoming modern and liberated.

Beal Obenchain is the idiosyncratic villain of the novel. He is presented rather dispassionately and objectively, but his inability to live in society is everywhere clear. Obenchain's inhumanity is even more insidious because of his intelligence and education. He in fact builds his power game against Clare Fishburn on Nietzschean philosophy.

Clare Fishburn, along with John Ireland Sharp, is the most sympathetically presented character in the novel. He is a man of feeling, aspiration, depth, and responsibility who, because of Obenchain's plot against him, changes markedly as he learns what is valuable in life. He faces death and stares it down, releasing himself from fear and intellectual tyranny back into life.

Themes and Meanings

The Living is less a repository of meaning than it is a reclaiming of the experience of the early Western settlers. Dillard investigates the relation of individuals to their past and their heritage as well as to the strange, novel, synthetic society that begins to form them anew. She recounts the incidents in such a way that the reader begins to perceive the recurring patterns of nineteenth century life in Bellingham Bay: racial hatred and tyranny, personal loss, both human and economic, and the ways in which characters respond to and internalize the landscape.

Dillard immerses readers sensually into the Western milieu. Readers smell the omnipresent smoke of smoldering tree trunks, feel the mist and fog that shroud the mountains during most of the year, mire down in the mud of the town and the woods, and feel the horror of the exotic in the discovery of a badly mummified native corpse or the unknown perils of going about daily business (as when a tree falls and kills a child).

Similarly, the portrait of each character shows the internal mental workings, the particular slant that this individual gives to interpreting the new Western life. Telling philosophical patterns recur. Several characters display a strange combination of social conscience and desire for seclusion, symbolized respectively by Mt. Baker (as hope, aspiration) and by the canopy of evergreens that entraps and isolates. All the characters feel that the West offers them both an opportunity and a test of their personal mettle. The novel is simultaneously about the changes that individuals can and do make in the long run and also about how impervious nature and history are to these minuscule personal efforts. Patience, suffering, and hope are embodied in recurring biblical and poetic quotations that emerge at crucial points and give the novel its title: "I believe that I shall see the goodness of the Lord in the land of the living." Human effort is always new and admirable; it is also never original and doomed to be stunted by perverse human nature and the impersonal forces of history, time, and landscape.

Critical Context

Annie Dillard has been well received and highly acclaimed. Her work includes *Holy the Firm* (1977) and *Pilgrim at Tinker Creek* (1974), which are responses to nature in the transcendentalist tradition; *An American Childhood* (1987), her early autobiography; *Tickets for a Prayer Wheel* (1974), a collection of poems; and *Living by Fiction* (1982), which discusses in essay mode concerns of the modern writer. *The Living* is her first novel. Reviews of the novel have been full of praise for the scope and humanity of *The Living*, for its ability to invoke in seamless prose the atmosphere of its inhabitants, and for its skillful weaving together of the seemingly disparate plot lines.

Although *The Living* has no real models, it resembles in intent other fictionalized historical epic narratives, such as Barbara Tuchman's *A Distant Mirror* (1978), and it perhaps imitates the naturalistic fiction of the turn of the twentieth century. Dillard's novel, however, is remarkable for being an American epic and for focusing on a specific area not often centrally included in the story of the building and settling of America. The novel is also animated by her personal experience of life in the area and is reinforced by extensive historical research.

In *The Living*, Annie Dillard proves her diversity as a writer who has mastered the grand epic sweep of imagination. She is fast becoming a stalwart of American letters, having won grants from the Guggenheim Foundation and the National Endowment for the Arts as well as the Pulitzer Prize, the Washington Governor's Award, the New York Press Club Award, and the Ambassador Book Award in Arts and Letters from the English-Speaking Union.

Bibliography
Albin, C. D. "What the Living Know in Bellingham Bay." *The Christian Century* 109 (October 7, 1992): 871-873. Focusing on the omnipresence of death and hardship in the novel, Albin sees the characters' responses to the land as an education in how to accept the random irony of suffering. Albin praises Dillard's techniques for revealing the inner lives of the characters. This is an admiring review, which ultimately decides that readers are strengthened by participating in the epic struggle.
Ames, Katrine. Review of *The Living*, by Annie Dillard. *Newsweek* 119 (June 8, 1992): 57. An enthusiastic review. Ames focuses on the authentic effect of the nineteenth century writing style that Dillard emulates. She compares Dillard to E. L. Doctorow in terms of the romantic sweep of the novel.
The New Yorker. Review of *The Living*, by Annie Dillard. 68 (July 6, 1992): 80. Notes how Dillard's attitude toward the natural world differs from its treatment in her earlier works: Here, nature is antagonistic to humans rather than in harmony with them. The reviewer deplores the many deaths in the novel as well as what is perceived as weak plot and character development.
Scheese, Don. Review of *The Living*, by Annie Dillard. *The Georgia Review* 47 (Spring, 1993): 193-197. Scheese tries to contextualize the novel in light of Dillard's own body of work and in light of the turn-of-the century fiction by Theodore Dreiser and Frank Norris. His primary observations concern Dillard's use of the ideas of Social Darwinism and Manifest Destiny. He believes that the land is a major character in the novel and that Dillard has written her own self into the piece. Finally, Scheese praises the deep religious response that the novel evokes.
Stewart, Albert B. Review of *The Living*, by Annie Dillard. *The Antioch Review* 50 (Fall, 1992): 772. Stewart praises Dillard for the power of her details in the novel. He finds enough matter in *The Living* for twelve novels and admires the way Dillard has synthesized the many stories into a patterned whole. The details bring the novel a sense of reality and genuineness, a historical accuracy. With wit and subtlety, Dillard reveals many of her characters to have spiritual energy to overcome the inertia of overwhelming loss and death.

Sandra K. Fischer

THE LONE RANGER AND TONTO FISTFIGHT IN HEAVEN

Author: Sherman Alexie (1966-   )
Type of work: Short stories
Locale: The Spokane Indian Reservation in Washington State
First published: 1993

> *Principal characters:*
> VICTOR, the main character, sometimes the narrator, in most of the stories
> VICTOR'S FATHER, a heavy drinker
> JAMES MANY HORSES, a mystic and seer, nearly a Christ figure
> THOMAS BUILDS-THE-FIRE, a storyteller, symbol of Native American tradition
> JUNIOR, another "typical" Indian youth, a diabetic

The Stories

Set on the Spokane Indian Reservation in eastern Washington State, *The Lone Ranger and Tonto Fistfight in Heaven* is a collection of loosely related stories featuring a recurring cast of characters. In these twenty-two stories, the young male protagonists, usually in their late teens or their twenties, struggle with poverty, alcoholism, and the despair of everyday life on and off the reservation. They also try to come to grips with what it means to be Indian (as the characters exclusively refer to themselves) in the late twentieth century.

Though these stories have no chronological order, vary wildly in style, and use different narrators, the author manages, with thin plots, sketchy characterization, and "artless" language, to build stories of great cumulative power and understanding. The reader is well advised to read the book through to experience the full effect.

The first story in the collection, "Every Little Hurricane," describes a New Year's Eve party as seen through the eyes of nine-year-old Victor. Images of bad weather metaphorically represent the emotional storms of the party, where Victor's drunken uncles, Adolph and Arnold, fight viciously for no apparent reason. "He could see his uncles slugging each other with such force that they had to be in love. Strangers would never want to hurt each other that badly." A flashback then recounts a Christmas of four years before, when there was no money for gifts and Victor had seen his father cry in despair. The narration then moves back to the party, with the emotional storm prompting other memories of pain, poverty, and humiliation among the partygoers. In the final scene, Victor crawls between the unconscious forms of his parents, passed out in their bed. He feels the power of love and the family there, and the power of survival.

Another story that explores Victor's family relationships is "Because My Father Always Said He Was the Only Indian Who Saw Jimi Hendrix Play 'The Star Spangled Banner' at Woodstock." A series of family memories in this plotless sketch describe Victor's relationship with his father, his father and mother's unusual love story, and

Victor's father's relationship with alcohol. All of this is set against the ever-present background of the Native American's relationship with modern America.

In "This Is What It Means to Say Phoenix, Arizona," Victor and his lifelong but estranged friend Thomas Builds-the-Fire travel to Phoenix to collect the personal effects of Victor's father, who has died of a heart attack. In the course of the journey, some episodes in the earlier life of Victor and Thomas are recounted, and their friendship is reborn. Thomas, a visionary storyteller and link to traditional Indian ways, suggests that they throw Victor's father's ashes in the Spokane River so that he can "rise like a salmon . . . and find his way home." In the story, therefore, three things are, like the phoenix, reborn from the ashes: the relationship of Victor and Thomas, some small part of Indian tradition, and Victor's father's Indian spirit.

Many of the themes and symbols of the book are brought together and underscored in the final story of the collection, "Witnesses, Secret and Not." Thirteen-year-old Victor accompanies his father on a trip to the Spokane Police Department to answer questions about a man who had disappeared ten years earlier. In the car, they discuss those who have died and those who have disappeared into the cities, but a dangerous near-accident on the ice goes unremarked. They see a drunken Indian man that they know, give him a couple of dollars, and leave him "to make his own decisions." They are treated cordially but with little respect by the police, who have called the father in to the police station for little reason, requiring a long journey on dangerous, icy roads. Returning home, they join their strong and apparently happy family, the redeeming quality of their lives. The story is simple, even superficial, but in the course of it, the issues of white-Indian relationships, alcoholism and personal responsibility, death and disappearances, and the warm bond of the family are subtly yet effectively explored.

Other stories deal with the narrator's relationship with a white woman ("The Lone Ranger and Tonto Fistfight in Heaven"), the trials of schooling ("Indian Education"), illness and death ("The Approximate Size of My Favorite Tumor"), and alcoholism ("Amusements"). Still others adopt a more mystical tone and experimental style to examine the art of storytelling ("A Good Story," "The Trial of Thomas Builds-the-Fire"), alternate history ("Distances"), and dreams of the future ("Imagining the Reservation").

The Characters

Victor is either the narrator or the main character of most of the stories in the book. He becomes the reader's eyes and ears in the world of the Spokane Reservation, from the first glimpse of the disturbing New Year's party when Victor is nine, to the quiet summing up of the themes of the book in the final story. He is perhaps the "typical" Native American youth, recounting his view of his society and his struggles with identity, alcohol, and family relationships.

Thomas Builds-the-Fire is a near mythical character, a storyteller and thus a symbolic link to the past. The stories he tells are usually historical, casting one of his present-day friends into a historical situation—as in "A Drug Called Tradition," in which he starts a round of storytelling by imagining his friend Victor raiding the camp of a rival tribe to steal a horse named Flight. In other stories, Thomas is ridiculed for telling too many stories, stories that the others do not want to hear anymore. Thomas' strongest appearance is in the surrealistic piece "The Trial of Thomas Builds-the-Fire." In it, he "testifies" by telling stories, casting himself first as a horse among a herd captured by the cavalry in 1858, then as a warrior in a similar battle. Though he is originally charged with "telling the truth," by the end of the trial, his crime is the murder of two soldiers in the story he told of events of a century before. Thomas represents the pull of tradition among Native American people. He becomes the scapegoat for the "crimes" of the past and is the nagging conscience of modern Native Americans, reminding them of the past and the traditions that they often do not want to remember.

James Many Horses is the mystic of the stories, the fountain of wisdom and guidance. His near divinity is revealed in the title of his first story: "Jesus Christ's Half-Brother Is Alive and Living on the Spokane Indian Reservation." He was born near Christmas, and his mother claimed to be a virgin, "even though Frank Many Horses said it was his." The infant James survives a fire that kills his parents and is adopted by the anonymous narrator of the story. James fails to develop normally and cannot walk, talk, or even crawl, but he is a supportive companion to the narrator through years of physical trials and alcoholism. James finally begins speaking at age eight, but his comments could possibly be only in the imagination of the narrator. The boy is wise and prophetic; his visions and counsel support the narrator for much of his life. In a poetic, visionary story, "Imagining the Reservation," an "Indian child," apparently James, figures strongly, counseling the anonymous narrator to "break every mirror in my house and tape the pieces to my body," a marvelous metaphor for the act of becoming a writer who reflects his environment. In "The Approximate Shape of My Favorite Tumor," an adult James Many Horses faces death from cancer with humor and love. James indeed becomes a Christ figure in life and death.

Themes and Meanings

The Lone Ranger and Tonto Fistfight in Heaven deals primarily with the Native American quest for identity. The characters in the stories constantly run up against what it means to be an American and an Indian, with the twentieth century cultural icons of soft drinks, television, and convenience stores played off against the Native American values of family, community, and tradition.

In the story "The Lone Ranger and Tonto Fistfight in Heaven," Victor lives with a white woman in Seattle, and the story chronicles the inevitable failure of the relationship as well as the suspicion he faces and the dislocation he feels in the city. In "Crazy Horse Dreams," the question becomes one of trying to live up to the model of an ideal Indian. Victor's relationship with an unnamed Indian woman fails because she wants the ideal. She is "waiting for Crazy Horse," while Victor finds that he must tread the steeper path of being "just another Indian."

The broader issue of the Native American quest for a cultural identity is also a major theme of these stories. The Indian society portrayed here is caught between two worlds. On one hand, Indians desire the modern America of fancy cars and cable television, even though they realize that this is a world in which they will never feel at home. At the same time, they feel a mixed nostalgia and embarrassment toward the pull of their Native American heritage and the ingrained values and traditions of thousands of years. This double ambivalence stops the characters in their tracks at every turn.

Alexie pulls these complex emotions together in simple symbolic sentences. For example, in "This Is What It Means to Say Phoenix, Arizona," Thomas, the storyteller who annoys the people with his incessant historical or mystical tales and is thus the symbol of traditional culture, gets in a fight with Victor when both are fifteen years old. Alexie writes, "That is, Victor was really drunk and beat Thomas up for no reason at all." Under the influence of the white cultural symbol of alcohol, Victor, the young Indian everyman, attacks the symbol of thousands of years of Native American tradition.

Indeed, alcohol nearly becomes another character throughout the stories. Characters in one story measure their lives by whether events happened before or after they had their first taste of alcohol. Alcoholism is accepted fatalistically: It is simply part of life, an irresistible temptation. In a subtle but powerful scene in "All I Wanted to Do Was Dance," Victor has recently been paid and is standing in front of the beer cooler in a store. A bystander comments that it seems that Victor has been standing there his whole life; another says that he thinks it has been five hundred years. The Native American culture has been corrupted with money and alcohol since the arrival of the first Europeans, almost exactly five hundred years before the writing of the story.

In spite of all of this, Alexie opens the door for rays of hope. At the end of several stories, characters are left wanting, or intending, to change the world. Other stories close with the family together in love, even if drunk or in tears, waiting for the future.

Critical Context

The Lone Ranger and Tonto Fistfight in Heaven is Sherman Alexie's first full-length work of fiction. His previous books, all published between 1991 and 1993, consist of two volumes of poetry and two books of poems mixed with short prose pieces. His conversational style and major themes are common to all of his work, and even some of the characters in *The Lone Ranger and Tonto Fistfight in Heaven* are introduced in earlier books.

Alexie's concern with the issues of contemporary Native Americans—their search for identity in modern America and their often ambivalent feelings about their disappearing traditional culture—places him in the mainstream of Native American fiction at the close of the twentieth century. Though this genre has emerged as a significant literary force only since the 1960's, Indian writers are working with and against a heritage of thousands of years of oral literature. The structure of this traditional literature was quite different from the European tradition into which most modern writers try to fit. The oral Indian tale was generally authorless, passed down through generations from storyteller to storyteller, altered and personalized, but never claimed. The storytellers "cared for" the stories, but never owned them. The stories therefore tended to be mythical and timeless, descriptive of the culture as a whole, as opposed to character studies of individual people. Alexie refers often to this tradition of storytelling, and his work, too, seems to consist of timeless stories of rather generic characters who confront problems, feel pain, and experience joys common to many people, yet in many ways unique to the situation of Native American culture.

Out of this tradition, then, Sherman Alexie has risen to present his view of life on the modern reservation. His stories show the young Native American man, in conflict with himself and the world in which he finds himself, getting by on love and trust and treading the narrow line between the past and the future.

Bibliography

Bogey, Dan. "The Lone Ranger and Tonto Fistfight in Heaven." *Library Journal* 118 (September 1, 1993): 218. This review takes note of Alexie's use of irony and humor to capture the absurdity of life on a reservation.

Owens, Louis. *Other Destinies: Understanding the American Indian Novel.* Norman: University of Oklahoma Press, 1992. The introduction to this study of Native American novels sheds light on Alexie's stories, though his work is not mentioned in the book. Owens describes the cultural roots of Native American literature and the historical context from which it emerges. The unique problems (including writing in what is essentially a second language) and the common themes of Native American fiction (notably the search for identity and belonging) are outlined.

Price, Reynolds. "One Indian Doesn't Tell Another." *The New York Times Book Review*, October 17, 1993, 15-16. Price, a short-story writer himself, finds moments of monotony and obsessive gloom in some of Alexie's stories. He also expresses disappointment at the spare plots and lack of detail, which others might consider Alexie's mythic voice. Finally, though, he praises the "lyric energy" and "exhilarating vitality" of these stories and looks forward to a more mature, broader vision from the writer.

Schneider, Brian. "The Lone Ranger and Tonto Fistfight in Heaven." *Review of Contemporary Fiction* 13 (Fall, 1993): 237-238. This review focuses on Alexie's use of myths and mythmaking to describe and support the Native American culture. Schneider especially praises Alexie's ability to juxtapose humor and pathos with brutally honest prose.

Throm, Lindsay. "The Lone Ranger and Tonto Fistfight in Heaven." *Booklist* 90 (September 1, 1993): 31. Throm notices that Alexie does not glorify Native American life on the reservation but questions and challenges cultural assumptions of Indians and whites alike.

Joseph W. Hinton

LONESOME DOVE

Author: Larry McMurtry (1936-   )
Type of plot: Western
Time of plot: The late nineteenth century
Locale: The Great Plains of the United States, from South Texas to Montana
First published: 1985

> *Principal characters:*
> AUGUSTUS MCCRAE, a former Texas Ranger, the co-owner of the Hat Creek Cattle Company in Lonesome Dove, Texas
> WOODROW F. CALL, also a former Texas Ranger and co-owner of the Hat Creek Cattle Company
> JAKE SPOON, a former Texas Ranger and old friend of Augustus and Woodrow
> LORENA WOOD, the town prostitute of Lonesome Dove
> CLARA ALLEN, a housewife, the former lover of Augustus
> JOSH DEETS, a black trailhand and longtime friend and companion of Augustus, Woodrow, and Jake
> NEWT, a teenage trailhand, Woodrow's unacknowledged son
> BLUE DUCK, an evil Indian raider

The Novel

Lonesome Dove is the story of a cattle drive from far South Texas through the central Great Plains and hostile Indian country to virgin grazing land in Montana. Along the way, the characters either grow and change or deepen to reveal further elements of themselves.

Part 1 introduces the characters and begins the cattle drive. Augustus McCrae and Woodrow Call are two middle-aged former Texas Rangers who for several years have been operating a cattle ranch headquartered in the town of Lonesome Dove on the Rio Grande River. Lorena Wood, the beautiful town prostitute, works at the Dry Bean saloon; most of the men are in love with her. Lorena herself is fond of Jake Spoon, also a former Texas Ranger and friend of Augustus and Woodrow, who has drifted into a life of grifting and low companions. Jake, who is on the run from Arkansas, where he killed a man accidentally, turns up in Lonesome Dove and renews his relationship with Lorena. Jake proposes to Woodrow that they enlarge the cattle herd and take it to Montana, where there is choice unused grazing land. In fact, Jake wants to stay on the run and be near his former ranger friends so that they will protect him if the law catches up with him. Lorena makes Jake promise that he will take her to San Francisco, and she plans to accompany the herd for part of the way. Woodrow and Augustus also have hidden reasons for going on the drive; Woodrow wants to see and conquer new territory for one more time in his life, and Augustus hopes that he will meet his great love, Clara Allen, along the way.

Woodrow and Augustus increase the number of their herd by raiding a Mexican ranch across the river and rustling the stock of a Mexican bandit who has stolen from them in the past. Among the hands who go on the trail drive are Josh Deets, a black cowboy who rode with Woodrow and Gus in their rangering days; Dish Boggett, who is in love with Lorena; the Irish immigrant O'Brien brothers; Newt, Woodrow's son by a prostitute; and the cowhands Jasper Fants and Pea Eye. The men begin the drive with the ominous knowledge that they have a long way to go and will be beset by dangers both unknown and known (most obviously hostile Indians, including the psychopathic loner Blue Duck).

Part 2 introduces a major subplot. July Johnson, the young sheriff of Fort Smith, Arkansas, knows that the killing Jake committed was accidental; Jake fired his gun in self-defense but missed and hit the victim, July's brother Ben. Ben was the mayor of the town, however, and his wife Peaches forces July to track Jake down. To do so, July must leave his recent bride, Elmira, who has already grown tired of July and is happy to see him leave. July is joined on his trek through Texas following Jake's trail by his middle-aged deputy Roscoe Brown, Joe Boot, who is July's stepson, and a young orphan girl, Janey. While July heads southwest into Texas, Elmira, who is pregnant, leaves Fort Smith and goes northwest in search of her former lover, Dee Boot, who is Joe's father.

As soon as the cattle drive begins, tragedies and disasters overtake the cowboys. While the cattle ford a river, one of the O'Brien brothers rides into a nest of water moccasins and is bitten to death. Hailstorms, rain, and drought alternately plague the herd and its owners. Blue Duck, the Indian Woodrow and Augustus had dreaded they would meet, kidnaps Lorena and takes her away to a gang rape by Indians and comancheros. Augustus rescues Lorena from her captors, and in response, she falls in love with him. July Johnson and his friends also run afoul of Blue Duck, who kills all of them except July.

Jake, ashamed that he has allowed Lorena to be taken, runs away from his friends and begins to ride with a group of outlaws who are not only thieves but murderers. When Woodrow and Augustus catch up with Jake, they have no choice but to hang him with the rest of the criminals, a shocking event that ends part 2.

Part 3 features the end of a number of relationships and the flowering of new ones. Elmira, July, Augustus, and Lorena all wind up in succession at the farm of Clara Allen, which is conveniently located where many trails cross. Elmira has her baby there and then goes to the nearby town where Dee is awaiting hanging. After his death, she heads back across the plains, but she is killed by Indians. July arrives, and Clara, whose husband lies dying after having been kicked in the head by a horse, tries to convince July that Elmira's baby is his and that he should stay on the ranch and help her run it. Augustus and Lorena come to Clara's house, and Clara refuses Augustus' romantic overtures. Augustus leaves Lorena at Clara's for her recuperation.

When Augustus rejoins the herd, the novel moves to its climax. Deets is suddenly and mistakenly killed by an angry Indian. While Augustus and Pea Eye are out exploring, they are attacked by a band of hostile Indians. Augustus is seriously wounded by an arrow in his leg, and he sends Pea Eye back to the herd for help. Augustus makes it to a town, where his leg is amputated, but gangrene has set in, and he begins to die. Woodrow, whom Pea Eye reaches, is there for the death of his friend, and he promises Augustus that he will return Augustus' body to a spot by a river in Texas where Augustus had a memorable picnic with Clara.

When the herd reaches Montana, Woodrow selects a site for a ranch, and both cattle and men prosper, with Newt gaining more and more responsibility and growing into a man in the process. When spring comes, Woodrow begins to fulfill his pledge to Augustus; before leaving, he gives his beloved horse, the Hell Bitch, to Newt. He also stops at Clara's, where she castigates him for not living up to his responsibilities to Newt. Woodrow also witnesses the demise of Blue Duck, and when he returns to Lonesome Dove after burying Augustus, he finds that the owner of the Dry Bean has burned it down, disconsolate over the loss of Lorena.

The Characters

Augustus McCrae is the dominant and most memorable character in *Lonesome Dove*. An engaging combination of rustic philosopher and confidence man, Augustus displays both humor and an adaptability to any circumstances, including physical danger, that make him likable and trustworthy. Augustus talks more than anyone else in the novel, a point about which his taciturn partner, Woodrow, reminds him frequently, but Augustus is not all blarney; when he rescues Lorena from a gang of desperadoes, he kills several men in a matter of seconds. When Augustus dies, it is as if a pillar supporting the structure of the novel has been removed.

Woodrow Call is similar to Augustus only in his ability to handle any physical trouble. Trouble of the other kind, devils of the mind and relations with other people, paralyze Woodrow. At the end of the novel, it is clear why Woodrow has been so quiet and withdrawn throughout; this behavior is a retreat from involvement and a defense against those who need him. He is friends with his apparent opposite, the affable Augustus, because both share a sense of honor and integrity, as well as many years and miles.

Jake Spoon shows what might happen to a person with the rough frontier skills of Woodrow and the slyness of Augustus but without the sense of principle that defines his former ranger pals. Jake uses Lorena, since he has no plans to take her to San Francisco; furthermore, he abandons her in her hour of greatest need. When Jake falls in with a gang who murder for fun, he knows that he will be blamed for riding with them, but he is too cowardly either to confront them or to break away. This weak behavior leads to his death at the hands of his best friends.

Clara Allen is the pioneer woman par excellence; when her husband falls into a coma, she takes over and runs their ranch more efficiently than he did. She is the only person capable of standing up to both Augustus and Woodrow. She refuses to renew her relationship with Augustus for a classic reason: She admires Augustus for his independence, and a lengthy romance would hurt either her (because Augustus would roam) or him (because his basic personality trait would be smothered). She also chastises Woodrow for his failure to live up to his responsibilities to Newt, and she is successful in making July stay with his son.

Lorena is, like Woodrow, a frozen character. While in Lonesome Dove, she is indifferent to the men who pay her for sex (except for Augustus, whom she finds amusing), behavior that may be an emotional defense. Her desire to go to San Francisco with Jake reveals her dissatisfaction. She does not care much for Jake, but he is a ticket to a more exciting life. Traumatized after her abduction and rape by Blue Duck, she hardly speaks again, but her actions and passionate attachment to Augustus show that she has found what she needed all along—understanding, tenderness, and protection.

Newt slowly emerges from the background characters to become, at the end of the novel, the strongest character. A boy as the drive begins, Newt gains more and more knowledge and ability. When Woodrow savagely beats a soldier who attacked Newt, Augustus tells Newt that Woodrow is the boy's father. Just before Woodrow leaves to take Augustus' body back to Texas, he turns over the operation of the ranch to Newt, and this time Newt is able to handle a physical challenge to his authority by himself. Yet Woodrow's failure to accept Newt as his son leaves Newt bitter.

Themes and Meanings

Hidden behind the stock Western novel device of the epic trail drive are basic themes of the novel, love and death. Several of the characters are either seeking lovers or are haunted by absent lovers. (This motif explains the title; doves mate for life, and a lonesome dove is one that has lost or is searching for its partner.) Elmira thinks that she can find happiness with Dee Boot, and she leaves both husband and baby in a search for a reprobate who will be hanged the day after she is reunited with him. Dish Boggett hangs around Lorena, to whom he is devoted, like a panting puppy. Even the remarkably resourceful and self-contained Augustus rides hundreds of miles to plead his case to Clara. Although Lorena reveres Augustus as a rescuing knight, she fails to understand that Augustus really is a knight: He helps her not because he has designs on her body or soul but because she is in danger, so he saves her as a good knight or Texas Ranger should. Dish Boggett's passion for Lorena is a reminder that emotion alone cannot sustain deep love. Lorena's attitude toward Dish passes from indifference to annoyance to scorn, perhaps because in Boggett she sees a reflection of her own moon-eyed pining over Augustus. Lorena is too weak to inspire more than affection in Augustus. He can only love someone who is as strong and independent as himself—and for that reason, ironically, there can be no permanent relationship between Clara and Augustus, since they are too strong for each other.

Lonesome Dove is also a reminder of mortality. The deaths begin as soon as the drive begins, when the O'Brien brother is bitten by the snakes. Because this character had scarcely been introduced, his death is more shocking than affecting. The deaths continue to come, however, and to characters of more significance; the deaths of Deets and Augustus are almost unbearable. Since the drive itself moves through ever-changing and unpredictable circumstances, the deaths are the final test of the characters' ability to change and adapt. The novel thus is an account of what happens when a group of people whose characters and relationships are fixed are placed in new circumstances and forced to adjust. Malleable and fluid characters such as Augustus thrive; those whose characteristics are set and unchangeable are destroyed or suffer reduction.

Critical Context

Much of Larry McMurtry's work is a continuing examination of life in modern Texas, both rural (as in *The Last Picture Show*, 1971, and *Texasville*, 1987) and urban (as in *All My Friends Are Going to Be Strangers*, 1972, and *Terms of Endearment*, 1975). Much of the remainder, including *Lonesome Dove*, is an attempt to understand the frontier past. Other McMurtry novels set in the nineteenth century include *Anything for Billy* (1988), an account of the life of Billy the Kid, and *Streets of Laredo* (1992), a sequel to *Lonesome Dove*.

The characters Augustus, Woodrow, and Deets are based on the real plainsmen Oliver Loving, Charles Goodnight, and Bose Ikard. Many of the features of the trail drive are suggested by events described in Teddy Blue's *We Pointed Them North* (1939), but McMurtry's novel is an ironic account of these lives and adventures. McMurtry's modern Texas novels are filled with a sense of frustration and dissatisfaction, as if Texas had once been a place where one could find fulfillment but, because of the collapse of frontier values, one no longer can. *Lonesome Dove*, most of the characters of which remain frustrated, suggests that the root of the problem may lie not in historical changes but in the male psyche, since Clara, with her self-reliance and her happiness in her involvement in the lives of those around her, is the most fully developed and fulfilled character.

Bibliography

Graham, Don. "*Lonesome Dove*: Butch and Sundance Go On a Cattledrive." *Southwestern American Literature* 12, no. 1 (1986): 7-12. Graham, an expert on films about Texas, finds parallels to *Lonesome Dove* in both film and literature. By writing this book, Graham notes, McMurtry does not follow his own prescription that Texas literature should concentrate on the contemporary urban scene. A helpful article for those also interested in the film version of *Lonesome Dove*.

Mogen, David. "Sex and True West in McMurtry's Fiction: From Teddy Blue to Lonesome Dove to Texasville." *Southwestern American Literature* 14 (1989): 34-45. Traces the sources of *Lonesome Dove*, particularly Teddy Blue's account of an old-time cattle drive. Mogen also relates the book to the rest of McMurtry's work.

Reynolds, Clay. "Back Trailing to Glory: *Lonesome Dove* and the Novels of Larry McMurtry." *Texas Review* 8, nos. 3-4 (1987): 22-29. Reynolds takes a critical view of the book, pointing out some of its deficiencies in plot and character. He also places the novel in the context of McMurtry's other work.

————, ed. *Taking Stock: A Larry McMurtry Casebook*. Dallas: Southern

Methodist University Press, 1989. An exhaustive survey of McMurtry's career up to 1989. Contains a section on *Lonesome Dove* that includes the essays by Graham, Reynolds, and Sewell mentioned here.

Sewell, Ernestine P. "McMurtry's Cowboy-God in *Lonesome Dove.*" *Western American Literature* 21 (November, 1986): 219-225. Discusses archetypal patterns in *Lonesome Dove*. A Freudian analysis suggests that Augustus, Woodrow, and Jake represent the three-part Freudian division of the personality.

Jim Baird

THE LOST LANGUAGE OF CRANES

Author: David Leavitt (1961-   )
Type of plot: Family
Time of plot: The mid-1980's
Locale: New York City
First published: 1986

>   *Principal characters:*
>   PHILIP BENJAMIN, a twenty-five-year-old gay man who edits paperback
>   romances
>   OWEN BENJAMIN, Philip's father, the dean of admissions at a prestigious
>   boys' school
>   ROSE BENJAMIN, Philip's mother, a copy editor at a small literary publish-
>   ing house
>   ELIOT ABRAMS, Philip's lover, a young, wealthy, and enigmatic entrepre-
>   neur
>   JERENE PARKS, Eliot's roommate, an African American lesbian and pe-
>   rennial graduate student

The Novel

The Lost Language of Cranes is a naturalistic, contemporary novel about a small, upper-middle class intellectual family in New York City in which the son's acknowledgement of his homosexuality transforms his parents' marriage in unexpected ways.

The novel is divided into four sections: "Voyages," "Myths of Origin," "The Crane Child," and "Father and Son," with the third significantly shorter and the last significantly longer than the others. The section titles are thematic; chronologically and stylistically, the novel flows as a unified whole. It is presented in a third-person narrative voice that often enters the thoughts and feelings of the main characters.

As the novel opens, the reader sees Owen and Rose Benjamin in their separate exploits on a Sunday afternoon. They are a happily, or at least tranquilly, married couple who have comfortable jobs and live in a rent-controlled apartment on New York City's posh Upper East Side. The security of their shared life is threatened by news that their building is to become a cooperative apartment house, leaving them the equally unattractive options of buying or moving out.

The reader then meets their son Philip, a twenty-five-year-old editor who is in love with a golden and capricious young man named Eliot. Philip dotes on Eliot but always feels uncertain and unsatisfied; he is also uncomfortable with the secrecy of his homosexuality and the distance it creates between him and his parents.

The novel weaves in and out of the Benjamins' lives as they travel the streets of New York, share meals, work, converse, make love, and face challenges large and small. Along the way, readers observe Owen in his secret life, furtively frequenting adult motion-picture houses where he indulges in homosexual fantasies and barely resists constant temptations. Readers are also introduced to Jerene, Eliot's roommate, an African American graduate student estranged from her parents because of her lesbianism.

Leavitt fills in details through flashbacks—about the Benjamins' marriage, Rose's extramarital affairs, Philip's childhood and sexual development—and constantly shifts among the characters to establish the connections between them and their stories. The novel's background is a New York populated by cab drivers, doormen, and street people and a media culture defined by television shows, books, and celebrities. Leavitt portrays his protagonists intimately, penetrating the isolation of their separate lives.

The main story lines of the book develop simultaneously. Philip's love for Eliot, and his fascination with Eliot's adoptive father Derek, ultimately result in Eliot's sudden departure. The real-estate dilemma creates a sense of despair in the Benjamin's apartment. Desperate and in search of love and identity, Philip seeks his old friend Brad and faces his need to be honest with his parents about himself. Jerene meets and becomes involved with a new woman, and she feels the need to seek out her parents once again. Owen finds it harder and harder to suppress his homosexual desires.

In the novel's critical scene, Philip informs his parents of his homosexuality. Rose responds with pain and a sincere effort to understand; Owen closes off and sobs silently to himself. Both know implicitly that Philip's is not the only sexuality at stake, and that his honesty unwittingly threatens the fragile foundation of their marriage.

In the brief third section of the novel, Leavitt explores a case study from Jerene's research in linguistics. The case involves a neglected, possibly retarded, teenage boy who was fascinated by some distant construction cranes and who would interpret and respond to their movements as if in a strange language. The case provides the novel's title and a central metaphor about the need for communication and love.

After encountering the Crane Child, Jerene seeks out her paternal grandmother Nellie in a Long Island nursing home. The reunion, a brief encounter in which she portrays her life as secure and normal for her simple, doting grandmother, is Jerene's first step toward reestablishing a link with her past and her estranged family.

The last section focuses on Owen and Philip, their individual transformations, and the growing affinity between them. As the gap between him and Rose widens and his homosexual yearnings grow, Owen looks to Philip, ironically, as a role model. A family dinner at which an English teacher from Owen's school is guest of honor invokes telling behavior and triggers the mostly silent but painfully honest confrontation between Rose and Owen, where his secret is acknowledged by both and the peace of their coexistence is irrevocably shattered. In the end, Owen seeks comfort and refuge in Philip's apartment.

The Characters

Philip is the central and most sympathetic character of the novel. His story is a coming-of-age and a "coming-out" tale, and he is the main conduit for emotional understanding. Philip is a sincere and sensitive young man whose journey takes him from self-doubt and obsessiveness toward self-knowledge and authentic love. It is through a more rigorous examination of his lovers and his parents that Philip ultimately finds himself. At the same time, he provides an interesting foil and gloss to Owen; at numerous points, scenes from their lives—meals, sexual encounters, phone conversations—are effectively juxtaposed.

Owen, an older, more confused, and more repressed man, is much more enigmatic. While on the surface potentially despicable for his deception and indecision, Owen is not an unsympathetic character, for Leavitt is careful to convey Owen's pain, guilt, and sincere desire to do what is right for both himself and those he loves. He is portrayed as a man lost and confused, a representation of the bluntness that results from the repression of desire and honesty.

Rose, though not as repressed or deceptive, has also been living with lies. While seemingly a victim, she is also a wife guilty of infidelities who prefers to avoid confrontation. She is a sympathetic character, but one with a complex layering of feelings, thoughts, desires, and self-deceptions. That her journey is determined primarily by the desires and actions of others indicates the passive nature of her personality.

Jerene provides both a contrast to the Benjamins, in her distance from them and the different issues that concern her, and a touchstone by which to understand their stories. The account of her parents' response to her lesbianism creates a tension in anticipation of Philip's eventual disclosure to Rose and Owen. Her interest in lost languages amplifies the significance of the characters' private worlds.

The narrative voice rarely penetrates the other characters, but they provide valuable links in the overall structure of the novel. The sharp contrast between Eliot and Brad helps to define Philip's emotional growth. Winston Penn, the dinner guest, becomes, essentially, a lens through which Rose confirms Owen's true nature.

Leavitt also uses character to establish the complexity of New York life, through a variety of serendipitous, and often undiscovered, connections. When Owen desperately calls a hotline for advice, Jerene is the volunteer who answers. Eliot's adoptive father Derek is one of Philip's favorite childhood authors, one whose books Rose edited. Owen discovers that the cinema he frequents is one Philip has visited as well. These links heighten the tension, irony, and emotional logic of the novel and contribute to the sense of complexity throughout.

Themes and Meanings

The Lost Language of Cranes is a novel, above all, about identity and empathy. The main characters face the challenges of defining themselves as clearly and honestly as possible and of choosing the terms, the aspects of life—relationships, jobs, sexuality, race, gender—by which their sense of self is established.

For Rose and Owen, marriage and home are implicit to identity. When they tell Philip that they might give up their apartment, he says that he simply cannot imagine them living anywhere else. Rose examines herself in the mirror, imagines herself in others' situations, and thinks about how people perceive her. While she and Owen both know that their intimacy has faded, neither is willing to question the basic value of their relationship.

For Philip and Owen, homosexuality is the issue through which identity is explored. In his secret life, Owen assumes the anonymity provided by gay film houses and bars; his self-image merges with those of the sex-driven men in the pornographic films he watches. He is painfully aware of playing roles in his marriage and job, of hiding his true identity in subtle but telling ways.

Philip at first locates his identity wholly in his love for Eliot, a love that is self-degrading and ultimately based in fantasy. It is only through the process of understanding himself and, more important, expressing himself more honestly to the world around him that he arrives at a way of loving that does not destroy his sense of self.

Communication becomes important as the manner in which identity is expressed. When Owen builds enough courage to call a man whom he encountered anonymously, the man misunderstands Owen's name and calls him "Bowen"; the mistake symbolizes the inevitable distortion of identity that comes with repression and deception. Philip searches through Derek's books for clues to Eliot's elusive identity. Jerene's false description of her life to Nellie is both poignant and pathetic; it is the only real language she can use.

Language, then comes to define the individual. In describing Jerene's response to the Crane Child case, Leavitt gives the novel's clearest and most compelling articulation of this theme:

> How wondrous, how grand those cranes must have seemed to Michel, compared to the small and clumsy creatures who surrounded him. For each, in his own way, she believed, finds what it is he must love, and loves it; the window becomes a mirror; whatever it is that we love, that is who we are.

Furthermore, identity becomes a question of finding one's place. Philip is strikingly conscious of where he and Eliot spend their nights together. For Rose and Owen, the imminent change in living situation is a metaphor for the challenges that their marriage faces. The home that was once safe for Owen has become a place of danger, yet it is still preferable to living on the street, an unlikely scenario that he and Rose both fear. Early in the novel, Philip and Rose step over a homeless person asleep in Philip's entryway; at the end of the novel, Philip comes home to find his father in the same spot. Yet Owen's descent to such figurative poverty represents liberty and clarity, not bankruptcy. He becomes one with, and brings empathy to, the many poor and nameless face of urban life.

Such a transformation suggests the empathetic understanding that suffuses the novel. As the characters face their own needs and idiosyncrasies in the pursuit of authentic identity, they need more than anything the empathy of others. *The Lost Language of Cranes*, despite the highly emotional nature of the conflicts and situations it examines, never explodes into anger, hatred, or vitriol. Rather, Rose, Philip, Owen, and the others consistently extend compassion to others; they strive not to judge but to understand.

This theme is underlined in various smaller events of the novel. At one point Rose, frustrated by incessant phone calls from opportunistic real-estate agents, lashes out at one caller only to receive an overpowering description of the caller's own miserable life. It is a reminder that all have burdens to carry, and that the best one can do is to accept others as they are. Such empathy can be the key to understanding such very human phenomena as homosexuality, infidelity, poverty, and emotional need.

It also can be the key to functioning in the complex and confusing society of the modern cityscape. Leavitt's New York is not merely a backdrop but a character in itself that constantly challenges and reflects on the protagonists. It is a world so vast and overwhelming that knowing one's place in it requires the utmost honesty, energy, generosity, and commitment.

Critical Context

At the age of twenty-three, David Leavitt burst on the American literary scene with a collection of short stories entitled *Family Dancing* (1984). The stories dealt with issues of sexuality and terminal cancer. *Family Dancing* received the PEN/Faulkner Award and was a finalist for the National Book Critics Circle Award. Because of his youth, Leavitt received much attention and was hailed by some as the new voice of his generation.

Two years later, *The Lost Language of Cranes*, Leavitt's first novel, appeared to mixed reviews. Focused more clearly on homosexual themes and characters, it established him as a gay writer. During the mid-1980's, the gay rights movement was well into its second decade and approaching a certain maturity; Leavitt's novel was noted for dealing with gay themes in a very accessible and universal manner. Despite the critical response, *The Lost Language of Cranes* spent many weeks on best-seller lists and was a popular success. In 1992, the British Broadcasting Corporation filmed an adaptation of the novel, transferring the story to London.

Leavitt's other works include *Equal Affections* (1988), a novel about a family facing its matriarch's slow death; a second collection of stories, *A Place I've Never Been* (1990); and a novel set in wartime England entitled *While England Sleeps* (1993). Leavitt has lived in Europe, and his work enjoys great popular and critical success there.

Bibliography

Hubbard, Kim. *"The Lost Language of Cranes." People Weekly* 26 (November 3, 1986): 19-20. After a brief synopsis of the novel, Hubbard considers the humorlessness of the characters and their preoccupation with sexual identity. The reviewer also questions the novel's lack of attention to AIDS.

Jones, Adams-Mars. *"The Lost Language of Cranes." New Republic* 195 (November 17, 1986): 43-46. A balanced appraisal of the novel on several levels. Jones examines the larger themes and metaphors and the use of pathos, irony, tone, and tempo. He criticizes Leavitt for underdevelopment of certain characters and the lack of a mature central protagonist.

Leavitt, David. *"The Way I Live Now."* *The New York Times Magazine* 138 (July 9, 1989): 28-32. Inspired by Susan Sontag's story *"The Way We Live Now,"* Leavitt discusses AIDS with candor and conviction. He looks at AIDS in his own writing and reviews the history of AIDS activism. Includes criticism of society's stereotypes in fighting the epidemic.

Lopate, Phillip. *"Sexual Politics, Family Secrets."* *The New York Times Book Review*, October 5, 1986, 3. Lopate favorably reviews the novel, commending Leavitt's female characters and the freshness and suspense of the story. He takes issue with the novel's emphasis on sexual identity and politics. The review is accompanied by an interview box in which Barth Healey quotes Leavitt's views on the novel.

Staggs, Sam. "David Leavitt." *Publisher's Weekly* 237 (August 24, 1990): 47-48. An intimate article based on an interview with the author. Leavitt discusses his work from a dispassionate, objective viewpoint. He also comments on the challenges of youthful success, his popularity in Europe, and his responsibility as a gay writer in the AIDS era.

Barry Mann

LOVE IN THE TIME OF CHOLERA

Author: Gabriel García Márquez (1928-   )
Type of plot: Romance
Time of plot: The late 1870's to the early 1930's
Locale: A fictional Caribbean coastal city in northern Colombia
First published: El amor en los tiempos del cólera, 1985 (English translation, 1988)

Principal characters:
  FLORENTINO ARIZA, a lovesick poet and president of the River Company
    of the Caribbean
  FERMINA DAZA, the wife and later widow of Dr. Juvenal Urbino
  DR. JUVENAL URBINO, a member of the aristocracy whose accidental
    death occurs at age eighty-one
  JEREMIAH DE SAINT-AMOUR, an Antillean-born refugee and friend of
    Urbino
  TRÁNSITO ARIZA, Florentino's mother
  LORENZO DAZA, Fermina's father
  AMÉRICA VICUÑA, the elderly Florentino's young female charge

The Novel

The first novel to be published by Gabriel García Márquez since he was awarded the Nobel Prize in Literature in 1982, *Love in the Time of Cholera* chronicles the nearly sixty-year relationship between Florentino Ariza and Fermina Daza, who finally consummate their love in old age during a boat trip down the Magdalena River in Colombia.

Love in the Time of Cholera is divided into six lengthy, discursive chapters, ranging in form from the chronologically linear to frequent flashbacks and reprises. The novel has a single narrative voice that relates certain events in duplicate order to capture the overlapping experiences of its protagonists: Florentino, Fermina, and her husband of some fifty years, Dr. Juvenal Urbino.

The book begins with the bizarre suicide (by gold cyanide) one Pentecost Sunday of Jeremiah de Saint-Amour, the elderly Urbino's longtime friend and chess companion, an event that coincides with the silver wedding anniversary of Urbino's most eminent medical student. Urbino's own accidental death later the same day (he falls while trying to retrieve his wife's pet parrot from a mango tree) sets in motion a second level to the narrative. Since this deceased physician had been one of the sleepy provincial capital's most prestigious residents, mourners from town swarm the Urbino household to console his widow, seventy-two-year-old Fermina Daza. One of those visitors is seventy-six-year-old Florentino Ariza, the president of the River Company of the Caribbean, who repeats to Fermina the vow of eternal love that he first expressed to her more than a half-century earlier.

This chain of events becomes the catalyst for the rest of the novel, which flashes back to tell the story of Florentino's passionate three-year courtship of Fermina Daza when they were still teenagers. Their romance is conducted entirely through clandestine letters and the complicity of Fermina's spinster aunt and her coquettish cousin, but Florentino's swooning preoccupation and progressive physical distress over Fermina arouse the concern of his mother, Tránsito, and his Uncle Léo XII. Florentino's romantic love remains unrequited, however, since the beautiful but fickle Fermina abruptly jilts him and later marries Urbino, a member of a fading aristocratic family.

Subsequent chapters of *Love in the Time of Cholera* account for the contrasting backgrounds of Florentino, Fermina, and Urbino, who together represent a stereotypical three-cornered love relationship. A broad temporal and spatial perspective registers the main social developments that shape the postcolonial community, and the book also surveys the political history of Colombia since its independence in the early nineteenth century. Yet even after Fermina has wed Urbino, at the coaxing of her father, and settled down into a life of social ostentation and domestic boredom, Florentino remains in the city of their star-crossed romance, a setting that is a social and racial microcosm of a formerly prosperous Spanish city situated at the mouth of the Magdalena River. The action of the novel centers on this provincial capital, a rough composite of Cartegena de Indias, Barranquilla, and other locations on the Caribbean coast.

Despite the fact that Fermina has married another man, the doctor famous for ending the ravages of cholera in the region, and has learned to cherish if not altogether love him, Florentino never abandons his devotion to the love of his youth and dedicates his life to preparing for Fermina's return. This is not to say, however, that he has forsaken heterosexual love during his half-century wait for her: In fact, while many of the townspeople suspect him of homosexuality because of his secretive ways, Florentino has earned a reputation as the lover of widows, shop clerks, madwomen, and even schoolgirls in his effort to find a substitute for Fermina. If he has resolved to keep himself spiritually pure for the day when he will possess Fermina, he nevertheless amasses and records in his diary hundreds of liaisons and sexual adventures with other women. Both he and Fermina hence cross the line into old age leading parallel lives in the same locale. Florentino has risen over the years from lowly messenger to president of the prosperous River Company (and continues his sexual exploits, despite the failings of his body and the tragic murder, by a cuckolded husband, of one of his mistresses), while Fermina endures her husband's infidelity, obsessiveness, and patriarchal domination to achieve at least the guise of conjugal contentment.

The final chapter of the work circles back to the beginning, or to the elderly Florentino's repeated vow to Fermina on the first night of her widowhood and her initial rage at and outright rejection of him. Yet because of a lifetime of experience and a maturer perspective tainted by intimations of his own mortality, Florentino persists in his veneration of her, and the meditational letters he now writes to Fermina are tempered, sympathetic, and comforting in the first years following the death of her husband. Eventually, against social conventions and disabused of their earlier illusions, Florentino and Fermina fulfill their desires on the *New Fidelity*, an aptly named boat that sails them endlessly up and down the Magdalena River. Thus, their dogged achievement over old age, fate, and the prejudices of their society stands as a final affirmation of life, hope, and persistent love.

The Characters

Florentino Ariza, whose lifelong obsession with Fermina motivates the narrative, is the stock figure of a solitary, lovesick poet who, like many a Romantic hero, finds refuge in sexual relations with other women to help replace or try to forget his youthful passion. After being rejected by Fermina, he becomes both a pathetic character whom adult females regard compassionately and a timid, nervous wretch whose idealistic pretensions are subject to ridicule. His sentimental romanticism includes writing interminable love letters and playing violin serenades to Fermina, whose callous abandonment of him drives Florentino to bouts of distraught melancholy and insomnia. His reunion with Fermina in old age, however, is premised upon his more realistic assessment of love and commitment.

Fermina Daza, who weds the pretentious Urbino after throwing over Florentino, displays a down-to-earth pragmatism and acceptance of her increasingly mundane domesticity, quickly forgetting Florentino and any melodramatic desire she may have possessed in her youth. Having married above her class, Fermina comes to embody the social snobbery of Urbino's shabby-genteel lifestyle, a position she maintains until her husband's death. Her return to Florentino as an elderly widow suggests too that requited love is only possible after one is disabused of idealistic illusions, in Spanish an experience called *desengaño*.

Dr. Juvenal Urbino, a member of one of the city's most prominent but now fading families, epitomizes professional objectivity and aristocratic reserve, but he marries Fermina, as they both later admit, more out of social expectations than passionate love (despite his final pronouncement, just before dying, to the contrary). His accidental death precipitates the eventual consummation of the half-century-long love of Florentino for Fermina.

Jeremiah de Saint-Amour, or the "prophet of love," kills himself at the opening of the novel, revealing the extent to which secretive love and the depression of old age can lead someone. A respected children's photographer and accomplished chess player, Jeremiah had kept a mulatto mistress for half of his life, the revelation of which shocks his friend Urbino into an awareness of the complicity of love and fate.

Tránsito Ariza, Florentino's mother, pities her son's lovesickness and helps him to overcome his grief by directing him toward business and other love interests. Her senile decrepitude and then death leave Florentino mourning his closest confidante in matters of the heart.

Lorenzo Daza, Fermina's father, is a shady businessman whose criminal activities eventually get him expelled from the country. He actively discourages Florentino's suit for his daughter and instead coaxes Urbino to court and marry Fermina, an event

Lorenzo hopes will give respectability to his dubious character.

América Vicuña, the young female charge of the elderly Florentino, commits suicide after Florentino has pledged to reunite with Fermina. As her guardian, Florentino deflowers América at the age of fourteen, but her maniacal love for the old man cannot withstand what she sees as his betrayal of her in favor of Fermina.

Themes and Meanings

The novel is a balanced portrayal of romantic love, irrespective of age and in a variety of forms, and devotion against all odds, even the threat of impending death. It highlights the themes of marriage and old age, human dignity and compassion, and sensual pleasure in defiance of prejudicial societal constraints, as Florentino and Fermina must overcome countless obstacles before their eventual reunion. Such consummation of love in old age rejects the idealism of youth and is based instead upon a fatalistic brand of humanism that rests on a mature recognition of social and personal realities, including the certainty of mortality.

The novel is also underlaid with feminist and "Americanist" themes and motifs. Fermina's marriage, while ultimately fulfilling, reveals the strictures placed on women's freedom and sense of individuality in a patriarchal society. In essence, Fermina is a slave to her husband's and family's demands, and she finds liberation and self-empowerment only in widowhood. Furthermore, the novel's postcolonial setting implies the theme of America: García Márquez's considerations of history, politics, race, class, and culture are conveyed in both literal and symbolic terms. The era of Spanish rule has left the city an open cesspool "forgotten" by the rest of the world, and the postcolonial milieu is evoked in the once-aristocratic Urbino family's economic and social decline. Yet the vital potential of the town's impoverished mulattos contrasts with the *criollo* class's decadence, thus celebrating the possible revival of Latin American peoples (despite the death of América Vicuña, who may allegorically represent the natural and political life of the continent).

Critical Context

Love in the Time of Cholera, unlike García Márquez's phenomenally successful *Cien años de soledad* (1967; *One Hundred Years of Solitude*, 1970), diverges from the Magical Realism that marked the author's early development and that of other "Boom" generation Latin American writers of the 1960's and 1970's. While the novel does experiment with fictional techniques, such as temporal flashbacks and simultaneity, it remains more in the tradition of the *follétin*, the lachrymose, sentimental nineteenth century love story. In this respect, García Márquez's work is similar to fellow Colombian Jorge Isaacs' *Maria* (1867), which enjoyed wide popularity with readers in Europe and the Americas. Yet García Márquez's novel is also more a pastiche of the *follétin* genre, since the book's verbal clichés, character types, and narrative situations finally transcend the melodramatic through an acute sense of irony and tragicomic style. The novel's thematic emphases upon love, solitude, old age, and death, however, place it well within the context of García Márquez's other fictions, including *El coronel no tiene quien le escriba* (1961; *No One Writes to the Colonel*, 1968), *El otoño del patriarca* (1975; *The Autumn of the Patriarch*, 1976), *Crónica de una muerte anunciada* (1981; *Chronicle of a Death Foretold*, 1982), and *El general en su laberinto* (1989; *The General in His Labyrinth*, 1990). Perhaps the most recognized Latin American writer, García Márquez has achieved a range and empathetic flexibility in his work that make him one of the most important novelists of the twentieth century.

Bibliography
Buehrer, David. " 'A Second Chance on Earth': The Postmodern and the Post-apocalyptic in García Márquez's *Love in the Time of Cholera.*" *Critique* 32 (Fall, 1990): 15-26. Buehrer analyzes García Márquez's novel from the perspective of its "postmodern" traits. Contends that García Márquez transforms the "inevitablist and fatalistic tendencies" of postmodernism into a novel expressive of "humanistic finality and hope."

Fiddian, Robin. "A Prospective Post-Script: Apropos of *Love in the Time of Cholera.*" In *Gabriel García Márquez: New Readings*, edited by Bernard McGuirk and Richard Cardwell. New York: Cambridge University Press, 1987. Provides an overview of the generic and thematic features of the novel, including its appropriation of the *follétin* form. Concludes with an analysis of "possible avenues of approach" to the book, such as its humanist, feminist, and Americanist motifs, which future critics might explore more thoroughly.

McNerney, Kathleen. *Understanding Gabriel García Márquez.* Columbia: University of South Carolina Press, 1989. A comprehensive treatment of the writer and his work, including a chronology and useful bibliography. Chapter 3 analyzes *Love in the Time of Cholera* from its thematic perspectives of romantic love, the aging process, and class differences. Also reveals García Márquez's autobiographical influences and self-reflexive allusions in the novel.

Minta, Stephen. *Gabriel García Márquez: Writer of Colombia.* London: Jonathan Cape, 1987. In chapter 4, "After Success," Minta explores the social and political underpinnings of *Love in the Time of Cholera*, including the postcolonial class structure capable of creating figures like Juvenal Urbino and Fermina Daza.

Palencia-Roth, Michael. "Gabriel García Márquez: Labyrinths of Love and History." *World Literature Today* 65 (Winter, 1991): 54-58. Compares the novel to García Márquez's *The General in His Labyrinth.* Analyzes the novel's "poetic realism" and "narrative traditionalism," as well as its myriad portrayals of love.

David Buehrer

LUCY

Author: Jamaica Kincaid (Elaine Potter Richardson, 1949-   )
Type of plot: Autobiographical
Time of plot: The 1980's
Locale: New York City and the Great Lakes
First published: 1990

> *Principal characters:*
> LUCY, the novel's narrator, who has come to New York from Antigua
> MARIAH, Lucy's well-meaning but insensitive white employer
> LEWIS, Mariah's husband, who falls in love with Mariah's best friend Dinah
> DINAH, Mariah's best friend, an insensitive woman to whom Lucy is "the girl"
> HUGH, Dinah's brother, who briefly becomes Lucy's lover
> PEGGY, Lucy's "bad" friend, who introduces her to the darker side of city life

The Novel

A roughly autobiographical novel, *Lucy* deals with the experiences of a young Antiguan woman who, like Jamaica Kincaid herself, comes to New York City to work as a nanny in an effort to escape her repressive family and the narrow island life in which she has grown up. Her experiences in the city disillusion her, but while she copes with her disillusionment, she must come to terms with her family back in Antigua.

The episodic action of the five chapters of *Lucy* is narrated by Lucy herself, beginning with her first morning on her new job in New York. Even when the family was driving her home from the airport and pointing out famous sights to her, Lucy recalls, her feelings were a sort of sadness. What she discovers is the difference between her romantic expectations and the gritty reality of the city. The difference is made even more powerful by her memory of warm, sunny Antigua, a place she had never expected to miss, for when she was at home she felt in constant conflict with her family. Now, however, she identifies this surprising sadness as homesickness for foods of home such as green figs and pink mullet, for a cousin, even for a favorite nightgown from her childhood.

The family she works for is kind to her, and Lucy admires their blonde good looks and happy informality. They recognize Lucy's unhappiness, however, and Lewis, the husband, begins to call her "Visitor." One night, Lucy tells the family a dream full of sexual images she dreamed about Lewis. Mariah and Lewis are obviously uncomfortable, but to Lucy, the dream simply indicates that she has made Mariah and Lewis important people in her life.

In early March, Mariah, knowing how Lucy longs for warm weather, describes the beauty of daffodils to her. The description makes Lucy remember how in school she had had to recite a poem about daffodils (evidently William Wordsworth's famous "I Wandered Lonely As a Cloud"). She recited it perfectly, but underneath she was angry about the task and the poem, which to her represented Great Britain's colonization of Antigua. Her anger emphasizes the gulf between Lucy and Mariah.

While Mariah plans a trip to her family home on the Great Lakes, Lucy is thinking about her own family. Her mother's letters are filled with threats and warnings of the city's dangers. This makes Lucy remember her mother's disreputable friend Sylvie, a woman who had a scar on her cheek from a human bite and who had spent time in jail, a powerful contrast to Mariah's inoffensive beauty. At the chapter's end, the family has arrived at the family summer home at the Great Lakes. Lucy is unimpressed and is angered by Mariah's claim that she is a good fisherwoman because she has Indian blood. To Lucy, the boast is the sort that only a victor can make, and she asks, "How do you get to be the sort of victor who can claim to be the vanquished also?" Mariah, however, does not understand Lucy's anger.

At about this time, Mariah's best friend, Dinah, arrives at the lakes. Lucy dislikes Dinah, who clearly sees Lucy as only a servant. Lucy also sees that Dinah is a vain woman who is envious of Mariah's possessions, even of her family.

Lucy is rather isolated while the family is at the lakes; she misses her disreputable friend Peggy, a young woman whose gaudy clothes, heavy smoking, and rebellious behavior have made Mariah forbid Lucy to bring her around the children. Loneliness makes Lucy interested in Dinah's brother Hugh, an attractive and worldly man who sees Lucy as an individual and who soon becomes her lover.

While at the lakes, Mariah decides to write a children's book about the environment. Lucy is rather amused at Mariah's naïve inability to see any relationship between the threatened environment and her own high standard of living. At about this time, too, Lucy recognizes that Lewis has begun a love affair with Dinah.

Back in New York again, Lucy enters a period of change. She stops her nurse's training. She takes a new lover, Paul; ironically, as she and Peggy grow apart, they begin to plan to find an apartment to share. Mariah asks Lewis to leave the household. Most important, Lucy receives a letter marked "urgent" from her mother. She ignores it as she has her mother's previous letters, until at last a cousin comes to her in person to tell her that her father has died, leaving her mother destitute.

Angry with her mother for marrying an unfaithful man who cannot manage money, Lucy nevertheless sends her some of the money she has saved toward the apartment. Shortly after that, she quits her job with Mariah, takes work as a photographer's assistant, and moves in with Peggy. At the novel's end, Lucy seems to have severed almost all of her emotional ties to others; in the last scene, she writes her name in a new journal and records her longing to love someone, a statement that makes her feel overcome with shame.

The Characters

Lucy is the narrator and central character of the novel. Her voice and her sensibilities lead the reader through the book's rambling episodes. The contradictions in Lucy's character are the contradictions that adolescence seems to create. On the one hand, Lucy is a keen and sometimes satiric observer of her new world. She laughs at American excesses and pities American provincialism. She also has insight into others' motivations. She suspects the affair between Dinah and Lewis long before Mariah knows about it, and she understands her mother's advice about siding with women rather than men to mean that she should never get involved with another woman's husband. In many ways, Lucy understands herself. She knows that she will not be sorry to part with Hugh; she knows that she cannot tell Peggy about her artistic interest in photography. What she does not understand completely is her relationship with her mother. She does not see that although she may refuse to read her mother's letters, may refuse all contact with her, she will always be her mother's daughter, just as her mother predicted.

Mariah functions as the means by which Lucy is introduced to American life and ideas. In that way, like Peggy, she serves as a foil to Lucy. Wealthy, beautiful, naïve about the world outside her own sphere, she is the object both of Lucy's admiration and of her scorn.

Dinah is scarcely developed as a character in the novel. She exists just fully enough to represent the sort of bigotry and ignorance that Lucy despises. She thinks of Lucy as "the girl who takes care of the children" and doesn't even know where she came from, referring to Antigua as "the islands." That is enough to earn Lucy's contempt, but Dinah also betrays her friend, an unforgivable act to Lucy.

Peggy, Lucy's dark self, is also a foil to her. Peggy's flashy clothes, her sexy language, and her use of marijuana become means by which Lucy acts out her rebellion against her past, even while she sees through Peggy's shallowness. Lucy knows herself well enough to recognize that their friendship is based on mutual convenience rather than any real affection.

Lucy's two lovers, Hugh and Paul, both exist almost as stick figures in the novel. Neither has really engaged Lucy's deeper emotions; both mainly serve her sexual appetites. The casualness with which they are introduced and dismissed suggests how little importance they carry for Lucy.

The episodic, looping organization of the novel's slender action and its heavy use of flashback may remind readers that this work really is a portrayal of Lucy's character. No other character is developed with the depth and attention to detail that Lucy is given.

Themes and Meanings

The central theme of *Lucy* concerns Lucy's coming of age in a new land. That process forces her to define her relationship with Mariah, her mother, and her homeland, while at the same time she must learn to recognize her self. In some ways, Lucy seems always to have had a clear understanding of who she is and what she wants, but her anger at her mother dramatizes her real confusion.

From soon after Lucy's arrival in New York, it becomes clear that she was very angry when she left her homeland and family. She says that she had never expected to miss them and that they had never shown regard for her feelings. She ridicules the fears of New York that her mother expressed in the few letters that Lucy opened, just as she ridicules the paltry news of island life that her mother is able to report. In the course of the novel, readers also see Lucy's anger at her father for his endless infidelities to her mother, as well as her anger with her mother for enduring the succession of mistresses and illegitimate children his love affairs have produced. All that anger boils over when, after months of refusing to open her mother's letters, Lucy learns of her father's death. She is angry at her father for being the sort of man he is and at her mother for putting up with him, for allowing herself to end up widowed and penniless. Although Lucy sends her mother money, she accompanies it with a harsh letter. Later, she sends a kinder one, but she also tells her mother the wrong address for her new apartment.

The cousin who came to tell Lucy about her father's death says that Lucy looks and acts like her mother. Lucy is surprised, and she rejects that idea, saying that they are not at all alike, just as she rejects Mariah's urging her to reconcile with her mother. Nevertheless, it is obvious that the two probably are alike. In fact, much of Lucy's information about the world and about how to get along with people originates with her mother, as Lucy herself admits. Moreover, whatever pain keeps Lucy from reaching out to her mother also affects Lucy. Indeed, she acknowledges that the anger and sadness she feels before she leaves Mariah's house is a sort of mourning for the end of the only true love affair—that is, the love she has had for her mother—she will ever know.

This ambivalence accounts for Lucy's relationships with Mariah and Peggy. Lucy says several times that Mariah reminds her of her mother. Their conversations and Mariah's concern for Lucy at the novel's end recall a sort of idyllic mother-daughter bond, the sort of relationship Lucy wishes that she and her true mother had shared. At the same time, Lucy finds her "bad self," the self neither her mother nor Mariah could approve of, in her friendship with Peggy. Peggy's casual acceptance of marijuana and sex and her dislike for intellectual activities allow Lucy to indulge her own rebellion against the Lucy her mother intended to create.

Antigua is Lucy's other parent and the object of her other rebellion. In the United States, she is forced to face what "Third World" means, and she is alternately defensive about her homeland and angry about the debilitating effects of British colonial rule in Antigua.

Critical Context

Lucy is an autobiographical novel, loosely representing the events of Jamaica Kincaid's life during her first year in the United States: Like Lucy, she worked as an au pair for a wealthy family that split up; like Lucy, she started school and quit; and like Lucy, she developed an interest in photography. At the end of *Lucy* there are slender hints that Lucy is about to discover an interest in writing, just as Kincaid herself did.

Kincaid's first novel, *Annie John* (1985), was also autobiographical, telling the story of a young girl growing up in Antigua. At the end of that novel, Annie John, having suffered a serious break with her mother, is leaving home, evidently forever. She is going to England, where she will go into nurse's training. In that respect, *Lucy* seems to take up where *Annie John* left off. The two works also share themes concerning mother-daughter relationships, sexual awakenings, and the debilitating effects of British colonial rule on the former colony. The books also share the same narrative style; both are told in the first person by a narrator who is more interested in developing a series of pictures and anecdotes to create an atmosphere than in telling a conventional linear story.

Kincaid's essay about Antigua, *A Small Place*, was published in 1988. It is reflective of the political anger that forms a theme of *Lucy*. In *A Small Place*, Kincaid details the ruinous effects of British rule on Antigua, attributing to colonialism a legacy of political corruption, racism, poverty, and ignorance. That same indictment forms a thematic element of *Lucy*. Just as Lucy must recognize herself as inevitable inheritor of some of her mother's being, so she is also heir to the island that gave her birth, to its beauty as well as to its pain.

Bibliography
Als, Hilton. "Don't Worry, Be Happy." *The Nation* 252 (February 18, 1991): 207-209. Als is particularly interested in *Lucy* in reference to Kincaid's position as a black writer from a Third World country. He understands Lucy as a budding artist, and he understands her at the end of the novel to be on the verge of interpreting the Antiguan people she loves. He gives some discussion to *A Small Place*.

Austin, Jacqueline. "Up From Eden." *Village Voice Literary Supplement* 34 (April, 1985): 6-7. Austin analyzes the themes of *Annie John* as logical culminations of the themes of Kincaid's short stories. Particularly, she sees them as asserting that the present is always tied to the past that gave it birth. She also gives attention to Kincaid's lyric style.

Garis, Leslie. "Through West Indian Eyes." *The New York Times Magazine* 140 (October 7, 1990): 42. A meaty biographical essay. Kincaid is quoted at length, particularly concerning her early lack of intellectual encouragement from family or teacher. Garis concentrates especially on Kincaid's life in the United States and talks about her relationship with *The New Yorker* magazine. Photographs.

Jaggi, Maya. "A Struggle for Independence." *The Times Literary Supplement* (April 26, 1991): 20. Jaggi relates *Lucy* to Kincaid's short-story collection *At the Bottom of the River* (1983) in its style and themes. Jaggi concentrates on analyzing Lucy's relationship with her mother and says that the novel's lack of linear narration weakens it.

Tyler, Anne. "Mothers and Mysteries." *The New Republic* 189 (December 31, 1983): 32-33. Tyler's review of *At the Bottom of the River* concentrates on two themes in the stories: the power of mother-daughter relationships and the mystery embodied in the ordinary. Tyler praises the lyric beauty of Kincaid's lush prose, but, except for the universally admired "Girl," she calls the stories "almost insultingly obscure" in their lack of narrative.

Ann D. Garbett

THE MacGUFFIN

Author: Stanley Elkin (1930-   )
Type of plot: Psychological realism
Time of plot: The 1990's
Locale: An unnamed major American city in the Midwest
First published: 1991

> *Principal characters:*
> BOBBO DRUFF, a fifty-eight-year-old neurotic who serves as commis-
> sioner of streets in a large city in the Midwest
> THE MACGUFFIN, Druff's second self—the devil within
> ROSE HELEN DRUFF, his sixty-year-old wife
> MICHAEL DRUFF, their thirty-year-old son
> MARGARET GLORIO, a buyer of fashionable men's clothing who becomes
> Druff's mistress
> DICK and DOUG, Druff's chauffeurs
> SU'AD AL NAJAF, an illegal Lebanese immigrant who is ostensibly a rug
> buyer

The Novel

Set in a large unnamed American city in the Midwest that seems much like St. Louis, *The MacGuffin* is the story of some two days in the life of Bobbo Druff, commissioner of streets. The novel successfully functions on many levels; it exhibits a multifaceted complexity in that it is the story of a family, a love intrigue of the husband with mistress, a murder mystery, a tale of smuggling, and a political state-ment. While being all of these, it is mostly about Bobbo Druff and "The MacGuffin," his psychological other and controlling self.

The MacGuffin has no chapter or sectional divisions; Elkin unfolds the narrative entirely by relating the thoughts and actions of Bobbo Druff during a Friday and Saturday of some unspecified weekend in the early 1990's. Even so, the novel is structured around some six to eight episodic adventures, determined primarily by Druff's physical location. Great portions of the novel are internal monologues, many of which are between Druff and The MacGuffin; other internal monologues occur as well, and there are also interchanges in dialogue with other characters.

When the novel opens, readers learn almost immediately of the recent mysterious death of Su'ad al-Najaf, a young college student and an illegal immigrant from Lebanon who sold rugs and dated Druff's son, Michael. Su'ad had died some forty hours before the beginning of the present action, having been repeatedly run over by an automobile. Druff somehow understands that he is connected with the death, but he does not know how. It is not clear if Druff is merely neurotic and paranoid or correct in his suspicions. The reader has many reasons to believe Druff is not mentally balanced: He continues to get high on coca leaves throughout the novel, and his mind wanders hopelessly, revealing him to be unacceptably solipsistic and at least a borderline psychotic. Too, the highs from the cocoa leaves are mixed with the effects of numerous prescription medicines.

In the second main episode of the novel, Druff meets Margaret Glorio, a buyer of men's clothing for department stores who claims to be forty-four years old but later acknowledges that she is "fifty, more or less." Witty, worldly, and experienced, the two soon agree to a liaison that night. Druff, who is fifty-eight years old and has never been unfaithful in his thirty-six-year marriage to Rose Helen, quickly and guiltlessly goes to Margaret's apartment, where the whole affair is enacted humorously. Both characters banter in what becomes a satire on sex and adultery.

Druff returns home to wife and son early the next morning and sleeps until noon. Meanwhile, Elkin provides the only significant flashback of the story as he relates the courtship and marriage of Bobbo and Rose Helen, describing in great detail their college years in the 1950's. Again, the author satirizes courtship and sexual relations, but this time his target is youth. The narrative is replete with rather stock situations (jokes about fraternities and sororities, escapes from housemothers who would catch them in the act, intrigues at hotels and in rented rooms, and the like), but there is a fresh perspective. Somehow, these events have meaning, as they help to explain Druff's present character and to make credible his MacGuffin.

On Saturday morning at home, Druff awakens mistakenly thinking it is another workday, and he dresses and heads off to work. Soon after discovering his mistake, he meets up with Hamilton Edgar and three other Jews who invite him into a synagogue. They have a conversation that feeds Druff's paranoia and the realization that he is somehow connected with Su'ad's accidental death. From a political context as well as a racial one, Jews are satirized as being like all other Americans: selfish, materialistic, and given to vice. They enjoy their breakfast of ham and eggs; and in the study of the synagogue—so Druff and the reader will eventually learn—are Arab rugs (presumably, Islamic prayer rugs) smuggled into the country and knowingly purchased by these men at the synagogue. The reader should quickly realize that Elkin is not particularly attacking Jews here; rather, he is attacking Jews as mainstream Americans who have the same vices as others, especially Druff himself, whose graft and political corruption have been self-acknowledged from the beginning.

Later in the afternoon, Druff has a series of conversations with acquaintances he happens to meet, all of whom reveal information or somehow indicate that Druff himself is involved with Su'ad's death. He begins to feel that he is to be the victim of some conspiracy and that this will be the day of his own death.

Druff returns late that afternoon to Margaret Glorio's apartment, where all the furniture and surroundings have been changed overnight. They have another sexual encounter, again enacted with humor paired with hopelessness. Significant to the plot, Glorio's apartment, so Druff now sees, has several Oriental rugs lying about. Druff learns that his newly acquired mistress had been friends with Su'ad and knows his own son Michael.

Death itself does not escape satire either. Druff leaves Glorio's apartment to go to the wake of Marvin Macklin, a city official who has just died. Druff is not quite sure who Macklin is, but he shows up anyway to give condolences to the widow and family. To his surprise, other persons who have been feeding his paranoia throughout the day are also present, including Dick and Doug (his two chauffeurs), the three Jews from the synagogue, and the mayor of the city. American death rites are satirized with both bitterness and comedy as Elkin describes the activities of the wake.

The novel's last episode occurs when Druff returns home to wife and son and unravels the events of the day so as to determine the truth about Su'ad's death. With funds from the Jewish bankers whom Druff had met at the synagogue, Su'ad had been smuggling rugs to make money to finance terrorist operations for Arabs in the Middle East. Druff's own son had been her driver when she delivered the smuggled rugs. The Jewish bankers had had her killed when she was unable to pay off loans to them. Druff's son had been driving Su'ad in Druff's car, and he had let her out onto the street moments before she was intentionally run over. Moreover, stolen goods are even yet in Druff's car trunk. Having learned all of this, Druff simply goes to bed to sleep.

The Characters

Bobbo Druff, the narrator and main character of the story, is truly the only subject of this complex novel that has so many other threads and aspects. He represents the modern American, and his life embodies, for Elkin at least, life in America in the 1990's. He is materialistic and corrupt; he is neurotic, psychotic, and schizophrenic (and, importantly, justly so); he is intellectual, witty, and smart; he is hopelessly middle-class; he finds relief in life by incessantly getting high on cocoa leaves and taking at least four different prescription medicines; he is both humor and pathos—a strangely correct mixture.

The MacGuffin is never seriously defined in the novel, yet Druff himself describes him several times in different ways. The MacGuffin is the alter ego, the devil within, the id and the ego, the conscience gone over to the other side. He is a kind of generally harmless "Sam" telling "Son of Sam" what to do. Recognizably, though, The MacGuffin is not localized to Druff's character but is present in everyone. The MacGuffin and Druff have conversations, but The MacGuffin never directly tells Druff what to do.

Rose Helen Druff is Bobbo's wife of thirty-six years. Her most significant role in the novel is during the flashback to her courtship and affair with Druff when they were college students in the 1950's. Thus we see two Rose Helens: the gifted young college student, extremely intelligent but slightly deformed by a childhood disease, and the housewife she has become some forty years later whose main concern is to get batteries for her hearing aid. Elkin's point is to create a character suitable to provoke guilt in Druff himself, given his new mistress. This does not occur. Druff covers up his actions and lies about them, but there is no feeling of guilt or remorse.

Michael Druff satirizes procreation. Thirty years old and still living at home, he is consistently described as a hopeless adolescent, one who will never grow up no matter what and will be perpetually dependent upon his parents even after their deaths.

Michael is the next generation of "Druffism": That is, he is Druff himself, who cannot make his way in the world because he lacks maturity and intelligence. Thus, Michael knowingly becomes the driver for a woman smuggling stolen goods, apparently oblivious to possible consequences.

Margaret Glorio's character permits Elkin to satirize yet another commonplace of American life: the liberated career woman who has made her way into the "man's world" by becoming "masculinized." She is Druff's equal in every way, perhaps more so. She is smarter than he and quicker with her tongue. Moreover, she is more successful in her profession and more secure in her personhood, identity, and activities. Nevertheless, she is given to all the vices of modern Americans; the fact that she controls and manipulates the system does not excuse the immorality of her behavior.

Dick and Doug, Druff's two chauffeurs, initially serve as Druff's confidants. As the story unfolds, however, it is clear that they are part of the political intrigue and satire. They are associates of those who know and suspect that somehow Druff is connected to Su'ad's murder—and they sell him out.

Su'ad al-Najaf, although a smuggler serving the Arab cause and terrorism in the Middle East, is yet another character who embodies the hopeless nature of politics in the 1990's. On the one hand, she publicly claims to favor the "final solution"; on the other, she does business with her enemies without reserve. Her existence, profession, and death reveal the complexities and hopeless entanglements of contemporary political problems, as well as of life itself.

Themes and Meanings

Stanley Elkin's main purpose is to reveal the hopeless and meaningless entanglements of life in the United States in the 1990's—for the thinking and thoughtless alike. There is no escape from problems, no solution to them, only an awareness of facts that add up to craziness (a matter blended with humor and bitterness) in a world in which borderline insanity is necessary for survival. Bobbo Druff is not, however, insane; he is victimized by society and politics and legalities—but yet entirely by self. Survival requires some control of the system in which one lives. For Druff and other characters, that system is corrupt, somehow defunct yet going on anyway.

Elkin reveals these themes through numerous metaphors. Most important of these is Druff's job as commissioner of streets: Life is a maze full of potholes, and nothing can be done about it. The maze will always be there, for all must travel the streets of life, which are replete with curves, stop signs, stoplights (which may or may not work), detours, traffic jams, and, most significant, inescapable potholes.

In coping with these streets of life, Druff creates, perhaps discovers, The MacGuffin—a metaphor for the lies that characters must tell themselves in order to excuse and justify their own behavior and to make some sense of the world around them. The MacGuffin, who exists only in Druff's mind, is nevertheless no less of a character.

Elkin's main point is not that life has no sense or values. Rather, the novel poses the question of what happens when one makes sense out of life. What happens then? Druff succeeds, with the help of his MacGuffin, in making sense of the events of Su'ad's murder, but he, like the reader, is left to discover if knowledge of actual events is enough to force order onto the world. Elkin is not clear about this point. On the one hand, numerous questions are left about all of the main events of the plot: What will happen to the stolen goods in Druff's trunk? Will Su'ad's murderers be exposed? Will Druff and Michael escape being implicated? On the other hand, Druff, having learned what he wants to know, simply goes peacefully to sleep, not so much because he is tired but because he has accomplished all that he can. He has learned answers to the questions of the day, but he has not found any solutions to them.

This novel is a modern-day night journey, a visit to the dark night of the soul. Perhaps there is no soul here other than that of The MacGuffin; Elkin certainly suggests as much, if not by explication then by derivation. Druff journeys into self in his inner monologues, in his internal dialogues with The MacGuffin, in his taking of a mistress, and, finally, in his pursuit of knowledge of the facts of Su'ad's murder. All of these are carried out for selfish and corrupt reasons. In the end, Elkin's use of psychological realism in such a way as to make the facts of Druff's character and actions match those of the nonpsychological world is not so much pointless as unexplained. All people are Druffs who harbor MacGuffins within.

Critical Context

The MacGuffin succeeds in making significant and correct statements about modern politics. The global situation is so involved that even such traditional enemies as the Arabs and Jews cannot disentangle themselves from the complexity of the various problems. They depend upon one another to have someone to hate, to have an enemy; just as certainly and more important, however, they depend upon one another to fund and sustain their own problems and hatreds.

Local politics, as exemplified by Druff, the mayor, other commissioners, and even the two chauffeurs, parallels the mess and havoc of larger problems. No one can be trusted in a world were friends serve the causes of enemies and, conversely, enemies serve the causes of friends—all knowingly, but never openly.

It is internal politics with which Elkin is doubtless most concerned. This is represented in Druff's family life with both his wife and son, and with his relationship with himself and The MacGuffin. The context of family politics finally makes it impossible for Druff to make sense out of the entanglements around him, even when he has full knowledge of all the facts. In *The MacGuffin*, Elkin's goal is to make a statement not merely about problems in the Middle East (he is actually little concerned about relations between Jews and Arabs) but rather about problems in self-definition facing all readers.

Bibliography

Edwards, Thomas R. "*The MacGuffin*." *The New Republic* 204 (May 20, 1991): 44-47. One of the best reviews available. Edwards finds Elkin's main character Druff to be a "cultural dinosaur" who is nevertheless successful as a comedian. The critic sees in the novel Elkin's attempt to define what it is to be an American in the 1990's.

Elkin, Stanley. Interview by Miriam Berkley. *Publishers Weekly* 227 (March 29, 1985): 74-75. This recorded interview, though brief, serves well to reveal Elkin's warped, dry humor. Although the review appeared some six years before *The MacGuffin*, the author's outlook on life is made clear, and his statements have bearing on the later novel.

Emerson, Ken. "The Indecorous, Rabelaisian, Convoluted Righteousness of Stanley Elkin." *The New York Times Magazine*, March 3, 1991, 40-43. Emerson playfully takes Elkin to task for the humor, irony, satire, and distancing between self and audience in Elkin's work. The critic appreciates these qualities of the writer while questioning the validity of some of Elkin's themes.

Koenig, Rhoda. "*The MacGuffin*." *New York* 24, (February 25, 1991): 113-114. This review, though brief, is particularly critical and revealing of the novel's main character. Koenig also draws attention to instances of the humor in the novel.

Moore, Lorrie. "*The MacGuffin*." *The New York Times Book Review*, March 10, 1991, 5. This early review of the novel draws attention to its main qualities. Lauds the work for its ability to provide humor about the contemporary American scene.

Carl Singleton

MACHO!

Author: Victor Villaseñor (1940-   )
Type of plot: Bildungsroman
Time of plot: The late 1960's
Locale: Mexico and California
First published: 1973

> *Principal characters:*
> ROBERTO GARCIA, the eldest son of poor Tarascan (native Mexican) farmers, who leaves his village for work in the United States
> JUAN AGUILAR, the leader of the village *norteños*, men who seasonally work in the United States
> PEDRO, a *norteño* and sworn enemy of Roberto
> ESPERANZA, Roberto's progressive and independent-minded sister
> DON CARLOS VILLANUEVA, Roberto's employer, a successful Mexican farmer

The Novel

This fictional account of approximately a year in the life of a young man dramatizes the real plight of the migrant Mexican farmworker attempting to enter and work in the United States. *Macho!* is divided into three major parts, each labeled as a book and further subdivided into chapters. Books 1 and 3 are short, with the action set in the rural Mexican village of the principal characters; book 2 chronicles the odyssey of the protagonist, Roberto Garcia, into the violent underworld of the illegal migrant farmworker. Although the omniscient third-person narrator occasionally reveals thoughts of other characters, the narrative perspective is almost entirely Roberto's.

In addition to the main fictional narrative, each chapter begins with a brief quasi-historical preface, designed to inform and to persuade the reader. The first and longest of these prefaces describes the dramatic 1943 appearance of the volcano Paricutin one hundred miles from Roberto's village and the volcano's far-reaching effects. Through these prefaces, Villaseñor suggests that the natural threat of Paricutin, a blessing in disguise for Roberto's community, has been replaced by the less visible, more insidious threat of airborne industrial pollution. The threat of pollution lingers before being dismissed summarily, like dirt in the wind, at the story's end. Most of the novel's remaining prefaces indict American agribusiness interests for exploiting cheap Mexican migrant farm labor and chronicle César Chávez's challenge to the status quo during the tumultuous 1960's.

The novel itself begins well into Roberto's seventeenth year, during the planting season of his native Mexican village. Roberto's father has over the past year begun drinking heavily, leaving Roberto, as the eldest child, to support his mother and seven younger siblings. Although Roberto is humiliated by his father's weakness, he can do nothing to change it; he must simply work hard and well, for his culture does not allow him to complain—or even to think about complaining. It would not be respectful or manly. It would not be *macho*.

Roberto's strength of character is revealed immediately, not only through his uncomplaining silence in response to his father's behavior but also by his interaction with the nine older men he works with and oversees. For example, on the morning the story begins, Roberto, on his way to the fields, falls into an irrigation channel with his horse and nearly drowns. Arriving for work but a few minutes late, dripping wet, he denies, when taunted by one of the other men, that anything untoward had happened. A man's personal condition should be of no concern to another. Yet his responses to the older man must tread carefully between nonservile amicability and nonprovocative bravado. Too much servility would cost him his job (not to mention his self-respect); too much arrogance would cost him his life.

The need for balance between servility and arrogance, dependence and independence, is emphasized again and again throughout the novel—along with the impossibility of maintaining perfect balance in a world of violent passion and conflict. Moving Roberto and the other *norteños* into an American setting adds further conflict, in the form of different cultural expectations, while simultaneously placing them in the middle of the ongoing farm-labor conflict.

In addition to the obvious intercultural conflicts of the novel are the conflicts between the traditional local farmers and the village *norteños*, who at great risk become temporarily wealthy (by local standards) by leaving the community and journeying north to work on U.S. farms. Although the *norteños'* dissolute and violent lifestyle does not appeal to Roberto, a persuasive offer from the *norteño* leader, Juan Aguilar, to travel north in the coming work season and thus provide for Roberto's family draws Roberto reluctantly away from his home and traditional way of life.

As book 2 begins, the novel explodes into violence with an episode that forces Roberto and the *norteños* to leave abruptly for the United States. Among the *norteños* is Pedro, Juan's companion of the past ten years. Pedro, who had already earned Roberto's enmity for publicly humiliating his father, continually goads Roberto. Although Juan keeps peace between the two for some time, Pedro and Roberto eventually clash openly and decisively. Final resolution of their conflict, however, must wait until the setting returns, in book 3, to the village in Michoacán.

The Characters

Roberto personifies what it means to be *macho*, without bluster or crude language (though the language of others is occasionally blunt). The desperate situations into which he is drawn neither oversimplify nor glamorize that ideal: a fight with a thief; the clash with Pedro; a barroom rescue; and finally, the novel's climactic confrontation. Although Roberto outwardly displays the Mexican cultural ideal of fierce arrogance, he also uses his intellect to question tradition and to preserve both life and honor.

Finally, it becomes clear that the central struggle in *Macho!* is not simply one of peace versus violence but of the struggle to reconcile tradition with change. Roberto succeeds not merely because he can endure the old ways of violence, but because he is willing to challenge his cultural traditions with the tools of change (reason), to create new roles that are both more honorable and more productive than death by violence.

Juan Aguilar, prematurely aged by his life as a *norteño*, at first impresses the reader with his knowledge of the road to fortune beyond the Mexican border. As the novel unfolds, however, Juan shows, not only by his speech and actions but also by comparison with more sophisticated migrant workers, that his knowledge of American culture and customs is as limited as his possibilities in and perhaps for life.

Juan's role as Roberto's protector is also flawed, for that relationship is based almost exclusively on Roberto's potential to contribute to Juan's continued success. Throughout the novel, Juan's role alternates between that of parasite and protector: His mercenary impulses conflict with his growing image of Roberto as the son he never had. Until the very end of the novel, suspense results from the uncertainty over which impulse will win out.

Pedro, the hardened *norteño* companion of Juan who is Roberto's sworn enemy, brings an image of pure violence to the novel. Pedro is not even identified by last name, making it easier for him to remain a faceless personification of evil. Despite his decisive defeat at Roberto's hands, Pedro's continued behind-the-scenes presence illustrates the pervasive and persistent nature of human violence and, in the end, ultimately refutes the axiom of live and let live.

Esperanza, who has a North American counterpart in the less well-developed character of Gloria Sanchez, represents progress through education and reason. Education and reason, long the principal tools of progress and the primary means by which tradition may be successfully challenged, also represent hope. (Esperanza's name, fittingly, means "hope"). Without hope there can be no progress toward a better world and society.

Don Carlos Villanueva, aged local landowner and farmer, has successfully combined traditional principles with progressive practices. He alone had the insight to see that the changes brought by the volcano could be beneficial. Although his bearing and presence are regal, his advanced age will soon force him into oblivion. Unless others such as Roberto are willing to continue in his stead, the good that the old generation offers the new may also be lost.

Themes and Meanings

Paralleling the narrative plot is the novel's larger political conflict, one which directly affected—and still affects—all United States farmworkers, legal or otherwise. The battle had presumably been resolved in 1963, when legal importation of braceros (migrant farmworkers) from Mexico into the United States was stopped, largely because of the efforts of farm-labor organizers such as César Chávez. Yet the end of the bracero program had what should have been predictable results: an increase in the demand for cheaper Mexican workers by American agribusinesses and an increase in the incentive for Mexicans to enter the United States illegally. Men south of the border grew so desperate for work in the United States that they fell easy prey to those who promised to get them across in any way possible—in many cases, to be deported soon anyway.

As political lines were being nobly drawn, the issues for the starving Mexican workers remained so basic that political ideologies were irrelevant. One must work to eat. Who among the poor Mexcians ever heard of refusing to work in order to improve their working conditions? If offered a fair wage, why not take it and perform uncomplainingly? For to the Mexican worker, American wages, no matter how low, were always better than Mexican wages. Is it Roberto's fault that he was born a poor Mexican farmer? Can it be expected that he should see an American problem through American eyes? He is by circumstances concerned, above all else, with providing food for his family. Abstract ideological concerns are for him a luxury beyond comprehension. The reader accepts Roberto's limited understanding but also sees the larger context as a moral dilemma of which Roberto is unaware: that better pay and working conditions for American workers, however much needed, may penalize humans born elsewhere (in this case, Mexico).

Villanseñor's resolution of Roberto's plight may not completely satisfy those who want an American success story or those who like perfect resolutions to difficult problems. Yet the ending does provide the reader with a sense that both the protagonist and the reader have learned and matured, that the power and the immediacy of life itself, though it may at times depend on political expediency, ultimately transcends political boundaries.

For Roberto, whose physical journey ends with a cyclical return to his origins, the passage to manhood is complete. He has survived the initiation rites of his male society, rites shared by the male warrior/worker (here one and the same) of many, perhaps all cultures: the Japanese samurai code of *bushido*, the Finnish tacit and unyielding *sisu*, the Roman warrior's stoicism, and the American marine's code of death before dishonor. Arguably, none of those masculine traditions may be fully appreciated or fully defined except by those who have lived them. Yet Victor Villaseñor offers the reader a glimpse of understanding through the eyes of Roberto Garcia.

Critical Context

Macho!, published under the name Edmund Victor Villaseñor, was the author's first novel. Part of a larger outpouring in the 1960's and 1970's of Latin American literature, it was critically acclaimed when it appeared in 1973.

Each chapter of *Macho!* begins with a prefatory sociopolitical comment on the times immediately preceding (and including) the turbulent American milieu of the late 1960's. Villaseñor's intent is to heighten the reader's awareness of the historical context within which the novel's fictional characters come to life. The novel's main character, serious and intelligent but naïve, endures the type of coming-of-age conflicts that young men in many societies have traditionally encountered. The resulting story dramatizes the struggles of the migrant Mexican farmworker in much the same way that John Steinbeck dramatized the plight of the displaced Okies in *The Grapes of Wrath* (1939).

Villaseñor's later works also rely heavily on dramatization of history. In 1977, Villaseñor's account of the trial of the convicted California serial murderer Juan Corona stirred even more controversy. At issue was the concern that Villaseñor's interpretation of historical events was more creative than current authorial conventions allowed.

Having captured the public's attention, Villaseñor's dramatic talents were given full rein in his 1981 television screenplay *The Ballad of Gregorio Cortez*, which won first place in the National Endowment for the Humanities television drama category that year. The film was subsequently released to theaters and on videocassette. More recently, Villaseñor's 1991 *Rain of Gold*, the story of his family's immigration from Mexico to California, is also historical, yet charged with the author's fictionalized personal drama.

Although Victor Villaseñor has established himself as an important and principled chronicler of the Mexican American experience, he has received relatively little critical notice to date. Part of the reason may be that he writes in English about people whose first language is Spanish. Yet that argument may be put to rest by his readers, who immediately recognize the universal appeal of his *Macho!* hero, a hero who challenges the limited stereotypical image of the Latino male. That appeal lifts Villaseñor's work beyond narrow regional or linguistic boundaries, to a genuinely international level of human understanding.

Bibliography

Barbato, Joseph. "Latino Writers in the American Market." *Publishers Weekly* 238 (February 1, 1991): 17-21. Discusses the obstacles facing Chicano authors and the troubled publishing of Villaseñor's *Rain of Gold*. Also includes an interview with Villaseñor, who gives his side of the publishing debate.

Guilbault, Rose Del Castillo. "Americanization Is Tough on 'Macho.' " In *American Voices: Multicultural Literacy and Critical Thinking*, edited by Dolores LaGuardia and Hans P. Guth. Mountain View, Calif.: Mayfield, 1992. Guilbault provides a sociolinguistic framework and a more complete understanding of the original Hispanic meaning of *macho*. (This book also contains an interview with Victor Villaseñor originally printed in the *San Jose News*.)

Hartman, Steven Lee. "On the History of Spanish *macho*." *Hispanic Linguistics* 1, no. 1 (1984): 97-114. Deals with one of the most misunderstood loan words in contemporary American society. The transmogrification of *macho* from positive to negative ideal is chronicled, with reasons for the change outlined.

Rocard, Marcienne. *The Children of the Sun: Mexican-Americans in the Literature of the United States*. Translated by Edward G. Brown, Jr. Tucson: The University of Arizona Press, 1989. A general literary history that discusses works by Anglo and Mexican American writers. The descriptions of stock type characters are helpful in understanding Villaseñor's work. A good introduction to the subject.

Sandoval, Ralph, and Alleen P. Nilsen. "The Mexican-American Experience." *English Journal* 63 (January, 1974): 61. Sandoval suggests that while verisimilitude may be strained in parts of this first book by Villaseñor, the drama portrays empathetic characters who may have real-life counterparts. Moreover, the novel is compelling and powerful, told in language the reader will recognize as realistic and direct. (Some language is very direct.)

William Matta

MACHO CAMACHO'S BEAT

Author: Luis Rafael Sánchez (1936-   )
Type of plot: Social satire
Time of plot: The early 1970's
Locale: San Juan, Puerto Rico
First published: La guaracha del Macho Camacho, 1976 (English translation, 1980)

> *Principal characters:*
> THE HEATHEN CHINKY (THE MOTHER), a lower-class mulatto prostitute
> SENATOR VINCENTE REINOSA (THE OLD MAN), a wealthy, corrupt, and lascivious government official
> GRACIELA ALCÁNTARA Y LÓPEZ DE MONTEFRÍO, the aristocratic, neurotic, and sexually frigid wife of Reinosa
> BENNY, the pampered son of Reinosa and Graciela
> DOÑA CHON, a representative of traditional values
> THE KID, an encephalitic, retarded child

The Novel

Macho Camacho's Beat is a fictional portrait of life in San Juan, Puerto Rico, at a time when the country is inundated with the sound of Macho Camacho's *guaracha*, or dance tune, "Life Is a Phenomenal Thing." Framed by a notice that reveals the subject of the novel and an appendix that provides the reader with the entire text of the *guaracha*, *Macho Camacho's Beat* is a montage of fragmented narrative sections interrupted by a series of radio announcements that track the meteoric rise in popularity of the rhythmical and irrepressible Afro-Antillean tune.

The entire plot of *Macho Camacho's Beat* occurs within the few minutes before, at, and just after five o'clock on a steamy Wednesday afternoon. As an immense traffic jam paralyzes San Juan, the novel's characters are depicted in the act of waiting. With the accumulative fragments of sounds, images, thoughts, and experience, the reader is able to piece together a composite picture of Puerto Rican culture.

The Heathen Chinky (whose name is never mentioned) is introduced through the device of an omniscient third-person narrator whose relation with each of the characters in the novel is so intimate as to allow the narration to pass fluidly between the third- and first-person voices. As she awaits the arrival of her lover, the Old Man (Senator Vincente Reinosa), the Heathen Chinky indulges in sexual fantasies of her virile triplet cousins, Hughie, Louie, and Dewey and anesthetizes her body with a sea of alcohol and her mind with the incessant, insistent, and sensual salsa beat of Macho Camacho's *guaracha*.

Senator Vincente Reinosa swelters in his Mercedes-Benz, stuck in the enormous traffic tie-up, impatient to meet his sultry and accommodating dark-skinned mistress (the Heathen Chinky), who waits for him every Monday, Wednesday, and Friday afternoon in a studio apartment rented specifically for convenient fornication. The news of a bombing at the university in San Juan interrupts the senator's lustful fantasies and political self-aggrandizements only long enough for him to worry whether he will lose votes in the next election. As the occupants of the hundreds of immobilized automobiles that surround him dance in the street with a frenzied abandon brought on by the *guaracha*'s irresistible beat, the senator's thoughts quickly return to the schoolgirl he has been ogling, and he wonders if he has time to make her his next conquest.

The senator's aristocratic wife, Graciela Alcántara y López de Montefrío, waits for her appointment with her trendy psychiatrist, Dr. Severo Severino. In her elegant compact mirror, Graciela scrutinizes her face to detect signs of aging and dwells on the absolute abhorrence she has of sexual relations with her husband. Graciela flips through the pages of *Time* magazine, deliberately ignoring the ugly reality of the war in Vietnam and concentrating instead on photographs of Elizabeth Taylor, Richard Burton, and Jacqueline Kennedy Onassis. Finally driven to distraction by the vulgar receptionist who constantly plays the vulgar *guaracha* on her transistor radio, Graciela, in an uncontrollable fit of temper, rails against the devastating reality that she can never be truly like her ideal, Jackie O.

The Mother, by a number of similarities—the desire to be Iris Chacón, the affair with the Old Man—is identified as being one and the same person as the Heathen Chinky. In this guise, she is shown in her own home, apparently moments before leaving to keep her appointment with the Old Man. Because the Mother cannot bring her encephalitic three-year-old son, the Kid, with her, she leaves him alone to "sunbathe" on the steps of a basilica in a nearby park—a treatment that the Old Man himself has prescribed. The Mother's neighbor, Doña Chon, agrees to pick the Kid up after the Mother offers to share the money she receives from the Old Man. Before Doña Chon arrives at the park, however, the Kid, cruelly abused by the neighborhood children, runs away from them into the street. Doña Chon arrives just in time to see the Kid hit by a speeding car.

Benny, spoiled son of the Reinosas, is also stuck in the five o'clock traffic. He sits in his beloved Ferrari, frustrated and furious at being compelled to keep his foot on the brake and restrain the power of his high-speed sports car, the object of his sexual fantasies. Benny's thoughts return obsessively to ways in which he can convince his father that what Puerto Rico's youth really needs are cars and fast tracks on which to race them. When Benny finally breaks free of the traffic, he roars down a narrow side street. The threads of the plot are tied together as Benny, privileged son of the wealthy and aristocratic Reinosas, hits and kills the deformed and retarded son of his father's poverty-stricken, lower-class mulatto mistress.

The Characters

The characters in *Macho Camacho's Beat* are grotesques, allegorical rather than fully rounded, and are defined primarily by their obsessions and a desire to be what they are not.

The Heathen Chinky/The Mother, representative of the masses as her generic labels suggest, is obsessed with sex and her desire to be television's sex symbol, Iris Chacón. Barraged on all sides by mass-media hype, her self-perception is so distorted that it seems quite reasonable to prostitute herself for the price of a new linoleum floor. She believes herself to be a good mother because she fondles the Kid and sings to him, just as she has seen mothers do in Mexican films. To maintain her delusions of happiness, the Heathen Chinky eagerly subscribes to the pop philosophy of Macho Camacho's *guaracha*, which insists, in spite of all evidence to the contrary, that "Life Is a Phenomenal Thing."

Senator Vincente Reinosa is obsessed with sexual fantasies involving black and mulatto women and fancies himself a modern-day Don Juan. He sexually exploits women whom he would never acknowledge in public and embezzles public funds to pay the cost of keeping them. He uses his political clout to keep his budding terrorist son out of jail (and out of the headlines), and he bilks the government for the price of a brand-new Ferrari to appease the boy. Reinosa wants Puerto Rico to become a part of the United States. He represents the desire of the wealthy to maintain the status quo by embracing American consumerism and eschewing the nationalist movement for an independent Puerto Rican nation.

Graciela is obsessed with the desire to be Jacqueline Kennedy Onassis. As her last name (Montefrío, which means "cold mount") suggests, she is sexually frigid and completely devoid of warmth and humor. She constantly tries to re-create herself in the image of an ideal promoted in trendy European and American magazines. Anything native to Puerto Rico, herself included, is repulsive to her. Graciela is the quintessential class snob and the model of Roman Catholic sexual repression.

Benny is obsessed with lust for his Ferrari. The product of his environment, Benny is spoiled, racist, lazy, fat, and soft. Still a teenager, he has already committed arson and probably murder. When Benny runs the Kid down with his Ferrari, the outlook for the future of Puerto Rico is clear: The hypocritical and materialistic upper class will continue to exploit and crush the nation's poor without remorse.

Doña Chon, seemingly the last bastion of kindness in all of San Juan, is representative of cultural tradition: She cooks Creole food, and she keeps her house full of images of Jesus Christ and the Roman Catholic saints. She is the only adult in the novel who is not obsessed with sex, and she seems impervious to Macho Camacho's *guaracha*. Even Doña Chon cannot avoid corruption completely, however; she accepts money earned by the prostitution of her neighbor in return for picking up the Kid. Delayed by her own affairs, Doña Chon arrives at the park a moment too late to save him. What little goodness exists in Puerto Rican society, it seems, is ultimately ineffectual.

The Kid, like his mother, is a generic representative of the masses. Apparently born quite normal, the child has been deformed by his environment. Helpless, he is tortured mercilessly by healthy neighborhood children, who all the while sing, "Life Is a Phenomenal Thing." When this child of Puerto Rico is forced to confront his own image in a fractured looking-glass, he flees from his monstrous self to find his own destruction.

Themes and Meanings

Macho Camacho's Beat is a razor-sharp, deep-cutting indictment of Puerto Rican culture. Sánchez's prose is rich with the colorful and often obscene language of the streets, loaded with the language of consumerism, and abundant in references to the lifestyles of the rich and famous, fictional and otherwise. The fragmented, baroque surface of Sánchez's highly allusive prose is a brilliant reflection of the kaleidoscopic confusion caused by the indiscriminate acceptance of the material values espoused by a profit-oriented consumerist society. Language defines thought, and in this novel, language is the product of a largely American-controlled mass media. The resulting inability to communicate on an intimate, personal level creates in the reader a sense of the moral and spiritual poverty of Sánchez's characters.

Macho Camacho's Beat clearly calls for a radical reformation of Puerto Rican society and of the ways in which individuals perceive themselves. The political push to Americanize Puerto Rico and the corruption of government officials is exemplified in the character of Reinosa. The moral decay of the population is sardonically expressed in the Mother's prostitution and Benny's love affair with his Ferrari, which supersedes his affection for any human being. Even the personal physical reality of the people is being transformed, Americanized, foreignized. This is clearly expressed in Graciela's obsession with makeup, hair, and fashion, in her social life, and in her absurd proposed design for typical Puerto Rican dress: a tailored suit in spotted calfskin.

The key metaphor of the monstrous traffic jam symbolizes the stagnation of a Puerto Rican society that constantly denies its own seedy reality as it becomes obsessed with the fleeting distractions offered by a sensationalist media and subscribes to the seductive but clearly false philosophy of the seductive *guaracha*. No element of Puerto Rican society is immune from Sánchez's irreverent and biting sense of humor. The sins of elitism, racial discrimination, and denial of self are laid bare before the grotesque feet and obtuse minds of the sinners. Just as the Kid is forced to confront his ugly and deformed reality reflected in the surface of a fragmented mirror, Sánchez compels his fellow Puerto Ricans to confront themselves in the fragmented and glittering surface of *Macho Camacho's Beat*.

Critical Context

Luis Rafael Sánchez's first full-length novel, *Macho Camacho's Beat* was written after Sánchez had already been acclaimed as an important Puerto Rican playwright. A critic of literature and the arts, Sánchez has published many articles in newspapers and magazines and has also published a collection of short stories under the title *En cuerpo de camisa* (1966; in casual dress).

Macho Camacho's Beat was an immediate best-seller. Sánchez's use of language and symbol, his irreverent sense of humor, his incisive social criticism, and his ability to explore a culture that is uniquely Puerto Rican has led some critics to consider *Macho Camacho's Beat* the single most important Puerto Rican novel of the twentieth century. In his second novel, *La importancia de llamarse Daniel Santos* (1989; the importance of being named Daniel Santos), Sánchez continued to explore mass culture and society. This second novel goes beyond Puerto Rico to include Latino communities in the United States, Central America, and South America as well as the Antilles, a much broader scope than that of the distinctly Puerto Rican *Macho Camacho's Beat*.

Bibliography

Agüra, Helen Calaf. "Luis Rafael Sánchez Speaks About *Macho Camacho's Beat*." Translated by Jo Anne Englebert. *Review* 28 (January-April, 1981): 39-41. An interview with the author in which Sánchez speaks about the critical reception of his work and his own intentions in writing the novel. Sánchez gives insight into his use of street language and his attempt to "portray the spiritual decomposition of Puerto Rico." He also discusses his novel as the expression of "a need to transform colonial reality in all spheres—political, moral, even in the realm of the physical."

Cruz, Arnaldo. "Repetition and the Language of the Mass Media in Luis Rafael Sánchez's *La guaracha del Macho Camacho*." *Latin American Literary Review* 13 (July-December, 1985): 35-48. This well-written and interesting article explores the ways in which the techniques of repetition and language act as distancing techniques, enabling the reader to approach the work with a critical eye. Interesting in its assessment of Sánchez's use of language as social analysis. Cruz has some interesting insights into the aesthetic effects of Sánchez's prose.

Guinness, Gerald. "Is *Macho Camacho's Beat* a Good Translation of *La guaracha del Macho Camacho*?" In *Images and Identities: The Puerto Rican in Two World Contexts*, edited by Asela Rodriquez de Laguna. New Brunswick: Transaction Books, 1987. Explores the techniques of Gregory Rabassa's translation of the novel. An interesting assessment of the loss of certain aesthetic values in a work so distinctly defined by language. Guinness offers some insightful alternatives to Rabassa's translation.

Schlau, Stacey. "Mass Media Images of the *Puertorriqueña* in *La guaracha del Macho Camacho*." In *Literature and Popular Culture in the Hispanic World: A Symposium*, edited by Rose S. Minc. Gaithersburg, Md.: Hispamerica, 1981. Explores the effects of mass-media advertising, focusing on the women in the novel. The Heathen Chinky and Graciela are looked at in terms of how their self-esteem and self-perception are defined by commercial advertisement and consumerism.

Waldman, Gloria F. "*La guaracha del Macho Camacho* as Popular Culture." In *Literature and Popular Culture in the Hispanic World: A Symposium*, edited by Rose S. Minc. Gaithersburg, Md.: Hispamerica, 1981. Waldman writes about the specifics of Puerto Rican popular culture and explores the *guaracha* as the "ultimate equalizer." An interesting, although brief, introduction to the nonfictional elements in Sánchez's fictional world.

Diane Almeida

MAMA DAY

Author: Gloria Naylor (1950-   )
Type of plot: Melodrama
Time of plot: The 1980's
Locale: Willow Springs, a fictitious island off the coast of South Carolina and Georgia, and New York City
First published: 1988

> *Principal characters:*
> OPHELIA (COCOA) DAY, a young woman who has left her family and heritage on Willow Springs to live in New York City
> GEORGE JOHNSON, an African American man Cocoa meets in New York
> MIRANDA (MAMA) DAY, Cocoa's great-aunt, who has powers of prophecy
> ABIGAIL DAY, Cocoa's grandmother
> RUBY, a mysterious woman with supernatural powers
> JUNIOR LEE, Ruby's shiftless husband

The Novel

Mama Day, Gloria Naylor's third novel, tells the story of Ophelia (Cocoa) Day and George Johnson, who later becomes her husband, and her initiation into the Day family. The novel is divided into three parts and opens with a brief prologue in which an anonymous, omniscient narrator sets the date as August, 1999; the rest of the novel is therefore a series of flashbacks. The prologue also tells the genealogy of the Days, the most important family of Willow Springs, an isolated island; although claimed by both South Carolina and Georgia, it is ignored and allowed to set its own laws and be independent of any outside control. Originally a slave plantation, the island was owned by Bascombe Wade, who in 1819 purchased a slave named Sapphira. He subsequently fell in love with her and took her for his wife. Four years later, after persuading him to free his slaves and deed the island to them, she killed him. That year—1823—marks the beginning of time on Willow Springs, and all local history is dated from it.

Sapphira had a reputation as a conjure woman, a woman who could work spells and control nature. By persons unknown, she bore seven sons; the youngest, Jonah, who later took the surname "Day," had seven sons as well, including a youngest named John-Paul. An African legend, continued in the South, holds that the eldest daughter of the seventh son of a seventh son would be unusually blessed with "conjure" powers, and this held true as the first of John-Paul's daughters, Miranda (born in 1895), became the matriarch of Willow Springs. Because she has the gift of prophecy and the ability to work with nature to heal the sick or defeat evil, she is called "Mama Day" by the islanders. The other two daughters of John-Paul were Abigail (born in 1897) and Peace. While Mama Day never married, Abigail did and subsequently bore three girls. The middle daughter, Grace, had one daughter, Ophelia (born in 1953), who is nicknamed "Cocoa." After her mother's death, Mama Day and Abigail reared Cocoa.

Following this prologue, both sections of *Mama Day* have three voices: Cocoa and George, who conduct a dialogue about their relationship, and the omniscient narrator, who focuses on Mama Day and Abigail. Later in the novel, it is revealed that George has died and that the conversation between himself and Cocoa is spiritual, not physical. The initial section tells that Cocoa left Willow Springs in 1974 to go to New York. In the summer of 1980, however, she meets George, a design engineer who spent his childhood in an orphanage and never had a family. The contrast between these two people cannot be greater; Cocoa possesses a link with her African heritage through her family, while George seems to have no connections left with Africa because he lacks a family. The two have a stormy relationship, but there is a magnetism between them that suggests they cannot live without each other. They marry six months after they begin dating, and four years later, in 1985, they go to Willow Springs so that George can meet Mama Day and Abigail. Their crossing of the bridge from the mainland to the island ends the first section of *Mama Day*.

While Cocoa and George are on the island, a hurricane strikes, destroying the bridge and all telephone lines. Furthermore, because Cocoa has been falsely accused of trying to seduce Junior Lee, his wife Ruby—an obese woman who has supernatural powers—poisons Cocoa and places a spell on her. Cocoa ultimately survives, but in saving her through Mama Day's magic, George dies. The exchange of her husband's life for her own satisfies the curse on Cocoa. She eventually leaves Willow Springs for Charleston, South Carolina, and remarries, but she now understands the truth about her family. Cocoa sees that the line of the Days has culminated in her. Spiritually, she is both Sapphira and herself; she is her own mother as she is also Mama Day. The novel ends with her realization of her family's heritage, which she is determined to pass on to her youngest son.

The Characters

Ophelia (Cocoa) Day, the protagonist of the novel, is the most interesting character in the book. She grows from an immature young woman into a person with exceptional personal insight. By the end of the story, she has learned not only about human nature but also about her family and herself. Her role in the novel suggests that of an "everywoman," a character intended to stand as a microcosm for the female African American experience. Although Naylor has argued that her fiction is not didactic, it is hard not to see a moral in the lesson that Cocoa learns.

George Johnson, the most important male figure in the novel, is a well-developed character. Readers are able to see all facets of him, his flaws as well as his virtues. It is easy, however, to sympathize with him throughout the novel, because a reader learns about Willow Springs and the Day family just as he does.

Miranda (Mama) Day, who made a cameo appearance in Naylor's second novel, *Linden Hills* (1985), is a marvelous creation. She can be profane and funny as she talks about sex, or sad and introspective as she reflects on her family's many tragedies. With Mama Day, Naylor has created a character who has a life outside the novel. She comes alive and remains with readers long after the book's covers have been shut.

Ruby, the only truly evil person in the novel, is little more than a stereotype of an African American witch. She acts in predictable ways, and her character is not developed because it does not need to be.

Themes and Meanings

The primary theme of *Mama Day* is the education of Cocoa, the woman whose destiny it is to continue the line of Days. Although she leaves Willow Springs after George's death and later remarries, in a sense she will become "Mama Day" after her great-aunt's death. In other words, Cocoa has now gained the responsibility of self-knowledge, through which she is initiated into the matriarchy of the family. Symbolizing this responsibility is an intricate wedding quilt that Mama Day makes for Cocoa. The quilt is made from fragments of cloth from all of the female Days, from Sapphira through Cocoa herself, and is intended to give her a tangible object from which to draw strength. The pages explaining the making of the quilt, as well as the pages showing Cocoa's reaction to it, are central to the novel.

Secondary to Cocoa's education, but still important, is the education of George. Early in the novel, he is seen as a product of New York, which means he has little faith in anything other than himself. George does not respect and honor his heritage as an African American man; in short, he lacks a soul. Mama Day tries to educate him into the ways of his ancestors, but he lacks faith in her and in her magic, leading to his death. Although he saves Cocoa, he cannot save himself.

It is possible, according to some critics, to see allusions to William Shakespeare in *Mama Day* as another theme. One critic finds many asides to *Hamlet* (1600-1601), especially in the character of Cocoa, whose given name is "Ophelia," also the name of the young woman in Shakespeare's play. Another critic finds the novel more reminiscent of *The Tempest* (1611), since Willow Springs is an isolated, magical place "ruled" by a person who can control the elements. It is worth noting that Mama Day's given name is Miranda, which is also the name of the daughter of the sorcerer of *The Tempest*. Clearly, though, Naylor did not intend for these Shakespearean threads in the novel to take precedence over her primary theme. Instead, they merely serve as a counterpoint to the theme of Cocoa's initiation into the matriarchy.

Critical Context

Gloria Naylor's first novel, *The Women of Brewster Place* (1982), caused an immediate sensation upon its publication. Only thirty-two, she was hailed by critics as one of the most important young voices in American literature. The book, a collection of connected stories centered on one inner-city neighborhood, went on to win the American Book Award for First Novel and was adapted into a popular television film. Her next novel, also reviewed favorably, was *Linden Hills* (1985), which is set in a middle-class black neighborhood in which the surface calm fails to reflect the tensions underneath. A character in the story, Willa Prescott Nedeed, is the cousin of Cocoa Day, providing a link with *Mama Day*, Naylor's third novel, which was also praised by critics. Her fourth novel, *Bailey's Cafe* (1992), tells the stories of a group of characters, who frequent a restaurant owned by a man named Bailey; the cafe also receives passing mention in *Mama Day*.

Each of these novels features well-developed characters. Naylor has an unusually precise knack for fleshing out a character in a few carefully chosen words, and her characters breathe and live. Naylor attributes this quality to the fact that she allows her characters the freedom to develop their own lives after she first creates them. Rather than dictate the plot, she records what happens when the characters encounter one another. For her, characters such as Mama Day and Cocoa are as real as nonfictional people.

Bibliography
Andrews, Larry R. "Black Sisterhood in Gloria Naylor's Novels." *College Language Association Journal* 33 (September, 1989): 1-25. Andrews argues that *Mama Day*, like Naylor's two earlier novels, shows how crucial the sense of community is among black women. By passing this sense of community down through generations, black women can help to give themselves strength in a world so often dominated by men. This tradition, however, is threatened by the modern world, in which women forget their heritage and consequently lose a bridge with the past and a link with the future.
Boyd, Nellie "Dominion and Proprietorship in Gloria Naylor's *Mama Day* and *Linden Hills*." *MAWA Review* 5 (December, 1990): 56-58. Boyd contrasts Naylor's second and third novels to find that they have different approaches toward a character who leads a community. In *Mama Day*, Boyd finds that Mama Day—the spiritual leader of Willow Springs—acts as a sort of benevolent dictator. She compares her to William Shakespeare's Prospero in *The Tempest* in the sense that she serves as the "island's conscience."
Mukherjee, Bharati. "There are Four Sides to Everything." *The New York Times Book Review*, February 21, 1988, 7. This insightful review of *Mama Day* states that the title character is the most interesting and most authentic character in the novel. On the other hand, Mukherjee finds the romance between Cocoa and George to be trite because neither character comes to life. Included with the article is a short interview with Naylor in which she discusses how she relates to her characters.
Naylor, Gloria, and Toni Morrison. "A Conversation." *The Southern Review* 21 (Summer, 1985): 567-593. Although at times this "conversation" sounds like an interview of Morrison by Naylor, it usually functions as a dialogue illuminating the fiction and lives of the two authors. Their discussion is wide-ranging, touching on everything from their affection toward the characters who people their novels to their ideas about love and marriage. Of most interest to those studying Naylor and her work would be her comments about the intentions behind her fiction. In short, Naylor condemns didactic art and argues that fiction, if it is to be accepted as art, must be honest but must not force a "message" on its readers.
Saunders, James Robert. "The Ornamentation of Old Ideas: Gloria Naylor's First

Three Novels." *The Hollins Critic* 27 (April, 1990): 1-11. Saunders argues that Naylor, like many other African American authors, uses classic texts as a springboard for the points she would like to make in her own work. In other words, in Naylor's first novel she builds on Ann Petry's novel *The Street* (1946) to illuminate the characters in her own *The Women of Brewster Place* (1982), while her second novel, *Linden Hills* (1985), uses the work of Dante Alighieri as a guide to its structure. Similarly, Saunders adds, Naylor relies on Shakespeare's *Hamlet* to give additional meanings to the characters and plot of *Mama Day*.

Wagner-Martin, Linda. "Quilting in Gloria Naylor's *Mama Day*." *Notes on Contemporary Literature* 18 (November, 1988): 6-7. This short article explicates a central image in *Mama Day*: a quilt made by the title character for Ophelia out of remnants of cloth from the women of the family. As Wagner-Martin shows, Naylor intends for her readers to see the quilt as a tangible symbol of the spiritual inheritance given to Ophelia through Mama Day. In fact, the quilt shows that one generation of black women has an effect on subsequent generations.

Jim McWilliams

THE MAMBO KINGS PLAY SONGS OF LOVE

Author: Oscar Hijuelos (1951-   )
Type of plot: Family
Time of plot: The 1950's to the 1980's
Locale: New York City
First published: 1989

>   *Principal characters:*
>   CESAR CASTILLO, the founder of the Mambo Kings orchestra, the older
>   and more extroverted of the Castillo brothers
>   NESTOR CASTILLO, the younger and more introverted of the Castillo
>   brothers
>   EUGENIO CASTILLO, the son of Nestor and Delores, the narrator of the
>   novel's prologue and epilogue
>   DELORES CASTILLO, Nestor's wife, the mother of Eugenio and Leticia
>   DESI ARNAZ, a historical Cuban musician and actor who is presented in
>   the novel as a fictional character

The Novel

   The Mambo Kings Play Songs of Love is the fictionalized story of two Cuban brothers, Cesar and Nestor Castillo, who emigrate to New York City from Havana in 1949 hoping to succeed as musicians.

   The novel is divided into five sections, three of which are extensive and tell the main story in detail; the other two are very short and appear as a prologue and epilogue to the narration. An omniscient third-person narrator tells the story in the three large sections, while Eugenio narrates the prologue and epilogue in the first person.

   The book begins in 1980. Eugenio recalls how in 1954, when he was not yet five years old, his father Nestor (now deceased) and his uncle Cesar (now old and disenchanted with his life) had appeared on the *I Love Lucy* television program as Ricky Ricardo's singing cousins fresh from Cuba. For Eugenio, this moment is more than just the high point in Nestor and Cesar's musical career; it is "a beautiful night of glory, beyond death, beyond pain, beyond all stillness." Nevertheless, this great moment of success does not reveal the many sorrows that the two brothers experience after their arrival in New York in 1949 (this is also the year when the two Castillo brothers form the Mambo Kings, an orchestra that is relatively successful for a time in nightclubs, dance halls, and theaters along the East Coast). Nestor is never happy after leaving Cuba; he is obsessed with the memory of a former girlfriend named María who broke his heart. It is precisely this sad memory that inspires Nestor to compose the Mambo Kings' most successful song, "Beautiful María of My Soul."

   Nestor dies in a car accident in 1957. Although Cesar and one of his girlfriends are also in the car when the accident occurs, they are not injured. Cesar, who has always seemed happy, concerned only with music, women, and drinking, starts to become as unhappy as his late brother. Cesar feels responsible for Nestor's death, and these feelings of guilt cause him to become an alcoholic. After Nestor's death, Cesar becomes very close to Nestor's wife, Delores, and their children, Eugenio and Leticia. Cesar attempts all kinds of solutions and escapes in order to overcome his great sadness: He goes back to visit his family in Cuba; he joins the merchant marine for eighteen months; he tries to revive his musical career; he continues his obsessive womanizing; and above all, he keeps drinking more and more heavily.

Yet the richness of *The Mambo Kings Play Songs of Love* stems not only from the story of the two immigrant brothers, but also from the book's detailed descriptions of life in New York City. The discussion of historical events and the use of real names of important Latin musicians and other public figures of the time help to re-create the ambiance of both New York City and Cuba. The events of the Cuban Revolution of 1959 and the resulting waves of exiles from Cuba to the United States are an important part of the novel's second section.

Near the end of the novel, readers learn about Cesar's death. In the epilogue, Eugenio tells how he went to Los Angeles one year after Cesar's death to meet Desi Arnaz, who had sent Eugenio a letter of condolence. Desi ended this letter with an invitation to his home, where he receives Eugenio affectionately. As the two men recall days gone by, their reminiscing gives way to Eugenio's intense daydreaming of a fantastic, wonderful world where he, his father, and his uncle are blissfully happy.

The Characters

Cesar, the central character of the book, undergoes a deep personal transformation after Nestor's death. This transformation, as well as Cesar's personality and his relationships with the other characters of the novel, constitutes the main narrative thread that weaves together the entire story. Cesar is the one who makes most of the decisions for the two brothers, including the critical choice of emigrating to New York. Cesar also becomes the chief organizing force of the Mambo Kings orchestra. His passions are sex, drinking, and music, passions that make him appear quite happy before Nestor's death. Afterward, however, Cesar's behavior reveals a deeply troubled personality. It becomes clear that even his compulsive womanizing is the product of a profoundly low self-esteem, largely the result of his father's abusive behavior toward him during his childhood. At the end of his life, Cesar realizes that his obsessive womanizing was the paradoxical result of his low self-esteem and his very good looks; it was only because many women admired him that he temporarily felt that he was worth something. This poor self-image explains both the extroverted, energetic side of his personality and his sudden and lasting transformation after his brother's death, which plunges him into a great unhappiness. Cesar's dependence on his good looks also explains his deepening sadness as he grows older and less attractive. Cesar, however, is particularly generous, even tender, in most of his relationships, especially with his brother Nestor, his sister-in-law Delores, and his nephew Eugenio.

Nestor, the more passive and melancholy of the brothers, functions in the novel as the regressive force; he is always longing for what he no longer has. Nestor's personality is dominated by a sense of loss, a feeling that is represented mainly by his obsession with his lost love, María. At times, however, Nestor also longs for his mother (also named María), his childhood, and his native land. Actually, the novel gives several indications that Nestor has unresolved Oedipal desires that make him relate the memory of his mother with his passion for his lost girlfriend. In spite of his regressive role, however, Nestor also functions in the novel as the object of the caring side of Cesar's personality.

Eugenio, although apparently a secondary character, plays an important role. He is the first-person narrator of the prologue and epilogue, perhaps suggesting that he functions as the alter ego of Oscar Hijuelos. Eugenio is also the final important recipient of Cesar's affection and care. Ultimately, Eugenio becomes an active participant in a new, although brief and final, twist of the novel in which he and Desi Arnaz are the main characters.

Desi Arnaz represents the ideal realization of the American Dream for Cubans and other Latin immigrants of the 1950's and 1960's. Desi appears in the novel as a fictitious character with the same characteristics as the historical Cuban musician and actor, who became famous in the 1950's as "Ricky Ricardo" on the television program *I Love Lucy*.

Delores does not play as important a role as Cesar, Nestor, Eugenio, or Desi, but she is worth mentioning. She represents the option of a normal and happily married life that Nestor was never able to choose for himself.

Themes and Meanings

From a psychological point of view, the main meaning of Cesar and Nestor's story has to do with the disastrous results of being reared in an abusive environment. Cesar and Nestor are unable to overcome the low self-esteem produced by the abuse their father inflicted upon them. Nevertheless, the novel has another main theme that transcends the psychological or individual perspective: the search for the American Dream. In the novel, however, the American Dream appears void of any meaningful fulfillment. The two Castillo brothers search in vain for happiness; American society does not provide more than a materialistic solution for most of their human aspirations. Consumerism—manifested in cars, carnal pleasures, and a sense of financial prosperity—is all that the American Dream has to offer the Castillo brothers.

The story of the two musician brothers and their Mambo Kings orchestra coincides with a historical, worldwide increase in interest in Latin music and culture. This fact gives special importance to the events narrated in *The Mambo Kings Play Songs of Love*, because the Latin music of the Castillo brothers introduces the reader to an important historical period in the relationship between American and Latin cultures. During the three decades covered by the story, moreover, both U.S. and Cuban society underwent radical changes; the novel thus helps to vivify such epochal developments as the Cuban Revolution and the U.S. Civil Rights movement.

Critical Context

The Mambo Kings Play Songs of Love, Oscar Hijuelos' second novel, was his first commercial success; his first novel, *Our House in the Last World* (1983), although welcomed by critics, did not sell well. Nevertheless, Hijuelos won the Rome Fellowship in Literature of Arts and Letters in 1985, mainly on the strength of *Our House in the Last World*. One of Hijuelos' main concerns as a writer is a deep desire for an understanding of his parents' lives prior to his birth; in his first book, Hijuelos tried to penetrate the Cuban cultural world in which his parents lived.

The Mambo Kings Play Songs of Love is a sort of continuation of Hijuelos' search for his parents' lives and culture. This time, however, Hijuelos concentrates his artistic imagination on fictionalizing a generation of Cubans in New York City in the 1950's. The character Eugenio is a kind of alter ego of Hijuelos himself. Eugenio appears as the author of the novel's prologue and the epilogue, and there are some suggestions in the rest of the work that Eugenio might have written the entire story of the Castillo brothers.

The Mambo Kings Play Songs of Love enjoyed enormous critical and commercial success. The novel won Hijuelos the 1990 Pulitzer Prize in fiction, the first such prize won by a Cuban American writer, and was adapted to film in both English and Spanish.

Bibliography

Frost, Laura. Review of *The Mambo Kings Play Songs of Love*, by Oscar Hijuelos. *Review* 42 (January-June, 1990): 64-65. Describes the novel as a narrow, male-dominated text in which women play secondary roles.

Jefferson, Margo. "Dancing into the Dream." *The New York Times Book Review*, August 27, 1989, 1, 30. An enthusiastic review. Jefferson connects *Our House in the Last World* with *The Mambo Kings Play Songs of Love*, explaining how both novels deal with the fictionalization of a Cuban family. Praises the novel for alternating between everyday language and the language of longing.

Kanellos, Nicolás. Review of *The Mambo Kings Play Songs of Love*, by Oscar Hijuelos. *The Americas Review* 18 (Spring, 1990): 113-114. A laudatory review of the novel. Asserts that *The Mambo Kings Play Songs of Love* is the best Hispanic book published by a commercial press.

Pérez Firmat, Gustavo. "Rum, Rump, and Rumba: Cuban Contexts for *The Mambo Kings Play Songs of Love*." *Dispositio* 16, no. 41 (1991): 61-69. Studies the novel from the point of view of the interplay of the contradictory imperatives of tradition and translation. Pérez Firmat argues that the great success of *The Mambo Kings Play Songs of Love* results from the fact that the novel, although showing traces of Spanish American literary and cultural tradition, separates itself from, or translates that culture.

Shacochis, Bob. "The Music of Exile and Regret." *The Washington Post Book World*, August 20, 1989, 1-2. Gives the general context of the novel, especially in terms of Cuban American novels written after the Cuban Revolution of 1959. Emphasizes the intertwining of music and remembrance as the most important aspect of the novel.

Emilio Bejel

MARKED BY FIRE

Author: Joyce Carol Thomas (1938-   )
Type of plot: Bildungsroman
Time of plot: The 1950's and the 1960's
Locale: Oklahoma
First published: 1982

Principal characters:

ABYSSINIA "ABBY" JACKSON, the protagonist, an African American girl
  born in an Oklahoma field
MOTHER BARKER, Abby's neighbor, a family friend and folk doctor
PATIENCE JACKSON, Abby's loving and understanding mother
STRONG JACKSON, Abby's father, who temporarily deserts the family after
  a tornado destroys his business
LILY NORENE JOHNSON, Abby's best friend, who becomes the young
  mother of three children and is beaten to death by her husband
SISTER LIGHTSEY, a neighbor and family friend, the mother of thirteen
  children
BROTHER JACOBS, a deacon in the local church who is imprisoned after he
  rapes Abby
TREMBLING SALLY, a crazy woman possessed by evil

The Novel

Marked by Fire, the first novel by Joyce Carol Thomas, tells the story of the first twenty years in the life of Abyssinia Jackson, a black girl born in the fields of Oklahoma in 1951 as a tornado goes through. Set entirely in Ponca City, Oklahoma, the work captures the experience of a young woman coming of age in rural America in the 1950's and 1960's.

Marked by Fire is divided into thirty short chapters, each designated not by title or number but by calendar date. The narration is entirely from the third-person point of view, although the story is always concerned only with Abby's experiences, thoughts, and development. All the main characters in the novel are black; hence, Abby's problems are never directly related to racial discrimination or prejudice. Her enemies are two other blacks, Trembling Sally and Brother Jacobs, and nature itself.

The organization of the novel and story is entirely chronological. Abby's life is momentous from her birth because of the tornado, which is viewed by her family and friends as an omen. This fictional biography chronicles some twenty years in her life, during which she overcomes problems few young people must face.

The setting of the small Oklahoma town frames the activities of Abby's family. Abby enjoys listening, then telling, stories in the folk tradition; she sings hymns at church and at home; she excels in school as a reader; and she learns the art of folk medicine from her older friend and mentor, Mother Barker.

One of the most important developments of the plot occurs early in the story. After Thomas records numerous instances of the peace and desirability of Abby's early life, a second tornado comes to town—one which destroys the barbershop of Strong Jackson, Abby's father. Devastated, he inexplicably runs away from home and family, giving no reasons. This desertion leaves the family without income and in conditions that are otherwise worse than could have been foreseen.

The central event of the novel occurs during the father's absence when Abby is ten years old. After being entrusted by Mother Barker with the secrets of making a pound cake for a church social, Abby takes a piece to Brother Jacobs, a deacon. He rapes her in his wife's absence, and the child is left traumatized physically, emotionally, and spiritually. It is of little comfort to Abby, her mother, and their friends that Brother Jacobs is tried and imprisoned for several years for the terrible deed.

During Abby's recovery from the rape, the other villain of the novel, Trembling Sally, makes an appearance. Without reason or explanation, this woman inflicts harm on Abby on several occasions. There is no understanding Sally's conduct: She functions as evil and insanity, acting only against that which is good. Thus, finding Abby alone in bed after the rape, she lets wasps into the bedroom to do additional harm to the child. Fortunately, friends return in time to rescue Abby.

Slowly, Abby returns to her new life, one in which her childhood is gone forever. Following a flood, yet another natural event that wrecks the economy of the black community, Abby plays in the water at the river. There she is attacked a second time by Sally, who is intent upon drowning her. Fortunately, Abby's father returns in time to save her from death.

During her childhood, Abby's chief pleasure in life is singing, both at home and in public. After the rape, she is at first unable to talk, but this ability is restored; however, she is not able to sing. Thoughtlessly, school officials assign Abby the task of singing at the Christmas play during her junior year in high school. She is unable to do so, and in her own estimation, at least, she makes a fool of herself.

Toward the end of Abby's teen years, Mother Barker, herself always the family friend and one especially close to Abby, takes the girl to be her apprentice in the practice of folk medicine. Abby thrives in this new role, learning quickly and truly enjoying not so much the mastery of the art as the fact of helping others with both physical and emotional problems. Mother Barker dies, leaving Abby her house and business. At about the same time, Lilly Norene Johnson, Abby's best friend during her early years, also dies after being beaten by her husband. Abby takes care of her friend's three daughters, saving them from a fire in which their house burns down. The novel ends on a positive note, with Abby secure in her profession as community folk doctor, in her role as a do-gooder helping the children of her dead friend, and in her maturity after having overcome the effects of the rape. At twenty years of age, she is therefore established in her society and equipped to proceed with her life.

The Characters

Abby, the central character of the story, is the subject of the novel throughout. Her experiences and thoughts are recorded by the novelist so that readers always know what is proceeding with her development. Abby must survive in a world where events from nature—tornadoes, floods, and fires—continue to threaten her life and well-being. Yet two other members of the black community, Brother Jacobs and Trembling Sally, cause her the most harm. Essentially, Abby stands as an innocent, one who never commits more than playful mischief herself but who is victimized by the physical elements and by other persons. Her role is that of the sensitive thinker, one who does not escape evil and calamity, but who does succeed in dealing with these.

Mother Barker is the chief matriarch of the black community. She seems in charge of the other women at social events, and in her role as folk doctor commands special respect from all. Mother Barker's essential goodness is portrayed to the reader through her actions: She is always ready to help others, particularly Abby, with her wisdom and medicine. She helps the young girl recover from the rape and then goes on to establish her in life. Mother Barker stands as a counterforce to Brother Jacobs and Trembling Sally.

Strong Jackson, Abby's father, is an important character. A man of seeming dignity and integrity, his sense of humor is revealed through stories he relates at his barbershop. His importance in the novel, however, mostly stems from his absence. Unable to go on against forces of nature that inflict harm and poverty upon his family, he deserts them. It is his return, however, that highlights Abby's own return to some sense of normalcy after the rape.

Lily Norene is Abby's only close friend during their school years. Lily marries at a young age and has three children, but her lot in life is to be beaten, repeatedly, by her husband. Eventually she dies, and Abby, who seemingly will not marry, is left to take care of her friend's offspring.

Brother Jacobs, a deacon in the community church, is a rapist and coward. The novel gives no explanation for his actions; before the rape, he is regarded by all as a leader of the blacks, an upstanding Christian and citizen. Abby fears him even while he is in prison, and she is comforted when, after his release, he decides not to return to Ponca City.

Trembling Sally's actions, always evil, are similarly never explained by the author; evil simply seems to exist in human nature just as it does in physical nature. Her character is revealed in part through dialogue but primarily through actions. Trembling Sally curses Abby at an early age, lets loose wasps upon the child (whom she blames for tempting Brother Jacobs), and attempts to drown her. Members of the community know and understand Sally, however, and choose to go on living with her.

Themes and Meanings

The novel is most specifically the story of Abby Jackson. As a character of fiction, she is never made to be representative of her race, gender, or time; rather, Thomas writes to depict the development of one character during her youth. This is not to say that Abby's story is not relevant to black identity; indeed, her race and gender, as well as the society in which she lives, do work to define her being and maturation.

The novel's main theme has to do with accepting evil as fact—and then overcoming it. Thomas does not delve into the origins of evil or try to understand it; there is no explanation, for example, for Abby's rape by Brother Jacobs or her attempted murder by Trembling Sally. The novelist sees the universe as one in which learning to cope with problems, and not explaining them, is the chief concern.

It is noteworthy that Thomas does not make the rapist a white man or Trembling Sally a white woman. Hence, the novel is not about racial problems, but about the black experience in America.

Pervasive and unresolved throughout the work is the question of God's existence: Is Abby alone in a meaningless and godless universe? Are the tornadoes, floods, and fires sent from (or, at least, permitted by) God to victimize the innocent and helpless, or do these calamities occur in God's absence? Abby never answers these questions for herself, and the reader is left in a world where life is at least partially governed by bitterness and cynicism as a consequence. The novelist does not answer questions raised by her own main character. Abby simply moves on with her life, whether God is helping her or not.

Critical Context

First published in 1982, *Marked by Fire* is a work that indicates the maturity of black literature in the United States. African American writers have generally written about black experiences, and most prominent African American works describe problems that directly or indirectly relate to race. In this work, however, Thomas avoids discussion of racial issues not so much by omitting any white characters of importance but simply by writing about her own fictional creation, Abby Jackson.

The chronological events of the work end in early 1971, and the main action occurs in the 1950's and 1960's; the novel was written and published some ten years later. The temporal distance gives the novelist an opportunity to look back at the social upheavals and turmoils of the earlier decades and write not about them but after them. Her focus and attention are on what it means to be black, what it means to mature (or, more correctly, to have matured) in black America, and what it means to define and establish identity. *Bright Shadow* (1983), a sequel, shows Abby attending college. *Water Girl* (1986) depicts the adventures of Abby's daughter.

Bibliography

Childress, Alice. "*Marked by Fire*." *The New York Times Book Review* 87 (April 18, 1982): 38. Childress discusses the main characters in the novel, particularly Abby's mother and Mother Barker. She points out that the plot does have weaknesses in that some events are not believable. The matter of belief in God is also taken up

Randall-Tsuruta, Dorothy. "*Marked by Fire*." *The Black Scholar* 13 (Summer, 1982): 48. Randall-Tsuruta reads the novel in its social context, finding that it calls for realization of certain horrors in society at large. She discusses the style of the writing, finding it to be lyrical. Trembling Sally is seen as the personification of the devil.

Rochman, Hazel. "*Marked by Fire*." *School Library Journal* 28 (March, 1982): 162. Rochman discusses the novel as it reveals the functions and activities of the black community in rural Oklahoma. She finds in the work "mythical overtones" that may prevent some readers from appreciating it. She also reads the work as being primarily by and for women.

Thomas, Joyce Carol. *Bright Shadow*. New York: Avon Books, 1983. In this sequel to *Marked by Fire*, Thomas continues the story of Abby Jackson. Now in college and in love, Abby has more tragedies strike her life. Another madman appears, and Thomas records an incredibly horrible murder.

Wray, Wendell. "*Marked by Fire*." *Best Sellers* 42 (June, 1982): 123-124. Wray interprets the novel primarily as a folk tale; he finds in the novel itself qualities and characteristics of Abby's own ability to render tall tales. Like other critics, he also finds similarities to the works of Maya Angelou.

Carl Singleton

THE MARTYRED

Author: Richard E. Kim (Kim Eun Kook, 1932-   )
Type of plot: War
Time of plot: June, 1950-May, 1951
Locale: Korea
First published: 1964

> *Principal characters:*
> CAPTAIN LEE, an intelligence officer in the army of the Republic of Korea (ROK) who is assigned to investigate the execution of twelve Christian ministers
> THE REVEREND MR. SHIN, a forty-seven-year-old Christian minister suspected of betraying his twelve colleagues to save his life
> CAPTAIN INDOE PARK, the best friend of Captain Lee and the son of one of the executed ministers
> COLONEL CHANG, the chief of ROK Army Political Intelligence
> THE REVEREND MR. HANN, a twenty-eight-year-old Christian minister who, with Mr. Shin, was spared execution
> CHAPLAIN KOH, a Christian minister in the army
> MAJOR MINN, a doctor in the army
> MAJOR JUNG, a Communist army officer and the executioner of the ministers

The Novel

The title of *The Martyred* refers to twelve North Korean Christian ministers who are shot to death by Korean Communists early in the first year of the Korean War. Intelligence officers of the South Korean forces seek to establish, for propaganda purposes, that the ministers died as true martyrs in defiance of their captors' attempts to win their allegiance to Communism. The narrative develops two movements in counterpoint; one is physical and historical, the other psychological and spiritual.

The historical movement is the first year of the Korean War. The North Korean Communist regime had sought to bring all of Korea into the Communist sphere. South Korea resisted the military and political takeover, and its capital, Seoul, was captured. The South Korean and United Nations troops drove the invaders back and captured the North Korean capital, Pyongyang, which is the scene of most of the action in *The Martyred*. A dreary and dispiriting winter of occupation is followed by the evacuation of Pyongyang and a retreat before the new advance of Communist forces.

As the physical situation of territorial command deteriorates, the spiritual situation of faith versus unbelief simultaneously moves toward resolution. The focus of the spiritual matter is the Communists' execution of twelve Christian ministers and their sparing of the lives of two others. Captain Lee, the narrator of the story, is assigned by Colonel Chang to interrogate the survivors, Mr. Shin and Mr. Hann, to ascertain that the twelve died as true martyrs, presumably betrayed by Shin and Hann.

The question of faith and unbelief arises from the uncertainty about the manner of the ministers' deaths. Captain Lee has learned that one of the ministers was the father of his good friend Captain Indoe Park, whose hope is that his father had died in a failure of faith. In life, the Reverend Mr. Park had been an exemplar of the truly faithful and had sought to constrain his son within a doctrine of spiritual correctness. The son rebelled, however, and the father disowned him. Lee's investigation discloses that the father had in fact lost his capacity for prayer. Captain Park's reaction leads to his own discovery that he himself is, and has always been, a believer. Throughout, Captain Lee, an atheist, remains firm in his unbelief.

Major Jung, a captured Communist officer who had presided over the execution, makes it clear before he is shot that all twelve had died in a betrayal of their faith, begging for their lives. The young Hann had been spared because he had lost his reason, while Shin, having spat in the major's face, had been spared because he alone of the fourteen had shown courage.

Shin insistently pretends that the twelve had died as courageous martyrs. Although he himself, as it turns out, has been unable to attain faith, he treasures the Christian faith and wants the populace, inspired by the martyred, to grow stronger in faith. His motives coincide with those of Colonel Chang, who wants the populace, enraged by the executions, to intensify their hatred of the Communist enemy. At a memorial service held for the slain ministers, Shin, the nonbeliever, delivers a eulogy that lifts the crowd to new heights of belief. Colonel Chang, despite his contempt for the "martyred" and his personal conviction that Shin had betrayed them, is delighted. Captain Lee, who has favored honest exposition of the truth, whatever it might entail, respects Chang and Shin for their actions but not for their motives. Ironically, both Lee and Chang are baptized Christians who hold no Christian belief and abhor Christianity.

Subsequent to the climactic evacuation of Pyongyang, Colonel Chang goes underground and is eventually killed in a raid that he engineers and in which he voluntarily takes part; Captain Lee is wounded in action and is hospitalized; and Captain Park, dying of wounds heroically received in combat, is, at Lee's request, given Christian burial. Shin, captured after refusing to leave Pyongyang, is reported to have been publicly executed, but accounts of his continued activity translate him into a legend.

The novel concludes with Chaplain Koh's Christian church service. Lee does not join in the prayers, but after leaving the church, he joins a group of refugees humming a song of homage to their homeland and feels "a wondrous lightness of heart."

The Characters

Captain Lee is the author's persona. Like Lee, Richard E. Kim, dislodged from academic life when the Communists entered Seoul, became an officer in the army of the Republic of Korea. Lee's observations of war and civilian suffering reflect Kim's personal experiences.

Lee is drawn in the text as one committed to truth but tolerant of religious beliefs that he cannot share. He is sustained in his conduct by his growing realization of a profound love that comprises friendship, devotion to homeland, a deep sense of duty, and compassion.

Mr. Shin is the novel's focal character. He is a minister whose faith is not in the God of his preaching but in the faith itself of the people to whom he preaches. His faith in the reality and efficacy of faith, as opposed to faith in the reality and solicitude of God, has various parallels in modern literature: These include Søren Kierkegaard's knight of infinite resignation; Albert Camus's Tarrou in *La Peste* (1947; *The Plague*, 1948) Pär Lagerkvist's Tobias in *The Pilgrim*, who, like Lagerkvist himself, is *en troende utan tro* (a person of faith without faith); and, especially, Miguel de Unamuno y Jugo's Saint Manuel, a Christian priest who nurtures in his parishioners the faith that he does not himself have.

Colonel Chang, a fashioner of propaganda, wants the people to be strengthened in their faith, but only in the interest of political unity. Lee's attitude toward Chang is initially one of dislike and distrust, but he comes to understand and appreciate Chang's human side and is, at last, not surprised to learn of Chang's heroic death in action beyond the call of duty.

Captain Indoe Park is representative of the believer, or the person of faith, whose opposition to the trappings of organized religion, as embodied in his affectedly righteous clergyman father, imbues in him the conviction that he does not have faith. The conviction is shattered when his father's hypocrisy is exposed; Park then makes his father's faith his own.

Chaplain Koh is a Christian whose faith, not being tested or challenged, is not made his own. A man of no faith with faith, he is the reverse of Shin, a man of faith without faith. It is significant that he abandons his military uniform and works with civilians as one of them.

Major Jung is the enemy officer. His role in the novel is to expose the executed ministers as cowards and to recognize Hann's lapse from sanity and Shin's remarkable courage. Jung himself, villainy aside, displays the same kind of courage toward his executioner, Colonel Chang, that Shin had shown when Jung was the executioner.

Themes and Meanings

Kim's dedication of his novel to Camus' memory, and his epigraph from an unfinished play by Friedrich Hölderlin expressing a spiritually familial love of one's homeland, constitute an overture to the novel's theme of the human need for religious belief or its equivalent. Kim, like many twentieth century writers, recognizes the modern insufficiency of traditional religions to satisfy this need. In the novel, Captain Lee and Mr. Shin exemplify, respectively, two means of satisfying this ineradicable need.

Captain Lee does so by identifying his individual self with his existential situation. He is heir to the transcendent happiness of Camus' Sisyphus, who makes his futile situation his own by contemplating the noble absurdity of the situation as he descends the hill to retrieve his rock. Lee also is like Camus' Dr. Rieux, for whom the futility of a fight does not justify giving it up. Camusian "nostalgia," which is the longing to return to a nonexistent heaven and which can be satisfied by a profound experience of one's homeland within one's heart, marks Lee's coming to terms with existence by finding his homeland within himself.

Mr. Shin satisfies his longing to find the Kingdom of God within himself by learning, like Lagerkvist's pilgrim Tobias, that his very longing is his homeland. Like Unamuno's Saint Manuel, he translates his quondam faith in God into an active faith in faith itself. Again, like André Malraux's oppressed worker in *Man's Faith* who seeks his salvation in the very humiliation from which he has terminated his attempt to escape, Shin seeks his salvation in the very loss of the faith that he has terminated his attempt to experience.

Critical Context

The Martyred, Kim's first novel, was followed by *The Innocent* (1968), a sequel of sorts, which continues the activities of Lee, Koh, and others and which opens with the end of the Korean War in 1953. In subsequently published works, he extended his investigation into the psychological fabric of his homeland. *Lost Names: Scenes from a Korean Boyhood in Japanese-Occupied Korea* (1970) offers, in novelistic fashion, his perspective of his country from his second through his thirteenth year, during the period from 1933 through 1945. Concurrent with his return to Korea from 1983 through 1985 as a Fulbright Scholar at Seoul National University, he wrote a book with the Proustian title *In Search of Lost Years* (1985).

The Martyred encapsulates the texture and mood of all of Kim's writing, namely, metaphysical self-discovery derivative from deep personal loss, expressed in a style imitative of the simplicity of Camus and Lagerkvist. *The Martyred* initiates a body of work that reflects not only the two worlds of spiritual faith and secular faith but also the two worlds of a Korean national writing in English as an American citizen.

Bibliography

Freund, John B. "Martyrs, Pilgrims, and the Memory of Camus." *The Minnesota Review* 4 (Spring, 1964): 483-485. Freund compares *The Martyred* to two other works published in 1964, translations of a novel by Lagerkvist and a play by Rolf Hochhuth. *The Martyred* is rated well below the other works and is described as an inelegant imitation of Camus.

Galloway, David D. "The Love Stance: Richard E. Kim's *The Martyred*." *Critique* 24 (Winter, 1964-1965): 163-171. An essay on the Camusian concept of the absurd is followed by a critical estimate of *The Martyred* as creatively evocative of Camus' fiction, particularly *The Plague*. Galloway is perceptive in pointing out the title as initially referent to those considered to have been martyred and finally referent to the only true martyr, Mr. Shin.

Valdés, Mario J. "Faith and Despair: A Comparative Study of a Narrative Theme." *Hispania* 49 (September, 1966): 373-379. Valdés likens the theme and narrative structure of *The Martyred* to Unamuno's *San Manuel Bueno, mártir* (1933; *Saint*

Manuel Bueno, Martyr, 1956). His observations of the similarities of Kim's story to Unamuno's intensify a reader's appreciation of both.

Walsh, Chad. "Another War Raged Within." *The New York Times Book Review*, February 16, 1964, 1, 35. Walsh places *The Martyred* within "the great moral and psychological tradition of Job, Dostoevsky and Albert Camus."

Roy Arthur Swanson

MAUD MARTHA

Author: Gwendolyn Brooks (1917-   )
Type of plot: Bildungsroman
Time of plot: The 1920's to the 1940's
Locale: Chicago, Illinois
First published: 1953

>   *Principal characters:*
>   MAUD MARTHA BROWN PHILLIPS, the protagonist, a sensitive, dark-
>   skinned African American woman
>   HELEN BROWN, Maud Martha's lighter-skinned sister
>   HARRY BROWN, Maud Martha's only brother
>   BELVA BROWN, Maud Martha's mother
>   RUSSELL, Maud Martha's first beau
>   DAVID MCKEMSTER, Maud Martha's second beau
>   PAUL PHILLIPS, Maud Martha's husband
>   PAULETTE PHILLIPS, Maud Martha's daughter

The Novel

Maud Martha is a lyrical, impressionistic series of episodes and vignettes narrating the life of Maud Martha Brown, a young African American woman born into a struggling working-class family. It is clear from the beginning that she is sensitive, aware, and deeply affected by color prejudice both outside and inside her home. The reader follows her through her development from a seven-year-old child into young adulthood. Much of the novel is loosely autobiographical.

The novel is divided into thirty-four brief chapters, each delineating a moment in Maud Martha's life. The narration is in the third person, but events are seen from Maud Martha's point of view. The first five chapters take readers quickly through her childhood, touching on her family life with reference to quarrels between her parents, a description of her schoolyard, the death of her grandmother, and the experience of being visited, and patronized, by a white child.

The sixth chapter begins to explore the young woman, beginning with a visit to a theater that results in Maud Martha's making the decision that what she wanted was "to donate to the world a good Maud Martha." The next few chapters explore three events significant in the heroine's life not only as individual occurrences but also as representative of the kind of traumas she deals with throughout the novel: the death of her Uncle Tim, the near loss of the family home; and the preference of a young man for her younger, lighter-skinned sister Helen, which makes Maud Martha realize that even her beloved father favors Helen. Helen tells her sister that she will never get a boyfriend "if you don't stop reading those books."

The following chapters prove that statement false, as they describe Maud Martha's "first beau," Russell, her "second beau," David McKemster, and Paul Phillips, the "low yellow" man who is to become her husband. Although at this point she is dreaming of going to New York City, her symbol for what life ought to be like, at the age of eighteen she settles for Paul partly because she is flattered that a man of his complexion would be interested in her. He becomes a challenge, a creature to be "hooked." He is also a man with desire to better himself materially; unfortunately, his aspirations are not equaled by his ability to provide.

Descriptions of the small, roach-infested apartment, a trip to a musicale through which Paul sleeps, Maud Martha's encounter with a mouse whose life she spares, a trip to a "white" theater, and Paul's invitation to the Foxy Cats Club, which results in a bout of jealousy on the part of the pregnant Maud Martha, all establish the tone of the marriage. At the dance, Maud Martha realizes that the marriage is in serious trouble; when she contemplates scratching and spitting at the "high yellow" woman in whom Paul is interested, she thinks: "But if the root was sour what business did she have up there hacking at a leaf?"

Chapter 20 deals with the birth of her first child, Paulette. The chapter ends with a moment of recognition between the new mother and her daughter that leads to musings on her life, now changed by the birth of Paulette, and her attempt to establish traditions for her new family, an attempt thwarted by Paul. The following chapters show Maud Martha's growing awareness of the world outside her apartment: first with the people in her building, then in an encounter with David McKemster, the second beau, a sycophant to the white academics whom he wishes to impress, and last when Maud Martha is shocked as a white saleswoman insults the owner of her beauty shop and the owner fails to respond.

In the following chapters, Maud Martha deals with a fear of dying (she is convinced she has a tumor, which turns out to be a pulled muscle) and with Paul, who is disappointed in his life, his wife, his job, his baby, his failure to be invited into the Foxy Cats Club. She realizes that all that matters is life itself. A chicken that she must disembowel herself leads her to an understanding of "brotherly love." All of this leads up to chapter 30, in which Maud Martha stands up for herself at the home of a white family where she has gone to work as a maid. This vignette captures perfectly the unconscious dehumanization that occurs when one people believes that another exists to serve them. Here, Maud Martha truly comes into her own by refusing to be treated as less than a fully human being.

The final four chapters concern her musings on tragedy ("If you got a good Tragedy out of a lifetime, one good, ripping tragedy . . . you were doing well," she says), a visit from her mother, a run-in with a racist Santa Claus, and the end of World War II. The book ends with the beginning of a new life for the again-pregnant Maud Martha.

The Characters

Maud Martha Brown is a sensitive, intelligent, and poetic child of seven at the start of the novel. As the novel is told from her point of view, readers see her grow, both literally into a young woman, a mother, and an adult and also in knowledge of herself and the world that she inhabits. By the end of the novel, Maud Martha has matured in many ways; she has learned to accept the limitations of her world that she cannot change, but she also has learned to create change where it is possible, and she knows her own abilities both to accept and to alter, depending on circumstances. She is a strong, compassionate, and in many ways wise woman by the end of the novel, as she contemplates the coming arrival of her second child.

Helen Brown, Maud Martha's lighter-skinned sister, appears as something of an antagonist in the early part of the novel, although often through no fault of her own. Helen is the preferred child, even by Maud's beloved father, and it is only as an adult that Maud can begin to appreciate Helen's toughmindedness.

Harry Brown, Maud Martha's only brother, is a minor but important character. He is the male element in her young life, separate and unequal.

Belva Brown, Maud Martha's mother, plays a more important part in the novel than does her father, although the father's influence in some ways is greater. She is a realistic character, both heroic and, at times, silly. Her behavior during the birth of her granddaughter first reinforces Maud Martha's sense of separation from her mother, but then is contrasted with the connection she feels with her own newly born child.

Russell, the first beau, is only briefly described. He is an attractive young man, but he is more than aware of the fact. Although he attracts Maud Martha, she does not fall completely under his spell, recognizing that if he had to choose between being great and grand, he would without hesitation choose the latter.

David McKemster, the second beau, is notable for being a young African American scholar who would prefer to be an English country gentleman. When Maud Martha meets him again after her marriage, she finds he has become not only the worst kind of pedant but also a sycophant, desperate for the acceptance and approval of his white colleagues. The encounter helps her to refuse to place her identity on the altar of white approval.

Paul Phillips, Maud Martha's husband, is the "low yellow" in the chapter of that title; he is light-skinned, ambitious in a rather limited, materialistic way, selfish, and self-centered. Maud Martha must outgrow him.

Themes and Meanings

Maud Martha is a celebration of black womanhood. At the same time, the book examines the difficulties and trials of growing up African American and female. Such trials include both the universal problems of life and those specific to Maud Martha's race and sex: race and color prejudice (the first from Caucasians, the second from her own people, including her family and her own husband); expectations rooted in racism and sexism; and the difficulties experienced by a sensitive, intelligent woman when there is no outlet for her abilities and talents.

The novel moves between inward-looking chapters to those that stress the outside world. For example, following the birth of Paulette, which allows Maud Martha a moment of recognition as she gazes at her daughter, Brooks describes the other people who live in the building. It had been a difficult birth, attended to by a neighbor, Mrs. Cray, whom Maud Martha had not even known before, and by her mother, who prides herself on the fact that she manages to last out the whole experience without fainting. Paul returns with the doctor only after the birth is over, when Maud Martha is already feeling "strong enough to go out and shovel coal." The chapter serves the purpose of establishing the environment in which Paul and Maud Martha live, but it also shows, from her point of view, Maud Martha's reactions to these people and perhaps, in a limited way, a broadening of her interest in the world outside her own small space.

This is followed by the chapter in which David McKemster works hard to ingratiate himself with his white university colleagues, efforts that are neatly compared with the actions of Sonia Johnson, the owner of a beauty shop, who capitulates to the racist expressions of white people. Sonia remains silent in the face of a white saleswoman's use of the phrase "work like a nigger" in Sonia's own shop. At first, Maud Martha cannot even believe that she has heard the woman correctly, as Sonia fails to respond to the phrase, but after the woman leaves, Sonia acknowledges the insult, trying to rationalize her failure to respond. Maud Martha says nothing, but she is realizing the forces at work in her world. This leads naturally to the chapter in which she rejects the maid's job offered by a white family, refusing to allow herself to be patronized or demeaned.

Thus, the novel describes and explores the coming of age of a sensitive, aware, yet not extraordinary young African American woman. What is extraordinary is Brooks's ability to sketch with few words not only the quality of that experience, but also the varied places and people who shape and affect—but do not control—the conscious-ness of Maud Martha.

Critical Context

Maud Martha, Brooks's only novel, has received little critical attention, which is regrettable, as it is one of the first novels by an African American woman focusing on the black female experience. The book's major precursor is Zora Neale Hurston's *Their Eyes Were Watching God* (1937). Brooks's novel was to have an important influence on Paule Marshall, who remarked that she considered it the finest portrayal of an African American woman at the time it was published.

This critical void may result from the fact that Brooks is mainly recognized as a poet; indeed, the novel itself reads like poetry, a fact that may have discouraged its wider acceptance. Barbara Christian, in her essay "Nuance and the Novel," argues that to Paule Marshall, Brooks's contribution was a turning point in African American fiction because it presented for the first time a black woman "not as a mammy, wench, mulatto or downtrodden heroine but as an ordinary human being in all the wonder of her complexity."

Christian also claims that the novel was not more widely acknowledged because it was published at the end of the 1960's civil rights era, when the stress was on integration, and just before a new awareness arose that "black is beautiful" and that women, especially black women, faced particular difficulties.

Bibliography

Brooks, Gwendolyn. *Report from Part One*. Detroit: Broadside Press, 1972. Brooks's autobiography covers the period of the novel's writing and allows the reader insights into the autobiographical portions of the book. Brooks writes that "an autobiographical novel . . . is a better testament, a better thermometer, than a memoir can be."

Kent, George E. *A Life of Gwendolyn Brooks*. Lexington: University Press of Kentucky, 1990. This biography provides a history of the composition of *Maud Martha* as well as the story of its publication. Emphasizes the autobiographical elements of the novel. The author provides both comments on the novel from the publisher and his own criticism of the work.

Lattin, Patricia H., and Vernon E. Lattin. "Dual Vision in Gwendolyn Brooks's *Maud Martha*." *Critique: Studies in Modern Fiction* 25 (Summer, 1984): 180-186. A positive analysis of the novel, which points out the lack of critical analysis up to the time of the article and explores the reasons for its neglect. Also discusses the novel as, in many ways, a comedy.

Melhem, D. H. *Gwendolyn Brooks: Poetry and the Heroic Voice*. Lexington: University Press of Kentucky, 1987. Melhem provides a brief biographical chapter, then proceeds to in-depth analysis of individual books. She describes *Maud Martha* as a "little appreciated masterpiece of classic simplicity and poetic precision."

Mootry, Maria K., and Gary Smith, eds. *A Life Distilled: Gwendolyn Brooks, Her Poetry and Fiction*. Urbana: University of Illinois Press, 1989. A collection of essays on Brooks's work, including two essays on *Maud Martha*: "Nuance and the Novella: A Study of Gwendolyn Brooks's *Maud Martha*," by Barbara Christian, and "*Maud Martha*: The War with Beauty," by Harry B. Shaw.

Shaw, Harry B. *Gwendolyn Brooks*. G. K. Hall, 1980. A typical Twayne production. Contains a chronology, a brief overview of Brooks's life, and a discussion of her work. Includes an insightful chapter on *Maud Martha*.

Mary LeDonne Cassidy

MEAN SPIRIT

Author: Linda Hogan (1947-   )
Type of plot: Magical realism
Time of plot: 1922 and 1923
Locale: Watona, Oklahoma
First published: 1990

Principal characters:

>MICHAEL HORSE, an Osage Indian water diviner and protector of his people's fire who records the events occurring in Watona
>LILA BLANKET, a Hill Indian river prophet who sends her daughter Grace to town to learn white ways
>GRACE BLANKET, Lila's daughter
>BELLE and MOSES GRAYCLOUD, the heads of the Graycloud family, who take in Grace for Lila and care for Nola after Grace's murder
>NOLA BLANKET, Grace Blanket's young daughter
>JOHN HALE, a white oil baron
>JESS GOLD, a white sheriff
>STACE RED HAWK, a Lakota Sioux who works as a government investigator

The Novel

A historical novel based on actual occurrences on oil-rich Oklahoma Indian lands, *Mean Spirit* tells a story of exploitation and murder committed against Native American Indians as they struggle against the greed that threatens their lives and the survival of their culture.

The background of the novel's action is provided by Lila Blanket and her daughter Grace. Repeating the warning the Blue River has "spoken" to her, Lila tells the other Hill Indians that white people are going to intrude upon the tribe's peaceful ways; to prevent their own downfall, she says, they must send some of their children to town to learn the white ways. Lila sends Grace to live with her friends the Grayclouds, hoping she will grow up and protect the Hill people with her knowledge. Grace, however, takes little interest in the old Indian ways, acquires an allotment of land, and strikes the richest oil vein in the territory. Her discovery of oil in the territory does indeed save the Hill people, as the current building of a dam on the Blue River is discontinued. Yet the riches that come to the Indian community also destroy it.

Near the beginning of the novel, Grace Blanket is murdered. Grace's thirteen-year-old daughter Nola and her friend Rena, hidden in the river mud, witness the brutal killing and watch as the unidentifiable murderers arrange Grace's body to suggest suicide. Because the killers are unaware of the witnesses, Belle and Moses Graycloud keep the children's knowledge secret in hope of protecting Nola, who, though she is constantly guarded by four mystical hill "runners," also brings a threat to the entire Graycloud family.

Grace's murder is only one of many that have recently occurred in Watona and is the first of many murders and atrocities to be committed in the plot of the novel. Grace's sister, Sara, is blown up, and Benoit, her husband, is wrongfully arrested. The local hermit dies of seemingly natural causes on the same night that John Thomas is shot after running madly into town yelling that he knows who killed Grace Blanket. Additionally, the government agency reduces the Indians' payments for oil profits and leased land, supposedly because of the Indians' inability to spend their money wisely. Unable to pay their bills, the Grayclouds, among many, are slowly driven into poverty. Letters are written to Washington requesting an investigation into a possible conspiracy, but all the murders have thus far occurred on private land, and until a crime is committed on Indian land, the federal agency has no legal jurisdiction. Scandalous events continue: Indians who owe John Hale money and who, in payment, allow him to take out life insurance policies on them mysteriously die. After more letters are sent, Stace Red Hawk becomes involved in the still-unofficial investigation.

That winter, two weddings take place, both shrouded in sorrow. Nola and Will Forrest, the son of Benoit's white lawyer, marry, but Nola doubts Will, believing only that she is more valuable to Will alive than dead. Letti Graycloud, one of Belle's daughters, marries Benoit; although Benoit is imprisoned, they are allowed a hotel wedding and a wedding night. The next morning, however, Benoit is discovered hanging from his own belt inside his jail cell. Spring temporarily brings some sense of hope. Joe Billy, a Baptist preacher who has returned to Indian ways, practices Bat Medicine along with Belle in the Cave of Sorrow. Stace meets Michael Horse in the cave, and the two cling to the land even as they try to unravel the mystery. Lionel Tall, from Stace's homeland, holds healing ceremonies that more and more Indians attend. All the characters gravitate back toward traditional ways, and even non-Indians begin to take up Indian ways and dress as means of mental survival amid the horrors.

When the white lawyer Forrest learns that Hale was involved in at least one killing, he too is murdered. His murder, at least, opens the door for federal prosecution. Belle is then shot—though not killed—by Sheriff Gold, and this revelation aids in launching a trial. Hale is tried for the multiple murders, by first state and then federal court, but both are imbued with corruption. Overwhelmed and misled by false rumors, many Indians from the town sell their land and move. The Grayclouds had planned to remain on their farm, hoping all would return to peace. Moses, responding to a feeling that his twin sister, Ruth Graycloud Tate, is in great danger, runs to Ruth's house, where he discovers that his sister has been murdered and that John Tate, his brother-in-law, is part of the corruption. Moses kills John Tate and, in fear of the law, the Grayclouds flee by horse and wagon in the middle of the night. Stace departs with them, also on horseback, and knows he will now return to his people in South Dakota.

The Characters

Belle Graycloud is established very early on as the matriarchal figure in the novel, and her ties to the people, the traditions, and the earth make her a vital character in the development of the novel's theme. She is compared to Lila Blanket, the river prophet of the Hill people, who, the reader is told, is a powerful matriarch of the Hill settlement. While Lila nurtures the Hill settlement, Belle nurtures the town of Watona. Lila trusts Belle with her only child, Grace, who Lila hopes will learn the ways of the white people and help to save the Hill settlement. Lila is the biological mother of Nola, and Belle becomes the nurturing mother of the believed savior of the people. Though Grace does not follow in her mother's footsteps, Nola—in essence, granddaughter to both women—will prove to be a river prophet, a fact suggested by her understanding of the water's messages near the end of the novel. Faithfully, Belle follows the traditions of her heritage. She performs the corn ceremony during planting season while other Indians use fertilizer; she wears traditional clothing and practices traditional medicine. She also protects and communes with the sacred animals of the earth—eagles, bats, buffalo, and bees—proving a vigilant warrior when these animals are threatened or desecrated. Hogan's characterization of Belle works to unite the earth, the people, and their traditions. When the traditions are not observed and the earth and its animals are injured, the people too will suffer.

Stace Red Hawk also has strong emotional ties to his people, traditions, and earth, though when the novel commences he has unintentionally weakened these connections. Stace became a reservation police officer against the advice of his mother, and that job leads to his eventual placement at the Bureau of Investigations. Stace's intentions were noble, as he hopes to aid his people through legal methods within the white system; however, this move literally removes him from his homeland and those things most important to his Native American culture. Through this depiction of Stace, Hogan comments on the dangers of complete assimilation. Stace, no longer with his Lakota people, feels the pull toward helping other Indians and becomes emotionally involved in what might have been just another case. He never ceases his ritual patterns, even while in Washington, D.C., but once back in a Native American community, he feels the strength of his culture and increasingly turns back toward it and away from his government life. Additionally, Stace becomes increasingly compelled to be outside, in the natural world. By the end of the novel, he sleeps outside constantly, and he chooses to return to his people via horse.

Themes and Meanings

Mean Spirit's central theme is the recognition that the survival of Indian culture is dependent on the survival of the natural world. The discovery of oil and the subsequent intrusion of whites into the Indian life of Watona initiates the deterioration of the community. The obsession with material goods, drinking, and gambling separates the Hill Indians from those living in town. Grace, who has little interest in old ways, desires electricity and china. When her daughter Nola, feeling threatened by the frequent murders and pervasive greed, marries Will, she too chooses to live in a European-style house; she buys numerous glass figurines, although her husband prefers earth and clay artifacts. Grace is murdered, and Nola experiences a complete nervous breakdown, ending only after she has murdered her own husband.

Drinking is invariably connected with gambling, initially showing the Indian culture's lack of emphasis on material goods. Hogan says that the novel's Indians have no concern about losing their possessions and merely enjoy the game of gambling; however, the pleasure in betting grows out of control, until men are gambling away their sacred pipes and women their sacred dancing shawls. The moral deterioration of the community is followed by many murders, a literal extinction of the people. Seventeen murders in six months have occurred near the start of the novel, and numerous characters die during the story. The Indians in town simply disappear. Originally, the town had belonged to the Indians, but now the still-living characters of the novel walk the streets of town surrounded by all peoples but Indians.

This crumbling of the Indian community is paralleled and intertwined with the desecration of the earth. As Hogan sets the scene in the first pages of the novel, the oil pumps rise and fall in the continual draining of crude oil from the earth, and a burned forest stretches across the horizon in the morning light. Right across the road is Belle Graycloud's house. Grace Blanket's "Barren Land" becomes "Baron Land"; the earth, originally believed poor and useless, is actually pulsing with an undercurrent of rich oil. Hogan elucidates the irony as the land, suddenly viewed as rich, is drained of its resources and made poor again. The drilling creates huge craters in the surface that Belle sees as gouges and wounds. Fires and explosions are common occurrences, destroying the earth and its creatures as quickly as greed destroys the Indian people. An explosion wakes the Catholic priest Father Dunne one night as he is sleeping outside; sure that the Earth is singing some glorious message, he goes to Michael Horse to confer. Horse, sadly, knows that the priest is mistaken and that the Earth merely cries out in pain.

Horse all along writes the happenings of Watona down in his journals, but he is also writing "the Gospel according to Horse," for he desires to "correct" the omission of some things. The priest repeatedly goes to the Hill Indians with his personal revelations, revelations that even the children of the Hill settlement have known as truths all along: "The snake is my sister," he says, and a child replies, "Yes, but what did you learn that is new?" Horse's gospel begins "Honor thy father sky and mother earth. . . . Live gently with the land." A belief in dominion over the Earth and a blindness to its destruction are characteristics Hogan attributes to the white culture. The destruction of the Earth brings the destruction of the Indian people and their culture and eventually threatens all people. Endurance and continuance are key to the cyclical pattern of existence. The bats survive, the bees return, and, though the Grayclouds are forced to flee in the middle of the night, they survive.

Critical Context

Linda Hogan is an established poet who has published several short stories, but *Mean Spirit* is her first novel. Of mixed-blood Chickasaw descent (not Osage as are the characters in *Mean Spirit*), Hogan was inspired to tell the story of "the great frenzy" because of her father's ancestral ties to Oklahoma. She is similar to Joy Harjo, a Creek Indian contemporary poet, in her impressive ability to incorporate spiritual beliefs into her poetry. This talent carries over into her prose; she communicates eloquently the continuance of traditions and the endurance of the Native American peoples.

Hogan's historical novel is written in a style much like that of Gabriel García Márquez and Jorge Luis Borges, two twentieth century Latin American writers. Her novel contains realistic description combined with strong components of the supernatural or the bizarre, placing her novel in the genre of Magical Realism. Many happenings in *Mean Spirit* seem bizarre: the swarming crickets that attack Nola (the event that pulls Nola out of her depressed, nearly catatonic state); the swarming bees, that attack and kill the sheriff after he attempts to shoot Belle; the speaking river, which foretells the devastation that the new dam will bring; the amazing meteorite that saves Belle's life. Hogan uses this technique to connect animals or the Earth with people and to connect traditional beliefs with contemporary Indians. The integration of the realistic and the bizarre facilitates Hogan's effort to merge ritualistic ceremony with her political interest in revealing suppressed Native American history.

Bibliography
Allen, Paula Gunn. "Let Us Hold Fierce: Linda Hogan." In *The Sacred Hoop: Recovering the Feminine in American Indian Traditions*. Boston: Beacon Press, 1986. Allen discusses Hogan's awakening to her own spirit-based ideology and how Hogan incorporates this vision in her work. Hogan, an activist, uses her work to educate readers on the politics of Indian survival. Allen examines the fusion of spirituality and political commitment that dominates Hogan's work.
Bonaham, R. A. "*Mean Spirit.*" *Studies in American Indian Literatures: Newsletter of the Association for the Study of American Indian Literatures.* (Winter, 1992): 114-116. Bonaham outlines the setting, events, and characters of the novel. He then examines the "spare phrasing and power of visualization" that Hogan, as a poet, brings to her prose. In conclusion, Bonaham attributes the power of *Mean Spirit* to Hogan's integration of traditional ritual and historical fact.
Lang, Nancy Helene. "Through Landscape Toward Story/Through Story Toward Landscape: A Study of Four Native American Women Poets." *Dissertation Abstracts International* 52 (September, 1991): 918A. Lang examines Hogan's poetry in regard to its emphasis on land and the significance land holds in tribal tradition. She compares a group of women poets who all write about their Native American culture and create through that connection. The piece is intended for academic readers.
Miller, Carol. "The Story Is Brimming Around: An Interview with Linda Hogan." *Studies in American Indian Literatures: Newsletter of the Association for the Study of American Indian Literatures* 2 (Winter, 1990): 1-9. This interview gives insight on Hogan's personal views and theories and her intentions in incorporating them into her writings. Hogan claims literature should, since history does not, explore historical fact.
Smith, Patricia Clark. "Linda Hogan." In *This Is About Vision: Interviews with Southwestern Writers*, edited by William Balassi, John F. Crawford, and Annie O.

Eysturoy. Albuquerque: University of New Mexico Press, 1990. Smith explores Hogan's position as an American writer focusing on Southwestern culture. She also looks at Hogan's themes and their niche within this group of writers.

Tiffany Elizabeth Thraves

MEDICINE RIVER

Author: Thomas King (1943-   )
Type of plot: Social realism
Time of plot: The 1980's
Locale: Alberta, Canada
First published: 1989

Principal characters:

WILL SAMPSON, the narrator and protagonist of the book, a forty-year-old
Native American

HARLEN BIGBEAR, Will's best friend and basketball teammate, an assertive, often dominating person

LOUISE HEAVYMAN, a woman courted by Will

ROSE SAMPSON, Will's mother, long abandoned by her husband

JAMES SAMPSON, Will's father, a mysterious and elusive figure

JAKE PRETTY WEASEL, a friend of Will who commits suicide

SUSAN ADAMSON, a former girlfriend of Will

DAVID PLUME, a Native American militant

The Novel

Medicine River chronicles the lives of a group of contemporary Native Americans
in Western Canada. The novel is divided into eighteen short chapters. The story is
recounted by the protagonist, Will Sampson, in an amiable, conversational fashion,
with frequent flashbacks to earlier portions of his life.

The novel begins with an encounter between Will and Harlen Bigbear. Harlen is an
entrepreneur who has set Will up in his own photography business. Harlen is Will's
best friend, but there is something unpredictable about him. Harlen is much more
dynamic than the stolid Will, and he lives life at a faster and more stressful pace.
Beneath Will's placid exterior, though, all sorts of psychological depths simmer.
These are hinted at as Will remembers contemplating letters written long ago by his
long-vanished father to his mother, Rose. Rose catches Will reading the letters and
reprimands him. Will realizes that his life will remain unsettled until he comes to
terms with the enigma of his father.

Harlen speaks to Will again soon after. This time, Harlen attempts to recruit Will to
play on a local basketball team, the Medicine River Friendship Centre Warriors. The
team's star player, Clyde Whiteman, cannot play at the moment, and Harlen urges Will
to substitute for him. Will is skeptical, doubting his own ability. His brother James, a
gifted artist, seems to have all the talent in the family, whereas Will sees himself as
merely an ordinary person who somehow muddles through life. Notwithstanding his
fears, Will agrees to join the team. At forty, he is not exactly in championship-quality
shape. Yet with the help of some coaxing from Harlen, he fits well onto the team.

Harlen also helps to activate Will's private life. He points out that Louise Heavyman, who is the tax accountant for both men, is an attractive woman. None too subtly,

Harlen urges Will to court Louise. Will is almost persuaded when, shockingly, he learns that Louise is pregnant by another man and is about to give birth. Whereas most men would be dissuaded at this point, Will takes the news in stride. He asks Louise for a date, not even mentioning her condition.

Soon, Louise calls Will to drive her to the hospital when her labor begins. There seems to be an unspoken understanding between Will and Louise that, despite the unusual circumstances of their relationship, they are both comfortable with the situation. The baby is born and is named Wilma, but Will jokingly calls her South Wing. This sounds like a traditional Indian name, but in fact it is derived from the south wing of the hospital, where the baby is born.

Jake Pretty Weasel is one of the best players on the basketball team, but it is also known that he beats his wife, January. When it is learned that Jake has shot himself, some people suspect that January has in fact murdered her husband, whether in retaliation or in self-defense. Because of Catholic prohibitions against suicide, a Mormon clergyman officiates at the funeral; the Canadian headquarters of Mormonism, Cardston, is quite near the fictional Medicine River. It turns out that Jake has in fact shot himself, but that January has forged a suicide note because she knew that people would suspect her. When January explains this to Will and Harlen, they are accepting and compassionate. After a while, Will and Harlen forget the tawdry and painful end to Jake's life, and they retain their fond memories of him as friend and teammate.

The basketball team is becoming a more close-knit, cohesive fraternity, but Will's feelings about his vanished father are still unresolved. He reveals that, for years, he has lied when asked about his father, saying that he is an engineer, photographer, or lawyer. These lies are an attempt to evade the embarrassment and hurt that Will feels at his father's abandonment of him. As time goes on, Will's fantasies become more elaborate. Will's mother once gave him a photograph of his father, but this sample of reality did not assuage his emotional disquiet.

As the basketball team tours the western areas of Canada and the United States, Harlen pressures Will to contact Louise again. Will recalls a former relationship with a Toronto woman, Susan Adamson, who attempts to draw Will into the urban excitement of contemporary Canadian culture. Will begins a relationship with her. Yet when he calls her at home, to his shock her daughter answers, revealing that Susan is married. Beneath Susan's facade of sophistication are qualities that the novel exposes as hypocritical and immoral.

Will and Harlen drive down to the site of the defeat of General George Armstrong Custer, the most famous event in Native American history, but it is closed for the night. Their basketball team is improved by the return of the gifted Clyde Whiteman, but Whiteman soon leaves the team again when he is jailed for stealing a car.

Will becomes closer to Louise and her daughter, prompting Harlen to comment that Will should marry Louise. As the two become closer, Will again flashes back to the end of his relationship with Susan Adamson and further reveals to the reader that his mother died when he was living in Toronto.

David Plume, a member of the militant American Indian Movement (AIM), is arrested after a man who had taunted him has been shot. Will believes that David committed the crime, but he sympathizes with his predicament. Louise goes into Edmonton to see Harold, the father of South Wing. Will worries that she will marry him. Louise, however, returns to Medicine River and Will. The reader gets the impression that the happiness Will experiences with Louise and her daughter will finally heal the wounds inflicted upon him by his vanished father.

The Characters

Will Sampson is a Native American professional photographer. He is forty and unmarried. The disappearance of his father has left him with unresolved emotional tensions. He is not only the narrator of the book but also the emotional center of the subtle social milieu of Medicine River. The other characters are defined by their interaction with Will. They establish an interpersonal atmosphere in the book that establishes a community whose whole is greater than the sum of its individual parts.

Harlen Bigbear is Will's best friend. He is energetic and innovative and often motivates Will to do things he otherwise would not do.

Louise Heavyman is courted by Will. She has a daughter, South Wing. Louise is an imperfect yet sympathetic character. She communicates largely through subtle, indirect hints, though her emotional language is readily understood by Will.

Rose Sampson, Will's mother, knows that Will has been affected by the disappearance of his mysterious and enigmatic father. She attempts to heal her son's emotional wounds, but she can never quite succeed during her life. She has died when Will sets up his photography business in Medicine River, so she is presented exclusively in flashback.

Jake Pretty Weasel is an abusive husband who commits suicide. His fate highlights by contrast Will's warmth toward Louise.

David Plume, a Native American militant, provides a contrast to the softspoken, nuanced character of Will. He also is a symbol of the lingering discontent felt among contemporary Native Americans.

Susan Adamson, a sophisticated Toronto woman who once was Will's girlfriend, is an unsympathetic character who helps the reader to recognize the positive values held by Will and Louise at the end of the book. She is presented exclusively in flashback.

Themes and Meanings

Medicine River is preoccupied with Native American themes, but this preoccupation is voiced with an almost spectacular unobtrusiveness. Prominent Native American writers of the late twentieth century have stressed the need to dispel degrading and condescending stereotypes of contemporary Native Americans. Works such as Louise Erdrich's *Love Medicine* (1984) and James Welch's *The Indian Lawyer* (1990) defy conventional notions of Native Americans as mere hapless, residual victims, lingering on in reservations after the near-obliteration of their culture by triumphant Europeans. Welch and Erdrich show Native Americans flourishing and thriving in markedly contemporary contexts, living lives much like the rest of mainstream Americans, yet these characters are never totally assimilated. They never forget (nor are they allowed to forget) their distinctive heritage.

This variety of representation is King's goal as well. King, though, weaves the themes of modernity and assimilation so deftly into the fabric of the book's plot that he does not even need to be overt about it. Will, Harlen, Louise, and the other residents of Medicine River are unmistakably Native American. Yet their guiding pursuits in life—eating pizza, watching football on television, and playing basketball—are dramatically antithetical to received expectations of Native American interests. The people of Medicine River participate as thoroughly in the modern world as do any of their Europe-descended neighbors.

At a party Will attends with his then-girlfriend Susan during his Toronto years, he meets someone who is surprised that Will is a photographer. This is because the partygoer has been exposed to widely disseminated canards about Native Americans, who ostensibly fear that photographs will capture their souls. The fact that Will is a photographer by profession is a striking indicator of how King's characters are at home with technology and do not fear or repudiate it. The symbol of the photograph also represents the preservation of the past through time. This is illustrated when Rose gives Will a photograph of his father in order to stem his bewilderment about the man who abandoned him.

Although Will lacks the militancy of his friend David Plume, he is sensitive to his own heritage. This is evidenced by the poignant attempt he and Harlen make to visit the site of Custer's defeat. That this site is closed may symbolize the way the characters remain rather distant from their people's past. More pressing to Will are dilemmas only accidentally connected to his heritage, such as the enigma of his father or his relationship with Louise. These questions of love and family occur in the lives of everyone. King's portrait of his characters' concerns is thereby ingratiating and authentic. The combination of the mellow social comedy of the surface plot and the questions of Native American identity that lie not far below lend the novel a relaxed and evocative atmosphere. The novel uses humor and understatement in order to treat potentially tumultuous situations with reserve and warmth.

An interesting facet of *Medicine River* is its Canadian setting, The characters relate more to American professional sports (for example, the National Football League) than to such partly Canadian professional sports as basketball and hockey. In this way, they are a part of a common North American culture, as shown in much of their everyday lives. Yet the reader is always reminded of the Canadian setting of the action. Louise goes to Edmonton to visit her baby's father. Will met his sophisticated former girlfriend in Toronto. Canadian writers such as Leon Rooke are mentioned prominently in the novel. Native Americans, however, live in both the United States and Canada, and lived in the areas now occupied by those nations before either existed. In addition, Native Americans often have dual loyalties to their own nation or tribe and to the Native American people as a whole. These competing loyalties are compounded when, as is often the case, ancestry can be traced from several different tribes and, more often than not, from Europeans as well. (Thomas King, for example, is partly of Greek and German descent. His Native American heritage comes from the Cherokee nation, which is not native to Western Canada.) Thus, the people of *Medicine River* can be said to belong to no one nation or tribe.

Critical Context

Medicine River was published in Canada in 1989 and released in the United States in 1992. It was King's first novel and was enthusiastically received in both countries. King has since published another novel, *Green Grass, Running Water* (1993), a more expansive look at many of the same themes and questions that concerned him in his first work of fiction. King's second novel delves more fully into the visionary potential of the Native American past and present than does *Medicine River*.

King is now counted as one of the leading contemporary Native American writers. He teaches in the departments of American and Native American Studies at the University of Minnesota. King is a Canadian-born man teaching in the United States whose work centers on a Native American identity common to both countries. In this way, King's life summarizes the contradictions that animate and nourish the lives of his characters.

Bibliography

Hemesath, James B. Review of *Medicine River*, by Thomas King. *Library Journal* 115 (August, 1990): 143. Addresses the novel's use of humor and characterization, as well as its engagement with Native American concerns.

King, Thomas. "Godzilla Versus Post-Colonial." *World Literature Written in English* 30 (Autumn, 1990): 10-16. Supplies some of the crucial intellectual background to the novel. King discusses the necessary differences between an inside and outside perspective on Native American concerns. King critiques the "postcolonial" approaches prevalent in current literary discussions of works by minorities, charging that they slight the full historical amplitude of Native American experience.

―――――――――. Interview by Constance Rooke. *World Literature Written in English*, Autumn, 1990, 62-76. King places himself in Canadian, Native American, and literary contexts.

Weaver, Jace. "Thomas King." *Publishers Weekly* 240 (March 8, 1993): 56. This interview emphasizes the themes of social comedy in King's two novels. King makes valuable comments on how he is influenced by ideas of oral tradition.

Nicholas Birns

MEN AND ANGELS

Author: Mary Gordon (1949-   )
Type of plot: Psychological realism
Time of plot: The 1980's
Locale: Selby, Massachusetts
First published: 1985

Principal characters:

LAURA POST, the nanny to the children of Anne and Michael Foster
ANNE FOSTER, the holder of a doctorate in art
MICHAEL FOSTER, Anne's husband, a professor on sabbatical
JANE WATSON, the elderly widow of Caroline's son, Stephen
ROSE CORCORAN, a brain-damaged woman
ED CORCORAN, Rose's husband and the Fosters' electrician

The Novel

Men and Angels illustrates the possible consequences of parental rejection and implies that people need religion to be complete. The story begins when Laura Post, a twenty-one-year-old drifter, becomes a live-in babysitter for the two children of Anne Foster, who is writing a lengthy catalog on the works of the late artist Caroline Watson, to be used at an exhibition being arranged by Anne's longtime friend Ben Hardy. Since Anne's work is time-consuming and since Michael, a professor, is teaching in France that year, she needs someone to tend the children and the house.

Anne hires Laura because her original sitter has changed plans and no other suitable person can be found. Yet she takes an instant disliking to the younger woman, for which she tries to compensate by doing small favors for Laura, such as making her cocoa in the mornings, taking her to lunch, and baking her a birthday cake. Anne's dislike of Laura is augmented by the latter's religiosity and her frequent reading of the Bible. Anne, on the other hand, has no conscious religious life. She and Michael do not attend church, and she has never told her children, Peter and Sarah, ages nine and six, respectively, about hell and the devil, thinking these supposedly questionable doctrines might frighten them. While Anne is not an avowed atheist, her highest objects of worship seem to be her spouse and children, whom she keeps safe and secure in their upper-class home.

Although Laura appears to be mentally stable, her lifelong deprivation of parental love (especially from her mother, who seems to hate her) has caused her to embrace religion (of no particular denomination) to the point of madness. She has convinced herself that human love, especially the love of family, is worthless and that the love of the "Spirit" (a term she never clearly defines) is the only love worth having. She guards herself from all close human encounters and owns only absolutely essential material items. Moreover, Laura fancies herself the Chosen One of God, sent to "save" Anne from materialism by destroying her maternal attachment. Without realizing it, however, she develops a love for Anne similar to a daughter's love for her mother. Unfortunately, this love is not reciprocated.

During the first six months of her employment, Laura is watchful of the children, but her first act of negligence—letting them slide on a deep, partially thawed pond while she sits behind a rock reading the Bible (a possible scheme for their deaths, which will forever sever them from Anne)—is her downfall. Furious with the sitter for endangering her children's lives, Anne fires her immediately. This abrupt dismissal is too much for Laura. The only way she can now "save" Anne and obtain her love is by offering herself as a sacrifice. While Anne takes the children out to supper, having told Laura to be packed and gone by the time they return, Laura slits her wrists and bleeds to death in an overflowing bathtub. By letting the water run, she knows she is beginning to rescue Anne from her preoccupation with the material, as the water, flooding the upstairs hall and dripping through the downstairs ceiling, destroys much of the Fosters' beautiful house.

While tragic, the young woman's suicide has redeeming effects. At last, Anne is able to feel some tenderness, if not love, toward Laura. Furthermore, her dormant spirituality begins to surface. After Sarah explains to Peter that the lifeless form the police have removed was not really Laura—only her body—Anne asks her daughter, "Where do you think she is now, sweetheart?" It is as if Anne is contemplating the afterlife for the first time. Later, at the cremation service, she understands from the words of Psalm 121 ("from whence cometh my help? My help cometh from the Lord, which made heaven and earth") that she is not completely autonomous; she must learn to appeal to a higher, divine being. Finally, Anne realizes that she cannot protect her children from all the pain and tragedy in life. Therefore, the death of Laura, tragic as it is, provides a growing experience for both Anne and her children.

The Characters

Caroline sets the novel in motion. Had Ben not arranged an exhibition of her works, he would not have asked Anne to write the catalog; hence, Anne would not have hired Laura.

Laura is the catalyst for Anne's religious development, while her strangeness lends interest to the novel. Her physical appearance is significant, as it is one reason for her mother's rejection. While not unattractively large, Laura is tall, with a sturdy bone structure. Her hair is red, her eyes blue, and her complexion fair. Laura's mother, in contrast, is dark and petite. Moreover, Laura has a sister who is a replica of her mother and who thus has received all the mother's attention and affection.

Anne, the protagonist, is the one character who develops to any extent. A woman who considers religion unnecessary and somewhat disquieting, she becomes marginally aware of this missing element in her life through her contacts with Laura and Jane Watson. After Laura's death, she realizes that there is something higher than the material world and her children. In addition, she develops as a mother by letting her children experience tragedy instead of trying to protect them. Like Laura's, Anne's looks are important, for she too is tall, red-haired, and blue-eyed. Coincidentally, she is thirty-eight, the same age as Laura's mother. Anne's age and their similarity in appearance probably contribute to Laura's love for her employer.

Jane exemplifies the practice of religion. A churchgoer, she can nevertheless form meaningful human relationships. For example, she is the lover of Ben, a divorced man. She also befriends a woman whose battered children have been taken from her. Since the formerly abusive mother regrets her behavior and has received therapy, Jane gives her another chance by entrusting her with the care of Anne's children for a few hours. Additionally, Jane becomes a mother figure to Anne, who, like Laura, is the less beloved of her own mother's two children.

Rose Corcoran, who developed an inoperable brain tumor during her second pregnancy, is permanently impaired both physically and mentally. Although she appears only once, she seems to represent the acceptance of fate and divine will. Not fooled by the comments of others that she is getting well, Rose regards herself as a "cripple" and wishes to be photographed on a particular hill, so that she might resemble a crippled girl in a painting she admires. When she says she would be better off dead, Laura replies, "If the Lord wanted you to be dead, you'd be dead in the blink of an eye." While Anne is shocked by the callousness of this remark, Rose is not offended. "That's what the priest says," she agrees. "He says I'm alive for a reason."

Ed Corcoran is an attractive man who loves his wife unconditionally. Physically drawn to Ed, Anne attempts to seduce him, but he declines her proposition on the grounds that he could never be unfaithful to the wonderful woman he married, despite her infirmity, which is not her fault. Thus, Ed stands for adherence to the marriage vow, "for better or for worse," and to a firm moral code that does not alter with circumstance.

Themes and Meanings

Gordon focuses on two interrelated themes, family and religion, which she conveys chiefly through characterization. First, she examines the strength of the traditional, ideal family by presenting three different groups: the Posts, the Corcorans, and the Fosters. Although the Post family is structurally traditional (two parents, two children), it is clearly destructive, by virtue of the parents' conscious rejection of one child, who eventually becomes psychotic. The Corcorans are not destructive, yet they are a less than ideal family in that the wife and mother is an invalid, unable to perform her domestic and maternal duties. In effect, Ed has become a single parent, since he must take full charge of his four-year-old son. Finally, the Fosters seem to match the stereotype of the ideal American family: two highly educated and devoted parents, a pleasant physical environment, and a home atmosphere that shelters the children from harsh realities. After Michael leaves for France, however, the Fosters' family strength begins to falter. Anne tries to seduce her electrician, an action she would never take were her husband at home. Moreover, she lies to Ed that Michael is having an affair himself.

Until Laura's suicide, Anne, the ideal mother, is able to protect her children from all things unpleasant or frightening. On the other hand, the little Corcoran boy lives each day with a nonfunctional, brain-damaged mother whose very appearance is somewhat grotesque. Yet whenever Ed brings his son to Anne's home (he must often take Brian on his jobs, when there is no one to watch him), the child seems happy. Apparently, living with an "imperfect" mother is a situation he takes for granted, rather than one that is troubling or deleterious. Through Laura Post and Brian Corcoran, Gordon implies that although children must be loved in order to remain mentally well, love does not necessitate blinding them to all pain. The Corcoran child, deeply loved by his father, illustrates the resilience of children exposed to conditions that are less than ideal.

Closely related to the theme of family is that of religion. For Ed Corcoran, religion may provide a standard of morality. Because Rose has mentioned conversing with a priest, it can be assumed that the family is either Roman Catholic or Anglican, or at least acquainted with one of these faiths. It may be Ed's religious convictions, then, as well as his love for Rose, that enable him to resist the advances of Anne and other women for whom he works.

Laura misuses religion as an escape from the pain of parental rejection. For her, human love and spirituality cannot coexist. At the other end of the pole, Anne disregards religion entirely, feeling that a stable family environment is all one really needs. Jane represents the middle ground, for she can both worship God and relate to human beings.

Gordon, a Roman Catholic, regards religion as an essential ingredient in the lives of families and individuals. During childhood, however, Gordon was surrounded by a religious atmosphere that dichotomized spirit and body, insisting that the flesh must be subdued. This division of spirit and flesh she could not accept. The body and the world, she insists, are parts of religion—a belief she exemplifies through the character of Jane, a woman who has suffered, turned to religion, and finally extended her love for God to the people around her.

Critical Context

Men and Angels demonstrates Gordon's growth and maturity as a writer. This novel, unlike her earlier *Final Payments* (1978) and *The Company of Women* (1980), moves beyond the subculture of Roman Catholicism, extending the theme of religion into society at large. Some critics, in fact, see Gordon's work as moving from the genre of "women's fiction" to that of religious literature. Moreover, her characters are older (with the exception of Laura) and less stereotypical. Isabel Moore, the protagonist of *Final Payments*, and Felicitas Taylor, heroine of *The Company of Women*, are thirty and twenty, respectively; Anne, however, is thirty-eight, and Jane is in her seventies. When the novel begins, Anne is already settled as a wife and mother, and Jane has come to terms with God and the world.

The characters in *Final Payments* and *The Company of Women* seem to be stock types, Catholics or privileged persons rebelling against their upbringing. Anne and Laura, on the other hand, are more complex. Anne conscientiously divides her time between work and motherhood. She feels ambivalent toward Caroline Watson, an artist who neglected and never truly loved her son—and worries over her own inability to love Laura, whose psychosis appears to be only eccentricity.

The theme of love, prominent in both *Final Payments* and *The Company of Women*, continues in *Men and Angels*. Yet those people whom the earlier protagonists cannot love are unlovable for obvious reasons: Margaret Casey in *Final Payments* and Muriel Fisher in *The Company of Women* are embittered spinsters, seething with envy and spite, while the Habers in *The Company of Women* are a filthy, coarse, and indigent family. Laura Post, however, is young, strong, and on the brink of life. Her unlovability, therefore, is more pathetic. Thus, the issue of love is more problematic in *Men and Angels*.

The novel also looks deeply into the issue of motherhood, probably because maternity had become central to Gordon's life. When she wrote *The Company of Women*, her first child had not yet been born, but while writing *Men and Angels*, she was pregnant with her second baby and was the mother of a three-year-old. The focus on motherhood and family, as well as the expansion of religion, probably makes Gordon's third novel attractive to a wider and more mature audience than her earlier works.

Bibliography
Mahon, John. "The Struggle with Love." In *American Women Writing Fiction*, edited by Mickey Pearlman. Lexington: The University Press of Kentucky, 1989. Mahon discusses characters' inabilities to give and receive love. He also points to the frailty of the secular family, which, he says, in times of crisis easily disintegrates.
Morey, Ann-Janine. "Beyond Updike: Incarnated Love in the Novels of Mary Gordon." *Christian Century* 102 (November, 1985): 1059-1063. Morey observes that Gordon's novels show religion from a feminine viewpoint. For example, Anne is concerned about nonsexual human love, an issue not found in the works of most male writers.
Seabury, Marcia. "Of Belief and Unbelief: The Novels of Mary Gordon." *Christianity and Literature* 40 (Autumn, 1990): 37-55. Seabury analyzes Gordon's works in terms of the inseparability of spirit and body. She observes that Laura's warped religiosity is juxtaposed with Anne's repressed spirituality.
Suleiman, Susan. "On Maternal Splitting: A Propos of Mary Gordon's *Men and Angels*." *Signs* 14 (Autumn, 1989): 25-41. Suleiman notes that working mothers may be jealous of mother substitutes and compensate by finding the substitute "bad." Laura's strangeness is the "badness" that aggravates Anne's animosity.
Wymward, Eleanor. "Mary Gordon: Her Religious Sensibility." *Cross Currents* 37 (Summer/Fall, 1987): 147-158. Wymward comments that in Gordon's fiction, individuals must find salvation within the world; however, they need faith in something higher. Laura evokes Anne's latent spirituality.

Rebecca Stingley Hinton

MIDDLE PASSAGE

Author: Charles Johnson (1948-   )
Type of plot: Adventure
Time of plot: 1830
Locale: Aboard the slave ship *Republic* in the Atlantic Ocean
First published: 1990

> *Principal characters:*
> RUTHERFORD CALHOUN, the narrator, a young black man freed from slavery, a stowaway aboard the *Republic*
> EBENEZER FALCON, the captain of the *Republic*, a slave trader and a dwarf
> JOSIAH SQUIBB, the cook aboard the *Republic*
> PETER CRINGLE, the first mate of the *Republic*
> ISADORA BAILEY, Rutherford Calhoun's girlfriend
> NGONYAMA, an African of the Allmuseri tribe, leader of the slave mutiny on board the *Republic*

The Novel

Winner of the National Book Award for fiction, *Middle Passage* is a fanciful account of the misadventures of a twenty-two-year-old black man, a freed slave who ends up aboard a ship bound for Africa to take on a cargo of slaves. *Middle Passage* is divided into nine entries made by Rutherford Calhoun in a ship's log. The first entry is dated June 14, 1830, and the last is dated August 20, 1830. Calhoun narrates each entry.

The book's action begins in New Orleans, where Rutherford Calhoun has drifted after being freed from slavery by his master, a preacher in southern Illinois. Calhoun, mischievous by nature, becomes involved in petty crime and ends up deep in debt to Papa Zeringue, a Creole gangster. Rutherford has also entered into a platonic relationship with Isadora, a young schoolteacher. Papa offers to forgive Calhoun his debts if he will marry Isadora, but for young Rutherford, any thought of marriage is too constricting even to contemplate. To escape, he stows away on a slave ship, the *Republic*. The ship puts to sea before he is discovered.

After he has been found, he is brought before the captain, Ebenezer Falcon, a strange but philosophical man, misshapen both in physique and in morality. Falcon turns out to be both a dwarf and a monster, but in his first interview with Calhoun, there are only intimations of this monstrosity. Falcon decides to allow Calhoun to work aboard the ship without compensation. For the rest of the voyage to Africa, Calhoun befriends the crew and learns about the ship, which is not in good condition and is constantly being repaired.

The ship drops anchor in the African port of Bangalang. There, Rutherford observes the captain buy a cargo of slaves and a huge, mysterious crate that becomes the object of much speculation among the crew. Curious to know more about the captain,

Rutherford resorts to his burgling skills in order to break into the captain's cabin. He rifles the captain's effects and reads from the captain's journal. Falcon returns, however, before Rutherford can leave. To the young man's surprise, the captain engages him in a philosophical discourse and then recruits Rutherford to be his spy among the crew, who the captain believes are plotting against him.

The *Republic* sails from Africa, and Rutherford soon befriends Ngonyama, a member of the Allmuseri tribe from whom the ship's slaves have been taken. Ngonyama has been made an overseer, and he is charged with ensuring that the slaves cooperate. A quick learner, Ngonyama masters English well enough to begin explaining to Rutherford some aspects of Allmuseri life. Rutherford also learns that the crew is planning a mutiny, and he is invited to participate. After Rutherford reveals the mutiny plot to Falcon, the captain tells Rutherford that the mysterious cargo carried in the ship's hold is the god of the Allmuseri, a creature that "has a hundred ways to relieve men of their reason." Caught in the middle, Calhoun participates both in the mutiny and in Falcon's attempts to thwart it.

Before this conflict can be brought to a resolution, however, the slaves stage their own mutiny, which is successful. Many of the sailors are killed, but Rutherford (himself spared because he is black) succeeds in convincing them not to kill Falcon or Peter Cringle, the first mate, since someone must guide the ship. Rutherford has one last conversation with the battered captain before Falcon kills himself. In this conversation, Falcon reveals that one of the ship's financial backers is Papa Zeringue, the gangster whose blackmail had sent Rutherford on his misadventures. Rutherford is shocked to learn that a black man is dealing in slaves. Falcon also charges Rutherford with the duty of keeping the ship's log, the entries of which make up the novel. The ship continues to drift in the Atlantic, the situation becoming so desperate that the passengers resort to cannibalism. Finally, a hurricane destroys the ship.

Adrift in the ocean, Calhoun is rescued by a pleasure ship. By coincidence, Isadora is aboard. She is about to be married to Papa Zeringue, a circumstance that Rutherford redresses by revealing that Papa Zeringue was a financial partner in the slaving venture. The blackmail works, leaving Rutherford and Isadora to contemplate their future together.

The Characters

Rutherford Calhoun, the narrator of the novel, is an engaging and likeable guide to the action despite his propensity for amoral (and sometimes immoral) behavior. For example, Rutherford leaves New Orleans solely to escape any kind of commitment to Isadora—a woman who clearly cares deeply for him—and yet he explains away his behavior humorously and with enough self-deprecation to keep the reader from judging him too harshly. The same holds true for Rutherford's numerous questionable actions—thieving, stowing away on a ship he knows to be a slaver, informing on his shipmates, and so on. Curiously, Rutherford has received a broad and liberal education from his former owner, a minister who had Rutherford read from the classics of Western philosophy. As a narrator, Rutherford employs this learning in numerous allusions that range from the Greek philosopher Paramenides to the Christian theologian Thomas Aquinas to the English poet Lord Byron. Similarly, Rutherford draws upon a vast and unusual vocabulary; it is clear that he has not been reared as a common slave. Despite this education, Rutherford is unable to make routine moral choices, and he continues to act purely out of self-interest until he meets the Allmuseri and learns something about their distinctly non-Western philosophy. Toward the end of the narrative, Rutherford has matured significantly, though the story ends before it is certain whether these changes are profound enough to last.

Captain Ebenezer Falcon is also a complex character. Rutherford's research (reading Falcon's journal) reveals that Falcon is the son of a minister and domineering mother, born on the day the Colonies declared independence. Calhoun sees Falcon as a Puritan with a utopian and expansionist vision for the country that was born when he was. In his conversations with Calhoun, Falcon displays a command of philosophy that borders on sophistry. At the core of Falcon's philosophy is the belief that conflict is the driving force in human affairs. War is thus the most human of activities, and a subject-object dualism is the basic structure that the human mind imposes on reality. Falcon's "dark counsel" represents the philosophical amorality and social authoritarianism (in the tradition of English philosopher Thomas Hobbes) that Rutherford is learning to reject. The presentation of Falcon's character calls to mind the dark broodings of Ahab, the whale-hunting captain of the novel *Moby Dick: Or, The Whale* (1851) by the American novelist Herman Melville.

Of the novel's minor characters, the first mate on the *Republic*, Peter Cringle, is the most interesting. Cringle is a man out of his element. He is a competent sailor, though less rugged than the rest of the crew. Cringle is also a moral, even pious, man in a world (the ship at sea) where, as Captain Falcon says, there are no rules, and the only authority is that of the stronger man. Cringle is the ship's "feminine air," a voice of tolerance and compassion amid intolerance and cruelty. Significantly, the dying Cringle offers himself as a sacrifice and is cannibalized by the starving crew.

Josiah Squibb, the ship's drunken chef, is a survivor by nature and thus is the only crew member to survive the hurricane with Rutherford. Squibb hones his ability to survive by focusing on practical actions. Unlike the novel's philosophical characters, Squibb dwells "on the smallest details of his chores" to deflect his mind from brooding, and this keeps him from descending into the madness and paralysis of other characters.

Themes and Meanings

Like many sea adventures, *Middle Passage* operates on one level as an allegory, the ship being, as Falcon tells Calhoun, "a society . . . a commonwealth." The name of the ship, the *Republic*, and the fact that its captain was born on July 4, 1776, are strong suggestions that the society allegorized is that of the United States. The novel touches on many themes from U.S. history, including slavery, equal opportunity, and race riots. Many of these references are anachronistic—that is, they are themes and issues that did not exist in 1830. While it is difficult to explain how a narrator writing in the nineteenth century could have knowledge of some of these things (such as the vocabulary of affirmative action), Johnson seems to be suggesting the interconnectedness of U.S. history. In other words, the slavery of the country's early days and the civil strife that Falcon foresees in his apocalyptic death dream ("I saw riots in cities") are connected in their origins. In this regard, the fact that the *Republic* is a ship constantly coming apart and constantly being remade metaphorically suggests that the United States is a society in process, undergoing constant upheaval and renewal. Following the beliefs of its captain, the shipboard society is governed by an essential dualism and characterized by a deep fissure, an "ontic wound" in Falcon's words, that necessitates slavery and strife.

Contrasting with this society of pluralism and division are the mysterious Allmuseri, the African tribe from which the slaves aboard the *Republic* have been captured. The Allmuseri, Rutherford learns, are a mystical people who have powers of sorcery. At least, that is how they have appeared to Western eyes. The Allmuseri stress the unity of all things and see disunity as the source of strife and madness. The slaves' mutiny on board the *Republic* is in part a rebellion against the pluralism that they see in the white society (as represented by the ship's crew). They cannot and will not tolerate being taken to such a world. Captain Falcon, who asserts that strife and division are fundamental driving forces in human relations, represents an opposing viewpoint. When the slaves mutiny and take over the captain's quarters, Rutherford notices that things are strangely altered; even though they appear to be the same objects that had belonged to the captain, Rutherford senses that there is something different about them. He senses that they have been transformed by Allmuseri possession; they are different because they have been touched by the Allmuseri worldview, with its emphasis on unity. Though Rutherford does not understand exactly what has happened, he realizes that the Allmuseri bring a different outlook to the material world, and this outlook is both disturbing and attractive to the young man.

A coming-of-age theme, the passage of a boy to manhood, is common in sea stories. Johnson makes use of this convention in *Middle Passage*. Rutherford, an immature young man with an undeveloped ethics, learns much about life and about himself on the voyage of the *Republic*. The most important lesson for Rutherford has to do with his identity. As a result of this voyage, he realizes that he is neither part of the Western or the African world and that he cannot be entirely part of one or the other. He must navigate between the two somehow, a figurative middle passage that parallels the physical middle passage the ship is making between Africa and America. In other words, it is up to Rutherford to find some common ground between the worlds of Falcon and the Allmuseri. Whether he is successful is a question left open at the novel's end, though Rutherford's reconciliation with Isadora and his adoption of the orphaned Allmuseri girl suggest that he has found some sort of middle ground on which he can build the rest of his life.

Critical Context

Middle Passage, the third of Johnson's novels, is an extension of his previous work.

Both of his previous novels, *Faith and the Good Thing* (1974) and *Oxherding Tale* (1982), are highly charged works of philosophical fiction, and yet, like *Middle Passage*, both are also highly readable novels that appeal to general readers. Johnson's works all feature historical themes, narrative inventiveness, and characters who must make moral choices under difficult, often perplexing, circumstances. One of Johnson's goals is to develop "a genuinely philosophical black American fiction," and with that goal in mind, he places his characters in situations in which their ethics must come under close scrutiny. Such scrutiny eventually reveals shortcomings not only in the characters' understanding of ethics but also in the various ethical programs proposed by Western philosophy. Johnson and his characters confront the inconsistencies inherent in traditional Western ethics and are driven to form their own moral visions from what is left to them after their experiences have forced them to deconstruct their received ethical understanding.

The narrative of *Middle Passage* is conscious of its debt to other sea stories, especially those of Herman Melville. Many of the characters in Johnson's novels are parodies or revisions of the great characters in Melville's works. Falcon, for example, resembles Ahab; Rutherford is a black Ishmael; Squibb acts much like Stubb; even the cabin boy Tommy parallels Melville's Pip. Johnson's intention in borrowing Melvillian archetypes is to re-present the self-destructive obsession of Ahab/Falcon in terms of a conflictive dualism the American manifestation of which is slavery. Just as Ahab is obsessed with the whiteness of the whale, Falcon (and by extension all white Americans) is obsessed with his own whiteness, and this obsession is played out in the violent repression of those who are, by appearance, the opposite of that whiteness: Africans.

Another Melville tale is subverted and recast by *Middle Passage*. "Benito Cereno" (1856) is the story of a slave rebellion aboard a Spanish ship. The captain of that ship is saved by an American, Amaso Delano, who after a lengthy confusion about what has occurred aboard Cereno's ship eventually captures the leader of the rebellion, a slave named Babo. Babo and his henchman Atufal are also aboard the *Republic* and involved in that mutiny. From this coincidence, Johnson develops what in Melville's tale is only a minor theme: Namely, that an institution such as slavery can be maintained only through extreme cruelty, a repression that can never be relaxed. Those who practice it must commit themselves to this cruelty or face rebellion. Falcon formulates a philosophy that justifies his, and America's, involvement in the slave trade. The rebellion of the Allmuseri shows that even Falcon's cruelty is not severe enough. Ultimately, then, *Middle Passage* responds to canonical American literature by offering a black deconstruction, or undermining, of traditional themes and contexts.

Bibliography
Iannone, Carol. "Literature by Quota." *Commentary* 91 (March, 1991): 50-53. A mostly critical examination of Johnson's novel. Iannone, former head of the National Endowment for the Arts, responds to the novel's tone and characterization.

She finds the tone too jocular and the characters too obviously symbolic. Her conclusion is that Johnson's novel is "hard to take . . . seriously as literature."

Johnson, Charles. "National Book Award Acceptance Speech." *TriQuarterly* 82 (Fall, 1991): 208-209. Johnson discusses his novel in terms of racism and the literary accomplishments of African Americans. These topics are also addressed in his book *Being and Race: Black Writing Since 1970* (1988).

Rushdy, Ashraf H. A. "The Phenomenology of the Allmuseri: Charles Johnson and the Subject of the Narrative of Slavery." *African American Review* 26 (Fall, 1992): 373-394. A study of the mysterious tribe in *Middle Passage*. The article discusses the Allmuseri philosophy and the points on which it counterbalances and contradicts the worldview of Captain Falcon and the other whites in the novel.

Schultz, Elizabeth A. "The Heirs of Ralph Ellison: Patterns of Individualism in the Contemporary Afro-American Novel." *College Language Association Journal* 22 (December, 1978): 101-122. This study of Johnson's early novel *Faith and the Good Thing* discusses Johnson's debt to Ralph Ellison. Johnson's work is considered part of a tradition that began with Ellison: the conscious exploration of philosophy from the African American perspective.

Wills, Garry. "The Long Voyage Home." *The New York Review of Books* 38 (January 17, 1991): 3. Wills rejects arguments that Johnson's novel did not deserve the National Book Award. Specifically, Wills considers the book an artistic achievement that is not beholden to a particular ideology. Thus, he contends, the book was selected on merit and not because of its "message."

Stephen Benz

THE MYSTERIES OF PITTSBURGH

Author: Michael Chabon (1963-   )
Type of plot: Bildungsroman
Time of plot: The early 1980's
Locale: Primarily Pittsburgh, Pennsylvania
First published: 1988

> *Principal characters:*
> ART BECKSTEIN, a recent college graduate uncertain about his future and
>   confused about his sexual identity
> JOSEPH (JOE THE EGG) BECKSTEIN, his father, a gangster
> ARTHUR LECOMTE, Art's male lover, a stylish idler whom Art seeks to
>   emulate
> PHLOX (MAU MAU) LOMBARDI, Art's female lover
> CLEVELAND ARNING, Art's friend

The Novel

The Mysteries of Pittsburgh follows Art Beckstein, the narrator, from the time of his graduation from college through a summer. During those months, the direction of his life is determined, through a series of intense, interlocking relationships with three other young people.

As the narration begins, Art is particularly vulnerable. He is without the structure provided by his educational experiences, faces the unappealing prospect of becoming part of the adult world of responsibility, and sees the possibility of a fulfilling existence as vague and elusive. His sense of himself rests on a shifting, unsteady foundation of injunctions from his stern father. He has an ambiguous but insistent inclination to spend this last summer of relative freedom "fluttering ever upward," but he has no idea of what this would entail, nor of what he needs to learn about himself and the world. He is nevertheless determined to permit "novel and incomprehensible situations" to absorb him. When he is invited to join a group of revelers by an intriguing young man, Arthur Lecomte, he has few qualms about accepting. Arthur's speech, style of dress, and patterns of pleasure imply excitement. Art does remain wary of Lecomte's apparent homosexuality but is drawn by its implications of participation in the realm of the forbidden.

The social nexus into which Art is drawn centers on Lecomte and two of his acquaintances, a young woman, Phlox Lombardi, who works in the university library while studying French, and Cleveland Arning, a young man who has been living on the edge of society. Arning is rebellious, courting danger and espousing defiance. Art, who has been a dutiful son guided by the wishes, suggestions, and various forms of subtle coercion exercised by his father, a gangster, finds the unpredictable, spontaneous rhythms of his new friends exciting. He begins to develop, in the course of their adventures and escapades, a particular relationship with each of the three. He remains linked to old habits of responsibility through his contacts with his father and his work at a mass-market book dispensary that mocks his love for literature with its commercial method of operation. The lure of the apparently freer, more genuine, more gratifying lives of his new friends opens a door that Art sees as an entrance to a cosmos of infinite possibility. One of the most appealing aspects of this different life is the opportunity for explorations of intimacy in terms of intense friendship and sexual experimentation. Art is uncertain of his inclinations in these areas. The summer he spends with Arthur, Cleveland, and Phlox becomes a quest for his true self.

As the summer progresses, Art is lifted in a whirl of excitement and exhilaration, living in a movable feast of food, drink, appreciation of others' clothes and wit, and expressive gestures of aesthetic sensibility. With little regard for the remainder of the human race, the self-selected elite to which Art belongs amuses itself by outrageous acts toward hopelessly square parents, drones in dumb jobs, and anyone who is not attuned to the somewhat outré literary ambience that guides them. At the root of their actions, Art begins to realize, is a fear that they will be absorbed and reduced to normality by the drab, often dysfunctional, world. The expanding uncertainty and dread gradually undermining Art's delight in his summer escapades is compounded by a growing sense of sexual confusion, as he finds himself both fully involved in a satisfying sensual relationship with Phlox and a thrilling but unsettling erotic adventure with Arthur.

Art's eventual discovery of the facts behind the façade of manner that Arthur has constructed, along with the intermingling of his own uneasiness about his family's income from crime with Cleveland's involvement in the same criminal organization, leads to the climactic episode of the novel. Cleveland is killed while fleeing from the police in a setup engineered by Joe Beckstein, Art's father, to teach Art a lesson about power, control, and obligation. The effect of this episode is to sever all of Art's connections to his previous life and to his dreams of a summer of "greater lust and hopefulness." He decides to follow Arthur to Europe but does not stay with him for long. At the novel's conclusion, he recalls the events of the months just passed with a mixture of fond, indulgent nostalgia and a rueful sense of wisdom recently acquired that does not completely obliterate his innocent expectations.

The Characters

Art Beckstein, whose mind is the source of the narrative consciousness of the novel, is the focus of the story. It is essential that he immediately and powerfully control the attention, curiosity, and sympathy of the reader. His compelling blend of aspiration and yearning, held just beneath a protective shield of studied sophistication, is established through a control of tone and language that recalls the singular voices created for Mark Twain's Huck Finn and J. D. Salinger's Holden Caulfield, other young men uncertain about the survival of their integrity as they enter a menacing world of adult demands and entrapment.

The mysteries of Pittsburgh that Art engages are the mysteries of existence, and the tentativeness and hesitancy of Art's explorations, both within the city and within his psyche, are testament to the candor of his accounts. Because everything is presented through Art's perspective, it is crucial that his judgments are conveyed with complete sincerity, so that even when he is clearly mistaken, his honesty remains unquestioned.

Despite his concentration in economics, which he refers to as "a sad and cynical major," and his distaste for the library, Art cultivates the sensibility of a literate outsider and is susceptible to the lure of Arthur Lecomte and Cleveland Arning. They appear to be of a world diametrically opposed to that of his father, which demands prudence and control. Although Art gradually discovers that both of his new friends are hiding the brutal circumstances of their early lives, the energy and intelligence of their created selves are compelling and have become integral parts of both young men's personalities.

Lecomte has fashioned a veneer of decadence, dressing with a self-conscious extravagance, speaking with an arch and dismissive wit, and charming those he wishes to influence or ingratiate while manipulating everyone else. Art is overwhelmed by his seemingly effortless manners and grace and is attracted to him sexually, hoping to emulate him and perhaps to acquire his characteristics through physical contact. Chabon presents Lecomte effectively from Art's point of view, so that even as his weaknesses and faults become apparent, he remains sympathetic and appealing.

Arning is a post-Beat, protopunk dazzler, so perceptive, self-assured, and exuberant that he is irresistible to Art. Arning's doom-driven recklessness, his sneering contempt for sham, his mixture of poetic responsiveness to beauty and toughness, and his genuine affection for Art make him a sympathetic character as well. His eventual destruction helps to explain Art's withdrawal at the novel's conclusion.

Although Phlox Lombardi and Joe Beckstein are important characters, both are essentially static if convincing. Beckstein is seen from the outside, remaining a formidable but unfathomable presence for Art and the reader. Phlox is described in considerable detail regarding appearance and objects. Her reactions to Art, however, are the determining means of her characterization; she tends toward a generic "good woman" stereotype.

Themes and Meanings

Although he is not sure that his attraction to Arthur Lecomte is final proof of a homosexual orientation, Art does find tremendously appealing the seemingly spontaneous, unstructured, impulsive pattern of living that Lecomte and his circle have evolved. At the completion of his senior year of college, he senses that he is about to be captured by the world of his father, a controlled, fundamentally serious, and frighteningly powerful man. Art respects, warily admires, and uneasily "loves" his father, but he believes that he is likely to lose the nascent elements of his own individual consciousness if he succumbs to his father's subtle pressures. He fears never becoming a complete and self-sufficient person, like his father, unless he permits the hazards of change to enter his world.

Already prepared for a form of outlaw aestheticism by his eclectic reading, Art launches himself into a "life" that can be assessed and appreciated as a work of art in which he is the hero, Art's awareness of his role as a player in this construction serves to sharpen his perceptions; his initial exhilaration at his admittance into the elite cadre of "extraordinary" people eventually shifts to a wiser, wider perspective that permits him to begin to see the shallow, almost desperate aspects of Lecomte's gestures and Arning's bursts of manic energy.

Art needs both his elevation into a realm of heightened experience and the gradual awareness of his friends' uneasiness to begin to develop an understanding of his own relationship to his family. Art seems to realize that his father was forced into a criminal position because his Jewish background made him a permanent outsider. This realization helps him to understand his own refusal to accept bland assimilation. Art's determination to preserve his poetic sensibility parallels his father's decision to maintain the freedom to act as an individual. His father has come to terms with his choices, and as the novel closes with Art looking in reflective satisfaction on his impulsive, romantically expectant plunge into what he now recognizes as a "lovely, dire summer," his decision is ratified. He needed the disruption and the thrill of chaotic agitation to grow beyond the silence and ill will that held him in a clutch of fear at the novel's onset.

Critical Context

Publication of *The Mysteries of Pittsburgh* immediately established Chabon as one of the most promising young writers in the United States. He was given an unusually large payment for his hardcover contract as well as the opportunity to prepare a screenplay adaptation of the novel. In addition, short stories he had published in various journals were collected under the title *A Model World* (1991).

Amid a considerable outpouring of positive commentary, which compared Chabon to J. D. Salinger and Jack Kerouac, several reviewers emphasized the parallels with F. Scott Fitzgerald's work, noting the similarities in sensitivity of Chabon's narrator and Nick Carraway of *The Great Gatsby* (1925). Chabon's treatment of sexual ambiguity and multiplicity extended more traditional considerations of the nature of love and erotic attraction from the realm of familiar heterosexual experience toward the less rigid demarcation of sexual attraction that became an important element of postmodern literary ventures.

Bibliography

Banks, Carolyn. "Bright Lights, Steel City." *The Washington Post Book World*, April 24, 1988, 5. Compares Art Beckstein with his literary precursors Huck Finn and Holden Caulfield and contrasts the comic motifs of the book with its sad side. Summarizes stylistic highlights.

Kaveney, Roz. "As They Mean to Go On." *New Statesman* 116 (May 13, 1988): 34-35. Considers the novel as a *bildungsroman* about writing a novel. Identifies attributes of Chabon's style that permit him to transform unlikely situations into plausible scenarios.

Keates, Jonathan. "The Boy Can't Help It." *The Times Literary Supplement*, June 23, 1988, 680. Discusses the meaning of the "mystery" of the title, evaluates claims made for Chabon's talents, and demonstrates how Chabon transforms familiar formulaic devices.

Lott, Brett. "Lover in a World Too Full for Love." *Los Angeles Times Book Review*, April 17, 1988, 1. Sets the literary context in which the book appears ("jaded young writers") and shows how Chabon surpasses his peers by going deeper into the nature of love and friendship. Assesses the book's weaknesses and virtues and examines Chabon's use of sexual identity as a psychic checkpoint.

McDermott, Alice. "Gangsters and Pranksters." *The New York Times Book Review*, April 3, 1988, 7. Points out the novel's limitations of some weak characters and unclear relationships and mentions that these are balanced by Chabon's language, wit, and ambition.

Leon Lewis

THE NARROWS

Author: Ann Petry (1908-   )
Type of plot: Psychological realism
Time of plot: The 1930's to the early 1950's
Locale: Monmouth, Connecticut
First published: 1953

> *Principal characters:*
>> LINCOLN (LINK) WILLIAMS, a Dartmouth graduate and bartender at the Last Chance Saloon, the adopted son of Abbie Crunch
>> ABIGAIL (ABBIE) CRUNCH, a seventy-year-old widow who prides herself on her New England Puritanism, immaculate appearance, and racial piety
>> CAMILLA TREADWAY SHEFFIELD, the internationally known heiress to the Treadway Munitions Company, who becomes Link's lover
>> BILL HOD, the owner of the Last Chance Saloon, who becomes a father figure to Link
>> FRANCES JACKSON, a successful black undertaker and Abbie's best friend

The Novel

The Narrows takes place in Monmouth, Connecticut, and tells the story of an interracial love affair between Lincoln (Link) Williams, a twenty-six-year-old black man, and Camilla Treadway Sheffield, the beautiful wife of Captain Bunny Sheffield, heiress to the Treadway Munitions Company, and daughter of Monmouth's most prominent white family. The complexity of the novel, however, makes it more than a novel of romance. Through an omniscient third-person narrator, flashbacks, introspective monologues, and memories, Petry discusses the impact of racism on the lives of her characters.

Link Williams, the adopted son of Abbie Crunch and Theodore Crunch—known as the Major—was happy with his life until one Saturday afternoon when he was eight years old. The Major, looking seriously ill, had been sent home by Bill Hod. The Major, however, smelled of whiskey, and because Abbie had a strong aversion to drinking, she did not listen to Bill's warning to get the Major a doctor soon. The Major had a stroke and died two days later.

Abbie, overwhelmed with guilt, blames herself for her husband's death. In her deep grief, she forgets Link's existence. Link tries to get Abbie's attention during and after the Major's death, but he fails. Frances, who is there to comfort Abbie, keeps telling Link to run along and play for fear he will disturb his mother. Link is too young to survive this double tragedy: It seems that he has lost both father and mother at once. He feels alone, abandoned, and betrayed. He has to find something or someone to make up for this great loss.

Link leaves the silent, dark, and grief-filled house. His sees Bill standing in front of his saloon across the street, and he gets food, shelter, and a job at the Last Chance

Saloon. He stays there for three months; it takes Abbie that long to notice his absence. When she and Frances finally go to the Last Chance to claim Link, he refuses to go home with them. It is only after Frances and Bill work out an arrangement to allow Link to go on working at the saloon that Link agrees to go home with Abbie, but things will never be the same again. Now Link has two rival authority figures in his life: Abbie and Bill.

Link grows up amid conflicting views of black people. Abbie, African American herself, is always finding fault with other blacks; the Major, on the other hand, enjoys telling stories about his family, the "swamp niggers." At the Last Chance, Bill and Weak Knees, the cook, try hard to instill racial pride in Link; Link's high-school history teacher, a white person, encourages him to read more about slavery in America so that he will not be ashamed of being black. Link goes on to Dartmouth College to major in history, and he is graduated with a Phi Beta Kappa key four years later.

Link is in the process of researching a book on the history of slavery in the United States when he meets Camilla, who is white, on a foggy night at the dock in the Narrows. Despite the taboo against interracial relationships, the two fall in love. The society in which they live dooms their romance. Link is accused of rape by Camilla when he tries to talk her out of their poisoned relationship. In a desperate act to save their reputations, Mrs. Treadway and Captain Sheffield, Camilla's mother and husband, kidnap Link and murder him. Mrs. Treadway is stopped by the police when she tries to dump Link's body in the river.

The Characters

The character of Link Williams is presented through his relationships with other characters in the novel. Link has suffered many scares that are detrimental to his psychological development. At the age of eight, Link is rejected by Abbie—his adoptive mother and the center of his boyhood—who, in her grief and guilt over the recent death of her husband, has completely forgotten Link's existence. In elementary school, Link is embarrassed by his teacher, who assigns him the role of Sambo in a class presentation. When Link is sixteen, Bill Hod—who has been a surrogate father to Link—betrays his trust and love by almost killing Link the first time Link disobeys him. When he is twenty-six, Link is betrayed by Camilla when he decides to end their relationship. Ambivalence marks all three relationships: Link's feelings toward Abbie, Bill, and Camilla mix love and hate, happiness and suffering, gratification and disappointment.

Abbie evokes the sympathy as well as the intolerance of the reader. Her disdain for black people, her embrace of white ideologies, and her adoption of aristocratic values greatly endanger Link's psychological well-being, indirectly cause the Major's death, and prevent her from enjoying life and loving Link. The author uses Abbie as an example to show that the internalization of the oppressor's values will bring only confusion and self-destruction. Still, Abbie proves that she is able to change. At the end of the novel, she transcends her racial bias and the painful loss over the death of Link to protect Camilla.

Camilla is a beautiful and wealthy young woman, loving at times but murderous when her authority is challenged. She is a spoiled child who must have her own way. She is so rich that she acts as if she owned the world, and Link is in many respects simply another one of her possessions. When Link ceases to be a kept man, Camilla is outraged; she simply has to destroy him. Though she and Link have shared a love that seems to have crossed the color line, Camilla is in no position to abandon her privileged status. Her eventual betrayal of Link shows her to be a product and victim of a racist society.

Bill Hod is a complex character who cannot be defined simply as either "good guy" or "bad guy." He has his dark side: He operates whorehouses, engages in smuggling illegal Chinese immigrants, has an affair with a married woman, and threatens to cripple Link if he ever disobeys him. On the other hand, he knows how to survive a racist world with body and soul intact. Above all, he has a strong sense of racial pride. He has no patience with Abbie's sense of racial inferiority and takes responsibility for teaching Link about black people: their history, their beauty, and their cultural heritage.

Frances Jackson is a woman with a man's build and mind. She is thin and tall, and she works in a profession that was traditionally a man's: undertaking. Being a successful entrepreneur, Frances is able to escape the daily humiliations of the poor and working-class blacks. She has been instrumental in nursing Abbie back to a normal life after the Major's death. Like Abbie, though, Frances has played her own role in miseducating Link about African Americans. She has been hardened by the racial discriminations she encountered when growing up. She is no longer bothered by the word "nigger." This indifferent attitude is not what Link needs in a racially hostile society.

Themes and Meanings

The Narrows is a complex work of literature that touches on several crucial issues in the lives of black people in a small New England city. The reader sees the deterioration of a neighborhood: The area in Monmouth where Abbie and Link live was once a mixed neighborhood of Irish, Italians, Finns, and Poles. Now it is a black ghetto called the Narrows, Eye of the Needle, the Bottom, Little Harlem, Dark Town, and Niggertown. Racism has taken its toll on the black people who live here: Abbie is ashamed of being black; Link is confused about his racial identity and learns to take pride in his heritage only through painful experiences; the black butler at the Treadway mansion, Malcolm Powther, becomes a Judas by pointing Link out to his master. The interracial love affair between Link and Camilla brings out the worst in people in Monmouth. Mrs. Treadway refuses to say Link's name but refers to him as "the Nigger"; she and Captain Sheffield have to kill Link to clear their names and save Camilla's reputation; the black population is more interested in Camilla's involvement in the scandal than in Link's fate; Bill Hod, upon Link's death, is ready to take the law into his own hands and kill Camilla in revenge.

Miss Doris—a character in the novel—says that Link's death is everybody's fault.

In a sense she is correct, but racism comes closer to being the primary cause of the evil. The novel makes clear that racism poisons people's thinking, prohibiting toleration and understanding of any deviation from established norms. As a result, Link is murdered for breaking the taboo against interracial love. Nevertheless, the author is not content merely to present this particular racial conflict. She goes a step further, making it clear that societal violence has to be stopped before a society can progress. It is symbolic that Abbie is chosen to break through this cycle. Her decision to protect Camilla shows that forgiveness is stronger than hatred. Her willingness to take care of J. C.—a little black boy who has been largely neglected by his parents—reveals that Abbie has come to terms with Link's death and her own neglect of him at the age of eight: She is not going to abandon this son and lose him to a racist world.

Critical Context

The Narrows, Ann Petry's third work of long fiction, is also her most complex one. Published seven years after her first book, *The Street* (1946), *The Narrows* has largely been neglected by critics and overshadowed by the success of her first novel. Both books are about racial themes and the impact of racism on the lives of her black people. Her second novel, *Country Place* (1947), on the other hand, deals with the devastating effects of World War II on the social and moral structures of a small New England town.

Petry is often set apart from black writers who are from the Deep South or from the black communities in the North. To some, her growing up in a small, predominantly white Northern town seems to have disqualified her to write about the experiences of black people. *The Narrows*, however, is very much a novel about black people's experience in America; it is about the development of Link Williams, a black youth, and his relationships with his family and the black community. The book is also concerned with the past: Link, a history major whose ambition is to write a book on American slavery, knows that the cause of his imminent execution by the Treadways reaches back to the first shipment of enslaved Africans that landed in Jamestown in 1619. In this respect, Petry has joined Zora Neale Hurston as a model for a later generation of black women writers—Alice Walker, Toni Morrison, and Gloria Naylor, to name just a few—in understanding the historical context of slavery in America and its legacy to the American people as a whole.

Besides writing novels, Ann Petry has written several historical books for young readers including *The Drugstore Cat* (1949), *Harriet Tubman: Conductor on the Underground Railroad* (1955), *Tituba of Salem Village* (1964), and *Legends of the Saints* (1970). Her collection of short stories entitled *Miss Muriel and Other Stories* (1971) demonstrates her remarkable versatility.

Bibliography

Bell, Bernard W. "Ann Petry's Demythologizing of American Culture and Afro-American Character." In *Conjuring: Black Women, Fiction, and Literary Tradition*, edited by Marjorie Pryse and Hortense J. Spillers. Bloomington: Indiana University

Press, 1985. Critical analysis of American cultural myths such as the American Dream, the city and small town, urban success and progress, and rural innocence and virtue in Petry's novels, including *The Narrows*.

Bontemps, Arna. "The Line." *Saturday Review* 36 (August 22, 1953): 11. Bontemps concedes that Petry's *The Narrows* is "a novel about Negroes by a Negro novelist and concerned . . . with racial conflict." This initial critical comment on the novel has served as a point of departure for later interpretations of this complex work.

McKay, Nellie Y. "Ann Petry's *The Street* and *The Narrows*: A Study of the Influence of Class, Race, and Gender on Afro-American Women's Lives." In *Women and War: The Changing Status of American Women from the 1930s to the 1950s*, edited by Maria Diedrich and Dorothea Fischer-Hornung. New York: Berg Publishers, 1990. From a feminist perspective, this essay takes a critical look at how class (Abigail Crunch and Frances Jackson in *The Narrows* are independent, middle-class black women, while Lutie Johnson in *The Street* is a working-class black woman), together with gender and race, affect the lives of black people in general and black women in particular.

Weir, Sybil. "*The Narrows*: A Black New England Novel." *Studies in American Fiction* 15 (Spring, 1987): 81-93. Focusing on the characterization of Abbie Crunch, Weir discusses convincingly how Petry's own New England heritage shaped *The Narrows*. Abbie's ambivalence toward her own people (black) and her obsession with aristocratic values (white) make her a victim of the racist New England culture.

Wilson, Mark. "A *MELUS* Interview: Ann Petry—The New England Connection." *MELUS* 15 (Summer, 1988): 71-84. Recalling the racial discrimination that she and her family encountered in their hometown, Old Saybrook, Connecticut, Petry remarks that she has difficulty calling herself a New Englander. Her comments on her life and work in general and *The Narrows* in particular are illuminating.

Weihua Zhang

NO-NO BOY

Author: John Okada (1923-1970)
Type of plot: Historical realism
Time of plot: The late 1940's
Locale: Seattle, Washington
First published: 1957

> *Principal characters:*
> ICHIRO YAMADA, a twenty-five-year-old Japanese American
> MR. YAMADA, Ichiro's father
> MRS. YAMADA, Ichiro's mother
> TARO YAMADA, Ichiro's brother
> KENJI KANNO, a former schoolmate of Ichiro
> EMI, Kenji's friend and Ichiro's lover
> FREDDIE AKIMOTO, Ichiro's schoolmate

The Novel

Spanning only a few days shortly after the end of World War II, *No-No Boy* portrays the experiences of a second-generation Japanese American returning to his hometown after two years in an internment camp and an additional two years in prison for refusing to swear loyalty to the United States. Ichiro Yamada, one of thousands of Japanese Americans imprisoned for refusing to say "yes-yes" to questions twenty-seven and twenty-eight of the government loyalty test administered in 1943, returns to Seattle to find his whole society a prison plagued with poverty, distrust, racism, and despair.

Ichiro is captive to an unhappy family, captive to the revulsion of his brother and his former friends who disapprove of his choice not to serve, captive to the racism of the society, and captive to his own self-hatred. In rapid succession, Ichiro is confronted with the passivity and drunken escapism of his father, the demented patriotism of his mother, rejection by his brother, the venom and ennui of former schoolmates, the mental and physical anguish of his friend Kenji, job discrimination, and the racism of the entire society. Briefly, Ichiro thinks that a return to prison might offer him a better future. The deaths of Kenji and Ichiro's mother on the same afternoon leave Ichiro with both more perspective and more freedom of choice. The emotional support of his married lover, Emi, and the offer of a job at the Christian Rehabilitation Center present Ichiro some prospect of personal comfort, though both are refused ultimately. A third death, the death of fellow no-no boy Freddie, who had been dissipating his life in idleness and self-loathing, leaves Ichiro feeling what he had long sought, a "glimmer of hope."

No-No Boy consists of eleven chapters that follow Ichiro from his arrival at his parents' tiny storefront through ever-widening circles of his world. Ichiro visits other families, old friends, pool halls, nightclubs, workplaces, a university, Chinatown, the suburbs, and a veterans hospital, then returns to Seattle and is confronted by three deaths in rapid succession. The author's choice of omniscient third-person narration distances the reader from the protagonist's pain and modulates the melodramatic qualities of the plot line. Like Ichiro Yamada, the reader is an outsider, observing, looking for some positive aspect of this time and place in history.

Ichiro's pain is depicted vividly in both inner reflection and speeches to family and friends, but the powerful constraints of his situation in life are revealed most fully in the contrasts between his feelings and his choices and those of his parents and peers. Mrs. Yamada is fanatically dedicated to the prospect of return to Japan; she cannot accept the idea that Japan has lost the war and that its people are suffering greatly. She is driven to suicide. Mr. Yamada appears dazed by the experience of relocation, unable to cope with the humiliation of their meager existence eking out a few dollars a day selling stale bread and cigarettes. He drinks too much. Taro Yamada turns eighteen, drops out of school, and enlists in the military days after his elder brother's return. He cannot bear the shame of his brother's "disloyalty" to America, and he tries to compensate with his own life.

Old schoolmates of "Itchy," Kenji Kanno and Freddie Akimoto, take different positions on the loyalty issue but suffer similar consequences. Kenji served in the armed forces, was decorated for valor, and lost part of a leg. He now has a pension, a big car, college tuition, and a recurring infection requiring repeated amputations. Only a few days after his reunion with Ichiro, Kenji dies. Freddie, like Ichiro, comes home to the scorn heaped on those who chose prison over the draft. Depressed and demoralized, he sleeps, gambles, and drinks. As Ichiro looks on, this young man, whose situation is so like his own, is killed fleeing a barfight in the final scene of the novel. One young man, Ralph, reenlists because it is easier than returning. Another, Gary, retreats into a self-protective shell where he paints and does little else.

Although Okada himself served in the U.S. Army during the war, the preface to the novel suggests that the book's origin is to be found in his memory of a friend who refused service because the government would not let his family live together in the same internment camp. Neither the "patriotic" choice nor the "disloyal" choice made a Japanese American's life any more bearable during or after the war; saying "yes-yes" yielded no better result than saying "no-no." The Japanese Americans in the novel have no good choices, no morally unimpeachable positions, no satisfactory consequences.

The Characters

Ichiro Yamada, known as "Itchy" to his school friends in happier days, is the "no-no boy," the Japanese American who refused, while in an internment camp deprived of his civil rights, to sign a loyalty oath and be drafted. After two years in prison, he does not choose expatriation to Japan or a new life elsewhere in America; he returns to his hometown, Seattle, where anti-Japanese sentiment is still strong.

Ichiro's first few days home reveal that his "no-no" was not done out of loyalty to Japan, for he considers himself an American through and through; nor was his refusal made out of outrage at injustice done to his race. His identity as a "no-no" is not the result of principled action but the upshot of a muddled state of mind and a vague loyalty to his mother's obsessive nationalism. His profoundest sense of shame and worthlessness arises not from the hatred directed at him but from his feelings that he has betrayed himself. Ichiro is not so much a resistor as a confused and empty man without hope. As he moves through the tangled, tense world of Japanese Americans in Seattle, however, he rejects his family, others' lifestyles, college, and several jobs in his search for the right place and a ray of hope. Through these "nos," Ichiro appears to arrive at a place of promise for himself.

Mrs. Yamada has always expected to return to Japan, so she has never learned English, never made friends. She has worked hard, saved her money, and waited to return. Her longtime determination becomes obsession after the war, as she denies the reality of newspapers and letters describing the condition of her homeland. In despair, she drowns herself. Mrs. Yamada has held powerful sway over her sons, and Ichiro feels that if it had not been for her fanaticism, he would not have made the choice he did. Her death, he senses, is freeing.

Mr. Yamada has become fat, cheerful, and spineless after years with his controlling wife. Her death seems to free him, too, but not to do anything new. He offers Ichiro a job in the store, but Ichiro gently rejects the offer. Mr. Yamada's helplessness contrasts sharply with the gentle strength of Kenji's father, Mr. Kanno.

Taro Yamada rejects his brother and his brother's choice totally and enlists as a point of honor. He is so ashamed of his brother that he actually helps other young men to ambush and attack Ichiro. Not only does brother turn against brother, but in these strange circumstances, two men from the same household choose diametrically opposed paths. The irony is that, like Taro, Ichiro regards himself as totally American.

Kenji Kanno, the wounded war hero, serves as yet another contrast to Ichiro. When they meet near the university, they have a debate about which of them has it worse. Is it worse to be dishonored and a social pariah, or to have honor but only one leg? Eventually, Ichiro admits he would not change places with Kenji. Kenji's physical and emotional pain and his approaching death allow Ichiro to see his own position in a more positive light.

Freddie Akimoto, "Shorty," also spent two years in prison as a no-no boy. Now he lies around all day and debauches all night. He is not searching, as Ichiro is, for a new start, for a glimmer of hope and a wisp of promise. His death in the final scene of the novel is associated with a moment of pain and compassion that seems to be the start of Ichiro's healing spirit.

Emi is a young Japanese wife whose husband has abandoned her by suddenly reenlisting. She befriends Kenji, and she and Ichiro become lovers in their mutual loneliness. Ichiro fantasizes about making her husband, Ralph, jealous enough so that he will return to her.

Mr. Carrick, the owner of an engineering firm in Portland, Oregon, offers Ichiro a job apparently out of sympathy with his plight and out of guilt about what has been done to the Japanese. Ichiro refuses the job, but he recognizes the man's compassion and sees him as a metaphor for the best qualities in human beings. Mr. Carrick shows Ichiro that rejecting America is not the way to reclaim his own life.

Themes and Meanings

The no-no boy is the central metaphor of the novel. The man who refused an oath of loyalty, whatever his reason, represents self-hatred and pride simultaneously. The no-no boy, like Ichiro, is empty. The literal and metaphorical "mother" of the no-no is insane, the family is insane, the society is insane with fear and prejudice, the world insane with war. In many ways, this is the typical story of the young man in search of his place and his goals. Ichiro, however, has to find not only a mate, a job, a family, a direction in life, but he has also to find to what culture he belongs, to what country he belongs.

The novel is certainly a vivid picture of the experiences of Japanese American men and women in the 1940's. The bleakness of the Japanese Americans' dilemma is striking, because no one can be "right." Both those who went to war and those who went to prison are living dead. Even those who escaped both horrors are victims of a society in the grip of fear. Whether no-nos or not, all are aliens, outsiders painted with the broad brush of racism.

Although Ichiro, as a no-no, is disdained by Japanese and Americans equally, he is also a hero, a sensitive, intelligent young man on an existential quest for personal identity, hope, and escape from his psychic prison. The question "who am I?" is most profound for a man without a country.

The novel has several aesthetic flaws, such as the implausibility of its condensed time frame, its intensely coincidental plot line, its mechanical patterns of character and contrasting foil, and a distinct leaning toward melodrama in presenting three death scenes in four chapters. Yet the book's language is often quite eloquent, particularly in Ichiro's interior monologues. Though consistently dark, the novel is not polemical. In fact, one way of accounting for the critical neglect of *No-No Boy* is that the book is disturbing exactly because of the coolness of its narrative and the indeterminacy of its exploration of issues raised to the light. Ichiro and Kenji seem to be counterpart images of the good and thoughtful man in physical and spiritual hell. The novel shows a vast landscape of social hatred and a tragic inner life of self-hatred.

Critical Context

No-No Boy is now identified by literary and social historians as the first novel to break through the pervasive anti-Asian sentiment of the 1940's and 1950's and be published by a major publishing company. That the Charles E. Tuttle Company had publishing facilities in Japan also may well have been a factor in making publication possible. The novel received little positive response, even from Japanese Americans. The work was perceived as an unflattering and disturbing portrait of the situation of Japanese Americans, and after publication, the novel vanished quickly and completely.

No-No Boy was the first and only novel by John Okada, who died at forty-seven years of age working as an unknown technical writer in the aerospace industry. Dramatist Frank Chin, in his afterword to the reissue of the novel, recounts how Okada's wife offered her husband's manuscripts and his unfinished second novel to a university library, only to have the documents rejected as worthless. She burned them.

In the early 1970's, Okada's novel was discovered and publicized by the young Asian American writers Frank Chin and Lawson Fusao Inada. The novel has been reprinted several times since, and excerpts are often anthologized. In spite of its historical importance, however, *No-No Boy* has received little scrutiny as a work of literature, and it has not become a standard part of the accepted canon of minority literature. Perhaps the coolness of the narrative and the indeterminacy of its exploration of problematical personal and social issues still keep it from extensive study and critical acclaim.

Bibliography

Chan, Jeffery Paul, Frank Chin, Lawson Fusao Inada, and Shawn H. Wong. "An Introduction to Chinese-American and Japanese-American Literatures." In *Three American Literatures: Essays in Chicano, Native American, and Asian-American Literature for Teachers of American Literature*, edited by Houston A. Baker, Jr. New York: Modern Language Association of American, 1982. The authors establish a strong historical, social, and literary context for Okada's work. They make an excellent case for the literary quality of his uses of language as rooted in the oral tradition and expressive of both the conflicts and the coherence of the Japanese American experience.

Chin, Frank, et al., eds. *Aiiieeeee! An Anthology of Asian-American Writers*. Garden City, N.Y.: Anchor Books, 1975. An excerpt from *No-No Boy* is prefaced by a biographical essay and a discussion of some of the early critical responses, including one from the Japanese community asserting that the novel is not literature. The longstanding exclusion of Okada's work from the American literary canon is pointed out by the editors.

Inada, Lawson Fusao. "The Vision of America in John Okada's *No-No Boy*." In *Ethnic Literatures Since 1776: The Many Voices of America*, edited by Wolodymyr T. Zyla and Wendell M. Aycock. Lubbock: Texas Tech University, 1978. Inada offers a glowing tribute to Okada's pioneering work and laments the author's early death. In a running commentary on Ichiro's situation and experiences, he points out the protagonist of the story, though a "no-no boy," is not so much in a state of rejection of loyalty to either his family or his nation as in a state of emptiness.

James, Thomas. "Loyalty and Its Lessons." In *Exile Within: The Schooling of Japanese Americans, 1942-1945*. Cambridge, Mass.: Harvard University Press, 1987. Although Okada's work is not discussed directly, this chapter offers a detailed account of the administration of loyalty oaths in the camps and the complex responses given. The descriptions of the conflicts experienced by interned Nisei correspond precisely to those represented in *No-No Boy*.

Kim, Elaine H. "Japanese American Family and Community Portraits." In *Asian*

American Literature: An Introduction to the Writings and Their Social Context. Philadelphia: Temple University Press, 1982. Kim suggests that the war between Japan and the United States had a "cathartic effect" on Japanese Americans and that the war and the experience of internment and rampant racism have dominated Japanese American literature. The loyalty oath that is central to the dilemma of *No-No Boy*'s protagonist is discussed as a powerful metaphor for the profound conflicts between Japanese and Japanese Americans, between self and society, between family and nation.

Virginia Crane

THE OLD GRINGO

Author: Carlos Fuentes (1928-   )
Type of plot: Historical realism
Time of plot: 1913-1914
Locale: Chihuahua, Mexico
First published: El gringo viejo, 1985 (English translation, 1985)

> *Principal characters:*
> HARRIET WINSLOW, a spinster from Washington, D.C., who goes to Mexico to work as a governess but finds herself in the midst of a revolution
> AMBROSE BIERCE, a famous writer and journalist, the "old gringo" of the title, who goes to Mexico seeking Pancho Villa, adventure, and a heroic death
> GENERAL TOMÁS ARROYO, a firebrand revolutionary torn between his loyalty to the revolution and his desire for the land he considers his birthright
> PANCHO VILLA, the revolutionary leader, who has to resolve the political dilemma caused by the old gringo's murder

The Novel

The Old Gringo is a novel fashioned as a tribute by one writer to the memory and courage of another, the cynical American journalist and storyteller Ambrose Bierce; the book offers a fictive speculation about Bierce's mysterious disappearance in Mexico in 1913 during the civil war. Carlos Fuentes imagines that Bierce, at first referred to only as the "old gringo," went to Mexico seeking Pancho Villa. His motives for going are ambiguous. He is seeking a new frontier and the adventure of fighting for the revolution, but what he seems to be seeking most is a heroic death. As Fuentes repeatedly states, the "old gringo came to Mexico to die," preferably with dignity.

The story is grounded in a factual framework. Bierce crossed the border at El Paso, Texas, in November of 1913. On December 26, he wrote that he intended to ride a troop train to Ojinaga seeking Pancho Villa. He was never heard from again. According to one legend, Bierce found Villa, became a senior staff adviser, and was later shot as a deserter, alienated by the bandit's cruelties. Fuentes works a variation on this legend.

Though named for the old gringo, the novel is mainly the story of Harriet Winslow, a spinster who leaves her mother in Washington, D.C., and goes to Mexico to work as a governess for the wealthy, landowning Miranda family, teaching English to the three Miranda children. She is seeking liberation, adventure, and independence, but she is manipulated by the Miranda family. They put her in the middle of the revolution by summoning her to their hacienda as they are making plans to depart themselves; the family uses her to create a diversion. She is also manipulated by General Tomás Arroyo, who uses her to gain entry to the Miranda estate. The Mexicans who exploit her consider her a fool. The story is framed by Harriet's memory.

The old gringo has concluded, to his shame, that he had also been manipulated and exploited during his career as a muckraking journalist by his employer, William Randolph Hearst. Bierce has contempt for his own accomplishments, done in the service of a millionaire who has profited by his talent. He describes himself as a "contemptible, muckraking reporter at the service of a baron of the press as corrupt as any I denounced in his name." He also considers himself a personal failure and blames himself for the deaths of his sons. He has turned his back on his country and on his former life. He is a would-be idealist, as Fuentes imagines him, who carries in his saddlebags a copy of the story of Don Quixote. Significantly, though, he has not yet read the book as he leaves El Paso to go tilting after windmills in revolutionary Mexico.

The gringo goes looking for Pancho Villa but instead finds General Tomás Arroyo, whom he antagonizes with his brutal honesty. His courage is unquestionable, and he is useful to Arroyo during the siege of the Miranda hacienda. Arroyo, himself a bastard son of the Mirandas, is conflicted. His quest to kill his father, Miranda, is frustrated by the family's escape, but after he has conquered the estate, he is derelict in his duty to return his army to Villa. He discovers Spanish documents that he believes to be sacred, for he thinks that whoever possesses the documents owns the land. The gringo has a more sophisticated understanding of political power than Arroyo, and he attempts to teach Arroyo that the documents are in fact worthless. When Arroyo refuses to believe him, the gringo burns the papers, and Arroyo, in a rage, shoots him in the back, killing his spiritual father, which the gringo has become.

Harriet Winslow is also searching for a father. Her own father deserted the family to serve in the Spanish-American War and never returned. Harriet confesses to the gringo that her father had not died in combat, as her mother prefers to believe, but remained in Cuba to live with a black woman. She and her mother had reported him dead in order to collect his pension: "We killed him, my mother and I," she confesses, "in order to live."

Harriet, too, becomes conflicted in Mexico; she is torn between the young Arroyo and the seventy-one-year-old gringo, who treats her with both respect and affection. She surrenders herself to Arroyo, claiming that she did so to save the gringo's life, a rationale that the gringo refuses to accept or believe. His humor is always to force those around him to face the truth. Arroyo, therefore, has exploited Harriet sexually, and she comes to hate him for that. She gets her vengeance, however, by reporting the gringo's death to the United States consulate, claiming that the gringo was her father, and demanding that his body be returned to Arlington National Cemetery for a military burial.

This lie creates a political problem for Pancho Villa, who is liable to be held responsible for the death of a captain of the United States Army. Politically, Villa and his allies will need the support of the United States government if their revolution is to succeed, and Villa must take measures to rectify the situation. The body of the gringo is exhumed, propped up against a wall, and shot by a firing squad at Villa's command. Arroyo is ordered to administer the *coup de grace*; he is then executed by the same firing squad. Harriet claims the body of the gringo and takes it home, where she continues to live with her memories. "She sits and remembers," Fuentes explains repeatedly.

The Characters

None of the major characters fully captures the sympathy of the reader in this story of revolutionary fervor, partly, perhaps, because they are symbolic stereotypes borrowed from the American Western: The outlaw (Arroyo), the gunfighter (the gringo), and the schoolmarm (Harriet). The fact that the characters seem to belong to a popular and familiar genre may, however, help to explain the novel's popular success.

Both Tomás Arroyo and the old gringo are defined by their courage and integrity. The gringo, an erstwhile cynic, is also a would-be idealist trying to rectify the mistakes of a lifetime. He is admirable in his dedication to truth and uncompromising in his determination not to let others be self-deceived. He forces Harriet to admit that she gave herself to Arroyo out of passion and desire. He forces Arroyo to take action by burning the Spanish documents that Arroyo considers his birthright. The gringo's death is a natural consequence of his actions, but his death is hardly to be pitied, since by his own admission he came to Mexico to die. His death serves a purpose; it puts Arroyo back on the revolutionary track.

If Arroyo's course is derailed, finally, it is because of Harriet's vindictiveness, not because of the old gringo. Just as the gringo represents age, wisdom, truth, and integrity, Tomás Arroyo represents unspoiled Mexican machismo. He is a pure revolutionary uncompromised by politics, unlike Pancho Villa, whose actions in the gringo affair are ultimately dictated by a concern for U.S. foreign policy. Arroyo could be a sympathetic icon of the oppressed Mexican minority, but his motives are flawed by a personal agenda. His revolutionary purpose is stalled. He cannot decide whether to be a Miranda or to continue fighting for the revolution. He presents all that is hopeful and virile in the new Mexico, but he is undone by his own past, by his virility, and by the Americans. He is a strong leader, but his misdeeds cause problems for Villa. Arroyo pays for these mistakes with his life, but he dies bravely, shouting "Viva, Villa!" Even so, at the final moment, his face is "the living image of pain and disbelief." He is a simple man driven by complex psychological motives he cannot fully comprehend. His innocence is carefully balanced against the cynical wisdom and experience of the old gringo, who becomes a father figure to him.

Harriet Winslow, the schoolmarm from the East, is made interesting by the conflict between her idealism and her sexual repression. She is sympathetic in that she is given a taste of an exotic and adventurous life in which she knows she cannot fully participate; her bitterness and vindictiveness, though, finally alienate her from the reader. She cannot forgive Arroyo for showing her a life that is not hers for the taking after he has inflamed her passion. Her punishment after her brief adventures in Mexico is to live a life of regret as she "sits and remembers." Her memories provide the dominant framework for the story, which is mainly her story.

Themes and Meanings

The novel is a cross-cultural meditation that demonstrates the differences between the Mexican and North American national temperaments. The freedom fighter Arroyo is an innocent undone by the inexperienced Harriet and the experienced gringo, both of whom make demands that he is unable to satisfy. In the novel's preoccupation with Mexico and Mexican history, apart from the way it explores the relationship of Mexico and the United States, *The Old Gringo* resembles Fuentes' earlier novel *La muerte de Artemio Cruz* (1962; *The Death of Artemio Cruz*, 1964).

The two novels also share a tendency to experiment with nonlinear storytelling, shifting points of view, consciousness, and structure. In earlier novels, Fuentes had experimented with multiple narrative voices. The point of view of *The Old Gringo* is predominantly third-person omniscient, but Fuentes rapidly shifts the focus from character to character without regard to linear chronology. Sequences and conversations started earlier in the novel are continued later, after the reader has developed a better and more complete sense of context. The narrative technique is sophisticated and challenging.

In the novel, the elegant Miranda hacienda becomes a symbol of the old order, which must be destroyed but which casts a hypnotic spell over Arroyo, who has links to the family, and threatens to seduce him from his revolutionary purpose. This could partly explain his sexual attraction for Harriet as well, since she is linked to the world of the Mirandas. The hacienda is a repository of historic memory and fantasy, its many mirrors serving as windows to the past. The peasants gaze into these mirrors and are enjoined by Arroyo to "see themselves," but the mirrors can also distort what they reflect. Harriet Winslow, a city woman from another culture, looks into the mirrors but can only see herself. For her, the mirrors cannot have the same cultural significance, since they will not reflect her history. What she sees is a thirty-one-year-old Gibson Girl in a Mexican setting.

The novel has been praised for its vivid treatment of the peasants' revolt against their masters but it has also been criticized for its mannered, dreamlike surrealism and its portentous symbolism and rhetoric. The legend of Ambrose Bierce is a dominant symbol. Bierce represents uncompromising honesty, which drives him out of the United States but is also not tolerated in Mexico, where his honesty is the destroyer of dreams. Harriet Winslow seems to represent both American innocence and American duplicity. The lesson she learns is that she cannot adjust to the "other," to a simple life in a different culture.

The novel is shot through with irony: Harriet and her mother have been living a lie in the United States, and Harriet goes to Mexico to find a new life; there, she finds only death and disappointment, and she returns to the United States to live another lie. Arroyo is obsessed with the idea of murdering his actual father, but he pays with his life for murdering his spiritual father. The old gringo wants to be put up against a wall and shot by Pancho Villa; he gets his wish, but only after he is already dead, shot ignominiously in the back by Arroyo. Harriet's journey to Mexico is framed as a spiritual quest, but the novelist turns it into a sexual one. She is not honest with the gringo or with herself about her sexual surrender to Arroyo.

The theme of children searching for fathers and a father searching for his children is carefully crafted but ultimately overworked. The theme of memory and its consequences and the notion that one's home can only be found through one's memories is interestingly developed.

Critical Context

The Old Gringo was first conceived as a film project. Although the story was effectively simplified and clarified by the film version directed by Luis Puenzo and produced by Jane Fonda in 1989, the film was a box-office failure, perhaps because the novel's value resides not so much in its story and relatively wooden archetypes as in its psychological complexity, which cannot conveniently be brought to the surface and visualized. The film makes the story more easily comprehensible—the identification of the gringo with Ambrose Bierce is made clear to the viewer from the very beginning, for example—but it cannot be as well understood, except on the most superficial level.

The Old Gringo is more than merely a colorful and passionate revolutionary epic that resembles a classic Western featuring archetypal characters. It is both a psychological novel and an intercultural meditation disguised as popular fiction that seems to exploit sensuality, romance, and adventure, and its varied strengths made it the first novel by a Mexican writer to become a U.S. best-seller.

Bibliography

Brown, Georgia. "A Woman's Work." *The Village Voice*, October 17, 1990, 90. Brown evaluates both the film adaptation and the novel, pointing out that even before the novel was published, Fuentes had assured Fonda that the novel would contain a part for her. Brown criticizes the novel as silly, but she tends to overlook the book's psychological complexity.

Kearns, George. "Revolutionary Women and Others." *The Hudson Review* 39 (Spring, 1986): 129. States that Fuentes has written a "colorful historical novel, filled with vivid, often moving scenes of the peasants' revolt against their masters." Kearns objects, however, to the "portentous symbolism and rhetoric" with which the novel is loaded.

Meacham, Cherie. "The Process of Dialogue in *Gringo viejo.*" *Hispanic Journal* 10 (Spring, 1989): 127-137. Asserts that three principal characters of the novel "achieve their being through a dialogue that examines barriers between generations" and barriers between "cultures, genders, and levels of self." Harriet and Arroyo are linked by their youth and idealism, by his "animal dynamism" and her "repressed sensuality"; both are contrasted to the older gringo's cynicism.

Talbot, Stephen. "On the Run with Carlos Fuentes." *Mother Jones* 13 (November, 1988): 20-25, 46. Talbot surveys Fuentes' life and career, paying particular attention to the writer's ambiguous feelings toward Americans. The United States is "a country of immigrants and pioneers, a country of extreme mobility," Fuentes is quoted as saying, "while Mexico is a country that never moved until the revolution."

Tittler, Jonathan. "Gringo viejo/The Old Gringo: The Rest is Fiction." *Review of Contemporary Fiction* 8 (Summer, 1988): 241-248. Tittler is concerned about the "untranslatability" of the Spanish original, which "does not maintain a word-to-word (or even page-to-page) correspondence with its English translation." Tittler notes that the Spanish version reverses the order of some chapters and adds an author's note that comments on Bierce and the novel's historical setting.

Updike, John. "Latin Strategies." *The New Yorker*, February 24, 1986, 98-104. Updike complains that Bierce, in real life the "writer of a thousand sardonic jokes," in the novel lacks a sense of humor. He also argues that the reader learns little about Mexico, even though the novel "goes through the motions of establishing geographical and historical authenticity," and dismisses the book as "mere mannerism."

James M. Welsh

ON DISTANT GROUND

Author: Robert Olen Butler (1945-)
Type of plot: Psychological realism
Time of plot: 1975
Locale: Baltimore, Maryland, and Saigon, Vietnam
First published: 1985

> *Principal characters:*
> DAVID FLEMING, an Army captain about to be court-martialed for setting
> a Viet Cong officer free
> JENNIFER FLEMING, David's wife, who gives birth to their son during the
> trial
> CARL LOMAS, David's Army lawyer
> KENNETH TRASK, a CIA officer who helps David return to Vietnam
> PHAM VAN TUYEN, the Viet Cong officer David set free
> NGUYEN THI TUYET SUONG, David's lover in Vietnam
> KHAI, David's Vietnamese son

The Novel

On Distant Ground is the fictional account of Army captain David Fleming and his internal and external conflicts with his experiences in Vietnam during the Vietnam War. Within the novel, Robert Olen Butler has not used formal chapter breaks; rather, white space divides one section from the next. The first two-thirds of the novel alternates between scenes in present time and scenes from Fleming's time in Vietnam. It is in these flashbacks that the reader is given the background for Fleming's court-martial.

The novel begins with the preliminary stages of David's trial and the birth of his and Jennifer's son, David Junior. David is being tried for aiding the enemy. He kidnapped Pham Van Tuyen, a known Viet Cong officer, from Con Son, the island where Tuyen was being held prisoner by the Army of the Republic of Vietnam (ARVN). Carl Lomas, David's lawyer, seems more concerned about the trial than David and tries to get him to think of anything he might be able to say in his own defense. David cannot think of anything; he freed Tuyet out of compassion when he saw the words "hygiene is healthful" written on Tuyet's vacated cell at the interrogation center in Bien Hoa.

During the preliminary trial stages, Jennifer and David's son is born, and David realizes that he now has another responsibility, that of a family. Both he and Jennifer become brittle as the pressure surrounding David's position and the real possibility of a prison term become more real to them. Adding to the tension is David's sudden realization that he has a son in Vietnam. He has no concrete knowledge of this situation, but he sees the news reports about children of American servicemen being evacuated from Vietnam and realizes that the reason Suong, his Vietnamese lover, disappeared was because she was pregnant. Suddenly obsessed, he realizes that he must return to Vietnam and bring his son home before Saigon falls to the Communist government.

David's trial and his growing concern about his son occur simultaneously. He sets up a meeting with Kenneth Trask, his Central Intelligence Agency (CIA) contact, and apprises him of the situation. Trask informs him that he can do nothing about the outcome of the trial; if David is not sent to prison, however, there is a chance that Trask could arrange for him to return to Vietnam to try to locate his son. Rather than a prison term, David is given a reduction in rank, a loss of pay, and a dishonorable discharge from the Army.

Trask arranges for David to return to Vietnam using a Canadian passport and other false identification papers. He is warned that Saigon will fall to the Communists in three days at the most. Once he is in Saigon, David begins the near-impossible task of locating Suong or part of her family. Her house in Saigon has been taken over by squatters, and the family home in the country is in disrepair. One servant is left, and she tells David that Suong has disappeared and her mother, Madame Trung, is still in Saigon. David returns to Saigon, and the Communists soon take over the city.

David locates Madame Trung and his son, Khai. He also learns that Suong had openly opposed the government of South Vietnam and had been in prison in Saigon for a year. Convinced that the Communist government would free her, he goes to the prison in search of information. He is taken to the office of Pham Van Tuyen, who is now the director of security for Saigon. Tuyen apparently does not recognize David, and since David is supposedly working for a Canadian organization that has Communist leanings, he agrees to try to find out what he can about Suong.

David returns to Madame Trung's the same evening and learns that a soldier had delivered Suong's ashes and some of her possessions earlier in the evening. Madame Trung convinces him to take his boy back to America and gives him the final payment for the illegal trip out of the country she had been planning.

David leaves during the night with Khai and makes his way to the rendezvous point. Unfortunately, the Communist officials have arrested Mr. Quang, the boat captain who was going to smuggle them out of the country. David is knocked out and wakes up in prison. From there, he is taken to a private audience with Tuyen.

Tuyen does, in fact, know who David is. Through a long interrogation, David does convince Tuyen that he is not a CIA spy and that his only motivation for returning to Vietnam was to find his son and take him back to America. Possibly in gratitude for David's freeing of him, Tuyen allows David and Khai to leave Vietnam and return to America.

The Characters

David Fleming, an Army intelligence captain, is not, at the beginning of the novel, a sympathetic character. He has, by his own admission, allowed a known Viet Cong officer to escape from a South Vietnamese prison. Through David's own thoughts, the reader is able to learn why he did what he did. There is a great sense of helplessness that is conveyed when David tells his attorney, Carl Lomas, that he can think of no way to explain his actions; the motivations are too complicated. David does, however, exhibit tremendous integrity. The moment he realizes that he has a child in Vietnam, he contacts Kenneth Trask and has him work out a plan for David to return to Vietnam to find his child, who he is sure is a son. While there are aspects to David's character that the reader might find unappealing, he is an honorable man. Butler refuses to have a stock Vietnam veteran as his main character. Rather, Fleming is a sensitive, complex man for whom there are no easy answers.

Jennifer Fleming, David's wife, is seen, more often than not, through the eyes of her husband. The reader is immediately sympathetic toward her because she is pregnant and vulnerable. Her husband is being court-martialed, and there is a strong possibility that she will be rearing their child while he is in prison. The reader is impressed by her strength throughout the ordeal. In addition, she will vent her frustrations and fears to David. Jennifer is a strong character, but she is not a martyr. She is, after some consideration, able to accept David's son from his affair with Suong and finally encourages him to go back to Vietnam.

Kenneth Trask is the typical CIA operative. He is secretive and constantly seems to lurk in shadows. His character is developed through his actions. While he admits that there is no way that he can alter the outcome of David's trial, he is willing to make arrangements for the documents that will allow David to enter South Vietnam even though the country is about to fall to the Communists. While little is revealed about Trask, he is the one character who seems immediately to understand David's need to return for his son.

Pham Van Tuyen is the Viet Cong officer whom David releases from the South Vietnamese prison. He is a complex man who is seen at the bottom and top of his career. The reader first meets him when he has escaped from his jailers on Con Son Island. As a result of the torture he has endured, Tuyen is weak and unable to function well. It is unsure how much of the situation he understands; however, he allows David to take him to a helicopter and back to his home. The next time the reader sees Tuyen, he is the director of security for the new Communist government in Saigon. Ironically, it is he who now has David's fate in his hands. Through his actions, he reveals that he, too, is a complex man who does not see actions as all black or white. Possibly to the surprise of the reader, he does allow David to maintain his cover as a Canadian and return to America with his son.

Themes and Meanings

On Distant Ground is a critique of the American military and its presence in Vietnam. The events transpire during the fall of South Vietnam to the Communist north after the departure of the U.S. military in 1975. The novel is also a poignant reminder of the number of children in Vietnam who have American fathers and who are ridiculed by their society because of their mixed background.

On Distant Ground is also about confusion. Throughout the work, Butler points out that there are no easy answers to any situation. While there may theoretically be black-and-white answers to any question, this is seldom true in reality. While David Fleming does aid the enemy, he does not do so in order to betray his country. Rather, he knows that it is only a matter of time before the Americans will leave. His rescue of Tuyen is, if anything, motivated by a possibly misplaced sense of compassion.

Butler also reminds the reader that no one has a blameless past. While David has married Jennifer in good faith, he has done so knowing that he has had an affair with another woman, even though the affair with Suong was over before he and Jennifer met. He must, in the context of the novel, now tell Jennifer that he has had an affair and, more difficult, that he wants to retrieve his son and bring him to America. Again, there are no easy solutions. While Jennifer is, after her initial outrage and shock, understanding, David is asking her to do something that anyone would be reluctant to do—rear a child from a spouse's past relationship.

The overriding theme of the novel does seem to be that good triumphs over evil. The author does, however, give an old theme a new angle. The good and bad characters are not absolutes. All the characters have good and bad traits, a condition that is more realistic, but perhaps also more difficult for the reader to accept.

Critical Context

On Distant Ground was Butler's fourth novel. The novel served to place Butler firmly within the ranks of Vietnam authors such as Tim O'Brien, Lynda Van Deventer, W. D. Ehrhart, and Larry Heineman, who, like Butler, helped to give the reading public a new, realistic view of the Vietnam War.

In the novel, Butler experiments with flashback, through which device nearly all Fleming's experiences are told. Butler also eliminates the traditional chapter breaks, relying on white space to signal his changes and giving the novel the feel of a seamless narrative. While the story is told in the third person, the main focus of the novel is on David Fleming, and it is through him that the reader receives most of the information about events and characters.

All of Butler's books have received critical acclaim. His collection of short stories about Vietnamese refugees living in Louisiana, *A Good Scent from a Strange Mountain* (1993), received the Pulitzer Prize in 1993. That work and the remainder of his impressive canon have made Butler one of the important voices in late twentieth century American literature.

Bibliography

Beidler, Philip D. *Re-Writing America: Vietnam Authors in Their Generation*. Athens: University of Georgia Press, 1991. In this thought-provoking book, Biedler places Vietnam authors within their generation, which provides the reader with the appropriate context for reading Vietnam fiction. In addition, there is a very good section on Butler that places his novels within the genre. Biedler also establishes and discusses the relationship between Butler's *The Alleys of Eden* (1981), *Sun Dogs* (1982), and *On Distant Ground*, which make up a trilogy about the Vietnam War.

Butler, Robert Olen. "The Process of Writing a Novel." *The Writer* 95 (April, 1982): 11-13. Butler describes the process he used to write *The Alleys of Eden*. Clifford Wilkes, who has a minor role in *On Distant Ground*, is the main character in *The Alleys of Eden*. In addition, it is useful to see the process Butler went through to gather and organize his material for the novel.

Klein, Joe. "Soldiers and Doctors." *The New York Times Book Review*, April 12, 1985, 26. Klein places *On Distant Ground* within the canon of Vietnam fiction. In addition, he writes that the story's "pyramiding absurdities seem not merely plausible, but inevitable."

Olshan, Joseph. "Louisiana: 'God, It's the Mekong Delta!' " *People* 39 (May 31, 1993): 22. In this interview, Butler talks about his experiences in Vietnam and how they influenced him and his writing. He also recalls his first view of Lake Charles, Louisiana, and how much it reminded him geographically of Vietnam.

Victoria E. McLure

OPERATION SHYLOCK
A Confession

Author: Philip Roth (1933-   )
Type of plot: Novel of ideas
Time of plot: 1988
Locale: The United States and Israel
First published: 1993

> *Principal characters:*
> PHILIP ROTH, the author, who dominates the book as a character and
> relates its events in the first person
> MOISHE PIPIK, ("Moses Bellybutton"), the narrator's double
> GEORGE ZIAD, a college friend of Roth who has become an anti-Israeli
> Palestinian
> JINX POSSESSKI, Moishe Pipik's voluptuous girlfriend
> AHARON APPELFELD, an Israeli novelist who is Roth's friend
> SMILESBURGER, an undercover agent employed by Israel's secret service
> JOHN DEMJANJUK, a Cleveland auto worker on trial for allegedly having
> been a monstrous death-camp guard

The Novel

Operation Shylock is Philip Roth's most complex, convoluted and baffling novel, in which he uses the device of the literary double to parallel his identity and history in the text's two leading personages. He thereby causes the reader to ponder the provocative and probably insoluble conundrums of fiction's relation to reality and of autobiography's role in the working of the literary imagination.

Not only does the protagonist-narrator appear under the name, personal history, and likeness of the author as Philip Roth, but from the book's opening chapter, another man obtrudes with the same name and in the same likeness, with the same gestures and in identical attire. The narrator, Philip, decides to name his double Moishe Pipik, Yiddish for Moses Bellybutton, a comical shadow and fall guy in Jewish folklore.

Philip is recovering, in his Connecticut home, from withdrawal symptoms after having discontinued taking pills to overcome severe pain resulting from knee surgery. In January, 1988, seven months after coming off the drug, he is informed, by a friend, the Israeli writer Aharon Appelfeld, that a Philip Roth is lecturing in Jerusalem's King David hotel on the topic, "Diasporism: The Only Solution to the Jewish Problem."

Philip phones his impostor, pretending to be a French journalist, and receives a long-distance lecture on Diasporism: It is Pipik's plan to move all Jews of European descent out of Israel and back to their ancestral countries in the hope of averting a second, Arab-organized Holocaust. Israel, Pipik insists, has become the gravest of threats to Jewish survival because of the Arabs' resentment of Israel's expansion. Were European Jews and their families resettled in the lands of their cultural origins, however, only Jews of Islamic descent would be left in Israel. The nation could then revert to its 1948 borders and could demobilize its large army, and Arabs and Israelis would coexist amicably and peacefully.

Philip objects that Pipik's proposal is wholly naïve, since Europe's hatred of Jews persists. Pipik responds that Europe's residual anti-Semitism is outweighed by powerful currents of enlightenment and morality sustained by the memory of the Holocaust. Hence, a Diasporist movement would enable Europeans to cleanse their guilty conscience. Philip's most caustic rebuttal to Pipik's argument occurs later in the book:

> When the first hundred thousand Diasporist evacuees voluntarily surrender their criminal Zionist homeland to the suffering Palestinians and disembark on England's green and pleasant land, I want to see with my very own eyes the welcoming committee of English goyim waiting on the platform with their champagne. 'They're here! More Jews! Jolly good!' No, *fewer* Jews is my sense of how Europe prefers things, *as few of them as possible.*

Flying to Jerusalem, Philip begins a searching interview, to be continued on several occasions in the book, with the distinguished Appelfeld, a Holocaust survivor whom he admires as a spiritual brother to his better self. (This interview was published by *The New York Times* in February, 1988.) He then attends the trial of John Ivan Demjanjuk, the Ukrainian-born auto worker accused of being the monstrous guard "Ivan the Terrible" Marchenko at the Treblinka death camp. (Israel's Supreme Court declared Demjanjuk's identity as Marchenko unproven five months after publication of the novel.)

Roth then comes face to face with his *Doppelgänger*, shocked to find him dressed in his own preferred outfit of blue Oxford shirt, khaki trousers, V-neck sweater, and herringbone jacket. The perfection of Pipik's duplication infuriates the original, whose charge of personality appropriation meets a rush of fawning verbosity, with Pipik assuring Philip that he is his greatest admirer. Philip's response to this bizarre doubling is a mixture of outrage, exasperation, fascination, and even amusement.

Hours later, Pipik sends Philip a pleading note: "LET ME EXIST. . . . I AM THE YOU THAT IS NOT WORDS." Its bearer is a wondrously voluptuous, mid-thirties blonde, Wanda Jane "Jinx" Possesski, an oncology nurse who has become Pipik's loving companion. In due time, Jinx delivers her life story: hateful, strictly Catholic parents, then a runaway hippie life, abusive men, Christian fundamentalism, a nursing career. She became an anti-Semite out of envy of Jewish cohesion, cleverness, sexual ease, and prosperity. Then she met Pipik as a patient for cancer, now in remission. Thanks to him, she is a recovering anti-Semite, saved by an organization he founded, Anti-Semites Anonymous. When Jinx reveals that Pipik had a penile implant so he could satisfy her, Philip cannot resist the temptation to outdo his double by implanting his unassisted virility on Jinx.

Pipik and Jinx leave Israel and end up in Roth's Hackensack, New Jersey, where Pipik expires of his cancer hours after the first Iraqi missiles explode in Tel Aviv in January, 1991. In the hope of resuscitating him, Jinx makes love for two days to his penile implant. She relates these events in a letter to Philip that concludes with the defiant comment, "I was far nuttier as a little Catholic taking Communion that having sex with my dead Jew." In his reply, Philip disciplines his senses enough to renounce the opportunity of repossessing Possesski. His letter to Jinx remains unanswered.

The Characters

Philip Roth's career as a novelist has long featured the self-revealing and self-reflexive concerns that pervade *Operation Shylock*. He has repeatedly invented avatars of himself in his protagonists, straddling the borderline between fiction and autobiography; after all, this novel is subtitled "A Confession." In the first chapter, Philip, after having been informed of Pipik's impersonation, muses, "It's Zuckerman, I thought . . . it's Kepesh, it's Tarnopol and Portnoy—it's all of them in one, broken free of print and mockingly reconstituted as a single satirical facsimile of me."

Alexander Portnoy is the protagonist of Roth's most popular novel, *Portnoy's Complaint* (1969). Peter Tarnopol is the central character in *My Life as a Man* (1974). David Alan Kepesh is the Kafkaesque victim of *The Breast* (1972). Nathan Zuckerman, Roth's most identifiable surrogate, stars in *Zuckerman Bound* (1985), which brings together three sequential novels, *The Ghost Writer* (1979), *Zuckerman Unbound* (1981), and *The Anatomy Lesson* (1983). Zuckerman is virtually a Rothian clone, author of a successful, controversial novel, *Carnovsky*, that closely resembles *Portnoy's Complaint*. This tetralogy is probably Roth's most varied, thoughtful, playful, and altogether best fictive performance.

"Philip Roth" as the protagonist of *Operation Shylock* is far more aggressive than Nathan Zuckerman. Roth the novelist has created in this Philip his most vivid character: fiercely comic, exuberant, stubbornly reasonable, and, on occasion, unreasonably stubborn. Above all, Philip is immensely curious, about others as well as himself.

Philip's impostor, Moishe Pipik, is a brilliant mimic or an authentic refraction of the narrator; he is also a liar, a charlatan, a wild obsessive, and an extravagant megalomaniac. To be sure, Pipik belongs to the literary tradition of the double, but Roth insists on making Moishe's relation to fictional self-reflexivity more prominent than any grand psychological resonance. The author construes the double not as the embodiment of the hidden self but rather as the far less threatening reinvention of the self for fictive purposes.

Roth features two other characterizations. One is that of an old friend of Philip from his University of Chicago days, George Ziad, who has become an official of the Palestine Liberation Organization (PLO) after having returned to his native Ramallah. Ziad calls himself "a word-throwing Arab," full of distress and anger at Israeli occupation of Palestine. He sees the current Israel as an arrogant, provincial, mediocre Jewish Belgium, "without even a Brussels to show for it." He characterizes Israeli politicians Menachem Begin and Ariel Sharon as Holocaust-mongers and gangsters. Philip is astounded to see the formerly suave, debonair Ziad a victim of his consuming rages, spluttering anti-Israeli harangues.

As an emblematic contrast, Roth features an Israeli secret agent, Smilesburger, a smooth-talking father figure who mixes ruthlessness with tact, pragmatism with wisdom. He persuades Philip to undertake a spying mission, "Operation Shylock"—presumably against the PLO—in Athens. Then, in the book's postscript, Smilesburger persuades a reluctant Philip to delete, for security reasons, a book chapter describing the espionage. "Let your Jewish conscience by your guide" is the epilogue's last line.

Gradations of humor tint the characterizations, including farce, burlesque, parody, and lampoonery. Roth stages a verbal vaudeville, with the characters often talking heads attached to frenzied monologues and excessively melodramatic, zany gestures. Thus, Jinx Possesski is a comic-book version of Jewish masturbatory fantasies centering around a delectable and available shiksa. Smilesburger is a tongue-in-cheek salute to John le Carré's fictional master spy Smiley. Pipik is ludicrous as well as deranged. In a bedroom conversation with Jinx, Philip expresses his sense of being trapped in a farce: "It's *Hellzapoppin'* with Possesski and Pipik, it's a gag a minute with you two madcap kids. . . . Diasporism is a plot for a Marx Brothers movie—Groucho selling Jews to Chancellor Kohl!"

Themes and Meanings

Operation Shylock is a very Jewish version of the use of the literary double. Roth establishes this theme in his two prefatory mottoes. The first translates Genesis 32:24: "So Jacob was left alone, and a man wrestled with him until daybreak." Roth suggests that the first split self in literature may have been the mysterious stranger, possibly the Angel of Death, who represents the fate Jacob fears at the hands of his vengeful brother, Esau. Could Pipik be an Esau, threatening Jacob-Philip?

The second epigraph is from Søren Kierkegaard:

> The whole content of my being shrieks
> in contradiction against itself.
> Existence is surely a debate. . . .

"Against itself" is Roth's evaluation of his nature, his art, possibly his life. For this is a confessional and self-reflexive novel, pointedly exposing Roth's own history and the text's structure as fictive artifice. Like his Philip, Roth is a brainy, funny, self-consciously Jewish writer with affectionate memories of his boyhood in Newark, New Jersey, with a wife whose first name is Claire (the British actress Claire Bloom), with a farmhouse home in Connecticut, and with Appelfeld his good friend. Like his Philip, Roth attended John Demjanjuk's trial. As he states in a final note, he used verbatim the minutes of one of the morning sessions to provide the courtroom exchanges in his ninth chapter. Thus Roth is not only preoccupied in this book with such issues as the course of Israel's evolution, the grievances of displaced Palestinians, and Jewish self-affirmation in opposition to a resurgence of anti-Semitism. He is, above all, preoccupied by himself.

Roth's first-person voice goes back to the youngest of his twenty books, *Goodbye,*

Columbus (1959), and has informed almost all of them. He parades the fact that a writer's life is his basic instrument of perception, possessing an authenticity and intimacy that can convey reader acceptance and conviction. He construes the double as the reinvention of the self for the purpose of fiction. Yet which self? The novel is one contentious self-on-self wrestling match. There is Philip, who is flattered by George Ziad as a model non-Israeli Jew, by Israeli students as an eminent, oracular author, by Jinx as a great lover and leader, by Smilesburger as both an outstanding writer and brilliant spy. Yet there is also Pipik, his Dostoyevskian *Doppelgänger*, zealous, paranoid, pathetic, both idealistic and mad. Then there is the manic part of Philip, or Roth himself, which has him impersonate Moishe and his Diasporist dementia as he plays at being Pipik for a credulous Ziad. "You just say everything," Philip tells himself, as he mockingly compliments Irving Berlin for having turned both Christmas and Easter into nonreligious, schlocky occasions with his songs. "We have been intertwined for decades in a thousand different ways," Pipik assures Philip. So, of course, have been the identities of John Demjanjuk and Ivan Marchenko. Moral ambiguity oozes through the book.

Critical Context

Operation Shylock is vulnerable, despite its wit, learning, intelligence, and eloquence, to the charges of hostile critics that Roth is trapped in narcissistic, sermon-ridden reveries whose tone is overly argumentative and whose vision is enslaved to his personal experiences and obsessions. In his defense, Roth could cite the long-established tradition of introspective writing originated by such classics of Romanticism as Jean-Jacques Rousseau's *Les Confessions de J.-J. Rousseau* (1782, 1789; *The Confessions of J.-J. Rousseau*, 1783-1790) and William Wordsworth's *The Prelude: Or, the Growth of a Poet's Mind* (1850). One direct influence on Roth's autobiographical texts is surely Fyodor Dostoevski's *Notes from the Underground* (1864), the first-person narrator of which resembles his creator in temperament and history yet remains a creature of fiction. A century later, Albert Camus used the same searingly subjective device in *La Chute* (1956; *The Fall*, 1957).

In less direct form, many of modernism's greatest novels and stories by such writers as Thomas Mann, Franz Kafka, and James Joyce present material from the author's life. Many others, including Dostyevski, Kafka, E. T. A. Hoffmann, Edgar Allan Poe, Nikolai Gogol, Joseph Conrad, Robert Louis Stevenson, and Vladimir Nabokov, have employed the literary device of the double.

Operation Shylock is thus both postmodern in its uses of self-consciousness and traditional in its exploration of the divided self. It is a masterful accomplishment by one of America's most important writers.

Bibliography

Alter, Robert. "The Spritzer." *The New Republic* 208 (April 5, 1993): 31-34. Alter teaches Hebrew and comparative literature at the University of California at Berkeley. This review stresses Roth's gift for what Jewish comedians call "spritz":

stand-up comedy that engages urgent political ideas and issues of identity.

Bloom, Harold. "Operation Roth." *The New York Review of Books* 40 (April 22, 1993): 45-48. Bloom, Sterling Professor of the Humanities at Yale, has long admired Roth's writing. He particularly praises the novel's narrative exuberance, moral intelligence, and high humor.

Gray, Paul. "A Complaint: Double Vision." *Time* 141 (March 8, 1993): 68-69. Gray likes the novel's "comic abandon" and broad social and historical range. He finds the book to be "a lot of fun."

Rodgers, Bernard F., Jr. Philip Roth. Boston: Twayne, 1978. Even though dated, the best of several books written on Roth. Rodgers emphasizes Roth's capacity for combining moral seriousness with comic insight. The chapter on *The Breast* gives this novella much higher marks than most Roth critics have done.

Updike, John. "Recruiting Raw Nerves." *The New Yorker* 69 (March 15, 1993): 109-112. As a novelist, Updike is in many ways Roth's opposite: coolly disciplined, WASPish, never boisterous. Yet he is an astute and generous critic, and his review praises Roth highly for his evocative style and ingenious plotting. Updike, however, does complain that the book has too many long monologues and that Roth is "an exhausting author to be with."

Gerhard Brand

THE OTHER SIDE

Author: Mary Gordon (1949-   )
Type of plot: Family
Time of plot: 1895-1985
Locale: New York City and Ireland
First published: 1989

> *Principal characters:*
> ELLEN COSTELLOE MCNAMARA, the matriarch of the McNamara family, who is dying of a stroke
> VINCENT MCNAMARA, Ellen's husband, who is returning home after a ten-month stay in a nursing home
> MAGDALENE MCNAMARA, Ellen and Vincent's oldest daughter, an alcoholic beautician who has not left her room in fifteen years
> THERESA MCNAMARA DOOLEY, the middle child, a medical secretary and religious fanatic
> CAMILLE (CAM) MCNAMARA, Magdalene's only child, a divorce lawyer
> DAN MCNAMARA, Cam's cousin and law partner

The Novel

The Other Side traces an Irish American family, the McNamaras, through five generations, from the "old sod" to "the other side," as the Irish called America. Framed by the events of one day, August 14, 1985, the story spans ninety years, weaving the memories of various family members throughout to tell the tale. The book consists of five sections: The first and last parts introduce the family members and set the scene in the present; the second relates Ellen McNamara's memories of her life; the third explores the lives of second-, third- and fourth-generation McNamaras; and the fourth recounts the past from Vincent's point of view.

The novel opens as Vincent McNamara recalls the night some ten months earlier when his wife Ellen, ninety years old and cruelly debilitated from a series of strokes, rises from her bed and strikes out at him in a senseless rage. She knocks him down, breaking his hip and leaving him helpless as she wanders into the street in her nightclothes. Vincent, who summons help by hurling family heirlooms through the window, spends ten months in a rest home recuperating, while Ellen continues to fluctuate between rage, fear, and sleep under the care of a domineering nurse at home. The story returns to the present as the family gathers to celebrate Vincent's return from the nursing home.

As Ellen drifts closer to death, her memories of the past become stronger than her grip on the present, and she relives her life. Her idyllic existence as the only child of a beautiful mother and handsome, successful father degenerates into a nightmare as her mother is transformed by a series of miscarriages and stillbirths into a fat, gibbering madwoman while her father takes up with another woman. The remainder of Ellen's childhood is spent caring for and concealing her mother, nourishing a profound hatred for her once-beloved father, and plotting her escape to America by stealing from her father's business. Leaving her mother in the care of a hired girl, she arrives in America, taking jobs first as a lady's maid and later as a seamstress. Her anger and resentment are further nourished by servitude and miserable working conditions, and she becomes passionately interested in the union movement and politics. She falls in love with and marries Vincent McNamara and begins her life as wife and mother.

Vincent also escapes a miserable, poverty-stricken childhood in Ireland by emigrating to America. He accepts the first position he is offered, an unspeakably miserable job digging the New York City subway system, although he trained as an ironworker in Ireland. He later works as a signal repairman and machinist and becomes actively involved in union organizing until a heart attack forces him to take up a less stressful occupation and give up union activity.

Ellen and Vincent, although devoted to each other, fail as parents. Ellen dislikes her daughters and lavishes all of her attention on her only son, John. The oldest daughter, Magdalene, marries hastily in search of the affection she missed at home, is widowed early, and becomes an alcoholic, self-imposed invalid, leaving the responsibility of rearing her daughter, Cam, to her parents. Theresa, the second daughter, is cold, judgmental, and filled with hate. She passes her mother's coldness on to her own children. Their son John impregnates a girl and must marry her before going off to be killed in the war. Ellen intimidates her daughter-in-law into leaving the child, Dan, for her and Vincent to rear. It is only with these grandchildren, Dan and Cam, that Ellen is able to provide the maternal love that was withheld from her own children. Dan and Cam grow up much closer than most brothers and sisters, and they are loving toward and protective of their surrogate parents.

As the novel returns to 1985, Cam picks up a reluctant Vincent at the nursing home to return him to care for Ellen and to keep the promise made early in their marriage that she will die in her own bed. Dreading the ties of family obligations and complications after the easy sociability of the nursing home, Vincent nevertheless realizes as he enters the house and sees his wife again that home is where he belongs.

The Characters

Ellen McNamara embodies many of the worst aspects of Irish culture and experience. Although she is bright, opinionated, and outspoken by nature, her childhood taught her concealment, shame, insularity, and anger. She has not adopted the American Dream, the pursuit of happiness: "She'd never believed in happiness. The mention of it put her in a fury." Although a voracious reader, passionately interested in the outside world, she shrinks her own universe to claustrophobic dimensions, allowing none but family and the closest friends inside her home.

Vincent, on the other hand, embodies more positive aspects of the Irish character. Despite a difficult childhood in the old country, plagued by an older brother who hated him and drove him from home, he did not carry anger and bitterness with him to the new world. Although not as sharp and quick as his wife, he is kinder and more decent.

Outgoing and friendly, he finds life at the nursing home refreshingly sociable and relaxed after his intense and confined life with Ellen.

Theresa Dooley is the product of Ellen's coldness and indifference as a mother. A medical secretary and a charismatic Catholic, she poisons everyone around her with bitterness, anger, and jealousy. Believing she is blessed with the power to heal, she spitefully withholds this "gift" from her dying mother. Her children—John, a Vietnam veteran unable to hold a job or a marriage together; Sheila, an unlikeable, self-despising former nun; and Marilyn, with three failed marriages behind her—are heirs to the hatred and bitterness that flow through the family's bloodlines.

Her sister Magdalene has been ruined by this familial poison as well. Pretty and soft, the antithesis of her mother, she has become a professional invalid, a role in which she can both receive sympathy and have control over her surroundings. Equipped with a big-screen television with remote control and bedside microwave oven, she interacts with the world on her terms, gossiping on the phone, entertaining visitors, and perusing her wardrobe in the safety of her room.

The two favored grandchildren, Cam and Dan, have also been poisoned by the family hatreds, jealousies, and feuds, but they fare somewhat better than their parents' generation. They receive the love, attention, and interest that their grandparents withheld from their own children, and they thrive academically and professionally. Both, however, have failed marriages, Dan is divorced, and Cam is married in name only. Dan grieves for the family that might have been and the time lost with his daughters, and although he has lived with a woman for fourteen years, he does not marry again. Cam, a prisoner to her own "good girl" instincts, lives with and cares for her self-pitying "invalid" mother and cannot bring herself to leave the husband she pities but no longer loves. She has finally met a man she loves, but her feelings of duty to her mother, her grandparents, and her husband prevent her from committing herself to him.

Themes and Meanings

In *The Other Side*, Mary Gordon explores the dynamics of Irish American families, examining the characteristics that set the Irish American experience apart from that of other immigrants and their descendants. While visiting Ireland for the first time Dan McNamara thinks of his family that "they could never be happy, any of them, coming from people like the Irish. Unhappiness was bred into the bone, a message in the blood, a code of weakness."

Although they cannot escape their heritage, Ellen and Vincent represent two different reactions to it. Ellen rails against her past and everything connected with it, condemning the church, mocking her husband's fondness for Irish music, and reviling anyone who romanticizes Ireland or the Irish. Vincent, on the other hand, although he came from poverty and a hard family life, has not let hatred poison his life, and he has fond memories of Ireland and the Irish. He has allowed his background to enrich his life in the new land rather than poison it. He has accepted the new, but he has not forgotten nor rejected the old.

The Irish heritage has power over even the third and fourth generations of American McNamaras. Cam and Dan, who visit the "old country" together as adults along with Dan's children, Darci and Staci, have strong reactions to the "old sod." Dan, accepting and forgiving like his grandfather, does not like Ireland. He sees it as a source of anger, hate, and unhappiness, as does his daughter Staci. On the other hand, Cam, who like her grandmother is rigid and unforgiving, feels a strong attachment to the country of her grandparents' birth.

The novel's concerns transcend those of the Irish American family, however; the book addresses the more universal theme of the dynamics of family life. As the experience of several generations of McNamaras illustrates, family cannot escape the ties that bind; everyone in some way is "in bondage" to their family. Ellen never escapes the effects of her miserable childhood, passing them on to her children, who pass them on yet again. The struggle for individuality within the family unit never abates. Cam, feeling duty-bound to her mother, her husband, and her grandparents, cannot be herself. She feels tied to their image of her rather than to her own image of herself. Dan also takes upon himself the burden of putting up a good front and hiding his real emotions for the sake of keeping the family's image of itself alive.

Critical Context

Mary Gordon's work can be placed in three literary traditions: the Catholic novel, the Irish American novel, and the feminist novel. Each of her novels exemplifies at least one, and sometimes more than one, of these genres, but Gordon is most often considered a Catholic novelist. Her first two books, *Final Payments* (1978) and *The Company of Women* (1980), are the most explicitly Catholic of her work, dealing with the protagonists' struggles to reconcile their own spirituality with the traditions and dictums of the church hierarchy. Her third book, *Men and Angels* (1985), can be classified as a religious but not specifically Catholic novel, as the protagonist struggles with her relationship to a fanatical fundamentalist Christian.

Most of Gordon's work can also be seen in feminist terms. Both *Final Payments* and *The Company of Women* feature women not only questioning their relationship with the church hierarchy but also struggling against their dependence upon the strong male figures in their lives. In *Men and Angels*, the protagonist struggles to come to terms with the conflict between her career and her children, and *The Other Side*, while not directly confronting feminist issues, features several strong female characters.

Much of Gordon's work can be placed squarely in the tradition of Irish American fiction, alongside the works of such writers as James T. Farrell, Jimmy Breslin, John O'Hara, John Gregory Dunne, and Edwin O'Connor. *The Other Side*, in particular, concentrates on the Irish component of the Irish Catholic experience in America. Gordon's work conforms to critic James Liddy's characterization of Irish American fiction as "a dramatic, easily accessible story in which men and women with divided loyalties and sensibilities work out their fate." In a controversial 1988 article published in *The New York Times Book Review*, Gordon accounted for what she saw as a shortage of Irish American novelists by discussing the Irish traits of concealment, sexual puritanism, and fear of exposure, traits, she wrote, that contributed to this shortage. Many critics and writers, however, have disagreed with her assessment and have argued for the recognition of a rich tradition of Irish American literature.

Bibliography

Cooper-Clark, Diana. "An Interview with Mary Gordon." *Commonweal* 107 (May 9, 1980): 270-273. In this early interview, Gordon discusses *Final Payments* as a Catholic novel and examines the religious novel in general. She considers issues relevant to *The Other Side*, including the Irish Catholic immigrant experience in America. She also reveals her own preferences in literature, her reaction to her critics, and what she likes best about her own work.

Gordon, Mary. "Radical Damage: An Interview with Mary Gordon." Interview by M. Deiter Keyishian. *The Literary Review* 32 (Fall, 1988): 69-82. Gordon discusses her collection of short stories *Temporary Shelter* (1987). Commenting on writing about women and children, she asserts that "to write about women and children is to be immediately ghettoized. . . ." She also reveals her own literary likes (which include Marguerite Duras and the German writer Christa Wolfe) and dislikes (which include Joseph Conrad and John Updike).

Liddy, James. "The Double Vision of Irish-American Fiction." *Eire-Ireland* 19 (Winter, 1984): 6-15. An examination of Irish American fiction; helpful in understanding Gordon's work. Liddy discusses those writers he classifies as Irish American (James T. Farrell, Edwin O'Connor, Jimmy Breslin, and Mary Gordon) as well as those he does not (F. Scott Fitzgerald and Flannery O'Connor).

Mahon, John. "Mary Gordon: The Struggle with Love." In *American Women Writing Fiction: Memory, Identity, Family, Space*, edited by Mickey Pearlman. Lexington: University Press of Kentucky, 1989. A study of *Final Payments*, *The Company of Women*, and *Men and Angels* in terms of their religious motifs. Includes a bibliography of Gordon's work, including books, poems, articles, reviews, and stories, and a bibliography of writing about her.

Ward, Catherine. "Wake Homes: Four Modern Novels of the Irish American Family." *Eire-Ireland* 26 (Summer, 1991): 78-91. An examination of four Irish American novels by women, including *The Other Side*. Ward reveals "how later generations try to escape the stultifying ties to family and church that had served the needs of their parents and grandparents but now threaten to overwhelm them." A straightforward evaluation of the novel as a study of the Irish American family.

Mary Virginia Davis

OUR HOUSE IN THE LAST WORLD

Author: Oscar Hijuelos (1951-   )
Type of plot: Family
Time of plot: 1929-1975
Locale: Cuba and New York City
First published: 1983

Principal characters:

> ALEJO SANTINIO, the father of the family, a violent man with a propensity for alcohol and womanizing
>
> MERCEDES SORREA, his wife, a superstitious woman who lives in a fantasy world
>
> HORACIO SANTINIO, the family's eldest son
>
> HECTOR SANTINIO, the younger son
>
> BUITA, Alejo's sister
>
> LUISA, Mercedes' sister

The Novel

Based in part on the author's own experiences growing up in New York City during the 1950's, *Our House in the Last World* is a fictional memoir that follows the fortunes of the Santinio family over several decades, first in Cuba and then in the United States.

Divided into fourteen unnumbered chapters that cover events between 1929 and 1975, the novel begins with the meeting of Hector's parents, Alejo and Mercedes, in Holguín, a small town in Cuba's easternmost province. Mercedes, whose family's fortunes have declined sharply after her father's death a few years earlier, lives with her mother and works as a ticket girl in a theater. Alejo is a tall, robust man and something of a dandy; he lives in a neighboring town and makes a living as a mail carrier. The romance begins in the theater on a Sunday afternoon and culminates in marriage several years later. Although Alejo and Mercedes do not seem particularly suited for each other, they enter upon their new life full of dreams and hopes.

Shortly after their marriage in 1943, Alejo decides to to try his luck in the United States. At first, he and Mercedes live with his sister Margarita and her husband Eduardo, but soon they get a small apartment of their own. After trying several odd jobs, Alejo lands a position as a cook in a large New York hotel, where he works for the rest of his life. The Santinios' first son, Horacio, is born in 1945; the second son, Hector, in 1951. Several years after Hector's birth, the Santinios go back to Cuba to see their families; during the stay, Hector contracts a mysterious infection that nearly kills him. Back in the United States, Hector spends a year in a hospital for terminally ill children. Because the hospital is in Connecticut, his mother visits him infrequently. During his long stay in the hospital, Hector is forced to learn English by one of the nurses, who locks him in a closet and refuses to release him unless he asks to be let out in English. Eventually, he gets well and rejoins his parents in their New York apartment.

The Satinios' life in New York is not a happy one. Alejo likes his job as a cook, but he feels frustrated that he is not doing as well as some of his relatives. He makes plans to buy a store and go into business for himself, but his plans never come to fruition. The high point of Alejo's career as a cook occurs one day when Soviet premier Nikita Khrushchev has dinner at the hotel and Alejo brings the food out. The next day, a picture of Alejo standing alongside Khrushchev appears in the newspaper, and Alejo becomes a celebrity in the neighborhood for a few days.

Mercedes is no happier than her husband. Constantly pressed for money, she hunts for bargains and rummages through the neighbors' castoffs in search of usable clothes for her children. Alejo and Mercedes fight endlessly. Alejo criticizes her for not being a good wife and mother; she criticizes him for being a drunk and for not providing adequately for the family.

Horacio and Hector grow up in the midst of constant battles between their parents. Often, when Alejo comes home drunk, Horacio and Hector have to undress him and help him into bed. After they go to bed, they hear their parents screaming in the next room. Horacio reacts to this unhappy situation by becoming a tough, street-smart kid. Spending as little time as possible in the apartment, he is defiant of his parents and neglectful of his brother. When he gets his girlfriend pregnant, he quits school and enlists in the Air Force.

Hector, who lacks his brother's toughness, is an obese and sickly boy who is tortured by his home situation but cannot do anything about it. Because his mother fears for his health, she does not let him out of her sight. Seeing him as his mother's ally, his father ignores him until Hector reaches adolescence. Alejo then seeks him out and tries to get to know him, but Hector wants to have nothing to do with his father. In the mid-1960's, Hector spends several months with his Aunt Buita, who lives in Miami. In Miami, though, Hector feels equally out of place; he cannot speak Spanish like the other Cubans, who mistake him for an American. Much as he tries, Hector cannot act and sound Cuban. In Miami, he falls in love with a Cuban American girl named Cindy, but she does not pay any attention to him. When Alejo collapses unexpectedly at work, Hector returns to New York for the funeral.

The novel concludes with an excruciating description of Alejo's funeral and the family's reaction. After Alejo's death, Mercedes retreats into a fantasy world of Cuban ghosts. Although she hated Alejo in life, once he is dead, she cannot seem to live without him; she pretends that he visits her in the middle of the night. Hector lives for a while with his mother, but eventually he moves out and enrolls in a university.

The Characters

Alejo is the dominant presence in the novel. Because he is seen primarily through the eyes of his sons, Alejo appears as a larger-than-life figure, fearsome and imposing. To the reader, though, it is clear that in spite of his monumental physique, Alejo is a weak man, lacking in discipline and initiative. While his relatives save their pennies in order to better their lives, Alejo is content to spend his salary drinking and womanizing. His generosity with friends verges on the foolish. He expects his children and his wife to be deferential, but he does little to earn their trust and affection. On one occasion, he takes Hector with him to visit his mistress. Yet the reader also feels a little sorry for this man who came to America with large dreams but who was incapable of fulfilling them.

Mercedes, his wife, offers a similar case. Although she cannot be blamed for her husband's excesses, she certainly does little to encourage him to achieve. Instead, she seems to relish his every failure and does not spare any opportunity to reproach him for their dingy apartment and impoverished life. Openly hostile, Alejo and Mercedes do not even pretend to be cordial toward each other. As the years go by and the frustrations mount, their fights become more bitter and more violent. The result is an unfortunate situation that seems not to have a remedy. Alejo and Mercedes cope with their unhappiness by finding artificial means of escape. Alejo escapes with alcohol; spirits of a different sort provide escape for Mercedes.

Hector and Horacio, the two sons, are a study in contrasts. Although the novel pays more attention to Hector, Horacio is the more attractive character; he seems to be the only one in the family who is capable of taking charge of his life and changing it for the better. Like his father, Horacio is a fighter, but in a positive way. Just as he does not let his father terrorize him, he does not allow the neighborhood bullies to take advantage of him. Given Horacio's aggressive character, it is no surprise that he eventually joins the Air Force. Horacio comes to terms with his parents. He does not fear his father enough to be rendered incapable of loving him; but he does not let his love for his father blind him to Alejo's many faults. Horacio has a similar relationship with Mercedes, whom he treats with affection but keeps at a distance.

Hector is a different story, for he can neither escape his parents nor come to terms with them. Even at the end of the novel, his feelings for his parents remain a jumble of unresolved contradictions. He accuses his mother of having killed his father, yet he blames his father for his mother's unhappiness. He resents his father for his violent temperament, yet he feels that he is not half the man his father was. To a large extent, *Our House in the Last World* is Hector's story. His feelings are the emotional center of the book. Even though he is not the narrator (the novel is told from the third-person-omniscient point of view), his attitude and outlook color the entire account. Because Hector grows up to be a writer, the novel may even be considered a transposition of the journals in which he records events and feelings.

The cast of significant characters is rounded out by several relatives, especially the two aunts, Luisa and Buita. They too are contrasting characters: Luisa is the good aunt, kind and loving; Buita is the nasty aunt, who tries to poison Hector and Horacio's feelings toward their mother.

Themes and Meanings

This novel tells the story of the disintegration of a family. Somber and unsparing, the narration details the miserable existence of the Santinios as they try to adapt to life in a new country. Almost every chapter chronicles a new misfortune—a child's illness, an episode of drunkenness or adultery, a violent squabble between husband and wife or father and son, a new setback for the family's finances. The reader emerges with a painful portrait of a troubled family on the way toward dissolution. There is little love or tenderness here, either between spouses or among parents and children.

At the center of it all is Hector. The great theme of Hector's childhood and adolescence is becoming a Cuban man like his father. Over and over, Hector harps on the fact that he is not as Cuban as Alejo or Horacio. He does not speak Spanish, he is blond, he is frail, and he is a mama's boy. Unlike Horacio, who follows in his father's footsteps by becoming a hard-drinking, brawling, macho womanizer, Hector develops into a shy and overweight "American" teenager. Making things worse is Hector's striking physical resemblance to his father. As he grows up, Hector develops the conviction that he is a defective replica of his father, a reproduction exact in outward details but lacking Alejo's Cuban spirit. Too Cuban to be completely American but hardly Cuban enough to resemble his father, Hector sees himself as freakish and deformed.

An important facet of Hector's struggles with his father is language. For Hector, Spanish is his father's tongue, a language that he both desires and abhors. When Hector speaks Spanish, he becomes Alejo; when he becomes Alejo, he turns into the monstrous man who comes home drunk in the middle of the night. Since the Spanish language focalizes his ambivalent feelings toward his father, it is a wound, a handicap. When he tries to utter a Spanish sentence, he feels as if the words wrap themselves around him like hospital tape. Spanish immobilizes him, ties him up in knots; try as he might, he cannot speak it fluently.

The circumstances in which Hector learns Spanish certainly shape his pathological view of the language. The most wrenching scenes in a book full of wrenching scenes are those that describe Hector's prolonged stay in the sanatorium (Hijuelos suffered a similar illness when he was four years old). During his convalescence, he sees his mother intermittently and his father not at all. Separated from his parents, he comes under the care of nurses who make him speak English. Hector enters the sanatorium as a Cuban boy; by the time he is released a year later, Spanish has become identified with the illness he caught in Cuba. In the five-year-old boy's mind, Spanish is disease, and English is health. This feeling was to stay with him for many years. Like other immigrant memoirs, *Our House in the Last World* is a conversion narrative, for it narrates a character's passage from one culture to another. What is unusual is that the conversion takes place in a hospital and is portrayed as a cure.

Our House in the Last World is best seen as a valedictory to Cuban culture. The voice that speaks in this novel, and which may be close to that of Hijuelos himself, is that of someone who retains some ties to Cuban culture but who is no longer Cuban. The novel pays tribute to Cuban culture even as it bids it farewell. As the title makes clear, Cuba is the "last world," a world that the characters have left behind. This work is Hector's complex and conflicted valedictory to the Spanish language, to his Cuban parents, and to the island's customs and culture.

Critical Context

Our House in the Last World, Hijuelos' first book, has been overshadowed by the success of his two subsequent works, *The Mambo Kings Play Songs of Love* (1989), which won the author the Pulitzer Prize for fiction, and *The Fourteen Sisters of Emilio Montez O'Brien* (1993). For this reason, although the book was well reviewed upon publication, it has received scant critical attention. Yet *Our House in the Last World* is certainly a significant accomplishment in its own right. As a sensitive and moving portrait of an immigrant family's difficult adaptation to life in the United States, it ranks with the best immigrant memoirs written by U.S. Hispanics.

Bibliography

Augenbraum, Harold. *Latinos in English*. New York: Mercantile Library, 1992. Provides bio-bibliographical information about Hijuelos and places his work in the context of the English-language literature produced by U.S. Hispanic writers.

Hijuelos, Oscar. Interview by Sybil Steinberg. *Publishers Weekly* 236 (July 21, 1989): 42-43. Hijuelos discusses his life and fiction up to *The Mambo Kings Play Songs of Love*.

Hoffman, Roy. "Two Tales of Culture Clash." *The Philadelphia Inquirer*, July 17, 1983, 8. Hoffman looks upon Hijuelos as an "urban poet" who vividly renders scenes in both small-town Cuba and big-city North America. In the reviewer's opinion, this is a "vibrant, bitter and successful first novel."

Milton, Edith. "Newcomers in New York." *The New York Times Book Review*, May 15, 1983, 12. Milton discusses the themes of identity and acculturation, concluding that the novel is "not just a literary exercise but a loving and deeply felt tribute" to the author's Cuban roots.

Pérez Firmat, Gustavo. *Life on the Hyphen: The Cuban American Way*. Austin: University of Texas Press, 1993. Pérez Firmat studies the novel in the context of Cuban American culture. Considering this novel in tandem with *The Mambo Kings Play Songs of Love*, he concludes that Hijuelos' work shows an "anglocentric bias" that Pérez Firmat identifies with second-generation Cuban Americans.

Gustavo Pérez Firmat

OUTERBRIDGE REACH

Author: Robert Stone (1937-   )
Type of plot: Adventure
Time of plot: The 1990's
Locale: Connecticut; New York City; the yacht *Nona* in the South Atlantic
First published: 1992

> *Principal characters:*
> OWEN BROWNE, the protagonist, a man seeking to reaffirm his manhood, lost youth and lost dreams
> ANNE BROWNE, Owen's wife of twenty years, still in love but disturbed by his changes and fascinated by Strickland
> MAGGIE BROWNE, the Brownes' teenage daughter
> RON STRICKLAND, a documentary filmmaker engaged to record Browne's round-the-world sailing adventure
> PAMELA KOESTLER, Strickland's prostitute girlfriend and film subject
> HARRY THORNE, an honest businessman half in love with Anne
> MAD MAX, a ham-radio operator, Owen's human connection for much of his voyage

The Novel

Building on his knowledge of the sea gleaned as a member of the U.S. Navy, a merchant marine seaman, and a yachtsman, Robert Stone in *Outerbridge Reach* tells an exciting but disturbing story of the challenges of transoceanic yachting, the heights and depths of human daring, the class conflicts beneath democratic façades, and the difficulty of fully understanding the behavior and motivations of others. The book is also a story of betrayal: of self, of family, of personal and corporate dreams.

The novel begins with Owen Browne testing a forty-five-foot Altan Marine sloop and having trouble with failing parts. Such weaknesses, the result of cutting corners and substituting cheap, unreliable materials for solid craftsmanship, will later prove his undoing on the long sea voyage he ultimately undertakes. He is inexperienced and uncomfortable at sea. Nevertheless, when the Hylan Corporation's head executive mysteriously disappears and therefore will not represent Altan in an around-the-world one-man yacht race, Owen decides to fill the gap, advertise the Altan product, and possibly win the race. Although he is undertaking a foolhardy venture, he convinces himself that this is the only way to regain his lost sense of self, the youthful self-awareness and self-pride of his military days. His wife, a far better sailor than he, doubts his ability to make the stressful voyage but supports his venture in hope that it will help him to regain the vigor and confidence of their early marriage. Superficially a perfect couple, they are estranged and drifting apart. Owen's humble origins have kept him far more aware of the class distinctions of the yachting crowd than she. The Browne's daughter sees her parents' deception of self and spouse and refuses to bless the farcical voyage, avoiding her father, refusing to see him off, and escaping telephone calls during the voyage—yet weeping for him. Owen, in turn, reveals ineffectiveness with the cabinetmaker and others hired to prepare his boat. Harry Thorne and his colleagues, the behind-the-scene movers considering how to save the sinking parent company, decide that Owen is the only Altan representative worth saving and give his voyage the go-ahead.

Before Owen leaves, he is interviewed and filmed by a mean-spirited, embittered, but clearly talented filmmaker, Ron Strickland, who is hired by Thorne to record the preparation for the voyage, set up cameras for Owen to self-record his adventures, and turn the whole into an advertisement for Altan yachts. Strickland, however, has other film goals. A cynical, professional skeptic whose films destroy their subjects' pretensions, he sees Owen epitomizing the self-deluding officer class he had earlier satirized in a film about the Vietnam War. He plans to expose the upper-middle-class emptiness of Owen's family life, social position, and self. The novel alternates between the Brownes and Strickland; the former are led to believe in his objectivity, while conversations between Strickland and his former film subject, Pamela Koestler, a prostitute and drug user, reveal the real, destructive effect of the scenes. Strickland also becomes sexually obsessed with Anne Browne and determined to break through her upper-middle-class façade. While Owen is at sea, Strickland finally seduces and falls in love with her. His love for her and her betrayal of Owen make Strickland see Owen in a new light, and his sense of his film begins to change. She, in turn, feels that she cannot telephone Owen at sea and as a result never speaks to him again, although she works hard to maintain the role of devoted wife.

In the meantime, at sea Owen faces repeated problems (including a lockjaw scare). Yet he falls into the rhythms of the sea and gains confidence and strength. Missionary programs enacting biblical stories, especially ones related to betrayals and concealment, and Morse-code communication with a blind South African adolescent, Mad Max, give Owen human contact. Thoughts of the boy's darkness make Owen think of the whole world in hiding, concealed and concealing. He and his ship *Nona* lead the race until furious driving rain and winds off Argentina reveal the internal flaws of his craft: plastic instead of wood and a failing mast. When Owen realizes the dangerous deception of his cherished advertising copy and his inability to complete the voyage because of his faulty ship, he anchors off a small South Atlantic island and goes ashore. The bleached bones of whales and the haunted house of nineteenth century whalers make for an eerily surreal, hallucinatory experience.

By the time Owen renews his journey, he has opted for deception. Because of satellite transmission difficulties, the *Nona* is no longer trackable, so Owen begins a devious course of misleading reports of distances covered to make those back home think he is still ahead of the race when, in fact, he is almost motionless in the water. He prepares two sets of nautical logs, one truthful, the other a fiction. Yet he realizes that "he could no more take a prize by subterfuge than he could sail to the white port city of his dreams" and that the strange confusions of Vietnam, where truth had been "a trick of the mind that confounded logic," continue. Employing "instruments of rectitude" such as compass, sextant, and rule to lie, he concludes, would "erode the heart and soul." He decides that there is no way out, that "there would always be something to conceal." After a final entry in his log, he steps overboard; as his ship sails on, he drowns.

When his deception and fate are discovered, the world rejects Owen as a cheat. Only Strickland sees into the heart of the matter and understands his basic honesty. This insight drives Strickland to try to make a film to restore Owen's reputation, but ironically, Anne and her company protectors steal back from him everything he could have used to redeem Owen. Only too late does Anne understand what Strickland could have shown the world: a man doing his best to meet the larger challenges of life but continually defeated, not by a lack of inner drive but by social concealment and deception that encompass everything from his boat to his own wife and daughter. Harry Thorne, the sponsor of Owen's voyage, one of the few honest men in the company, concludes that his trust has been misplaced. The novel ends with Anne considering making the voyage her husband failed and writing a novel about it.

The Characters

An Annapolis graduate and Vietnam veteran, Owen Browne was one of the golden boys of his generation. For him, the war years were the best years of his life, a time of excitement and danger but also of intense commitment, clear-cut purposes and loyalties, and a daily challenging of self physically, psychologically, and intellectually. Everything has been downhill since. He resigned his Navy commission to write advertising copy for a yacht brokerage in Connecticut. Though he excels at sales and copy, he has lost his self-respect and the respect of his wife and daughter. He feels estranged, isolated, discontent. Browne sees the round-the-world yacht race as an opportunity to experience the excitement and danger of his wartime years and to regain his self-respect. His inexperience sailing the high seas alone does not diminish his desire to do so.

Anne Browne, a lovely, intelligent woman from a wealthy nautical family, has been faithful but is hurt and disturbed by an unfulfilling sex life and by Owen's psychological distance from her; she longs to recapture the love of their youth. A successful, serious writer, she feels contempt for his advertising career. Though not convinced Owen can survive the voyage, she does nothing to stop him. Anne is trapped between loyalty to her husband and the fierce, fascinating sexuality of Strickland's continued and insistent attentions. Strickland's intensity, his driving sensuality, the sense he communicates of being on the edge, of dealing with harsh realities, both attract and repel Anne, and she ultimately succumbs. Yet she worries about appearances and proprieties; she is strong enough to reject Strickland when she thinks Owen is returning, and she later agrees to his being robbed and mugged to prevent him from finishing his film about her husband. She is a survivor who recoups financially at the end and who toys with redemption through repeating Owen's maritime struggle. When she reads a romantic quotation she had included in her final, unsent note to Owen, she cannot imagine the person she had been.

Maggie Browne, the teenage daughter of Anne and Owen, is a silent presence throughout, fearful, pouting, embarrassed, refusing to acknowledge her father's affection, but deeply loving him. She takes after Owen both physically and in her upright sense of character and fortitude. She is embarrassed and disappointed by his pretenses and lies and is heartbroken at his demise.

Ron Strickland is central to the testing of and understanding of Owen and Anne. He is an aging, embittered hipster filmmaker, obsessed by the Vietnam War, instinctively detecting pretense, hypocrisy, and human foibles. He prides himself on being able to see through "uptight" manners and find the core of darkness. Yet he is also an artist who can capture on celluloid the essence of the human condition, twisted and weak but somehow also pathetic and worthy of sympathy. He begins his film with the idea of tearing down the Browne family and showing the emptiness, fakery, and hypocrisy of their inner selves, but he ends up falling in love with Anne, admiring the innocence and vulnerability of Maggie, and vowing to do everything necessary to redeem Owen, to restore his honor by showing the integrity behind his lies and death.

Pamela Koestler, the star of one of Strickland's films, accompanies him during much of the filming. In fact, Strickland delights in introducing a kinky degenerate into the homes of what he considers "uptight" puritanical types. Pamela feels comfortable with Strickland's obsessions. Through her, readers see his darkest side.

Themes and Meanings

Outerbridge Reach is the story of a man staking his and his family's fate on a single decision that will either make or break him, pitting himself against the sea, society, and self, pushing himself to his limits—and failing. In the tradition of Joseph Conrad, Herman Melville, and Ernest Hemingway, Owen's battle against the sea represents all of humankind's challenges. In the harsh geometry involved, the sea, sky, and sailor form a triangle, with other concerns completely removed, all emphasis being placed on the ethics of winning and losing. Ultimately, Anne's final musings make clear the symbolism of the voyage: "The ocean encompassed everything, and everything could be understood in terms of it. Everything true about it was true about life in general." Within this tradition, Owen is the believer, the idealist shattered by the harsh discovery of emptiness and delusion. One of the final entries in his diary is from Melville's *Moby Dick: Or, The Whale* (1851): "Be true to the dreams of your youth."

Like Robert Stone's other novels, *Outerbridge Reach* questions the cost of pursuing the American Dream: Success turns to ashes, lives disintegrate, and nightmares come true. It is a story of failures of responsibility, of loyalties challenged and betrayed, of human weakness and limitation, the shattering of "lovely illusions." As such, it is meant to be a portrait of its time, an exploration of the deceptions and self-deceptions in the service of success that are commonplace in society, the workplace, and even the home. Owen's father taught him the importance of concealment and lies, a lesson with which he was never really comfortable. His Vietnam experiences were exercises in misleading statistics and lying as a mathematical art. His experience in the Hylan Corporation is with the illusions of advertising, illusions accepted so wholeheartedly that he believes them himself, staking his life and future on them, only to be faced with the fact that the beautiful ships he has praised in such glowing terms lacked the craftsmanship to endure. The deceptions are reinforced by the mysterious disappearance of the corporate head and the failure of the company in the wake of shady dealings and financial scandal. The love of his life fails him in his time of need, betrays him with another man, and ultimately founds her success on his failure. She asks her daughter not to judge Owen harshly, since few men ever test themselves the way he did, but even this is a lie of sorts. The story ends with cover-ups, deceptions, and self-delusions.

Mad Max, the blind shortwave fanatic tapping away to unknown listeners in Morse code, epitomizes the human condition—hopeful, optimistic, yet limited and somehow doomed. Blindness about motive and reason is quintessential Stone.

Critical Context

The excited reception of *Outerbridge Reach* suggests that many critics consider Robert Stone America's leading novelist, at least in the arena of the "big issue" novel that takes up the moral problems of the age. After a brilliant beginning to his career with *Hall of Mirrors* (1967) and *Dog Soldiers* (1974), his *A Flag for Sunrise* (1981) and *Children of Light* (1986) left some enthusiasts disappointed and hopeful that a new novel in the man-against-the-sea tradition would have substance enough to carry the weight of Stone's themes. Critics in general seem to feel this hope was justified, and while Stone has been criticized for windiness, he has also been praised for his balance—counterweighting his customary social deviants with citizens solid to a fault—his lively and interesting prose, his evocation of place, and his masterful plotting of doomed relationships. Thus *Outerbridge Reach* gave new hope that a mature Stone would deliver the crowning works his youth promised, and that this sensitive recorder of the 1960's generation's angst and fears would produce new surprises and insights in coming years.

Bibliography

Jones, Malcolm, Jr. "A Good Novelist's Glum Cruise." *Newsweek* 119 (February 24, 1992): 69. Jones believes Stone's great themes, convincing characters, and scenes "as sharp as rusty fishhooks" are marred by attempts to imitate the moral dramas of Nathaniel Hawthorne and Herman Melville. *Outerbridge Reach*, Jones writes, is best when Owen is fighting off insects, haunted by icebergs, beset by fervent radio preachers, and undone by sloppy craftsmanship that turns his boat into a coffin.

Pritchard, William H. "Sailing Over the Edge." *The New York Times Book Review*, February 23, 1992, 1, 21, 22. Pritchard finds Stone's usual preoccupation with the underside of American life toned down in *Outerbridge Reach*, though Strickland, with his ability to penetrate to the false heart of pretentiousness and to expose ideals as trumpery, is typical Stone. Allusions to Melville, William Shakespeare, and nineteenth century poems add depth and irony, while the symbol of Outerbridge Reach "reaches further and deeper than anyone could have thought."

Stone, Robert. "The Genesis of Outerbridge Reach." *The Times Literary Supplement*, June 5, 1992, 14. Stone discusses the degree to which he based his story on personal experiences sailing in the Antarctic regions. He also describes the historical case of David Crowhurst, who decided not to sail around the world but to claim that he had.

Sutherland, John. "In Dangerous Waters." *The Times Literary Supplement*, May 22, 1992, 28. Sutherland places *Outerbridge Reach* in the tradition of Stone's other fiction, discusses his Navy and sailing experiences, and tendentiously considers the degree to which Crowhurst and others influenced Stone.

Weber, Bruce. "An Eye for Danger." *The New York Times Magazine*, January 19, 1992: 6, 19-24. Weber summarizes Stone's life, including his friendships and adventures with Ken Kesey and the Merry Pranksters, his canon, the influence of Samuel Beckett, the serendipity of some Stone characters, the influence of the Crowhurst story, and Stone's spiritual quest as he studies perplexed men unsure of right.

Andrew Macdonald
Gina Macdonald

OXHERDING TALE

Author: Charles Johnson (1948-   )
Type of plot: Bildungsroman
Time of plot: 1843-1865
Locale: South Carolina
First published: 1982

> *Principal characters:*
> ANDREW HAWKINS, the narrator, a slave
> GEORGE HAWKINS, Andrew's father
> MATTIE HAWKINS, George's wife and Andrew's stepmother
> JONATHAN POLKINGHORNE, Andrew's first owner
> ANNA POLKINGHORNE, Jonathan's wife and the biological mother of Andrew
> EZEKIEL SYKES-WITHERS, a Trancendentalist and Andrew's tutor
> FLO HATFIELD, Andrew's second owner and lover
> REB, an older slave who befriends Andrew
> HORACE BANNON, The "Soulcatcher," who captures runaway slaves
> PEGGY UNDERCLIFF, Andrew's white wife

The Novel

   Oxherding Tale describes the education a young slave, Andrew Hawkins, receives from a variety of people. It is through synthesizing the different views from these people that he becomes a complete person.

   The novel itself opens with "the Fall," which is how Andrew describes his conception. During a bout of heavy drinking, Jonathan Polkinghorne, the owner of a South Carolina plantation named Cripplegate, and his favorite slave, who is also his butler, decide to swap wives for one night. The master slips into the slave's quarters, while the slave (George Hawkins) goes to the Polkinghornes' bedroom. The deception is uncovered by Anna Polkinghorne during the act of intercourse, and although she immediately screams, causing George to run from the bedroom, Anna has been impregnated. This act forces her husband to send George to work in the fields, thus causing him to fall in stature from a house slave to a field slave. George's new occupation is that of an oxherd.

   Even though Jonathan would like the baby to be brought up as the Polkinghornes' own son since they are childless, his wife insists that Andrew be placed in the slave quarters as though there is no connection between the master and his slave. Consequently, Andrew is reared by George and his wife, Mattie, though Jonathan allows the boy to receive an excellent education with the promise of someday being free.

   To tutor Andrew, Jonathan hires an itinerant philosopher named Ezekiel Sykes-Withers. Ezekiel professes to be a Transcendentalist, which means that he is more interested in theory than in real life. Andrew learns his lessons well from Ezekiel—mathematics, languages, abstract reasoning—but something is missing. Andrew finds what is lacking from his life in the person of a girl named Minty. When he asks Jonathan for his freedom so that he may purchase Minty and marry her, however, Andrew is sent to work for a woman, Flo Hatfield.

Flo, owner of a mine named Leviathan, takes the handsome boy as a lover and teaches him the philosophy of hedonism. Andrew enjoys the privileges of being Flo's lover for a year before he sickens of it. He escapes with another slave, Reb, a coffin-maker, who has become a father figure to him. On the road north, they meet Horace Bannon, the "Soulcatcher," who captures runaway slaves by emptying his own soul to allow the essence of the runaway to fill it. In other words, Horace—who is also a psychopathic killer—becomes "black" himself, taking on the characteristics and personality of his prey. He does not kill the runaway, he tells Andrew and Reb, until the slave begs for death because he can no longer stand the pressure of being on the run, of never fitting into a white society.

At Spartanburg, South Carolina, Andrew takes a job as a teacher. This is possible because his light complexion allows him to "pass" as white. Reb stays with Andrew for awhile, but finally he leaves for Chicago. Meanwhile, Andrew finds himself trapped into marrying the daughter of a local doctor. He comes to love Peggy Undercliff, however, and seems to be settled into Spartanburg as a respectable member of the white community.

Ironically, just as he feels safe, Andrew learns that Horace has set off to catch and kill Reb. Further complicating matters, Andrew attends a slave auction and discovers a very ill Minty. He buys her, but she soon dies. As he stands by her deathbed, Andrew feels forlorn and wonders how long he can continue the charade in Spartanburg. It is then that Horace appears. Andrew willingly accompanies the Soulcatcher to the woods, expecting to be killed. Instead, Horace tells Andrew that he could not catch Reb because the coffin-maker had gradually emptied his soul during his captivity; he had learned to expect nothing and to desire nothing. Reb had freed himself, literally and figuratively, by never attempting to fit into white society. Because he had finally encountered a slave he could not capture, Horace tells Andrew that he has retired from the slave-catching profession, leaving the schoolteacher to return to his life in Spartanburg. Andrew does just that, but he is wiser having learned from all his teachers—George, Ezekiel, Flo, and especially Reb.

The Characters

Andrew Hawkins, the narrator of *Oxherding Tale*, is an extremely intelligent, pragmatic man. He is always eager to experience all aspects of life and to learn from others. Although he comes across as a prig early in the novel—he feels himself superior to all the slaves and most of the masters—by the end of the story he has grown into a character with whom a reader can empathize. Charles Johnson certainly intended this feeling of empathy, as the readers of *Oxherding Tale* are to learn from Andrew's experiences just as Andrew himself learned from them. Andrew is not to be seen as a "real" character, however; instead, Johnson intends his protagonist to stand as a metaphor, a character whose adventures are allegorical. Woven into the character of Andrew are various philosophical threads that reinforce points Johnson wants to make in his novel. All this taken together means that Andrew never comes to life or seems like a real person.

George Hawkins, Andrew's father and first teacher, is nothing more than a stereotype in the novel. A radical black nationalist convinced that all whites are evil, he eventually leads a slave revolt at Cripplegate. Horace Bannon tracks him easily because George's soul is so full of hate that he can never hide. In the end, he begs Horace to kill him because the hate he bears is too much to carry any longer.

Ezekiel Sykes-Withers, Andrew's second teacher, is portrayed as a fool because he lives only for the abstract. He is devastated, for example, when he meets Karl Marx and finds that the German philosopher fails to share his own pessimism. Marx tells Ezekiel to enjoy life, to find a woman with whom he could be happy. Ezekiel, however, is "happiest" when miserable because he is convinced of the stupidity of the human race.

Flo Hatfield, Andrew's lover and third teacher, is a stereotype as well. Her only interest is in seeking all forms of pleasure. She indulges in excesses of food, drugs, and sex in an attempt to kill the pain of existence. For a time, this sort of life seems appropriate to Andrew, but he soon realizes that it is ultimately just as empty as the life led by Ezekiel.

Reb, a father figure for Andrew and his fourth teacher, is a member of the Allmuseri tribe from Africa. The Allmuseri, apparently a creation of Johnson's, believe that it is the duty of each individual in a society to immerse himself in the society as a whole, that individuality is, if not an outright illusion, at least an act of selfish egoism. Reb has learned that to survive in an alien culture he must eliminate his individuality through self-denial; he lives for each moment and for himself, in contrast to the other characters in the novel. Through the way he leads his life, Reb serves as an exemplar for Andrew. By the end of the novel, Andrew has learned his lesson well; it is understood that he, just as Reb had done years earlier, has freed himself.

Horace Bannon, the "Soulcatcher," represents the sum of all the people Andrew has met and the sum of all the lessons that Andrew has learned. Horace has a tattoo on his chest and arms, revealed to Andrew at the end of the novel, in which the entire story is seen in microcosm. It is through viewing this tattoo that Andrew realizes how Reb freed himself, for it is in the tattoo that Andrew sees the meaninglessness of physical life.

Themes and Meanings

Oxherding Tale is clearly not to be read as a novel about the brutality of slavery in the American South, although that element is certainly very evident. Instead, Charles Johnson would like his readers to see the novel as a parable about one man's attempt to free himself—both literally and figuratively—from a life full of traps. In other words, this is a novel that explores the existential truth of trying to lead an honest life, one that allows a person to be free spiritually. After experiencing many different "lives," Andrew comes to realize that Reb's philosophy is the most suitable for living in this world. His philosophy, which one critic has called "the phenomenology of the Allmuseri," is similar to Eastern religions in that it holds that the path to freedom lies through negation of the self.

Reinforcing this theme of finding one's true self is Johnson's style in the novel. It can best be termed "metafiction" because it eschews the traditional conventions of fiction—such as an author who remains aloof from the world he has created—in favor of experimentation. For example, there are two philosophical digressions in *Oxherding Tale* about the very nature of slave narratives and first-person narrators. These digressions seem to undercut the story itself, until a reader places them within the context of the overall fable that Johnson is relating. It is then that the true purpose of the digressions—their function as an "objective" commentary upon Andrew and his story that allows the reader to see the novel in a different light—becomes clear. In short, Johnson's metafictional techniques enable the reader to search for the true meaning of *Oxherding Tale* just as Andrew searches for the true meaning of his life. In summary, Johnson would like the novel as a whole to serve as a microcosm of human life; slavery in *Oxherding Tale* is meant to represent metaphorically the captivity in which human beings live until they manage to set themselves free through self-negation.

Critical Context

Charles Johnson started his career as a cartoonist and published his work in newspapers and magazines. Two collections of his cartoons and drawings were subsequently published, *Black Humor* (1970) and *Half-Past Nation Time* (1972). Eventually, however, he turned to fiction as a means of artistic expression. As he completed his master's degree in philosophy at Southern Illinois University in the early 1970's, Johnson studied with novelist John Gardner. He wrote and rewrote under Gardner until he produced what would become his first novel, *Faith and the Good Thing* (1974). That novel can be read as a folktale in which a woman named "Faith" sets out on a literal and figurative journey to find the meaning of her existence.

Following *Faith and the Good Thing*, Johnson published *Oxherding Tale*, which received favorable reviews from both popular magazines as well as from literary journals. He followed his second novel with a collection of short fiction, *The Sorcerer's Apprentice* (1986), and with a book of literary criticism, *Being and Race: Black Writing Since 1970* (1988). His growing reputation as one of America's most important writers was solidified in 1990 when he published *Middle Passage*, which was accepted by most critics as his best novel and which won the National Book Award. *Middle Passage* is the story of Rutherford Calhoun, a thief who meets members of the Allmuseri tribe who are being taken into slavery. He comes to admire their fortitude in the face of captivity and wants to learn how they deal with adversity. The novel then shows Rutherford's slow progress toward renunciation of materialism in favor of self-negation under the guidance of the Allmuseri.

A common thread throughout these novels is an interest in exploring the limits of human knowledge. Johnson, with his training as a philosopher, wants to know what is possible for people to understand about their own existence. Exactly why, Johnson asks, do we act and think the way we do? Although answers are not always readily available, Johnson argues persuasively in his fiction that to neglect to ask such questions, to go through life always accepting the way things are, is to live with blinders. According to Johnson, it is up to each individual to question his own existence in order to lead a full, free life.

Bibliography

Crouch, Stanley. "Charles Johnson: Free at Last!" In *Notes of a Hanging Judge: Essays and Reviews, 1979-1989*. New York: Oxford University Press, 1990. Crouch's insightful review of the novel shows that Johnson has created, using the nineteenth century genre of the slave narrative, a fascinating protagonist in Andrew Hawkins. Crouch finds Andrew and his search for some truth in his existence to be reminiscent of characters created by authors such as Herman Melville or Mark Twain, in that Andrew is a character of mythic proportions. Also, Crouch points out that much in the novel satirizes contemporary stereotypes—held by whites and blacks both—about African Americans.

Hayward, Jennifer. "Something to Serve: Constructs of the Feminine in Charles Johnson's *Oxherding Tale*." *Black American Literature Forum* 25 (Winter, 1991): 689-703. Hayward attempts to demonstrate that *Oxherding Tale* can be read as a metaphor in which polar opposites (white/black, master/slave, male/female) are reconciled through Johnson's use of metafictional techniques and African American tradition. She argues, for example, that deliberate "anachronisms"—places where the fictional guise is dropped—are crucial to the novel because they remind the reader that *Oxherding Tale* is to be read as a parable about finding freedom. Hayward, however, is troubled by what she perceives as misogyny in the novel.

Johnson, Charles. "Philosophy and Black Fiction." *Obsidian: Black Literature in Review* 6 (Spring/Summer, 1980): 55-61. Johnson looks at the world of African American fiction and finds it lacks freshness. In other words, he finds a one-dimensional world populated with caricatures. Johnson goes on to argue that African American fiction writers should feel an obligation to strip away the "presuppositions" about black life in order to see the complexities that lie beneath. This prescription for African American fiction, of course, outlines what Johnson himself does in *Oxherding Tale*. Johnson later expanded on the opinions in this brief essay in a critical book about African American fiction, *Being and Race: Black Writing Since 1970*.

Little, Jonathan. "Charles Johnson's Revolutionary *Oxherding Tale*." *Studies in American Fiction* 19 (Autumn, 1991): 141-151. Little's excellent essay argues that *Oxherding Tale* breaks the constraints usually placed on African American fiction by dealing with issues, such as one man's struggle to find meaning in his own life, not normally seen in works by African American writers. Little points out that the novel, rather than serving as a simple polemic against racism, for example, deals with problems of metaphysics and ontology.

Rushdy, Ashraf H. A. "The Phenomenology of the Allmuseri: Charles Johnson and the Subject of the Narrative of Slavery." *African-American Review* 26 (Fall, 1992): 373-394. Rushdy's essay is one of the best critical pieces written about Johnson's fiction and is the logical place for students of *Oxherding Tale* to begin. His thesis, one he proves decisively, is that all of Johnson's fiction about slavery is connected through the "phenomenology" of the Allmuseri, an African tribe mentioned repeatedly in Johnson's stories. Essentially, Rushdy contends that the Allmuseri believe that a man only becomes whole by submerging himself into society and losing his individual wants. Through this process of submerging, he can then free himself. This process is illustrated in *Oxherding Tale* by the character of Reb.

Jim McWilliams

PACO'S STORY

Author: Larry Heinemann (1944-   )
Type of plot: Magical Realism
Time of plot: The early 1970's
Locale: Vietnam and the American Midwest
First published: 1986

> *Principal characters:*
> PACO SULLIVAN, a seriously wounded Vietnam veteran looking for work
> and a new life after hospitalization and discharge
> GALLAGHER, the raconteur company mate of Paco, capable of almost any
> cruelty
> ERNEST MONROE, a World War II veteran and proprietor of the Texas
> Lunch, where Paco briefly works
> JESSE, a hitchhiking Vietnam veteran with whom Paco is compared and
> contrasted
> CATHY, a college student and rooming-house neighbor whose sexual
> teasing torments Paco

The Novel

Based in part on Larry Heinemann's experience in the Vietnam War, *Paco's Story* tells a representative tale of the brutality of war and the subsequent problems of a veteran's adjustment to life in small-town America. Heinemann presents this material though a narrative that focuses on Paco Sullivan's arrival in, partial adjustment to, and departure from the typical American crossroads town of Boone, a river town in the American Midwest. This strand of the narrative is punctured by scenes of the massacre of Paco's company at Fire Base Harriet, Paco's rescue and recovery, and earlier war incidents in which Paco was involved.

The novel, however, begins not with Paco but with a virtuoso introduction by and to the unnamed narrator, whose hip but elegant manner provides much of the novel's special flavor. The narrator insists that people do not want to hear another war story, and he is rather specific about just what they do not want to hear and why. Still, stories such as Paco's must be heard, and the narrator, who has cornered a listener whom he addresses as James, must tell it. Readers soon learn that the narrator is the ghost of a soldier who served with Paco in Alpha Company and who lost his life with all the others at Fire Base Harriet.

Paco arrives at the outskirts of Boone by bus, washes up at the Texaco station, and begins a hobbled walk toward town. Befriended by the garage mechanic, he begins a search for work and a place to stay. The townspeople are curious about Paco, and also suspicious. His faraway gaze (he is heavily medicated) and his cane-aided limp make him something of a freak; his presence brings the unpleasantness of the Vietnam War, about which few seem to know anything, into their midst. Most of the townsfolk— those he meets at Rita's Tender Trap and Hennig's Barbershop—respond ungenerously to his requests for information about work. Soon, however, Paco meets Ernest Monroe, who gives him the job of dishwasher at the Texas Lunch and helps him find lodging at the nearby Geronimo Hotel (no doubt an ironic allusion to the serviceman's labeling Vietnam as "Indian Country").

The early scenes of Paco's progress in Boone, along with a detailed description of his wounding and rescue at Fire Base Harriet, underscore the various levels at which the war continues to effect Paco. Crippled and pain-riddled, he carries the physical consequences of the war everywhere he goes. He cannot leave it behind, because it has reshaped him. Although he wishes to get on with his life, to move forward, he carries his memories with him as well. Moreover, the war has shaped how he is to be perceived by others.

He remains a freak to most, not only because of his physical appearance but also because such a vision allows others to remove themselves from any connection with America's involvement in Vietnam. Ernest, an ex-Marine who survived World War II battles at Guadalcanal and Iwo Jima, is a fortuitous, benevolent presence through whose own story Heinemann is able to universalize his concerns with the human capacity to make war and survive it. Paco's earlier encounter with Mr. Elliot, a mildly crazed refugee from World War I Russia who runs the town's fix-it shop, also serves to establish a context for approaching the meaning of Paco's experience in and after Vietnam.

As Paco learns and repeats the harsh routine of his work at the Texas Lunch, it becomes clear that this unfriendly work helps him to hold himself together psychologically. The scalding water and irritating chemicals are nothing to what he has already endured, and the long hours of busing tables, soaking, rinsing, and scrubbing help to keep his memories and behavior under control just as much as the depressant drugs do.

The routine of Paco's short career at the Texas Lunch is disturbed by two encounters. One night, minutes before closing, a drifter named Jesse comes into the restaurant. Jesse has been on the road a long time, and he tells Paco and Ernest of his restless wanderings across the length and breadth of the United States. After Paco tells him (as he must tell everyone) about how he got his wounds and his limp, Jesse says that he, too, served in Vietnam, though at an earlier period of the war. Though he has suffered far less physical trauma than Paco, Jesse cannot settle down. He has spent the intervening years trying to discover America and, as he puts it, "looking for a place to cool out." As Jesse sounds off about the military-industrial complex and about the kind of memorial that might be appropriate for the Vietnam war, his rage pierces through his good-natured manner. He heads back to the road after giving a lesson on hitchhiking.

Even before Jesse shows up, Paco had noticed that his neighbor at the Geronimo Hotel, a college girl named Cathy, had been spying on him. Over a period of weeks, she pursued a tormenting game of allowing Paco to see her in various provocative stances and daring him to approach her. To his mind (and to the narrator's), she had even encouraged her boyfriend to a noisy lovemaking that would disturb and entice

Paco. This sadistic teasing culminates with a stealthy visit to Paco's room. When Paco discovers that Cathy has visited his room in his absence, he decides to return the favor. Once there, he discovers a diary in which she has set down her observations and fantasies about him. He reads about her dream in which, after lovemaking, he peels his scars off, laying them on her body, where they tingle and burn.

The diary entry wakes Paco from his own dream of belonging. He knows now that this is not the place to find what he needs. Taking the pay he is owed and leaving Ernest a thank-you note, Paco heads back to the Texaco station and boards a west-bound bus.

The events during Paco's brief sojourn in Boone are accompanied by formal flashbacks (Paco's memories) and by less formal interjections of antecedent action by the narrator. Key scenes involve Paco's company-mate, Gallagher. Readers learn how Gallagher selected his tattoo and how he led his comrades in the gang rape and killing of a young woman who was a member of the Viet Cong. In one scene, Gallagher is allowed to tell a story of his own. In another, the medic who discovered Paco is placed in a bar, years later, to tell his version of Paco's story. In yet another background scene, Paco is shown in action as the company booby-trap man. In this way, Paco's life in Alpha Company is threaded through the events in Boone, counterpointing them and suggesting relationships between the present and the past.

The Characters

Paco Sullivan is soft-spoken, withdrawn, and polite. He wants peace, but he is unlikely to find it. Though the reader learns that (in war) Paco is capable of violence, the knowledge comes as a paradox about Paco and about humankind in general. While Paco's suffering, past and present, evokes the reader's sympathy, especially since many townspeople reject him or belittle him, that sympathy is checked by knowledge of his participation in the gang rape. His present state—in which his every movement brings pain, his dreams torment him, and drugs only make life tolerable—is perhaps overdrawn to the point of sentimentality. Paco's survivor's guilt is more successfully, because more subtly, handled. Paco lives just as much among the ghost of Alpha Company as he does among the living.

Ernest Monroe serves as a father figure and as a connection to America's war-riddled history. His present situation of responsibility and his active compassion suggest that the transformations of war need not be permanent. Ernest cannot forget, but does not live within, the traumas of his World War II experiences. He serves as one possible future for Paco.

Jesse is more obviously a foil for Paco. They have seen the horrors of the same war, and they have returned to the same inhospitable homeland, a country that does not seem to have a place for them. Heinemann employs the loquacious Jesse to articulate those perspectives of the Vietnam veteran that tight-lipped, drug-slowed Paco cannot or will not. A somewhat comic character, Jesse is also the conscious incarnation of a Vietnam veteran cliché. His tall-tale drifter manner has connections with frontier literature and legend.

Gallagher, prominent in the Vietnam flashback scenes, is a streetwise Chicagoan who is defined as the company killer and the company clown. For Gallagher, it seems natural to put on the attitudes and behavior that war demands. He seems made for it.

Cathy, the niece of the couple who run the Geronimo Hotel, is the most prominent female character in the novel. She, like the others, is defined (and defines herself) as a sexual object. Such portrayals of women are a perplexing ingredient in Heinemann's first two novels. Her diary provides one of the several versions or pieces of a story that Paco himself never fully tells.

Themes and Meanings

The devastation of war, its human toll, is one of Heinemann's primary themes, as is the arbitrariness of life and death in the combat arena. Paco's miraculous survival from an otherwise complete massacre cannot be seriously attributed to his will to live. The terms of his survival render him ghostlike, suggesting that in certain ways he remains among the dead whose spirits haunt him. Indeed, the dead quality of Paco's existence is heightened by the animated voice of the narrator, himself a ghost. Ironically, this story is one that only the dead can tell. There is a static and ghostlike quality, too, to Boone itself, as if Heinemann means to suggest that the United States has murdered or drugged itself, lost contact with its own most vital meanings and purposes. Technically, the ghost narrator provides the authority of a first-person (witness) narration along with the Olympian omniscience of third-person perspective. By defying (through blending) the pure conventions of narrative choice, Heinemann complicates his compact novel with concerns about how Paco's experience can be made sharable.

Critical Context

Though following his combat novel, *Close Quarters* (1977), at some length, *Paco's Story* fulfilled anxious critics' expectations that Heinemann was a major literary talent. By winning the National Book Award for fiction, *Paco's Story* assured itself a permanent place in the Vietnam War canon and perhaps first place in the important subgenre of the returned veteran. Moreover, with *Paco's Story*, Heinemann proved himself a stylist capable of a range of effects. The naturalism of *Close Quarters* is one ingredient in *Paco's Story*, in which fantasy and an intriguing narrational gamble figure importantly, as does a precise rendering of the material aspects of American culture. Heinemann is a master at blending the ordinary and the extraordinary in his evocation of the workingman's Vietnam and the workingman's America.

Bibliography

Anisfield, Nancy. "After the Apocalypse: Narrative Movement in Larry Heinemann's *Paco's Story*." In *America Rediscovered: Critical Essays on Literature and Film of the Vietnam War*, edited by Owen W. Gilman, Jr., and Lorrie Smith. New York: Garland, 1990. Anisfield argues that while the typical war narrative, including that of the returned veteran, depends on a violent, apocalyptic ending, *Paco's Story* defies this convention by closing with a largely passive, internal event. The rejection of apocalyptic closure allows thoughtful examination of the war and its consequences.

Beidler, Philip D. *Re-Writing America: Vietnam Authors in Their Generation.* Athens: University of Georgia Press, 1991. Beidler examines the "complex experimentalism" through which Heinemann raises questions about the nature of storytelling. By puzzling the reader with a ghost narrator and a named but still unspecified listener, Heinemann dares himself and the reader to find the terms by which to value another Vietnam story. Beidler also comments on the relatively self-contained nature of each chapter as a partial exploration of how the war reaches into the unfolding present, changing the historical vision of Americans and America.

Bonn, Maria S. "A Different World: The Vietnam Veteran Novel Comes Home." In *Fourteen Landing Zones: Approaches to Vietnam War Literature*, edited by Philip K. Jason. Iowa City: University of Iowa Press, 1991. *Paco's Story* is the linchpin in Bonn's analysis of how veterans' fictions reflect the unusual conditions of return for participants in this unpopular war. Bonn compares Paco's situation to that of Philip Dossier in Heinemann's *Close Quarters* and Chris Starkmann in Philip Caputo's *Indian Country* (1987), exploring how these novels treat the limits and terms of reintegration.

Jeffords, Susan. "Tattoos, Scars, Diaries, and Writing Masculinity." In *The Vietnam War and American Culture*, edited by John Carlos Rowe and Rick Berg. New York: Columbia University Press, 1991. Jeffords finds a sinister pattern in which masculine suffering seeks retribution and relief in the raping of women. The polarization of women and victims turns women into oppressors. Jeffords makes fascinating connections among the various images of scars, tattoos, and other inscriptions.

Myers, Thomas. "Dispatches from Ghost Country: The Vietnam Veteran in Recent American Fiction." *Genre* 21, no. 4 (1988): 409-428. Myers observes that while consistency is hard to find in the popular and literary representation of the Vietnam veteran, there is agreement that the Vietnam veteran's experience differs from that of the veterans of other wars. *Paco's Story* is viewed by Myers as a minimalist narrative, a study of stasis. To the extent that Paco remains hidden, unrevealed, Heinemann's subject becomes more and more the ways in which Paco is perceived (or ignored) by others.

Philip K. Jason

THE PALACE OF THE WHITE SKUNKS

Author: Reinaldo Arenas (1943-1990)
Type of plot: Family
Time of plot: The late 1950's
Locale: Holguín, a small provincial town in the rural Oriente province of Cuba
First published: Le palais des très blanches mouffettes, 1975 (English translation, 1990)

Principal characters:

> FORTUNATO, the protagonist, an adolescent trying to escape from the misery of his family life during the time of the Cuban revolutionary struggle
>
> POLO, Fortunato's grandfather, an embittered old grouch fed up with life who refuses to talk to any of the members of his family
>
> JACINTA, Fortunato's superstitious and blasphemous grandmother, who is desperately searching for answers to explain life's hardships
>
> CELIA, Fortunato's aunt, who is driven to madness after her only daughter poisons herself
>
> DIGNA, Fortunato's aunt, who has been abandoned by her husband
>
> ADOLFINA, Fortunato's aunt, a spinster desperate to lose her virginity
>
> ONERICA, Fortunato's unmarried mother, who abandons him and goes to the United States

The Novel

The Palace of the White Skunks is a stylistically rich experimental novel that tells of the desolation, despair, and vicissitudes of a Cuban family prior to the 1959 Cuban Revolution. The novel, which deliberately and systematically undermines the conventions of the realistic novel tradition, is centered on Fortunato, a sensitive and restless young man living through a turbulent political period in Cuban history: the insurrectional struggle against the dictatorial government of Fulgencio Batista. Desperate to escape the disappointments and cruelties of his family (whom he refers to as "creatures" and "wild beasts"), as well as to escape from Holguín, a small, conservative rural town, Fortunato attempts to join Fidel Castro's revolutionary forces. This flight for freedom, however, ends tragically when the young man is arrested, tortured, and executed by the government police.

The novel is divided into three parts: "Prologue and Epilogue," "The Creatures Utter Their Complaints," and "The Play." In the fourteen pages that make up part 1, "Prologue and Epilogue," the reader is introduced to the self-pitying and squabbling voices of each character, all members of the same family. At this point, the crisscrossing of voices is so entangled that it is extremely difficult to decipher during a first reading. These fragments of voices, however, will be contextualized and expanded during the second and third parts of the novel. With the (con)fusion of what is traditionally the first word (prologue) and last word (epilogue) of the traditional novel, the suggestion is made that there is no first or final word on any given matter; rather, discourse is open-ended, without a finalizing period.

Part 2, "The Creatures Utter Their Complaints," constitutes the major portion of the novel. This section is divided into five "agonies" in which each family member takes turns articulating his or her own intimate sufferings. These accounts are presented as a rambling of voices that often conceals the identity of the speaking subject. Temporal-spatial realities are filtered through the turbulent voices of the family members, who do not concern themselves with providing objective reference points. It appears as if the same state of instability and crisis that is assaulting the country exists internally in each family member.

Part 2 also introduces fragments from newspaper accounts, bulletins of guerrilla activity, advertisements, film announcements, and beauty magazines; these fragments are juxtaposed alongside and serve to parallel the babel of voices of the family members. In "Fifth Agony," there appear twelve versions of the two most significant episodes within the novel: Fortunato's decision to escape from home to join the Castro-led rebels, and Adolfina's unsuccessful attempt to lose her virginity during a night on the town. The contradictions in the different versions of these two fruitless quests reveal the difficulty of attempting to record any reality faithfully. Yet this lack of precision is quite irrelevant to the emotional intensity, dreams, and desires of both characters. In the end, any reader searching for objectivity in *The Palace of the White Skunks* will be at a loss and will consequently miss the artistic and creative intensity of the novel. To appreciate this text, one must surrender to its hallucinatory situations, implausible incidents, and disjointed digressions.

In part 3, "The Play," the reader discovers the insertion of a play within the novel. This change of genre (from novel to drama) is accompanied by a significant change from interior monologue to dramatic dialogue. In this phantasmagoric theatrical representation, the family members become performers who reenact their own lives and obsessions. Immediately following the play, there appears "Sixth Agony," which recounts yet another version of Fortunato's escape. The omniscient narrator of this last agony describes the young man's torture and death at the hands of government soldiers. Earlier, however, this same omniscient narrator, traditionally a reliable voice, had expressed doubt over whether Fortunato had ever joined the rebel forces. Regardless of what indeed happened, it is significant that no version denies Fortunato's basic reasons for wanting to escape from home: hunger, poverty, repression, lack of opportunities, and the suffocating demands of his family.

The Characters

The Palace of the White Skunks is the story of Fortunato and of the young man's eccentrically frustrated and obsessive family: Polo, Fortunato's grandfather, who considers himself cursed for having engendered only daughters; Jacinta, Fortunato's superstitious and crazed grandmother; Digna, Celia, Onerica, and Adolfina, Polo's and Jacinta's daughters, all marginalized figures who desperately search for a space, either real or imaginary, in which to forget the misery of their existence. Together, on a structural level, the sisters function to articulate a psychotic and paranoic discourse that identifies the passive role assigned to women in Hispanic society. Their frustrated attempts to escape their suffocating fate only add to their sense of desperation. The sisters' children, Esther (Celia's daughter), Tico and Anisia (Digna's son and daughter), and Fortunato (Onerica's son), are all fatherless. On a spiritual level, Digna, Celia, Onerica, and Adolfina also are fatherless, since Polo rejects them because of their gender. Throughout the novel, these characters—or, rather, voices, for the text is constructed as a cacophony of voices—are given the opportunity to recount their own obsessive stories of despair.

In the novel, Fortunato pursues writing as a means to survive the continual oppression of his family and the conservatism of his hometown. He fabricates and invents imaginary refuges that take him away from his asphyxiating situation. The young man steals paper from his grandfather's small vegetable and fruit shop in order to write in secret, a labor of passion that he faithfully carries out under the most oppressive conditions. His wish is to record his family's experiences. For his identification with other oppressed individuals, however, he must pay a price. Fortunato's desire to bear his family's suffering, to understand, to feel their intimate pain and frustrations, places him on the path to destruction. The adolescent poet, whose existence is already marked by isolation and hopelessness, begins to fragment under the weight of misfortune. *The Palace of the White Skunks* challenges the notion of a single reliable voice that can faithfully telegraph reality to the reader, for the audibility of Fortunato's voice, a voice that wishes to sees itself as the authentic representative of the family, is incessantly drowned out by the multiplicity of voices of other family members eager to tell their own sides of the story. Although first-, second-, and third-person narrative voices are utilized in *The Palace of the White Skunks*, the first-person point of view predominates within the text. This narrative "I" is shared by all the family members, producing a cacophony of voices in which each voice, at times unrecognizable, struggles in vain to be heard. Multiple narrative "I's" contradict one another, in this way not granting referential stability to any speaking subject. Thus, the text is reduced to a crisscrossing of affirmations and contradictions, denying the concentration of veracity into a single authoritative voice. In this Tower of Babel where no one understands anyone else, personal agonies are fated to echo and reecho within the chambers of the novel. That the characters, prisoners of their own suffering, yearn in desperation to find a receptive listener only underscores their alienation.

Themes and Meanings

The Palace of the White Skunks is embedded in a concrete historical event, the fight of the Sierra Maestra rebel forces against the Batista regime that culminated in Fidel Castro's revolutionary victory of 1959. Yet, the presentation of the characters' other levels of experience is never sacrificed for any type of accuracy or transparency, any hope to reproduce historical reality faithfully at a referential level of language. Arenas' concern is not to rewrite history but to subordinate history to fiction, thus allowing free inquiry into the nature of human existence. The novel does not support the concept of an "official" history of a collective consciousness that simplifies human experience by reducing it to facts or figures; rather, the book examines the enigma of individual human existence.

The ironic and ludicrous title, *The Palace of the White Skunks*, already alerts the reader to the unconventional story that follows. In this novel, the notion of a well-structured plot is subverted by the presentation of a narrative time-space of multiple possibilities that invites the reader to sort out the various narrative threads and, thus, to work out a larger meaning. The text requires a flexible approach to reading, a letting go of traditional expectations. The reader is asked to make the text intelligible in spite of its violations and transgressions, to accommodate the shifting codes of a multifarious reality. Hence, the initial image of death riding on a bicycle around the family home is presented as being equally "real" as the protagonist's frustrated attempt to join the revolutionary struggle. Fortunato's walking on the roof while stabbing himself, Esther and Fortunato's chats beyond the grave, demons and spirits dancing in the living room, the extreme poverty of the rural town, the insurrectional struggle against Batista, the grandmother's blasphemies and insults, Adolfina's sexual frustrations—all are presented side by side and contribute equally to the novel's textual validity.

Utilizing a narrative strategy that fragments the story into bits and pieces, *The Palace of the White Skunks* invites the reader to re-create a bewildering collage that, although it at first disorients, ultimately reforges the life-art connection on the level of the imaginative. In this, his third novel, Arenas provides the reader with a disturbing portrait of the poverty and misery that were present in rural Cuba shortly before the triumph of the revolution. While many Cuban novelists during the 1970's were writing testimonial realistic works that idealistically presented the revolution as the decisive moment that radically transformed Cuban society for the better, Arenas, undermining this rather utopian vision of history, portrays the revolution as the catalyst responsible for the death of his protagonist and the emotional destruction of a family.

In *The Palace of the White Skunks*, Arenas clearly had no intention of writing a closed, linear text that presented a coherent, objective representation of the empirical reality. The novel is a daring compositional experiment that subverts and challenges authoritarian and reductionist attitudes toward literature as well as life.

Critical Context

While living in Cuba, Arenas published only one novel, *Celestino antes del alba* (1967; *Singing from the Well*, 1987), and a few short stories. The author's refusal to articulate revolutionary propaganda in his writings forced the cultural policymakers of the Cuban Revolution—individuals who defined the function of literature as political and of immediate practical utility—to censor his texts and designate them as counterrevolutionary. After Arenas' fall from favor with the Cuban government, his work was no longer published on the island; moreover, his manuscripts were repeatedly confiscated and destroyed by the Cuban secret police. As a result, Arenas secretly began to send his manuscripts abroad. *The Palace of the White Skunks* thus first appeared in 1975 in French translation before appearing in its original Spanish version, *El palacio de las blanquísimas mofetas*, in 1980.

The Palace of the White Skunks is the second novel of a five-book sequence—*Singing from the Well, The Palace of the White Skunks, Otra vez el mar* (1982; *Farewell to the Sea*, 1986), *El color del verano* (1991; the color of summer), and *El asalto* (1991; the assault)—that constitutes a unique intradependent unit within the author's total novelistic productions. This quintet, which the author insisted on calling a *pentagonía* ("pentagony")—a playful but revealing neologism that underscores the despair and *agonía* (agony) suffered by the characters in each novel—reflects different historical periods of Cuban society as well as provides an imagined futuristic vision of the Cuban island and its people. In each novel of the series, the main character is destroyed—only to be resurrected under a new name in the subsequent text, where he suffers a whole new set of ordeals. With *The Palace of the White Skunks*, Arenas continued the family saga that he had initially begun with *Singing from the Well*. *The Palace of the White Skunks* explores the protean main character's adolescent world, a chaotic world of torment and spiritual hardship played out against a backdrop of revolutionary upheaval.

Bibliography

Olivares, Jorge. "Carnival and the Novel: Reinaldo Arenas' *El palacio de las blan-quísimas mofetas*." *Hispanic Review* 53, no. 4 (Autumn, 1985): 467-476. Analyzes Arenas' novel within the liberating aesthetics of carnivalesque literature as studied by Mikhail Bakhtin and Julia Kristeva. Olivares claims that the novel "exhibits a carnival logic; it does so in the form of a family saga that lacks the authoritative presence of its founding member—the patriarchal figure."

Rozencvaig, Perla. "Reinaldo Arenas's Last Interview." *Review: Latin American Literature and Arts* 44 (January-June, 1991): 78-83. Arenas' last interview, granted shortly before his death in 1990, in which he talks at length about the novels of the *pentagonía*. The reader gets a sense of the author's humor and subversive spirit, essential elements of his writing.

Santí, Enrico Mario. "The Life and Times of Reinaldo Arenas." *Michigan Quarterly Review* 23 (Spring, 1984): 227-236. One of the first overviews in English of Arenas' life and work. Santí rates *The Palace of the White Skunks* as Arenas' most experimental work.

Stavans, Ilan. "An Irredeemable Clan." *The New York Times Book Review*, January 20, 1991, 20. Stavans clearly observes how despair and desolation permeate the entire text, concluding that Arenas' characters, "like those of William Faulkner, are irredeemable, destined to suffer . . . we hear their tormented screams as they succumb to the perverse joke that has been played upon them by fate."

Wood, Michael. "No Sorrow Left Unturned." *The New York Review of Books* 38 (March 7, 1991): 21-23. A lengthy review of *The Palace of the White Skunks*. Wood states that Arenas "hasn't written any of this book ironically; he has written it lyrically . . . making excess and stylistic risk a kind of signature."

Francisco Soto

THE PASSION ACCORDING TO G. H.

Author: Clarice Lispector (1925-1977)
Type of plot: Philosophical realism
Time of plot: The 1960's
Locale: An apartment in Rio de Janerio, Brazil
First published: A Paixão Segundo G. H., 1964 (English translation, 1988)

>*Principal characters:*
>G. H., the middle-aged sculptress who tells the story, a gregarious and
>outgoing woman who shies away from intimate relationships
>JANAIR, G. H.'s maid, who has abruptly quit and decamped
>A COCKROACH, an insect who lives in Janair's wardrobe and whose
>appearance precipitates G. H.'s spiritual crisis
>THE CRYING MAN, a vaguely described ex-lover of G. H. to whom she
>imagines she is telling her story

The Novel

Though the book is heavy with Christian allusions, especially to the Old Testament, what *The Passion According to G. H.* presents is a completely secular description of a spiritual rebirth. The trivial act of squashing a cockroach as she cleans her maid's room strangely rattles the story's narrator and leads her into a cascade of profound reflections on the scheme of things.

The book centers on a few hours in the life of the narrator, who is identified only as G. H., as she sits in her servant's room and thinks. The bulk of the text is taken up with a precise delineation of her thought processes as she reevaluates her life. This reevaluation, however, is not of the sort found in psychological novels, in which a character might reconsider past actions and resolve to make up for past lapses. What concerns G. H. is not any specific incidents but rather the tenor of her life. Thus, for example, thoughts on the animality of the cockroach lead her to ponder her own humanness, which, she learns, can be truly appreciated only by understanding its linkage to nature. This facet of her existence she has previously overlooked.

Abstruse as such a concentration on abstract issues may seem, the heroine's spiritual journey is correlated with the specifics of her present lifestyle, her relation to her maid, and her past history. Concurrent with the unraveling of her previous, faulty spiritual constructions occurs a gradual revelation of her material circumstances.

G. H.'s life is ripe for enlightenment because it is one of extreme artificiality. She is a rentier, that is, one who lives off the dividends of her investments. She sculpts, not as serious artistic activity but to pass the time. Her friends are fellow idle bohemians, isolated from the daily life of the average Brazilian, and G. H.'s relationships extend no further than friendships. She has no relatives or long-term interpersonal commitments. She is without real work, hobbies, or intimacies with others.

Such facts are scattered throughout the story, but G. H.'s connection to her maid, Janair, is given in a lump at the beginning. Though the servant had been employed for some time, G. H. knows nothing about her and has not been in her quarters since she was hired. Going into the room to clean up after the maid has abruptly left, G. H. is startled to find that the occupant had stripped the place of its clutter and sketched rude, primitive pictures on the wall, depictions that reveal Janair's hatred for her mistress. Finding her superficial understanding of her employee totally exploded sufficiently disorients G. H. so that she can begin a reconsideration of her relations with the world.

Forced to see one relationship in a new light, the narrator is enabled to more purposefully allow herself to look at major events from her past in a new light. Her casual killing of a cockroach in the maid's wardrobe leads her to remember an abortion she had undergone just as casually. Her quiet moments in the servant's quarters lead her to think back to quiet times with an ex-lover and to acknowledge for the first time the depth of the love they had, which was expressed best in silence. In keeping with the novel's philosophical bent, however, G. H. thinks of her abortion not to blame herself for the choice she made in eliminating her unborn child but rather in order to condemn herself for the offhanded, thoughtless manner in which she made the decision. This condemnation links to the central spiritual perception with which she leaves the room at the end: She must henceforth try to live without preconceptions so that she can approach every moment with heightened authenticity.

To crown and close this chapter in her life, these few hours in which she has thought and functioned more intensely than ever before, G. H. bends down and eats the cockroach. In this bizarre act of "communion," G. H. both thanks the bug for being the guide to her spiritual reinvigoration, and, more important, physically acts out her new rejection of traditional social stereotypes, such as the belief that insects are inherently disgusting. After this ritual, G. H. is ready to leave the room and confront life with an altered and enriched perspective.

The Characters

The Passion According to G. H. has an extremely tight focus. From G. H.'s viewpoint, the novel recounts what happened one morning while she worked and sat alone in her flat. Nothing about G. H.'s life is reported unless a memory of it turns up in this space of time—the reader learns nothing about the narrator's childhood, for example, since none of her mental associations lead to thoughts of it—and other characters are sketched only to the degree that they occur in her reminiscences. Aside from her maid, other people who appear in the book are not even named. The fact that the speaker laconically calls herself G. H. is thus a relative matter, since even this slight designation gives her more substantiality than is granted to other figures in the book. Lispector's strategy for describing her main character, then, is to keep personal details to a minimum without eliminating them altogether.

G. H. has had a shallow life, according to the details that do appear to describe her. Her life is taken up with such insignificant pursuits as gossiping and partying. Though she is a sculptress, she does not labor seriously at her art; though she is a social butterfly, she has no special confidantes or long-term love relationship. Yet she has, on occasion and only for brief spans, longed for a more profound connection to the universe. These details serve to anchor the character firmly in reality, so that what happens to her seems neither unbelievable nor an experience that would happen only to an extraordinary personality. On the other hand, Lispector's restrained use of specifics, so that next to nothing is told about G. H.'s current status or her life's former chronology, acts to direct readers' attention to what is of paramount concern to the writer: describing the gradations of consciousness that G. H. goes through in encountering a nova of philosophical epiphanies.

A cockroach, ironically, is the second most prominent character in the book. Like other characters in the novel, the insect is only described insofar as it is a contributor to G. H.'s awakening. Few details are given about the cockroach's looks or behavior. Rather, it is described generically. It is mentioned, for example, that the cockroach has a long pedigree, having been on earth since the time of the dinosaurs, and this thought draws G. H. into a lengthy reflection on history.

Janair, G. H.'s maid, is also incompletely known. The main information given about her is that she has rather grotesquely redone her room. The room changes do not cause G. H., who tells the story, to try to plumb the servant's motives; instead, G. H. merely observes how the shock of finding the changes affects herself.

Other characters without names, such as the doctor who performed G. H.'s abortion, are even less distinctly drawn. A single moment when they were in contact with G. H. is recalled, with neither the background to the scene nor its aftermath filled in.

Themes and Meanings

Before writing this novel, Lispector had lived extensively outside her homeland of Brazil, in the United States and in European countries, and she had a cosmopolitan, nonsectarian outlook. In depicting G. H.'s epiphany, though Lispector draws on Christian imagery and citations available to her from her unbringing, she presents the situation nondenominationally. She translates religious terminology into a secular vocabulary. In G. H.'s moment of truth, the name of God frequently comes up, but "God," G. H. explicitly states, is a word she is using to name the constantly emergent life force of the world, not a higher being attached to some religious creed. To someone like G. H., who has lived out of touch with nature and her own animal side, an awareness of this life force strikes with as much power as a religious revelation.

Part of the reason for Lispector's desacralization of this experience is to remove it from its doctrinal trappings. Above all, she wants to bring spiritual exaltation down to earth and make it seem realizable for anyone. Through such techniques as the use of homely details and realistic characterization, Lispector strives to indicate that every person who has ever thirsted for a richer life has the potential to undergo a genuine rebirth. Stated obversely, the book argues that no one has the right to shrug off such intangible events as are captured in the volume, since every person is liable to vital renewal.

Metaphysical experiences are often described by those who went through them in unconvincing and unsatisfying ways. Lispector confronts the issue of the possibility of representing near imperceptible happenings head on by having G. H. keep a written record. Everything in the novel describes the events of the narrator's extraordinary morning, but without revealing what has occurred since then, G. H. tells the reader that it is the day after her revelations; she is trying to write down what took place so that she will never forget the particulars. She runs into manifold problems in trying to find the words to embody what are resolutely nonverbal experiences. This is where redefinition comes in. Many words that she used to use, such as "God" and "love," no longer seem meaningful according to her new understanding of reality. Also, her wrestling with expression provokes her to constantly draw on biblical imagery, as when she describes the maid's room as a desert where a saint is tested. She does this not because the experience is especially Christian but because this imagery accurately conveys the subtleties of mental nuance felt by those undergoing spiritual ordeals.

Thus, though Lispector is intent on showing readers how close anyone is to mystical discovery, this does not persuade her to downplay the complexity or ambiguity of such discovery. The writer is unflinching in accepting the challenges of attempting to put the ineffable into words.

Critical Context

The Passion According to G. H. can be connected to two intellectual currents of the period. The first was the rising prominence of "liberation theology" in Latin America. This theology was a Christianity, largely Catholic, that had become more concerned with social justice and trying to ensure the poor an adequate life than with getting them to take the sacraments and register doctrinal purity. This religious trend partook of some of the spirit of the Cuban Revolution and of the urban guerrillas who fought corrupt dictators in many South and Central American countries, though it differed fundamentally from these movements in choice of means. Where the guerrillas depended on firepower, the liberation church eschewed violence in favor of preaching and having its leaders set examples of simple, dignified living in the communities of the impoverished. Though Lispector does not directly promote such ideas in her book, she shows she is influenced by them in her double act of translation. She places a woman's moment of life-shattering vision in a mundane setting, and she drops religious phraseology in favor of everyday language. She translates a moment from specialized religious experience to place it in the common stream of life. By this tactic, she follows the wave of liberation theology in an insistence on the relevance and worldliness of spiritual concerns.

Second, Lispector is inspired by Continental existentialism, to which she had been exposed in the fiction of the twentieth century French philosopher and novelist Jean-Paul Sartre. Sartre's novel *La Nausée* (1938, *Nausea*, 1949) is highlighted by a scene that recalls the one in which G. H. is transfixed by a cockroach. Sartre's protagonist is struck and horrified by the roiling, inexhaustible life revealed to him by a tangle of tree roots. Though his feeling is one of revulsion, Sartre suggests that such moments are constructive, since one can live in authenticity and freedom only if one breaks the brittle surface of conventions—conventions that would ignore, for example, the life force in the tree and see it as merely another object. Lispector shares

Sartre's belief that the passageway to authenticity leads through a realization of the estranging foreignness of the natural world, though her vision is not so unrelievedly dark as his.

This novel continued to add to Lispector's reputation as a writer's writer. She did not garner as much popular support, as did many of her contemporaries in Latin American fiction. Though some of them, such as Julio Cortázar, and, to a lesser extent, Mario Vargas Llosa, were as tenaciously experimental as she was, their works had more conventional plots (though they were not always unfolded in a traditional way) and seamier themes, being concerned with such matters as sex or political corruption. Yet Lispector's reputation has continued to grow, as discriminating readers increasingly appreciate the exquisiteness of her writing and the depth and precision she brings to her treatment of philosophical and aesthetic issues.

Bibliography

Fitz, Earl E. *Clarice Lispector*. Boston: Twayne, 1985. Fitz situates Lispector's work in relation to the Latin American writing scene (in which she broke experimental ground for others), to authors such as Virginia Woolf, and to existential philosophy. He also links *The Passion According to G. H.* to the general stylistic traits and themes of Lispector's other fiction.

Lowe, Elizabeth. *The City in Brazilian Literature*. Rutherford, N.J.: Fairleigh Dickinson University Press, 1982. Discusses how the urban experience is represented in Brazilian fiction and pinpoints Lispector as an important contributor to this tradition. *The Passion According to G. H.*, set in an impersonal high-rise building, is given special consideration.

Monegal, Emir R. "The Contemporary Brazilian Novel." In *Fiction in Several Languages*, edited by Henri Peyre. Boston: Houghton Mifflin, 1968. Gives an overview of the development of Brazilian literature to the late 1960's. Lispector is given pride of place as being one of the handful of originators of the new novel in Brazil. Focuses on *The Passion According to G. H.*.

Patai, Daphne. "Clarice Lispector and the Clamor of the Ineffable." *Kentucky Romance Quarterly* 27 (1980): 133-149. Patai finds that the language used to describe G. H.'s mystical and irrational experiences is, at different times, too "grandiloquent" or too logical. The overrationality, Patai argues, derives from the narrator's tendency to try to work out new definitions for concepts, such as love, that have been problematized by her experience.

_____ . *Myth and Ideology in Contemporary Brazilian Fiction*. Rutherford, N.J.: Fairleigh Dickinson University Press, 1983. Patai looks at different works of Brazilian fiction to show how they play with universal patterns of myth. She selects *The Passion According to G. H.* for extended treatment because of the heroine's mythical imagining of a sojourn in the desert. She finds that the novel, though rooted in myth, also deals with Brazilian social relations.

James Feast

PICTURING WILL

Author: Ann Beattie (1947-   )
Type of plot: Family
Time of plot: 1989
Locale: Charlottesville, Virginia; New York City; Florida
First published: 1989

>   *Principal characters:*
>   WILL, a five-year-old boy around whom the story revolves
>   JODY, his mother, a talented and promising photographer
>   WAYNE, Will's unstable father, divorced from Jody
>   MEL ANTHIS, Jody's lover, devoted to Will
>   MARY VICKERS, Jody's friend
>   WAGONER, Mary's son and Will's best friend
>   D. B. HAVERFORD (HAVEABUD), a New York City art-gallery owner
>   SPENCER, the seven-year-old son of Haverford's former client
>   CORKY, Wayne's current wife
>   KATE, Wayne's lover

The Novel

In *Picturing Will*, the author presents the lives of three family members—mother, father, and son—in the late twentieth century. The first major section of the novel, "Mother," introduces Jody, who has managed to bring her life back to normal after her husband, Wayne, walked out and left her with their infant son, Will. Jody lives in Charlottesville, Virginia, and supports herself as a photographer specializing in weddings. She is an attractive and energetic woman for whose work the demand is increasing, but she is also an artist with an eye for the out-of-the-ordinary. She is on the verge of success, an obvious candidate for the attention of an art capital such as New York. Jody's devotion to Will is genuine. As she herself admits, he has been her salvation during the difficult days after Wayne's departure.

Enjoying the success of her photography business, Jody considers the proposal of Mel, her lover, to marry him and move to New York City. She hesitates to jeopardize the security of her present life and her independence as a single woman, but Mel is a good man who has developed an exceptionally close relationship with Will, and a move to New York would rescue her from routine photographic work. In many ways, Mel is even more understanding of Will than is Jody, while his sympathy for her work keeps prodding her to the challenge of New York. Judy's friend Mary Vickers, in a bad marriage herself, admires Mel and urges Jody to accept his offer. While Jody and Mary share the experiences of young motherhood, Mary poses for a photograph destined to show Jody's genius beyond doubt, and their sons Will and Wagoner become best friends.

With the intention of persuading Jody to move to New York, Mel arranges to show her work to art-gallery proprietor D. B. Haverford, who immediately sees the appeal of her photographs and agrees to a public show in his gallery. When they meet, he is as fascinated by her as by her pictures. She sees him as a mere businessman whose name she cannot bother to remember, so he is always "Haveabud" to her and to the reader, but she perceives that he could be the key to her professional future.

The second major section of the novel, "Father," centers on Will's father Wayne, now living in Florida with his third wife, Corky. It was the birth of Will, after he had unsuccessfully urged an abortion, that made life with Jody intolerable for Wayne, but as Will's father he of course retains visiting rights.

While Jody is absorbed in furthering her career in New York, Mel has willingly assumed the responsibility of driving Will to visit his father. This time, however, they are accompanied by Haveabud (whom Will is told he must tolerate because he is important for his mother's work) and Haveabud's young friend Spencer. Haveabud, once the promoter of Spencer's father, is sexually exploiting the seven-year-old boy. Will's only interest in the trip is the opportunity to visit Wagoner, now living in Florida with his mother, Jody and Mel having arranged for their reunion.

Wayne anticipates Will's visit with apprehension and dread, while Corky, trying to persuade Wayne that they should have a child, welcomes the opportunity to show him what a good mother she will be. She greets Will enthusiastically, amuses him with shopping, and carefully prepares his clothes and meals. Wayne makes the effort to please Will by taking him and Corky to the pool of a wealthy client whose garden he maintains, but he becomes more interested in having an affair with the wealthy owner. Wayne's most intense though brief affair during Will's visit, however, is with Kate, a mysterious woman who suggests that they conceal their last names from each other. It is this liaison that is his downfall. The police discover a pillbox with Corky's name that Wayne had accidentally let fall from his pocket into Kate's car; at the same time, they find a sizable amount of heroin in the abandoned car. From a window, Will sees his father being led away in handcuffs. As soon as his father is taken, he leaves for New York at once, without achieving the promised visit with "Wag" that was so important to him.

The final, brief section of the novel, "Child," presents Will twenty years later. The future of the family is revealed: Will has a self-absorbed, very successful mother and a devoted stepfather, Mel, Wayne having disappeared. Will himself now has a wife and son. As the novel ends, Will imagines that he is photographing himself and his son playing with the ball Mel has given them.

The Characters

This novel defines family members by their relationships to one another. All of their lives revolve around Will, both parents measuring themselves by their relation to, and responses to, their son. Because Will himself is too young to understand their motives, the reader sympathizes with him in his bewilderment, viewing the parents through Will's eyes even as the author allows the reader to see how the boy has changed their lives. He is a likable five-year-old who remembers his mother's counsel and tries to be a good son. He responds to Mel's love, appreciates Corky's kindness (they remain correspondents over the years), and ultimately becomes a loving husband and father. Throughout most of the novel, however, he is a child hoping to be reunited with his friend but unable to initiate the action.

Readers appreciate the difficulties of Jody's predicament and admire her determination to forge a new career and yet remain a functioning mother to Will. Gradually, though, her manipulation of others becomes apparent: She accepts Mel's love with reservations until the opportunity in New York persuades her to marry him, and she unhesitatingly photographs the private life of a real friend, Mary Vickers. Having made the mistake of marrying Wayne, she at first apprehensively and then more and more singlemindedly determines to realize her life as an artist. She sees only potential subjects for her camera. Even Will becomes mainly a subject for the cover of *Vogue*. Her selfishness transforms Mel from ardent lover to sacrificial husband. Haveabud she has shrewdly manipulated to forge a career. Like Mel and Will, the reader accepts her for the artist she is and the mother she has tried less successfully to be.

Wayne's deficiencies as a parent of course exceed Jody's coolness and self-serving calculation, for he is weak and despicable, a man totally unable to meet the responsibilities of fatherhood. Recognizing his own unsuitability as a father, he nevertheless blames Jody for insisting that Will be born. He reveals his inferiority when he accuses Jody of making it difficult for him to finish college, and he can only regard himself as victimized. Wayne's preeminent weakness, however, is women; he himself suspects it of bordering on addiction. Not surprisingly, it is a woman, Kate, who is his undoing.

Mel is Wayne's opposite. He has the decency and dependability that makes the family unit work. Will responds to him early, even before Jody is ready to make a commitment. Mel gives of himself, from the art show in New York that he initiated, to his protection of Will during his trip to Florida, and through the years that follow.

The character most like Mel is Corky. She tries to make Will's visit a happy one, and she displays wifely virtues that Wayne can never appreciate, particularly a determination to make family life work. Mary and Wagoner Vickers are serviceable friends to Jody and Will. Mary helps Jody to further her career, while Will remains a true friend until Wagoner's early death.

Haveabud is an opportunist ready to take advantage of anyone naïve enough to trust him, while Spencer is merely Haveabud's victim. Abandoned by both parents, he is a vulnerable child with no strong Jody and loving Mel to save him.

Themes and Meanings

The overriding theme of *Picturing Will* is surely the destruction of family life in the modern world. Beattie labors not only to present each member of a family but also to set the scene authentically with photographic detail. Her choppy sentences and rapid sequence of sketchily presented scenes reflect the fragmentation of a family. The scenes are mere flashes, like those from Jody's camera. A scene depicting grotesque masqueraders at a Halloween party that Jody is snapping, juxtaposed with that of a deer struck and killed by Mary Vickers' car on her way home, epitomizes the unpredictability of the moment, which Jody is quickly on the scene to record with her camera. As scenes keep changing rapidly, the reader is left, like Will, to decipher their significance. Will tries to fathom Haveabud's rape of a child and, later, his own father's arrest. Does his childhood amount to such experiences or to a photograph of himself and his mother taken for *Vogue* and persisting as a prominent display in his mother's home?

By the presentation of unconnected scenes, the author suggests that modern urban life is like a series of random pictures. Her splashes of realistic detail vivify the often excruciating relationships of Mel and Jody, of Haveabud and Spencer, of Wayne and Kate. The nature of Jody's art inclines her to see life as snippets, even her son as something to "picture." With good intentions, she becomes more and more a mere provider for her son, more like the hardworking but distant father of an earlier time. Is it possible, the reader wonders, for such a woman to succeed as a mother under such circumstances?

In its third section, the novel affirms the possibility of stable family life by telescoping twenty years, in the process establishing a sense of continuity to counter the staccato effect of the prior scenes, although the brevity of the section arguably diminishes its effectiveness. Also contributing to the sense of stability, however, are the characters of Corky and, in particular, Mel. They demonstrate the possibility of integrity and cohesion even amid the disintegrating forces at work in a megalopolis corrupted by too many versions of Wayne and Haveabud and increasingly served by people who, like Jody, fall short of the challenge of combining responsible parenthood with professional success.

Critical Context

Picturing Will was Ann Beattie's eighth book of fiction and fourth novel. She and her typical protagonist belong to what is sometimes called the Woodstock Generation. Their detachment and characteristically unfocused rebellion against the society their elders bequeathed them do not so much mellow as atrophy in middle age. Twenty years beyond the point of not trusting anyone over thirty, they face the ordeal of trusting themselves to be forty. They often can accept neither the commitment and responsibilities of parenthood nor the other miscellaneous obligations that society— now the society that they had a substantial part in forming—imposes on them. Yet if Jody's contemporaries in *Picturing Will* are the Woodstock Generation, the third section of the novel, in leaping to Will's adulthood, projects a hypothetical future, as if the author cannot wait for enough "real" time to elapse to make Will an art historian at Columbia University.

The six-page excursion into Will's future seems to suggest that if Will and his generation will not prevail, at least they will endure. Beattie's critics argue inconclusively about whether her photographic techniques work as well in long fiction as in her short stories. *Picturing Will* is a kind of album, perhaps suffering somewhat from the typically unselective nature of albums, but some of the pictures are vivid and true. They are not all beautiful by any stretch of the imagination, and some, such as the homoerotic scene Will is compelled to witness on the trip to Florida, are disturbing, but some, such as Will's discovery of Mel's diary, are touching. It is to Beattie's credit that she finds shards of hope among the wreckage of her generation, even as she avoids easy solutions to the problems arising from their improvisational lifestyles.

Bibliography

Beattie, Ann. "An Interview with Ann Beattie." Interview by Steven R. Centola. *Contemporary Literature* 31 (Winter, 1990): 405-422. This discussion ranges over Beattie's work up to and including *Picturing Will*. Her disclosures that the rough draft of this short novel required three years and that she discarded "at least fifteen chapters" provide an idea of the distillation involved. Centola's questions generally solicit useful information about Beattie's literary aims and techniques.

Friedrich, Otto. "Beattieland." *Time* 135 (January 22, 1990): 68. Friedrich disagrees with the critical consensus (for example, Will and his friend Wag are for Friedrich "the only really likable characters"). He also faults Beattie's admitted practice of beginning her novels without knowledge of the way they are to end. It should be pointed out, however, that many of the most successful nineteenth century novelists, including the great Charles Dickens, often began serializing their work periodically before they settled on a conclusion, and that many of Beattie's contemporaries have admitted similar uncertainties en route.

Hulbert, Ann. "Only Disconnect." *The New York Review of Books* 37 (May 31, 1990): 33-35. Hulbert sees Beattie as striving for "greater certainty" and more "authorial control" in this novel than in her previous books. The principals are less inclined to float aimlessly but have acquired a sense of duty. To a considerable extent, however, their liberation from the trammels of an earlier generation leaves them lonely and uncertain.

Murphy, Christina. *Ann Beattie*. Boston: Twayne, 1986. Although published before *Picturing Will* appeared, Murphy's book is valuable as the only one on Beattie to date. It is a typical Twayne book—compact, readable, and orderly. A biographical chapter is followed by one on Beattie's "literary milieu," another on her early fiction, a chapter each on her six books before 1986, and finally one assessing her achievement. To Murphy, Beattie captures her age in fiction as successfully as J. D. Salinger, John Cheever, and John Updike did a somewhat earlier one.

Wyatt David. "Ann Beattie." *The Southern Review* 28 (Winter, 1992): 145-159. Wyatt assesses Beattie's fiction from a more recent perspective than Murphy. His verdict is a largely complimentary one, though *Picturing Will* comes in for some negative criticism. Wyatt sees the novel as focusing on the cost of choosing art as the work of one's life, but he finds Beattie's presentation of art and life "too binary to satisfy."

Robert P. Ellis

PIGS IN HEAVEN

Author: Barbara Kingsolver (1955-   )
Type of plot: Social realism
Time of plot: The 1990's
Locale: The Southwestern United States; Seattle, Washington; and the fictional town of Heaven, Oklahoma
First published: 1993

> *Principal characters:*
> TAYLOR GREER, a young white woman, fiercely independent and devoted to her adopted daughter Turtle
> TURTLE GREER, a six-year-old Cherokee girl
> ALICE GREER, Taylor's sixty-one-year-old mother
> JAX THIBODEAUX, Taylor's devoted live-in boyfriend, a rock musician
> ANNAWAKE FOURKILLER, a young, idealistic lawyer for the Cherokee tribe
> LEDGER FOURKILLER, Annawake's uncle, a wise medicine chief
> JOHNNY CASH STILLWATER, a fifty-nine-year-old Cherokee who becomes Alice's lover
> BARBIE, a young woman who devotes her life to emulating a children's doll

The Novel

The third novel by Barbara Kingsolver, *Pigs in Heaven* is a warm, humorous, and thought-provoking story of the conflict between an adoptive mother and a Native American tribe over the destiny of an adopted Cherokee girl. The novel covers a time span of about six months and is divided into three parts: "Spring," "Summer," and "Fall." Generally, Kingsolver uses a third-person-limited point of view. Each scene is presented in the author's folksy third-person voice, and the view of the action is usually limited to the perspective of one of the five main characters, Alice, Taylor, Jax, Annawake, or Cash. At times, however, Kingsolver presents a scene from the perspective of a minor character (such as Annawake's coworkers Jinny Redbow and Franklin Turnbo) or briefly enters into the consciousness of a second character (such as Turtle or Lucky Buster) in a scene that is described mostly from a major character's point of view.

Pigs in Heaven is an unusual and provocative sequel that calls into question the moral certitudes of Kingsolver's first novel, *The Bean Trees* (1988). In that book, as the plucky young protagonist Taylor Greer drives southwest from Kentucky, she has a three-year-old girl thrust upon her during a stop on Cherokee land in Oklahoma. In this earlier novel, Taylor's act of accepting and rearing the girl seems unquestionably heroic, since the girl's mother is dead, Taylor has no desire to acquire a child, and, particularly, since it is revealed later in the novel that the girl has been sexually abused.

Much of *The Bean Trees* focuses on the special, nurturing love that develops between Taylor and the Cherokee girl, whom Taylor names Turtle because the girl attaches herself to her new mother with the tenacity of a turtle's jaws.

Pigs in Heaven, on the other hand, presents a different and unexpected perspective on the situation: that it might be better for Turtle (now six years old) to be taken from Taylor (who has settled in Tucson) and returned to Turtle's Oklahoma tribe. Annawake Fourkiller, a young Cherokee lawyer, is on a crusade to test the legality of adoptions that have taken numerous Cherokee children out of the tribe and into non-Indian homes. Annawake's legal weapon is the Indian Child Welfare Act of 1978, which gives individual tribes the right to rule over the legality of such adoptions—and even to take children back from families that have been rearing them for years.

Kingsolver leads into this central conflict with a dramatic and moving prologue. While Taylor and Turtle are visiting Hoover Dam, Turtle glimpses a man falling down the spillway, and Taylor and Turtle become national celebrities when the man is found and rescued. That national fame brings trouble, however, when Annawake hears about their appearance on a television show and begins to investigate the legality of Taylor's adoption of Turtle.

When Taylor feels her hold on Turtle threatened by Annawake's inquiries, she impetuously flees with Turtle from their Tucson home. Taylor's mother, Alice Greer, who was about to leave her unsatisfying marriage in Kentucky anyway, flies to Las Vegas to bolster her daughter's morale. As they are about to leave Las Vegas, the Greers acquire a bizarre traveling companion named Barbie. Alice then travels to the Cherokee nation to reconnect with a childhood friend and to try to bolster Taylor's legal claim to Turtle. Meanwhile, Taylor, Turtle, and Barbie head on to Seattle, where Barbie betrays their trust and Taylor is left struggling to eke out a living as a working single mother.

In addition to this main plot line, Kingsolver also develops two other plot threads involving Jax Thibodeaux and Cash Stillwater. Back in Tucson, Jax is badly depressed over the absence of Taylor and Turtle and has an affair with his landlady, Gundi, an eccentric bohemian artist. After two years in Jackson Hole, Wyoming, Cash Stillwater regrets his departure from the Cherokee nation (which he left out of grief and shame over the deaths and losses in his family) and eventually returns to Oklahoma.

As Alice is drawn in by the warmth of the Cherokee people and by a ceremonial "stomp dance" in Heaven, Oklahoma, she feels increasingly comfortable with the Native American way of life. Meanwhile, Annawake, who discovers that Cash is Turtle's grandfather, surreptitiously plays matchmaker to Alice and Cash, hoping that a romance between them will help to resolve the conflict over Turtle. The romance does develop, and Alice convinces Taylor to bring Turtle back to Oklahoma for a custody hearing. When Alice learns of Annawake's matchmaking, she feels manipulated and indignant, but despite this minor snag, Turtle's case is harmoniously resolved. Under a joint custody settlement, she will spend school years with Taylor and summers with Cash. This compromise is further sweetened by the novel's final developments: Taylor plans to marry Jax, and Alice will marry Cash.

The Characters

Alice is the folksy, down-to-earth matriarch who embodies and repeatedly reflects upon a key issue for Greer females: their stubborn self-sufficiency. From Alice's mother Minerva Stamper (who ran a hog farm by herself) through Alice (who leaves two husbands) to Taylor (whose main goal in leaving Kentucky was to avoid the small-town girl's common fate of early pregnancy), Alice sees her female line as holding so tenaciously to their independence that it is difficult for them to establish and sustain relationships—particularly with men. The reader, however, takes pleasure in watching Alice reach out to provide maternal support for Taylor, Turtle, and even Barbie. Once Alice arrives in Heaven, she plays the role of an observer from the white world who enables the reader to appreciate the rich human and spiritual interconnectedness of the Cherokee culture.

Taylor, the chief protagonist in the novel, earns the reader's admiration for her independence, her pluck, and her devotion to her daughter Turtle. Early scenes involving the Hoover Dam incident establish the purity and power of this mother-daughter bond, as Taylor's staunch belief in her daughter's integrity enables her to prod disbelieving male officials into conducting a search for the accident victim her child has seen. Yet the reader also sees that Taylor's admirable qualities have their shadow side. Her self-reliance takes her out on a dubious limb when she flees with Turtle, disregarding the legal consequences and abandoning her support network in Tucson. The turning point in the novel comes for Taylor when she realizes that she and her daughter cannot be self-sufficient; Taylor agrees to bring Turtle back to the Cherokee nation and to submit to legal procedures that will determine what is best for her daughter.

Annawake Fourkiller is an idealistic young Cherokee lawyer who becomes the antagonist to Taylor, by virtue of Annawake's crusade to test the legality of adoptions of Cherokee children taken out of their tribe. Ironically, Taylor and Annawake share many character traits: stubborn independence, remarkable physical beauty, an indifference to that beauty and to the prospect of a committed relationship with a man, an intense bond with one other person, and ultimately the wisdom to listen to an older mentor. Parallel to Taylor's intense bond with Turtle is Annawake's deep feeling for her brother Gabriel, who was adopted off the reservation into a white family, was subjected to racist misunderstanding and abuse, and became a chronic criminal. Annawake's legal zeal is clearly traceable to her determination to prevent other Cherokee children from suffering as her brother has. The turning point comes for Annawake when her Uncle Ledger advises her to go beyond her tribal zeal and to consult her heart—the source of her eventual sympathy for Taylor and Alice.

Jax Thibodeaux and Cash Stillwater, though dissimilar in age and race, are alike in many of the traits that make them the obvious good choices of Taylor and Alice for their husbands. Both men are handsome, insightful, communicative, gentle, and humorous. Both are artists: Jax a rock musician with a band called the Irascible Babies, Cash a craftsman who keeps his senses and memories alive by stringing colorful beads in traditional Cherokee patterns. Both have a melancholy streak, partly the result of their sad family histories, and both are warm and attentive lovers. Finally, in keeping with the feminist tone of the novel, both extend themselves beyond the limitations of traditional male roles: Jax is a softhearted homemaker who misses not only Taylor but also Turtle, and Cash's enjoyment of cooking is a revelation to Alice.

Themes and Meanings

The conflict between Taylor and Annawake, between the interests of motherly love and tribal community, provides Kingsolver with the foremost dramatic issue of the novel. From the beginning, the reader's sympathies are strongly with Taylor, fueled by her staunch belief in Turtle during the Hoover Dam episode and by the ways in which Taylor and Turtle have clearly become the central foci of each other's lives.

On the other hand, it is one of the greatest strengths of Kingsolver's writing that she makes the reader feel that the claims of Annawake and the Cherokee nation are not merely a matter of legal abstraction or political correctness but are also heartfelt concerns for both the tribe and the child. Kingsolver makes the reader realize that the unfortunate case of Gabriel is far from an isolated incident when Annawake cites the statistic that as late as the 1970's, a third of all Native American children were still being taken from their families and adopted into non-Indian homes. With children being removed in these numbers, the tribe's concern that such adoptions threaten its strength, and even its very existence, is clearly legitimate. Annawake makes the further points that there are invariably Cherokee extended-family members who want such children returned and would make good homes for them and that even if Cherokee children are being reared in loving non-Indian homes, such children would lack the strong sense of cultural identity that would strengthen them to confront the inevitable racism and stigmatization of white society.

The Cherokee position that Turtle may be better off with the tribe also gains strength from Kingsolver's treatment of the theme of poverty. Once Taylor and Turtle are on their own in Seattle, the reader sees that in white urban society, a single mother working a minimum-wage job faces virtually insurmountable odds in trying to pay for housing, food, medical care, and day care. In white society, poverty also brings Taylor the emotional burdens of isolation and guilt. In the Cherokee nation, on the other hand, poverty is no disgrace, and to ask for and receive help from others is the cultural norm.

Kingsolver's ultimate theme in *Pigs in Heaven* is that even though in its material poverty Heaven, Oklahoma, might appear to be anything but a heaven, it actually holds rich emotional and spiritual fulfillment for those people whose spirits are generous enough to see it. Her title refers to the Cherokee myth in which six greedy boys are turned into pigs and then into a star constellation as a warning about the dire consequences of selfishness. The novel suggests that when people hold too tightly to what they consider theirs, they risk ending up miserable and might even appear to be greedy swine. On the other hand, when they open their hearts to realize that everyone's interests can be reconciled, they then find themselves to be the happiest of creatures in a heaven on earth.

Critical Context

The ascension of *Pigs in Heaven* to national best-seller lists for a number of weeks testifies to growing interest both in Barbara Kingsolver as a writer and to the literary movement of ecofeminism that she represents. The distinctive focus of Kingsolver's books is on people who are marginalized by American society and on their struggles for economic, cultural, and emotional survival. Further, drawing on her academic training in environmental science, Kingsolver often focuses on her people's connections to the land and on the disastrous consequences that heedless abuse of the land can bring. Kingsolver's novels have been grouped with other works that draw connections between the exploitation of women and of the environment and that promote the healing that can occur when women are empowered and the Earth receives reverence and care. In addition to *Animal Dreams* and *Pigs in Heaven*, other notable ecofeminist novels include *Always Coming Home* (1985) by Ursula Le Guin, *Tracks* (1989) by Louise Erdrich, and *Mean Spirit* (1991) by Linda Hogan.

Even in the company of such distinguished writers, however, Barbara Kingsolver stands out by reason of the remarkable entertainment value of her fiction. Born and reared in Kentucky, she is a born raconteur, heir to the rich oral literary tradition of the South. Even as she is sharpening the reader's awareness of weighty social issues and profound literary themes, her narrative voice never ceases to entertain as a humorous and engrossing storyteller, a gifted creator of heartfelt characters, and a witty and poetic stylist.

Bibliography

Berkinow, Louise. "Books." *Cosmopolitan* 214 (June, 1993): 32. Berkinow praises the novel for its "breathtaking" story and racial themes. Among its many "unforgettable" characters, she particularly admires Alice for her "country-plain, nononsense sensibility." Overall, Berkinow finds the novel "profound, funny, bighearted."

Karbo, Karen. "And Baby Makes Two." *The New York Times Book Review*, June 27, 1993, 9. Karbo praises Kingsolver's ability to "maintain her political views without sacrificing the complexity of her characters' predicaments." On the other hand, she faults the author for not pursuing the issue of responsibility for Turtle's abuse.

Koenig, Rhoda. "Books." *New York* 26 (June 14, 1993): 99-100. Koenig praises Kingsolver's "lovely eye (and nose) for details" and judges her to be "a nice, well-meaning woman." Koenig, though, criticizes the novel for its "dopey benignity." According to Koenig, by making her major characters so well-meaning and good, Kingsolver eliminates her chances for suspense and for meaningful treatment of serious issues.

Lehmann-Haupt, Christopher. "Community vs. Family and Writer vs. Subject." *The New York Times*, July 12, 1993, C16. Lehmann-Haupt praises the novel for its "appealing homespun poetry" and "down-home humor." He also admires the "generosity and spiritedness" of its characters. On the other hand, he comments that "there isn't much conflict or tension in the story" and that "the reader begins to suffocate in all the sweetness."

Shapiro, Laura. "A Novel Full of Miracles." *Newsweek* 123 (July 12, 1993): 61. Shapiro praises Kingsolver for avoiding polemics and creating "a complex drama." On the other hand, she remarks that the novel is "less deftly plotted" than Kingsolver's earlier fiction because its resolution "relies on a somewhat unwieldy coincidence." Overall, however, Shapiro concludes that the novel "succeeds on the strength of Kingsolver's clear-eyed, warmhearted writing and irresistible characters."

Terry L. Andrews

PLATITUDES

Author: Trey Ellis (1962-   )
Type of plot: Romance
Time of plot: The 1980's and the 1930's
Locale: New York City and rural Georgia
First published: 1988

> *Principal characters:*
> DEWAYNE WELLINGTON, an unpublished novelist
> ISSHEE AYAM, a successful novelist trying to revise Dewayne's novel
> EARLE TYNER, a shy New York teenager, the main character in Dewayne's novel
> EARLE PRIDE, a shy Georgian farmboy in Isshee's revision
> DOROTHY LAMONT, a popular, even wild girl in Dewayne's version, who is modest and innocent in Isshee's
> MAYLENE, Earle's mother, an urban socialite in Dewayne's version and a hardworking farm woman in Isshee's
> DARCELLE, Dorothy's mother, the owner of a Harlem restaurant in Dewayne's version and an educated Southern woman reduced to prostitution in Isshee's

The Novel

Platitudes consists of two novels in progress and the correspondences between their respective authors. Both writers are African American, as are most of their characters. Dewayne Wellington's writing style is postmodern, hip, and urban. Isshee Ayam, whose work includes such titles as *My Big Ol' Feets Gon' Stomp Dat Evil Down*, *Hog Jowl Junction*, and *Heben and Chillun o' de Lawd*, is more traditional in terms of both her narrative style and her preference for what Dewayne refers to as "Afro-American glory-stories." She bears more than a passing resemblance to such authors as Toni Morrison and Alice Walker, while Dewayne is somewhat similar to novelist Ishmael Reed.

Dewayne's novel is about two black teenagers in 1980's New York City, both in private school: Earle, a shy, upper-middle-class "nerd," dreams of love and eagerly awaits his first sexual experience; and Dorothy, who frequents the city's hottest clubs, experiments with drugs and sex and hopes to get rich and leave Harlem. When Dewayne, stuck in the writing of his novel at chapter 6, solicits Isshee's advice, she disgustedly condemns his work as sexist. She also sends him a chapter based on his characters but reflecting her own beliefs about the appropriate functions and components of African American literature. This chapter, and those that follow, is located in rural 1930's Georgia, with Earle and Dorothy recast as farm children, poor but proud, who walk fifteen miles to school each day. In both works in progress, the two teenagers become friends and, eventually, lovers. Although the two authors have radically different styles and political agendas, they are headed for the same goal, and their chapters work in parallel to tell the story of Earle and Dorothy's rocky courtship and, later, Dewayne and Isshee's personal relationship.

In Dewayne's story, Earle, who seems to have no deeper connection to his African American heritage than watching reruns of *The Jeffersons* on television (his mother is a spokeswoman for South African Airlines), is led by chance and curiosity to explore Harlem. There, he finds himself in Dorothy's mother's soul-food restaurant. For middle-class Earle, Harlem is a dangerously exotic place where he must make an effort to conform to the stereotypes of black behavior he has learned from television. For Dorothy, who hums the theme song of *The Jeffersons* on the subway, Harlem is the place where she serves grits to her mother's customers while dreaming of getting out and becoming more "booj" (bourgeois) than her white friends.

Although Earle does not immediately impress Dorothy, her mother Darcelle tries to play matchmaker between the two, and when he gets a job in the neighborhood registering voters, Darcelle sends Dorothy out to deliver free sodas and encouraging words to the enamored Earle. Earle is not popular and has a number of typical adolescent problems, so when one of the popular girls in school invites him to a party, he is pleased and surprised. He is even more surprised when Dorothy, who goes to another school, is also at the party. Unfortunately, she has a date, but Earle's hopes remain high. In the following weeks, he and Dorothy begin to spend time together, going to films and amusement parks. The slowly developing romance between Earle and Dorothy is being paralleled in the correspondence between Dewayne and Isshee: He invites her to have dinner with him during the upcoming Black American Authors convention, and she accepts. Both Earle and Dewayne are hopeful and expectant, but when Isshee stands Dewayne up to go out with another novelist, he retaliates by writing a chapter in which Earle catches Dorothy with another man, having sex that is described in deliberately brutal and demeaning terms. As the lines between writers and written texts gradually blur, Dewayne punishes Isshee through Dorothy. Isshee's apology, a chapter in which her Earle and Dorothy make love tenderly and romantically, arrives and is accepted, clearing the way for Dewayne and Isshee to meet. They have dinner and talk, then go back to his apartment and begin to make love, but Dewayne finds himself unable to consummate this real relationship until he has resolved the romantic desires of Earl and Dorothy. Finally, after his characters have reconciled and made love, he is able to do the same with Isshee.

The Characters

Dewayne Wellington, the author of the more substantial of the two novels in progress, is revealed primarily through his writing and the ways that his novel reflects events in his personal life. It gradually becomes clear that despite the juvenile habits of his characters, Dewayne is a committed artist attempting to write with sensitivity and humor about the problems of teenage identity, sexuality, and love. It also becomes apparent that, in part because of a recent and bitter divorce, Dewayne harbors some resentment against women, perhaps black women especially. Earle and his novel are, in part, Dewayne's way of working through his own feelings about trust and intimacy; when Earle is finally able to reconcile and make love with Dorothy, it is a healing experience for Dewayne as well, freeing him to pursue a relationship with Isshee.

Isshee Ayam is initially contemptuous of Dewayne's work in progress. She calls him a "No-Rate Hack," urges him to "learn a trade," and calls his writing "puerile, misogynistic, disjointed, and amateurish." She also stands him up for dinner and threatens to co-opt his novel, and her initial apologies are rather casual. She eventually begins to gain the reader's sympathy with a subsequent, more heartfelt apology. Just as important, it becomes clear that her initial dismay at reading Dewayne's first chapters reflects her sincere concerns about the portrayal in literature of African Americans in general and of black women specifically. When she realizes that Dewayne does not share Earle's sexism or indifference to his black heritage, she begins to read his work differently and to find more of merit in both the novel and the novelist.

Earle Tyner's experiences in high school and his first romantic encounters are believable and familiar, if somewhat predictable. Hiding pornography under his bed and dreaming of falling in love, Earle is an apt mixture of teenage awkwardness and maturity, hope and fear, love and hormones. Earle Pride, Isshee's farmboy version of this character, is somewhat more sensitive and less obsessed with sex, but the two characters are more similar than different, both looking for love and trust, like their creators.

In both versions of the novel, Dorothy is more confident and experienced than Earle. In Dewayne's version, while she enjoys slow dates with Earle, she also craves the fast life of New York clubs and college boys. In Isshee's version, she is both more innocent and better educated than Earle. She is not quite so fully developed a character as Earle, especially in Isshee's version, but the reader can gain some insight into her feelings about her life and dreams and about being black, poor, and pretty.

Earle's mother Maylene is a rather sketchily developed character. Her chief function seems to be to provide Isshee with an opportunity to rewrite her as a traditional black super-mother, in contrast to the nagging, self-justifying socialite in Dewayne's version.

Dorothy's mother is considerably more fleshed out in Isshee's version than in Dewayne's: The powerful black farm mother seems to be one of Isshee's main themes as a novelist. Like Maylene Tyner, Darcelle is transformed in Isshee's version into an indomitable life force, enduring poverty and the humiliations that go with it without losing sight of either her own dignity or her duty to her children.

Themes and Meanings

Generally speaking, *Platitudes* is about love, trust, and the trials of growing up. Earle's struggle to make friends, his teenage sexual fantasies, and his dismay at this mother's nagging are familiar elements of contemporary adolescence. So are Dorothy's mixed feelings about her mother's unglamorous business, her hopes of escaping poverty and its restraints, and her conflicting desires for romance and glamor. Other issues under examination include Dewayne's emotional problems as he moves past the resentment of his divorce and Isshee's tendency to have adversarial relationships similar to those she depicts in her novels.

On one level, this is a straightforward story of boy meets girl and the difficulties that arise when people with complex lives and conflicting desires begin to move toward one another. Romance requires obstacles, whether poverty and venal landlords or ex-wives and competing careers, and the fact that one of these couples is inventing the other two can be read simply as an elaborate courtship ritual.

Platitudes can also be read as a dialogue among different ways of representing, perceiving, and experiencing life for and by African Americans. The fact that most of the characters in Dewayne's novel ignore or actively reject their identities as African Americans is not an oversight on Trey Ellis' part. This indifference is consistently contrasted with Isshee's almost obsessive glorification of every aspect of the lives of her black characters, even their "weathered but jubilant and noble handmade cedar outhouse." Ellis uses gentle satire to make each position seem empty, both for the characters and the novelists who envision black identity so narrowly. Finally, as Dewayne and Isshee come to appreciate one another more, both as novelists and personally, a more balanced perspective, a middle ground, seems possible.

The dialogue between Dewayne and Isshee about African American literature, its traditions, purposes, and responsibilities, is carried out explicitly in the course of their correspondence as well as implicitly in their rival versions of Dewayne's novel. In an early letter, Isshee contemptuously dismisses Dewayne's "postmodernist, semiological sophism" and asks him if he has read James Baldwin or heard of "narrative and continuity." Dewayne responds not by defending his literary style but by revealing his marital and financial woes. This has the desired effect, however, of convincing Isshee that he is a "heartbroken human being" rather than an "insensitive cretin," and she concludes by revising her opinion not only of his novel but also of experimental or postmodern fiction in general, even confessing some envy for its "stylistic liberty." It is in this same letter that she suggests that they meet at the upcoming literary conference, suggesting a connection between their literary and personal lives that will continue and become complete by the end of the novel.

Critical Context

Trey Ellis' style in this, his first novel, is not identical to Dewayne's but is also postmodern and experimental. In addition to its postmodern flair, the book is obviously influenced by the development of the African American novel. While Ellis questions and gently parodies some of the assumptions and approaches of the more traditional African American novel, he also pays homage to it: Dewayne is a fan of Isshee's mainstream novels, while she lists James Baldwin, Alice Walker, and Toni Morrison (as well as T. S. Eliot and F. Scott Fitzgerald) among those writers who have influenced her most.

Ellis' purpose is not to reject or condemn literature that focuses on aspects of African American life but rather to argue that literature by and for African Americans need not focus exclusively on issues of race. In a 1989 article, Ellis describes the "New Black Aesthetic," a new literary trend being developed by black artists to whom he refers as "cultural mulattoes." These artists can embrace both African American culture and mainstream "white" culture, both Geoffrey Chaucer and Richard Pryor, "both Jim and Toni Morrison." Elsewhere, Ellis has stated, "In the past some wanted to force Black artists to only write about jazz and Africa and poverty. Black folks deserve and crave more choices." By contrasting Earle and Dorothy's suppression of their identities as black Americans and Isshee's obsession with blackness and black experience, Ellis seems to be suggesting that neither extreme is a tenable position, that both result in gaps and missed opportunities, and that a middle ground should be sought or created.

Bibliography

Ellis, Trey. "The New Black Aesthetic." *Callaloo* 38 (Winter, 1989): 233-243. Ellis describes the art and philosophy of art being produced by a new generation of black artists. Ellis calls these artists, including himself, "cultural mulattoes," able to appreciate and function in both white and black culture. He states that such an aesthetic is "not an apolitical, art-for-art's-sake fantasy" but a redefinition of "the black aesthetic as much more than just Africa and jazz."

Hunter, Tera. "It's a Man's Man's Man's World: Specters of the Old Re-Newed in Afro-American Culture and Criticism." *Callaloo* 38 (Winter, 1989): 247-249. Hunter perceives the black art world (and Ellis' criteria for the New Black Aesthetic) as male-dominated and misogynist. She comments that Ellis' article on the New Black Aesthetic disregards most class and gender differences among black artists, but she nevertheless praises his article for opening "a discourse with far-ranging implications."

Lott, Eric. "Hip-Hop Fiction." *The Nation* 247 (December 19, 1988): 691-692. Lott addresses the dialogue between literary styles in *Platitudes*, calling it Ellis' "call for a truce in the black literary world." He concludes, however, that the debate between Dewayne and Isshee is unbalanced and that Dewayne's "tale is the one finally endorsed; the various jokes on Isshee go unanswered."

_____ . "Response to Trey Ellis's 'The New Black Aesthetic.'" *Callaloo* 38 (Winter, 1989): 244-246. Lott chides Ellis for oversimplifying complex literary movements and discussing authors with significant differences as if they were in complete agreement. Lott also states that Ellis' article largely ignores class differences among black artists and intellectuals.

Morrison, Toni. *Playing in the Dark: Whiteness and the Literary Imagination.* Cambridge: Harvard University Press, 1992. Morrison's book does not discuss Ellis or *Platitudes*; however, it does provide valuable insight into relationships between black and white culture, especially as reflected in American literature. Morrison's central argument is that white American literature, culture, and identity are defined, in part, in contrast and opposition to what she calls "the Africanist presence."

Nelson, Dana D. *The Word in Black and White: Reading "Race" in American*

Literature, 1638-1867. New York: Oxford University Press, 1992. Like Morrison, Nelson focuses on literature produced by white Americans and on the results of the construction and fetishization of race and difference. Nelson argues that race is an ever-changing political construction that members of dominant cultures evoke "as a means of delineating and oppressing groups of people."

Catherine Carnell Watt

THE PLUM PLUM PICKERS

Author: Raymond Barrio (1921-   )
Type of plot: Social criticism
Time of plot: The 1960's
Locale: The Santa Clara Valley, California
First published: 1969

> *Principal characters:*
> RAMIRO SANCHEZ, the protagonist, a Chicano farmworker who fights
> exploitation by the growers
> MANUEL GUTIERREZ, a Chicano farmworker from Texas whose endless
> labor barely keeps his family alive
> LUPE GUTIERREZ, his wife, who dreams of a middle-class life
> MORTON J. QUILL, an overseer who is murdered
> FREDERICK Y. TURNER, the owner of the Western Grande migrant com-
> pound
> JEAN ANGELICA TURNER, his wife, a delusional failed actress

The Novel

Detailing the daily lives of Chicano migrant farmworkers trapped in low-paying, dead-end, back-breaking roles within the corporate agricultural system, *The Plum Plum Pickers* protests their exploitation and degradation. While exploring the hierarchy of oppression, the novel attacks the greed, racism, and injustice leveled against workers and reveals the unfulfilled hopes of the workers, who suffer from self-deception, disillusionment, and self-destruction.

Written with a loosely framed narrative but carefully designed coherent structure, the novel consists of thirty-four chapters that are like fragments in a collage of episodes, broken by graffiti, picking instructions, newspaper articles, radio broadcasts, popular songs in both Spanish and English, and government announcements to the pickers. The reader not only receives a complete description of daily routines in the migrant compound and of the pickers' futile labor in the fields of plums and tomatoes but also feels immersed in the emotional tension between hope and despair and engulfed by the juxtaposition of a lush landscape with the brutality of harsh, racist exploitation.

As the novel opens, Morton J. Quill, the Anglo manager of the Western Grande migrant compound, receives an anonymous death threat. Quill, behaving more like a merciless plantation overseer than a competent manager, fears the ruthless power of his boss, Frederick Y. Turner, the compound's greedy owner. Blind to the squalor in which the migrant children live, Quill measures his success by the number of boxes of fruits and vegetables; the less overt resistance from the pickers, the greater Quill believes his status to be. To insulate himself from confrontations with the pickers, he relies on Roberto Morales, his Mexican assistant.

Much of the novel proceeds not so much by plot as by unabashed—even didactic—social protest that documents migrant pickers' routes from state to state, their desperate and self-deceptive dreams, their self-destructive conflicts among themselves, their increasing entrapment by the growers and their political allies, and their increasing rage. Manuel and Lupe Gutierrez recall their brutal treatment at the hands of the Texas Rangers and try to believe that their life in California's Santa Clara Valley is really better. Manuel works himself to exhaustion and fears never being able to provide his wife and three children with a stable life of human dignity and worth; Lupe, however, dreams of a bigger house, regular schools, and greater opportunity for her children. Although she can sustain her fantasies of freedom and security during her own daily grind amid the harsh conditions, she must often be awakened from nightmares of seeing her children plowed alive under the earth by the noisy tractors.

When the pickers seek a Saturday night escape at the Golden Cork, their frustration, fueled by alcohol, erupts into a near brawl. Zeke Johnson, an Anglo mechanic and sometime picker from the South, provokes Ramiro Sanchez, a vocal critic of the system from Texas, with racist taunts. He passes out before fists fly, and Sanchez's crew unceremoniously carries him outside and dumps him in the garbage.

Throughout the narrative, Manuel and the other pickers move closer to embracing the collective bargaining power of the farmworkers' union and the threat of strikes. Turner and his cohorts, such as the bigoted, right-wing radio announcer Rat Barfy and the governor Howlin Mad Nolan, continue to assert their paternalistic delusions that they are preserving the freedom of the pickers and their right to work without government interference. Any reform, in their minds, would mean the arrival of communism.

Meanwhile, Turner's wife, Jean Angelica Turner, becomes trapped in her own isolating fantasies of a career on the stage. To hold back the stark reality of suffering that surrounds her lonely mansion, she "acts" as an organizer of the rich growers' wives to provide hollow deeds of charity.

When Quill, his ego inflated by a meager raise, decides to confiscate some of the pickers' few possessions to pay off their food and rent debts, his own nightmare of death becomes reality. Seized by unidentified vigilantes during the night, he is lynched behind his own apartment. When Turner arrives at the compound, he is greeted by Lupe's scream announcing discovery of the body twisting in the sun. Despite the workers' rage, little has changed, save that their nightmare existence has emerged into daylight.

The Characters

Barrio balances fully rounded characters with stock types in order to integrate his themes with the psychological development of his strongest characters. The novel achieves its significance and power more through skillfully constructed characters than through the elaboration of a linear plot. Barrio relies heavily on a combination of precise description, blatant polemic, and insistent dialogue. These elements find common ground in the speech patterns of characters and the third-person narration.

Reproducing rhythmic dialect of his protagonist pickers, highlighting the bark of clichés from Barfy and Turner, and crafting the affected diction of menial workers in the compound who have deceived themselves into thinking that they have improved their lives because they no longer depend on picking for their low wages, Barrio uses parallel syntax, arranging English in a typically Spanish word order, and provides immediate translations of Spanish words and phrases. His switching between Spanish and English within paragraphs or even sentences echoes the larger thematic conflict between Chicano pickers and Anglo growers.

Manuel, an innocent man who believes in the dignity of his labor but struggles with despair, internalizes this conflict. When Morales pushes Manuel's crew to the brink of collapse, Manuel resists by proclaiming himself a man like any other in the hierarchy—owner, overseer, crew boss, or picker. Setting the tone for eventual resistance to exploitation, he wins the respect of his crew and realizes his own qualities of leadership. Turner's system permits no development of Chicano leaders, for that inevitably would mean reform and an end to his profiteering at the expense of human lives.

Ramiro is Barrio's spokesman. He is willing to engage in any resistance rhetoric and to give it flesh in any revolutionary act. He knows that Turner's greed has made slaves of his people and that such enslavement not only diminishes their present lives in their exploited poverty but also degrades their heroic heritage and robs their children of the future. He is often keenly astute in his analyses of the exploitive system, but he seldom indulges in revolutionary jargon, preferring ordinary language of authentic change.

Pepe and Sarafina Delgado, having escaped the picking crews to become custodial attendants at the compound, embrace the stereotypes of Turner and Barfy. They believe that the pickers are lazy and ungrateful, pursuing only a good time through alcohol, marijuana, and meaningless sex, yet Pepe embodies the stereotypes more than any of the pickers. The Delgados serve as the deceptive model that Lupe Gutierrez hopes to imitate: They have a house, their children go to school, and they maintain the pretense of upward mobility.

Morton Quill, the manager, regards Turner alternately with awe, as the outlaw hero Black Bart, and fear, as his own sense of vulnerability wakes him with every sound in the night. He is as likely to ignore acts of vandalism by the pickers as he is to test his derived power by directly challenging such resistance. Most of all, he fears that the death around him will become his own; by the novel's end, his body has replaced the straw effigy of Black Bart that twists ominously from the hangman's tree in the compound.

Against these rounded, complex characters, Barrio juxtaposes several type characters. Zeke Johnson represents the poor Southern white man who depends on his presumed racial dominance for his higher sense of place in the pecking order of the pickers. He abandons his wife's illegitimate child in a stark gesture of his own inhumanity. Similarly, Chuck and Olive Pope, in an ironic reversal of the stereotype they seek to perpetuate, are too lazy to work, too ignorant to change, and too inept to pursue any trade but selling drugs on the compound. Phyllis Ferguson, the compound prostitute whose fat body but alluring seductions both repel and attract Quill, represents the objectification of the exploiter and the exploited. She easily seduces the young pickers out of their money, but she becomes a sobbing, dirty object in her own eyes as she pursues her "easy" money.

Themes and Meanings

The Plum Plum Pickers closely parallels the historical exploitation of California farmworkers, whether Mexican, Chicano, or Anglo. Both the fiction and the history testify to the paradox of abundance that buries the humanity of those who have the least and are exploited the most. Barrio strips the mask from the face of a ruthless capitalism that crushes the pickers and proclaims its own benevolence, convincing those businesspeople and politicians who are prone to believe in their own racial superiority that the agricultural corporate combines are the guardians of lesser human beings than themselves. The owners of plum and apricot orchards or of vast acres of tomatoes see only the green of profits, denying the reality of rotting human lives in deference to the appearance of a lush green paradise. They convince many of the pickers either that their lives are meant to end in futility or that their salvation rests in copying the corrupt success and fraudulent goodness of the rich.

What the greedy owners do not see is their psychological and spiritual self-destruction. Quill lives in suspended terror, never sure whether he is alive and dreaming of death or instead living death and dreaming of having a life that he can call his own. Despite his power and influence, Turner isolates himself in fantasies of his days as a Hollywood extra in cowboy roles, obsessively constructing his own false reality by turning the Western Grande compound into an absurdly "authentic" old Western town, complete with false fronts on the migrant shacks.

In the process of revealing that slavery inevitably leads to revolt, Barrio shows that the pickers, once forced to act against their enslavement, achieve a higher human dignity and self-worth than any imagined by the owners. In their struggle to overcome physical misery, the Chicano pickers find humanity precisely in the struggle for a self-determined identity and a fragile existence. They see themselves in the cycles of life and death that surround and threaten them. Their unshakeable faith is symbolized by Lupe's careful watering of the avocado plant she nurtures in her shack. Their faith in themselves is defiantly symbolized by Lupe's refusal to accept Jean Turner's old dresses and her implicit condescension.

The novel does not indulge in blind optimism, for although hope may survive, it does so in the ambiguity of Barrio's principal symbol of the omnipresent summer sun. The symbolic sun is both destruction and resurrection, reality and appearance, futility and hope. Rising with the sun, Manuel feels the hope of a new day, but he knows the reality of the searing sun that waits in the fields. That ambiguous reality is too dark to accept fully but too bright to deny completely.

Critical Context

Having its origin in Barrio's friendship with a migrant family that he met in Cupertino, California, *The Plum Plum Pickers* failed at first to reach publication. Although Barrio wrote at the time that César Chávez's movement to unionize farm-workers was making national news, every major publishing house to which he submitted the novel rejected it as too didactic, too narrow in its topic, or too regional in its significance. He was forced to publish it himself. Only after the novel had sold more than ten thousand copies through five printings in less than two years did Harper and Row inquire about purchasing publishing rights. The novel emerged as an underground classic, its impact spreading largely by word of mouth.

The Plum Plum Pickers serves as a foundation in the development of the Chicano novel over the next twenty-five years. The first Chicano novel to explore social issues through literary innovation and experimental techniques, its forerunners are the North American proletarian novels of the 1930's, the literary extravagance of the Beat poets in the 1950's and 1960's, and the early 1960's Magical Realism of South American writers. Now widely acclaimed and more anthologized through brief excerpts than almost any other Chicano fiction, the novel is one of the first issued in the Chicano Classics series published by the Bilingual Press. Despite its favorable reception in brief reviews, the novel has received scant in-depth analysis and focused critical attention.

Barrio has continued publishing, though none of his subsequent works has gained the reputation of *The Plum Plum Pickers*. His interest in the visual arts resulted in a collection of essays on art, *Mexico's Art and Chicano Artists* (1975). In *The Devil's Apple Corps: A Trauma in Four Acts* (1976), he cast Gore Vidal as the public defender in a mock trial of Howard Hughes, perhaps the industrial parallel to the fictional Turner. Barrio makes it clear that he remains a harsh critic of those who exploit the rank and file of American workers. His editorials in *A Political Portfolio* (1985) consistently attack exploitive figures from all professions; among the pieces in this collection are three selections from the novel *Carib Blue* (1990). That novel further develops, in broader contexts, the potential for aesthetic experimentation to reveal the exploitation behind the masks of the practical approaches to resolving social issues.

Bibliography

Geuder, Patricia A. "Address Systems in *The Plum Plum Pickers*." *Aztlán* 6 (Fall, 1975): 341-346. Geuder explores the complex relationships among the Chicano pickers and between them and the Anglo bosses through a classification of the ways in which characters address one another. Writing to sociolinguists, she analyzes the ways in which power relationships are embedded in direct address, concluding that the pickers shape a sense of community through their use of language while the Anglos are formal and distant in their relationships. She argues that social status and self-image of both groups rest in the monolingualism of the Anglo growers and the bilingualism of the Chicano workers.

Lattin, Vernon E. "Paradise and Plums: Appearance and Reality in Barrio's *The Plum*

Plum Pickers." Selected Proceedings of the Third Annual Conference on Minority Studies 2 (April, 1975): 165-171. Lattin argues that the essential tension in the novel, both within the characters and between them, is the juxtaposition of the bountiful landscape against the squalid realities of the pickers' existence, supporting this thesis through analysis of Barrio's techniques of characterization and symbolism. Concludes that the novel ends in ambiguity, setting the tone for later criticism of the novel.

Lomelí, Francisco A. "Depraved New World Revisited: Dreams and Dystopia in *The Plum Plum Pickers." Introduction to *The Plum Plum Pickers*. Tempe, Ariz.: Bilingual Press, 1984. Lomelí extends and elaborates Lattin's premises by detailing the living conditions of migrants and the self-deceiving strategies of both Chicanos and Anglos. Emphasizing the ironies of decaying lives spent in harvesting the ever-ripening fruit, he analyzes the economic system that perpetuates the promise of greater wealth while creating the impossibility of its reality. Lomelí's thorough discussion is the most significant critical study yet published.

McKenna, Teresa. "Three Novels: An Analysis." *Aztlán* 1 (Fall, 1970): 47-56. Although minimal in its assessment, McKenna's study does seek to place Barrio's novel in the historical moment. She notes the promise of social realism to detail migrant conditions and comments on the aesthetic difficulties in reading the work, implying that Barrio's novel may suffer from its aesthetic experiments.

Ortego, Philip D. "The Chicano Novel." *Luz* 2 (May, 1973): 32-33. Ortego claims that Barrio mediates his social protest with fantasy constructions that collapse back into social realities. He notes the dilemma of the Chicano writer in finding a medium between Spanish and English, applauding Barrio's ability to shape both into a coherent fictive whole. He also realizes that Barrio has established a new artistic direction for the Chicano novel.

Michael Loudon

POCHO

Author: José Antonio Villarreal (1924-   )
Type of plot: Bildungsroman
Time of plot: 1923-1942
Locale: Santa Clara, in the Imperial Valley of California
First published: 1959

> *Principal characters:*
> RICHARD RUBIO, the only son of Juan Manuel and Consuelo Rubio
> JUAN MANUEL RUBIO, a soldier in the Mexican Revolution who becomes
>   an itinerate laborer and conflicted family man
> CONSUELO RUBIO, the wife of Juan Manuel, the mother of eight daughters
>   and one son
> JOÃO PEDRO MANÕEL ALVES, a Portuguese aristocrat and poet who
>   befriends young Richard
> RICKY MALATESTA, Richard's Italian American school friend
> THOMAS NAKANO, a Japanese American schoolmate of Richard who is
>   sent to an internment camp
> ZELDA, a neighborhood tomboy and bully who becomes Richard's girl-
>   friend
> MARY MADISON, Richard's Protestant friend and fellow enthusiast for
>   reading and writing

The Novel

Pocho recounts the lives of Mexican migrant farm laborer Juan Rubio, his wife, and their nine children as they attempt to hold their family together, survive the Depression, and adjust to American culture. As family bonds disintegrate, the only son, Richard, defines himself against both Mexican and American cultures and affirms his determination to become a writer. The first of eleven chapters introduces Juan Rubio, a colonel in Pancho Villa's army, and depicts his grief over the Mexican Revolution's failure, his flight from Mexico, and his resettlement in California; the chapter ends with the birth of Juan's only son, Richard. Richard's background and development from childhood to young adulthood in chapters 2 through 9 strongly resemble experiences of José Antonio Villarreal's own life. The division of each chapter into two or three sections emphasizes the tensions, conflicts, and multiple perspectives associated with the construction of Richard's personal identity: family, church, school, language, sex, friendship, career, money, prejudice, injustice, and, most important, dual cultural allegiances. Dramatic events of chapters 10 and 11 (including Juan's leaving home, Richard's high-school graduation, and his enlistment in the U.S. Navy) move Richard to the brink of adult responsibility and an uncertain future as a man and as a Mexican American.

As early as age nine, Richard is aware of his attraction to books and his interest in writing. In contrast to his soldier father, he shrinks from fights and sex and finds shelter in reflection and escape in reading and imagination. He is in love with words, words such as "sundries," which is painted on the window of his home, an abandoned store, and he shifts easily between English and Spanish as his context requires.

As Richard matures, he consciously rejects large parts of his Mexican heritage, including some of the "macho" privileges offered him by his father, his mother's faith in God, and obedience to religious dogma; at the same time, he rejects pressures in Anglo culture to devalue his own intelligence, neglect his own education, and settle for menial and meaningless labor. Such negations are in fact affirmations of his own self-worth and his own aspirations to be a writer. Free of many of the ideological constraints of both cultures, he may at last be able to write his novel and his life.

Although Richard's liberation of consciousness as man, Mexican American, and artist is in the foreground of the novel, the backdrops to his personal growth include the dissolution of the traditional Mexican family, the chaos of a nationwide depression, a vast panorama of social unrest and prejudice, and, finally, world war.

The Characters

Richard Rubio, whose development is the central focus of the novel, is presented in a third-person-omniscient narration that seems reflective, distant, neutral, even blandly indifferent to characters' struggles. This mode of presentation is a strange contrast to the frequent episodes of passion experienced by the hero and his family. This portrait of the artist as a young man is more typical, however, in its depiction of its writer-hero as a sensitive child, a contemplative, curious, and voracious reader, observant and self-conscious. It seems *Pocho* is this boy's own story and testament to the successful realization of his boyhood dream to write. Richard's movement away from traditional values and roles contrasts vividly with his father's conscious clinging to connection with his homeland and native culture. Richard is last seen entering war, not on a horse but on a ship, motivated not, like his father, by patriotic fervor but by desire to escape his own fierce inner conflicts and sense of personal loss.

The Juan Manuel Rubio shown in chapter 1 is a famous colonel in Villa's revolutionary army. He is also a cold-blooded killer and a ruthless exploiter of women who is callous to the pain he causes. Yet he weeps profusely and grieves deeply when told of the assassination of his idol Villa. After flight to the United States and reunion with his wife and children in California, Juan appears to be a different man. He gives up gambling, women, and violence for manual labor, family closeness, and generosity to those in need. The patriarch of the Rubio family is a man of contradictions, but in one thing he is consistent: He never relinquishes the romance of return to his homeland, even while buying a house in California. As he sees his wife and children assimilate, he is at last driven to abandon them entirely and reaffirm his ties to Mexico.

Consuelo Rubio, loving and dutiful wife and mother of nine children, discovers that American law protects her from physical abuse and, even more surprisingly, finds that she loves her husband and enjoys sex. The novel suggests that these new awarenesses lead directly to new freedom, new jealousy, and new demands on her husband that culminate in the disintegration of her marriage and her family. She dotes on Richard and indulges him totally, but she is ashamed of her own inadequate education and her inability to guide him in the world and respond to his intellectual needs. Abandoned in midlife by her husband, she is bitter; she refuses to divorce to spite him and seems destined to a lonely and sour old age.

João Pedro Manõel Alves is a forty-year-old social outcast, scorned by his aristocratic Portuguese family for apparent sexual indiscretion. Living reclusively in Santa Clara, he has only two friends, the boy Richard and twelve-year-old Genevieve. Richard is shocked and grieved by the accusation that Alves impregnated the girl and by Alves' commitment to a hospital for the insane.

Ricky Malatesta, Richard's best friend in school, differs in values and goals. His character is a foil to Richard's and helps to distinguish some of Richard's unusual qualities. Ricky is a scrapper, an egotist, a charmer, a pragmatist, and a materialist.

Thomas Nakano is a Japanese American schoolmate whose internment dramatizes the prejudice and racial fear that pervade American society.

Zelda is one of the few females in Richard's social existence. As a child, she is a cruel bully who dominates the boys with violence and willfulness. At adolescence, she suddenly becomes the object of their sexual exploitation. Richard claims her as his own sexual object in his teens, and she is submissive and docile.

Mary Madison is three years younger than Richard and enjoys the same passion for reading and writing. She has a teenage crush on him and declares that she intends to marry him, though she and her family are moving out of town.

Themes and Meanings

Three concerns dominate *Pocho*: What is a "man"? What does it mean to be Mexican in American society? How does a writer come to be? For Richard Rubio, answers to each are found in negations. Richard finds his manhood not in the esteemed tradition of fighting but in feeling and weeping, and he finds his male dignity not in acts of valor but in reading and thinking. To define himself in an alien culture, he negates the macho tradition of his father's world, refuses the comforts of insularity in a Mexican barrio, rejects the reassurances of religious faith, and opts for joining the "melting pot." As a writer, he immerses himself in the books and the language of Anglo culture and relinquishes dependence on the language of his forefathers. Yet he rejects as well Anglo social pressure to make do, to leash his dreams and settle for the life of a welder or a policeman. Without support or encouragement, he affirms for himself the less conventional aspiration to write, to labor with head and heart rather than hands. Ironically, Richard seems less a Mexican American than a man without a country. What is, after all, the origin of a man's nationality? Is it the accident of his place of birth or the geography of his residence? Is a man's nationality determined by his past, by his present or by his future? What physical or mental borders separate a Mexican from an American identity? Shedding gender, familial, religious, linguistic, and social skins, Richard slowly builds a liberty of mind and perception that frees him to be an artist.

The title *Pocho* suggests one of the major themes of the novel: the complexity of the immigrant's dual existence in language, culture, and values. The term *pocho* has many resonances. Among loved ones, it can be a term of affection acknowledging the practical and emotional difficulties of surviving as an alien in an alien world. Used by a stranger, the term is an ethnic slur or a shaming label suggesting a Mexican who is a would-be gringo. As a descriptive term, it can mean the hybrid language used by the immigrant or it can mean the man himself, a kind of hybrid, who lives with simultaneous powerful attachments to two cultures. This one word and Richard, the *pocho* of the novel, represent the many tensions in personal identity that exist in a man undergoing the metamorphosis of acculturation.

Although Richard is a *pocho*, a man who thinks in two languages and lives in two cultures, the language of the novel itself is very much English, a relatively formal and academic English at that. Richard the writer was never Ricardo, and the language of his novel is never *pocho*, never hybrid. Its language bespeaks total assimilation.

The dominant tone of the novel is elegiac. An adult evokes his lost youth, innocence, parents, and culture. This is a tale of exile characterized by a profound sense of loss. Loss of homeland, loss of culture, loss of language, even loss of family, faith, and friends, pervade every chapter. It is small wonder that lamentations, profuse weeping by men and women alike, occur repeatedly. Richard's personal sacrifices and negations of his heritage are only a solitary, individual portion of one family's disintegration, of Mexico's impoverishment, of America's panoply of social ills and racial fears, and of worldwide poverty, prejudice, and cataclysmic violence.

Critical Context

Pocho is widely recognized as literary landmark; it was the first novel in English written by a Mexican author about the Mexican experience of the United States to be printed by a major publisher. At its publication in 1959, however, the novel received little attention and went quickly out of print. After the social activism of the 1960's, the novel was reprinted, and discussion focused on the book's social and political import.

Pocho was Villarreal's first novel. His second, *The Fifth Horseman* (1974), takes Mexico for its setting and deals with interpretation of the Mexican Revolution. While in that work Villarreal decried the excesses of the Mexican Revolution and affirmed its spirit, in *Clemente Chacón* (1984) he showed how high the cost of success in the United States can be for the Mexican immigrant.

Bibliography

Bruce-Novoa, Juan. "*Pocho* as Literature." *Aztlán* 7 (Spring, 1976): 65-77. Claims that *Pocho* deserves careful literary analysis instead of the sociological, historical, and political responses given it for fifteen years. Argues that the book's literary stature arises from its exploration of themes that are not culture-bound but are of universal appeal: the individual's struggle for identity, search for moral direction, and need to contribute to the world.

Grajeda, Rafael F. "José Antonio Villarreal and Richard Vasquez: The Novelist Against Himself." In *The Identification and Analysis of Chicano Literature*, edited by Francisco Jiménez. New York: Bilingual Press, 1979. Asserts that the significance of *Pocho* lies in its historical status as the first novel by a Mexican American depicting the cultural identity of Mexican Americans. Perhaps because of this, it is in fact an unmistakable "failure"; obvious, sentimental, flat of character, and stylistically "flaccid."

Luedtke, Luther S. "*Pocho* and the American Dream." In *Contemporary Chicano Fiction: A Critical Survey*, edited by Vernon E. Lattin. Binghamton, N.Y.: Bilingual Press, 1986. An exploration of the social context of this "typical American story" follows an excellent summary of the novel. Luedtke offers many insights into the mythos of the immigrant experience in the United States and the literary powers of *Pocho*.

Paredes, Raymund A. "The Evolution of Chicano Literature." In *Three American Literatures: Essays in Chicano, Native American, and Asian-American Literature for Teachers of American Literature*, edited by Houston A. Baker, Jr. New York: Modern Language Association of America, 1982. A tracing of the origins of Chicano literature that acknowledges the historical importance of Villarreal's work. Asserts that though *Pocho*'s subject is important, its treatment of issues such as abuse of women and the role of Catholicism is oversimplified.

Tatum, Charles M. "Contemporary Chicano Prose Fiction: A Chronicle of Misery." In *The Identification and Analysis of Chicano Literature*, edited by Francisco Jiménez. New York: Bilingual Press, 1979. Discusses how Villarreal's novel portrays the *pocho*, the Mexican male who retains connection to tradition while adapting to and integrating into Anglo culture, in a positive light.

Virginia M. Crane

POSSESSING THE SECRET OF JOY

Author: Alice Walker (1944-   )
Type of plot: Psychological realism
Time of plot: The 1930's to the 1980's
Locale: Africa, the United States, and Europe
First published: 1992

Principal characters:

TASHI (EVELYN JOHNSON), an Olinka African woman executed for killing a tribal medicine woman

OLIVIA, the child of African American missionaries to Tashi's tribe and friend of Tashi

ADAM, the child of African American missionaries, Tashi's husband and Olivia's brother

M'LISSA, a tribal wise crone whom Tashi murders for her part in performing female circumcisions

LISETTE, the white French lover of Adam and mother of Pierre

PIERRE, the son of Lisette and Adam

BENNY (BENTU) MORAGA, the learning-disabled son of Tashi and Adam

RAYE, Tashi's American female therapist, who helps her identify the real source of her madness

AMY MAXWELL, a Southern white American "lady" whom Tashi meets in a mental hospital

THE DOCTOR, an unnamed male psychoanalyst

The Novel

When their missionary family arrives at the tribal village of the Olinka, young African Americans Adam and Olivia Johnson see Tashi, the main character of *Possessing the Secret of Joy.* They observe the six-year-old girl weeping silently alongside her mother; readers later learn that Tashi's favorite sister, Dura, has just died from complications of a ritual clitoridectomy, performed on all village girls as they approach puberty. The novel weaves back and forth between the early memories of Tashi, Adam, and Olivia, cycling forward as Walker chronicles Tashi's later American/Western European life, her madness and struggle to accept the horror of female mutilation. While the Johnsons work as missionaries to the African Olinkas, Tashi recounts folktales of female power and plays with Olivia. In Tashi, Adam meets the woman whom he will later make his wife.

The novel pieces together fragmentary reminiscences of the main characters, stories that move toward Tashi's eventual murder of M'Lissa. *Possessing the Secret of Joy* does not provide a straight chronological narrative, only fragments of a story seen from the perspectives of different characters. Not until the novel's conclusion, when Tashi has returned to her native Olinka and is executed for M'Lissa's murder, does the story make sense in a traditional way.

When Adam makes Tashi his bride, she changes her name to Evelyn; she undergoes a gradual external transformation into a Westernized black woman. Much of Tashi's story—and, by extension, the stories of her husband, his lover, and the other main characters—serves as Walker's means of telling Tashi's interior story, her confrontation with the source of her madness: the excision of her external genitalia, including the clitoris and labia, which was done to her as part of a tribal rite when she was a young woman.

As Evelyn, Tashi seeks help to recover from the trauma induced by the death of Dura and her own mutilation by becoming the patient of a European disciple of Sigmund Freud; this doctor sees her "madness" as an aberration caused by repressed or "unnatural" sexual appetite. Interwoven with the European doctor's and Tashi's accounts are observations from Adam, Lisette, and the two boys, Benny and Pierre. These fragmentary narratives provide additional insight into the difficulties Tashi experiences in articulating the sources of her "madness." Furthermore, the voices of the others show how Adam deals with his damaged wife: by seeking companionship with Lisette, a white French woman. In part, at least, his long-term affair lets Adam abandon not only his fragile wife but also their son, Benny, who needs Adam as much as Tashi does, since he suffers from moderate mental retardation.

Ironically, Pierre, the son of Adam and Lisette, tries to unravel the mystery of Tashi's pain. The young man works as a cultural anthropologist, taking as his subject female circumcision. Raye, Tashi's second psychiatrist, a woman, also helps Tashi to name her wound and explore the forms of psychic circumcision that the physical surgery and death of her sister have caused her. While in a psychiatric hospital, Tashi meets a white American woman, Amy Maxwell, who had been circumcised as a treatment for her "excessive" sexual curiosity. It is at this point that Tashi begins to understand the extent to which women, and not just black African women, have had their identities cut away from them; Tashi begins to see clitoridectomy and infibulation as a means of controlling females. Tashi's anger turns outward, finding as its focus M'Lissa, the Olinkan woman who circumcises the female children of her tribal village.

Returning to Olinka, Tashi at first nurses M'Lissa and then murders her. The book ends with Tashi's execution; she is accused of destroying a great cultural hero, M'Lissa, who fought alongside the males of her village as they struggled to throw off European oppression.

The Characters

Tashi/Evelyn, the central character, is a woman caught between the world she knew as a child—tribal Africa—and the European and American cultures. As a woman who symbolically bridges these two worlds with her marriage to Adam, Tashi cannot cope with nor understand what has been asked of her as a woman of the Olinka tribe: to give up her sexual identity through the removal of her clitoris and labia, a ritual that was meant to bond her to her tribal sisters but that also separated her from her complete self through the erasure of her ability to respond sexually. Nor can Tashi fully transform herself into an American black woman, because she carries her Africanness with her in ways that her American-born husband cannot fathom. Her madness stems not only from her circumcision but also from her situation in an alien white culture that cannot understand who she is. In changing her name to Evelyn, Tashi attempts to become another woman, to cut the Africanness out of herself, thus denying herself full expression as a black African woman. Tashi's strength comes when she sees what she and her two cultures have done to her; her solution is to choose to kill M'Lissa, the woman who circumcised her. The murder enables Tashi to recapture her femaleness by obliterating the person who destroyed its outward symbols.

Like his wife, Adam is a person caught between worlds. As an African American, he represents the legacy of slavery. His time in Africa as the child of missionaries introduces him explicitly to his blackness, and he seeks in the African Tashi a reconnection to that heritage. Ironically, Tashi has been circumcised so that she could be the wife a tribal African male would prefer. It is clear, however, that Adam is a split person, divided forever from his Africanness by his slave heritage and by his acculturation in a predominantly white society. Adam's desire to become truly blended with the white culture that has oppressed him expresses itself in his liaison with Lisette, the young, white Parisian woman with whom he strikes up an ongoing sexual relationship that endures for decades and produces Adam's illegitimate son, Pierre. Like the other characters in the novel, Adam eventually learns to "see" Tashi for the complete woman she is and to understand and value her because of her identity—as black, as a sexual female, as African, as libidinous, as circumcised against her will.

The two half-brothers, Benny and Pierre, represent the outcome of Adam's and Tashi's forced blendings. Benny (whose African name is Bentu Moraga) is the product of Adam's insistence on returning to the Africa inside himself. A gentle, retarded young man, Benny will never survive alone. Ironically, it is Pierre who comes to his rescue; like Benny, and like Adam before him, Pierre (ironically named after Lisette's father) is a person who does not "fit." His blackness is muted; he has fair skin and hair, and it is the knowledge of his difference that drives Pierre to become a cultural anthropologist. Furthermore, both young men bear the stigma of their mothers' sexuality: Benny is something other than what the dominant culture would define as an adult male; he retains an emotional and sexual innocence that will, like Tashi's literal circumcision, forever keep him from realizing his full potential. Similarly, Pierre's mixed racial heritage will keep him forever between the African and the white worlds.

The roles of the village crone, M'Lissa, and the male psychoanalyst parallel each other. Both persons serve to maintain their "tribe's" status quo: M'Lissa by rendering women docile through the removal of their source of sexual joy; the male psychiatrist by defining depressive, sexually unsatisfied, or frigid women as mad, thereby removing them as sources of power.

It will take the female psychiatrist, Raye, and a white, female victim of circumcision, Amy Maxwell, to facilitate Tashi's healing. Both women can be seen as more fully realized aspects of Tashi herself: Women who have recognized exactly what female circumcision does to and takes from a sexual woman. Most powerfully, it is the white American Amy who helps Tashi to name her oppression. Until well into her adult life, Amy did not even realize what had been done to her, did not even remember that she had been circumcised; thus, she had been removed from the company of fully sexually expressive women and not even known it. By talking to Amy and hearing her story, Tashi learns to name her own pain and is empowered to choose a path by which she can make herself whole again. The path she takes is the murder of M'Lissa, who symbolizes Tashi's oppression.

Themes and Meanings

Possessing the Secret of Joy is foremost an exploration of female sexuality and the way that that aspect of a woman's self-identity is managed on a grand scale—not simply in Third World cultures but also in supposedly progressive societies in Europe and America. Walker equates the position of women in every culture with that of a castrated male; female circumcision is the equivalent to castrating a male, since both surgeries destroy a person's ability to attain sexual release. In the case of the female, one of the chief locuses of sexual pleasure, the clitoris, is excised. The circumcision of Tashi stands for her personal enslavement to a patriarchal world. In such cultures, women's needs and women's desires are not only passed off as unimportant but also considered to be unhealthy aberrations. This is certainly true in the case of Amy Maxwell, whose mother had her young daughter circumcised for masturbating.

Possessing the Secret of Joy is an angry novel. Walker focuses her attack on European colonialism, in its metaphoric castration of Africa and the silencing of Africanness in slaves excised from their mother countries. She also condemns the excision of femaleness from every woman that is performed by patriarchal cultures. Walker clearly parallels these two lines of argument by drawing all of her female characters as needing strong or oppressive males for their validation. For all the women, these relationships diminish their capacity to become complete, independent, strong women. In the case of Lisette, for example, her father dominates her young life, treats her like a fragile blossom, and prevents her from becoming a fully realized, independent adult. In Tashi, the parallels are obvious, but they also exist for M'Lissa, the Olinkan medicine woman who circumcises the female children of the village. Although circumcision itself is repugnant to Walker, the male Olinkan rebels co-opt and use even this person, the strongest tribal female, for their own purposes. M'Lissa cooperates to gain their protection and approval during the rebellion; she cannot exist as a woman alone. M'Lissa must allow herself to be used by the men of her tribe.

The metaphoric relationship between African and European cultures creates a similar master/slave dependency, which can be interpreted as a metaphoric castration, clitoridectomy, or rape. Even though the Olinka have gained their freedom, they have, like the mutilated women, lost their integrity—that of their culture. The forced imposition of European Christian values has irreversibly altered their culture; this shift can be seen, for example, in the tribe's adoption of European dress. A more telling form of castration is the excision of the Olinkas' African names: M'Lissa, who is originally known as Mzee, renames herself during the fight for independence, taking as her new name a contracted form of the European name Melissa. She has cut out her female as well as her Olinkan identity—first literally, because she has been circumcised, but also metaphorically, because she has cut off her given tribal name. The same set of circumstances surround Tashi, and, because she physically relocates herself by marrying an American and living in his home country, her loss is more extensive. Unlike M'Lissa, Tashi loses all of her Africanness, her roots as well as her femaleness.

Critical Context

The purpose of *Possessing the Secret of Joy* is not only to indict the practice of female circumcision but also to make the physical removal of the clitoris a metaphor for many other forms of oppression and diminishment. Walker's novel is a powerful feminist expression as well as a forceful consideration of tyranny, no matter what shape it takes, and is equally applicable to both genders. As such, it deserves to be read from both perspectives.

Walker earlier explored the nature of being black and being female in such novels as *The Color Purple* (1982). Of equal importance in her fiction is the black struggle for identity in a white-dominated culture, a theme taken up not only in *Possessing the Secret of Joy* but also in her earlier novels *Meridian* (1976) and *The Third Life of Grange Copeland* (1970). In *The Temple of My Familiar* (1989), Walker examines African American spirituality, a theme that in part also informs *Possessing the Secret of Joy*. Throughout Walker's distinguished career as a writer, women and women's roles, ambitions, psyches, and sorrows have occupied a central place in her vision. In her nonfiction analysis of the African American female literary tradition, *In Search of Our Mothers' Gardens: Womanist Prose* (1983), Walker seeks to identify the many women whose voices inform hers and those of other contemporary African American women writers.

Bibliography

Benn, Melissa. Review of *Possessing the Secret of Joy*, by Alice Walker. *The New Statesman and Society* 5 (October 9, 1992): 36-37. Offers an analysis of the rite of female circumcision. Also makes the point that Walker is really looking at human barbarism, no matter the culture: in Africa, in the contemporary psychiatrist/witch doctor's office, or in the symbolic circumcision rendered by male infidelity.

Butler-Evans, Elliott. *Race, Gender, and Desire: Narrative Strategies in the Fiction of Toni Cade Bambara, Toni Morrison, and Alice Walker*. Philadelphia: Temple University Press, 1989. Although this book was published before the publication of *Possessing the Secret of Joy*, it contains much insightful material on Walker's fiction. This scholarly treatment is also useful because it considers Walker alongside two other important contemporary African American writers, Toni Cade Bambara and Toni Morrison. The discussions of race and class as they shape the fiction of African American women writers are particularly enlightening.

Hospital, Janette Turner. Review of *Possessing the Secret of Joy*, by Alice Walker. *The New York Times Book Review*, June 28, 1992, 11. Points out the nature of the taboos Walker includes in her fiction and the various strategies she selects to structure her text. Interesting consideration of the ways in which the narrative structure of the book shapes it as myth and archetype rather than as a conventional novel.

Watkins, Mel. Review of *Possessing the Secret of Joy*, by Alice Walker. *The New York Times*, July 24, 1992, p. B4. Discusses the novel as a feminist clash with racism and sexism. Describes the book as mythic in tone and structure, in particular because of its use of multiple narrators and shifting points of view. Characterizes the novel as a polemic against female genital mutilation as well as other forms of sexism and racism.

Whitaker, Charles. "Alice Walker: *Color Purple* Author Confronts Her Critics and Talks About Her Provocative New Book." *Ebony* 47 (May, 1992): 86-89. Interview with Walker in which she addresses criticism she has received for her allegedly negative portrayals of African American men. Walker defends her right as an author to depict less than admirable characters.

Winchell, Donna Haisty. *Alice Walker*. New York: Twayne, 1992. Although this book does not directly address *Possessing the Secret of Joy*, it provides an excellent introductory treatment of her writing career. Included are discussions of Walker's life, novels, poetry, and nonfiction. A bibliography is also included.

Melissa E. Barth

PRAISESONG FOR THE WIDOW

Author: Paule Marshall (1929-   )
Type of plot: Psychological realism
Time of plot: The 1940's to the 1970's
Locale: Tatem, South Carolina; Carriacou, a small island in the Caribbean; White Plains, New York
First published: 1983

> *Principal characters:*
> AVEY (AVATARA) JOHNSON, a widowed, middle-aged African American woman
> JEROME (JAY) JOHNSON, Avey's late husband
> CUNEY, Avey Johnson's great-aunt
> LEBERT JOSEPH, the proprietor of a bar on the island of Grenada

The Novel

In *Praisesong for the Widow*, Paule Marshall explores the dynamics of the West Indian cultural landscape as well as its African heritage. The title of the novel reflects the author's attempt to celebrate both cultural transition and African continuity.

Praisesong for the Widow is a novel of healing, as its structure emphasizes. Dedicating the work to her ancestral figure, Da-duh (Alberta Jane Clement), Marshall divides the book into four parts that delineate the journey from disease to health for those affected by the contradiction of being "old" in the "New World."

In the first section, "Runagate," named for African American poet Robert Hayden's poem about the flight of a runaway slave, Avey Johnson feels the burden of being a slave to materialism when, on her annual cruise to the Caribbean, she dreams of her great-aunt Cuney. In this first section of the novel, as throughout the work, Marshall uses ritual as an opening to a hidden worldview that is antithetical to the values proclaimed by the elite of the Americas. "Runagate" recalls slavery times, when threats of corporal punishment precipitated slaves into flight.

The first section of the novel opens with sixty-two-year-old Avey Johnson, the protagonist, a black woman widowed one year previously. Avey is frantically packing her six suitcases for flight from her luxury liner, barely five days after setting sail on a two-week cruise in the Caribbean. Agitated and bewildered, she has no concrete reason to offer for her behavior. She can hardly recognize her own image in the mirror. A self-doubt triggered by her daughter's criticism of the cruise has escalated into hallucinations after a vision of her long-dead great-aunt Cuney, who seems determined to force Avey to confront her past, her roots, and her heritage. Cuney directs Avey to the highly symbolic Ibo Landing in Tatem, which is a key to that heritage. At the end of this section, Avey misses her flight back to New York and stays at a hotel on the island of Grenada instead.

In "Sleeper's Wake," Avey, in a dream, recalls her husband, her marriage, and the events leading to its spiritual death. In this section, "wake" represents both a ritual of death and an awakening. Literally, it might be the wake for Avey's husband, Jerome Johnson. More likely, it is a wake for Jay Johnson, the man Avey married, whose spirit died unnoticed—along with the marriage—one Tuesday in 1945. It could also be a wake or funeral for the close relationship between Jay and Avey, which was killed off by their materialistic ambitions. "Sleeper's Wake," in another sense, refers to the awakening of a sleeping Avey—from the stupor of her bourgeois mentality to a sudden realization of all that she has lost, all that she and her late husband had sacrificed in terms of happiness and life-giving values in order to acquire a house in a white neighborhood.

In "Lavé Tête," the next section, destiny intervenes in the form of Lebert Johnson, the proprietor of a local bar on the island of Grenada. He convinces Avey to take a brief excursion to the annual festival of the "out-island" people—people of the smaller island, Carriacou—who live and work in Grenada. The excursion back to their native land (Carriacou, and, by way of myth/ritual, Africa) is in fact their annual rite of rejuvenation, their rite of the eternal return, their form of communication with the African past and its sacred forces.

This section of the novel chronicles a cleansing ritual, a head washing, as well as a shedding of false image or worldview. The sudden awareness and tragic sense of loss that make Avey mourn Jay's death force her into a violent confrontation with the root cause of the loss: her bourgeois values. The rejection of those values is rendered symbolically and dramatically through Avey's excruciating vomiting fits. Ironically, it is in her moments of greatest weakness that she finds the greatest sympathy and moral support from her fellow passengers. None is repulsed. Their support of the purgation reveals that the process is natural and even anticipated. This communal support echoes the African communal involvement and deep empathy with young initiates during their rites of passage.

"Beg Pardon," the final section, is, as the title implies, the final stage in the growth process of awareness, when Avey, the cultural prodigal, comes home to beg the pardon of her offended ancestors. In preparation for the feast and celebration that mark all initiations, Avey is thoroughly bathed, oiled, massaged, and dressed. Psychologically, she is now ready, willing, and eager, and is no longer persuaded or coerced. Avey has finally understood the significance of her heritage.

The Characters

Avey Johnson, affluent and ready for retirement from her supervisory job at the state motor vehicle department, lives in a fashionable section of New York. Her late husband, Jerome, literally worked himself to death to attain this affluence. The novel relates an experience on the level of the psyche toward which Avey's whole life has been pointed. The movement of the novel is a gathering together, the achievement of linkages in time and place, linkages of the disparate elements of the individual self as it merges with the collective self.

In her journey, Avey fulfills the promise of black women in the twentieth century.

In *Praisesong for the Widow*, Marshall emphasizes that the fulfillment of promise cannot be achieved without a true understanding of the past. In the character of Avey, myth and history, place and consciousness unite in her struggles to become fully human.

Jay Johnson, Avey's late husband, is depicted as a hardworking, dependable family man who spends time with his family and whose wit and sensibility keep the love between him and Avey alive. The novel makes it clear that the confidence and contentment in this marriage comes from acceptance of self and one's roots. The schism between the couple starts with a slow but steady movement away from all the rituals that held their family life together. Endless work demanded by new ambitions takes Jay away from his family and away from love. The yearly trip south to their relatives and heritage is forgotten, as are old friends and values. At this point in his life, Jay insists on being called Jerome. He cuts himself and his family off from their roots. Avey's journey will bring her back to those roots.

In gaining an understanding of the past, Avey is guided by two elders. The first is her great-aunt Cuney from Tatem, South Carolina, long dead before the action of the novel begins. When Avey was young, her great-aunt used to take her to a place called Ibo Landing, where slaves were said to have walked across the water back to Africa. Avey's dream of her great-aunt and of the place takes hold of her consciousness in such a profound way that past and present unite in her spiritual journey. On the island of Carriacou, Avey finds her roots as a member of the Arada people of Carriacou and accepts her identity as "Avatara," the name her great-aunt had insisted she use as a child. Her discovery prompts her plan to sell her house in White Plains and move to her girlhood home in Tatem for at least part of the year, so that she, like her great-aunt before her, could instill in her grandchildren the history of their people.

The second spiritual guide on Avey's journey is Lebert Joseph, the proprietor of a bar on Grenada who lives in Carriacou. He plays a leading role in redirecting Avey's journey and is Marshall's artistic reincarnation of the Yoruba deity Legba, the liaison between man and the gods. He is vital to numerous rituals, both in West Africa and in the New World. In this role, Lebert Joseph links the spiritual and the physical worlds, the ancestors with the living and the unborn. Lebert meets Avey at her crossroads and firmly but gently leads her back to her roots, to a unified African worldview. Avey soon begins to remember the oral narratives and folk tales she heard as a child from her great-aunt, and she joins in the islanders' dances and rituals.

It is precisely because Avey responds to the call of her spiritual guides, because she undergoes her physical and spiritual journey, that she comes to deserve her praisesong. Only then can she recognize her true name and become an elder whom others can respect and from whom others can learn.

Themes and Meanings

In *Praisesong for the Widow*, Marshall suggests that the journey through the African diaspora must be rooted in an understanding of the past, which must be continually sung, continually reiterated in the present. The novel is about a woman reclaiming her story in a context in which storytelling becomes part of a larger project of self-actualization.

For Africans, a praisesong is a particular kind of traditional heroic poem. Sung in various communities over the entire continent, praisesongs embrace many poetic forms but are always specifically ceremonial social poems, intended to be recited or sung at public occasions. When sung as a part of a rite of passage, they mark the advancement of a person from one group or stage to the next. This novel, therefore, celebrates for the widow her coming to terms with her widowhood—a reconciliation that has greater implications than coming to terms with the loss of an individual husband alone. The entire narrative in itself acts as a "praisesong" for the widow, with the narrator as the griot (the oral historian/genealogist/musician of traditional African society). The title also refers specifically to the communal song and the dance of the "beg pardon" at the end of the novel, which itself becomes a praisesong for the widow in homage to her homecoming. Through the healing of one of Africa's lost daughters, a scattered people are made whole again.

In this work, storytelling is not only a metaphor for cultural self-possession and wholeness but also a literal injunction. The quest on which the widow is embarked culminates in her taking upon herself the burden, bequeathed by Cuney, of telling the story of the African slaves at Ibo Landing. This story serves in the text as the representation of spiritual understanding and the will to survive and triumph. In taking it upon herself to perpetuate the story, the widow finds a meaning to her own personal journey, which then also transcends the self and the family. Storytelling, like singing, becomes a cultural metaphor and the carrier of cultural meaning. This is Avatara's true inheritance and legacy.

Critical Context

In her first novel, *Brown Girl, Brownstones* (1959), Marshall felt compelled to make a spiritual return to her sources, a return she believes is necessary for all African Americans. At the end of the book, the heroine, Selina Boyce, leaves the United States in order to return to the Caribbean. In her second novel, *The Chosen Place, the Timeless People* (1969), Merle Kinbona completes the voyage to the Caribbean only to depart for Africa at the end of the novel. Those two novels, together with *Praisesong for the Widow*, in which Avey Johnson also makes the mythic return to the Caribbean, form a trilogy.

In a note to a reprinting of her 1967 story "To Da-duh, In Memoriam," Marshall explains that Da-duh is an ancestral figure who appears in various forms throughout her work—from the character Mrs. Thompson in *Brown Girl, Brownstones* to Cuney in *Praisesong for the Widow*. Like Alice Walker and Toni Morrison, Marshall believes in the significance of ancestors and celebrates them in her fiction; they are the ground upon which she stands.

In focusing on such an unlikely heroine as Avey Johnson, Marshall once again charted new territory in the area of African American women's literature. Older women, such as Eva in Toni Morrison's *Sula* (1974) or Miss Hazel in Toni Cade

Bambara's story "My Man Bovanne" (1978), had been represented in fiction. In the 1980's, moreover, African American women writers—for example, Toni Morrison in *Tar Baby* (1981) and Gloria Naylor in *Linden Hills* (1985)—had increasingly approached the question of class schisms in contemporary African American society. Yet no writer had fashioned a "praisesong" for a character such as Avey Johnson, whose life journey explores issues of age and class in relation to the racial, cultural, and political issues of her society.

Bibliography
Busia, Abena P. A. "What Is Your Nation?: Reconnecting Africa and Her Diaspora Through Paule Marshall's *Praisesong for the Widow*." In *Changing Our Own Words: Essays on Criticism, Theory, and Writing by Black Women*, edited by Cheryl A. Wall. New Brunswick, N.J.: Rutgers University Press, 1989. Discusses the work as a novel that has as its focus the act of women reclaiming their stories; in this context, storytelling becomes part of a larger project of self-validation.
Christian, Barbara T. "Ritualistic Process and the Structure of Paule Marshall's *Praisesong for the Widow*." *Callaloo* 6 (Spring-Summer, 1983): 74-84. Christian examines *Praisesong for the Widow* as an African ritual that shows the relationship between the individual and the community.
Eko, Ebele O. "Oral Tradition: The Bridge to Africa in Paule Marshall's *Praisesong for the Widow*." *The Western Journal of Black Studies* 10, no. 3 (1986): 143-147. Demonstrates the way in which Marshall integrates oral traditional elements into her novel to achieve unity of plot as well as unity and contrast of characters.
Pollard, Velma. "Cultural Connections in Paule Marshall's *Praisesong for the Widow*." *World Literature Written in English* 25 (Autumn, 1985): 285-298. Discusses *Praisesong for the Widow* as a diaspora novel that dramatizes the cultural similarities between the communities of Africa, the Caribbean, and black America.
Reyes, Angelita. "Politics and Metaphors of Materialism in Paule Marshall's *Praisesong for the Widow* and Toni Morrison's *Tar Baby*." In *Politics and the Muse: Studies in the Politics of Recent American Literature*, edited by Adam J. Sorkin. Bowling Green, Ohio: Bowling Green State University Popular Press, 1989. Reyes views Marshall and Morrison as two writers deeply concerned with personal experience as it illuminates external history.

Genevieve Slomski

A PRAYER FOR OWEN MEANY

Author: John Irving (1942-   )
Type of plot: Bildungsroman
Time of plot: 1952-1968 and 1987
Locale: Gravesend, New Hampshire, and Toronto, Canada
First published: 1989

> *Principal characters:*
> JOHN WHEELWRIGHT, an expatriate who recollects his youth in Gravesend, New Hampshire
> OWEN MEANY, John's childhood friend, whose death gives John faith in God
> HARRIET WHEELWRIGHT, John's eccentric grandmother, a small-town matriarch
> TABITHA WHEELWRIGHT, John's loving mother, whose one brief affair resulted in John's birth
> DAN NEEDHAM, John's stepfather, an amateur drama coach
> HESTER EASTMAN, John's cousin, who loves Owen Meany and becomes a rock singer famous for songs related to Owen's death
> LEWIS MERRILL, John's father, a guilt-ridden minister

The Novel

A Prayer for Owen Meany is the story of John Wheelwright's relationship with his childhood friend Owen Meany, a midget with a high, squeaky voice, whose life and death move John to have faith in God. Despite his size, Owen has a commanding presence that directs John's life. Owen comes to symbolize a moral intensity that John finds sorely absent from American life.

In 1987, John Wheelwright, a forty-five-year-old English teacher living in Canada, is finally able to write about his experiences with Owen Meany in the 1950's and 1960's, when they were growing up in Gravesend, New Hampshire. John's narrative is disjointed and nonsequential, oscillating between past and present, intermixing current news events, historical statistics, and cultural commentary with personal recollections. Unable to adjust to Canadian life and outraged at the moral malaise in the United States, John is drawn back to his youth in New England. His recollections focus on his illegitimate birth to a single mother, his mother's marriage and untimely death, and his close relationship with Owen Meany.

Tabitha Wheelwright, John's mother, had an affair during one of her overnight trips to Boston that resulted in John's birth. She never tells John the identity of his father. Tabitha rises above town gossip and rears John in the stately house of her mother, Harriet Wheelwright, whose ancestors go back to the *Mayflower*. Tabitha is devoted to John. She later marries Dan Needham, a Harvard graduate and a teacher at Gravesend Academy. During Tabitha and Dan's wedding, an ominous hailstorm breaks out. As Tabitha offers a ride to Owen, whom she loves almost as much as her son, a hailstone hits her on the head. Owen apologizes for the accident.

This part of the wedding scene carefully mirrors the scene of Tabitha's death. During a boring Little League baseball game that is already lost, Owen hits a foul ball that strikes Tabitha on the head, killing her. This scene propels John on his quest for his father. John believes that his mother was waving to his father when she was hit. The baseball, which the local policeman calls the murder weapon, mysteriously disappears. Owen is convinced that he is God's instrument. Overcome by a sense of destiny, Owen believes that he frightened the angel of death away from John's mother one night and thus was ordained to be the instrument of her death.

Owen Meany's father owns a granite quarry that primarily engages in manufacturing tombstones; his mother is reclusive and unstable. Owen becomes a dominant figure in the life of John and his family. Although a diminutive young man with a screechy voice, Owen creates an overpowering presence. He directs the Christmas pageant, stuns the audience with his performance in the role of the Ghost of Christmas Future in *A Christmas Carol*, and becomes the leading spokesperson for student rights at Gravesend Academy. Brilliant, attractive to women, and able to beat off bullies, Owen helps John through school, stays back with John when he repeats the ninth grade, teaches John how to read, inspires John to become an English major, practically writes John's master's thesis, amputates John's finger to keep him out of the Vietnam War, and tells John to go to Canada to escape America's moral exhaustion.

Owen Meany also directs John on his quest to find his biological father. Owen, who sees everything and forgets nothing, leads John to discover that his mother was a supper-club singer called "The Lady in Red." After Owen's death, Owen's spiritual voice directs the Reverend Lewis Merrill to pull the missing baseball out of his desk drawer and to admit that he is John's father. Merrill waved at Tabitha during the fatal baseball game and wished her dead; when she was killed, he wallowed in remorse and guilt. Owen, however, kept Tabitha's dressmaker's dummy with her red dress. John uses it to convince Merrill that he is seeing an apparition of Tabitha and to shock him into a renewal of his faith.

Owen himself directs the key plot line of the second half of the novel. As a young boy playing the Ghost of Christmas Future, he sees his own name and the date of his death on Scrooge's tombstone. Later, in a dream, he sees himself bloodied and wounded after saving a group of Vietnamese children. Owen joins the Army so that he will be sent to Vietnam. Instead, he is appointed as casualty officer with the task of delivering bodies to bereaved families in Arizona. He invites John to Phoenix to spend some time with him. Owen promises that no harm will come to John but becomes concerned as the day of his heroic death (July 8, 1968) approaches. On that date, he is not in Vietnam but in a Phoenix airport. As a group of Vietnamese orphans deplanes, the nuns with them ask Owen to take the boys to the airport's makeshift restroom. Dick Jarvits, a drugged and deranged young man wearing military fatigues and contraband weapons, throws a grenade to John, who throws it to Owen. Within seconds, John lifts Owen up to a window as the grenade explodes. The children are saved, but Owen loses his arms and dies. John realizes how elements fit into place: Owen's lightness that tempted people to lift him, his undeveloped voice that matched the voices of the children who listened to him, and Owen and John's game in which John lifted Owen to slam dunk a basketball. All these attributes and skills were ordained for a purpose. Realizing now that Owen had foreseen his own death, John becomes a believer.

John realizes that Owen Meany was a man of faith living in an age of doubters. The older John, struggling with his own faith and disillusion, asks God to give him Owen Meany back.

The Characters

Owen Meany is both a realistic and a symbolic character. His diminutive size and screechy, undeveloped voice contrast with his powerful presence. As his name, Meany, implies, Owen believes that all actions and objects have meaning. In an indecisive world that has lost its sense of purpose, Owen sees all actions as purposeful. He processes all information, forgets nothing, and saves everything. He believes in strong moral leadership in a country of flawed leaders and morally righteous hypocrites who value public relations above human relations.

Owen is also a Christ figure. In Sunday school, he endures the other students raising him overhead. He is hung on a coat rack like a crucified Christ, and his parents tell him that he is the result of a virgin birth. Playing the Christ child, he disturbs the complacent churchgoers. Owen's life also focuses on death and resurrection as he absorbs appropriate quotations from Scripture, hymns, and the works of William Shakespeare. He carves gravestones and later delivers the bodies of dead soldiers. Owen knows that he must sacrifice his life to save others, both physically and spiritually. He also proclaims the resurrection of the dead. Raised overhead as a young man, elevated as a Christmas angel, lifted up to slam dunk a basketball, and thrown up to a window to shelter children from a grenade, Owen is connected with resurrection even in the moment of death, as he sees himself raised above the palm trees. Owen is a Christ figure and a hero in an age that has lost its belief in heroes.

John Wheelwright is the disciple of Owen Meany and creates gospel versions of Meany's life and death, highlighting Meany's words in capital letters. John, however, is not heroic. Outraged at political scandals, he criticizes American foreign policy from a safe distance. Owen casts him in the Christmas play as Joseph, a witness to the miraculous but not a participant. John is an alienated, detached parade-watcher who has escaped real suffering. When lost for words, he proclaims what Owen would have said. A detached and celibate Christian, he clings to his faith in Owen. Both are victims of the Vietnam era, Owen as a heroic martyr and John as an alienated defector.

Minor characters symbolize family life, politics, and religion. Harriet Wheelwright, the *Mayflower* aristocrat, holds on to her antiques and her preserves as she and her generation drift into senility. Fathers are also significant figures. Dan Needham is a caring stepfather who shows John the meaning of friendship. Paul Meany cares for Owen, but is a detached father. The victims of the Vietnam era include Hester

Eastman, a rebellious and promiscuous girl who turns into a street revolutionary proud of her scars and becomes an aging rock star, converting her suffering into a mixture of sex and violence. Harry Hoyt, bitten by a poisonous snake, dies in front of a Vietnam whorehouse. Buzzy Thurston takes drugs to dodge the draft and kills himself in a car accident. A variety of members of the clergy are satirized. The novel thus features a broad range of eccentric characters separated into several social and religious configurations.

Themes and Meanings

The novel principally concerns faith and the ability to hold on to it in a collapsing world. It is about young Americans growing up in an age of innocence and faced with the terrors of war abroad and senseless violence at home. The novel also chronicles the history of a lost generation and the failure of American leadership. At each New Year's celebration, John rolls through the death count in Vietnam. When Defense Secretary Robert McNamara says that America is winning a war of attrition, Owen comments wryly that such a war is not the kind that one wins. In some ways, America's guilt goes deeper than Vietnam. As he dies, Owen recalls the name of the Indian chief who sold his land to John's ancestors, thus connecting Owen's death to the genocide of the Indians. Owen also connects the fate of America to the abuse of women. Like Marilyn Monroe, America has become the plaything of powerful men.

Set in a world in which leadership is breaking down, the novel is also about the absence of the father. This theme is brought to the fore in the novel's climactic scene. Dick Jarvits, a crazed and violent teenager whose father is dead, throws a grenade to John, a young man who does not know who his father is. Owen Meany, a truly fatherless young man who believes he is the result of a virgin birth, saves John and a group of orphans.

The novel also depicts a cultural wasteland in which television renders disasters entertaining and Liberace turns serious music into kitsch. Biblical epics turn religion into soap opera while rock videos present a mindless mixture of sex and violence. Owen uses the term "made for television" to comment on any absurd incident.

Critical Context

A Prayer for Owen Meany is postmodern in its approach, blending the grotesque and the comic with the mysterious and the realistic. It views a declining civilization through the eyes of an alienated narrator. In the tradition of American novelist Kurt Vonnegut, Irving reduces minor characters to short biographies, forecasting their ironic deaths, such as Harry Hoyt's death by snakebite in Vietnam. Like Vonnegut, Irving mixes statistics and historical events with the lives of characters, even pointing out the ironic fates of real people. Although Liberace supposedly died from acquired immune deficiency syndrome (AIDS), for example, the official press release said that he overdosed on watermelons.

Despite its modern tone, the novel is closely connected to the traditional romantic American novel. It is heavily weighted in the New England Calvinist tradition of predestination. John is named for John Wheelwright, the rebellious Puritan who believed in justification by faith and the grace of the Holy Spirit. The novel's secret sins, fated destinies, search for the father, mysterious dark-haired women, biblical allusions, and prominent symbolic objects all could come straight from the works of Nathaniel Hawthorne or Herman Melville. The novel clearly mirrors elements found in Hawthorne's *The Scarlet Letter* (1850). Tabitha Wheelwright, the good woman, is called "The Lady in Red," and her red dress becomes the symbol of her illicit sexual relationship with the Reverend Merrill, a guilt-obsessed minister who eventually confesses to John. Even the scandalization of the town matrons at Tabitha's wedding and their belief that divine justice had been done at her death reflect the Puritan wives in *The Scarlet Letter*. Hester Eastman, a dark-haired, primitive woman, resembles Hawthorne's Hester Prynne. The Christ figure with the speech problem resembles Herman Melville's Billy Budd. Even the novel's interconnecting symbols are in the tradition of the classic American novel. The armless totem of the Indian chief who sold his land, the declawed armadillo, the armless dressmaker's dummy, and the statue of Mary Magdalene with her arms sawed off all reflect Owen's martyrdom when a grenade blows his arms off, just as the statue of Joseph with his missing hand forecasts the amputation of John's finger.

Bibliography

Kazin, Alfred. "God's Own Little Squirt." *The New York Times Book Review* 94 (March 12, 1989): 1, 30-31. Gives a detailed summary of the novel. Focuses on the political commentary. Praises Irving's craftsmanship but finds the book devoid of irony and sees its religious message as somewhat juvenile.

Pritchard, William. "Small Town Saint." *The New Republic* 200 (May 22, 1989): 36-38. Briefly traces the change in Irving's style, noting the lack of irony in Irving's later works. Also presents a detailed analysis of the novel and compares it to the works of J. D. Salinger.

Reilly, Edward C. *Understanding John Irving.* Columbia: University of South Carolina Press, 1991. Chapter 8 gives a thorough analysis of Irving's characterization and symbolism and a brief summary of critical reviews.

Sheppard, R. Z. "The Message Is the Message." *Time* 133 (April 3, 1989): 80. Sheppard finds the novel to be a stunning mixture of horror and humor and praises Irving's prose. The review is followed by a brief interview article.

Wall, James M. "Owen Meany and the Presence of God." *Christian Century* 106 (March 22, 1989): 299-300. Sees a profound theological message in the novel that secular critics are not willing to approach.

Paul Rosefeldt

RABBIT AT REST

Author: John Updike (1932-   )
Type of plot: Psychological realism
Time of plot: The late 1980's
Locale: 1990
First published: Southeastern Pennsylvania and southwestern Florida

> *Principal characters:*
> HARRY "RABBIT" ANGSTROM, a middle-aged, semiretired Toyota dealer with a faulty heart
> JANICE ANGSTROM, his wife, now an independent woman
> NELSON ANGSTROM, their perverse son and acting manager of the Toyota dealership
> TERESA "PRU" ANGSTROM, Nelson's wife
> JUDY ANGSTROM, Harry's eight-year-old granddaughter
> ROY ANGSTROM, Harry's four-year-old grandson
> THELMA HARRISON, Harry's secret lover
> RON HARRISON, Thelma's husband and Harry's childhood classmate
> CHARLES STAVROS, a retired car salesman

The Novel

   Rabbit at Rest is the final volume of John Updike's tetralogy recording the life and times of Harry "Rabbit" Angstrom during four decades, from the late 1950's to his final year of life in 1989. In his own thirty-year effort to chronicle Rabbit's life, Updike parallels events of the American experience from 1959 to 1989.

   The 512-page book begins in 1988 on the Gulf Coast of Florida, where Harry, now semiretired from running the Toyota dealership in Brewer, Pennsylvania, and his wife Janice spend six months every year. They await the arrival of their son Nelson and his family. Harry, once a high-school basketball hero, is overweight and unable to resist eating cholesterol-filled junk food. He now has a bad heart. His son's visit culminates with the fifty-five-year-old Harry being hospitalized following a heart attack, brought on by his attempt to rescue his granddaughter during a boating accident. Back in Brewer, Harry undergoes angioplasty to clear his coronary arteries, refusing a needed bypass operation. He is attended at the hospital by a young nurse who proves to be the daughter of his former mistress. The thought that the nurse may be his daughter intrigues him, but he chooses not to pursue it.

   Harry's physical concerns intensify his sense of mortality. In addition, his and his wife's peace and prosperity are threatened by their discovery that Nelson, who has been managing the family Toyota franchise, has been embezzling from the business to support a cocaine habit. Although Nelson eventually agrees to enter an addiction-treatment program and Harry returns from Florida to straighten things out, the corporation withdraws its franchise. Its Japanese representative trenchantly censures the American people for lack of discipline, Nelson for his immaturity, and Harry for inept parenting. A corollary to this outcome is that the protagonist constantly finds himself at odds with both his wife and his son, who take defensive positions on the matter of Nelson's perfidy and find ways to blame Harry for it. Nelson refuses responsibility for what he has done to the family business. Janice, unwisely ignoring evidence of her son's shiftiness, lets him remain in charge of the dealership until it is too late. Ensuing financial constraints pressure Harry and his wife to share a house with their son and his family. Harry's family unconsciously prepares itself to survive him, his wife and son making decisions about the family business that leave him out. Janice enrolls in real estate courses and emerges as energetically businesslike. Harry admires this but notices that she occasionally talks about him in the past tense.

Throughout the story, Harry is seen as a receptor of cultural and historical changes and events. References abound to the television sitcoms Harry watches and the news events he observes through broadcast media. Impressed by the limitless information offered by the media, he muses on news of China, ozone depletion, Panamanian leader Manuel Noriega, and the beginning of the fall of Communism; he becomes somewhat obsessed with such death-dealing events as the Lockerbie air disaster and the demise of television personalities. Thoughts of mortality pervade Harry's thinking. While still recuperating from surgery, Harry has a premonition of death while visiting an adoring former lover, Thelma Harrison, who is dying of lupus. As is true for other women with whom he has been involved, he is incapable of feeling deep affection for Thelma. He is later accurately accused of this when encountered by her husband as she lies close to death in a hospital.

In the penultimate portion of the novel, a depressed and demoralized Harry finds himself left alone one evening with Pru, his equally depressed daughter-in-law. Harry characteristically obeys his instincts, and the two end up in bed. When Janice finds out and angrily demands that her husband confront the family, he flees to his Florida condominium. His reaction is surprise at his wife's anger rather than shame. His family does not pursue him, and he maintains a lonely existence, eventually suffering a terminal stroke while playing basketball with a boy whom he does not know. Lying in a Florida hospital, unable to communicate with his family when they arrive, Harry dies at the age of fifty-six, never having taken control of his life.

The Characters

Harry "Rabbit" Angstrom has lived his life by trusting and gratifying senses, by selfishly following his instincts—like a rabbit—and running from serious emotional commitments and responsibilities. At the same time, he pursues a search for self-realization. The title character looks at a world that he will soon leave, a world constantly presenting him with images and premonitions of death. He finds that his wife and his family become increasingly independent of him, almost as if he has ceased to exist. Finding no joy in life and little faith to sustain him, Harry is a depressed and demoralized man. Earlier in life, trust in his instincts led to success as a high-school sports hero, an attracter of women, and a prosperous car dealer. He is nevertheless a failure, a lonely and empty man who can do little for himself. Although not unethical, he follows a moral code centered on himself. When confronted with the consequences of his own behavior, he runs. Despite Harry's egoism, immaturity, and other limitations, he is likable. His loneliness and vulnerability to chance are appealing, and readers may see bits of Harry in themselves.

Janice Angstrom is a somewhat unsympathetic wife and a mother who delays recognizing her son's waywardness, placing his concerns before those of her husband. One admires her newfound abilities as a decisive businesswoman and real estate agent who can stand on her own feet. Yet her concern for her husband has become secondary.

Nelson Angstrom is a selfish, spoiled, weak man consistently at odds with his father, whom he has not forgiven for being an absent and indifferent parent during a portion of his life, as depicted in *Rabbit Run* (1960) and *Rabbit Redux* (1971). His father holds no real liking for him. Bored with his responsible position at the family Toyota dealership, he becomes a cocaine addict, with disastrous financial consequences for the family and the business. He never apologizes for his deeds and only with great prodding admits that his addiction is a problem. Even when Nelson emerges from a treatment center bent on a career as a social worker, he does not enlist the reader's sympathy.

Pru Angstrom is a good mother to Nelson's children, a victimized wife properly censorious of her husband's addiction, denying him her bed but forgiving him when he seemingly overcomes his drug problem. Her own self-enforced abstinence allows readers to forgive her one night's dalliance with Harry. Her basic honesty and wifely love compel her to confess to her peccadillo. The confession forms the narrative climax hurtling Harry into Florida exile and the last episode of his life.

Judy Angstrom is Harry's granddaughter, representing for him the image of his dead daughter. She initiates the novel's first action that dramatizes Harry's weak heart. When a boat manned by Harry overturns, his exertions in rescuing her result in a heart attack, foreshadowing his eventual death. Harry recalls his infant daughter's drowning death almost thirty years earlier, resulting from young Janice's alcoholic carelessness, an incident detailed in *Rabbit Run*.

Thelma Harrison, a terminally ill former lover of Harry, makes only a brief appearance in this novel. As a woman deeply in unrequited love with Harry, she represents his attraction to women and his inability to love another. Thelma's dying is another intimation of mortality.

Themes and Meanings

The main focus of *Rabbit at Rest* is the title character, who has approached, in the late 1980's, the end of an unexamined life. Harry "Rabbit" Angstrom has pursued life instinctively, like a rabbit, hopping away from emotional commitments and responsibility, domestic and otherwise. His detached treatment of women, such as his wife and several mistresses—let alone his view of women as sex objects—reveals him as a person who does not know what it means to love another. Never having achieved self-realization or control of his life, Harry faces death—hastened by damaging an aging heart through indiscriminate eating—without faith and without consolation.

The central character approximates a representative American, displaying the typical American psyche of the Cold War era. Harry's former success as basketball star, womanizer, and car dealer is honored in a culture that rewards nerve more than ideas and hard work. At the same time, he is a failure. Neither unethical nor immoral, Harry has a moral code centered largely on himself and does not live in moral relation to other people.

Harry is the product of an America that believes in luck, valuing good instincts over brains and success over moral capacity. He embodies the novel's concern as to whether American egotism will leave its citizens empty and demoralized. By employing a flexible third-person narrative technique and the present tense, Updike allows the reader to experience Harry's observations, recollections, and expectations. His thoughts about contemporary culture reveal Harry as an American man with middle-class fears, lusts, and prejudices. That he accepts uncritically the unselective plethora of advertising, popular songs, and current events that pour into him from his television and car radio makes Updike's point. Moreover, Harry cannot adjust to the probable fall of Communism, remarking at one point, "If there's no Cold War, what's the point of being an American?" Through Rabbit Angstrom and his actions and attitudes, the author reveals his theme: the possible corruption and emptiness of the American Dream.

Critical Context

The publication of *Rabbit at Rest*, owing to the critical and popular success of its three predecessors, was a major event. Updike's history as a best-selling serious novelist brings broad and immediate attention to anything he produces. The novel swiftly became a best-seller and generated a range of critical reactions, from enthusiasm to dismissal. Bruce Bawer, surveying the entire tetralogy in *The New Criterion*, found the final book's episodes inflated and contemplated that Updike's career and art might have fared better had he turned to other projects after *Rabbit Run*. Garry Wills, surveying the tetralogy in *The New York Review of Books*, saw the Rabbit series as vacuous and increasingly implausible. He particularly faulted *Rabbit at Rest* for substituting excessive descriptiveness for analysis and mere length for moral pointedness. Contrarily, *Newsweek* writer Paul Gray described the tetralogy as "a grand trip, and this finale is one of Updike's best books." Certainly for many readers the novel is a fitting culmination of the Rabbit series, an apt requiem for the 1980's and for the title character in a time when his chauvinistic view of America could no longer comfortably exist.

Updike's reputation as a writer is firmly established and has been enhanced by the completion of the Rabbit tetralogy. He has given fiction a rich legacy in the character of Rabbit, a contemporary American, lost yet likable, a measure of his time. Updike has limned a finely textured, detailed, provoking portrait of America over four decades. *Rabbit at Rest*, as a contribution to the Updike canon and to American literature, will continue to be read and discussed.

Bibliography

Bawer, Bruce. "Updike's 'Rabbit' Novels." *The New Criterion* 9 (October, 1990): 30-39. Describes Updike's evolution of "Rabbit" Angstrom from *Rabbit Run* to *Rabbit at Rest*, offering informative synopses. Bawer observes that comparatively *Rabbit at Rest* is more verbose and less convincing in its treatment of its central character. Valuable for an overview of Rabbit in Updike's tetralogy.

Cooper, Rand Richard. "Rabbit Loses the Race: John Updike's 'Small Answer of a Texture.' " *Commonweal* 118 (May 17, 1991): 316-320. Identifies Updike as a realistic writer whose prolific descriptiveness is rooted in religious concerns. Follows Rabbit through the tetralogy from a young man engaged in an unresolved spiritual search to his end in *Rabbit at Rest*, facing the depressing realization that he and the whole world are "material." An enlightening look at the novel from a religious perspective.

Menand, Louis. "Rabbit Is Dead." *Esquire* 114 (November, 1990): 93-94. Perceives Rabbit in *Rabbit at Rest* as a metaphor for American culture. He is described as initially successful, through luck, but ending as a failure. Menand finds a parallel between Rabbit and an America, prosperous after 1945, that came to value fortune, instinct, and luck over intellectual and moral capacity.

Updike, John. "Why Rabbit Had to Go." *The New York Times Book Review*, August 5, 1990, 1, 24, 25. Discusses the evolution of the "Pennsylvania Tetralogy." Admitting sadness at his mother's death, Updike refers to *Rabbit at Rest* as "a depressed book about a depressed man, written by a depressed man." Illuminates Updike's thoughts about Rabbit.

Wills, Garry. "Long-Distance Runner." *The New York Review of Books* 37 (October 25, 1990): 11, 13-14. In synopsizing the Rabbit tetralogy, Wills points out that an angstrom is a unit of measure and deduces that Rabbit represents a measure of American beliefs over four decades. In *Rabbit at Rest*, Wills finds Updike softening his original aim to express some hard truths about America. Offers a helpful overview of Rabbit's background before the 1980's.

Christian H. Moe

THE RESURRECTION

Author: John Gardner (1933-1982)
Type of plot: Metaphysical
Time of plot: The early 1960's
Locale: San Francisco, California, and western New York state
First published: 1966

> *Principal characters:*
> JAMES CHANDLER, an associate professor of philosophy at the University of California at Berkeley
> MARIA CHANDLER, his wife, a caring and practical woman
> KAREN CHANDLER, their oldest daughter, age eight, already a thinker
> SUSAN CHANDLER, their middle daughter, age six, a game player
> ANNE CHANDLER, their youngest daughter, age two, who looks remarkably like James
> ROSE CHANDLER, James's mother, puzzled by her late husband and already mourning her son
> AUNT EMMA STALEY, a painter, now senile
> AUNT BETSY STALEY, a pianist and cultural leader of Batavia
> AUNT MAUD STALEY, a singer, now deaf
> VIOLA STALEY, the niece of the three Staley sisters, bitter and nearly insane
> JOHN HORNE, a lawyer, librarian, and lay philosopher

The Novel

The specific gravity of *The Resurrection* is very great. James Chandler, a metaphysician living in a time of analysis, feels that he was born out of time. Because of his interests, however perverse for this age, and because he is dying from leukemia, he might be forgiven for being concerned about important questions that, as a philosopher, he is prepared to discuss at an elevated level. Since James Chandler is a philosopher who comes from the mind of a novelist, he also might be forgiven for having an interest in aesthetics, though of course it is the novel itself that is Gardner's aesthetic response to very heavy questions.

Immediately after the diagnosis of his illness, Chandler decides to return to Batavia in western New York, the town in and near which he (and the author) grew up. He, his wife, and their daughters stay there with his mother, still alive though failing; his father, an undereducated man of intelligence who spent much of his time trying to perfect a perpetual-motion machine, has died. Also still alive are the Staley sisters, whom Chandler soon visits, all mediocrities but important in the town in their day: One was a painter, though she now is senile; one still gives piano lessons; and one, now deaf, was a singer. Their vestigial status says much about the culture of Batavia. Their niece, Viola, takes care of them and their house and, ill-used by them and by life, is bitter. She becomes much less so as she comes to love James Chandler, a pipe-smoking, fair-haired, owl-faced man with glasses, who—glasses excepted—resembles Gardner.

The sisters in their varying artistic ways are trying to order life, to make it conform to some rules. So are some students at a local institution for the blind, watched in fascination by the Chandler girls, as they try to play baseball. Of course, once the ball stops rolling, the players have no way to find it except by groping—a nice trope for the metaphysician the girls' father is. The girls themselves do something similar by playing a game that they have invented, the rules of which they occasionally violate. Meanwhile, Chandler dreams of a wizened old woman with a face like a monkey and a mouth full of blood—in his weakened state of mind, she often is not far away from him. The mind, he decides, cannot handle the idea of personal death and thus comes up with such images.

Marie, his wife, is a caring and practical soul who takes care of her family and tries to care for her husband, whom she loves. She is always in the background, but she shares few concerns with James, who has decided in his last days to "seize existence by the scrotum." On returning from a visit to the Staleys, he falls and is rescued, bleeding, by Viola. From then on, her concern for him grows.

When Marie visits her husband in the hospital, she meets John Horne, an attorney who never practiced as such, but rather gave himself to being a law librarian, a scholar, and a lay philosopher. He is a grotesque, misshapen, probably dying, and something of a mental patient. Mainly, however, he exists as a *deus ex machina* to ask the same sorts of questions Chandler does, though he comes up with a different answer—nihilism—than does the associate professor.

Like Chandler, however, he cannot be "cured" by logical positivism (a doctrine that assumes that any question is invalid if it cannot be analyzed by the senses; thus "God" and "afterlife," for example, are non-questions) from asking metaphysical questions. Horne confesses that he is in despair. He does get off some good lines—"Art is the self-sacrifice of a man incapable of sacrificing himself in real life"—a line that fits Chandler fairly well too. He repeatedly reminds himself that he has not involved himself fairly with his wife, his daughters, or, lately, Viola, and now he avoids Horne. Chandler begins his last work, "Notes Toward an Aesthetic Theory."

A country man tells the senior Mrs. Chandler that "Everything in the world was made to go to waste" and that "the only difference between people and trees is trees don't fret about it." Chandler, dying, has his mother drive him to Viola, where, bleeding and able only to crawl, he grasps her foot in expiation. His wife and children, meanwhile, are at Betsy Staley's last-ever recital, where the pianist bursts into no melody at all, "a monstrous retribution of sound, the mindless roar of things in motion, on the meddlesome mind of man." The audience stares at their feet "as if deeply impressed."

The Characters

James Chandler, who is dead at the beginning of the book, is a philosopher mainly concerned with metaphysics and aesthetics. Since the prologue opens with four women visiting his grave (his mother, his widow, his oldest daughter, and Viola Staley), one feels he was justified in asking questions about ultimate reality—indeed, from chapter 1, he has known he was dying. He is a man who loves, but he feels continually that he does not give people their due, especially those closest to him. His thoughts about various issues in his life's work intersperse the book, as do new thoughts raised by his immediate situation and by his visit to his old town, his former piano teacher, his father's workshop, and John Horne. Like John Gardner in appearance, Chandler also resembles him in his mystical tendencies and his interest in issues that logical positivists would say are nonsense.

Maria Chandler is an intelligent woman uninterested in her husband's work. She worries what meals will be nutritious for him in his last days and wonders where she will rear their daughters after his death. She is the sort who make the living of a decent life possible for the James Chandlers of the world.

Karen, Susan, and Anne Chandler are too young to do much more than be girls, though Karen already is showing signs of becoming serious-minded. She asks Viola if there is a God, and she notices much, including how people play various games, in some of which she leads her sisters. Anne is owl-faced like her father, and he worries that she may be like him in other ways.

Rose Chandler, James's mother, is an ordinary woman who has lived her life in and near Batavia. She has put up with a husband whose shop always just made it; James's father was himself a tinkerer, though with things rather than ideas, so there was precedent for their son.

The Staley sisters all are old maids now watched after by their brother's daughter, but they once were the artistic center of the old Batavia. Although the singing teacher is now deaf and the painting sister is demented, the pianist sister still gives lessons, and the preparations for her annual recital resonate through the book. Its occurrence serves as the novel's conclusion.

Viola Staley, a young woman stuck with taking care of her aunts, is bitter about her lot, but she is capable of growth and change after she finds in James Chandler someone to love, though he is long in realizing the importance of her gift. Through her association with the Chandler family, she reverses a dementia and reclusiveness that seemed at first inevitable.

John Horne is grotesque in every sense. His face is distorted by disease, and his mind is concerned with questions normally encountered only in college courses in philosophy. He serves to show that Chandler is not alone in his questionings. Also, he empties out the bucket of ideas that Gardner wants emptied, without having Chandler do it; such a role would overload the character of the professional philosopher. Horne will talk to anyone who will listen, or pretend to; through him, it all gets said.

Themes and Meanings

John Gardner was a mystic, three-quarters Welsh and proud of the skepticism that Welsh people have always had of the more literal-minded English. Chandler, a philosopher, can raise all the transcendental questions the author wants to, offering no final enlightenment about such matters, except insofar as Chandler is himself resurrected at the end of the book: Just before he dies, he makes loving contact with another person for perhaps the first time when he grasps the naked foot of the waiting Viola. She had only a short time before told him of her love, and he had suggested they have a cup of coffee; crushed, she had run away. Yet her love for him has resurrected her, too, from a life that was apparently spiraling downward, certainly into depression and perhaps into madness.

John Horne is a brilliant man who, like Chandler, is ill, but who in counterpoint comes up only with nihilism as a response. He is unable to break from the life of the mind to enter meaningfully into the life of the world; even his work had been as a librarian of law rather than as a practicing attorney.

Because Gardner writes *The Resurrection* mainly from the third-person-limited perspective but tells the story from multiple points of view, readers see that most people are not really aware of what they themselves need, of how they are perceived. Nor, the book shows, do people often communicate—enter communion—with anyone else, or with themselves.

Critical Context

The Resurrection was John Gardner's first novel. While the book was received more favorably than most first novels, Gardner's later works did better in that regard, and it was not until after the author's death that a critical reassessment of his work began. *The Resurrection* is now viewed as the novel in which Gardner sets forth his concern for the primacy of art, especially as a way of bringing apparent order out of apparent chaos. This is the "moral" task Gardner set for himself, a task he wished others also would follow.

Gardner's comparatively short career—he was killed in a motorcycle accident before he was fifty—was extremely prolific. He published widely in long and short fiction, wrote the libretto for an opera, did children's stories, and was a prominent critic, especially of medieval subjects.

Bibliography

Butts, Leonard. *The Novels of John Gardner: Making Life Art as a Moral Process.* Baton Rouge: Louisiana State University Press, 1988. Commentary on *The Resurrection* shares an entire chapter with discussion of Gardner's *Mickelsson's Ghosts* (1982). Butts notes that the former generally has been overlooked and often is condemned for being overly philosophical; however, he says, it succeeds where Gardner's *On Moral Fiction* (1978) fails, in that it convincingly asserts the primacy of art over philosophy.

Cowart, David. *Arches and Light: The Fiction of John Gardner.* Carbondale: Southern Illinois University Press, 1983. Gardner is seen as having tried through art to make the world a better place, focusing not on God as artist but on the human artist. If this is so, *The Resurrection* is a first statement of Gardner's intent, which his later works illustrate in one way or another.

Ficken, Carl. "Structure, Point-of-View, and Themes in John Gardner's *The Resurrection*." In *John Gardner: True Art, Moral Art*, edited by Beatrice Mendez-Egle. Edinburg, Tex.: School of Humanities, Pan American University, 1983. Ficken claims that the shifting from omniscient point of view to the limited third person is integral to the novel. Ficken also observes that Chandler's name (which means "candlemaker") suggests his desire to shed light and other niceties.

Gardner, John. *Conversations with John Gardner*, edited by Allan Chavkin. Jackson: University Press of Mississippi, 1990. A collection of twenty interviews from 1971 to 1980. Gardner discusses all of his works, including *The Resurrection*, and his remarks make clear how much James Chandler is like his creator.

McWilliams, Dean. *John Gardner*. Boston: Twayne, 1990. The basic events and dates in the author's life are surveyed here, as are his major works. In *The Resurrection*, McWilliams sees as particularly significant Gardner's dialogic approach.

Morris, Gregory L. *A World of Order and Light*. Athens: University of Georgia Press, 1984. An overview of Gardner's work that contains a lengthy chapter on *The Resurrection*. What Chandler is looking for, Morris argues, is design in creation—ironic for one dying of a disease caused by cells going mad. Morris sees Chandler's death at Viola's feet as a virtual suicide, totally egoistic, and unheeded by the girl, who is "catastrophe fleshed out."

J. H. Bowden

RESUSCITATION OF A HANGED MAN

Author: Denis Johnson (1949-   )
Type of plot: Psychological realism
Time of plot: 1980-1981
Locale: Cape Cod, Massachusetts
First published: 1991

> *Principal characters:*
> LEONARD ENGLISH, the protagonist, a man suffering from spiritual crisis
> LEANNA SOUSA, his bisexual lover
> RAY SANDS, the former police detective who hires Leonard
> PHIL, a local taxi driver whose occasional gossip fuels Leonard's paranoia
> GERALD TWINBROOK, the missing artist Leonard is hired to find
> BERRYMAN, the reporter Sands fires

The Novel

Resuscitation of a Hanged Man is a story about the search for faith and redemption in a chaotic and uncertain world. The book is divided into four sections, and Leonard English's quest for redemption follows some of the conventions of a detective story. The first section covers Leonard's arrival in Provincetown, on Cape Cod, at the end of 1980; the second covers most of the next year, during which time Ray Sands dies from a heart attack and Leonard becomes increasingly obsessed with the case of a missing artist named Gerald Twinbrook. In the third section of the book, "May-June," Leonard finds Twinbrook but fails to find the absolution he is seeking. Twinbrook died when he hanged himself, but without faith he cannot be reborn. In "Last Days," the final section of the book, Leonard finds salvation in jail, having tried to redeem himself in a failed attempt to assassinate the local bishop. In his punishment—imprisonment—he finds the order and certainty he has been seeking.

Leonard arrives in Provincetown, a popular summer resort, during the off season. His arrival is hardly propitious: He wrecks his car and has to be driven into town in a taxi. He has come to work at two part-time jobs, one as a radio announcer and the other as a private investigator. His boss, Ray Sands, a former police detective, runs both the radio station and a private-detective agency in town. Leonard is not only here for the jobs; he is running from his failed suicide attempt and a crisis in faith.

His first day in Provincetown reveals a town full of transvestites and homosexuals. Already, Leonard's shaky sense of self is challenged. He makes an unsuccessful confession at the local church, where he also meets Leanna Sousa, with whom he falls in love instantly. Leanna, however, is a lesbian and appears to be uninterested in Leonard.

Leonard's first assignment is to follow Marla Baker, who turns out to be Leanna's lover. Overcome with guilt and disgust at his own corruption, Leonard puts an end to the investigation by writing an anonymous note to Marla, letting her know that she is being followed. Shortly after that, Marla leaves town, and Leonard becomes involved with Leanna.

Through a reporter at the radio station, whom Ray Sands fires, Leonard hears about a paramilitary group called the Truth Infantry. After Sands dies, Leonard learns that he was the head of the Truth Infantry. Shortly after Sands's death, Leonard is inexplicably kidnapped and brutally beaten. Resuming his search for Gerald Twinbrook, he finds Twinbrook's notes on the 1870 resuscitation of a hanged man by two doctors. The man was a criminal, but reading the accounts of his resuscitation, Leonard wonders if he was really the victim.

Looking for meaning in unrelated events, he starts to see connections between the Truth Infantry, his kidnapping, Ray Sands, and Gerald Twinbrook. Leonard begins to believe that God is trying to get a message to him and that if Leonard can act on the "inner rebop," if he "can follow every impulse as if it started from God," perhaps he will be healed. Within this framework, he understands that nothing is a coincidence: Everything that happens is part of God's plan for him.

By the "May-June" section of the book, the beginning of the tourist season, Leonard is becoming more and more paranoid. He can no longer deal with Leanna, who has taken up with Marla again yet wants to continue seeing him. Leonard traces Twinbrook to Franconia, New Hampshire, the headquarters of the Truth Infantry. Trekking up to their campsite, Leonard finds Twinbrook hanging from a tree. He has succeeded where Leonard failed. From this moment on, Leonard crosses the thin line between spiritual fervor and insanity.

Leonard returns to Provincetown, dresses in Leanna's clothes, and goes to church to seek absolution one more time. Calling himself "May-June," he tells the priest that he is in disguise. By now, Leonard's assumptions—about his sexuality and his religion, about death and life—have been stripped from him. In one of the novel's more bizarre and hallucinatory scenes, replete with crucifixion imagery, Leonard makes his way to the water; in a final act of redemption, he shoots at the local bishop, but he misses.

The Characters

Leonard is characterized by his actions and thoughts. The story is told in the third person from his point of view. From the beginning, the reader understands Leonard as a desperate man, one who is searching for something he probably will not find. Although Leonard is not a saint—he is drunk when he arrives in Provincetown and wrecks his car—he is a spiritual innocent. He has lost his faith, yet he still believes that he can redeem himself and find forgiveness for his actions. Like Dorothy in the film *The Wizard of Oz* (1939), he has come from Kansas to a place seeking what he cannot find in himself; as in Oz, everything that is mundane and normal for Provincetown takes on a sinister meaning for Leonard. Leonard's greatest weakness and strength, as pointed out by a reader of auras, is his ability to empathize with others. His ability becomes a problem only when he starts to empathize with imaginary situations.

Leanna Sousa, one of Leonard's objects of redemption, is a local woman descended from Portuguese immigrants who settled the area. She runs a hotel, and while she initially tells Leonard that she is a lesbian, once Marla leaves town, she is quick to sleep with Leonard. As presented, this switch is not very convincing; Leanna is reduced to another element of Leonard's confusion. Leanna's bisexuality and the apparent ease with which she accommodates both Leonard and Marla in her life are unexplained; Leonard is unable to pin her down. The scenes between them best illustrate her elusiveness and the strangeness of their relationship.

Ray Sands, a former police detective, is seen by Leonard as two bosses—one at home, from where he runs his detective agency, and another at WPRD, the radio station. He seems to find nothing morally questionable about the spying he has Leonard doing, yet it is difficult for Leonard to judge him, especially after seeing the mild way he treats his unpredictable, possibly senile wife Grace. They have been married for forty-two years, and Sands knows how to "love without hope." Around the radio station, however, Sands behaves with the stupidity of "the boss," irrationally firing a reporter for no reason Leonard can see. Again, Sands is not what he appears to be; after his death, Leonard discovers three false passports in his desk and comes to believe that he was the head of the Truth Infantry.

Gerald Twinbrook is dead, but as a character, he functions as another paradox in Leonard's life. Like Leanna, Twinbrook is an object of redemption; if Leonard can find him, perhaps he will be able to make meaning of his own life. His obsession with death and resuscitation gives the novel its title and core; through his notes, Leonard finds a kindred soul, one who talks to him in his paranoid imagination, giving him the guidance for which he longs.

Themes and Meanings

There are many themes explored in the novel, most connected by biblical and religious references. Johnson's main point, around which all of Leonard's actions and discoveries evolve, is to question the purpose of life. For Leonard, the quest for personal redemption brings him to Provincetown and dictates much of what he does in the book. He cannot die until he has justified his life, found some meaning in his actions, and redeemed himself in the eyes of God. As a Catholic whose faith has failed him, however, he is searching for absolutes in a world, Provincetown, where everything is inverted. Men might be men, or they might be women dressed as men; the woman he falls in love with is a lesbian; Ray Sands, a former policeman and keeper of justice, is the head of a paramilitary organization and has three false passports in his desk; even the priest from whom Leonard seeks absolution is gay.

From Leonard's point of view, the town is both absurd and corrupt. Simple, mundane elements are magnified; he looks for significance where there is none, searching for meaning in external events that mirror his inner confusion. One of Leonard's first actions on arriving in Provincetown is to go to Mass and seek absolution, but he finds himself unable to make a "committed" confession. He falls instantly in love with Leanna, whom he meets at church. She is "strictly P-town," yet

Leonard pursues her. Perhaps he can redeem her, sexually, and in so doing redeem himself. His obsessive search for Twinbrook also shows how important redemption is to Leonard.

The issue of death, as part of life, is also important. The title for the novel comes from Leonard's investigation of Twinbrook. Twinbrook was obsessed with an experiment by two doctors in the nineteenth century who attempted to resuscitate a hanged man using electricity. Although the man is brought back to life—his heart beats, he breathes, and he responds to light—he cannot speak. He is alive, but he has not been reborn. A man who cannot speak or hear has no faith and therefore has no life. In this, Johnson questions the restoration of life to the dead and whether such a life is worth living. Leonard cannot articulate his reasons for committing suicide. He did die when he hanged himself, but he has not been reborn, because his assumptions about himself and his church have failed him.

Leonard experiences death on many levels—emotional death, moral death (when he finds himself spying on Leanna and her lover as part of an investigation), the death of his identity, and the death of his assumptions about the world. Johnson shows the thin line between religious fervor and insanity, and how a religious framework can be used to give meaning to seemingly random events. It is a dangerous impulse that can be used to justify the actions of saints and mass murderers alike, as Leonard shows in the end.

The metaphors and imagery in the novel reflect these concerns. Johnson relies on references to the Bible, Christ, and martyrs such as Simone Weil to develop Leonard's obsession. As Leonard comes to see himself as a Christ figure toward the end of the book, images of crucifixion and light come into play. The last section of the book, entitled "The Last Days," further echoes the last days of Christ, describing Leonard's final sense of redemption as he finds comfort and peace in the ordered life of the prison.

Critical Context

Resuscitation of a Hanged Man is Johnson's fourth novel and continues his exploration into the spiritual lives of characters living on the edge of mainstream America. Johnson's four collections of poetry and previous novels have focused on misfits, people who cannot speak for themselves or articulate their experiences of life.

Johnson began his career as a poet, receiving recognition at an early age. When he was nineteen, his first collection, *The Man Among the Seals* (1969), attracted substantial critical attention, and his third collection, *The Incognito Lounge and Other Poems* (1982), was a National Poetry series selection. Yet Johnson always wanted to be a novelist, and in 1983 his first novel, *Angels*, was published. *Resuscitation of a Hanged Man* firmly established Johnson as a serious contemporary writer remarkable for the complexity and depth of the material he tackles in his work. In 1992, he published a collection of short stories, *Jesus' Son*.

Johnson uses bizarre, freakish characters and incidents as more than trendy window dressing in his fiction. Through them, he explores the chaos and corruption of a modern society lacking a spiritual core. Johnson's skill lies in making characters such as Leanna and Leonard's crazed kidnappers transcend the absurd and sometimes incredible aspects of the novel.

Critics have remarked on Johnson's fascination with such grotesque characters, suggesting that it is perhaps gratuitous, serving no function in his work. Yet Johnson believes that his concerns about redemption, punishment, death, and rebirth are best explored with depictions of people who are not ordinary but who live on the edge, their lives unstable and transient.

Interestingly, Johnson himself did not have a religious upbringing. In fact, his childhood was marked by a distinct absence of any kind of discussion of spirituality. His sense of God as an "audience"—a "future agency" looking down on humanity, with understanding and forgiveness—grew over time, in relation to his writing. Johnson has said that the only thing worth trying "is to try to reconcile the ways of God to man." *Resuscitation of a Hanged Man* reflects Johnson's understanding of death, rebirth, heaven, and hell on this plane, rather than in some distant hereafter.

Over the years, Johnson's work has appeared in popular magazines such as *The New Yorker*, the *Atlantic*, and *Esquire*, and his popularity as a writer continues to grow. Johnson rarely grants interviews, preferring to let his work speak for itself.

Bibliography
Hull, Lynda, and David Wojahn. "The Kind of Light I'm Seeing: An Interview with Denis Johnson." *Ironwood* 13 (Spring, 1985): 31-44. A rare interview with Johnson, who discusses his development as a writer and talks about the religious themes in his poetry and fiction. Although the interview is dated, much of what he says is relevant to his more recent work.
Elie, Paul. "The Shape of Distant Things." *Commonweal* 118 (September 13, 1991): 522-523. Elie sees the novel as a provocative yet odd "work of religious art." He talks about the paradoxes in the story, the "double-edge of sanctity and insanity." The focus of the review is Johnson's skill as a novelist who refuses to distance himself from his characters.
Krist, Gary. "Cape Hell." *The New Republic* 204 (June 3, 1991): 41-42. Krist briefly analyzes the themes of Johnson's previous work, arguing that Johnson's concern with how the religious impulse "operates in . . . a context of spiritual catastrophe" is a recurrent theme in his work. Krist concludes that the novel "raises large doubts about the possibility of faith in any world like our own."

Geeta Kothari

ROGER'S VERSION

Author: John Updike (1932-　　)
Type of work: Novel
Type of plot: Novel of ideas
Time of plot: 1984-1985
Locale: An unnamed New England city
First published: 1986

>   *Principal characters:*
>   ROGER LAMBERT, a divinity-school professor
>   ESTHER LAMBERT, Roger's current wife
>   DALE KOHLER, a graduate student in computer science
>   VERNA EKELOF, Roger's niece, a single mother who lives in a housing
>   project in the same city as the Lamberts
>   PAULA EKELOF, Verna's illegitimate two-year-old daughter

The Novel

John Updike's long-standing interest in religious issues and his continuing fascination with human sexual behavior are combined in this novel set in New England, the landscape that admirably served an earlier American novelist, Nathaniel Hawthorne, for his investigation of similar subjects in his American classic *The Scarlet Letter* (1850). Told from the point of view of Roger Lambert, the novel presents an intriguing narrative of modern concerns with science and theology. Lambert, a divinity-school professor married for the second time and living happily in an older suburb near the university, is approached by Dale Kohler, a graduate student in computer sciences at the same institution. Dale wants Roger's support in obtaining funding for a most unusual project: He wishes to use the university's computer to prove the existence of God. After an impassioned conversation, Roger provides Dale with the information he needs to seek a grant from the theology school.

Dale has sought out Roger at the suggestion of Roger's niece, Verna Ekelof. The daughter of Roger's half-sister, Verna has fled the family home in Cleveland with her illegitimate mulatto child. Roger has had nothing to do with his niece, but at Dale's insistence, he visits her; he is immediately attracted to her sexually, and the worldly-wise Verna takes advantage of his interest to manipulate him throughout the novel.

Roger's efforts to help Verna finish her education provide him with opportunities to see her, and their family ties make it easy for him to invite her to Thanksgiving dinner. Dale receives an invitation, too, and Roger's wife Esther immediately takes a strong interest in the computer-science student. During the remaining months of winter, Dale prepares his materials to seek the grant, Roger continues to assist Verna in several ways, including financially, and—in Roger's mind, at least—Esther and Dale engage in an affair, using the third-floor studio in the Lambert home or the slovenly student apartment where Dale lives with his Korean roommate.

In February, the Grants Committee awards Dale his grant, and his search for the proof of God's existence begins in earnest. Roger imagines the graduate student seated before his computer screen, manipulating data, cross-referencing information, searching for patterns that might suggest an intelligent being at the seat of creation. Excited by the repetitions of certain combinations, Dale presses on until first a face, then a hand, emerges on the screen—then the computer overloads and shuts itself down.

While this investigation goes on, Verna's situation at home deteriorates. Lambert is called one evening in the spring to come immediately to Verna's apartment, because her daughter Paula is apparently ill. Roger discovers a clear case of child abuse; he takes charge of the situation, delivers mother and daughter to the hospital, and then tries to make excuses for Verna with the doctors and social workers. When Verna is forced to leave the girl overnight at the hospital, Roger takes her back to her apartment, and the two finally make love.

After the consummation of Roger's physical attraction to his niece, the novel moves quickly toward its conclusion. Dale decides to give up his project, claiming that it has eroded his faith; his affair with Esther seems to wane, too. Roger helps Verna come to the conclusion that it would be better for her to return to her mother in Cleveland. In the final scene, Roger and his wife have returned to what is for them a normal lifestyle; the twin crises in their lives, caused by the intrusion of the two young people who have placed unusual and competing demands on them, is apparently over. All is not as it was before Dale Kohler and Verna Ekelof entered the picture, however; Esther is pregnant, presumably with Dale's child. Roger is left to accept this permanent alteration in their lives.

The Characters

Roger Lambert is both narrator and principal subject of this novel. As narrator, he serves as the medium through which events in the story are filtered, and his unusual capacity for self-reflection allows readers significant insight into his character. It also nudges readers to adopt his opinions of other characters, however, which may be at variance with the truth. A former pastor and now divinity-school professor, he represents the attitude of many Americans toward religion: For him it has become a form of social psychology and an intellectual exercise, divorced from any of the fervor of faith that characterized believers in earlier ages. He is uncomfortable when a devout believer such as Dale Kohler accosts his complacency. Nevertheless, the author creates him with sufficient sympathy for the reader to see him as a typical Updike hero: a complex individual struggling with desires of both the spirit and the flesh.

Esther Lambert is less well developed, largely because she is seen only through the eyes of her husband. A woman possessed of courage, she is willing to brook social convention to steal Roger from his first wife (ruining his work as a pastor in the process) and then to take up with Dale to fulfill a sexual appetite that her husband cannot satisfy. Though certainly not devoid of intelligence, she serves primarily as a complement to Roger's overindulgence in intellectual pursuits.

Dale Kohler is a true believer in God; his passion for seeking the deity stands in contrast with Roger's cool, analytical approach to religious questions. The young computer-science student's idealistic—and ultimately unsuccessful—attempt to use scientific knowledge (in this case, the power of the computer) to demonstrate with certainty that God is not a figment of the human imagination is both a typical application of the scientific method and an extension of a long philosophical and theological proof for God's existence.

Verna Ekelof, like Esther, complements Roger's intellectual side in that she is almost totally sensual. A rebellious young adult who has defied parents and social custom by becoming an unwed mother through an interracial relationship, she serves as a living reminder to Roger that he has yearnings of the flesh that are as powerful as his desire to explore the ideas and idiosyncrasies of heretics who influenced the Christian church in its early centuries. She also reminds Roger that he has responsibilities to society that extend beyond the domain of the university at which he earns a comfortable living.

Though not a fully developed character, Paula Ekelof, Verna's illegitimate daughter, serves important functions in the novel. She plays a key role in the plot, since her presence drives Verna to the housing project. She is also the proximate cause of Roger's lovemaking with his niece, since Verna's abuse of Paula causes Roger to leave his home in the middle of the night to help his niece cope with her problem.

Themes and Meanings

In *Roger's Version*, John Updike develops a complex narrative interweaving several themes. Primary among them is the investigation of modern religious beliefs. It is no accident that Roger Lambert's specialty at the divinity school is the exploration of heresies. His comfortable view of God as totally Other and unknowable is challenged by Dale Kohler's curious brand of fundamental assent to the literal tenets of the Bible coupled with his conviction that God can be discovered through the use of sophisticated computer technology. The conflict is more than a simple test of wills between individuals: Kohler's approach to the proof of God's existence is an extension of the scientific community's method of discovering the nature of all reality. In exhibiting an intense dislike for Dale, and in manipulating the younger man's research efforts to discredit and discourage him, Roger is actually representing a religious community that still feels threatened by advances in science. He cannot accept the notion that science might in some way help support the tenets of theology.

The novel is also an investigation of modern domestic relations and of people's sexual needs. Roger appears on first meeting to be a happily married man; readers learn as the story progresses, however, that his earlier affair with Esther led to the breakup of his first marriage and to the loss of his position as a pastor. Nevertheless, Roger and Esther's conventional life in the quiet suburb near the university is set in contrast to that of his niece Verna, who lives as a single mother with her illegitimate mulatto daughter in a housing project populated by economically deprived African Americans. Though neither Roger nor Esther really feels comfortable with Verna, they find that they must take some responsibility for her welfare; they are the only family she has who can come to her aid when she is in need.

Additionally, each of the four main characters in the work is driven toward sexual gratification. Even though the novel is told from Roger's point of view, there is sufficient evidence that Dale, Verna, and Esther seek physical as well as intellectual satisfaction in their lives. Roger is preoccupied with sexual activity—his own and other people's. Try as he might to convince readers that he is an intellectual being, he proves by his thoughts—and later by his actions—that even a clergyman is a prisoner of his libido. The message from Updike is clear: Every person is both soul and body, and there is no escape from this inextricable linkage that makes people human.

Critical Context

Roger's Version is the middle novel in a trilogy Updike wrote as an extended commentary on Nathaniel Hawthorne's *The Scarlet Letter*. Hawthorne's story of religious intolerance and sexual repression is for Updike a profound commentary on the American character. Over a thirteen-year period, Updike wrote three novels, each focusing on these topics from the point of view of a character modeled on one of the three principal personages in Hawthorne's tale: the adulteress Hester Prynne, whose character is reprised in Sarah Worth in the novel *S.* (1988); her lover, the respected minister Arthur Dimmesdale, recast as Tom Marshfield in *A Month of Sundays* (1975); and the relentless persecutor of Hester and Dimmesdale, Roger Chillingsworth, the model for Roger Lambert in *Roger's Version*. As in almost all of his works, Updike focuses on the domestic scene, detailing the lives of everyday middle-class people struggling with their sexual desires and with a feeling of *angst* brought on by a modern world which has turned its back on God and is much the worse for having done so. The characters in this novel share many similarities with others in the Updike canon. In several ways, Roger is an intellectual version of Harry "Rabbit" Angstrom, principal character of four Updike novels which also examine people's preoccupation with their sexual desires and their anxieties about the significance of their lives.

Bibliography

Duvall, John N. "The Pleasures of Textual/Sexual Wrestling: Pornography and Heresy in *Roger's Version*." *Modern Fiction Studies* 37 (Spring, 1991): 81-95. A poststructuralist analysis of the novel focusing on Roger's unconscious erotic relationship with Dale. Duvall points out parallels between Roger's interest in theology and pornography. He also traces the novel's relationship to Hawthorne's *The Scarlet Letter*.

Greiner, Donald J. "Body and Soul: John Updike and *The Scarlet Letter*." *Journal of Modern Literature* 15 (Spring, 1989): 475-495. Greiner discusses the ways Updike uses Hawthorne's *The Scarlet Letter* as the basis for his discussion of modern American mores and interests in three novels: *Roger's Version, A Month of Sundays*, and *S.* He highlights similarities between Updike's hero and Hawthorne's Chillingsworth. Greiner argues that the novel is about "sexuality and the frantic effort to contain it."

Lodge, David. "Chasing After God and Sex." *The New York Times Book Review* 91 (August 31, 1986): 1, 15. Lodge remarks on five distinct strands in the novel: theological debate, interest in pornography, domestic behavior, physical description, and scientific inquiry. He believes that Updike blends these five strands into an interesting account of modern life but notes that there are some difficulties created by the use of the first-person narrator, who seems to know more than he should about events to which he is not privy.

Neary, John. *Something and Nothingness: The Fiction of John Updike and John Fowles.* Carbondale, Ill.: Southern Illinois University Press, 1992. Describes the reaction to the novel by several early reviewers. Neary argues that Roger is not really Barthian in his views; rather, the novel presents a Gnostic portrait of the deity. Though Roger manages to crush Dale's spirit, the younger man's optimism lives on in the transformation Esther undergoes.

Newman, Judie. *John Updike.* New York: St. Martin's Press, 1988. Newman briefly summarizes the main action and shows how Updike has carefully crafted his narrative strategies to highlight his themes, theology and technology. Though the story is told from Roger's point of view, Updike employs a "collective protagonist," mathematically opposing and combining the characters in a novel which stresses the mechanical nature of modern life. The work displays Updike's belief in the "indeterminacy of existence."

Sage, Lorna. "Narrator-Creator." *The Times Literary Supplement,* October 24, 1986, 1189. A brief review stressing the stylistic qualities of the novel and Updike's use of a self-reflective narrator. Sage comments on the novel's treatment of the godlessness of modern life. She believes that Updike is more concerned with style and technique than with writing a great novel.

Wilson, Raymond J., III. "*Roger's Version*: Updike's Negative-Solid Model of *The Scarlet Letter.*" *Modern Fiction Studies* 35 (Summer, 1989): 241-250. Wilson discusses the many parallels between Updike's novel and Hawthorne's romance. He delineates ways *Roger's Version* is more complex than its predecessor; he also demonstrates how Updike transforms Hawthorne's tragedy into a comic vision of life.

Laurence W. Mazzeno

ROLL OF THUNDER, HEAR MY CRY

Author: Mildred D. Taylor (1943-   )
Type of plot: Historical realism
Time of plot: 1933-1934
Locale: Rural Mississippi
First published: 1976

> *Principal characters:*
> CASSIE LOGAN, the nine-year-old only daughter of a black family in rural
>   Mississippi during the Depression
> STACEY LOGAN, the twelve-year-old eldest son in the Logan family
> CHRISTOPHER JOHN LOGAN, the cheerful, sensitive, and passive seven-
>   year-old middle son
> CLAYTON CHESTER LOGAN, nicknamed "Little Man," a bright six-year-
>   old boy
> MARY LOGAN, the mother of the four Logan children, a teacher
> DAVID LOGAN, the Logan children's father
> BIG MA, David Logan's sixty-year-old mother, who helps to care for the
>   children
> T. J. AVERY, a fourteen-year-old schoolmate of Stacey
> LILLIAN JEAN SIMMS, an adolescent white girl
> KALEB and THURSTON WALLACE, white brothers who run the local
>   grocery store by day and lead the Ku Klux Klan by night

The Novel

Based to a large extent on Mildred D. Taylor's experience as a child visiting relatives in Mississippi, *Roll of Thunder, Hear My Cry* depicts the many dimensions of the racism of the Deep South in the 1930's. The Logan family is a strong, close-knit black family struggling to keep their four hundred acres of land during the hard times of the Depression. Against the forces of national economic catastrophe and intense social prejudice, they fight for the survival of their nuclear family, for freedom from racially motivated attacks, and for better educations and adequate livelihoods.

In the first of twelve chapters that encompass a year in the family's life and in the community's turmoil, Cassie Logan and her brothers, in their Sunday best, take the several-mile walk to The Great Faith Elementary and Secondary School, the large segregated school where black children begin their new school year in October after the cotton picking is finished. Cassie's education in the harsh realities of the bigotry of her society begins. The open animosity of whites; the pervasive institutionalized racism in schools, commerce, and laws; and the nighttime violence of vicious vigilante gangs form the cultural context for her growth from innocence to experience. In the next few months of watching, listening, feeling, and thinking, she becomes aware for the first time of the importance that white people give to skin color, and she gradually recognizes how stifled the voices and lives of her family members truly are.

In the geography of racial hatred, rural Mississippi in the 1930's is both homeland and heartland. Terror rules the day-to-day lives of black men and women, from the small-time intimidations of the white children's schoolbus to the cold-blooded murders that go unacknowledged and unpunished. Cassie and her brothers seek what is "fair," and the innocent child's insistence on fairness grows into the adult's desire for social justice. Stacey finds some secret fairness when they ambush the schoolbus, and Cassie finds satisfaction in her carefully orchestrated but hidden revenge on Lillian Jean Simms. Public justice, however, for the Berry family, the Barnetts, or T. J. Avery cannot be achieved. Cassie learns and keeps unspeakable secrets. Nine-year-old Cassie tells her story in first-person narration; it is the story of her education in the dangerous consequences of speech and her lessons in when to keep silent.

The warm bonds of love in the Logan family, their pains and their hopes, their individual and collective strength, and their intelligence and principled behavior are particularly dramatic in a novel in which white characters are few and villainous. One black character, T. J. Avery, seems a scoundrel, but next to the heinous crimes of the white people—the Wallaces and the Simmses—T. J.'s crimes seem petty and child-like.

The new year, 1934, brings an escalation of violence in the community as David Logan, Cassie's father, is shot and his leg broken in a late-night Klan attack. The threat of danger to the Logan family has built continually, but through what seems to be a combination of cleverness and good luck they escape any more serious physical harm.

The climactic eleventh and twelfth chapters, in which T. J. is captured and beaten and is then saved from lynching by David Logan's arson, open with a preface that sounds like a traditional spiritual. The first lines are an invocation, the enigmatic phrases of the novel's title, "Roll of thunder/ hear my cry"; the last lines express determined defiance of the "Ole man" and his whip. This preface to the closing chapters connects the powers of physical nature with the eruption of personal pain into expression. The physical forces of fire and rain are connected in Cassie's mind to the unbearable onslaught of yet more violence and wronging of her race as she watches and responds to the terror of that last night of her childhood.

The Characters

Cassie Logan's innocence allows the reader to experience racial intolerance in the pure light of her naïveté and thereby to share her dawning consciousness of its violence, horror, and injustice. Expecting to gain knowledge of herself and others from books, she instead discovers "the way of things" in the physical and emotional violence of her racially dichotomous society. The reader follows her progress through a hazardous course in how to survive in a world hostile to one's very skin. Like many books for the young, this novel shows issues in black and white, but here that does not make them simpler. Cassie undergoes a rite of passage from the simplicity of family unity to the complexity of the fear and fury of racial discord. Yet the positive values instilled in her by her family live on. Her family's support and love seem to strengthen in the face of adversity. Paradoxically, with new experience and new knowledge gained, Cassie's loss is profound. Her closing words are elegiac; she weeps and laments both the injuries done T. J. and the injuries done the land.

Stacey Logan, Cassie's eldest brother, also matures in the course of this year. A moody, serious twelve-year-old, he is a typical enough young adolescent to be chagrined that his own mother is his seventh-grade teacher. He learns important lessons about loyalty, friendship, and responsibility. In his father's absence, he strives to be the head of his household. He evolves from acting according to a blind allegiance to his friends (as when he refuses to betray T. J.'s cheating at school) to reasoned accountability for his own actions, as when he confesses to his mother that he has broken his promise not to go to the Wallaces' store.

Christopher John Logan is unlike both his brothers and his sister in his passivity. Even on the night of T. J.'s beating and the fire on the Logan land, he refuses to budge from the house. He makes no waves; he sees no evil. Six-year-old Clayton Chester Logan, "Little Man," seems to have been born an adult. A compulsion for neatness in his personal grooming extends to an insistence on logic and order in the world around him. The incident of the dirty book on the first day of class not only reveals his intelligence, pride, and fierceness but also dramatizes Cassie's caring and generosity.

Mary Logan, a strong, protective mother, has worked for fourteen years as a teacher. She is horrified by the burnings of three members of the Berry family. She responds by organizing a boycott of the Wallace store, because the Wallaces seem to be behind such acts of violence. She is a positive role model for her children as a loving person, a well-educated professional, and a socially concerned member of her community willing to sacrifice for principles and the betterment of the community.

David Logan is a hardworking and gentle man forced to leave his family in order to support them. His greatest pride is the four hundred acres of "Logan land." The land holds the roots of his family and literally and figuratively nourishes their future. His children's love and admiration for him are boundless. His strength as a provider, his devotion to his family, and his cunning and courage in the face of mortal danger counter stereotypes of the irresponsible self-involved black male.

T. J. Avery, a fourteen-year-old con man and petty thief, gets into trouble when he falls for the exploitive flattery of two young white men. Although T. J. is disliked and distrusted by virtually everyone, his punishment far exceeds the weight of his crime. He is duped into helping to rob a store. His companions attack and kill Mr. Barnett, one of the owners, and then frame T. J. for the crime. After a bad beating and a narrow escape from lynching, T. J. is thrown in jail, in all likelihood to be hanged for murder. The final and greatest injustice of the novel is T. J.'s fate. Although T. J. is not guiltless, he is no murderer; the fact that he is a child and a dupe of the real murderers creates the kind of moral complexity that Cassie is coming to recognize and trying to understand.

Uncle Hammer Logan, David's brother, has fled the racism and poverty of the Deep South for the freer and more profitable streets of Chicago. Although he is hot-tempered, this Logan male also exemplifies positive qualities of caring, personal courage, and responsibility.

Themes and Meanings

The title *Roll of Thunder, Hear My Cry* symbolizes the novel's focus on the cataclysmic events which wash over the Logan family and their small rural community. Their pain, expressed in both cries of grief and cries of protest, comes from a rising consciousness of the oppression and injustice dominating their individual, family, and social existence.

Cassie's year-long transformation and her new awareness of injustice and modes of resistance prefigure the beginnings of a new society-wide consciousness and emerging resistance to oppressions. The acts of resistance to injustices by the Logan family and their neighbors foreshadow the nationwide active and vocal opposition to racial discrimination during the Civil Rights movement a few decades later.

Education is a central concern of this novel. Formal education is a travesty in Cassie's community. Authorial outrage is implicit in Little Man's rage at the condition of his book, and the cowardice and cruelty of his teacher speak for themselves. These children's education is separate but not at all equal to that of the white children a few steps away at Jefferson Davis County School, with its buses, sports field, and fluttering Confederate flag. The larger and more vital education for Cassie and her brothers takes place outside the classroom: They learn how dangerous their world is and acquire some strategies for staying alive.

The rising action of the plot builds a clear sense of threat to the well-being of the Logan family. Only in the last two chapters is the tension released in the frenzy of violence and fear at the Avery house, where all the disparate forces in the community confront one another. The sharecroppers are torn from their home and subjected to the blows of the night riders. The attack is led by the actual murderers of Mr. Barnett, now intent on destroying Avery.

The novel skillfully escapes sentimentality and predictability. Taylor's style and characterization, although accessible to young readers, are quite sophisticated. Although moral and social issues may be somewhat simplified (as they would be in a nine-year-old's perceptions), universal truths shine through. The novel's close does not sugarcoat the injustice and does not suggest that everyone will live happily ever after. With her eyes now opened, Cassie is entering a world of clear and present danger. What she has learned of racism in the classroom is on display on a large scale in her community's stores, streets, and churches. Black men can be lynched, torched, and beaten; they can be robbed of their livelihood, possessions, human rights, human dignity, and lives.

Critical Context

Roll of Thunder, Hear My Cry is the second in a series of semiautobiographical novels in which Mildred D. Taylor portrays the hardships and courage of African Americans in the South. At the time of its publication in 1976, the book was one of the few novels depicting minority experiences for young readers; it became a bestseller and is widely accepted as a classic. Taylor was only the second African American writer to be honored with the Newbery Award for the most distinguished contribution to American literature for children. In her acceptance speech in 1977, Taylor dedicated the award to her father. She attributed her inspiration to him and to memories of her childhood trips to Mississippi.

The joys and pains of these years of her life gave rise to the ambition to write a series of novels about a family in rural Mississippi. The first, *Song of the Trees*, a short, illustrated book for children, appeared in 1975. Subsequent works in the series include *Let the Circle Be Unbroken* (1981) and *Mississippi Bridge* (1990). A novel not about the Logan family, *The Friendship* (1987), is also set in the South in the 1930's; it focuses on the dynamics of a relationship between an elderly black man and a white shopkeeper. A novella, *The Gold Cadillac* (1987), recounts an Ohio family's visit to Mississippi in an expensive 1950's car and explores the hostility provoked by this symbol of affluence.

Bibliography
Dussel, Sharon L. "Profile: Mildred D. Taylor." *Language Arts* 58 (May, 1981): 599-604. The great strength of Taylor's work, Dussel notes, is its autobiographical ring of truth. Taylor is able to represent a child's painful growth from innocence to awareness, from openness to bitterness, from optimism to disillusionment.

Hannabuss, Stuart. "Beyond the Formula: Part II." *The Junior Bookshelf* 46 (October, 1982): 173-176. Hannabuss commends Taylor's work for its vivid representation of social issues central to American life—racial enmity, economic hardship, violence, educational inequities, and violations of human rights.

Huck, Charlotte S., Susan Hepler, and Janet Hickman. "Historical Fiction and Biography." In *Children's Literature in the Elementary School*. 5th ed. Orlando, Fla.: Harcourt Brace Jovanovich College Publishers, 1993. In an extensive review of types of historical fiction, Huck, Hepler, and Hickman place *Roll of Thunder, Hear My Cry* in literary context and assess the values of such fiction. Taylor's portraits of positive family experiences, they say, offset the overall grim hues of the tale's events. Brief discussion of the three others in Taylor's Logan family series is also included.

Rees, David. "The Color of Skin: Mildred Taylor." In *The Marble in the Water: Essays on Contemporary Writers of Fiction for Children and Young Adults*. Boston: Horn Book, 1980. Rees contends that several American authors for children, including Taylor, have confronted directly and honestly the fear, anger, and violence so often directed at people of color. This novel has strong characterization, narrative ease, and fresh, eloquent language. One limitation of the novel is the author's apparent protectiveness of both her child narrator and her young audiences.

Sims, Rudine. *Shadow and Substance: Afro-American Experience in Contemporary Children's Fiction*. Urbana, Ill.: National Council of Teachers of English, 1982. According to Sims, *Roll of Thunder, Hear My Cry* is a distinguished example of "culturally conscious" fiction. Strong connections between generations of a family, vivid language, and pleasurable portraits of unique customs and qualities of the culture are positive influences on young African American readers. Yet the tone does not suggest optimism about the possibility of black and white people living in harmony.

Virginia Crane

SALLY HEMINGS

Author: Barbara Chase-Riboud (1939-   )
Type of plot: Historical realism
Time of plot: 1759-1835
Locale: Paris, France; Virginia
First published: 1979

> *Principal characters:*
>> SALLY HEMINGS, a beautiful, white-skinned woman born into slavery who is mistress to Thomas Jefferson
>> THOMAS JEFFERSON, the third president of the United States and author of the Declaration of Independence
>> NATHAN LANGDON, a lawyer and census taker in Virginia, who befriends Sally Hemings after Jefferson's death
>> AARON BURR, a politician and enemy to Jefferson
>> JAMES and DOLLEY MADISON, the fourth president and First Lady, friends of Jefferson and abolitionists
>> JOHN TRUMBILL, an artist who paints portraits of important historical figures
>> ELIZABETH HEMINGS, Sally's mother, housekeeper and boss of Monticello
>> GEORGE WYTHE, Jefferson's former schoolteacher and sometime mentor
>> JOHN and ABIGAIL ADAMS, the second president and First Lady, friends to Jefferson who supervise Sally during her stay in France
>> MADISON and ESTON HEMINGS, sons of Sally and Jefferson
>> JAMES HEMINGS, Sally's brother

The Novel

Since Thomas Jefferson's lifetime, it has been accepted by many historians, though never officially proven, that the third president had for a mistress a slave who bore him several children. Barbara Chase-Riboud takes this matter as fact in writing the novel *Sally Hemings*.

The work is based in great part on facts that are substantiated by documentation and historical records. Essentially, however, the novel itself is fiction; dialogue, characterization, and plot are all creations of the novelist, who takes great license with what is known and established about Jefferson and his relationship with Sally Hemings.

The book is divided into seven chapters according to place and time; however, the arrangement is not chronological. Most of the story is told by the novelist herself, writing in the third-person-omniscient point of view. In a few of the chapters, though, Sally Hemings tells her own story from the first-person point of view.

The book begins in 1830 in Albemarle County, Virginia, after Jefferson's death. Monticello has been sold, and Sally Hemings is living as a freed slave (and white woman) with her two sons on a small farm near the president's old plantation. A census taker visits to get the facts of her existence for public record. Infatuated first with Sally's story and then with Sally herself, young Nathan Langdon becomes intrigued with her beauty (even though Sally is now an old woman and Nathan is much younger) and history, and they become friends. Nathan's curiosity about slavery, Jefferson's two families, and race relations provide the author with a way to engage and entice the reader into concern for Sally's circumstances. Sally's two sons, Madison and Eston, are naturally suspicious of the white man and his motives, but they are unable to prevent the friendship.

The novel then switches in time and location to Paris, France, in 1787. Here, young Sally and her brother James, functioning as servants, travel with the Jefferson family when Jefferson is serving as ambassador to France. Under French law, the two slaves are free and cannot be held against their will or forced to return to the United States, where they will once again be legal slaves. Jefferson himself seduces the two into returning, more or less by making promises to free them. This promise is not kept to James Hemings for another several years; Sally is freed only at Jefferson's death many years later. Be that as it may, the chief interest of this chapter is the relation between Jefferson and Sally, for it is in Paris where he first seduces the beautiful fifteen-year-old girl, falls in love with her, and makes her his lifelong mistress.

In the next section of the novel, Chase-Riboud again focuses on the United States. It is now 1833, and Nathan Langdon is trying to find all the information he can about the Jefferson and Hemings families. He interviews the artist John Trumbill, who knows the facts but will not tell them, thinking that the facts would only besmirch the name of the great Jefferson. Like all other major characters in the novel, white or black, and including Sally herself, no one is willing to tell the story directly. All remain silent, not only about Jefferson and Sally, but also about the institution of slavery itself and the way in which Jefferson's two families (the white one and the black one) lived together, loved one another, and otherwise conducted their affairs and familial relations.

The middle section of the novel records these family histories from 1795 to 1809. The author explores the ways in which two sets of children, one white and one black, could live together given the social hypocrisy and the legal implications of the various blood relationships. Similarly, slave life is depicted, and certain historical characters are introduced by the novelist in order to give differing points of view about what is going on at Monticello. Jefferson is described at length. Always, the most important matter is his love for Sally, which is returned. Sally bears children to Jefferson and suckles the offspring of her white sisters. One by one, her own children leave (some with their father's knowledge and blessing, some without) for the north and freedom, where they must thereafter live as whites and can have no contact with their parents.

In the last chapter of the novel, Chase-Riboud makes clear that her main purpose is an indictment of slavery and the people who perpetuated the institution, even would-be do-gooders such as Jefferson himself. As Jefferson became older, his finances deteriorated, and he was forced to sell off slaves to keep Monticello his own. With his death, the demise is complete: The plantation is sold, as are most of the remaining slaves, even though many of them are family members and blood relations to Jefferson. The cruelty of the actions here, all going back to Jefferson himself, do not succeed to balance, in Sally's life, her love for him or his love for her. She remains a victim of the economic system, but most of all a victim of Jefferson himself.

The Characters

Sally Hemings is the centerpiece of the novel in every way. It is she who commands the story, telling much of it. Victimized by slavery, Jefferson, love, and herself, Sally does not so much grow and mature as she becomes older; rather, she merely endures changes in her circumstances. Always, Sally is seen making choices: The novel opens with her deciding whether to talk to Nathan Langdon; in her youth, she must decide if she will remain in France and be free or return to Virginia and slavery; through the years, she repeatedly elects to stay with Jefferson and to love him; as Jefferson's death approaches, she must decide to what extent she can and will help her children escape slavery; finally, after Jefferson's death, she remains illegally in Virginia in order to live on a small farm near Monticello. The character is described by the author almost throughout; however, in three or four instances she does speak for herself in small subchapters given to her first-person point of view.

Thomas Jefferson is always depicted externally, as are most of the characters in the novel. Readers see him in action and hear him speak but seldom know what is occurring in his mind. The novelist, to her credit, does not attempt to debunk myths surrounding the historical Jefferson; his greatness is left intact, though readers will doubtless be disturbed by the omnipresent fact that Jefferson continued to own slaves and to live his life within the confines of slavery as an institution. His greatness and role in history are not undermined, but much of his hypocrisy is exposed. Chase-Riboud has assured this by prefacing the chapters with actual historical writings, documents, and letters, most of which are directly from Jefferson himself.

Nathan Langdon grows and learns more than any other character in the work. A Southerner himself, he fully understands the functions and techniques of slavery, but he is unable to understand how Thomas Jefferson could have had such a relationship with Sally Hemings. Langdon plays something of a proxy for the reader, for his questions to the various characters would likely be the reader's own questions. Inevitably, what he learns is that Jefferson is a hypocrite; he also learns that Sally acted out of love to cause her own destruction.

Madison and Eston Hemings, as the only surviving sons of Sally and Jefferson, live in a world where they are legally black but otherwise white. Fixed forever in this messy state of affairs, their circumstances serve to expose the evils and corruption of the society itself. Their primary action in the novel is to object to their mother's new friend, Langdon. They do not trust him, because he is white. Sally, too, comes to distrust him, though for differing reasons.

Aaron Burr is one of the most memorable characters in the novel. Again, Chase-Riboud's description does not significantly vary from the traditional picture of the historical man. As an enemy to Jefferson, he acts to expose him for his miscegenation at home. A political creature who has few morals, Burr is never silenced except by old age.

John Trumbill appears throughout the narrative in significant episodes. As the sensitive artist who has painted Sally Hemings and Thomas Jefferson as well as other important historical figures of the time, Trumbill knows what is going on in the personal lives of these people. According to propriety, he must remain silent and does so. Chase-Riboud makes important not so much what Trumbill says but what he remains silent about.

Sally's mother, Elizabeth Hemings, has in many ways lived the same life as Sally. With white skin, education, and manners, Elizabeth knows very well the trap into which her daughter is falling with her love for Jefferson; too, the mother knows and forewarns Sally that nothing good can come from it, that Sally will pay with her life. Elizabeth serves to prove to the reader, and Sally herself, that mistakes are passed from one generation to the next.

Themes and Meanings

First and foremost, the novel is the imagined story of Sally Hemings. The bare historical facts of her life remain intact; nevertheless, most of the story is a creation of fiction. The skeletal events of the novel are well established by historical documents and common knowledge. The excitement, intrigue, and suspense, however, are created by Chase-Riboud.

The dominant theme is simply the story of the forbidden and illegal love of Sally Hemings and Thomas Jefferson. The novelist explores the possibilities for love against all such obstacles and shows that it is real, something that both lovers give themselves to. At the same time, the story is an exploration of slavery. Chase-Riboud's intentions are not to expose the evils of slavery—this had been done, of course, a century earlier with such works as *Uncle Tom's Cabin, Or, Life Among the Lowly* (1852)—but to explore the conscience of the slaveholders. Chase-Riboud tries to show how the two races (literally of one blood) could live and survive together in one house, in one society, and in one Union. How could Jefferson have two families, one white and one black, and be at peace with himself, given the flagrant differences between the ways he treated them publicly and privately?

Intricacies of the legal system that permitted slavery are also attacked. The census taker wishes not only to know the facts of the Jefferson-Hemings lifelong love but also to understand how Jefferson could love Sally, her children, and other family members and yet treat them as he did. Moreover, after Jefferson's death, the society permits Sally to remain in Virginia as a free woman, even though it is illegal.

Critical Context

Sally Hemings is Barbara Chase-Riboud's first novel. First published in 1979, it is a statement about a fact of history: Thomas Jefferson's forty-year love relation with one of his slaves. Inescapably, the novel is important because of messages that have importance for contemporary race relations in the United States. Of first concern here is not the fact that a founding father had a black mistress, but that he loved her and kept her in servitude. The social meaning is clear: Those who control power cannot continue to want brotherhood privately but not publicly.

Sally Hemings indicates the maturity of the black novel in American literature. Published at a distance of some ten years after the Civil Rights movement of the 1960's, it makes clear that equality remains a goal—an ideal—for which the nation should work. Chase-Riboud's thrust is not to expose the evils of slavery but to relate a matter that explains something in the national character. This movement toward equality and human rights is depicted in a historical setting so as to emphasize that such social changes have not yet been realized.

Bibliography
Brooks, Valerie. Review of *Sally Hemings*, by Barbara Chase-Riboud. *New Republic* 181 (July 7, 1979): 38. Brooks emphasizes the historical elements of the novel and briefly questions the belief that Hemings was actually Jefferson's mistress. She retells the basic events of the plot, finding other matters to be accurate. This favorable review of the novel serves as a brief outline of its contents.
Crandall, Norma Rand. "*Sally Hemings.*" *America* 141 (November 3, 1979): 267. Unlike other reviewers, Crandall finds the novel to be primarily about Jefferson himself, rather than about Sally Hemings. Crandall focuses on Jefferson as states-man and politician, as he is depicted in the work. She also emphasizes his role as father to two families, one black and one white; similarly, she deemphasizes his role as slaveholder.
Giddings, Paula. "Word Star." *Essence* 19 (February, 1989): 30. In this short review, Giddings relates *Sally Hemings* to subsequent novels written by Chase-Riboud. Too, Giddings provides a glimpse into the personal life of the novelist herself. Briefly, Giddings discusses how Chase-Riboud uses history as a backdrop for her work.
"*Sally Hemings*' Author Wins Copyright Lawsuit." *Jet* 80 (September 9, 1991): 36. This unsigned article is essentially a report about a lawsuit that Barbara Chase-Riboud made against Granville Burgess for a play he wrote in 1982. The courts ruled that the play was in fact plagiarized from the earlier novel. All performances of the play were banned, as was its further publication.
Levin, Martin. "*Sally Hemings.*" *The New York Times Book Review*, October 28, 1979, 14. Explains some of the blood ties of Jefferson's two families, the white one and the black one. Levin finds the narrative itself weak and uneventful; he sees problems in Chase-Riboud's telling of events and judges the novel to be too impressionistic.

Carl Singleton

THE SALT EATERS

Author: Toni Cade Bambara (1939-   )
Type of plot: Expressionism
Time of plot: 1978
Locale: Claybourne, Georgia
First published: 1980

> *Principal characters:*
> VELMA HENRY, a black activist in her late thirties whose life has nearly ended in suicide
> MINNIE RANSOM, an ancient faith healer who may be able to restore Velma's mental health
> OLD WIFE, a querulous spirit whose folk wisdom and Christian belief guide Minnie
> FRED HOLT, an unhappy bus driver whose only friend has been killed
> OBIE (JAMES LEE HENRY), Velma's husband
> DOC SERGE, the director of the Southwest Infirmary, a man with a checkered past
> M'DEAR SOPHIE HEYWOOD, Velma's godmother and a potent force for good in her life

The Novel

The Salt Eaters tells the story of Velma Henry, a bone-weary, despairing black woman whose marriage is on the skids and who has begun to falter seriously as she attempts to juggle a commitment to social activism, a career, and life as a wife and mother. In addition to being the story of Velma, the novel tells a larger story of African Americans in the late twentieth century as they come to grips with themselves, their country, and the world.

The central action of *The Salt Eaters* occurs in the short space of time it takes for the "fabulous healer," Minnie Ransom of Claybourne, Georgia, to "bring through" her patient Velma, who that same day has attempted to take her own life. From three o'clock in the afternoon of an early spring day until the novel ambiguously concludes less than a half hour later, the two women sit facing each other on stools in the Southwest Infirmary, a century old black-founded hospital where modern medicine is practiced side by side with traditional healing arts handed down from slave and Indian times.

Velma has slashed her wrists and crawled head first into a gas stove. Now, the veteran political worker, civil-rights activist, and computer consultant sits quietly in a hospital robe as the ancient crone—abetted by Old Wife, her familiar, her guiding spirit—attempts to unravel the twisted psyche of the younger woman. Both are legends in the black community, Minnie for her supernatural powers and Velma for her organizational ability and aggressive self-confidence, now reduced to depression and confusion.

Those familiar only with her better-known short stories such as "Gorilla, My Love" and "Raymond's Run" will find Toni Cade Bambara's first and only novel very different. In its narration and style, the novel is indebted to such earlier authors as James Joyce and William Faulkner. Like Joyce's *Ulysses* (1922), *The Salt Eaters* is concerned with the events of a single day; like that novel and Faulkner's *The Sound and the Fury* (1929), Bambara's book makes use of stream-of-consciousness narration, jumps in place and time, and free associations. Because the narration plunges backward and forward in time, jumps about in the presentation of events, and frequently alternates perspectives, even the persistent reader may often encounter difficulties.

Velma occupies a central position inside the hospital; she is perched uneasily on a stool undergoing therapy and surrounded by a local prayer group of twelve elderly people known as The Master's Mind and by a number of curious hospital personnel. From there, the untraditional plot radiates out into the street, the surrounding neighborhood, and often to a bus approaching the city limits of Claybourne carrying among its passengers an interracial group of women led by Velma's sister. While Velma is being treated by Minnie, numerous people wander in, out of, and by the infirmary. Julius Meadows, a light-skinned physician, steals out of the room to walk the streets. Fred Holt, who has parked his bus, peers in at the curious ritual going on inside. Velma herself has a restless mind that leads her back to her childhood, to her husband Obie, and to her current lover Jamahl, a self-styled guru whom she cruelly but accurately dismisses as just "a jive nigger."

Little by little, the reader comes to see that the Black Power movement of earlier years has become a fragmented host of antagonistic parties, each making its impetuous demands on Velma. Her activities have taken a grievous toll on her marriage, so that she comes to reflect within herself the shattered state of her people, radicalized into factions that defy reconciliation.

Outside the hospital, the divided black community is preparing to celebrate a rite of spring, an ambiguous Mardi Gras-like festival that appears both boisterously merry and ominous. Though a carnival atmosphere exists in the streets, it is constantly undercut by allusions to the "Hoo Doo Man," by disconcerting encounters with transvestites, and by the recurring reminder that weapons stolen from an armory may be stashed at the Academy of the Seven Arts, Obie's community self-help center. The center, which conducts adult-education classes and has a well-equipped gym, is sponsoring a midnight parade that could easily turn into an armed uprising.

The academy, like the festival and like the strange storm that suddenly sweeps the streets with wind and rain, resists an entirely satisfactory interpretation. The outcome of Velma's treatment as the book comes to a close suggests that the first stage of healing has been reached, however, and that auspicious sign may well comment equally on the hope for the values of the community now in disarray.

The Characters

Velma is a take-charge woman, ever ready to adopt a new radical cause and careless of whom she offends. Committed to a number of civil rights projects, she has only recently become aware of environmental issues and seen an interrelatedness where previously she discerned none. She is convinced that Claybourne's largest employer, Transchemical, drives workers to early deaths and that its pollution is part of a global conspiracy of the privileged to enrich themselves through exploitation of the wretched of the earth, largely people of color. Just before her attempted suicide, she has been questioned about the destruction of Transchemical's computer records. Her disturbed state of mind makes her sketchy thoughts, including flashbacks to the recent past as well as to her childhood, often difficult to grasp, while her friends' recollections of her range from impatient and envious to unqualifiedly admiring. In perhaps Minnie Ransom's most difficult case, Velma is fighting for her life.

Minnie Ransom and Old Wife ought not to be considered separately but rather as a team. This old woman and her spirit mentor resemble a married couple whose impatience with each other cloaks deep affection. Although Minnie, a consummate herbalist, combines a variety of techniques in her healing, she relies mostly on commonsensical counseling combined with generous doses of love. Nothing about the low-key performance in the pleasant room suggests the bizarre. That these women, who probably represent body and soul—though which is which is often hard to say—are miracle workers is attested by a pregnant teenager, Nadeen, who sees the slashes on Velma's wrist vanish.

Fred Holt, an aging black Everyman, has no direct connection to Velma. He merely drives her sister's Third World sorority, The Seven Sisters, to Claybourne, where he is scheduled to pick up a charter group for extra money. Yet he represents the sort of man Velma must understand and even love if she is to love and help her people. Fred longs for his dead friend Porter, the only other African American at his company, although he could not mention his white wife to him and did not even see the man outside work. When Fred deliberately swerves to run over a raccoon, he is trying to kill the "coon" in himself, his alienated black identity.

Obie, a barely developed yet important figure in the novel, is the last to know that his wife is in the hospital—just as she was the last to know that he is "sleeping around." Who is to blame for the present state of their marriage is impossible to determine, but his claim that she has abandoned him and their twelve-year-old son makes a certain amount of sense, though Velma airily dismisses it. The masseur at the academy, where Obie once ruled unchallenged, tells the now-ineffectual cuckold that his body is a mass of knots.

M'Dear Sophie Heywood, the "auntie" with chiffon roses in her hat, has mythic dimensions that lift her from being merely Velma's godmother to something approaching a fairy godmother. She is to Velma what Old Wife is to Minnie, a guide through life, interpreting the omens that Velma fails to read. Sophie runs a celebrated rooming-house where Dr. Meadows is currently staying, and she never hesitates to mount the barricades in the cause of racial justice.

Doc Serge, half con-man, half saint, directs the infirmary, managing somehow to meet its bills and payrolls. His title is purely honorary; he has done many things in his day, even pimping. A flashy, street-smart survivor, he commands respect for his convictions and strength of character from people who know that the line between the criminal and ethical is not as clear to those on the fringe as it may be for others.

Themes and Meanings

The Salt Eaters poses questions: What has happened to the wonderful promise of the 1960's for African Americans, and can the movement of those days be brought back on course?

Although the novel was published in 1980, it was written in the late 1970's and depicts a time when the protagonist suffers not only a crisis in confidence and faith but also a mid-life crisis. The seemingly gratuitous references to Velma's menstruation are evidence that Velma is as concerned about lost youth as the lost promise of her cause. Many will ignore this aspect of the novel, though it in no way diminishes the larger theme of lost direction in the Civil Rights movement or the book's pervasive feminist concerns.

Velma and Obie were once glittering role models in the early years of the Black Power movement. Now, as forty looms, Velma has turned to a man she does not love, afraid, too, that she has lost the affection of her son, Lil James.

If *The Salt Eaters* proclaims that a woman can meet menopause and disappointment in relationships when offered support from those who love her, may not a similar answer apply to the fragmented cause of racial equality? Such a solution is offered in the novel's somewhat diffuse treatment of The Seven Sisters, women of color who unite amid their acknowledged diversity, presenting a solid front against oppression of all kinds, including militarism, environmental pollution, and the nuclear threat.

As a feminist, Bambara is often impatient with men—white men of authority in some places, but black men as well. In bitter pages, she describes the "boymen," a parasitical breed who live off women while avoiding all responsibility. They haunt the periphery of the black matriarchy, fathering children, pleading for money from their women, and wasting their lives in a haze of alcohol, drugs, and empty daydreams. More despicable yet are the "boymen's" successful brothers, vain self-serving peacocks who use the black community to boost their egos and establish their own importance. They too exploit women as footsoldiers in their political and civil rights campaigns, assigning them tedious jobs of organization and logistics while reserving for themselves glamorous roles of leadership and oratory. Often they reject their faithful female sisters, whom they treat as servants, for more alluring, less committed female companionship, even of another color.

Critical Context

Reviews greeting *The Salt Eaters* remarked on the book's difficulty. Even the title remains a bit murky, though "salt eaters" appear to be those with whom things are shared, such as traditional basic foods of bread and salt. Salt is also seen in the novel as an antidote to wounds, as a stancher of blood, and as a necessary ingredient to a salutory body chemistry.

Such opacity, however, is not the rare exception in Bambara's novel. Varied points of view, narrative interruptions, a multiplicity of characters frequently overwhelm the reader. Yet if *The Salt Eaters* is confusing, repetitious in its assertions, and strained in some of its dialogue, this unforgiving novel is still a tour de force, a mosaic of brightly colored tiles wherein elements of myth, folklore, local color, psychology, and impassioned exposition come together. A woman's odyssey offering a searching look into the African American psyche, *The Salt Eaters* influenced many of the prominent African American women writers of the 1980's.

Bibliography

Burks, Ruth Elizabeth. "From Baptism to Resurrection: Toni Cade Bambara and the Incongruity of Language." In *Black Women Writers (1950-1980)*, edited by Mari Evans. Garden City, N.Y.: Anchor Press/Doubleday, 1984. Burks shows that often "the language of the mind has usurped the language of action" in the novel, or that thoughts and imaginings of characters are presented as more real than actuality. Thus, Fred Holt does not actually drive his bus into the swamp, but only believes he has—a scene that has puzzled readers.

Byerman, Keith E. *Fingering the Jagged Grain*. Athens: University of Georgia Press, 1985. A helpful summary of the novel. Makes the point that "simply reversing the direction of oppressions" serves to perpetuate oppression and observes that harmony of life and mind is to be found within the unifying principles represented by Minnie's folk arts.

Hull, Gloria T. "What It Is I Think She's Doing Anyhow." In *Conjuring: Black Women, Fiction, and the Literary Tradition*, edited by Marjorie Pryse and Hortense J. Spillers. Bloomington: Indiana University Press, 1985. This reading of the novel takes a scatter-gun approach relying on highly subjective judgments. Yet the essay is helpful in understanding numerous details in a book that is almost certainly "autobiographically generated."

Lardner, Susan. "Third Eye Open." *The New Yorker* 56 (May 5, 1980): 169-173. This early review works appreciatively from Bambara's short stories to the novel. Lardner concludes that, though untidy, the book is "full of marvels."

Wideman, John. "The Healing of Velma Henry." *The New York Times Book Review* 85 (June 1, 1980): 14. A largely favorable review that revels in the book's "dislocations," turning what some saw as liabilities into assets. Wideman finds *The Salt Eaters* flawed but "persuasive."

James E. Devlin

SARAH PHILLIPS

Author: Andrea Lee (1953-   )
Type of plot: Bildungsroman
Time of plot: The 1960's to the 1970's
Locale: Philadelphia
First published: 1984

> *Principal characters:*
> SARAH PHILLIPS, an African American minister's daughter who matures
>   from a young child to an adult woman in the course of the novel
> HENRI, Sarah's French boyfriend during her college years
> THE REVEREND JAMES FORREST PHILLIPS, Sarah's father, the pastor of the
>   New African Baptist Church in Philadelphia
> GRACE RENFREW PHILLIPS, Sarah's mother
> MATTHEW, Sarah's elder brother
> LYN YANCY, Sarah's best friend in fourth grade
> LILY, EMMA, and MAY, aunts of Sarah
> GRETCHEN MANNING, Sarah's best friend in seventh grade
> MARTHA GREENFIELD, Matthew's white college girlfriend
> MRS. JELLER, an old convalescent taken care of by Sarah's mother
> CURRY DANIELS, a male friend of Sarah's at Harvard

The Novel

Sarah Phillips presents the experiences of an African American woman growing up in a middle-class environment. It covers the period from the early 1960's until the mid-1970's. The setting and themes of the book are similar to those of the author's own life.

Sarah Phillips is divided into twelve episodes. Each of these are a complete story in themselves but also develop the overall narrative. The story is told by a first-person narrator. It is recounted in the form of an autobiographical reminiscence.

The book begins with the narrator and protagonist, Sarah Phillips, living in France during a year abroad as a college student. Sarah is having an enjoyable time, reflecting with amusement on the French myths about America that come to the surface during her conversations with French people. When her French boyfriend, Henri, makes an insensitive racial joke, however, Sarah's sense of serenity and fun is shattered. She begins to realize that although she had previously thought that Europeans did not possess American racial stereotypes, these stereotypes are difficult for her to escape. Sarah is reminded anew of her racial background and identity. She begins to reflect back on her childhood days.

Sarah had been born the daughter of a prominent African American minister. Sarah is reared in a middle-class residential section of Philadelphia. At the age of ten, she sits on a summer Sunday in a pew of the New African Baptist Church, where her father preaches. The world of the church, where Sarah is surrounded by her extended family, seems all-encompassing to the young girl. The long hours of prayer and singing begin to bore Sarah, however, and she idly fantasizes about playing outdoors in a treehouse. Sarah feels both protected and stifled by the rich atmosphere of the church.

Despite his profession, the Reverend Phillips does not maintain a strict religious grip on the household. Sarah and her older brother Matthew grow up in a loose and relaxed spiritual atmosphere. Even so, Sarah feels that she cannot live up to her father's expectations of her as a good Christian. She is made particularly nervous by the rite of baptism. When her Aunt Bessie urges her to volunteer to be baptized, Sarah refuses. Sarah expects her parents to be angry, but their reaction is surprisingly mild. Her father's reluctance to punish Sarah makes an impression on her and becomes a major ingredient of her bond to her father. By not imposing his own expectation on her character, the Reverend Phillips permits Sarah to become her own woman.

On the surface, Sarah's childhood appears unexciting, but even the most ordinary people and places offer unexpected possibilities. Sarah's mother, who appears sedate and domestic, always exudes an air of the thrilling and the forbidden despite her prudish exterior. With her best friend, Lyn, Sarah is enthralled by tales of gypsies stealing children, and she is quite disappointed when the gypsies never come to perform their dark task.

Sarah's father is active in the Civil Rights movement. As the push for racial equality becomes more intense in the mid-1960's, Sarah's private life is increasingly affected by social changes. Sarah wants to attend a march in Washington led by Martin Luther King, Jr., but her father does not permit her. She watches the march on television with her family, feeling that she is missing out on taking part in a historic event.

When Sarah reaches the seventh grade, she enters an elite boarding school for girls in Pennsylvania. In the outside world, civil unrest rages, and the racial turmoil of the nation mounts, but Sarah's world at the school is placid and tranquil. With her best friend, Gretchen, who is white, she explores areas of the school grounds forbidden to them by authorities. On one of these expeditions, the girls stumble upon the sparse and dingy living quarters of the school's African American maids. Sarah is reminded that she leads a much more privileged life than most other African Americans.

Racial issues enter Sarah's life in a different way when Matthew brings home a white girlfriend, Martha Greenfield, during his first year at college. Sarah's parents treat Martha in a hostile way. They are used to a segregated world and are not ready to accept interracial dating. Sarah gains new insight into the predicament of African Americans as well as into the dynamics of her own family.

Sarah goes away to summer camp, where her life is dominated by a teenage gang called the Thunderbirds. As a good student from a prosperous family, she naturally feels different from this gang, but she is also attracted by their defiance of social regulations. At the end of camp, she is accepted in a way by the Thunderbirds, although she will always be different from them.

While Sarah is shopping for clothes with her mother, Mrs. Phillips takes her to visit Mrs. Jeller, an old convalescent who had been a parishioner at the Reverend Phillips' church. Mrs. Jeller tells a story about how, as a young girl, she had been forced by her pregnancy into a loveless early marriage. This had occurred long ago in a impoverished section of Kentucky, and the baby had died when it was only a year and a half old. Sarah feels that her comfortable middle-class identity is further questioned by this tale.

Sarah goes to Harvard University. There she meets Curry Daniels, a dynamic young photographer. Curry convinces Sarah to let him take photographs of her in the nude, but they never have a romantic relationship. In a way, Sarah is disappointed in this. Sarah's college years are filled with social and personal accomplishment, yet there remains an unsatisfying aftertaste about the entire experience.

Sarah is still at Harvard when her mother calls to tell her that the Reverend Phillips has had a stroke. Sarah rushes home, at once horrified by the news and feeling that it possesses a strangely unreal quality. Sarah returns to the scene of her nurturing childhood, this time not celebrating life but commemorating death. Seeing her former life through adult eyes, she comes to a new understanding of herself that enables her to accept her father's passing. Feeling she has at last begun to know herself, Sarah sets out back to Harvard. She has no idea what her ultimate destination is, but she feels that her individual journal has finally begun.

The Characters

Sarah Phillips, the heroine and narrator of the book, guides the reader on a tour of the various stages of her life. The other characters in the book function as auxiliary figures who fill in the outlines of Sarah's progress through the first two decades of her life.

Intelligent, sensitive, and observant, Sarah nevertheless doubts herself and her own capacity to come to terms with her experience. Sarah is grateful to her parents for their loving attention, but she never feels herself a part of their world. Attracted by the romantic appeal of the gypsies and the Thunderbirds, she is too straitlaced to stray far outside the middle-class contours established by her parents. At first oblivious to her racial identity, Sarah determines to come to grips with the contradictions of being a middle-class, educated African American.

The Reverend Phillips, Sarah's father, is a figure of great wisdom and power. Yet he uses his authority not to discipline Sarah and her brother but rather to make them feel protected and loved. Sarah feels somewhat distant from her father, whom she reveres but does not fully know. Reverend Phillips, however, clearly is the dominant figure in his daughter's life.

Sarah's mother, Grace Renfrew Phillips, is more elusive. Beneath her placid, bourgeois exterior lurks a far more exciting and illicit world of adventure and intrigue. Sarah's mother seems more traditional and self-effacing than her intelligent, ambitious daughter. Sarah, though, gets much of her questing spirit, her desire to encounter new realms other than the one into which she is placed by birth, from Mrs. Phillips.

Matthew, Sarah's brother, provides a male perspective on many of her childhood experiences. Sarah's aunts, Lily, Emma, and May, help to compose the comfortable church setting of Sarah's youth. They also point up traditional, socially endorsed behavior patterns of African American women from which Sarah sharply departs. Mrs. Jeller, an aging convalescent, indicates the vast differences between Sarah's well-off status in life and those of older African American women.

Sarah's friends, Lyn Yancy, Gretchen Manning, and Curry Daniels, are introduced in order to underscore certain stages in Sarah's development. They call attention to the ever-present factor of race in all of her personal relationships. Sarah's French boyfriend, Henri, initiates the narrative of the book through his racial insult.

In general, the characters other than Sarah are in the book to illustrate specific aspects of the novel's themes. They do not grow or develop. Sarah, on the other hand, progresses from child to adult as the novel proceeds.

Themes and Meanings

The novel's primary theme is the tension of growing up both African American and middle-class. Rebelling against the conventional stereotype of African Americans as constrained within a cycle of bleak poverty and crime, Lee presents a stable, loving, and prosperous family. Sarah defies traditional images of African American women by her assertiveness and intelligence. Sarah is not one of life's victims; she is a member of what the African American thinker W. E. B. Du Bois termed the "Talented Tenth" of African Americans.

Yet Sarah is also made constantly aware of the other ninety percent, those African Americans who do not get to go to prestigious boarding schools and colleges. Sarah realizes that her privileged life is possible only because of the struggles of the Civil Rights movement, largely accomplished by men and women of her father's generation. Sarah also realizes that for many African Americans who still have to endure poverty and discrimination, these struggles have yet to bear fruit.

The novel's focus is not, though, exclusively social. Sarah goes through private experiences common to the maturation process of any young woman. She loves her parents but feels that they do not understand her. She has close friendships but feels that there are many aspects of her character that her friends can simply never get to know. The novel is animated throughout by the tension between Sarah as an individual and Sarah as a type, a representative of the new generation of prosperous, educated African Americans that came to maturity in the 1970's.

Critical Context

It is interesting that the novel's title is the name of an individual person. This was a common practice in the nineteenth century, as evidenced by such books as Charles Dickens' *David Copperfield* (1850) and Leo Tolstoy's *Anna Karenina* (1877), but it has been far less common in the twentieth century. Lee's novel, like its nineteenth century counterparts, chronicles the tension between public and private experience. *Sarah Phillips* has an affirmative faith in the capacity of an individual to prevail against worldly obstacles. One of the novel's principal accomplishments is its skilled interweaving of personal and social realms. To some extent, Sarah is free to determine her fate, but the pressures of society and race are never minimized.

Andrea Lee first came to prominence with the publication of *Russian Journal* in 1981. That book, written in lapidary prose, was a candid account of Lee's personal experiences while visiting the Soviet Union during the "era of stagnation" presided over by Communist Party leader Leonid Brezhnev. Full of observant and idiosyncratic reportage, *Russian Journal* garnered praise from across the American critical spectrum. This feat was especially impressive in light of the fact that Lee was only twenty-eight at the time the book was published. After *Russian Journal*, Lee's readers eagerly awaited a novel from her. Their expectations were satisfied with the publication of *Sarah Phillips* in 1984.

Bibliography
Kapp, Isa. "The First Time Around." *The New Leader* 67 (December 10, 1984): 5. Discusses the insecurity felt by the title character and her dissatisfaction with the conflicts induced by her class privilege.
Murrell, Elizabeth J. Review of *Sarah Phillips*, by Andrea Lee. *Freedomways* 25 (Summer, 1985): 119. Examines the novel's African American consciousness and its contribution to awareness of racial issues.
Obolensky, Laura. "Scenes from a Girlhood." *The New Republic* 91 (November 19, 1984): 41-42. Discusses the potential for elitism in Sarah's self-portrait. A principal concern is Sarah's relationship with her father.
Shreve, Susan Richards. "Unsentimental Journey." *The New York Times Book Review* 89 (November 18, 1984): 13. Praises Lee's personal honesty and luminous style. Emphasizes the skill with which even minor characters are drawn.
Taylor, Linda. Review of *Sarah Phillips*, by Andrea Lee. *The Times Literary Supplement*, April 5, 1985, 376. Examines the novel's meditations on African American issues from a British perspective. Addresses particularly the question of style in the work.

Nicholas Birns

SEA GLASS

Author: Laurence Yep (1948-   )
Type of plot: Bildungsroman
Time of plot: The early 1970's
Locale: Concepcion, California
First published: 1979

> *Principal characters:*
> CRAIG CHIN, an overweight Chinese American of middle-school age
> CALVIN CRAIG, Craig's father, a storekeeper who wants his son to excel in sports
> JEANNIE CRAIG, Craig's compassionate and loving mother
> KENYON, a female classmate of Craig
> UNCLE QUAIL, Craig's great-uncle, a Chinese American who remembers the old days
> STANLEY, Craig's cousin who excels in sports
> SHEILA, Craig's cousin and classmate
> UNCLE TIM and AUNTIE FAYE, the parents of Stanley and Sheila
> RALPH BRADLEY, a friend and classmate of Craig

The Novel

Set in the Chinatown of Concepcion, California, in the early 1970's, *Sea Glass* is the story of a second-generation Chinese American boy who is struggling to find his identity as a Chinese, as an American, and—most important—as a person. Pressing against young and overweight Craig Chin are two seemingly overwhelming problems: His father expects him to excel in sports in order to achieve acceptance as an American, and, when the novel opens, Craig is undergoing troubles as the new boy at school. His family has just moved to Concepcion from San Francisco.

The novel is organized into ten chapters of approximately equal length and importance. Each is divided into shorter subchapters to give the work something of an episodic effect and substance. The work has only one narrator, young Craig Chin himself; thus the point of view is entirely that of the adolescent boy as he struggles with his problems and new surroundings. The setting of the novel, in its entirety, is Concepcion, California.

The book opens with Craig trying unsuccessfully to play football with some new acquaintances upon his arrival in the new town. Craig's father stands on the sidelines to shout instructions to Craig and the other players. Because Calvin Craig had been successful in high school as an athlete, he believes his son can achieve acceptance in American society only by becoming a sports hero at school. Craig is fat and uninterested in football or any other such activity; however, he cannot make his father accept these facts.

In the next chapter, Craig's father has changed the game from football to basketball, where the same pattern occurs again. Craig cannot play basketball well, no matter how hard he tries; he succeeds only at humiliating himself and his father, who relentlessly claims that enough practice and hard work will make Craig a star player. He claims this even when it is clear to everyone that it cannot possibly be the case.

In the middle sections of the novel, two other main characters are introduced and become central to the action. Craig's job at the family store is to deliver groceries to older people in the community, one of whom is Calvin's great-uncle, Uncle Quail. This older Chinese gentleman, who never trusts the "white demons," lives alone in a small cottage near a cove on the ocean. Through his regular Saturday visits, Craig and Uncle Quail become friends who enjoy swimming together in the ocean in their own secret place. At the same time Craig is befriending Uncle Quail, he strikes up an acquaintance with a classmate named Kenyon, the daughter of two extremely liberal parents. The father is a poet and the mother a political activist. Kenyon and Craig recognize in each other kindred spirits because of their differences from the other children at Dana Middle School: Craig is different because of his Chinese ethnicity; Kenyon is different because of her parents' liberal lifestyles.

Because of his relationships with Kenyon and Uncle Quail, Craig's life seems to be getting better. At least he has friends and companions whom he enjoys. Kenyon, however, elicits from Craig the promise to ask Uncle Quail's permission for her to swim in the cove. Uncle Quail is horrified; he does not want any white people on his property and is offended that Craig would even ask. Yet he gives in to Craig's pleadings that Kenyon is "different," and a date is set. Kenyon is unable to keep the appointment, and through a series of misspoken statements, Craig alienates himself from both Uncle Quail and Kenyon. In the middle of these events, Craig loses his ability to maintain feelings of respect for his father in the Chinese fashion, and he violates the social order by screaming at his father the truth—that he is no good at sports, does not like them, and does not want ever to play or pretend to play them again.

Thus Craig has only his mother left for affection and friendship. She counsels him simply to wait patiently for the father, the uncle, and the friend to reconcile. Eventually, Uncle Quail thaws toward Craig, whereupon he visits Craig's father and, as the elder Chinese gentleman of the community, tells him to let Craig pursue his own interests and activities. Kenyon, too, softens and reestablishes her friendship with the young man. The novel concludes with Uncle Quail, Craig, and Kenyon taking a swim in the secret cove and diving for abalone. Instead, they find "sea glass," broken pieces of glass that have been smoothed and shaped by many years in the sea. It is clearly a happy ending, as Craig Chin is now at peace with those around him and with himself.

The Characters

Craig Chin, the first-person narrator of the story, tells of events that are important to him as he finds identity and peace. This occurs on several levels, but the most important of these is his relationship with his father. Both father and son love each other in an unquestioned, unconditional way, yet problems occur because of the father's insistence that Craig become a sports star. At the same time, Craig experiences severe difficulties because of his birth and ethnicity. On the one hand, he is Chinese by looks and blood; on the other, his way of thinking, his central culture, and his own goals in life are distinctly American. Readers learn of these difficulties and their resolutions through the revelations of the main character's thoughts and actions.

Calvin Craig, Craig's father, is the most loving and helpful and understanding of all fathers except for one matter: He is unable to accept that his son will never be any kind of successful athlete. His attitude is revealed primarily through his actions. Always on the sidelines encouraging and advising his son in football and basketball, he fails to realize the torment he is working upon the person in the world whom he loves most. For Calvin himself, sports had been the ticket to acceptance in American life.

Uncle Quail is the stereotypical "last generation" from the Old Country. In one section of the story, Uncle Quail tells of the experiences of his own father's generation as they built the United States' railroads and performed other such tasks. Then he explains the discrimination against them that occurred once the rails had been laid. He survives as a "Chinaman" gentleman, one who clings to the old ways of life and will not trust the "white demons" again. This works to Craig's benefit when Uncle Quail visits Craig's father and plays the part of family sage, essentially instructing the father to leave the boy alone to pursue his own interests.

Kenyon is the female foil and counterpart to Craig. She has problems similar to those experienced by Craig, and both come to realize that these are not because of Craig's Chinese heritage. Both are outsiders to the society of middle-school children because they do not conform to some unspoken, unknown mold and code of behavior. Kenyon's character and relation with her own parents give Craig the example and strength to stand up to his father and finally to speak the truth: that he will never be an athlete no matter how long or hard he tries.

Craig's mother, Jeannie Craig, is in some ways a stereotypical gentle, caring mother figure. She listens, encourages, and directs, and she works to keep peace between father and son as well as to help Craig develop as a young man who is pointed in the right direction in life.

Stanley and Sheila, Craig's first cousins on his mother's side, are examples of Chinese Americans who have seemingly made the transformation to being mainstream Americans without difficulty. Stanley is something of the son Calvin wishes he had had, because Stanley does very well in sports. Sheila, because of her quickness and sense of humor, is similarly accepted by the American-born white children at school. In fact, Sheila is so much accepted that she feels free to ridicule Craig for his ethnicity, although both children are entirely of Chinese descent.

Uncle Tim and Auntie Faye similarly appear in contrast to Craig's own parents. Evidently, they live as Chinese Americans without problem or difficulty, fitting well into the society at large because they do not push their children to overachieve for the sake of social acceptance.

Ralph Bradley is the only new friend other than Kenyon that Craig makes in

Concepcion. Ralph represents in many ways that which is best of white Americans in terms of racial tolerance and acceptance of others. Ralph immediately understands why Craig's father pushes him on the sports field, and he does all he can to help Craig succeed in sports. His efforts fail, but their importance is in his attempts.

Themes and Meanings

Sea Glass is at once an ethnic novel and a novel of initiation. Craig Chin must grow up and find his place in the society around him—and he must do so as a Chinese, as an American, and as a Chinese American. The events of the book unfold so as to assure his success on all counts. Ironically, the only major obstacle to this attainment is his father, the person who would help him most because he truly loves him. To the credit of the author, Craig's problems are never really derived from the youth's Chinese ancestry (as the father would seemingly have it) or from the American society at large (as Uncle Quail would have it). Rather, the problems are primarily at home in the heart of the father who would dictate that his son become a sports hero whatever the cost.

Such thinking is not localized with Craig Chin's parents. The attempt to relive within the lives of children that which was not achieved by the parents is common to human nature. Sadly, Craig must become the worst of an American (that is, a disrespectful youth who would scream at his father and throw something of a tantrum) in order to make this point to his father.

The chief literary device used by the novelist is that of metaphor. Yep takes the commonplace knowledge that "life is a game" and shows human tensions and conflicts to be a series of ongoing "plays"—here, ones which are off the field. The real games in the story are the ones between father and son, between Uncle Quail and Craig, between Kenyon and Craig.

The overriding metaphor and symbol of the novel are indicated by the title. Life is like an ocean, and people as individuals are like broken pieces of glass. Persons can, in time, be shaped by the forces of nature and society into something smooth and beautiful—something like "sea glass."

Critical Context

Sea Glass was Laurence Yep's fourth novel to be published in the 1970's, and all dealt with problems of Chinese American childhood. These novels reveal a particular maturity and sophistication in that they do not simplistically blame white Americans for all the problems experienced by Chinese immigrants. Yep recognizes that the mainstream society may all too often be responsible for problems of racism and discrimination, but he argues that meaningful resolution of such difficulties finally lies within the selves of his characters.

Yep, himself a native-born American, is a product of the American 1960's. His sensitivity to the social turmoil and upheavals occurring during his own life are present in his work, if not through description of event then at least in attitude and perspective. Yep's books have won several awards. *Child of the Owl* (1977) won the *Boston Globe-Horn* Fiction Award; *Dragonwings* (1975) won recognition as the

American Library Association Notable Children's Book in 1975 and the Newbery Honor Book in 1976. He has continued to write novels, expanding his domain from ethnic fiction to works of mystery and suspense.

Bibliography
Burns, Mary M. "*Sea Glass.*" *The Horn Book Magazine* 55 (October, 1979): 542. The reviewer focuses mostly on conflicts between children and parents but also emphasizes the culture clash between American and Chinese in the United States. There is some discussion of Yep's narrative techniques, style, and structure in the novel.
Dinchak, Marla. "Recommended Laurence Yep." *English Journal* 71 (March, 1982): 81-82. Dinchak provides a thorough discussion of *Sea Glass* as well as three other novels by Yep: *Sweetwater* (1973), *Dragonwings*, and *Child of the Owl*. She makes valid comparisons among the teenage protagonist-narrators of the four works. In so doing, she takes up matters of adolescent conflicts, rebellion against parents, and communicating with others.
Fritz, Jean. "*Sea Glass.*" *The New York Times Book Review*, January 20, 1980, 30. Fritz's review focuses mostly upon the problems of Chinese Americans proving themselves as Americans. She explains Yep's purposes in retelling the story of a father-son conflict, finding the resolution of the plot to be less important than the characters themselves.
Kao, Donald. "*Sea Glass.*" *Interracial Books for Children Review* 11, no. 6 (1980): 16. Kao discusses the concept of achievement and success as it is understood by young Americans and as revealed in *Sea Glass*. He sets forth the idea that Craig is a "star" about things in life that are truly important and make sense. He identifies real-life problems and barriers as issues in the novel and discusses how "outsiders" to mainstream society deal with them.
Lenhart, Maria. "Finding the Courage to Be Oneself." *The Christian Science Monitor*, October 15, 1979, B11. This discussion is primarily concerned with the development of the main characters in the novel. The critic explains the faded dreams of the past (Craig's father) in the light of his own goals and expectations in life. She also discusses the dialogue of the first-person narrator, finding it credible.
Sutherland, Zena. "*Sea Glass.*" *Bulletin for the Center for Children's Books* 33 (February, 1980): 124. Sutherland gives perhaps the best discussion of *Sea Glass* as literature. She takes up the matter of the metaphor and symbol of "sea glass" itself, explaining how it relates to Craig. She also comments about changes within the main character.

Carl Singleton

THE SHARPEST SIGHT

Author: Louis Owens (1948-   )
Type of plot: Detective and mystery
Time of plot: The early 1970's
Locale: California and Mississippi
First published: 1992

>*Principal characters:*
>RAMON MUNDO MORALES, a deputy sheriff
>GLORIA MORALES, his wife
>ATTIS MCCURTAIN, a Vietnam veteran, part Choctaw and Cherokee, part Irish
>COLE MCCURTAIN, his brother
>HOEY MCCURTAIN, their father, part Irish, part Choctaw
>LUTHER, an aged Mississippi swamp dweller, Hoey McCurtain's Choctaw uncle
>ONATIMA, his friend, sometimes called Old Lady Blue Wood
>JESSARD DEAL, a tavern owner, also a Vietnam veteran
>LEE SCOTT, an FBI agent
>DAN NEMI, a rancher, the wealthiest landowner in the county
>DIANA NEMI, his daughter

The Novel

Although the plot of *The Sharpest Sight* involves a double murder mystery, the novel is far more than a whodunit, as it concerns several people of mixed ancestry who have to discover and come to terms with their identity, acknowledge their American Indian heritage, its values and meaning, and the position of Indians in a predominantly white society. The novel also deals with the trauma of the Vietnam War on its walking wounded.

The narrative opens with Mundo Morales, deputy sheriff of Amarga, California, driving his rounds on a night when it is raining so hard that the ordinarily dry Salinas River is flooding. Mundo thinks he sees a panther in his headlights, but when he gets out to investigate, he catches a glimpse of a dead body being tossed in the churning waters. It is his best friend, Attis McCurtain. They had grown up together, played basketball together, and gone to Vietnam together. While Mundo made a shaky adjustment back to American life, however, Attis cracked up, stabbed his girlfriend, Jenna Nemi, to death, and was institutionalized in the local hospital for the criminally insane. No one except Mundo, Attis' father and brother, and the murderer now believe that Attis is dead; everyone else with an interest in him insists that he escaped from the asylum and is on the run. Mundo cannot find the body, but he is sure that whoever cut the fence wires and helped Attis to escape did so in order to kill him. The likeliest suspect is Dan Nemi, the father of the murdered daughter. So thinks Hoey McCurtain,

Attis' father, who in turn is gunning for Dan to avenge his son's murder. Mundo therefore has to solve one murder while preventing another.

The authorities have vested interests in killing the case, however, and want Mundo to shut down his investigation altogether. Since Attis was a veteran and escaped from a veterans' hospital, the Federal Bureau of Investigation (FBI) enters the scene in the person of Lee Scott, a singularly obnoxious agent who boasts of being a Vietnam veteran who had no trouble adjusting to civilian life. The FBI and government seek to prevent any embarrassing negative publicity about Attis as a psychological casualty of the war, which is still going on. The sheriff wants to protect Dan Nemi, the wealthiest and most powerful man in the county, and threatens to discharge Mundo and send him back to his former job as janitor, the best work he could find after coming home from Vietnam. If Mundo is to pursue the case, he must do so on his own time.

Just as the Salinas River runs deep underground when it is dry on the surface, there are mysteries beyond the murder mystery, for Hoey McCurtain's Uncle Luther, an ancient Choctaw who lives in a swamp by the Yazoo River in Mississippi, has second sight that lets him know not only what has happened two thousand miles away but also what may happen in the future. Furthermore, Luther has a visitor in his cabin, the ghost of the murdered Attis, who cannot rest until his body has been found and given proper burial. In California, Mundo also receives occasional visits from the ghost of his grandfather. With these supernatural visitations, the novel moves from a Tony Hillerman-style murder mystery involving Indian heritage and part-Indian police into the realm of Magic Realism, as the living have dialogues with the dead and dream visions may be more real than waking sight.

Attis' younger brother, Cole, must visit that realm, both to discover his own identity and to enable his brother's spirit to rest. Cole has received a draft notice, but after his brother's experience, he resists going to Vietnam. His father sends him to Mississippi, both to find refuge in the swamp and to learn from Uncle Luther. Luther, in turn, learns from his college-educated friend Onatima, a venerable Choctaw whom he calls Lady Blue Wood, who blends traditional wisdom with that of great literature.

The title comes from a passage by the eighteenth century Puritan theologian Jonathan Edwards: "The arrows of death fly unseen at noon-day; the sharpest sight can't discern them." Despite his best efforts, Mundo never really proves who murdered Attis; probably it was not Dan Nemi. For a while, it looks as if it might be Dan's oversexed daughter Diana, who seduces Cole, tries to seduce Mundo, and boasts of having made love to Attis in the bed of Attis' lover, her murdered sister. Perhaps it is the psychopathic tavern owner Jessard Deal, another of the walking wounded from Vietnam, who periodically goes berserk and attacks his customers. The novel ends in an explosion of violence that leaves the question of Attis' murder moot. As the FBI agent says, it no longer matters who killed Attis any more than it does who killed the soldiers in body bags in Vietnam. Cole, however, succeeds in finding the body and taking it back to Mississippi so that his brother's bones can rest with his ancestors and his ghost can be released.

The Characters

Though much of the story is told from the perspective of Mundo Morales, he does not dominate it, for the narrative shifts back and forth among him, Cole McCurtain, and Uncle Luther; one chapter is even told from the point of view of the corpse. A veteran of Vietnam, Mundo has a shaky position as a deputy sheriff; his boss threatens to throw him back to being a janitor if he persists in asserting himself instead of being a docile subordinate. Despite opposition from all the authorities, he continues his investigation with intelligence and tenacity. Mundo's Mexican ancestors once owned all the land in the Salinas Valley; now most of it belongs to Dan Nemi, the chief suspect in the murder. Yet Mundo does not feel sorry for himself; he has a good marriage and self-respect, and he comes to appreciate the part-Indian ancestry that he shares with the McCurtains.

Hoey McCurtain's Irish father would not let him speak the language of his Choctaw mother and labeled him "white" on his birth certificate, but Hoey has chosen to consider himself an Indian and to direct his son Cole back to his roots. Cole could pass for white yet has not only a Choctaw grandmother but also a Cherokee mother; it is by learning the lessons of the Choctaw shamans that he finds himself and allays his murdered brother's troubled spirit. Diana Nemi, the white teenage princess, is addicted to having sex with Indians as a substitute for finding her own identity. The ghost of Mundo's grandfather calls her a witch, a "bruja." Hoey's Uncle Luther and his friend Onatima express most of the wisdom (as well as the humor) of the novel as they explore with Cole the significance of Indian values and the nature of the evil running amok in a world out of balance. Jessard Deal, the enormous, violent, poetry-quoting tavern owner, alludes to Jonathan Edwards, believes in innate depravity, and manifests it in his own actions.

Themes and Meanings

The Sharpest Sight champions the heritage of Native Americans and condemns their exploitation by a society that drafts them into the military and sends them to a senseless war in Vietnam, from which no one escapes without at least psychological trauma. There, Indians are given the most dangerous assignments, put "on point" because they supposedly have innate tracking skills. The government wants to hide Attis' tragedy, the way it has been hiding Indians on reservations "so they won't embarrass rich white folks by looking poor and hungry." Vietnam becomes a symbol of a world "screwy, cockeyed," of the circles broken, the balance destroyed. While soldiers die in Southeast Asia, students are shot at Berkeley and Kent State. Though Uncle Luther is trying to learn more about his people's history and in turn relate it to Cole, he concludes that there may be no difference between a warrior and a murderer; instead, he says, "We just kill each other over and over, forever." Just as ghosts visit him and Mundo, the ghosts of the dead haunt the jungles of Vietnam. Luther says the healing Indian medicine must go beyond the swamps, must go through the entire world, because "the whole world's out of whack and people like us Indians is the onliest ones that knows how to fix it." Such people will heal the world by respecting every part of it, treating it with care, not raping it as the whites have done. To do this, to live in balance, one must learn the stories of one's people. To prevent a blood feud from spreading, Luther sends Cole back to California to find his brother's body once Cole has learned what he needs to know.

There are many searches in the novel—for Attis' body, for his murderer, for vengeance, for identity, for insight, and for roots. Owens writes with sharp, precise imagery, dramatic dialogue, poetic description, and a vivid sense of place to produce a novel that is far more than a genre mystery.

Critical Context

The Sharpest Sight is volume 1 in the University of Oklahoma's American Indian Literature and Critical Studies Series, which also includes Louis Owens' *Other Destinies: Understanding the American Indian Novel* (1992). Owens, a professor of literature at the University of California at Santa Cruz, is a specialist on the work of John Steinbeck and coauthor with Tom Colonnese of *American Indian Novelists: An Annotated Critical Bibliography* (1985). *The Sharpest Sight*, his first novel, reflects his own mixed Choctaw, Cherokee, and Irish ancestry. In it, he combines ingredients from Tony Hillerman, John Steinbeck, William Faulkner, and the Magic Realism of Latin American novelists to come up with a work that is strikingly original.

The Indian protagonists and their cultural background resemble those of Hillerman, but with Choctaws and Cherokees rather than Navajos. The California episodes take place in Steinbeck country and show how the Chumash Indians had their lands stolen by Mexican settlers, who in turn were dispossessed by aggressive white invaders. In the Southeast, the five civilized tribes had their land stolen and were sent west on death marches in the 1830's. The Mississippi episodes not only take place in Faulkner country but also have Uncle Luther allude to Ikkemotube, or Doom, the Indian chief who features in a number of Faulkner's fictions.

Onatima brings Luther books of literature so that he will turn from Westerns to the stories that count, the ones that change the world. At the moment, she is reading Thomas Pynchon. She is worried that white people, with no homes, no roots, and no concern for the earth, make heroes of immature people who perpetrate senseless violence. Among the more amusing as well as enlightening parts of the novel are Luther's Choctaw explications of *Moby Dick: Or, the Whale* (1851) and *The Adventures of Huckleberry Finn* (1884). The Choctaws also have their own stories to give words to the spiritual dangers in the world. Yet literature is not enough, for Jessard Deal throws out allusions to poetry while committing atrocities. Attis believed that "we have to accept responsibility for our lives, for everything within us and around us." Tragically, Vietnam derailed him from doing this.

Bibliography

Jakowski, H. Review of *The Sharpest Sight*, by Louis Owens. *Choice* 29 (June, 1992): 1546. Though he calls the landscape a "palpable character" in the narrative, Jakowski misplaces the Mississippi sequences in Arkansas. He praises Owens' "lyrical prose" and calls the novel "a graceful literary production" that he compares to the poetry of Wallace Stevens, William Carlos Williams, and Hart Crane.

Mitten, Lisa A. Review of *The Sharpest Sight*, by Louis Owens. *Library Journal* 117 (January, 1992): 176. Mitten calls the narrative a voyage to discover the self and the false divisions between this world and the spirit world. She praises Owens' work as "a fine inaugural novel" for the beginning of the Oklahoma series on the American Indian.

Paulson, Gary. "Noonday Arrows of Death." *Los Angeles Times Book Review*, June 21, 1992, 12. Paulson, a novelist himself, praises Owens' novel as a mystery but shows how it extends the genre into a serious, even philosophical work that investigates "the relationship of Anglo literature to Native America." Yet he consistently confuses the Choctaw Indians of the novel with the Chickasaws.

Publishers Weekly. Review of *The Sharpest Sight*, by Louis Owens. 238 (December 20, 1991): 66. The anonymous reviewer finds resemblances between *The Sharpest Sight* and the fiction of Gabriel García Márquez in its use of mythic and fantastic elements but considers its style too "hard-boiled and turgid."

Seaman, Donna. Review of *The Sharpest Sight*, by Louis Owens. *Booklist* 88 (February 15, 1992): 1089. In its study of the destruction of the Indian nations and the evil of Vietnam, Seaman finds Owens' novel "a wise and poetic tale set to the seductively enigmatic music of magic and dreams."

Robert E. Morsberger

THE SHAWL

Author: Cynthia Ozick (1928-   )
Type of work: Novella and short story
First published: 1989

> *Principal characters:*
> ROSA LUBLIN, a survivor of a Nazi internment camp
> MAGDA, her infant daughter
> STELLA, her niece
> SIMON PERSKY, an elderly man interested in Rosa

The Novel

    The Shawl is the book publication of Cynthia Ozick's metaphorically complex and morally profound short story about the horrors of the Holocaust combined with her longer follow-up novella about the personal reverberations of that horror some thirty years later.

    "The Shawl" is a breathtaking story. In seven short, poetically terrifying pages, Cynthia Ozick compresses the unspeakable horrors of the Holocaust into a story that is as close to perfection as a story can be. The plot is thin to the point of nonexistence—a young Jewish mother loses her infant child to the barbarism of the Nazis. The characters are not so much real as they are highly compressed embodiments of tortured terror. It is therefore neither event nor persons that make this story so powerful, although history agrees that the cultural event described is the most shameful in modern life, and the characters in the story suffer more pain in a moment than most human beings will in a lifetime. Rather, as is typical of great works of art, it is the voice and language of the speaker that make this miniature narrative the powerful story that it is. Therefore, it is not possible to summarize its events without also referring to the words used to describe them.

    The style of "The Shawl" is a combination of short, unembellished descriptive and narrative sentences and nightmarish metaphors of human ugliness and transcendent beauty. The story opens with a march through a winter landscape toward a Nazi concentration camp. There are only three characters: Rosa, a young Jewish mother, her fifteen-month-old daughter Magda, and her fourteen-year-old niece Stella. The Nazi soldiers are monstrous mechanical abstractions that inflict pain and death rather than real human presences. Rosa is described as a "walking cradle" as she hides the baby between her breasts under her clothes. She feels in a trance, like a "floating angel." While Magda is like a squirrel in her nest, Stella, her knees like tumors on sticks, is jealous of her cozy safety.

    Ozick uses language to humanize and dehumanize her characters simultaneously. The face of the child is round, a "pocket mirror of a face"; one small tooth sticks up from Magda's bottom gum like an "elfin tombstone." The duct crevice of Rosa's empty breast is like a "dead volcano, blind eye, chill hole." For lack of physical nourishment, the child sucks on the shawl that gives the story its title—a shawl that Ozick calls magical, for it has nourished the child for three days and nights. Because Magda occupies herself with the shawl, never uttering a sound, she has so far been spared. On the horrifying day described in the story, however, Magda scurries into the prison yard crying loudly for her mother, for Stella has taken her shawl away from her. Although Rosa runs quickly to retrieve the shawl to quiet the baby, she is too late. When she returns to the yard, she sees Magda being carried over the head of a guard and thrown into the electrified fence of the camp: "She looked like a butterfly touching a silver vine." The story ends with Rosa stuffing Magda's shawl into her mouth to stifle her own screams so she will not also be killed.

The story is so powerful that the reader can hardly bear it, which is Ozick's point: Rosa, like the millions of others caught in the horror of the Holocaust, can hardly bear it. Yet bear it she must, and "Rosa," the second story in the collection, recounts how Rosa has borne it. This story is quite different from the first. It is less poetic, less compact, and more discursive; it is more focused on character and consciousness than on visceral and poetic impact. Thirty or forty years after the event of "The Shawl," Rosa is living in Miami, Florida. Just before the story begins, she has gone "mad" and destroyed her junk store in New York. She is now a middle-aged woman staying in a hotel that caters to the elderly. Her niece, Stella, who still lives in New York, sends her money.

The events of the story focus on a few days of Rosa's life in which the following events occur: She meets an elderly man, Simon Persky, who is interested in her and wants to get to know her better; she receives a request from a sociologist, Dr. James Tree, who wants to interview her as part of a study he is doing on Holocaust survivors; and she receives the "magical" shawl that she has requested that Stella send to her. Rosa meets Persky, whose wife is in a mental hospital, in a laundromat, where he often goes to meet women. When Persky asks her, "You ain't got a life?" she replies "Thieves took it." When Rosa goes home and discovers that she is missing a pair of her underpants from the laundry, she thinks that she has been the victim of another thief, believing that Persky has stolen them. While she is considering this violation of her privacy and person, she receives a more pointed invasion—a letter from Dr. Tree, who wants to treat her as a subject of study; he is developing a theory about survivors of the Holocaust.

Rosa's search for her lost underpants takes her on a journey into the heart of darkness of the Miami night. Accidentally wandering onto the private beach of one of the large Miami hotels—an ironic image of a Nazi concentration camp, but an enclosure that now harbors the analytical Dr. Tree—she cannot escape the barbed-wire compound that encloses her until she is thrown out by the manager. When she returns to her hotel room to find Persky waiting for her, and to find that her underpants have simply gotten mixed up with the rest of her laundry, she begins to accept Persky's interest and to make connections to the world outside. She gets her telephone reconnected, and she allows Persky to visit her. The story ends with the lines: "Magda was not there. Shy, she ran from Persky. Magda was away." This does not mean that

Rosa is finally free of her obsession, but it does suggest that she has begun to allow real people to replace the magical shawl of her memory.

The Characters

The only real character in these two stories is Rosa, for it is her conflict and her loss that is the focus of the first, and it is her isolation and her anguished efforts to "reconnect" that constitute the longer story that bears her name. In "The Shawl," the infant Magda is little more than the moon-faced creature of Rosa's womb that she hides between her dried-up breasts. In the second, Magda is the child of her fantasy, who she imagines is now a professor of Greek philosophy at Columbia University, and to whom she writes letters that she never mails. In "The Shawl," Stella is an unfortunate fourteen-year-old child who clings to life; even if she decides that she must sacrifice the infant Magda, her situation is so extreme that she cannot be blamed. In "Rosa," where the reader only meets Stella in letters and a telephone call, she serves as a reminder of the truth of the past to a Rosa who does not want to remember. Stella chastises Rosa for wanting to hold on to the past, as she wants to hold onto the talismanic shawl.

Because Rosa must bear so much, both as the symbolic Jewish mother of all those lost in the Holocaust in the first story and as one still stunned and entrapped in the past in the second story, she is more complex than any of the other characters, who exist primarily to reflect her complexity. Her efforts to protect her child and to survive, her inarticulate helplessness even to rage or grieve at the death of her child, her confused entrapment in the memories of the past, and her valiant effort to survive on her own terms without becoming the victim of those she fears will violate her further make her the powerful center of both of these stories.

The most significant aspect of Rosa's character is a stylistic one, for in the novella that bears her name she is not only a distracted and disoriented aging woman who is often irrational and neurotic, but she is also, when she writes to her imaginary daughter Magda, a sensitive and articulate spokeswoman of all that the Holocaust stole from its victims. Indeed, those parts of the story in which readers are privileged to read Rosa's letters to Magda, in which she invents fictions to retrieve her past, are the most powerful parts of the story.

Themes and Meanings

It is difficult to articulate any single thematic meaning for "The Shawl." Like Shirley Jackson's famous story, "The Lottery," with its mixture of myth and reality and its shocking climax, Ozick's story has an immediate visceral impact; moreover, it is structured with such consummate skill that it impresses one as a stylistic *tour de force*. When the story won first prize in the 1981 annual *O. Henry Prize Stories*, editor William Abrahams said in the introduction to that collection that "The Shawl" is one of those stories where one believes that the author has been inspired—has received the story and written it in a single go, without even pausing for the manipulations of craft. In reality, what makes the story so memorable is precisely that it is so well crafted it has the force of a breathtaking work of art.

What Ozick has achieved so brilliantly in the story is to capture the horrors of the Holocaust in one unforgettable symbolic scene and horrifying image. Writers have long known that to try to reflect the persecution of the Jews under Adolf Hitler by realistically depicting its magnitude is futile. The very immensity of the tragedy numbs the mind and freezes the feelings. Ozick uses the power of language to capture the horror in its quintessential reality. Even though in reality the death of a single child represents only one inconsequential event in the midst of the murder of millions, in Ozick's story all the accumulated sorrow and horror of that unbelievable historical tragedy is expressed by Rosa's stuffing the shawl into her mouth to prevent her own screams.

The meaning of the longer story "Rosa" is easier to discuss, for it contains more exposition and more direct emphasis on the themes of violation, exploitation, memory, and the human attempts to hold on to the past and yet to escape it. "Rosa" is quite emphatic about the very power that makes "The Shawl" difficult to discuss—the power of language. When Rosa writes to the nonexistent Magda, the pen unlocks her tongue, for she is immersed in language. Writing for her is the power to "make a history, to tell, to explain. To retrieve, to reprieve! To lie!" By giving Rosa's writing her own highly articulate voice, Ozick is able to present the writer as a maker of parables, one who tells fictions that have more truth value than the accounts of history: The stories the writer tells are concrete, specific, and powered by emotion and desire rather than by facts, figures, or abstract ideas.

Critical Context

Cynthia Ozick is a Jewish writer in the tradition of Bernard Malamud, for her stories, like many of his, are a special blend of lyricism and realism; they create a world that is socially immediate and recognizable while also being mythically mysterious and distant. She is also a Jewish writer in the tradition of Saul Bellow, for her fiction, like much of his, is powered by an underlying political and cultural vision. Ozick is a skilled novelist and poet as well as a powerful essayist on Judaism, art, feminism, and other subjects both contemporary and eternal. It is probably her short stories, however, that most significantly reflect her genius. When "Rosa" won first prize in the O. Henry competition three years after "The Shawl" did, William Abrahams said he would not hesitate to name her one of the three greatest living American writers of short fiction. "The Shawl" is one of those magical stories that so capture the imagination they become instant classics. Already, the story has been widely anthologized in college-level short story anthologies, where—with its eerie and unreal imagery, its distanced and transcendent point of view, and its horrifying climactic event—it will continue to shock and astonish readers for many years to come.

Bibliography

Knopp, Josephine. "Ozick's Jewish Stories." In *Cynthia Ozick*, edited by Harold

Bloom. New York: Chelsea House, 1986. A helpful discussion of the early Jewish stories from the point of view of the polemical concerns Ozick expresses in her essays. Focus is on such well-known Ozick stories as "The Pagan Rabbi" and "Envy, or Yiddish in America." Places her in the tradition of such Jewish American writers as Saul Bellow.

Lowin, Joseph. *Cynthia Ozick*. Boston: Twayne, 1988. A good overall introduction to Ozick's thought and art. Places her within the Jewish American literary tradition and discusses "The Shawl" within the context of her other short fiction. Reprints Lowin's article listed below as chapter eight. Also includes an annotated bibliography of additional criticism on Ozick.

—————— . "Cynthia Ozick, Rewriting Herself: The Road from 'The Shawl' to 'Rosa'" In *Since Flannery O'Connor: Essays on the Contemporary American Short Story*, edited by Loren Logsdon and Charles W. Mayer. Macomb: Western Illinois University, 1987. Lowin argues that, like the French symbolists, Ozick paints not the thing itself but its effect. Discusses how each of the three major characters uses the shawl as a life preserver. Describes "Rosa" as being within the tradition of Ozick's earlier midrashic writing such as "The Pagan Rabbi."

Scrafford, Barbara. "Nature's Silent Scream: A Commentary on Cynthia Ozick's 'The Shawl'" *Critique* 31 (Fall, 1989): 11-15. Claims that the short sentences of "The Shawl" and its concise syntax tell the story with a minimum of rhetoric. Argues that it derives most of its power from its ironic contrast between a barbarous place, where lives end, and motherhood, where life begins. The story is a skeleton itself, says Scrafford, for it is almost pure form, pure shape.

Strandberg, Victor. "The Art of Cynthia Ozick." In *Cynthia Ozick*, edited by Harold Bloom. New York: Chelsea House, 1986. Although this essay does not specifically discuss "The Shawl," it is an important analysis of Ozick's major themes. Discusses her power to elevate local materials to universal and timeless significance.

Charles E. May

SO FAR FROM GOD

Author: Ana Castillo (1953-   )
Type of plot: Impressionistic realism
Time of plot: The 1970's to the 1990's
Locale: Tome, a small town in New Mexico
First published: 1993

> *Principal characters:*
> SOFIA, a family matriarch who struggles to rear her four extraordinary daughters alone
> ESPERANZA, Sofia's eldest daughter, a former campus radical turned successful television journalist
> CARIDAD, the second and most beautiful daughter, a hospital orderly whose failed marriage leads her into a self-destructive lifestyle
> FE, the third daughter, whose preoccupation with appearances and securing the good life leads her to reject her family
> LA LOCA, Sofia's youngest daughter, gifted with supernatural abilities following her resurrection at age three
> DOMINGO, Sofia's wayward husband, a compulsive gambler whose inability to change dooms his marriage
> THE NARRATOR, one of Sofia's *compadres* or *comadres*, an opinionated storyteller who narrates, judges, and interprets, the events in the novel

The Novel

Medieval Christian mythology transformed the story of Sofia, the Greek goddess of wisdom, into the inspirational story of a heroic mother and her martyred daughters. *So Far from God* is Ana Castillo's modern reinterpretation of the lives and struggles of Sofia and her four daughters, Esperanza, Caridad, Fe, and La Loca. Set in contemporary New Mexico, the novel chronicles how this family, its neighbors, and their community confront and essentially prevail over the obstacles of racism, poverty, exploitation, environmental pollution, and war. The novel, covering two decades in the family's lives, unfolds through a series of flashbacks woven into the central narrative. Blending ironic humor with scathing social commentary, the novel is told from the perspective of a highly opinionated, omniscient third-person narrator.

Beginning with a flashback to the mysterious death and equally mysterious resurrection—*El Milagro*—of La Loca at age three, the narrative quickly shatters any boundaries between the real and the unreal, the natural and the supernatural. La Loca's miraculous resurrection and ascension to a church rooftop elevates the child to the status of folk saint. Left with an aversion to people, La Loca withdraws from the world and devotes her life to prayer and to the spiritual care of her family.

From this flashback, the novel moves into the more recent past as the narrator details the stories of Sofia and her daughters. Like their mother, Sofia's three older daughters have painful, failed relationships. While at college, Esperanza, a college activist, lived with her activist boyfriend, Ruben, who upon graduation elected to trade his Chicano cosmic consciousness for a *gabacha* (a white woman) with a Corvette. The most sensible of Sofia's children, Esperanza turns her failed relationship into the catalyst for an advanced degree and a successful journalistic career. Esperanza's younger sister Caridad also experiences problems in her marriage to her unfaithful high-school sweetheart, Memo. Rather than use that failure, the self-destructive Caridad resorts to alcohol and nightly anonymous sex to deal with the rejection.

Unlike her two older sisters, who seem doomed to failed relationships, Fe, the third daughter, appears fine until she receives a letter breaking off her engagement. Unable to cope with this loss, Fe suffers a nervous breakdown, and only a miracle eventually restores her. Before that miracle, Sofia, Esperanza, and La Loca have to deal with yet another crisis—the vicious attack, horrible mutilation, and near death of Caridad. The simultaneous miraculous restoration of Caridad and cure of Fe trigger a series of changes in the family. Following the incident, Domingo, the girls' wayward father, reappears and tentatively resumes his life with Sofia; Esperanza accepts a dangerous assignment to cover the Persian Gulf War; Caridad—now gifted with foresight and prophecy—moves out and apprentices herself to doña Felicia, an eccentric *curandera*, or witch woman; Fe also moves out and resumes her job at the bank. La Loca remains at home and prays.

While covering the war, Esperanza and her news crew disappear and are presumed captured in Saudi Arabia. Her unknown fate becomes the focal point for both her family and the media community until La Loca informs her mother that Esperanza has been killed. Without the attendant news coverage, Caridad also undergoes a profound, life-changing encounter: Accompanying doña Felicia on her yearly pilgrimage to Chimayo, Caridad falls in love with Esmeralda, a mysterious woman. Unsure how to deal with the effect of Esmeralda and with her renewed emotions, Caridad also disappears. The fate of Sofia's missing daughters is partially resolved when Caridad is discovered exiled in the desert. For a time following her return, Caridad is regarded as a local folk saint. Although severely tested by the fates that have befallen her daughters, Sofia, who continues to believe in the power of faith and in the principles of social change advocated by her war-hero daughter, decides to run for mayor of Tome. Protected from the world in the cocoon of her mother's *rancheria*, La Loca continues to pray.

Fe appears close to achieving her quest for the American Dream in her marriage to her cousin Casimiro. The epitome of middle-class consumer utopia—complete with a three-bedroom, two-car-garage tract home and new sedan—deteriorates into a horrid nightmare. In order to afford the amenities of the good life, Fe quits her dead-end job at the bank and takes a job with a mysterious chemical company; the result is her slow, excruciating death from toxic poisoning. While her sisters have been victims of misguided social policies, Caridad becomes the victim of the misguided obsession of one man, Francisco el Penitente. Viewing Caridad as his God-chosen mate, Francisco begins to stalk her. Completely unbalanced after he uncovers Caridad's friendship with Esmeralda, Francisco abducts and rapes Esmeralda. When he continues to stalk them, the women commit suicide by leaping from a cliff.

The final tragedy which Sofia must face is the death of her youngest daughter, La Loca, from acquired immune deficiency syndrome (AIDS). Facing death as she had lived, with courage and acceptance, La Loca, once again elevated to the status of saint, becomes the patron of her community. Rather than end tragically, the novel returns to the themes of survival, endurance, and heroic triumph in Sofia's founding of M.O.M.A.S., an eccentric organization for the mothers of martyrs and saints.

The Characters

Esperanza, the least developed of the main characters, is presented in the role of surrogate caregiver and stabilizing influence in the family. Representative of many modern women who recognize the difficulty of maintaining both a career and a meaningful relationship, Esperanza is a successful journalist struggling to reconcile her personal needs, her political beliefs, and her professional responsibilities. The most politically active of the daughters, Esperanza functions as the novel's social conscience. Her death while covering the Persian Gulf War transforms her into a heroic symbol of outrage at death without dignity. Esperanza is both a martyr to and a symbol of the consequences of the United States' misguided foreign policies.

Presented as the passive victim of an unfaithful husband, Caridad resorts to nightly drinking and anonymous sex to deal with her failed marriage. Her mutilation, restoration, and exile are all simply preludes to her ultimate discovery that "falling in love . . . now that was something else altogether." Caridad comes to embody the redeeming power of love as she voluntarily sacrifices herself for another. The principal thematic elements—the blurring of the lines between the mythic and the everyday, and the transforming power of heroism and love—come together in the final, simultaneously selfless and self-affirming act of Caridad and Esmeralda.

Initially the least sympathetic of the four daughters, Fe is also the most unlikely heroine. Superficial, distant, and immature, Fe is anxious to get out of Tome and to get away from her family. She is eager to disassociate herself from Chicano culture and to align herself with the dominant culture's values and beliefs. The hardships that Fe must face function as rites of passage that help her evolve beyond this psychological immaturity to the courage of self-responsibility and assurance. In the process of facing her own mortality, Fe develops into an assertive, independent, compassionate woman. Like Esperanza, Fe is also a martyr and a symbol; her death is a warning against the effects of racist environmental policies.

Woven into the narrative is the story of the miraculous life of Sofia's youngest daughter. Perceived by others as retarded, mentally ill, or soulless, La Loca is the spiritual center of her family and later the patron saint of her community. Defined by the tragedies and triumphs of her family, La Loca lives without fear, fully aware of the choices she has made in life. From La Loca, the reader sees that life is to be lived with courage and wisdom, with dignity and joy, with an appreciation of its mystery.

Throughout the novel, Sofia endures and triumphs over tragedy. Sofia's heroism is seen in her repeated efforts to understand; rather than fall victim to despair, she reaches into the depths of her spirit and her faith to prevail over the obstacles that confront her. Sofia represents the heroic qualities of *hispano* women—strong, courageous, resilient women who not only survive adversity but who also prevail, endure, and pass their strength and determination on to their children and communities.

Domingo, of the Clark Gable mustache and piercing eyes, is at once the love of Sofia's life and the source of her greatest heartache. Initially the family, the community, and the reader believe that Domingo abandoned Sofia and the girls. Only later, when, after his unexplained return, he gambles away the land and the house, does Sofia "remember" that she had thrown him out.

Themes and Meanings

So Far from God, a complex, multidimensional novel, blends elements of New Mexican mythology, Pueblo stories, and European Catholicism with home remedies, recipes, and Castillo's bitingly sardonic humor to tell the story of a remarkable family. The subtext of the novel examines the brutal poverty and discrimination faced by hispanic and indigenous peoples in the Southwest.

The novel is a probing critique of the racism, sexism, and materialism of American society in general and of social institutions such as the government, the church, and large corporations in particular. Woven into the narrative is a pointed examination of such contemporary issues as political oppression, economic exploitation, and environmental pollution. One of the novel's main thematic focuses is environmental racism and the lack of protection afforded to minorities and the poor by the policies and agencies intended to safeguard them. The powerfully poetic chapter 15 juxtaposes brutal sociopolitical realities with the deep religious feelings of people making a Way of the Cross procession, presenting a catalog of social and environmental ills: minority families living below the poverty level, growing unemployment, deaths from toxic poisoning, radioactive dumping on reservations, birth defects and cancers linked to uranium contamination. The critique is not limited to sociopolitical issues, for the narrative also examines the problems of socially defined sex roles, sexuality, and women's struggle for self-respect. Throughout the novel, women strive to define themselves outside restrictive, socially acceptable roles: Esperanza struggles to succeed in a typically male-dominated profession; Caridad struggles to reconcile her feelings for Esmeralda with her internalized expectations; Sofia struggles to keep her family together and her faith intact in the face of repeated challenges and tragedies.

The novel is also about interpersonal and family relationships; about loyalty, honesty, compassion, and love as the basis for successful relationships. A compulsive gambler who cannot control his addiction, Domingo nevertheless loves Sofia and his daughters; a victim of *susto* (shock) who cannot commit to a relationship, Tom clearly loves Fe; a nearly textbook-perfect *machista* (male chauvinist) who refuses to admit his feeling and vulnerabilities, Ruben finally realizes that he truly loves Esperanza. Although the men love the women, their relationships fail because they lack mutual respect, loyalty, and compassion. Yet, it is these very qualities that form the basis of the women's relationships with one another. Even Fe, who is originally estranged from her family, grows to appreciate the importance of compassion and acceptance.

Castillo's novel is also a powerful study of personal heroism, of honor, courage, and determination. *So Far from God* is a remarkable celebration of survival with dignity and joy. The power of the novel lies in the women's ability not only to survive adversity but also to triumph over it. In the midst of death and tragedy, Castillo affirms life and the human will that sustains it. Refusing to give into despair, the women discover that within themselves they have the power and the vision—both spiritual and political—of the saints they love.

Critical Context

So Far from God is Ana Castillo's third novel. The book's favorable reception by critics and public alike secured her place among the writers at the forefront of the wave of Chicana fiction that came to mainstream consciousness in the late 1980's and 1990's. The novel's publication marked the author's move from small presses to larger publishing houses.

In the novel, Castillo successfully continues the experimentation with literary techniques that characterized her previous novels, *The Mixquiahuala Letters* (1986), which received the American Book Award in 1987, and *Sapogonia* (1990). In *So Far from God*, Castillo uses a distinctive participating narrator, flashbacks, introspective asides, and digressions from the central narrative to create a rich, complex, mythic tale.

Internationally recognized as a poet, novelist, essayist, and translator, Castillo started as a "protest poet" and continues to explore the issues—racism, sexism, oppression, inequality—to which she first gave voice in her poems. In *So Far from God*, she also continues to explore the feminist themes that have been recognized as central not only to her other two novels but to her poetry and nonfiction as well.

Bibliography

Castillo, Ana. "A Conversation with Ana Castillo." Interview by Elsa Saeta. Texas College English 26 (Fall, 1993): 1-6. In this interview, Castillo discusses her development as a writer, her literary influences, and her philosophical perspectives. Helps to place Castillo's work in context by providing insights into the personal, philosophical, and political concerns that define her work.

—————————. "Massacre of the Dreamers—Reflections on Mexican-Indian Women in the U. S.: Five Hundred Years After the Conquest." In *Critical Fictions: The Politics of Imaginative Writing*, edited by Philomena Mariani. Seattle: Bay Press, 1991. In this critical essay, Castillo discusses some of the theoretical perspectives that influence her work. Castillo defines her poetics and examines Chicana writers' relationship to their culture, their language, and their history.

Kingsolver, Barbara. "Desert Heat." *Los Angeles Times Book Review*, May 16, 1993, 1, 9. Kingsolver's review suggests that the novel could be "the offspring of a union between *One Hundred Years of Solitude* and *General Hospital*: a sassy, magical, melodramatic . . . delightful novel." Kingsolver discusses the novel's strengths specifically: the characters and their development, the narrative voice, and Castillo's venture into North American Magical Realism.

Publishers Weekly. Review of *So Far from God*, by Ana Castillo. February 22, 1993, 81. Generally laudatory review that calls the novel "inventive but not entirely cohesive." Notes Castillo's combination of Magical Realism with a North American perspective.

Yarbro-Bejarano, Yvonne. "The Multiple Subject in the Writing of Ana Castillo." *The Americas Review* 20, no. 1 (1992): 65-72. An analysis of three of Castillo's works. Summarizes much postmodern and feminist criticism of Chicana writing.

Elsa Saeta

A SOLDIER OF THE GREAT WAR

Author: Mark Helprin (1947-   )
Type of plot: Bildungsroman
Time of plot: 1899-1964
Locale: Primarily Italy
First published: 1991

> *Principal characters:*
> ALLESANDRO GIULIANI, a professor of aesthetics
> NICOLO SAMBUCCA, a young factory worker
> SIGNORE GIULIANI, Allesandro's father, an attorney
> LUCIANA GIULIANI, Allesandro's sister
> RAFI FOA, a friend of Allesandro, Luciana's fiancé
> GUARIGLIA, a harness-maker
> ORFEO QUATTA, a copier in Signore Giuliani's office who later works in
>   the defense ministry
> ARIANE, Allesandro's wife, a nurse

The Novel

Mark Helprin's *A Soldier of the Great War* relates, through a long flashback, the early manhood of Allesandro Giuliani, particularly his life during World War I. Told in the third person, the narrative begins in 1964. Allesandro is journeying by streetcar from Rome to visit his granddaughter's family. A young factory worker, Nicolo Sambucca, futilely chases the car in an attempt to board. Allesandro demands that it be stopped. Refused reentry by the driver, Allesandro decides that he and Nicolo will walk the seventy kilometers to their respective destinations. They have little in common. Allesandro, from an old and successful Roman family—his father was an attorney—is a professor of aesthetics. Nicolo, a helper in a factory, is young, naïve, and uneducated. During their walk, Allesandro relates the crucial events of his life, centering on the years of World War I.

Life is idyllic for Allesandro before the war, centering on his family and their home in Rome. One evening, he hears singing in the garden of the French Academy. Entering, he sees three young girls. The youngest, at sixteen, and the most beautiful, is Ariane. He also saves the life of a fellow university student, Rafi Foa, who had been harassed because he is a Jew. Afterward, Allesandro introduces him to his passion for mountain climbing.

In the autumn of 1914, while millions of men are marching to war and death, Allesandro travels to Munich to view Raphael's portrait of Bindo Altoviti, a painting that had survived time; Allesandro comments that "he knew from Bindo Altoviti's brave and insolent expression that he was going to stay alive forever." There Allesandro first hears the thundering cannons of war. To avoid the carnage of the infantry, Allesandro joins the navy; instead of escaping the front, however, he is assigned as a river guard in the mountains he knows so well.

It is there that he meets Guariglia, a Roman harness-maker. Although unsympathetic to the war aims of his country—or any political or economic ideology—Allesandro becomes an excellent soldier. Later, he and Guariglia are transferred to Sicily to search for deserters. In the interim, Allesandro visits Venice, where he sees Giorgione's *La Tempesta*, a painting of a woman, a baby, a male figure that Allesandro believes to be a soldier, and an approaching storm. Paradoxically, while taking the captured deserters back to trial and execution, Allesandro and Guariglia desert. Allesandro returns to Rome, where his father is dying.

Hoping to get the medicine that might save his father, Allesandro turns to Orfeo Quatta, a copier of documents in Signore Giuliani's office before the war who is presently working in the defense ministry. Orfeo, who believes that the secret to the universe is the "blessed sap," initially seems merely madly eccentric. Then, however, he confides that he is directing the Italian war effort through his documents and that he has often reversed the orders of his superiors. It was he who had assigned Allesandro to the front lines, supposedly to protect him. Orfeo has become a demented *deus ex machina* to millions. He provides the medicine, but it does not help. Allesandro is arrested and sent to a military prison for eventual execution. At the last moment, he is reprieved thanks to Orfeo's intervention. He tries to give his life for Guariglia's because of the latter's children, but he is clubbed into unconsciousness.

Returning to battle, Allesandro is injured. He is cared for by a nurse who turns out to be Ariane, the girl from prewar days, and they fall in love. Ariane becomes pregnant, but as a recovered Allesandro marches again to war, an Austrian plane destroys the hospital. Back in the mountains, Allesandro retrieves Rafi's body from a cliff in the face of enemy fire and is captured. A prisoner in Vienna at the end of the war, Allesandro flees to Munich to kill the pilot who bombed Ariane's hospital, but he changes his mind because of the pilot's young child. There, he again sees Raphael's painting of Bindo Altoviti, taking consolation from the portrait that nothing is ever lost: All can be remembered, even Ariane.

After the war, with his father dead and his sister having emigrated, Allesandro becomes a gardener. Again he visits Venice to see *La Tempesta*, which he believes should have been the story of his life—a woman and child waiting for a soldier returning from war. The guard mentions that a woman with a baby had recently cried when she viewed the painting. Hoping it could be Ariane, Allesandro finally discovers his son sailing a toy boat in Rome.

The narrative returns to 1964, to the old Allesandro and the young Nicolo. Allesandro relates his life with Ariane, who had since died, and their son, who had been killed in World War II. At the end of their long walk, Allesandro feels death approaching. Dismissing Nicolo, he descends into a valley, recollecting again his life and art.

The Characters

Allesandro Giuliani dominates the novel, since it is his life he relates to Nicolo. Although a professor of aesthetics, Allesandro is not a typical academic. He rejects the traditional critical approach, claiming that critics "parse by intellect alone works that are great solely because of the spirit." Drawn to art, Raphael's portrait of Bindo Altoviti and Giorgione's *La Tempesta* help illuminate his life. So, too, does nature—the seas, skies, and mountains. As a counterpoint, war also has its lures; as in everything else, Allesandro excels on the battlefield. Opposed to the twentieth century "isms" of communism, fascism, and nationalism, Allesandro's pole stars are love and beauty.

The rest of the characters revolve around Allesandro, satellites to his world. Signore Giuliani, his father, is the great influence on Allesandro's life—his mother is almost absent from Allesandro's story—but he is a shadowy and somewhat symbolic figure who represents family, love, and stability in a universe torn by war. Luciana, Allesandro's sister, also remains a secondary figure; she too is an undeveloped character, of greater importance to Allesandro than to the reader.

Even Ariane remains obscure. When they meet in the hospital, she literally sits in the shadows, remaining nameless. She becomes the great love of Allesandro's life, and he seeks her in both art and life until he finds her. Yet the reader is left with little knowledge of Ariane except through Allesandro's own words and feelings, which illumine him but not her.

Nicolo, young, innocent, and uneducated, is an antithesis to Allesandro. Allesandro treats Nicolo as a professor might approach a student: imparting knowledge and wisdom and hoping that the lesson will have effect. In turn, Nicolo validates Allesandro's life, not only because he listens to the story but also because he will live into the future. Nicolo, because of his youth and innocence, is still malleable, and nothing is lost that can be remembered.

Guariglia is also Allesandro's antithesis. Guariglia is unattractive and uneducated; he works with his hands, not his head. Yet the furnace of war unites them in the same manner as the later walk unites Allesandro and Nicolo. Beauty is more than appearance, and Guariglia is sanctified by his love for his family.

Other than Allesandro, the most notable character is also the most fantastic: Orfeo Quatta. A repulsive dwarf who could populate the pages of Charles Dickens, Orfeo is mad. Convinced of the reality of the "blessed sap" and fearing that the advent of the typewriter will lead to civilization's demise, Orfeo at first seems a harmless eccentric. In the insanity of war, however, Orfeo's dementia takes a sinister turn; his is the perverse hand on the levers of power. Orfeo wants Allesandro to live—he transfers Allesandro to the front instead of allowing him to drown on a naval ship, and he aborts Allesandro's execution—but his megalomania and irrationality are a paradigm of the war itself. In the end, however, even he is a minor figure. It is Allesandro who is at the center of the novel's universe.

Themes and Meanings

"'I was born to be a soldier,' Allesandro said, 'but love pulled me back.'" For Allesandro, love and beauty are the essences of life, and one of the most obvious themes in Helprin's novel is its contrast of the beauty of art and nature and the love of family and friends with the evil, madness, and anarchy of war. Yet these polarities are also inseparable. Love comes with carnage and death: Ariane and Allesandro find each other in the darkness of a military hospital, and as he is about to be executed as a deserter, Guariglia's last words are "God keep my children." Allesandro's interpretation of Giorgione's *La Tempesta* conjoins the soldier, storm, woman, and child as a unity. On the night before he is to be executed, Allesandro, looking out his prison window, is overcome with the starlight, and his heart rises in response. After he leaves Nicolo, Allesandro's last sight is of a flight of swallows, "the unification of risk and hope," slaughtered in mid-flight by a hunter.

Love and beauty are not merely transcendent, they are redemptive. In prison in Vienna at the war's end, Allesandro is confronted by several socialists and anarchists who ask him if he believes in God. He replies that he does, since both nature and art affirm God's reality, but he denies that God's existence can be proved by reason; thus, he explains, he never followed the formalities of organized religion. He expects no afterlife, but he says that "I love God nonetheless, with every atom of my being, and will love Him until I fall into black oblivion." Still, Bindo Altoviti's portrait suggests that art can be eternal, and Allesandro's plaintive and hopeful last words are addressed to God: "I beg of you only one thing. Let me join the ones I love. Carry me to them, unite me with them, let me see them, let me touch them."

Allesandro's life consists of many journeys: from Rome with Nicolo at the end of the novel and his life, from the Edenic days of peace to the mayhem of war, from innocent youth to experienced old age, from the life of the many to the inevitable death of all, from this life to whatever might await after death. *A Soldier of the Great War* is thus a *Bildungsroman*, as Allesandro and his world receive a bloody education in the eternal necessity of morals and values in a twentieth century society seemingly dedicated to their eradication.

Helprin asks the great questions about goodness, beauty, and love in a world of madness and chaos. Allesandro can be compared with Voltaire's Candide: Allesandro's is not the best of all possible worlds, and after the war is over, he accepts employment cultivating his own family's former garden. Like Voltaire, Helprin can be ironic and satirical with many of his characters and their actions, but there is also a profound seriousness in his commitment to the realities of love and beauty. There are risks for a writer taking this path, but Helprin's brilliant use of language allows his themes to soar above the level of cliché and banality.

Critical Context

A Soldier of the Great War was Mark Helprin's third novel, following *Refiner's Fire* (1977) and *Winter's Tale* (1983). He has also published many short stories and has written for children. Many years in the writing, *A Soldier of the Great War* is the most ambitious of Helprin's works. A serious author who has attained best-seller status, he claims that he is basically a teller of tales who eschews the modernist literary concerns of introspection and alienation in his characters.

Helprin's first novel, *Refiner's Fire*, also uses the flashback technique, recounting the picaresque adventures of a widely traveled Israeli soldier who has been mortally injured in the Yom Kippur War of 1973. *Winter's Tale*, Helprin's second novel, is a surrealistic fantasy that relates the lives and adventures of a number of characters, including a horse who flies, in an idealized New York City. Popular with readers, the book received mixed reviews from critics. Helprin's father, to whom Helprin was very close and who died in 1984, suggested that he make his next work more realistic. As Helprin has noted, in contrast to the previous novel, there is "nothing that violates the laws of physics" in *A Soldier of the Great War*. It too became a best-seller.

All Helprin's novels have in common the struggle against mortality. In *Refiner's Fire*, Marshall Pearl, although apparently dying, exhibits the will to live as he rises from his bed. The same battle and victory is true of many of the characters in *Winter's Tale*. Although many characters physically die in *A Soldier of the Great War*, the spiritual, through art, beauty, and love, can and will endure. At times out of step with much of modern literature, Helprin's works are life-affirming, humanistic tales of heroic adventures.

Bibliography

Eder, Richard. "Radiance Is in the Details." *Los Angeles Times Book Review* (May 5, 1991): 2. Praises the novel for its magical radiance, which "claps together comedy and sudden beauty . . . as a gateway not to skepticism but to wonder." Argues that the battle scenes are less successful, however, for they are merely realistic and have been done before.

Edwards, Thomas R. "Adventurers." *The New York Review of Books* 38 (August 15, 1991): 43-44. Suggests that Helprin's novel may be part of a new literary trend, reacting against certain current expectations in art and life. States that the work exhibits a disillusionment with secular explanations but at times becomes portentous and abstract.

Keneally, Thomas. "Of War and Memory." *The New York Times Book Review* (May 5, 1991): 1. Keneally admires Helprin for asking the big questions and notes that the author's answers are sometimes banal but often illuminating. Keneally suggests that Anton Chekhov would have hated Helprin's work, but he points out that Chekhov disliked Fyodor Dostoevski's concern with God's mysteries.

Solotaroff, Ted. "A Soldier's Tale." *The Nation* 252 (June 10, 1991): 776-781. Noting that the tension in the novel is between the glory of war and its horror, Solotaroff finds Helprin's account more lyrical than dramatic. For Helprin to be a great novelist, Solotaroff argues, he must become less facile.

Wade, Alan. "The Exquisite Lightness of Helprin." *The New Leader* 74 (August 12, 1991): 19-20. Calling the work a marvelous fairy tale for adults, Wade claims that Helprin is the "most gifted American novelist of his generation." His gift, Wade says, is in creating great adventures, not complex characters or literary realism.

Eugene Larson

SOMETHING TO BE DESIRED

Author: Thomas McGuane (1939-)
Type of plot: Psychological realism
Time of plot: 1958 to the 1980's
Locale: Deadrock, Montana
First published: 1984

> *Principal characters:*
>> LUCIEN TAYLOR, an immature young man who has left his wife, his child, and his government job to come to the aid of a former lover who has shot her husband
>> EMILY, Lucien's strong-willed and hard-hearted former lover who has killed her abusive husband and is fleeing the police
>> SUZANNE, Lucien's strong-willed and tender-hearted former wife, who divorced him when he abandoned her and whose trust and respect he must work to regain
>> DEE THOMPSON, Lucien's unhappily married lover in Deadrock
>> WICK TOMPKINS, Emily's lawyer, who befriends Lucien
>> W. T. AUSTINBERRY, Emily's hired hand, whom she seduces and kills

The Novel

When Lucien Taylor in Thomas McGuane's *Something to Be Desired* abruptly leaves his wife, child, and job to aid a former lover who has shot her abusive husband, his motives are not purely altruistic. He is restless and still finds Emily attractive. Eventually, he realizes that he desires neither adventure nor Emily but the love of his family; as he sets out to reclaim it, he acquires self-knowledge and a sense that his life finally has a "center" that makes it rewarding.

Something to Be Desired is divided into twenty chapters. Filled with Lucien's memories, the third-person narrative is so closely focused on Lucien that it has the immediacy of a first-person tale.

In the first chapter, Lucien and his irresponsible father are entering the final, disastrous phase of their relationship. Long absent, the father has suddenly reappeared to take his son on an "adventure" camping trip. The boy and his father have been lost for two days. Before Lucien locates their campsite, they stumble upon and bathe in a hot spring.

Filled with self-pity, the father ends the trip abruptly. Lucien sees him pick up a prostitute along the way; the boy also watches him brutally strike his bitter and vengeful former wife before he leaves for good after a last drunken quarrel.

After years of living with his alcoholic and abusive mother, Lucien goes away to college, where he meets the other two women who will influence his life. Although he is obsessed with Emily's beauty and passion, she leaves him to marry the other man with whom she has been having an affair. Lucien then meets and marries the beautiful

Suzanne, who is as principled, generous, and stabilizing as Emily is unprincipled, selfish, and unsettling.

Common sense tells Lucien that Suzanne is Emily's superior. Nevertheless, he is troubled by a "lack of high romance in his life." When they learn that Emily has shot her husband, he abandons his family and goes to Emily's ranch near the spring in Deadrock. While he admits that his behavior has begun "the process of stain" in him, Lucien also sees himself as carrying out a mission, part of which is to have Emily love him again, a feat he thinks he can accomplish by rescuing her—paying her bail. The doubts of Emily's lawyer, Wick Tompkins, about her chances and character are confirmed when Emily disappears with W. T. Austinberry, the hired hand.

Left alone with the ranch, Lucien engages in a halfhearted affair with the unhappily married Dee. He begins to recognize that he is on the road to loneliness. After spending a year in a despairing, alcohol-induced daze, he announces that he is "going to start something tremendous." Encouraged by Wick, he decides to transform the ranch and its spring into a spa. When the resort is hugely successful, Lucien calls Suzanne to tell her. Cautious but hopeful, she agrees to bring James to visit Lucien, who is "head over heels in love."

Lucien continues the process of self-discovery. He reflects on his own mortality and on the importance of tradition and continuity. He realizes that he is not interested in making even more money, and his desire to provide his son with a sense of security continues to grow.

Lucien has other trials to undergo. Although James comes around, Suzanne does not. Dee announces that she is leaving, and Emily reappears, carrying a gun. Finally unmoved by her, aware that she could destroy his life, Lucien informs Suzanne of her arrival and tells Emily that she must leave. Partly in anger, Suzanne concludes her visit; while James twists around to wave goodbye, Suzanne "keeps her eyes on the road."

The Characters

Lucien's thoughts, actions, and language indicate that he finds it difficult, if not impossible, to make and to commit himself to choices that are clearly in his best interests. This Hamlet-like indecision seems to stem from his childhood. He was attracted by what he saw as the romance of his father's life and is often driven, like his father, by sexual desires he refuses to control. Lucien (whose name suggests the devil that often seems to control him) is saved from self-destruction, ultimately, by his fine ironic sense and by his willingness to find a center to his life in the form of his son.

A lover of well-told tales, he often sees his life unrealistically, in terms of a story. In college, he is torn between two girls sketched in outlines suited to tales of the Old West; they have old-fashioned names and seem to represent vice and virtue. Even though the values and codes represented by the myths of the Old West appeal to him, he is not a storybook hero. As he rushes off to "save" Emily, he abandons his own child.

When he feels that he can go no lower, he finds that he can turn to his advantage resources that he has used successfully before: his organizational skills, his business acumen, and his "willingness to please." He is a kind of fallen angel who starts to rise again as he begins to create a new life, this time one that he invests with meaning.

Suzanne is a stabilizing influence; she remains a wonderful wife and mother throughout. Suzanne rejected all other suitors to marry Lucien. Stung by his abandonment, she forces him to fight for her, as he did not before, until she considers him a responsible adult. Suzanne manages to occupy the moral high ground without appearing "sappy," as Lucien thinks her to be at one point. Even though her unhappiness hardens her and makes her able to shock Lucien, she is still, in many ways, an idealized character.

Emily is the other woman, the bad girl whose most notable characteristics are selfishness and amorality. She represents the Wild West at its wildest. When she kills a second time, she becomes not only a villain but also a literal outcast from American society. Emily represents a dislocation of body and soul; in chasing her, Lucien sees, he is courting death.

Lucien's father appears only in the opening chapter, but his presence haunts Lucien. He and his wife are the source of Lucien's instability. Alcoholic, childish, self-pitying, and abusive, he is impulsive, ignoring the consequences of his actions and leaving loose ends everywhere. He runs from problems and lies to himself, excusing his behavior by telling Lucien that "we are all animals." Lucien, sadly, recognizes that his father's childish and underhanded approach to fighting with his wife is "wholly characteristic." He is an antifather; a worse model is hard to imagine.

Dee's behavior provides a counterpart to Lucien's. Caught in an unhappy marriage, she has no illusions when she slips into an affair with Lucien. She surprises—and impresses—him when she breaks the slender tie that connects them to begin a new and independent life for herself. Dee is given a few sharp, ironic words to say; she appears mainly in the narrator's description of their sad, squalid encounters.

Wick Tompkins, Emily's lawyer, comes to like Lucien, and the obvious affection of this wise, amusing, and basically decent man for Lucien indicates that there is hope for Lucien's future.

With the absurdly grand name of W. T. Austinberry, Emily's hired hand is not even a cowboy in name only. He is another source of disillusionment to Lucien. A far cry from the idealized figure of the Old West, he has no love for the land. He is inadequate as a lover and contemptible as a sportsman; he dumps quantities of bleach into a river when he wants to catch fish.

Themes and Meanings

The themes of *Something to Be Desired* are traditional and typical of McGuane's work: the desire to be close to and to respect nature, the search for a way to deal with contemporary society's corruption and materialism, and the desire to find stability in an unstable world while maintaining a sense of individuality in a culture that encourages sameness.

McGuane believes that "authentic" modern fiction has as its vantage point dislocation, and a sense of instability and displacement pervades the novel. From the beginning, Lucien has difficulty securing a footing on the shifting grounds of modern life. The failure of his parents' marriage seems inevitable in a society where traditional moral and ethical codes of behavior are no longer in effect. He even finds his own happy marriage unsatisfying and seems to value it only when he must run enormous risks to regain it.

The theme of dislocation and instability is also apparent in Lucien's realization that the romantic image he had of the Old West, the last outpost of new beginnings, is now insupportable. Schooled in its myths, Lucien grew up admiring a variety of rugged individualists, heroes such as Lord Nelson, Vasco da Gama, Theodore Roosevelt, and the anonymous ranchers and cowhands who created new lives for themselves in the frontier. He has always valued an Emersonian self-reliance, and he occasionally tries to adhere to certain codes of behavior (he admires Suzanne for her stubborn belief in the value of such a code).

In Deadrock, however, the discrepancy between the myths and the reality is glaringly and often comically apparent. Lucien's ranch supports "sulphur taffy" rather than cattle; his most libidinous encounters are not with prostitutes but with vacationing nannies; the villain he must confront does not challenge him to a duel but overcharges him for seamless gutters. Lucien needs to find ways he can live in this new, "tame" West.

The novel is also about the relationship between fathers and sons. Lucien's unclouded memory of his "adventure" with his father reveals nothing about his feelings; the boy seems to be holding his judgment in abeyance, as if to deny what he is seeing and feeling. It is years before he can tell himself with some revulsion that in leaving his family he is repeating the pattern set by his father. Unlike his father, Lucien wants to be a hero to his son, and when he sees a copy of a book of "true tales of the old West" by the sleeping boy's bedside, he begins to sense that he has found his home.

Critical Context

Something to Be Desired, McGuane's sixth novel and seventh book, was not as well received as his earlier novels. Critics faulted McGuane for inconsistent control of the narrative, for stylistic artificiality, for "working hard" to achieve certain effects, and for depending on familiar approaches to characterization and thematic development.

Generally, however, critics agreed that McGuane was moving in a new direction. At first, Lucien seems to be like McGuane's other protagonists. They are nonconformists seeking personal fulfillment, often through unconventional means, and their searches usually end unsatisfactorily, if not disastrously. Lucien's problems, however, do not seem to be self-imposed. Unlike the parents in McGuane's earlier novels, Lucien's mother and father are unstable emotionally and financially. In addition, Lucien's unhappiness never brings him so low that he would willingly die. His comic sense is eventually accompanied by common sense, which in this case permits him to acknowledge his need for Suzanne and James.

The most obvious characteristics of McGuane's novels—the machismo exhibited by his protagonists, their yearning for adventure and romance, the impossibility of their finding an appropriately glamorous vehicle for succeeding in that search, the spare, tough dialogue, the particular beauty of the passages dealing with natural settings, the eruptions of violence, and the concern with place, especially Key West and Deadrock—all of these have caused McGuane to be labeled a follower of Ernest Hemingway and William Faulkner. Also apparent, however, are the effects of McGuane's early interest in the romance and adventure found in the works of W. H. Hudson and Ernest Thompson Seton, and of his study and enjoyment of the "serious" comedy of Aristophanes, Lazarillo de Tormes, Miguel de Cervantes, Mark Twain, and Evelyn Waugh. This greater comic exuberance, the softening of the protagonist, and Lucien's belief that "anything was possible once the center had been restored" indicate why McGuane has called *Something to Be Desired* a "positive" novel.

McGuane's skill at using dialogue to reveal character is apparent in the numerous screenplays with Western themes that he wrote during and after a stay in Hollywood. He is one of a number of new writers, such as David Long and Rick Bass, who are reshaping the New West as a landscape for other writers and new readers to explore. He is also a literary critic and the author of numerous essays on hunting and fishing.

Bibliography
Klinkowitz, Jerome. *The New American Novel of Manners: The Fiction of Richard Yates, Dan Wakefield, and Thomas McGuane*. Athens: University of Georgia Press, 1986. Useful in providing a sense of the literary and cultural context in which McGuane writes. Argues persuasively that since recent literary theorists treat social practices as if they are complex systems of signs in our linguistic system, novelists who do so are in effect creating a contemporary novel of manners. Lucien is a prime example of a character who uses a variety of "signs" to identify manners and provide models for his behavior.
McCaffery, Larry, and Sinda Gregory. "The Art of Fiction LXXXIX: Thomas McGuane." *The Paris Review* 27 (Fall, 1985): 35-71. Illuminating and immensely readable, this interview focuses on McGuane's style, themes, and comic vision. The authors find in *Something to Be Desired* less "rambunctiousness," more control over language, and more complex and subtle techniques of characterization than appear in the earlier novels.
Morris, Gregory. "How Ambivalence Won the West: Thomas McGuane and the Fiction of the New West." *Critique: Studies in Contemporary Fiction* 32 (Spring, 1991): 180-189. Excellent discussion of McGuane's use of the "New West." Argues that while both the language and the action of the novel illuminate Lucien's attraction to the landscape and to the myths of the Old West, his efforts to find a place for himself in the New West require him to deny acceptance of the old.
Neville, Jill. "Getting Away from It All." *The Times Literary Supplement*, May 17, 1985, 573. An interesting discussion that focuses not on the disappearance of the Old West but on Lucien's "odyssey," as he moves from being the son who refuses

to put away childish things to the man who ceases being self-destructive and yearns for "health, emotional stability, and Nature."

Roper, Robert. "Lucien Alone in Deadrock." *The New York Times Book Review*, December 16, 1984, 11. Asserts that *Something to Be Desired* is McGuane's best book. Roper comments that McGuane's comic gifts and lively style are well suited to conveying Lucien's struggle to understand himself, to accept his "softer qualities" as he matures.

Wallace, Jon. *The Politics of Style*. Durango: Hollowbrook, 1992. Argues that McGuane finds language "an end in itself." Although McGuane's characters' words and thoughts often seem incoherent or meaningless, Wallace claims, the mixed codes in his language reflect their fragmented sense of being and their attempts to bring themselves into being in a world without style or unity. Includes a useful bibliography.

Westrum, Dexter. *Thomas McGuane*. Boston: Twayne, 1991. An excellent overview of McGuane's work. Westrum sees *Something to Be Desired* as "championing a course for infinite possibility in the twentieth-century American West." Includes an annotated bibliography.

C. L. Brooke

SPIDERTOWN

Author: Abraham Rodriguez, Jr. (1961-   )
Type of plot: Bildungsroman
Time of plot: The 1990's
Locale: South Bronx, New York City
First published: 1993

> *Principal characters:*
> MIGUEL, a teenage crack runner, the main character of the novel
> AMELIA, Firebug's girlfriend, a crack user and college student
> CRISTALENA, also called Lena, Miguel's naïve girlfriend
> SPIDER, a young crack lord
> FIREBUG, a teenage arsonist, Miguel's roommate

The Novel

Spidertown is a *Bildungsroman* that recounts the intellectual and spiritual growth of a teenaged boy. Sixteen-year-old Miguel falls in love with Cristalena, a preacher's daughter who despises crack cocaine and the criminals who are terrorizing her neighborhood. Because he works for Spider, the local crack czar, Miguel fears that Cristalena will reject him. Consequently, he lies about his work, and his guilt and shame propel him on a journey of self-discovery and redemption.

As the novel opens, Miguel and his roommate, Firebug, are drinking and talking in their nearly unfurnished apartment. Firebug, a professional arsonist, invites Miguel to a "wienie roast," which is a euphemism for the torching of a building. Though he agrees to escort Firebug's girlfriend, Amelia, Miguel would prefer to stay home. He no longer enjoys the commotion of the crowd, the fire engines, and the flames. His relationship with Cristalena has shown him the perversion and ugliness of his world.

At the fire, Miguel and Amelia sit in his car and discuss his growing disenchantment with the drug culture. Amelia says that he has too much heart to be a criminal, confesses that she has fallen in love with him, and tries to explain her relationship with Firebug, who is incapable of love.

The next day, as he makes his usual deliveries for Spider, Miguel stops several times to call Cristalena, but she is unavailable to speak with him. Angry and dejected, he starts drinking heavily and gets behind in his deliveries. His tardiness almost costs the lives of several drug dealers, who have to dodge bullets to get to his car.

In the morning, Miguel visits Cristalena at the boutique where she works and learns the reason for her evasion. She has not yet told her parents about him, and they are very strict and watch her closely. Miguel proposes to Cristalena, and they make plans to celebrate her birthday in bed at his apartment.

At Spider's request, Miguel delivers ten thousand dollars to a police car parked across the street from his apartment building. One of the officers sticks a pistol in his face and threatens him. After this humiliating experience, Miguel walks to his car and discovers that the tires have been slashed by Spider's spies to prevent him from running off with the money. Enraged by Spider's lack of trust in him, Miguel resolves to quit his job at the right moment.

Starting another day of deliveries, he meets with Spider to pick up the crack. When Spider asks him to deliver more money to the police, he refuses. He does not take Spider's threats seriously because he intends to quit soon anyway. At his last stop, a group of street thugs, led by a boy named Richie, drag him from his car and beat him severely. It is Spider's way of teaching him a lesson. When he returns to his apartment, only Amelia shows sympathy for his bruises. That night, she drugs Firebug and sleeps chastely with Miguel in his bed.

In the morning, Miguel telephones Spider and informs him that he is quitting, but Spider refuses to believe him. When Miguel picks Cristalena up that night, he starts to tell her the truth about himself, but he is interrupted by Spider, who emerges from the darkness and pounds on the windshield. Miguel gets out of his car, and they argue. After Spider leaves, Miguel tries to tell Cristalena the truth about himself, but she says he is too late and runs back into her building.

Upset by Cristalena's reaction, Miguel visits Amelia; she takes him to her private apartment, where they finally have sex. Miguel still loves Cristalena, however, and resolves to win her back. Knowing that he must first straighten out his life, he goes to see his mother, Catarina, who is living with a well-to-do importer named Nelo. She agrees to let Miguel move in with them if he will submit unconditionally to their authority. He reluctantly accepts her terms. After begging for and receiving Cristalena's forgiveness, Miguel takes Cristalena to his apartment, and they have sex.

The next day, he encounters Richie, who tries to persuade him to betray Spider. Miguel refuses emphatically. When he gets back to his apartment, he discovers that Firebug is moving out. Firebug gives Miguel a gun for protection, tells him to meet Spider at a bar, and leaves. Wanting to break with Spider amicably, Miguel foolishly goes to meet him, and he is shot twice in the back during an attack on the bar.

At the hospital, Miguel is questioned by a police officer named Sanchez and visited by Amelia and Cristalena. After his release from the hospital, he moves in with his mother and Nelo. He decides to burn his car as a symbol of his independence from Spider. Amelia, Cristalena, and Miguel create a funeral pyre for the car and set it ablaze. As the three friends walk away from the fire, Sanchez drives up, and Miguel hands him a tape of Spider's life story, narrated by the drug lord himself.

The Characters

The main characters in *Spidertown* either strive to be like their fathers or struggle to be different. Firebug became an arsonist because his father revered fire, forced him to leap flames at community barbecues, and punished him by burning parts of his body. Amelia's "masculinity" is at least partly an attempt to earn her father's respect and love. She tries to be the son he always wanted. Cristalena is a victim of her father's religious fanaticism. She rebels successfully against his effort to make her "a little child of Christ," but she cannot completely liberate herself from his terrifying sermons on sin. Miguel reads voraciously because his father hated books. Spider strives to be the antithesis of his father, who plays dominoes outside the neighborhood market. Spider's ambition is a rejection of his father's mundane existence as well as a desperate quest for excitement and purpose in life.

The most corrupt characters, such as Spider and Firebug, have become insensitive to the suffering around them. Firebug contemplates Miguel's bruises with stolid curiosity. He is incapable of feeling sympathy for a friend or love for a woman. Interested only in business, Spider betrays his associates coldly, without remorse. Other characters such Amelia and Miguel are soft because of their compassion. Though she has learned to use people, Amelia still cares. Miguel, too, has too much heart to become a hardened criminal. He shows concern for Spider's safety even after Spider has betrayed him, and he feels guilty about the harm he is doing to his neighborhood. His conscience prevents him from developing the indifference necessary to survive in Spider's world.

Amelia and Cristalena function as reflectors for Miguel, who is both adult and child. Amelia, a twenty-one-year-old college student, represents the responsible, worldly adult, perhaps symbolic of platonic or intellectual love, while sixteen-year-old Cristalena represents the child in Miguel. Cristalena even refers to herself as a child. It is significant that the three characters walk away "arm in arm in arm" at the end of the novel. Amelia also functions as Miguel's confidante and counselor, allowing him to purge his anxiety and fear. In her role as therapist, she guides him to redemption, undergoing a parallel transformation herself as she returns to college. Cristalena and Spider represent good and evil, respectively, locked in a struggle for Miguel. Cristalena's name even suggests a divine being, capable of redeeming sinners. In his rhetoric, Spider is very much like the Devil, using flattery and deception to tempt Miguel to sin.

Rodriguez creates a colorful array of minor characters who give the novel depth and focus: giddy Rosa, Cristalena's cousin, who serves as a liaison between Cristalena and Miguel; eighteen-year-old Careta, an independent pimp who peddles young flesh and marijuana but avoids crack; Catarina, Miguel's mother, who yearns for a picture-perfect family; Nelo, Catarina's middle-class boyfriend, who personifies dullness and complacency; Richie, one of Spider's henchmen, who secretly despises Spider and plots to assassinate him; and Sanchez, the police officer who befriends Miguel after the bar massacre and tries to extract information about Spider.

Themes and Meanings

The theme of deception is central to the novel's meaning. With their lies and subterfuges, the characters weave hopelessly tangled webs and often snare themselves. Cristalena deceives her parents about her clothes, boyfriends, and parties. To sustain the deception, she must expend vast amounts of energy and creativity, even enlisting the aid of her cousin and aunt, who provide alibis and a refuge for the "little child of Christ." Fearful of losing Cristalena, Miguel lies about his profession, telling her that he works for a lumber company. He goes to great lengths to conceal the truth about himself; in the end, he almost loses Cristalena because of his deceit. By pretending to be estranged from Spider, Firebug deceives Miguel, but only for a short while. Eventually, Miguel figures out the truth on his own.

Deception is Spider's modus operandi. He lures children into his operation by promising them exaggerated wealth and power. He lies repeatedly to Miguel, first about the car tires, then about the beating. When he is caught in his lie, he reacts with insouciance and moves on to another deception, supremely confident in his abilities as a machinator. He summons Miguel for a meeting and has his thugs shower the bar with bullets. The betrayal, once realized, prompts Miguel to cooperate with Sanchez, and the cost to Spider's organization is potentially great, because Miguel can provide damaging and detailed information about the drug kingpin's operation.

At one point in the novel, Amelia talks bitterly of self-deception, accusing the people in Spider's world of deluding themselves with guns, stereos, and gold chains. They act like millionaires and generals and pretend to be important, yet they live in squalor. Like rodents and insects, they scurry from one abandoned building to another, dodging sunlight. Amelia blames white people for creating the illusion of success for blacks and Latinos and for encouraging them to deceive and kill themselves. Miguel used to revel in the "fringe benefits" of his job such as money, women, and drugs. When he realizes that it is all a "sick pretend game," however, he stops playing.

Deception perverts friendships, undermines trust, and fosters paranoia. It will inevitably cause Spider's destruction. More odious still, self-deception imprisons the soul and impedes individual growth and development. The only antidote for deception, of course, is truth. Miguel cures his self-deception by holding up a mirror to himself and seeing the truth.

Rodriguez uses Charles Dickens' *Oliver Twist* (1837-1839), which is also concerned with deception, as a model for *Spidertown*. Amelia reveals that she gave Spider a copy of the novel and that he devoured it. At their first meeting, Spider questioned Miguel about the book, and Miguel demonstrated his familiarity with it by comparing Spider to the crafty Fagin, who uses children to commit crimes, and himself to the Artful Dodger. In *Spidertown*, Miguel is actually more like the young Oliver than the Artful Dodger. Both Oliver and Miguel wander the streets of a big city until they are befriended by exploitive criminals. Because he arranges the first meeting between Miguel and Spider, Firebug is like the Artful Dodger, who introduces Oliver to Fagin.

Critical Context

Spidertown is Rodriguez's first novel but not his first book. In 1992, he published *The Boy Without a Flag*, a critically acclaimed collection of short stories about Puerto Rican Americans in the South Bronx. Several of the characters in *Spidertown* have prototypes in the stories. For example, Spider is a minor character in "Birthday Boy," and Careta makes an appearance in "The Lotto." Miguel is similar in many ways to Angel in "Birthday Boy" and to the narrator of "The Boy Without a Flag." Likewise, Cristalena resembles Dalia in "The Lotto." It is obvious that Rodriguez borrowed situations and characters from his first book to create continuity between the works.

As a *Bildungsroman*, or apprenticeship novel, *Spidertown* is a descendant of such established novels as Johann Wolfgang von Goethe's *Wilhelm Meisters Lehrjahre* (1795-1796; *Wilhelm Meister's Apprenticeship*, 1824), Dickens' *David Copperfield* (1849-1850), W. Somerset Maugham's *Of Human Bondage* (1915), James Joyce's *A Portrait of the Artist as a Young Man* (1916), and Thomas Wolfe's *Look Homeward, Angel* (1929). These novels all trace the youthful development of a male protagonist, often an artist or a writer.

By having his characters discuss *Oliver Twist*, Richard Wright's *Native Son* (1940), and Ken Kesey's *One Flew Over the Cuckoo's Nest* (1962), Rodriguez creates another context for his novel. These works depict the underbelly of society and constitute sophisticated protest literature, of which *Spidertown* is an example. It is interesting to note that the literary tradition represented by these works is distinctly male, though not exclusively white or American.

Finally, *Spidertown* belongs to a body of recent literature by Latino authors. As a New York Puerto Rican writer, Rodriguez has an affinity with Nicholasa Mohr and Piri Thomas, who also write about Puerto Rican Americans in the South Bronx. *Spidertown* has been compared to Thomas' *Down These Mean Streets* (1967), an autobiography of one man's struggle with drugs and crime in New York. Rodriguez's novel can also be grouped with the works of other Latino authors, such as Mexican American author Sandra Cisneros' *The House on Mango Street* (1989) and Cuban American author Oscar Hijuelos' *The Mambo Kings Play Songs of Love* (1989), which won the 1990 Pulitzer Prize in fiction.

Bibliography
Ermelino, Louise. Review of *Spidertown*, by Abraham Rodriguez, Jr. *People Weekly* 40 (July 19, 1993): 27. Summarizes and evaluates the novel briefly. Ermelino criticizes the street dialogue for being repetitive but praises the repetitiveness of the plot for highlighting the tension and desperation of the characters. She accurately describes the novel as a personal look at "teenage angst" in a war zone.
Dodd, David. Review of *Spidertown*, by Abraham Rodriguez, Jr. *Library Journal* 118 (April 15, 1993): 127. Recommends the novel highly. Dodd compares Rodriguez to Richard Wright and Fyodor Dostoevski because all three writers are willing to explore the darkest crevices of society. He praises Rodriguez's authoritative voice and vision.
Finn, Peter. "Tenement Romance." *The New York Times Book Review*, July 18, 1993, 16. Finn commends Rodriguez for allowing his characters to evoke pity but complains that allusions to Sartre, Dickens, and others tend to intrude upon the narrative.
Rosenthal, Lois. "Notes." *Story* 41 (Winter, 1993): 6. Rosenthal discusses her editorial relationship with the writer and reveals that she helped him find a publisher for his first book. She also notes that Columbia Pictures acquired the film rights to the novel.
Sammons, Jeffrey L. "The Bildungsroman for Nonspecialists: An Attempt at a

Clarification." In *Reflection and Action: Essays on the Bildungsroman*, edited by James Hardin. Columbia: University of South Carolina Press, 1991. Provides a context for understanding the novel. Sammons examines the etymology of the word *Bildungsroman* and attempts to define it precisely. In the course of his essay, he identifies characteristics of the form and cites several examples from German and British literature.

Edward A. Malone

THE SPORTSWRITER

Author: Richard Ford (1944-   )
Type of plot: Psychological realism
Time of plot: The mid-1980's
Locale: New Jersey, New York City, Michigan, New Hampshire, Vermont, and Florida
First published: 1986

> *Principal characters:*
> FRANK BASCOMBE, a divorced father and a writer for a national sports
>   magazine
> X, his ex-wife, a teaching golf professional
> VICTORY (VICKI) WANDA ARCENAULT, Frank's lover, a hospital nurse
> WALTER LUCKETT, a member of the Divorced Men's Club who forces his
>   friendship on Frank
> RALPH BASCOMBE, Frank's dead son

The Novel

In this first-person narrative, thirty-eight-year-old Frank Bascombe examines the tragedies and disappointments in his life without self-pity. Fascinated equally by the vast spectacle of life and the most mundane aspects of daily existence, Frank is satisfied by the choices life offers and the decisions he has made.

A few years out of the University of Michigan, Frank publishes a well-received book of short stories, marries a beautiful woman he refers to only as "X," and settles into a typical suburban existence in Haddam, New Jersey, midway between New York City and Philadelphia. Unable to generate the inspiration and motivation to continue writing fiction, Frank abandons literature to write for a national sports magazine. This life remains placid until nine-year-old Ralph, the oldest of his three children, dies from Reye's syndrome. A few years later, his marriage breaks up, and X becomes a teaching golf professional at the local country club. The breakup is initiated by X's discovery of letters written to Frank by a lonely woman he met on one of his sportswriting trips but with whom he has not had an affair. *The Sportswriter* opens with Frank and X meeting at Ralph's grave, as they do each year on his birthday. He begins to read Theodore Roethke's "Meditation," but X says she does not like or believe the poem: "Sometimes I don't think anyone can be happy anymore." The novel is essentially about Frank's belief not in the possibility of happiness but the necessity of it.

In the house where his family once lived happily, Frank lives alone except for Bosobolo, his boarder, a seminary student from Africa, while X and his two children live across town. X has adjusted to divorce much better than Frank, who thinks he is in love with Vicki Arcenault, a nurse, while wanting his wife (and normalcy) back at the same time. Despite telling himself he does not need such solace, Frank attends meetings of the Divorced Men's Club. One of the members, the pathetic Walter Luckett, whose wife has run off to Bimini with a water-skiing instructor, tries to force his friendship on Frank, who uneasily resists any intimacy, especially after Walter confesses a recent homosexual encounter with a business acquaintance.

Frank takes Vicki with him to Detroit, where he is to interview Herb Wallagher, a paraplegic former professional football player. Frank enjoys writing inspirational stories about the courage of athletes, but Herb, given to violent mood swings because of his medication, refuses to be a source of inspiration to anyone, preferring to seethe in self-pity. Back in Haddam, he finds the persistent Walter waiting. Unable to help himself, Walter wants some gesture of understanding from the sportswriter. Too tired for sympathy, Frank is shocked when the departing Walter kisses him on the cheek.

Frank's relationship with Vicki, whom he tells himself he loves and wants to marry, is already fragile before he spends Easter with her down-to-earth father, sullen brother, and effervescent stepmother, whom she jealously resents. As the day progresses, Vicki grows increasingly annoyed with Frank. Even news of Walter's suicide does not make her view him more sympathetically, and as he leaves, she punches him in the mouth.

Frank returns to Haddam to find the police suspicious of homosexual overtones related to Walter's death. Frank gets permission to visit Walter's apartment and convinces X to accompany him. While there, he attempts to seduce his ex-wife, who is repelled by the desperate absurdity of his suggestion. Frank goes to the local commuter train station to calm himself by watching his fellow suburbanites arrive home.

Seeing a woman he mistakes for Walter's sister arriving from Ohio, he flees to Manhattan and the camaraderie of the magazine staff gathered to complete an issue devoted to the upcoming National Football League player draft. When an attractive young intern, Catherine Flaherty, praises his work, they begin an affair. Frank soon goes to Florida in search of an illegitimate daughter whom Walter mentioned in his suicide letter, only to discover she is a figment of Walter's tortured imagination. Frank finds that he likes Florida and becomes an honorary member of a family named Bascombe.

The Characters

The events of his life might make Frank lonely, sad, and angry, much like Walter and Herb, but unlike them, he has adjusted to pain and regret, becoming surprisingly contented. His major conflict is resisting the state he calls dreaminess, meaning giving in to self-pity and despair, much as he does immediately following Ralph's death. The constantly self-analytical Frank posits a simple yet unsentimental optimism in numerous ways throughout the novel: "things sometimes happen for the best. Thinking that way has given me a chance for an interesting if not particularly simple adulthood." He claims to be willing to say "yes" to almost anything life presents. One of the problems with their marriage is X's resentment of his optimism.

Although he claims not to be searching for anything, Frank clearly longs for the stability of a traditional family. His father died when he was fourteen, and his mother treated him like a nephew. He loves his house in Haddam because it symbolizes the type of family life he seeks, even if only he and Bosobolo reside in it. Owning such a house without actually needing it provides an unusual comfort. He fantasizes about becoming part of the Arcenault family, who strike him as better than he expected. He allows himself to become addicted to mail-order catalogs, attracted not only by the products but also by "those ordinary good American faces pictured there."

Frank refuses to see people as either heroes or villains, even when he is writing about athletes. He writes an article about Haddam for a local magazine, saying that he works best if he lives in a "neutral" place, and he seems neutral about life, though not disinterested or indifferent. He attempts to offset the perception of himself as passive by claiming that he is "always vitally interested in life's mysteries, which are never in too great a supply." He is open to such mysteries without seeking them out, saying that "it may simply be that at my age I'm satisfied with less and with things less complicated." A man of contradictions, Frank loves the mystery of life but lacks curiosity about others, hence his discomfort with the confessions of Walter.

Frank's essentially optimistic view of the world lacks sentimentality because it is rooted in realism. He tells Walter that the hardest part of his job "is that people expect me to make things better when I come. . . . The fact is, we can sometimes not make things worse, or we can make things worse. But we can't usually make things better for individuals." He is reconciled to living his life a stranger to others.

Frank is impatient with Walter for not recognizing the individual's need to over-come life's disappointments: "Maturity, as I conceived it, was recognizing what was bad or peculiar in life, admitting it has to stay that way, and going ahead with the best of things." Frank, of course, does not always adhere to this philosophy, continuing to mourn for Ralph and hoping to start over with X. Just before attempting to seduce X in Walter's apartment, he tells her, "You can't be too conventional. That's what'll save you." Such inconsistencies make him believably human. Frank is alert to his frailties, and he harshly criticizes himself whenever he spots any deviance from his optimistic philosophy, as when he suspects himself of the cynicism inherent in his age and rampant among sportswriters in particular. When a retired baseball player who is going blind from diabetes wants Frank to write about him, Frank realizes that he would have nothing to say: "Some life is only life, and unconjugatable, just as to some questions there are no answers." Because of Frank's insistent belief in living in the present, Ford has him narrate his story in the present tense.

The other characters are mere satellites to the protagonist. *The Sportswriter* focuses on his sensibility, and the narrator would not presume to portray them in much detail. X's edginess contrasts with Frank's optimism: "She is still an opinionated Michigan girl, who thinks about things with certainty and is disappointed when the rest of the world doesn't." Worrying about getting older is only one example of X's refusal to live only in the present. Having also been through a divorce and death in the family, Vicki, like X, wants to exert control over life rather than simply observe its pageant, and she realizes that she cannot control Frank. Just before slugging him, she says, "You're liable to say anything, and I don't like that." Walter's desperation serves primarily to make Frank's relative normality seem more unusual. Frank's desire to have sex with X in the suicide's bed suggests his awareness of his kinship with Walter.

Themes and Meanings

Although *The Sportswriter* deals with such subjects as love, marriage, divorce, and death, it is primarily an examination of attitudes toward life. Ford refuses to sneer at or reject the conventions, however banal, of middle-class American existence. Frank's life and observations imply that there is something almost heroic about learning to live within the limitations imposed by these conventions. As Lynette Arcenault, Vicki's devotedly Catholic stepmother, observes, alienation is not a workable option. Frank argues forcefully against the randomness of life, saying that "down deep we're all reaching out for a decent rewarding contact every chance we get."

Frank also has much to say about the nature of literature, sportswriting, and sports. He abandons writing fiction for complicated reasons. His need to live only in the present makes him lose his anticipation for what will happen next, a must for the creative writer. He finds the seriousness required of the fiction writer too gloomy. He resent writers who turn people into stereotypes; he finds the real world engaging and dramatic enough. Frank credits marriage with saving him from this lonely pursuit: "I needed to turn from literature back to life, where I could get somewhere." Even the death of a beloved son and a divorce do not make this point ironic.

Since it deals with describing and analyzing real people and events, sportswriting, as defined by Frank, offers a freedom from the ambiguities and enigmas of literature, the need to impose meaning. Sportswriting is more impersonal in this sense, but it provides the companionship of fellow writers, which Frank finds highly desirable even though many of his colleagues are cynics. He also comforts himself in the knowledge that more people will read his feature articles and columns than would have read his fiction. Sportswriting appeals to him "not as a real profession but more as an agreeable frame of mind." Sports themselves appeal to Frank for bringing people together and offering a distraction from the unavoidable dreariness of life. He does not romanticize sports, however, being disturbed by the lack of individuality in athletics.

The suburbs, the other major subject of *The Sportswriter*, present a similar problem for Frank. While he feels comfortable with this way of life, he never quite fits in socially, especially after his divorce sets him apart from his more settled neighbors. Frank understands the latter attitude, since he feels at ease with the uniformity of suburban existence. He admires Haddam—and New Jersey as a whole—because it is dull, because he prefers the uneventful life and the lack of forced friendships. Most important for Frank are such comforts as "stable property values, regular garbage pick-up, good drainage, ample parking." *The Sportswriter* is not about the need to impose order on chaos but rather about the potential for finding order within chaos.

Critical Context

The Sportswriter is the novel that established Ford with critics and readers after his first two novels, though well received, sold poorly. It stands out from his other novels and stories, which feature characters who are more rootless and whose experiences are more violent and melodramatic.

Because the novel deals with the mores of contemporary American suburbia, it has been compared to the fiction of John Cheever, John Updike, and Richard Yates. Frank bears similarities to Cheever's characters in particular, resembling a saner version of the protagonist of "The Swimmer." For the most part, however, Ford's milieu is more subdued than those in typical examples of this literary subgenre.

Ford's novel stands apart from mainstream American fiction of the 1980's in several ways. His presentation of a protagonist who finds refuge in the ordinary, stubbornly refusing to give in to despair, is an anomaly in an age emphasizing alienated, often nihilistic characters. Creations such as Frank are usually presented as naïve and foolish. *The Sportswriter* is also unique in portraying Frank's optimism as stemming from his strength of character rather than from religious, political, or aesthetic values.

Bibliography
Bonetti, Kay. "An Interview with Richard Ford." *The Missouri Review* 10, no. 2 (1987): 71-96. Ford discusses the writing of *The Sportswriter*, explaining how Frank differs from him, why he made Frank a sportswriter, why the ex-wife is called X, and how the novel's religious elements can be misconstrued. He defends Frank's optimism as merely an openness to choices.
Dupuy, Edward. "The Confessions of an Ex-Suicide: Relenting and Recovering in Richard Ford's *The Sportswriter*." *Southern Literary Journal* 23 (Fall, 1990): 93-103. Analyzes Frank as a searcher for mystery in the ordinary. Shows how Frank, unlike Walter, survives by yielding to the vicissitudes of life. Explains that Frank gives up fiction by choosing reality over the power of language. Considers the influence of William Faulkner and contrasts Frank with Quentin Compson in Faulkner's *Absalom, Absalom!* (1936).
Gornick, Vivian. "Tenderhearted Men: Lonesome, Sad and Blue." *The New York Times Book Review*, September 16, 1990, 1, 32-35. This consideration of the way men are portrayed in works by Ford, Raymond Carver, and Andre Dubus shows how Frank is typical of Ford's lonely, confused, hurt protagonists. Analyzes Frank's relations with women. Argues that Ford is infatuated with Frank's depression.
Schroth, Raymond A. "American's Moral Landscape in the Fiction of Richard Ford." *Christian Century* 106 (March 1, 1989): 227-230. Admires *The Sportswriter* for reproducing a complex cross-section of middle-class America. Explains that the novel is about the modern American search for integrity through sports, art, religion, friendship, love, and daily obligations.
Weber, Bruce. "Richard Ford's Uncommon Characters." *The New York Times Magazine*, April 10, 1988, 50, 59, 63-65. This biographical profile explains how Ford's fiction differs from the dominant American fiction of the 1980's, which is minimalist in style, nihilistic in spirit. Argues that Ford's style is more lyrical than that of the minimalists and discusses the difficulty critics have categorizing Ford's work.

Michael Adams

STARS IN MY POCKET LIKE GRAINS OF SAND

Author: Samuel R. Delany (1942-   )
Type of plot: Science fiction
Time of plot: Far in the future
Locale: The planets Rhyonon and Velm
First published: 1984

> *Principal characters:*
>> RAT KORGA, the sole survivor of a destroyed planet
>> MARQ DYETH, a privileged member of the dazzling egalitarian future who forms an explosive bond with Korga
>> VONDRAMACH OKK, a tyrant of worlds, military genius, priest, and poet
>> JAPRIL, a senior official of the Web

The Novel

Stars in My Pocket Like Grains of Sand involves travel between various worlds and their diverse cultures, travel of mind and heart as well as body. The novel is structured by means of a prologue with an omniscient third-person narrator, followed by a series of thirteen monologues entitled "Visible and Invisible Persons Distributed in Space." Each is written in first-person narration and includes occasional memory flashbacks. The novel concludes with an epilogue, also with first-person narration.

The prologue narrates the experiences of Rat Korga as he undergoes the simple, voluntary operation offered by the Radical Anxiety Termination (RAT) Institute. The operation liberates him from his rage while preparing him to be docile and obedient. It resembles nothing so much as a high-tech lobotomy. The stupefied Korga then passes from job to job, his employers believing him incapable of sustained thought or feeling, until he is taken away briefly by a woman who lends him a General Information (GI) headset and allows him to rapid-read a slew of great poems and literary works. Korga now has a headful of ideas that no one knows he has or even could have. On the day of his planet's destruction, the temperature rises twenty degrees in ten seconds. During the next seventeen hours, all life on the surface of the planet is destroyed.

In the monologues and epilogue, Marq Dyeth of Velm, an Industrial Diplomat of high family, learns from a paid assassin that the planet recently destroyed, Rhyonon, was surrounded by the ships of the Xlv, an alien race, just before its destruction. He also learns that there was one survivor, that GI will refuse to divulge any information on the subject, and that the assassin will kill him if he pursues the matter.

Gradually, however, he learns more. He learns from Japril of the Web (the controllers of information) that the survivor, Rat Korga, has been rescued by the Web. Dyeth, a diplomat and person of high sensibility, discovers that he is Korga's perfect erotic object.

Korga sits in a Web life-restoration tank without blinking and demands that he be given a new world. Because of his operation, Korga lacks the precise neuronal connections that would allow him access to the advanced GI programs offered by the Web. He is therefore fitted with the rings Vondramach Okk had worn to restore her mental functioning after her own bout with a similar procedure. The rings have extraordinary power.

Korga is brought to Dyeth, and the attraction between them is consummated. Dyeth suggests that they go dragon hunting the next day. The secret in hunting dragons is to hunt one whose flight is beautiful, because one becomes the dragon one shoots, enters the dragon's being, and experiences with the dragon the dragon's flight. Delany explains, "The radar bow hooks on to a pretty complete mapping of the dragon's cerebral responses and, after a lot of translation, plays it back on your own cerebral surface." That is no more than the method. The magic is in the experience. Delany captures it exquisitely in what is the virtuoso passage of the novel.

Korga's extraordinary charisma begins to take effect, and crowds flock to see him. He is the one survivor of a world lost either to Cultural Fugue—a condition universally dreaded, in which a world's inhabitants render their entire planet uninhabitable—or to a first military encounter with the Xlv.

After an extraordinary formal dinner, at which members of the Thant family manage to upset all Dyeth's attempts at diplomacy and hospitality, Korga leaves Velm, in Japril's company. The Web has decided that it is not a suitable world for him, after all, as his presence comes close to provoking Cultural Fugue. There are even larger issues: The balance between Family and Sygn is threatened, and an Xlv fleet is circling Velm. Delany opens the door to a second volume, to be entitled *The Splendour and Misery of Bodies, of Cities*. "We can't have the two of you there," Japril says toward the end of *Stars in My Pocket Like Grains of Sand*. "We can't have the two of you together yet."

The Characters

In Marq Dyeth, Delany creates an open and forthright character to contrast with the enigmatic Rat Korga. Dyeth's education, privileged background, and nurturing family life serve as a foil to the ill-educated, abandoned social misfit Rat Korga. Even physically, the two are at odds: Dyeth is short and attractive; Korga is well over seven feet tall and disfigured. Perhaps most significant, Dyeth's successful career is based on his understanding not only of his home world but also of the myriad cultures of other planets, while Korga has never understood his home world and knows virtually nothing about any other. That these opposites are still strongly attracted to each other underscores Delany's cross-cultural and cross-racial themes.

Korga's life on Rhyonon has been one of institutional and personal servitude and exploitation. Misled by the RAT Institute to believe that he would be happy after undergoing the surgical procedure, Korga loses his freedom to an institution that strips away his dignity and profits from his mistreatment. As if his economic exploitation were not bad enough, Korga is illegally purchased by a woman—on Rhyonon only institutions can legally own slaves—and experiences sexual exploitation. Required to fulfill his new owner's erotic desires, the homosexually oriented Korga is obliged to imagine his female owner to be a man in order to perform sexually. Later, she sadistically abuses him for her own sexual satisfaction. The institution of slavery depicted in these predestruction scenes on Rhyonon comment pointedly on the institution of slavery.

Rat Korga's relationship with Marq Dyeth contrasts with the social and sexual slavery on Rhyonon. Custom on Velm promotes a relaxed sexual atmosphere in which erotic encounters between humans and evelm are culturally sanctioned. The capacity to see "the other" as erotic object is shown as a cornerstone for healthy individual relationships, fostering cross-cultural and cross-species understanding. Delany's sexually repressed Rhyonon may correspond to Earth, where gay and interracial relationships continue to face legal and social obstacles.

Themes and Meanings

Samuel Delany is interested first and foremost in spinning a fine yarn. He is a master storyteller, as he demonstrated in *Babel-17* (1966) and as he proves again in this novel. He is also a great lover of words and language, an excellent prose stylist with occasional experimental flurries.

Delany is more than this: He is also a person of minority sexual tastes and skin pigmentation in his own nation. It is perhaps his statistical "deviance"—both an unloaded, technical, and a loaded, pejorative term—from the norm that has made him a superlative anthropologist of far future, deep space, and other worlds.

To the extent that Delany has purposes other than storytelling woven into his stories—he would deny they were "themes"—those purposes commonly include arriving at an understanding of the alien, the strange, and the unusual by virtue of his sympathetic exploration of the varied thought processes, languages, customs, and sexualities of the worlds through which he leads his readers.

In *Stars in My Pocket Like Grains of Sand*, he contrasts two rival polities, each of which rules many worlds. The Family is "trying to establish the dream of a classic past on a world [the original Earth] that may never even have existed in order to achieve cultural stability, . . . with the Sygn committed to the living interaction and difference between each woman and each world from which the right stability and play may flower."

In the sentence just quoted, "woman" is the cue to another of Delany's themes, a questioning of gender roles. "In Arachnia as it is spoken on Nepiy, 'she' is the pronoun for all sentient individuals of whatever species who have achieved the legal status of 'woman.' The ancient, dimorphic form 'he' . . . has been reserved for the general sexual object of 'she' . . . regardless of the gender of the woman speaking or the gender of the woman referred to." As in Ursula Le Guin's *The Left Hand of Darkness* (1969), a shift in gender usage confronts and skews the reader's assumptions about gender identity.

The many varieties of sexuality is another of Delany's themes. With males, females, and neuters, and several very different "races," the possibilities for both variety and repression are endless. He describes sexual acts committed with "rats" such as the early Rat Korga, who will obey any command; "sex and sculpture" arcades; the sexuality of the winged evelmi, for whom taste is the predominant sense; worlds where sex between people of different heights, of whatever gender, was considered the ultimate taboo; and worlds where interracial heterosexuality is treated as a perversion. The hunting of dragons, too, may be some kind of elevated analog of sexuality. All are described with sympathetic attention and respect.

Cultural Fugue runs like a fugal theme through the book, as through a century beset by threats of nuclear or ecological world catastrophe. It is instructive that Delany treats it as an infrequent occurrence. As noted by critic Martha A. Bartter, if any issue connects this novel with today's world, it is Cultural Fugue. Delany's message is a reassuring one.

As befits a man almost Shakespearean in his love of language, and once married to the poet Marilyn Hacker, Delany returns here to his great theme of the poet. Vondramach Okk is the latest in a line of Delany's poets, running from Rydra Wong, poet captain of the ship Rimbaud in *Babel-17*, through Lobey, the alien Orpheus in *The Einstein Intersection* (1967), to The Singers of Worlds in "Time Considered as a Helix of Semiprecious Stones" in *Driftglass* (1971). Delany himself is the poet—the man ("woman") able to move between worlds, powerful by virtue of his eyes and all that they are open to perceive, by virtue of his love, by virtue of his language.

Critical Context

Stars in My Pocket Like Grains of Sand had been drafted in 1979 and expected for publication in 1981 or 1982. The novel was enthusiastically received by critics when it was published in December, 1984. The book's publication signaled a return to science fiction for Delany, who had previously published a series of fantasy novels. Delaney was recognized early as a talented writer, and two of his early novels, *Babel-17* (1966) and *The Einstein Intersection* (1967), won Nebula Awards while Delany was still in his mid-twenties. Delany's reputation as a serious novelist continued to grow, not only in the United States and England but also on the European continent, where he was won the praise of critics and fellow artists, among them Umberto Eco.

Delany has repeatedly acknowledged his interest in issues of gay, women's, and civil rights. *Stars in My Pocket Like Grains of Sand* reflects these interests and extends them into a fictive future world. Delany's investigation of institutional slavery and cross-racial barriers to communication reveals his intention to translate many of the issues of the African American experience to a future universe.

Bibliography

Barbour, Douglas. *Worlds Out of Words: The SF Novels of Samuel R. Delany*. Frome, England: Bran's Head Books, 1979. A good overview of Delany's novelistic production, though predating this novel. Useful for comparison of themes and fictional strategies.

Bartter, Martha A. "The (Science-Fiction) Reader and the Quantum Paradigm: Problems in Delany's *Stars in My Pocket Like Grains of Sand.*" *Science-Fiction Studies* 17 (November, 1990): 325-340. Suggests that Delany's fiction, especially this novel, subjects readers to something analogous to the paradigm of Heisenberg's uncertainty principle, with certain things unknowable. Strained in many details but provocative.

Delany, Samuel R. "Thickening the Plot." In *The Jewel-Hinged Jaw: Notes on the Language of Science Fiction.* Elizabethtown, N.Y.: Dragon Press, 1977. Delany's own account of the way in which he conceives his plots and writes his imaginatively detailed scenes. A brilliant introspection and excellent introduction to the craft for neophyte science fiction writers.

Massé, Michelle. "'All You Have to Do Is Know What You Want': Individual Expectations in *Triton.*" In *Coordinates: Placing Science Fiction and Fantasy*, edited by Eric S. Rabkin, Robert Scholes, and George E. Slusser. Carbondale: Southern Illinois University Press, 1983. Examines the role of desire in Delany's novel *Triton* (1976), which like many of Delany's novels has a strong sexual theme. *Triton* is similar to *Stars in My Pocket Like Grains of Sand* in use of technology to adapt people's thinking; in *Triton*, people can voluntarily change their sexual preferences as well as their sexuality.

Slusser, George Edgar. *The Delany Intersection: Samuel R. Delany Considered as a Writer of Semi-Precious Words.* San Bernardino, Calif.: Borgo Press, 1977. An analysis of Delany's style and use of language, using early works as examples.

Charles Cameron

THE STORYTELLER

Author: Mario Vargas Llosa (1936-   )
Type of plot: Philosophical realism
Time of plot: The 1950's to the 1980's
Locale: Lima, Peru; the Peruvian Amazon; and Florence, Italy
First published: El hablador, 1987 (English translation, 1989)

> *Principal characters:*
> THE NARRATOR, a Peruvian novelist and former television host
> SAÚL ZURATAS, a Jewish-Peruvian student, a long-lost friend of the narrator
> THE STORYTELLER, a Machiguengan man who travels the Amazonian jungles telling stories
> TASURINCHI, the Machiguengan creator, whose name also denotes each particular man in the tribe

The Novel

The Storyteller is an intriguing, often disturbing exploration of the Machiguengas, a real, indigenous, nomadic tribe in the Peruvian Amazon, and of the encroachment of modern life and values into their environment and culture. Mario Vargas Llosa frames this exploration as a quest for information about both the tribe and a Jewish student from Lima who may have been absorbed into it.

The narrator resembles Vargas Llosa himself. Like the author, he is a Peruvian novelist who vacations in Florence, Italy, and who once hosted a Peruvian television magazine. Although the narrator is never explicitly identified as Vargas Llosa, such identification is neither denied nor contradicted. Within the fictional world, many factual particulars of the novel suggest that it is written in the author's own voice.

At the beginning of the novel, the narrator, on vacation in Florence and immersed in a reading of the works of Dante, wanders into a photographic exhibit on the Machiguengas, an indigenous people of eastern Peru. The tribe has long fascinated him and once played a central role in an ongoing debate he had with a friend at the university, Saúl Zuratas. In one of the photos, the narrator sees a native storyteller who strongly resembles Saúl. This prompts an account by the narrator of the two students' friendship.

Saúl was an intense young Jewish man with an enormous purplish birthmark that covered half his face and earned him the nickname La Mascarita, or Mask-face. He was deeply concerned about the survival of indigenous peoples in Peru and had strong criticism for those who sought to evangelize, assimilate, or "culturally advance" such peoples under the guise of scientific, anthropological, and linguistic research. Saúl turned down a lucrative scholarship to study in France, choosing instead to remain with his aging father and continue his studies in Peru.

The narrator and Saúl shared discussions on many issues, including the Machiguengan people. The narrator found Saúl's views too strident. The narrator went to study in Europe; although he tried to maintain contact, he never heard from Saúl again. Upon returning to Peru, the narrator learned that Saúl and his ailing father supposedly had moved to Israel.

The account of the students' relationship is rendered in a speculative, impressionistic fashion. Few scenes or conversations are presented in detail; all is filtered through memory and, to a degree, emotion. Plot and action are outpaced by a wealth of information and meditation on the Machiguengas, Peruvian politics, and modern life.

Interwoven into the account of Saúl Zuratas are chapters written in the voice of the Machiguengan *hablador*, or traditional storyteller. In these chapters, Vargas Llosa employs a language that is at once naïve and wise, suiting Machiguengan lore, beliefs, and rituals. The storyteller describes Kientibakori, the spirit of evil; Kashiri, the sometimes benevolent; the seripigari, or wise men; the Viracochas, or dangerous outsiders; and Tasurinchi, the Machiguengan creator whose name is also used to refer to any Machiguengan man.

The storyteller chapters relate story after story of Tasurinchi after Tasurinchi: their family relationships, their lifestyles, and the lessons they have learned from the environment and animals that surround them. Some of the stories are amusingly scatological, while others clearly establish the Machiguengan cosmogony. The Machiguengan people come into focus as a loose society of wanderers, "the men that walk," believing that their walking keeps the sun in the sky. In addition, the storyteller relates his own experiences as the link among the scattered Tasurinchis.

As the novel alternates between the narrator's account and the storyteller's tales, the two sequences, already linked by the photograph in Florence, begin to merge. The narrator describes his interest in Machiguengan storytellers and the unavailability of pertinent information. In the early 1980's, as host of a television program called *The Tower of Babel*, he ventured back into the jungle to report on the Machiguengans. There he encountered the Schneils, a husband-and-wife team of American linguists working with the Summer Institute for Linguistics. He had met them once before: It was Edwin Schneil who had first mentioned Machiguengan storytellers to the narrator. During this later visit, to the narrator's amazement, Schneil described an "albino" storyteller with a large birthmark on his face. In speaking with a Jewish coworker, the narrator also discovered that Saúl did not go to Israel as rumored. After his father's death, he disappeared.

In the following chapter, the storyteller relates how he found that vocation. He refers somewhat cryptically to his birthmark, his previous life elsewhere, his acceptance among the Tasurinchis, and his transformation from a studious listener to an itinerant teller of stories. It is strongly suggested, though not explicitly articulated, that the storyteller is Saúl Zuratas.

By the end of the novel, the narrator returns to the present moment in Florence, where he repeatedly visits the photography exhibit to view the singular image. He contemplates his friend's destiny, puts together the pieces of the puzzle he has been investigating, and decides for himself that the storyteller in the photograph is none other than his lost friend Saúl Zuratas, La Mascarita.

The Characters

The Storyteller is an extended meditation rather than a compelling dramatic narrative. Thus, the novel's characters are more strongly developed in terms of the ideas they hold and represent than in their human desires and interrelationships. Vargas Llosa seeks to particularize the larger struggle of indigenous peoples against the encroachment of modern, technological influence by focusing on two students, their ill-fated friendship, and their different interactions with a fascinating tribe.

As a stand-in for the author, the character of the narrator pulls the reader into the novel by blurring the separation between the real and fictional worlds. Clearly, the tribe described is a real tribe, and many of the people, places, and incidents evoked in the novel are authentic. The use of a semifictional narrator demands complicity, asking the reader to participate in the ideological discussions and to form an opinion about the Machiguengas.

In the narrator's chapters, the characters are not fully fleshed out with complex behavioral patterns based on personal, emotional responses to external situations. Saúl is kept at a distance; his father, Don Salomón, is referred to but not seen; and the Schneils are barely developed beyond expository purposes. Likewise, the university professors, the television crew, the missionaries, Machiguengan leaders, and many other minor characters seem only to exist to help elucidate the novel's central question.

In contrast, the characters in the storyteller chapters, though united by the common name of Tasurinchi, are of flesh and blood, with human desires and functions and clear links to land and nature. The storyteller himself conveys his fears and vulnerability, and in the stories he tells he creates a Machiguengan world that is vibrant with life and its own natural logic.

Thus, in his use of character, Vargas Llosa subtly supports an ideology that is central to the novel's debate. The Western narrator and his world are dry, fact-based, single-minded, and extremely impersonal and cerebral. The world of the storyteller and the Machiguengans is, conversely, rooted in visceral functions, emotions, physical acts and phenomena, and chance and improbability. In each half of the novel, one of the storytellers expresses how he has come to puzzle out his universe, but their methods, reflected in their characters and the worlds they portray, could not be more different. This difference provides ironic commentary on implicit assumptions about the civilization of "civilized" society and the primitiveness of "primitives."

Themes and Meanings

The Storyteller questions the basic values of modern Western culture by placing it in direct juxtaposition with the Machiguengans. Organizations such as the Summer Institute of Linguistics (a real entity) are charged with the disruption of natural prerogatives. In researching indigenous peoples of the Amazon, they appropriate native languages and ways while imposing Christianity, technology, and the Spanish language. Also implicit is criticism of the destruction perpetrated on precarious natural habitats such as the Amazon jungle. Vargas Llosa offers an evenhanded examination of these issues and effectively avoids sentimentalizing the plight of indigenous peoples. The questions, nevertheless, loom large over the novel.

Balance is a key element in *The Storyteller*. The alternating narrative voices balance one another, as do their respective cultures. Saúl and the narrator are balanced in their friendship and discussions. Saúl, the arrogant, impenetrable Jewish university student, contrasts sharply with the wise, humble, and candid Machiguengan storyteller that he allegedly has become. Machiguengan history is compared to Jewish history, with the storyteller recounting Biblical cosmology in Machiguengan terms. The narrator's journey into the heart of Machiguengan culture is placed in relief against the often-unwilling journey of Tasurinchi into knowledge about the world outside the Amazon jungle. For Vargas Llosa, transformation requires balance; the worlds of modern Peru and the traditional Machiguengans can only meet through slow and mutual accommodation and respect.

The novel is concerned with what is right. In the same way as Saúl and the narrator search intellectually for ethical ways of interpreting their world, the various Tasurinchis and the Machiguengan people as a whole strive to make the world right. Their entire cosmology makes sense of a natural world often riddled with contradictions, and they are aware of how human words and acts put natural elements and heavenly bodies out of order.

In such a world, the storyteller is essential as a preserver of order. Among a people whose mandate is to wander incessantly, the storyteller is an important link to the past, to the environment, and to the whole community. He is also the retainer and definer of the indigenous language (even if he, as suggested, is not a native speaker himself). Storytelling becomes a much larger cultural institution: It is the foundation of society.

The power of storytelling grows further when considered in the context of the novel as a whole. Vargas Llosa, through his narrator, sets out to learn about the Machiguengans, to create a stylistically viable language for them, and to tell their story as part of his own. In doing so, he highlights his own role as a storyteller in Latin American culture. His invocation of Franz Kafka and his reading of Dante in Florence place his present writing in the tradition of Western literature. At the same time, he is asserting not only the need for inclusion (rather than appropriation) of native history and culture, but also the speculative quality that such inclusion must take. Vargas Llosa cannot solve the mystery for certain: If the storyteller is indeed Saúl, he is inaccessible to his old friend. Machiguengan stories are inherently incompatible with Peruvian novels, so the storyteller chapters are by necessity inventions, and the coincidences— the birthmark and the recounting of Jewish history among them—are, by the rules of the game, not clues encountered in the narrator's investigation but rather manufactured results of an intellectual process. Thus, Vargas Llosa's efforts to inform and stimulate certainly succeed, but whether the two worlds do or can meet—and whether the elusive Machiguengan storyteller is indeed a transformed Saúl Zuratas—is a question that the reader, like the narrator, must in the end decide.

Critical Context

Vargas Llosa has always drawn from personal experience to document the injustices and uncertainties of life in modern Peru. His earliest novels, *La ciudad y los perros* (1962; *Time of the Hero*, 1966) and *La casa verde* (1966; *The Green House*, 1968), explore themes of repression and corruption in the military academy of his adolescence and a small jungle town of his youth. *Conversación en la catedral* (1969; *Conversation in the Cathedral*, 1975) is a panoramic portrait of Peru in the 1940's and 1950's under the dictator Manuel Odria. In these early novels, Vargas Llosa began to experiment with an interweaving, nonlinear narrative style.

His next two novels, *Pantaleón y las visitadoras* (1973; *Captain Pantoja and the Special Service*, 1978) and *La tía Julia y el escribidor* (1977; *Aunt Julia and the Scriptwriter*, 1982), incorporate humor and farce and draw on the author's knowledge of military life and the television industry. Both use the technique of incorporating fictional documentary material into the body of the novel.

With *La guerra del fin del mundo* (1981; *The War of the End of the World*, 1984) and *Historia de Mayta* (1984; *The Real Life of Alejandro Mayta*, 1986), Vargas Llosa returned to his serious, political writing, focusing on turn-of-the-century religious zealotry in Brazil and contemporary radicalism in Peru. For Vargas Llosa, writing is a political act; in 1990, the author ran unsuccessfully for the presidency of Peru. *The Storyteller*, not surprisingly, gives evidence of the political leader that Vargas Llosa has become, concerned with the larger issues confronting Peruvian government, society, and culture.

Bibliography

Alter, Robert. "The Metamorphosis." *The New Republic* 202 (January 8, 1990): 41-42. In this review, Alter focuses on the Jewish themes, the light characterizations, and the links to Joseph Conrad's *Heart of Darkness*. He closely examines Vargas Llosa's craft in creating the style of the storyteller chapters.

Castro-Klarén, Sara. *Understanding Mario Vargas Llosa*. Columbia: University of South Carolina Press, 1990. Castro-Klarén traces the thematic evolution of Vargas Llosa's oeuvre. The well-developed but sometimes dense chapter on *The Storyteller* examines the work's ideological underpinnings and the power of the storyteller chapters.

Johnston, George Sim. "The Call of the Wild." *National Review* 42 (February 5, 1990): 56-57. Johnston's review is ultimately critical of the novel for its implausibility and incompleteness. He discusses Vargas Llosa's views of human morality, his sense of irony, and his European-style intellectualism.

Updike, John. "Writer-Consciousness." *The New Yorker* 65 (December 25, 1989): 103-104. Updike places Vargas Llosa in the postmodernist tradition of Italo Calvino, John Barth, and Vladimir Nabokov. He praises the author's inventiveness and the blending of the novel's real and imaginary worlds but bemoans the text's speculative quality and its lack of romance and sensuality.

Vargas Llosa, Mario. *A Writer's Reality*. Syracuse, N.Y.: Syracuse University Press, 1991. A collection of thoughtful and candid essays by the author, reflecting on his literary roots, his creative method, and his political beliefs. Although containing only a few references to *The Storyteller*, the volume is nevertheless a fascinating glimpse into the mind behind the novel.

Williams, Tamara. *"The Storyteller." America* 162 (March 24, 1990): 298-299. Williams discusses Vargas Llosa's didactic and political purposes in the novel, enjoying the story as a quest for a lost way of life. She also examines how the novel reflects on the author as a storyteller and chronicler of his culture.

Barry Mann

THE STREET

Author: Ann Petry (1908-   )
Type of plot: Naturalism
Time of plot: The mid-1940's
Locale: Harlem, New York City
First published: 1946

> *Principal characters:*
> LUTIE JOHNSON, an attractive black woman in her early twenties
> BUB, her eight-year-old son
> JONES, the superintendent of the building in which Lutie rents an apartment
> MIN, a middle-aged woman who lives with Jones
> MRS. HEDGES, a woman who operates a brothel on the first floor of the building
> JUNTO, a powerful white man attracted to Lutie
> BOOTS SMITH, a bandleader who owes Junto

The Novel

    The Street follows the foredoomed struggle of a young black woman to escape the street and to evade what the street threatens to do to her and to Bub, her young son. The street is 116th Street in Harlem. The time is the 1940's; World War II is not yet over.

    Lutie Johnson has not come to the street by choice. Lutie had taken work as a domestic with the Chandlers, a white family in Connecticut. The job required that she live apart from Jim, her unemployed husband. In her absence, Jim took up with another woman. Unable to turn to her alcoholic father for support, Lutie has had to do the best she can for herself and her son Bub. At the moment, this means a low-paying job and a walk-up apartment on the top floor of a dismal building.

    Three other inhabitants of the building play an important role in Lutie's story: Jones, Min, and Mrs. Hedges. Lutie senses at once the powerful lust of Jones, the superintendent. Her resistance generates in Jones a rage he takes out on Min, the most recent of a series of shapeless middle-aged women with whom he has lived. Min finally realizes that her only course is to leave him and to hope that some other man will take her. The repeatedly frustrated Jones is determined to get at Lutie somehow. He wins the trust of Bub, and when Jones's obsession with Lutie turns to hatred, he makes Bub his instrument in a plot to destroy her.

    Mrs. Hedges takes an immediate, even protective, interest in Lutie, but her interest is not innocent. Lutie represents interesting possibilities: A nice white man is interested in her.

    The white man is Junto, who operates the Junto Bar and Grill and a number of other enterprises in Harlem. He and Mrs. Hedges have been associates for a long time, ever since they met while both were picking through garbage. Junto has come a long way since them. He is now the power behind Mrs. Hedges's operations; he has powerful connections, and he knows what he wants. Ironically, Lutie's attempts to improve things for herself and her son make her vulnerable to Junto. Lutie has a fine singing voice, and when she is approached by Boots Smith, a bandleader, she dreams of a success that will take her and Bub away from the street. Lutie knows what Boots has in mind when he suggests that she should be "nice" to him, but she gambles that she will be able to handle Boots long enough to achieve independence by establishing herself as a performer.

What she does not know is that Boots is answerable to Junto. Not only does Boots owe much of his success to Junto, but it was also Junto who made it possible for Boots to evade military service in wartime. Although Boots is genuinely interested in Lutie—however limited and shallow that interest may be—he is unwilling to cross Junto.

Meanwhile, the influence of the street is working on Bub, and Lutie unwittingly reinforces that influence. Her pursuit of her goals leaves a frightened Bub alone at night, vulnerable to the false friendship of Jones. Moreover, her complaints about their poverty instill in Bub the notion that money is everything. After some hesitation, Bub agrees to make some money by assisting Jones in "detective work." In fact, Jones instructs Bub to steal letters from the mailboxes in the neighborhood, setting up the boy as a way of getting revenge on the mother.

Bub is arrested, and an unscrupulous lawyer tells Lutie that she needs two hundred dollars to pay for his services—although, in such a case, she does not need a lawyer at all. Desperate, Lutie asks Boots for help. He agrees, but when Lutie goes to his apartment she finds that Junto is there as well. The help she needs will be forthcoming only if she agrees to Junto's sexual demands. When Lutie refuses, Junto leaves. Defeated and angry, Boots attacks Lutie. When she hits him with a candlestick, Lutie is at first defending herself, but then she is striking out at all the forces that have conspired to crush her. She does not stop until Boots is dead.

In the eyes of the law, Lutie is sure, she has committed murder. With no one to turn to for help, she can only try to escape. This means abandoning Bub, the eight-year-old boy who is waiting for his mother to visit him in jail. Yet what hope can there be for Bub if he is saddled with a mother who has been branded a killer? On the train taking her to Chicago, Lutie hopes that Bub will remember that she loved him.

The Characters

In addition to being the protagonist, Lutie Johnson functions as the viewpoint character for much of the novel. Thus, readers come to know her in large part through her perceptions and the actions and reactions based on these. Readers see the street, the hallway, and the apartment through her eyes, and her dissatisfaction with what she sees reflects significantly on who she is. She is determined not to surrender to the street, but readers feel her anxiety and know how close she is to despair.

Other characters assume the role of viewpoint character for extended stretches.

Most of these characters are first seen through Lutie's perception of them, then through their perception of a world that includes Lutie. In Lutie's perception, Jones, the building superintendent, is frightening in the openness of his lust for her—and, indeed, her initial fears are justified by his attempt to rape her. Yet readers are also allowed to see something of how the world looks to Jones, and of the forces that have brought him to where he is. The result is not to make Jones a sympathetic character, but to suggest that one errs if one sees in him only the stock villain of melodrama.

Others function as viewpoint characters in the course of the novel. Of the principal characters, only Junto is excepted. Junto is depicted essentially on the basis of how others see him and in his effect on others. He protects Mrs. Hedges, as Jones finds out when he summons the law in an angry attempt to put her out of business. To Boots, Junto has given, and Junto can take away. Junto's desire for Lutie generates much of the action of the novel. Although Lutie manages to resist, this resistance forces her defeat.

The author also develops characters through comparison and contrast. Lutie, readers observe, has internalized the materialistic values of Mrs. Chandler, her white employer. Lutie's helplessness is shown in contrast to the varying, and ultimately unsatisfactory, sorts of resourcefulness represented by Mrs. Hedges and Min, each of whom might claim to be a survivor, but in a morally shrunken universe. Lutie is, by comparison, a morally vigorous character, but the negative power of the street is finally more than she can overcome.

Themes and Meanings

The Street is a novel about struggle and defeat. Lutie Johnson struggles against the limitations imposed upon her by circumstance, and she is destroyed in the struggle. Her defeat, when it comes, has about it an air of inevitability; readers respect her hopes but put no faith in them. Understanding the novel in which she appears may be a matter of understanding why a sense of hopelessness pervades a book that centers on a woman's hopes.

The novel begins with a description of the street. The author writes of the street as though it has a personality, and a malevolent one at that. The street works, consciously it almost seems, to defeat and destroy those within its influence. Moreover, readers know the street before meeting any human characters; when the humans are introduced, they are seen, as it were, in the shadow of the street. The result is to weaken the readers' sense of human moral agency.

When readers first meet Lutie Johnson, it is true, they are quickly made aware of the strength of her aspirations. At one point in the novel, Lutie half-seriously compares herself to Benjamin Franklin, the great American model of the self-made man. He has served as a model for many ambitious young Americans, and Lutie dares to suppose he may serve as her model, too. She is determined to forge a better life for herself and her son.

Yet if readers know the strength of Lutie's aspirations, they also know the weakness of her condition. That Lutie has come to 116th Street is not a matter of choice. She finds herself in an environment that is ugly to her and, she is convinced, dangerous to her eight-year-old son because this is what her circumstances demand. Her hopes are not linked to any realistic positive options, not because Lutie is unintelligent, but because the narrowness of her situation allows little room for the creative use of intelligence.

Lutie's hopes are given a more specific direction when her talent for singing brings the promise of a career as a performer. Yet there is, from the start, something not quite real about this. Lutie's "discovery" is reminiscent of the mythology of fan magazines, and the life of a band singer, under the best of circumstances, seems far removed from the stability for which Lutie had been looking. As it turns out, Lutie's talent, although apparently genuine, presents Junto with an opportunity for manipulation. Her talent, then, becomes part of the causal chain leading to her destruction.

Her attractiveness to men is equally destructive in its consequences. It is this attractiveness that arouses the interest of Junto and that drives the obsession of Jones. Jones's obsession motivates the scheme that leads to Bub's arrest, and Bub's arrest forces Lutie to look for help, making her vulnerable to Junto. Finally, Lutie's attractiveness has made her desirable to Boots, and in rejecting Boots's advances, Lutie performs the action that finally destroys her. It is significant that the action does not arise out of any conscious decision; Lutie is simply striking out against all that has conspired in her defeat.

The structure of the novel, especially Petry's use of a series of viewpoint characters, forcing readers to see the world as it appears even to the least sympathetic of them, seems designed to suggest that these other characters are no more free moral agents than Lutie is. Even Junto, who embodies so much power, is driven by desires he seems incapable of understanding. The consistent portrayal of characters as driven or determined by forces, social and psychological, that they can neither understand nor control is among the defining features of the naturalistic tradition that the novel represents.

Critical Context

Ann Petry was not the first novelist to explore aspects of African American life in naturalistic terms. Richard Wright's *Native Son*, published in 1940, was a great predecessor. Part of the significance of Petry's achievement was her success in applying the naturalistic approach to the story of an articulate woman, in contrast to Wright's inarticulate moral drifter.

The significance of literary naturalism for the African American writer is plain. To see characters in terms of the forces that shape them, to define the distorting effects of negative social forces, offers a possibility of explanatory power in the depiction of African American life. It also provides the materials of a strong implicit indictment of white America, which has, after all, largely created and maintained the world writers like Wright and Petry depict. Lutie Johnson has a lucid perception of the ways in which white power works to limit the options of black Americans, even though this lucidity does not enable her to escape the effects of what she knows.

Yet it is no denigration of what Petry has achieved to point out that naturalism is but one option open to African American novelists, and that other alternatives will appeal to those writers for whom the portrayal of black people as victims is ultimately not enough. The folk imagination of Zora Neale Hurston, manifested in *Their Eyes Were Watching God* (1937), and the Transcendentalist impulse of Ralph Ellison's *Invisible Man* (1952) suggest other models, to which younger writers have responded. Petry's fine novel takes its place in an African American literary tradition the richness of which readers and critics are still learning to appreciate.

Bibliography
Bell, Bernard W. *The Afro-American Novel and Its Tradition*. Amherst: University of Massachusetts Press, 1987. Bell comments that, in a novel of economic determinism, Petry demythologizes American culture and the African American character.
Gayle, Addison, Jr. *The Way of the New World*. Garden City, N.Y.: Anchor Press, 1975. The novel's major flaw, Gayle claims, is that it backs away from a denouement, failing to define the necessity for collective action. Gayle's criteria are essentially ideological, sometimes naïve, and often stridently expressed.
Gross, Theodore L. "Ann Petry: The Novelist as Social Critic." In *Black Fiction: New Studies in the Afro-American Novel Since 1945*, edited by A. Robert Lee. New York: Barnes & Noble, 1980. Gross sees Petry's concern as the oppressive details of ghetto life rather than black-white conflicts. Yet he comments that Petry does not let the reader forget that the white world has drawn the limitations and caused the bitter despair of black people.
Hernton, Calvin C. *The Sexual Mountain and Black Women Writers: Adventures in Sex, Literature, and Real Life*. New York: Anchor Press, 1987. Pays tribute to Petry's daring in depicting a black woman's killing of a black man because he is an oppressor; the novel looks forward to a later stage of consciousness in fiction by black women. Hernton naïvely treats fictional characters as if they were real people, with real histories beyond the books in which they appear.
Pryse, Marjorie. " 'Pattern Against the Sky': Deism and Motherhood in Ann Petry's *The Street*." In *Conjuring: Black Women, Fiction, and the Literary Tradition*, edited by Marjorie Pryse and Hortense J. Spillers. Bloomington: Indiana University Press, 1985. Pryse takes Petry's reference to Benjamin Franklin to suggest that Deism figures significantly in the thematic and ideological implications of the novel. The discussion is stimulating, if a bit strained; Pryse seems prepared to make "Deism" mean whatever fits her argument.

W. P. Kenney

SUNDOWN

Author: John Joseph Mathews (1895-1979)
Type of plot: Psychological realism
Time of plot: The 1880's to 1930
Locale: Osage Indian country, near the Oklahoma-Kansas border
First published: 1934

> *Principal characters:*
> CHALLENGE (CHAL) WINDZER, a mixed-blood Osage caught between
>   cultures
> JOHN WINDZER, Chal's optimistic father
> CHAL'S MOTHER, a traditional Osage woman
> COUSIN ELLEN, a stereotypically censorious white woman
> BLO DAUBENEY, a foolish female college student whom Chal idolizes
> RUNNING ELK, a friend whom Chal watches degenerate
> JEP NEWBERG, a leading merchant
> CHARLIE FANCHER, Chal's supercilious university pal
> PROFESSOR GRANVILLE, Chal's friend and later, flight instructor

The Novel

John Joseph Mathews' *Sundown* traces the disintegration of Chal Windzer's character. Chal is a mixed-blood Osage Indian torn by conflicts within Osage tribal values and confused by both the aggressiveness and the vices of the white Americans whom he encounters. The chronicle of Chal's life ends with his decline into boastful, passive dreaming, womanizing, and alcoholism. Chal becomes a sad caricature of the manhood exalted in the ideals of the Osage's warrior culture.

Chal's life of declining faith and growing insecurities unfolds through sixteen chapters. The first five of these cover his boyhood through his entrance into the university. Chal was born in the 1890's, when the great god of the Osage still ruled the land defined by the Caney and Arkansas rivers, centered on Pawhuska, near the Oklahoma-Kansas border. He enjoys an idyllic youth as part of an animistic culture. He interacts closely with prairie nature and leads a life nicely balanced between contemplation and action.

Even in boyhood, however, Chal's disillusionment is progressive. It is synonymous with his personal contacts with whites—merchants, teachers, Bible thumpers, government officials, and oilmen—drawn by opportunities to convert the "heathen," to exploit Indian lands, and to profit from the discovery and swift expansion of the Oklahoma oil fields after 1897. His disenchantment stems also from familial circumstances. His father is a sanguine white man with enduring faith in "the guv'mint" and his mother is a silent Osage woman who judges her son's character in the Osage way and sees little good in white culture.

As a mixed-blood, Chal also reflects a deep division with tribal ranks, one which had been confirmed by tribal councils in the 1860's and which thereafter consigned mixed-bloods to inferior position relative to full-bloods. In addition, by the time Chal reaches adolescence, the undreamed-of wealth accruing to the Osage from government annuities and (to a vastly greater extent) from oil royalties is wreaking its own havoc. Chal's youthful companions, like many Osage, lacking incentive and business acumen, become profligates. Chal's separation from them is widened by his entrance into the university, the subject of chapters 7 through 11.

Chal's university career has little to do with learning. Led on by his supercilious and patronizing "pal," Charlie Fancher, he succumbs almost immediately to the age-old frivolities: fraternities, football, cars, girls, drinking, and parties. Throughout these activities, he realizes that he does not fit; he is a curiosity, and he moves among people who smile with their teeth but not with their hearts. He is ensnared in a vapid, superficial world. Only his chance encounter with Professor Granville, a wise, understanding Englishman who represents what white culture could be like—but is not—affords a contrast to the inanities to which he has lent himself.

The American entrance into World War I offers Chal a way out when Granville suggests that Chal act on his plans to participate by joining the air service. He does so and wins his commission. More significant, in flying he finds a calling to which he is well adapted. He is reunited with Granville, who, having distinguished himself in the Royal Air Force, is Chal's flight instructor. Yet at war's end, despite his pride in his flying ability and his enjoyment of the notoriety brought to him by his commission, Chal finds little to do and resigns from the service. His father's death, meanwhile, has enriched him. He has no need to work, though he briefly toys with thoughts of business and investment. He watches the successful businessmen of his boyhood fail, however, and, with his own wealth in hand, he settles for a life of idleness. He spends his time driving through town in his "long, powerful red roadster," killing time with young people in the local drugstore, occasionally dating, and—as the years pass— succumbing to alcoholism. Chapters 13 through 16 are thus the final record of his decline, epitomized by his mother's silent judgment on his childishness and failure.

The Characters

Sundown is both a chronicle and a didactic exercise. Mathews' characters are thereby denied some of their potential dimensions so that the author can better convey his principal message: Namely that because of their values, the Osage are victims of the dubious concept of "progress" as embodied in white American society.

Chal, Mathews' mixed-blood protagonist, exemplifies the degradation that befell most American Indian cultures, unable as they were to maintain tribal integrity in the face of white incursions into their lands and values. Chal's heart looks in two directions. On the one hand, he profoundly enjoys and respects the fraternity with nature taught by the Osage's full-blooded elders; in a more specific way, he seeks to make his Osage mother proud of him within her traditional frame of reference. Yet on the other hand, he is drawn by the positive, confident, and assertive views of John Windzer, his white father, who doggedly persists in believing that the government will rectify the manifest injustices and dangers to which the Osage are exposed by the white people flooding into their midst. Chal is unsuited to function positively in either world, and he is confused by the attractions and repulsions of each.

While Chal's boyhood reactions to several white characters—merchants such as Jep Newberg and Mr. Fancher, teachers such as Miss Hoover, Christian do-gooders such as Cousin Ellen, and oilmen such as Osage Dubois—are negative, his serious distrust of whites comes after his entrance into the university. There he is taken in tow by Charlie Fancher, a know-it-all whom Mathews has created to emphasize the inanity and insincerity of wealthy, privileged white people. Lacking the substance to be genuinely bad, Fancher exposes Chal to continuous social exploitation. Fancher's female counterpart, the narcissistic Blo Daubeney, with whom Chal becomes infatuated, furthers his discomfiture in white university society by using him as a pawn in her dating and sexual gambits. Worse, Chal is soon abandoned to Fancher and Daubeney amid his growing disaffection with student life: Two of his boyhood Osage friends (like Chal they were recruited principally to play football) suddenly pack their trunks and depart for home.

The sole white character presented as engaging, strong, and admirable is Granville. Mathews uses him to underscore the perspective of Chal's mother—that white civilization had its virtues, but only at its European sources, before it was corrupted in its transition to America. Granville, the Englishman, is brave, gentle, courteous, and wise. He talks and smiles with his heart. Moreover, he leads Chal into his only positive experience in the white world: flying. Nevertheless, like all of *Sundown*'s characters, he tends to be a two-dimensional stereotype, the bearer of a heavy thematic burden.

Themes and Meanings

Mathews' objective, realized as far as his readers are concerned with some grace and a high level of interest, is to depict the victimization of a vulnerable American Indian culture by forces that a majority of non-Indian Americans historically have defined as progress. Repeated descriptions of the march of the oil derricks through Osage lands symbolically traces the flight of an arrow that lodges ever more deeply and fatally in the heart of Osage society.

As Mathews constantly reminds his readers, accompanying the inexorable march of the derricks came the white men who mined the earth. Whether motivated by good intentions aimed at bringing the Osage into conformity with mainstream American society or driven by witless adventuring and greed, their impact was devastating. During the latter part of the nineteenth century, as a consequence of intermarriages, whites had already divided the Osage among themselves. There were mixed-bloods, such as Chal, whose acceptance by full-bloods was at best grudging, however appreciative mixed-bloods were of the tribe's ways and the beauty of its perception of the world of the Osage gods. Children of intermarriage such as Chal were almost predestined to inferior status in the culture of each parent.

For the Osage, Mathews emphasizes, the fruits of white technological progress proved as catastrophic as did the planting of their personal seeds. Oil royalties appended to the annuities that the Osage already received from the federal government reportedly made them the wealthiest tribe in the world. In this regard, their situation differed dramatically from that of most American Indian groups. Most American Indians who clung to tribal customs were impoverished by contact with white society. The results of Osage wealth, nevertheless, were equally calamitous.

Mathews' descriptive powers evoke a sense of loss, a feeling that inevitable change is not necessarily for the better. The price paid for the Osage's share of progress was a loss of intimacy with the world of living things and sentient objects surrounding them. The fact that the choices between their traditional worldview and "the white man's road" confused and disillusioned many of the Osage reinforces Mathews' implication that white people too have frequently apprehended their losses and have often been confused and distraught by the many forks in the road.

Critical Context

Although *Sundown* is a semiautobiographical novel, its author did not follow the sad route of his protagonist, Chal Windzer. Mathews, like fellow Osages Clarence Tinker, Sylvester Tinker, and Maria Tallchief, distinguished himself in several ways. He was a pilot in World War I. Early in the postwar years, he was graduated from the University of Oklahoma and pursued study at Sewanee, the University of Oxford, and the University of Geneva. After a few years in ranching and real estate, he rejoined the Oklahoma Osage, became a tribal councilman, and was soon recognized as one of the Osage's principal spokespeople and their preeminent historian.

Publication of his *Wah'Kon-Tah: The Osage and the White Man's Road* (1932) brought him and the Osage national attention. It was the first university press book to be chosen as a Book-of-the-Month Club selection. (A paperback edition was republished by the University of Oklahoma Press in 1981.) Appearing two years later, *Sundown* was a literary plea for public acknowledgment of the Osage's fate and, by implication, of the plight of most American Indians. By the early 1930's, the Osages, like millions of other Americans caught in the grip of the Great Depression, had fallen on hard times, though they remained far less impoverished than most American Indians. The "Great Frenzy," the oil boom of the 1920's, had collapsed, and royalties had diminished to a trickle. A series of related and widely publicized murders, the "Osage Reign of Terror," deepened the pall over reservation life. However traumatic, these events posed opportunities for Mathews, since the entire nation was reexamining its traditional values.

Mathews' literary and historical skills, joined to the talents of others such as John Collier, an American Indian whom President Franklin Roosevelt appointed Commissioner of Indian Affairs, and Sylvester Tinker, helped to win substantial appropriations for Indian Emergency Conservation Work. Far more important, particularly since Mathews was keenly aware of his tribe's dissolution, were his contributions in setting the stage for passage of the Wheeler-Howard Bill, enacted in 1934 as the Indian Reorganization Act. Ostensibly repudiating past assimilationist policies, the act acknowledged the intrinsic worth of American Indian cultures and sought to reestablish tribal values and revitalize tribal life. To a considerable degree it was successful.

Meanwhile, Mathews continued with his Osage histories, which were completed in his beautiful and masterful *The Osages: Children of the Middle Waters* (1961), perhaps the finest American Indian history produced for any tribe.

Bibliography

Hunter, Carol. "The Protagonist as a Mixed-Blood in John Joseph Mathews' Novel: *Sundown*." *American Indian Quarterly* 6 (Fall-Winter, 1982): 319-337. Author Hunter, herself a mixed-blood Osage, here analyzes the experiences of Mathews that encouraged him to create Chal Windzer. Hunter, a specialist in Osage mythology, brings interesting insights to bear on this aspect of Mathews' work. A useful perspective, especially since Mathews was himself an expert on Osage myths.

Lodgson, Guy. "John Joseph Mathews: A Conversation." *Nimrod* 16 (April, 1972): 70-75. A rare pleasure. Articulate as he was, Mathews tells little about himself on the record. This is a valuable dialogue because Lodgson interviewed Mathews after he had completed his major writings. Charming and revealing.

Mathews, John Joseph. *The Osages: Children of the Middle Waters*. Norman: University of Oklahoma Press, 1961. A beautiful and masterful study. Drawing on recollections that he coaxed from tribal elders, Mathews skillfully reconstructs the ethnohistory of his people. It is therefore a history written from an Osage perspective, but a balanced and objective one. The symbolisms embodied in it allow comparisons with Joseph Campbell's studies.

——————. *Talking to the Moon*. Chicago: University of Chicago Press, 1945. This was Mathews' own favorite among his writings, and it is a delight to read. It is based on memories of his boyhood among the blackjack pine, the red bank lands, and the prairie wildlife in the Oklahoma-Kansas Osage country. Subtitled *Wildlife Adventures on the Plains and Prairies of Osage Country*, it was reissued in paperback by the University of Oklahoma Press in 1979, the year of Mathews' death.

Wilson, Terry P. "Osage Oxonian: The Heritage of John Joseph Mathews." *The Chronicles of Oklahoma* 59, no. 3 (1981): 264-293. This essay adduces all the reasons why Mathews, the distinguished warrior, intellectual, scholar, and tribal leader could serve as a role model for other American Indians. Not all of the Osage missed opportunities.

——————. *The Underground Reservation: Osage Oil*. Lincoln: University of Nebraska Press, 1985. An academic study that is well researched and well written. Its background materials include Mathews' contributions, but it goes beyond them. Mathews concluded his study with the opening of the twentieth century, while Wilson updates through the 1970's. Good information on the Oklahoma land rush, the "Great Frenzy," "the Osage Reign of Terror," the Depression, and federal policies relevant to the Osage.

Clifton K. Yearley

THE SURROUNDED

Author: D'Arcy McNickle (1904-1977)
Type of plot: Social realism
Time of plot: 1914, with flashbacks to 1854
Locale: Salish (Flathead) Reservation, Northern Montana
First published: 1936

> *Principal characters:*
> ARCHILDE LEON, the mixed-blood protagonist, who returns home after leaving the reservation
> CATHERINE LEON, his Salish mother, a Christian, who renounces her baptism before her death
> MODESTE, Archilde's blind uncle, the heir to tribal leadership
> MAX LEON, Archilde's Spanish father, long estranged from his mother
> FATHER GREPILLOUX, a founding missionary at St. Xavier
> LOUIS LEON, Archilde's fugitive brother
> MIKE and NARCISSE, Archilde's nephews
> SHERIFF DAVE QUIGLEY, an Indian hater
> GEORGE MOSER, a former Indian trader
> HORACE PARKER, an Indian agent

The Novel

The Surrounded is a synthesis of D'Arcy McNickle's autobiographical recollections and his research into the traditions of the Salish, or Flathead, people. The novel develops its plot in the historical tensions between the Native American Salish and the white settlement that begins with the founding of a mission, St. Xavier, in the Salish country of what would become Montana. On the surface, the story seems to unfold like a murder mystery: One Indian and two law-enforcement officers are killed, and the protagonist is wrongly suspected and eventually arrested. Beneath the action, however, McNickle constructs a much deeper second plot of personal discovery, cultural identity, and the renewal of Salish traditions.

The novel opens when the protagonist, Archilde Leon, returns home from Portland, Oregon, where he has been struggling to earn a living as a fiddle player while aspiring to be recognized as a violinist. He finds his family in disarray; his brother Louis is a fugitive, charged with stealing horses and hiding out in the mountains. His nephews Mike and Narcisse have run away from an Indian boarding school much like the one in which Archilde had had his Salish ways educated out of him. His father, Max Leon, and his mother, Catherine, continue to live in two houses on the same plot of land; estranged and barely communicating, they seem to inhabit two different worlds, one white and one Salish.

When Archilde returns to his mother's small cabin behind Max's big house, he is welcomed by Catherine, who organizes a feast in his honor. As the celebration of homecoming continues, storytelling provides a frame for recollections of the Jesuit priests' first arrival in 1854. Catherine relates stories about her father Chief Running Wolf's belief that the Salish had to learn from their enemies and her own baptism into Christianity. Modeste, her blind brother and tribal elder, tells of Salish origins, sparking Archilde's childhood memories and eventually provoking a half-conscious conflict between his Christian rearing and his earlier sense of Salish customs and values.

Max, who refuses to attend, and Father Grepilloux relate the same stories to the reader as the priest reads from his old journals. Archilde, although caught up in the presence of the people who are affirming their relationships with one another, still intends to help harvest Modeste's wheat and be on his way to Paris to study the violin. Archilde increasingly doubts Christian dogma, however, and in an epiphany in the church, conquers his fear of damnation. Ironically, he prays for help for his mother, who is increasingly bewildered by the failure of her faith to sustain the lives of her children, especially the troubled and troublesome Louis.

When Archilde agrees to take Catherine on a hunting trip, he discovers that he is caught between the two worlds of his heritage. On the one hand, he approves of the emergent modern commercial ranch economy of St. Xavier. People are changing; the old Indian trader George Moser has become the town merchant, and Archilde's father has become a successful rancher. On the other hand, Archilde begins to realize that the relative poverty of the Salish indicates a spiritual poverty that is far more devastating; indeed, for the Salish, they are the same, and Archilde admires their mutual struggle to overcome conquest and survive as a people.

Catherine and Archilde join Louis in his hideout camp, but Archilde cannot shoot his prey. Instead, Louis shoots an illegal doe. When the game warden Dan Smith appears and tries to arrest them, gunplay erupts, and Louis is killed. Before Archilde knows what has happened, the old woman has killed the game warden with a hatchet. Archilde buries his body, returns to Catherine's place with the body of Louis for a proper Salish burial, and is arrested but released for Smith's murder.

As Sheriff Dave Quigley swears to find the body and the killer, Archilde comes to reject both white and Salish visions of the world. Both seem to him to end in hopelessness. Father Grepilloux dies; Max, losing his only friend, makes an effort to reconcile with his son but belittles his mother in attempting to do so. Max dies, and Catherine moves into the big house. Meanwhile, Mike and Narcisse, returned by the Indian agent Horace Parker to the Oregon mission school once already, have returned home again.

In the healing ritual that Modeste uses to cure Mike, Archilde discovers that his world has come to be that of the Salish. His mother also moves further into the Salish worldview, and she asks to be forgiven for the game warden's murder, renouncing her baptism as she submits to a ritual whipping for atonement. Her return to her earliest identity, however, is unknown to Archilde, who tries to summon a priest as she lies dying. Her refusal of last rites helps Archilde to realize how much he has come to embrace the Salish values since he returned home.

Archilde tells Parker the truth about the game warden's murder, and the agent lets him remain at large to grieve. Archilde instead flees into the mountains with Elise La Rose, Modeste's granddaughter, who has fallen in love with him, and they join Mike and Narcisse at their camp in the mountains. Sheriff Quigley, however, finds them. As he prepares to take them all into custody, Elise kills him before Archilde can knock the rifle from her hand. Moved by Elise's defiant act to defend him, Archilde holds her while Parker and his Indian policeman move in to arrest them. As Archilde extends his hands for the cuffs, the agent tells him that Indians are fools to believe they can run away. Mike and Narcisse escape again into the mountains.

The Characters

Archilde, the moral center of the novel, must reconcile his mixed-blood heritage. Almost completely assimilated into the white world before he returns home, he gradually uncovers his own fear of damnation and conquers it with the help of Catherine's history and Modeste's stories. Learning through his love for his mother, Elise's love for him, and his own love for his father, his uncle, and his nephews, Archilde discovers his freedom in his ability to act out of his Salish values. His characterization allows the reader to explore both Salish and white perspectives, although he adopts a wholly Salish point of view by the novel's conclusion.

Catherine, a fully rounded character, provides the frame for both the historical context of the arrival of the Jesuits and the experience of being Salish. Her feast to honor Archilde is the beginning of the resolution of his ambivalence, just as she works to resolve her own sense of failure in having become a Christian in her childhood. Her storytelling at the feast, joining Louis at his camp, seeking atonement for the murder from Salish elders, and refusing last rites all affirm the sense of belonging and persistence through change that are at the core of Salish beliefs. Through her, Archilde returns to his mother and to his mother culture.

Modeste, though blind, represents the vision of the elders' wisdom. He recalls history from the Salish rather than the personal view, but his history is mythic, and his emphasis is on values rather than events. Modeste stands aloof from the white-Indian conflicts, affirming Salish ways and values rather than attacking those of the settlers.

Max Leon, Archilde's Spanish father, is a stock character who represents a white version of the American Dream. His own racial heritage prevents him from being a bigot, but he has never understood his wife or his sons. Although he leaves his ranch to Archilde, he never lets his son get close until it is too late. He dies with the same values that brought him to St. Xavier: Hard work without interference from familial and social entanglements would bring success.

Father Grepilloux, Max's only friend, is caught in his own paternalistic delusions. Ironically, the Salish word for "chief" is also "father," so when the people summoned him from St. Louis to help them survive by educating them in white ideas and religion, the priest responded to them as children. He dies fearful but unwilling to probe too deeply his emotional frustration that perhaps his entire life had been spent trying to achieve the impossible; the Salish ways remain as vital as they have ever been.

Louis Leon, horse thief and outlaw, shares the frustration of the old priest but from a Salish perspective. Louis has lashed out at all cultural codes, until even his Salish identity seems determined by his reactions to and defiance of the white world. For him, even the mountains, a natural spiritual refuge, have lost their power to heal.

Elise La Rose, a counterpart to Louis, redeems her Salish values through her love for Archilde. Her murder of the sheriff is an instinctive reaction to shield Archilde from further abuse at the hands of whites.

Themes and Meanings

McNickle's novel illuminates the historical conflict in the oppression of Native Americans and the erosion of their cultural identities. The book also affirms the self-determination of the individual and the enduring Salish values that give meaning to individuality. Archilde's situation at the end is only superficially as grim as it seems; while he is thwarted once again in his effort to escape the control of white authority, he resolves his cultural dilemma. He emerges from his ordeals knowing who he is and what he values.

By framing his flashbacks in both Catherine's and Modeste's storytelling, McNickle frames his narrative to revive the power of the oral tradition. His research into traditional Salish rituals and myths gives the novel authenticity and accuracy. In changing Modeste's address to the second person, moreover, the author challenges both Archilde and the reader to participate in the storytelling experience as a total, dynamic event. With protagonist and reader entrenched in the Salish perspective, McNickle then juxtaposes the written accounts of Father Grepilloux; consequently, the oral and written traditions are brought into relief one against the other. Thus the reader, like the protagonist, comes to see the white worldview from the point of view of the Salish.

Catherine's renunciation of her Christian belief further affirms the validity of Salish spiritual experience and endurance. In her retreat to her childhood as a Salish chief's daughter, Catherine realizes that she is also telling the story of Archilde and of the next generation, represented by Mike and Narcisse. When her death dream, with all the power attributed to it by Salish wisdom, promises her a heaven that is indeed a paradise, she still renounces her baptism and refuses last rites. She knows that the vision has been false to her historically and has imprisoned her personally in the authority of the white concepts of materialistic progress.

What fails has been the significance of personal relationships that sustain family, community, and culture. Through Catherine and Modeste, Archilde learns what is important: the people's love for and trust of one another. Although Archilde is told by Parker, just after Elise kills Quigley, that he has lost everything, all that he has lost is from the point of view of the agent's white concept of authority and material gain. Instead, Archilde gains everything just when he seems to have lost it.

No longer surrounded but literally captured by that authority, Archilde is arrested while he holds Elise in his arms. His immediate embrace of her after she has acted to save him is not the condoning of murder but the acceptance of their mutual responsibility for each other's lives. He kisses her and further deepens their intimacy as well as his own with the Salish people, thereby freeing himself to surrender not only his body to the agent, but also his heart to Elise and to the future of the Salish. As his grandfather Running Wolf had counseled, he overcomes his fear of change and discovers that his individuality is interconnected to the whole of the Salish people, past and present. Moreover, when Mike and Narcisse flee the final murder scene, Archilde seems symbolically to have acted to affirm their future as one of self-determination in the midst of cultural integrity. In Archilde's ironic loss of his literal freedom, he has found his spiritual freedom; in it, he finds himself, his family, and his people's future.

Critical Context

The Surrounded, McNickle's first published novel, was six years in the making, undergoing substantial revisions as the author radically altered plot lines and developed point of view through his characterizations of Archilde and Catherine. What began as "The Hungry Generations" in manuscript had Archilde released at the novel's close in a happy ending. By subordinating the plot of conflict between whites and Indians to the plot of his protagonist's self-discovery and by creating an ironic, ambiguous conclusion, McNickle became one of the first modern Native American novelists to explore the dilemma of the mixed-blood. His legacy of affirming tribal identity was to be carried forward by a renaissance of Native American writing through such novels as N. Scott Momaday's *House Made of Dawn* (1969), James Welch's *Winter in the Blood* (1974), and Leslie Marmon Silko's *Ceremony* (1977).

After the publication of *The Surrounded*, McNickle began a career with the Bureau of Indian Affairs (BIA), publishing a second novel, *Runner in the Sun* (1954), for adolescents. His third and final novel, *Wind from an Enemy Sky* (1978), was published a year after his death and continued to explore the near impossibility of resolving Anglo-Salish relations while affirming the enduring influence of tribal values in the modern world.

While serving in the BIA, McNickle wrote several histories that initiated a revisionist view of the Native American past. In *They Came Here First* (1949), *Indians and Other Americans* (1959), *The Indian Tribes of the United States* (1962), and *Native American Tribalism* (1973), he demonstrated his compassion for both sides of the historical genocide.

Bibliography

Owens, Louis. "The 'Map of the Mind': D'Arcy McNickle and the American Indian Novel." *Western American Literature* 19 (Winter, 1985): 275-283. Owens' overview provides a reading of *The Surrounded* and *Wind from an Enemy Sky* that sees little hope for resolving white and Indian relations. Focusing on the lack of communication that stems from conflicting worldviews, Owens is pessimistic that they can ever improve.
_____ . "The Red Road to Nowhere: D'Arcy McNickle's *The Surrounded*

and 'The Hungry Generations.'" *American Indian Quarterly* 13 (Summer, 1989): 239-248. Comparing McNickle's early version of the novel to its final published form, Owens traces changes made in plot and characterization that reveal the novel's artistry. He argues that Archilde's affirmation of Salish ways in the revision does not prevent his alienation.

Parker, Dorothy R. *Singing an Indian Song: A Biography of D'Arcy McNickle.* Lincoln: University of Nebraska Press, 1992. The first full biography of McNickle, Parker's work provides background on his early years, boarding-school experiences, and career as a BIA agent. She offers insights into the autobiographical elements of the novel and reports sufficiently on Salish practices and values for a reader to grasp McNickle's use of research in constructing his fiction.

Purdy, John Lloyd. *Word Ways: The Novels of D'Arcy McNickle.* Tucson: University of Arizona Press, 1990. Purdy's study, the first complete critical account of McNickle's fiction, grounds its argument in McNickle's autobiographical elements and supplies cultural contexts from the Salish. Noting particularly the techniques of characterization and point of view, he discusses extensively the revisions of "The Hungry Generations," and explicates McNickle's growth as an artist.

Ruppert, James. *D'Arcy McNickle.* Boise, Idaho: Boise State University, 1988. A substantial overview of McNickle's biography, career, and writings, this monograph discusses briefly not only *The Surrounded*, but also his other work. Ruppert concludes that McNickle is equally at home in both white and Salish worlds and is able to provide a compassionate synthesis of both perspectives.

Michael Loudon

SWEET WHISPERS, BROTHER RUSH

Author: Virginia Hamilton (1936-　　)
Type of plot: Psychological realism
Time of plot: The 1970's
Locale: A large American city
First published: 1982

> *Principal characters:*
> TERESA PRATT (TREE), the protagonist, a sensitive fourteen-year-old African American girl
> DABNEY PRATT (DAB), her mentally retarded brother
> VIOLA PRATT (MUH VY), their mother, a practical nurse
> BROTHER RUSH, Viola's dead brother
> CENITHIA PRICHERD, a homeless woman
> SILVESTER WILEY D. SMITH (SILVERSMITH), Muh Vy's business partner and lover

The Novel

Sweet Whispers, Brother Rush is the story of a black girl in her early teens who must deal with poverty, isolation, overhwhelming responsibility, disillusionment, and loss. That she survives and finally triumps is the result of her own strength and, as she finally realizes, her mother's never-failing love for her.

Sweet Whispers, Brother Rush is divided into seventeen chapters. Although the novel is written in the third person, the voice throughout is that of the protagonist, Teresa Pratt. Sometimes she is identified as the narrator; often, however, the author presents Tree's thoughts in the first person or in fragmentary form. The matter of voice becomes particularly complex when, through the magic of the ghost Brother Rush, Tree travels into the past. Then she speaks and thinks as her own mother, a woman with two children, Tree and Dab, while at the same time never forgetting that she is really Tree, the fourteen-year-old observer. Though such segments demand close attention from the reader, they are essential to the plot; through these ventures into the past, Tree is led to important truths.

The book begins with Tree's falling in love at first sight with a well-dressed stranger she sees while she is walking home from school. Tree's life is not easy. She lives alone in a small apartment with her older brother Dabney, who is "slow" and often ill. Their mother Viola sometimes does not see her offspring for weeks at a time. Tree does not even know how to contact "Muh Vy" in case of an emergency, but has to hope that she will turn up when there is no food or money left. So far, Muh Vy always has.

Tree's glimpses of her "dude" serve to bring some excitement into a life of poverty, loneliness, and frightening responsibility. It is not until the stranger appears inside the Pratt apartment, standing inside a table, that Tree realizes that he is a benevolent ghost through whose auspices she can walk into the past. On her first journey, Tree sees the young woman her mother once was, and she discovers that the ghost is her mother's favorite brother. Just before Tree returns to the present, she sees Viola collapse after being informed that Brother Rush has been killed in an accident.

Obviously, Brother Rush is not just a creature of Tree's imagination. In the days that follow, Dabney also mentions being transported into Brother Rush's world, and Cenithia Pricherd, who is cleaning the apartment, sees the figure in the table so clearly that she falls into a dead faint.

On her ventures into the past, however, Tree is making some troubling discoveries. One is that her mother never loved Dabney but, in fact, abused him heartlessly. Another is that Brother Rush deliberately chose to die.

When Muh Vy appears, along with her likeable lover Silverster Wiley D. Smith, Tree is prepared to confront her mother with her knowledge. Muh Vy and Tree, however, have a more immediate problem: Dabney is desperately ill. After Muh Vy rushes him to a hospital, Tree gathers that Dab's illness is probably porphyria, which Viola knew had caused the deaths of her brothers and which is aggravated by the use of alcohol and drugs. When Dab dies, Tree blames her mother, and indeed Muh Vy admits that she had never even bothered to have Dab tested, much less to keep him away from the drugs that to some degree were responsible for killing him.

In the final section of the book, however, Tree comes to terms with her grief and with her anger. Silvester Smith's son Don helps her to accept the fact that all human beings are flawed—including her mother, who, despite her inability to love her son, does love Tree. While she misses Dab, Tree finds some consolation in his being freed from his misery. At the end of the novel, she looks forward to a future with new friends and a new family.

The Characters

Tree is the narrator, the protagonist, and, finally, the heroine of *Sweet Whispers, Brother Rush*. Tree voices almost all the opinions in the novel and describes every event from her perspective. Furthermore, Tree has many of the qualities one expects in a heroine. In a difficult situation, she displays intelligence, self-discipline, an admirable sense of responsibility, and a deep, uncomplaining love for both her difficult brother and her absent mother. Yet there is another side to Tree. When the homeless Cenithia Pricherd comes to clean up the apartment, Tree judges her harshly, summing her up as a lazy, greedy old woman. Clearly, in everyone except Dab, Tree expects perfection. Therefore, when she finds out the worst about her mother, she is at first unforgiving. Not until she learns to separate the sinner from the sin, to feel compassion for Muh Vy and for Cenithia, can Tree be considered a true heroine. Of all the characters in the novel, it is Tree who changes most drastically.

The alteration in Viola is less dramatic. While she does what she can to save Dabney, she cannot bring herself to love him. Yet she does love Tree enough to break the habit of a lifetime. When she admits that she abused Dabney and neglected both of her children, Muh Vy for once is facing facts instead of running away from them. She, too, has become a better person.

Unlike Tree and Muh Vy, most of the characters in *Sweet Whispers, Brother Rush* remain the same throughout the novel. As Tree learns more about others, however, her readers share her new perceptions of them. For example, Tree finds an explanation for Dab's increasingly erratic behavior, as well as an index to his pain, when she discovers that he is addicted to drugs. Similarly, when she sees Brother Rush throw himself out of the car, Tree realizes that the glittering "Numbers Man," who seemed so carefree, was actually suffering so much that he took refuge first in alcohol and eventually in suicide. Tree also discovers that Cenithia is not greedy but actually hungry and that she is not a ridiculous old woman but a person who is both brave and proud.

Unlike these characters, Silversmith and Don are exactly what they appear to be. From the moment Silversmith appears at the apartment door, Tree intuitively trusts the big man, who, she notices, is so careful not to misuse his physical strength. It is evident that he loves Muh Vy; it is also evident that there is room in his generous heart for her daughter. Silversmith's function in the novel is twofold. By joining with Muh Vy to make Tree's life better, he assumes the role of the father for whom Tree has yearned and thus makes it possible for the book to end on a hopeful note. At the same time, the qualities united in his nature—strength and tenderness, respect for others and a sense of responsibility—make him a paradigm.

Don Smith, too, is important to both plot and theme. At Dab's funeral, when Silversmith is preoccupied with Muh Vy, it is Don who moves to console Tree, thus establishing a friendship that enables her to move out of her isolation. In addition, Don can be seen as a model for other young black men. The boys on the street corner, and even Tree's beloved Dabney, see girls as sexual prey, to be used and thrown away. In contrast, as he proves when he takes Tree on her first date, Don sees them as fellow human beings. Thus, like his father, Don is presented as an ideal.

Themes and Meanings

Sweet Whispers, Brother Rush is a story about growing up. Although Tree's situation is unusual, her uncertainties are not. Like all girls of her age, she is troubled about relationships with parents, with siblings, and with the opposite sex. In her parents' absence, she yearns to be part of a real family; when her mother is revealed as less than perfect, however, Tree distances herself and rejects Muh Vy's love. Similarly, while she has always made allowances for her brother, Tree is not happy about his sexual promiscuity, which seems no different from the behavior of the boys on the street corner, whose catcalls somehow make her ashamed of her own gender.

What makes this story so different from most young adult novels is that instead of rebelling against the standards she has been taught, the protagonist clings to them too rigidly. In the process of growing up, Tree must learn to temper two good qualities she possesses, her capacity for devoted love and her strong sense of resonsibility, with compassion for those who are deficient in those virtues. It is easy to idealize an absent mother; it is more difficult to forgive one who is present, admitting what seem like unforgivable faults. Fortunately, Tree already has some experience in accepting imperfection; what she must learn is to extend the tolerance she displays in her relationship with Dabney to others, like her mother, who are not so obviously flawed.

Finally, *Sweet Whispers, Brother Rush* emphasizes the importance of dealing honestly with the past. After Muh Vy's rejection and mistreatment of Dabney is revealed, it is obvious to the reader, though perhaps not yet to Tree, that Muh Vy's feelings of guilt are the reason she sees her children so infrequently, just as her habit of denial is the reason she has suppressed her memories of her brothers' deaths. It is interesting that the past, in the person of Brother Rush, chooses to approach Tree, rather than Muh Vy herself. One might say that, after all, this is a young adult novel, with a young adult protagonist. Yet it is more significant that by having Viola redeemed through her daughter, Virginia Hamilton has expanded the theme of responsibility. It is not just the obviously afflicted who merit concern, she suggests; everyone in a society or in a family has an obligation to everyone else.

Critical Context

Few writers for young readers are better know than Virginia Hamilton, who for decades has been delighting her public as well as winning high praise from critics. Among her many successful books are *The Planet of Junior Brown* (1971), a finalist for the National Book Award and a Newbery Honor Book, and her best-known novel, *M. C. Higgins, the Great* (1974), which won both the National Book Award and the Newbery Medal. After completing *The Gathering* (1981), the third work in a science-fiction trilogy, Hamilton returned to realism with *Sweet Whispers, Brother Rush*, another Newbery Honor Book.

While she writes in a genre that has fixed conventions—for example, the absence or the relative unimportance of parents, the focus on a young protagonist who functions as a savior, and the inevitable happy ending—Hamilton is not enslaved by custom. She places her characters in unusual situations; one thinks of M. C. Higgins, perched on a bicycle at the top of a pole, keeping watch over his mountain domain; of the time-travellers in *The Gathering* who are trying to rescue an unhappy computer; and of Tree, walking through Brother Rush's mirror into another world. Hamilton avoids the use of stock characters as religiously as she eschews humdrum plots. Each of her characters is distinctive, and many of them are memorable, in part because Hamilton often has them reveal their thoughts in poetic language, reflecting the rhythms of black dialect. Critics agree, however, that it is not her technical skill but her powerful imagination that keeps Virginia Hamilton at the top of her genre.

Bibliography

Bulletin of the Center for Children's Books. Review of *Sweet Whispers, Brother Rush*, by Virginia Hamilton. 35 (July-August, 1982): 207. Compares Hamilton's technique to that of a mystery writer who builds suspense by gradually revealing the truth. She is praised for her skill in combining elements of realism and of fantasy. The reviewer sees the central theme of the work as the "affirmation of the power of love."

Farrell, Kirby. "Virginia Hamilton's *Sweet Whispers, Brother Rush* and the Case for a

Radical Existential Criticism." *Contemporary Literature* 31, no. 2 (Summer, 1990): 161-176. A detailed analysis from a psychological perspective. Farrell argues that the novel has the same appeal as popular romances. By minimizing the protagonist's mother and killing off all the black males except two unrealistic, idealized characters, the author fulfills the fantasies of young black female readers.

Guy, David. "Escaping from a World of Troubles." *The Washington Post Book World*, November 7, 1982, 14. A lucid explanation of the ghost's significance in Hamilton's work. While the reviewer notes the effectiveness of this device, he believes that the formula of the young adult novel prevents the author from expressing her profoundest visions. Comments on her use of black dialect, which, though realistic, may confuse some readers.

Heins, Ethel L. Review of *Sweet Whispers, Brother Rush*, by Virginia Hamilton. *Horn Book Magazine* 58, no. 5 (October, 1982): 505-506. Despite occasional "lapses into obscurity," Heins comments, Hamilton is a superb writer, "daring, inventive, and challenging to read." With characteristic deftness, she creates a believable ghost, whom she then uses to reveal past history. The reviewer priases Hamilton for creating characters who are "complex, contradictory, and ambivalent."

Paterson, Katherine. "Family Visions." *The New York Times Book Review*, November 14, 1982, 41, 56. Asserts that unlike some of Hamilton's other novels, this book catches a reader's attention from the very first and keeps it to the last page. Paterson also remarks on the "unique black light" that Hamilton casts upon such conventional subjects of young adult fiction as the quest for identity, the perils of membership in a family, and the death of a loved one.

School Library Journal. Review of *Sweet Whispers, Brother Rush*, by Virginia Hamilton. 29 (September, 1982): 138. Observes that the "powerful center" of this book is the relationship between Tree and Dab. As she works through her grief over her brother's death, Tree learns to feel compassion for others and even to forgive her mother for abusing him and loving only her. This "poetic, many-layered" novel is "Hamilton at her best."

Rosemary M. Canfield Reisman

TAR BABY

Author: Toni Morrison (1931-   )
Type of Plot: Social Realism
Time of plot: The 1970's
Locale: The Caribbean; New York City; and Florida
First Published: 1981

> *Principal characters:*
> WILLIAM "SON" GREEN, an uneducated African American man
> JADINE "JADE" CHILDS, a well-educated African American model
> VALERIAN STREET, a retired white businessman
> MARGARET STREET, Valerian's wife
> SYDNEY CHILDS, Jade's uncle, the Street's butler
> ONDINE CHILDS, Jade's aunt, the Street's cook

The Novel

The tar baby in Morrison's title is Jade, an intelligent black woman, orphaned and Paris-educated, who at twenty-five stands poised between two worlds. The world into which she was born is that of her aunt and uncle, Sydney and Ondine Childs, servants to the affluent Streets. Impressed by Jade's unique abilities, the Streets have provided the wherewithal for her to study art history at the Sorbonne. Jade functions socially both in the world of the Streets and the world of the Childses.

Tar Baby, a polemical novel, projects Jade's two worlds effectively. Although legitimately a member of each world, Jade sometimes wishes that race were not a part of her social context. She wants to be accepted for the person she is inside. Much of the book is—on the surface, at least—concerned with Jade's attempts to establish her identity.

Isle des Chevaliers, the Caribbean island on which most of the novel is set, is a mystical place named for a shipload of legendary blacks who were struck blind at their first sight of the island. They were not sold into slavery, as had originally been intended, but were left to wander the island, as their descendants still do. The setting is idyllic yet ominous; spirits lurk in the deep jungle foliage.

Valerian Street and his wife, Margaret, a former beauty queen two decades his junior, came to the island from Philadelphia. Valerian has retired from his lucrative candy manufacturing business. Their faithful servants, Sydney and Ondine Childs, accompanied them to Isle des Chevaliers, Sydney as butler, Ondine as cook. The two, however, are not enthralled at being separated from their roots. Sydney dreams often of his native Baltimore. The Childses are exemplary servants. Their relationship is warm and touching.

Into this harmonious setting comes Son, the protagonist. A street-savvy black who has fled the United States after murdering a woman, Son, homesick and disheartened, sneaks off his ship shortly before Christmas and is borne by the currents to Isle des Chevaliers. He steals food from the Streets's kitchen.

When Son is caught, Valerian, rather than having him arrested, invites Son to eat at his table, where Jade and Son interact uncertainly; Son is not Jade's kind of black; to begin with, his skin is much darker than hers. He is unschooled. He believes that whites and blacks can work together, but—reflecting attitudes Morrison's own father possessed—he clearly thinks that blacks and whites should not eat, live, or sleep together.

Son and Jade become antagonistic to each other. Each obviously sees in the other something magnetically attractive yet inherently threatening. Their mutual attraction, however, prevails, and soon the two are openly enamored of each other.

Jade perceives her primitive roots in Son—what Morrison elsewhere calls the "true and ancient properties" of her race. Jade is to Son the fulfillment of his dreams, the tar baby that attracts him hypnotically but that can trap and destroy him utterly.

Shortly after Christmas, Son and Jade go to New York, where they cohabit for several months. They then journey to Florida, where Son was reared. During this trip, Jade realizes that she cannot be Son's "woman" in the dominating way he demands. Son knows he cannot accommodate Jade's way of life, where color lines are muted, where black and white commingle on equal terms.

Son pursues Jade when she returns to Isle des Chevaliers. In the novel's epilogue, however, Son is on the far side of the island, stumbling in the overgrown foliage, seeking the blind horsemen, the distant progeny of the original black settlers, who will help him renew his roots and escape the charms of the tar baby who has nearly robbed him of his manhood and ethnicity.

In the end, Valerian Street's way of life is eroded when he learns that his wife has abused their child, a secret Ondine has kept from Valerian and Sydney for many years. Sydney and Ondine essentially take control of l'Arbe de la Croix, Valerian's ironically named, idyllic estate, upon which the unrelenting tropical jungle encroaches steadily.

The Characters

Valerian Street, a good businessman who grew rich in the competitive world of manufacturing, married Margaret, recently crowned Miss Maine, when he was in his mid-thirties. Margaret was more a trophy than a wife. Valerian, more liberal and sensitive than the stereotypical cigar-chomping American businessman, accepts his servant's orphaned niece as a surrogate daughter. Valerian, however, does not realize that some blacks toward whom he directs his liberalism—notably Son and Sydney— do not share his egalitarian views of race and class. In the end, Sydney is more the master of l'Arbe de la Croix than Valerian can be; Son, having made his statement, flees the socially disordered household he has disrupted.

Margaret Street married too young. Her youth and beauty attracted Valerian and her major effort now is to preserve the fast-fading youth and beauty that first made her attractive to him. It is a losing battle. Margaret is terrified of Son, probably because he represents a smoldering, primitive sexual force that simultaneously attracts and repels her. Margaret apparently has no society outside her life with Valerian. She tried early in their marriage to establish a social equality, a camaraderie, between herself and Ondine, but Valerian discouraged it.

Sydney Childs has pride and dignity. He loves his wife deeply and touchingly. He massages her throbbing feet, but refuses to wear slippers when his bunions ache because he considers himself a first-rate butler who cannot be first-rate in slippers. Sydney is reminiscent of the title character in James Barrie's *The Admirable Crichton* (1902), the resourceful, highly competent butler, capable of taking over but—understanding class distinctions—willing to only when dire necessity makes it unavoidable.

Ondine Childs demonstrates the special bond that exists among women. She is Margaret's confidante, a role in which she proves herself completely trustworthy. She has not shared Margaret's darkest secret with anyone, including her husband. Ondine is the quintessential black matriarch. She and Sydney are, in essence, more capable of running l'Arbe de la Croix than the Streets are. Race, class, and gender are the major factors that keep Ondine in the kitchen for most of her life rather than in the drawing room, where, given Jade's opportunities, she might have landed. Ondine, like her husband, has inherent dignity and native intelligence.

Jadine Childs exemplifies the new black. Well-educated, refined, intelligent, upwardly mobile, the twenty-five-year-old Jade holds the world in the palm of her hand. She wants to overcome her blackness not because she is ashamed of it but because she believes that race is not a relevant factor in determining the worth of people. Her own accomplishments bespeak her contention. Jade, nevertheless, is drawn to the unschooled, primitive Son, who represents the pulsating call of the ancestral past.

Morrison's father might well have been the inspiration for Son's father. In racial matters, Son thinks the way Morrison's father thought. He distrusts whites and believes in the separation of the races. Son's attraction to Jade is perhaps based psychologically upon his desire to tame her, to return her to her racial roots. Jade attracts Son physically, but more as an object to be controlled and tamed than as someone with whom to share his life.

Two minor characters are also significant: Gideon, the yardman, and Thérèsa, the partially blind maid, both of whom function as a sort of chorus. Although free, they are treated like chattel—ostensibly free, but slaves nevertheless.

Themes and Meanings

In the *Tar Baby*, Morrison broaches the most pressing human conflicts in American society: rich versus poor, male versus female, black versus white, primitive versus civilized, old versus young. Most of the novel evolves against a backdrop of a primitive jungle that must be trimmed constantly to keep it from encroaching on and ultimately consuming the cultivated enclave the Streets occupy.

Morrison uses her characters to represent a similar conflict. Son represents the primitive, Jade the cultivated. Morrison's question is more whether the primitive should be tamed than whether it can be tamed. Her question is an essential one that goes beyond matters of race. It causes one to question how thick and durable is the socially accepted veneer of cultivation that defines society. The jungle, left unchecked, will reclaim everything in its path.

Morrison also considers the theme of ultimate worth. The Streets are richer than the Childses and are acceptable in venues where the Childses dare not tread, but are they better than their servants? Jade, left unattended, could have led the life her aunt and uncle led. She could have spent her life in a kitchen preparing meals for white people. Given Jade's opportunities, could not Sydney and Ondine be the social equals of the Streets—or even their social superiors?

The Streets, by rescuing Jade from such a fate, prove that native ability, when nurtured, can bring people to high levels of accomplishment. The question remains, however, of whether someone like Jade can function in the environment that her accomplishments have finally won for her. She wishes that she could be judged by her inner self rather than by her pigmentation. In the end, however, it is unclear whether she judge herself according to her own criteria.

Morrison deals with the universality of human needs and emotions. She uses metaphors related to feet to reflect the similarities of all people: Son loses his shoes when he jumps ship; Sydney suffers from painful bunions, Valerian from aching corns; Sydney massages Ondine's sore feet as an act of love; Sydney refuses, because of professional pride, to wear slippers on the job; Jade returns to Paris wearing high-heeled boots. The human condition is universal, but as society is structured— perhaps immutably—inequalities exist: This is what Morrison implies by this metaphor.

Tar Baby is presented from multiple viewpoints. Every character represents an individual point of view, and the two minor characters, Gideon and Thérèsa, represent the perspective of the native inhabitants of Isle de Chevaliers. Using a multiple viewpoint enables Morrison to heighten the conflict on which *Tar Baby* focuses. The introduction of Gideon and Thérèsa allows Morrison to articulate points of view that none of the major characters can represent convincingly but that require airing—if for no other reason than to lend credibility to Son's final retreat into the briars.

Critical Context

Reared in Ohio, Toni Morrison was in her thirties when the race riots of the 1960's raged. By then, she held a bachelor's degree in English from Howard University and a master's degree from Cornell University, had taught at two universities, had married, borne two sons, and had been divorced. By the end of the 1960's, she had taken a position as an editor at Random House. The events of the 1960's affected her deeply, even though she was not an activist.

Nevertheless, the social changes of the time had implications for all African Americans, causing Morrison to think hard about what it means to grow up black in America. Her first novel, *The Bluest Eye* (1970), is about a young black girl who longs to have blue eyes. Morrison's *Sula* (1973) and *Song of Solomon* (1977) explore some of the social problems Morrison pinpoints so sharply in *Tar Baby*.

Along with obvious matters of racial prejudice and stereotypes, Morrison's novels are concerned with black women's roles in male-dominated societies. Her works also focus on the social and economic questions of the poor in a society that is clearly affluent—one that is, paradoxically, equal yet glaringly unequal.

The social context of *Tar Baby* is enhanced by Morrison's choice of setting. Isle de Chevaliers is at once romantic and decadent, appealing and appalling, comfortable and terrifying, foreign and familiar. Despite its distance from the United States, this Caribbean island provides a microcosm that obviously represents the United States and that presents—often in exaggerated form—the most pressing social problems of Morrison's homeland.

Jade, in broad ways an autobiographical character, suggests many correspondences to Morrison's own life and to the adjustments she had to make as a member of a racial minority during a time of racial transition. Jade is, at least partially, on the road to becoming what Morrison became in society: a black woman, bright and educated, who could function well in the white world. Both have shaken loose their bonds of blackness in a segregated society and, by virtue of sheer intelligence and talent, have flourished in the broader social context. The inner conflicts that Jade experiences are conflicts with which Morrison had first-hand familiarity.

Bibliography

Awkward, Michael. *Inspiriting Influences: Tradition, Revision, and Afro-American Women's Novels*. New York: Columbia University Press, 1991. Awkward deals with Morrison's place among African American women writers. He compares her to Zora Neale Hurston, Alice Walker, Gloria Naylor, and others. He also reviews the history of the African American novel in the United States.

Bloom, Harold, ed. *Toni Morrison*. New York: Chelsea, 1990. This 247-page book has an introduction by its editor and extensive contributions from more than a dozen scholars of Morrison's work. The overall assessments are useful in placing Morrison within her literary context. The essays that deal directly with *Tar Baby* are thoughtful, sometimes profound.

Harris, Trudier. *Fiction and Folklore: The Novels of Toni Morrison*. Knoxville: University of Tennessee Press, 1991. The overall coverage of Morrison's fiction is solid. Harris pays particular attention to Morrison's use of African American folklore. She traces its roots to the West African origins from which it sprang.

McKay, Nellie Y., comp. *Critical Essays on Toni Morrison*. Boston: G.K. Hall, 1988. All the essays in this collection will be useful to readers interested in Morrison. Of particular note is Craig H. Werner's "The Briar Patch as Modernist Myth: Morrison, Barthes and *Tar Baby* As-Is." This piece considers Morrison in the light of modern critical theory.

Mobley, Marilyn Sanders. *Folk Roots and Mythic Wings in Sarah Orne Jewett and Toni Morrison: The Cultural Function of Narrative*. Baton Rouge: Louisiana State University Press, 1991. This book complements Harris' study (see above) nicely. Mobley shows how Jewett, a Maine writer of the nineteenth century, and Morrison, a black writer of the late twentieth century, used similar folk motifs. A controversial thesis, but an intriguing one.

Paquet, Sandra Pouchet. "The Ancestor as Foundation in *Their Eyes Were Watching God* and *Tar Baby*." *Callaloo* 13 (Summer, 1990): 499-515. Pacquet shows consistent patterns of character and plot development in two of the author's novels. This entire issue of *Callaloo* is relevant to Morrison scholars. The range of articles is broad.

R. Baird Shuman

TATTOO THE WICKED CROSS

Author: Floyd Salas (1931-   )
Type of plot: Social realism
Time of plot: After World War II
Locale: Golden Gate Institute of Industry and Reform, a prison farm in California
First published: 1967

> ### Principal characters:
> AARON D'ARAGON, a fifteen-year-old boxer and gang leader sent to the boys' prison farm for fighting
> BARNEYWAY, a former gang member and Aaron's good friend, also in prison
> BUZZER, a large black youth who is brutal and vengeful
> RATTLER, a follower of Buzzer
> JUDITH, Aaron's girlfriend
> BIG STOOP, a brutal giant, the commanding officer of the prison farm
> THE PRISON CHAPLAIN, a Protestant minister

The Novel

Floyd Salas' *Tattoo the Wicked Cross* takes place in a boys' prison farm. The novel is divided into ten parts. As Aaron D'Aragon enters the prison, he sees its sign: GOLDEN GATE INSTITUTE OF INDUSTRY AND REFORM. The prison looks almost like a cemetery, and the entrance resembles the "pearly gates" of heaven. Aaron has been sent to prison for gang fighting. The story encompasses approximately six months and shows the changes that Aaron goes through during that time. He changes from an idealistic, religious youth who believes in God and honor to one who learns that to survive he must change and learn a different code of honor. He learns that in prison there is a code that must be followed: One does not snitch, and one takes care of oneself.

Aaron is apprehensive when he arrives at the prison. His good friend Barneyway is in prison, and Aaron is looking forward to seeing him. Part 1 is titled "Dead Time," referring to the stage of a prison sentence during which an inmate is not yet acclimated to prison life. Aaron is placed in a cell with a limited view of the prison and other inmates. He hears people but cannot see them, and his food is brought to him. While in this cell, he discovers that someone has carved a heart with the message RICHIE DE LA CRUZ + EVA, Richard of the Cross and Eve. Along with the heart is a pachuco cross with three lines, suggesting rays of light emanating from it. From his initial contacts with other inmates, he learns about prison and also learns he must be cautious, especially when inquiring about his friend Barneyway.

In part 2 "Buddies and Bad Actor," he learns that Buzzer rules the prison ruthlessly and brutally and that he sodomizes whomever he wishes. When Aaron learns that Barneyway is one of Buzzer's victims and has become a "queen," he becomes determined not to be a victim.

In the third through eighth parts, Aaron learns of the brutalities occurring in the prison and must make decisions about how to respond. Aaron's family visits him and encourages him to do what they believe is right. They tell him to avoid trouble and do his time quietly. Aaron's girlfriend, Judith, gives him hope in a seemingly hopeless brutal place.

Aaron finds himself in a dilemma: How can he live up to his ideals and beliefs if he is beaten and sodomized by Buzzer? Aaron does not want to be a hapless victim like Barneyway. He wants vengeance but cannot seek it while remaining true to his Catholic faith.

Judith appears for one of her visits with a tattoo on her cheek. Because she has a tattoo, Aaron now views her as lost, no longer the ideal pure person who gave him hope. His faith was already slipping because he was angry with God for taking his mother; now his girlfriend has been taken away from him.

Part 9 prepares the background for the final chapter. Aaron is in the prison hospital recovering from a savage beating and rape by Buzzer and his gang. He is aware that he has been beaten badly but knows that he fought bravely. At this point he does not know that he has been "gang banged." When he is told, he does not feel anger; he only feels shame. He is asked for the names of the people who jumped him. He says he does not know. Barneyway visits Aaron, and Aaron says he must make sure that Buzzer does not bother them again. It is then that he decides he must have revenge.

Buzzer and his gang attack Aaron again. Hot with anger, he remembers that there is poison in the supply room to feed Buzzer and his gang. He pours the white powder into the soup. Buzzer dies a horrible death in the chapel, but Barneyway also dies of poisoning.

Tattoo the Wicked Cross ends with part 10, "Good Time." Aaron's revenge does three things for him: He has gotten back at Buzzer, has earned the respect of his fellow inmates, and will finally be left alone. He is a mass murderer, but because he is a minor, he is not sentenced to the gas chamber or a state prison. He will remain in the institute doing "good time," remaining on his best behavior.

The Characters

The story is told from Aaron's perspective. Aaron is the most developed of all the characters. He must pit his survival skills against the other youths and against the prison itself. He is an individual with convictions. His interior monologues let the reader know how he feels about his prison experience. Initially, he is cautious in his contacts with other prisoners. No matter how he feels inside, he does not let others know his inner feelings. His introspection and analysis of his circumstances moves the story along briskly.

Barneyway, Aaron's friend, has succumbed to prison life and become a "queen" as a result of Buzzer's brutish force. Although Barneyway is not the same forceful person he was outside prison, Aaron still wants him as a friend. He finds it painful to see what has happened to Barneyway. Barneyway's characterization shows the reader what happens to some youths in prison and the kind of adaptation sometimes necessary to survive.

Buzzer shows how cruel a person can become when there is nothing holding him back. Prison rewards Buzzer for his large size and lack of a conscience. The most developed characteristics of Buzzer are his cruelty and ruthlessness. He has acquired precisely those characteristics that the prison tries to eliminate. There is no pretense of rehabilitation for him. Buzzer's almost unchecked power is seen each time he comes into the reader's view. He is evil personified.

Although Rattler can strike and kill, and although he is sly and slick, he is only a follower of Buzzer. Rattler's role is essential in that he represents those who are loyal to power; Buzzer is the power.

Judith, Aaron's girlfriend, personifies influences outside the prison. Outsiders represent hope for those inside. Aaron loses hope after seeing Judith's tattooed cheek. She is no longer a symbol of the purity and virtue possible in the outside world.

Big Stoop, the commander of the institute, represents the brutal power of the institution. He provides the connection between the ultimate power of the institution and the inmates. He also represents the militaristic power of the state.

The prison chaplain represents false hope. It is through the chaplain's inaction that the reader learns what kind of person he is. He is supposed to, but does not, provide spiritual hope for the inmates. He proves to be a lackey for the prison, informing on the "flock" to the authorities.

Themes and Meanings

Tattoo the Wicked Cross is a complex novel with many themes and meanings. Ostensibly it is about what happens to a fifteen-year-old delinquent, Aaron D'Aragon, while in a boys' prison farm. The prison is supposed to teach him to be a "good citizen," to reform. Aaron and the other boys in prison have a different code of ethics, the ethics of the streets. Salas shows the reader that prison is a dehumanizing place, one that offers corruption instead of the promised rehabilitation. When Aaron enters prison, he is an "innocent" boy who still has beliefs and a sense of right and wrong. He soon realizes that he cannot hold on to his ideals. His good friend Barneyway is also in prison, and Aaron is eager to see him. He remembers Barneyway as a tough gang member but Aaron soon learns that he was not tough enough to withstand the brutality of Buzzer. Barneyway falls victim to Buzzer and thus to the system that created this cruel person.

Another theme is the loss of faith. Aaron tries to pray as he has been taught and tries to remain true to his Catholic faith. When he is beaten and violated by Buzzer and his gang, a dilemma develops. How can he remain true to his faith, which does not allow retaliation? How does one remain nonviolent in a violent world? Aaron finds it impossible to abide by his old moral code and makes a decision to take vengeance on his tormentors. Aaron poisons his tormentors, forsaking his faith and becoming a mass murderer.

The outside world and the visitors who once gave him hope have changed. Judith, his girlfriend, was once a symbol of purity and virtue, of love and goodness. Aaron sees her differently when she tattoos her cheek. She is now a symbol of fallen feminine perfection, no longer the biblical symbol that bears her name, "the praised one." She is also not the symbolic heroine of the apocryphal Book of Judith. Aaron becomes angry with God for taking away his mother and for allowing Judith to fall from purity. Even the death of Buzzer has religious overtones. Buzzer dies in the prison chapel, at the altar. It is ironic that Buzzer, the one who torments and "crucifies" Aaron, is now the crucified.

In the kind of prison system in which Aaron is placed, the murders elevate him. As a killer, he will be respected by his peers. Salas asks whether this is the kind of system in which youths should be placed.

Another main point made in the novel is that society destroys its "innocent" children under the guise of helping them. If these children are to be rehabilitated, this will not be accomplished by placing them in dehumanizing prisons with dehumanized authorities and dehumanized inmates. The result will be tragedy. Salas makes his point by chronicling the changes that the main character goes through during his first six months in prison.

Critical Context

Tattoo the Wicked Cross is an important novel because it deals with universal themes of honor, faith, good and evil, survival, and identity. Much of the fiction by Latinos and Chicanos during the 1960's deals with their experiences with authority figures such as the police, the church, schools, and parents. Fiction of that period also addresses issues of poverty, insufficient social and health services, lack of education, and discrimination. Although Salas' novel touches on some of these concerns, he has concentrated on the environmental factors that send young people to prison and what happens to those youths while they are incarcerated. Salas' novel speaks eloquently and graphically about the injustices of the penal system, especially as it concerns youthful offenders. Placing them in prisons does not rehabilitate them; it corrupts them. It turns youths into incorrigibles unfit for society.

Salas' book gives the reader a glimpse of the penal system that destroys youth. He speaks from some of his own experiences in a youth camp. Since publication of his books, there has been a movement to treat youthful offenders with an eye toward rehabilitation rather than punishment. Perhaps Salas' book has influenced some members of the penal and judicial system.

Tattoo the Wicked Cross, Salas' first published novel, set him apart from other Latino and Chicano writers of the time. The novel set the tone of his writing, which rebelled against the literary world. Two other works that show his rebellious bent are the novels *What Now My Love*, (1969) and *Lay My Body on the Line* (1978). He writes about issues that concern him, even though the resulting works may not readily find publishers. He remains true to himself and to his art.

Tattoo the Wicked Cross was honored with the Henry Joseph Jackson Award and Eugene F. Saxton Fiction Fellowship. The novel was reissued in 1981, and it was translated into French in 1969 and into Spanish in 1971. Salas' recognition as a writer goes beyond the sphere of Latino and Chicano writing, but his works are becoming part of the canon of Latino and Chicano literature.

In addition to writing Latino fiction, Salas has also published poetry and numerous essays on the craft of writing. In 1986, he edited *Stories and Poems from Close to Home*, a collection of writings by San Francisco Bay writers, and in 1992 he published *Buffalo Nickel: A Memoir*, an autobiography that reads like a novel. Although his roots are Latino, of Spanish stock, he has not limited his writings. He has contributed much to Latino literature, but his writings are truly contributions to the wider American literature.

Bibliography

Bruce-Novoa, Juan. *Chicano Authors: Inquiry by Interview*. Austin: University of Texas Press, 1980. In the introduction, Bruce-Novoa examines the position that Salas' novels hold within Chicano literature. The book as a whole offers a good perspective on Chicano literature and the concerns of Chicano writers.

Haslam, Gerald. *Forgotten Pages of American Literature*. Boston: Houghton Mifflin, 1970. The section titled "Viva La Raza: Latino American Literature" offers a good commentary on Salas' work within the framework of Chicano literature. Haslam discussed the problem of placing a Spanish American writer with Chicano writers even though the main character in *Tattoo the Wicked Cross* is depicted as a Chicano. The excerpt from Salas' book clearly shows the brutal conditions and relationships in prison.

McKenna, Teresa. "Three Novels: An Analysis." *Aztlán* 1 (Fall, 1970): 48-49. McKenna's analysis includes three writers: Richard Vasquez, Raymond Barrio, and Floyd Salas. Her analysis includes Salas' *Tattoo the Wicked Cross*, which she sees as concerning rites of passage. She also does an analysis of language use to show Aaron D'Aragon's inward perception. A good analysis for the reader who wishes to see how Salas uses language to develop the character.

Shirley, Carl R., and Paula W. Shirley. *Understanding Chicano Literature*. Columbia: University of South Carolina Press, 1988. Chapter 3 briefly discusses sixteen Latino writers who have had considerable influence on the contemporary Latino novel. It names Salas' *Tattoo the Wicked Cross*, *What Now My Love*, and *Lay My Body on the Line*. The chapter gives the reader a quick overview of the place of Salas' work within Latino literature.

Tatum, Charles M. *Chicano Literature*. Boston: Twayne, 1982. In the introduction to chapter 5, "Contemporary Chicano Novel," Tatum offers a brief historical overview of Chicano literature since 1959. Part of Tatum's discussion includes *Tattoo the Wicked Cross*. His comments center on the personality of Aaron D'Aragon, the inner conflicts of nonviolence as taught by his religious beliefs, and his survival in the brutal prison system. The book provides a synopsis of the Chicano novel and its development.

Marcus "C" Lopez

THE THANATOS SYNDROME

Author: Walker Percy (1916-1990)
Type of plot: Science Fiction
Time of plot: The 1990's
Locale: Feliciana Parish, Louisiana
First published: 1987

> *Principal characters:*
> TOM MORE, a psychiatrist who has just been released from federal prison
> LUCY LIPSCOMB, More's cousin, an epidemiologist who becomes involved in his investigation
> BOB COMEAUX, More's parole officer on the medical ethics committee, an instigator of the plot that More uncovers
> ELLEN MORE, Tom More's second wife, who has suddenly become a bridge expert
> JOHN VAN DORN, Ellen More's bridge partner and operator of the Belle Ame Academy
> FATHER SIMON RINALDO SMITH, a friend of Tom More who runs a hospice

The Novel

The Thanatos Syndrome is in some ways an extension of Walker Percy's *Love in the Ruins: The Adventures of a Bad Catholic at a Time Near the End of the World* (1971), also narrated by Tom More. In *The Thanatos Syndrome*, More confronts a plot to adulterate the drinking water for his area with heavy sodium. Although the chemical has the desirable effects of reducing crime rates and teenage pregnancy, it causes people to revert to childlike thinking and speaking patterns and also changes women's bodies from a menstrual to an estrous cycle. The novel's characters debate the issues involved in programs of social control in this primary plot as well as in a secondary plot involving a hospice.

As the novel opens, More has just returned to his home in Feliciana, Louisiana, after spending two years in federal prison for selling prescription drugs illegally. More, a psychiatrist, is asked by Bob Comeaux, his parole officer on the medical ethics committee, to examine a patient. More notices that Mickey LaFaye, formerly one of his patients, no longer demonstrates her former symptoms of agoraphobia and anxiety but now speaks in simple sentences and jumps from topic to topic. She also shows somewhat aggressive sexuality and an ability to recall obscure facts.

When More meets other former patients and acquaintances, he notices the same types of behavior and absence of former psychiatric symptoms. Even his wife, Ellen, is affected. She manifests her increased memory in her newfound skill at bridge, a game at which she has become an expert and won tournaments with her partner, John

Van Dorn. More suspects that something unusual is going on but receives no support in his investigation from Comeaux, who appears to want More to stop investigating. He offers More a lucrative government consulting job while simultaneously threatening to alter the conditions of his parole if he does not take the job.

Lucy Lipscomb, an epidemiologist and More's cousin, tells him that she thinks something peculiar is going on. She taps into government data banks and discovers that all the people in whom More saw changed behavior showed high levels of heavy sodium. More thinks that the behavioral changes result from cortical deficits caused by the chemical. Lipscomb and More quickly trace the sodium to a water intake valve coming from the local power plant.

When More, Lipscomb's uncle, and one of her friends investigate the intake valve, they are arrested for trespassing. Bob Comeaux bails them out and, in private, tells More that the heavy sodium is part of a government experiment to reduce crime. He reiterates his job offer, stating that More will be able to monitor the program from inside the system if he takes the job. In the meantime, Lipscomb discovers that no government agency formally acknowledges the heavy sodium program.

John Van Dorn, Ellen's bridge partner, also works at the power plant and runs the Belle Ame Academy, which More's children attend. More discovers that Van Dorn knows about the diversion of heavy sodium into the water supply and agrees with the short-term goals of the program. Lipscomb examines some of the children at the Belle Ame Academy, observing signs of sexual abuse and noticing that the children appear to expect sexual behavior from her toward them.

At this point, the primary plot is interrupted by a section entitled "Father Smith's Confession." More had known Father Simon Rinaldo Smith as a parish priest and had talked with him while Father Smith was in a counseling program for alcoholics near the prison where More was serving his sentence. Father Smith had abandoned his duties at the local parish and moved into a fire tower, refusing to come down, when government budget cuts forced the closing of his hospice. Comeaux wanted to convert the hospice into a center for euthanasia. In his confession, Father Smith discusses his time spent in Germany and confesses that if he had been German he would have joined the Schutzstaffel (SS), the Nazi secret police. This confession ties into the main story line by reiterating questions of the morality of social control through medical means and by reinforcing Comeaux's heavyhandedness in promoting his programs.

The climax of the novel comes when More, Lipscomb's uncle, and her friend return to the Belle Ame Academy and discover photographic evidence of sexual molestation of the children there. Knowing that this evidence may be dismissed in court and that some of the adults involved have already had charges of sexual abuse dismissed, More devises a plan to incriminate them. He forces them to drink water with an extremely high concentration of heavy sodium. He summons the sheriff, who witnesses their regression to primate sexual behavior caused by drinking the treated water. Arrests of all the adults who run the academy lead to its closure. More bargains with Comeaux to end the experiment and reopen Father Smith's hospice, with increased government funding.

The Characters

More is introduced as a character alienated from his society. He wonders, when he comes back to Feliciana, whether something really has changed or if he has simply misremembered life outside prison. Throughout the novel, he questions his beliefs in the way the world operates, wondering about the propriety of running the heavy sodium experiment on unknowing subjects, including the children at the Belle Ame Academy. His is the voice of a social conscience.

More's character is presented sympathetically. Even his conviction for selling prescription drugs is cast positively: He sold the drugs because he needed the money, but he also thought that they would help truckers to adjust to their schedules of long hauls without sufficient breaks to sleep. Readers will sympathize with the facts that his practice has all but disappeared and his wife no longer stays home, even though both are largely results of his own actions. His narration is friendly and informal, encouraging readers to like him.

The villains in this story do not appear in stereotype form. Their behavior appears to stem from humanitarian goals of reducing crime and, in Van Dorn's case, increasing abilities. He uses water treated with heavy sodium to improve the mathematical skills of children at the Belle Ame Academy. Comeaux thinks like a stereotypical government bureaucrat, concerned with outcomes but not bothered by the moral questions involved in his actions. His threats to More come in subtle forms, and he appears to be genuinely interested in getting More involved in his program.

More's patients are mostly one-dimensional. Percy uses them primarily as examples of unusual behavior that put More on the track of Comeaux and Van Dorn. Each, however, also has a small story of his or her own. Through these minor characters, Walker discusses religious communes, couples counseling and counselors, politics in El Salvador, people's desires to behave correctly (as defined in part by the false reality of television characters), and race relations.

Apart from More, Father Smith is the most developed character. Prior to Father Smith's confession, More establishes that he is mentally unsound. Percy uses Father Smith to question some of society's beliefs, asking whether it is Father Smith or instead the rest of society that is crazy. Father Smith believes that language has failed to "signify," that words no longer carry meaning, with the exception of the word "Jew." Ironically, More is unable to comprehend much of Father Smith's side of their conversations.

Father Smith's confession to More, coming just prior to the climax, highlights the issues raised in the novel. Father Smith chose the priesthood rather than a career in medicine because, as he says, one must choose between life and death. While in Germany, he witnessed doctors experimenting on and killing children in the name of helping humanity. He concludes that he would have joined the SS, as he saw sense in the German commitment to the state. The confession is the most direct statement of the idea that the world has entered what More calls "the age of thanatos," in which society collectively has a death wish.

Themes and Meanings

Percy's primary intent in *The Thanatos Syndrome* is to question the thinking behind programs of social control. He asks whether controlling socially undesirable behavior and killing children with genetic defects will destroy society. He presents his side convincingly, arguing through More and Father Smith that people should be left to behave according to their own free will and that all people are entitled to life. Percy allows his version of good to triumph over evil. The heavy sodium experiment is abandoned by the end of the novel, and Father Smith's hospice is receiving government funding and taking in patients who formerly would have been sent to the Qualitarian centers promoted by Comeaux, with euthanasia as their fate.

The theme of alienation is important in this work. More returns from federal prison unsure if society has changed or if, instead, he has lost touch as a result of his years in prison. His alienation and status as an outsider allow him to ask questions that no one else cares to. Father Smith, declared mentally unsound by More, appears to have a firmer grasp on morality than does society, as represented by Comeaux and Van Dorn.

Although the novel is in some ways structured as a thriller, the reader never gets the impression that More is in serious danger. The threats against him are subtle: implied loss of his favored parole status, arrests for trespassing, and a cable television van that appears to be following him. The subtlety of the threats underscores the idea that society as a whole can be attacked nonviolently, with damage done before anyone realizes the danger.

After its climax, the novel slips into comic moments, suggesting that all has ended well. Percy uses irony and satire to make some minor points. Van Dorn, for example, takes several months to recover from his dose of heavy sodium and retains primate characteristics during his recovery. More convinces the director of the Tulane Primate Center to take Van Dorn in and pair him with Eve, a gorilla who had learned sign language but no longer uses it. With Van Dorn as her companion, she again begins to use sign language and teaches it to him. Once he recovers, Van Dorn returns to human society and is convicted for his crimes. He is sentenced to ten years in prison, where he writes a book entitled *My Life and Love with Eve*. That episode ends with Van Dorn a celebrity, the director of the primate center appointed as a professor of semiotics at twice his former salary, and Eve returned to Zaire, where she is shunned by other mountain gorillas. Percy makes it very clear who benefits in contacts between humans and their supposed lessers.

The people of Feliciana recover from their treatment with heavy sodium, exhibiting their former psychiatric symptoms and increasing More's practice. The novel ends with More counseling Mickey LaFaye, who once again is anxious and has disturbing dreams in which a stranger is trying to tell her something. Percy appears to believe that this is a desirable state of affairs, that people should have doubts and questions.

Critical Context

Comparisons of *The Thanatos Syndrome* to George Orwell's classic *Nineteen*

Eighty-four (1948) and Aldous Huxley's *Brave New World* (1932) are unavoidable. All three novels discuss the morality of social control through medical means, each pointing out the dangers of going too far in trying to improve society. Percy's book adds religious content to the discussion and updates the social problems supposedly being solved.

The Thanatos Syndrome is Percy's last novel. It illustrates many of the themes common in both his fiction and his essays, themes of religious belief, racial relations, social control, and personal identity. Percy earned his M.D., but his practice was interrupted by an episode of tuberculosis, during which he began an intense study of philosophy that manifests itself in each of his novels. He turned his attention to writing and earned the National Book Award for his first novel, *The Moviegoer* (1961). That novel introduced the idea of people identifying more with films than with real life, a theme touched on in *The Thanatos Syndrome*.

The Thanatos Syndrome brings back the character of Tom More from *Love in the Ruins*. In the earlier book, More was declared crazy, and his first wife left him to join a religious cult, much as Ellen is attracted by the Pentecostals at the end of *The Thanatos Syndrome*. More waited for the end of the world and became an alcoholic in the earlier book; here, he appears to have conquered alcoholism, though he is still prone to knocking back a shot of Jack Daniels, and he takes positive action to save the world from itself.

Bibliography

Coles, Robert. *Walker Percy: An American Search*. Boston: Little, Brown, 1978. The first comprehensive study of Percy. Sections discuss Percy's philosophical roots, his essays, and his novels. This work predates *The Thanatos Syndrome* but is useful for its in-depth discussion of Percy's earlier work and his ongoing theme of alienation. Briefly discusses *Love in the Ruins*. Percy dedicated *The Thanatos Syndrome* to Coles, a child psychiatrist.

Gretlund, Jan Nordby, and Karl-Heinz Westarp, eds. *Walker Percy: Novelist and Philosopher*. Jackson: University Press of Mississippi, 1991. Several essays in this collection discuss *The Thantos Syndrome* or aspects of the novel. Other essays provide overviews of Percy's work, discuss his other novels, and explain his philosophy. "Father Smith's Confession" receives considerable attention and is the subject of one entire essay.

Hardy, John Edward. *The Fiction of Walker Percy*. Urbana: University of Illinois Press, 1987. Contains an introduction and one chapter for each of Percy's novels. Hardy treats each novel internally rather than relating each to Walker's background and overarching philosophy. Treats Percy's work as literature rather than philosophy or prophecy.

Lawson, Lewis A., and Victor A. Kramer, eds. *Conversations with Walker Percy*. Jackson: University Press of Mississippi, 1985. Dozens of interviews are arranged chronologically, beginning with 1961, and appear as originally printed (one is original). This leads to some minor repetition across interviews. Useful for understanding Percy's perspectives on his work, though none of the interviews discusses any of his books in great depth.

Percy, Walker. *Signposts in a Strange Land.* New York: Farrar, Straus and Giroux, 1991. This book of Percy's essays includes several that had not been published previously. Sections include Percy's thoughts on life in the South; science, language, and literature; and morality and religion. An epilogue includes an interview of Percy by Zoltán Abádi-Nagy and a self-interview.

A. J. Sobczak

A THIEF OF TIME

Author: Tony Hillerman (1925-   )
Type of plot: Detective and mystery
Time of plot: 1980's
Locale: New Mexico, Arizona, and Utah
First published: 1988

> *Principal characters:*
> JOE LEAPHORN, a member of the Navajo Tribal Police who is attempting
> to find a missing woman anthropologist
> JIM CHEE, a younger member of the Navajo Tribal Police who investi-
> gates mysterious and violent incidents involving pot hunters
> ELEANOR FRIEDMAN-BERNAL, an anthropologist tracing Anasazi pots
> who has mysteriously vanished
> RANDALL ELLIOT, an aristocratic anthropologist who violates protected
> sites and resorts to murder to protect his reputation
> JANET PETE, a lawyer with the Navajo Tribal legal services and friend of
> Jim Chee
> SLICK NAKAI, a likeable Navajo fundamentalist Christian evangelist
> involved in selling Anasazi pots
> HARRISON HOUK, a prominent Utah rancher who sells Anasazi pots
> BRIGHAM HOUK, Harrison's son, an insane recluse who lives in a remote
> canyon

The Novel

Set amid the Anasazi ruins of the American Southwest, *A Thief of Time* is an anthropological mystery in which Joe Leaphorn and Jim Chee, two members of the Navajo Tribal Police, work together to locate a missing anthropologist and to solve the murders of two pot hunters, "thieves of time" who ransack Anasazi graves to steal artifacts, thereby damaging the sites for researchers trying to understand the past. Narrated from the omniscient third-person point of view, most of the novel's chapters alternate between Leaphorn and Chee as they conduct parallel investigations, using their intimate familiarity with Navajo culture and the Southwestern landscape. Although solving the mystery provides the major physical action, both characters also deal with personal problems that add significant emotional tension to their investigations.

The novel opens with Dr. Eleanor Friedman-Bernal's nighttime arrival at an unexplored Anasazi ruin in southern Utah. Friedman-Bernal is looking for potsherds bearing the pattern of Kokopelli, the humpbacked fertility god of Indian myth. The pots are apparently the work of a single artist whose pottery was first unearthed at the Chaco Canyon site in New Mexico. Friedman-Bernal believes that this potter's work may help to explain the migratory patterns and mysterious disappearance of the Anasazi people seven centuries ago. Injured in a fall, the anthropologist discovers someone has already ransacked the graves, and the only episode featuring this character ends shrouded in mystery and suspense.

Leaphorn, depressed and grieving over the death of his wife Emma, agrees to help find the anthropologist, whose disappearance has puzzled and alarmed her coworkers at the Chaco Canyon site. On terminal leave and initially apathetic, Leaphorn finds his curiosity returning as he pieces together the puzzle of Friedman-Bernal's disappearance, beginning his search with clues from her appointment calendar. Learning of her research on the Anasazi pots with the Kokopelli design, he starts his hunt for the missing woman at a fundamentalist Christian revival conducted by the Navajo evangelist Slick Nakai, who tells Leaphorn he has an arrangement with Friedman-Bernal to show her and verify the origins of Anasazi pots with the peculiar pattern.

In trouble with Captain Largo for failing to guard a backhoe (stolen from a tribal storage yard while Chee helped a drunken relative), Chee links a suspect to Slick Nakai's revival, where he meets Leaphorn. Chee eventually discovers that the backhoe was stolen by Joe Nails, a white man, and Jimmy Etcitty, another Navajo who follows the "Jesus Way." Chee tracks the backhoe to a remote Anasazi ruin, where he finds that both men have been murdered while vandalizing graves. Since both pot hunters have ties to Nakai, Friedman-Bernal, and the Chaco Canyon anthropologists, Leaphorn and Chee agree to work together.

Harrison Houk, a Utah rancher, tells Leaphorn about an Anasazi pot with the Kokopelli design that he had sold to an art dealer in New York City. After tracing Friedman-Bernal's visit to the dealer and the collector in New York, Leaphorn returns to find Houk murdered, and he trails Friedman-Bernal to the Anasazi site near Houk's ranch. Meanwhile, Janet Pete, Chee's Navajo lawyer friend, helps him to discover Friedman-Bernal and Randall Elliot's mutual interest in the unexplored site in Utah.

At the site, Leaphorn finds the injured anthropologist in the care of Brigham Houk, Harrison's deranged son. Elliot also arrives, and Leaphorn learns the motives that drove the anthropologist to violence. Elliot has been digging up gravesites in search of genetically marked lower jawbones, documenting his finds until he could later get permits to explore the sites officially. Nails and Etcitty, his helpers, had been selling pots from the gravesites, thus attracting Friedman-Bernal's attention. To prevent her from destroying his reputation, Elliot killed his helpers and Harrison Houk and intends to murder Friedman-Bernal, but he is himself killed by Brigham. Chee, who had followed Elliot to the site, helps Leaphorn to rescue the anthropologist, while Brigham disappears into the canyon. The mystery solved and order restored, Leaphorn decides not to retire, and he asks Chee to sing a healing ceremony.

The Characters

Although *A Thief of Time* is built on the framework of the detective story, it is essentially a novel of characterization, a portrayal of the values and complex development of two Navajo tribal policemen, Joe Leaphorn and Jim Chee. The remaining cast of characters is subordinate to the portrayal of the two major characters, underscoring the fact that the novel's action derives from character.

Joe Leaphorn is a modern Navajo who functions as a mediator between cultures—comfortable with the ways of the dominant white culture, pragmatic, a bit skeptical and cynical about taboos (he does not believe in witches or evil ghosts), yet steeped in tribal traditions and at home in the Southwestern landscape. He accepts the basic metaphysical thrust of Navajo culture: *hozho*, the Beautyway, which implies harmony, cosmic orderliness, and the interdependency of nature and the Navajo people. Crime, therefore, is disharmony, disorder, a social and spiritual aberration. Keenly analytical, Leaphorn seeks the underlying pattern of events. His quest to solve the mystery of Friedman-Bernal's disappearance by connecting intricate links becomes a complex metaphor for his need to restore social and spiritual order, not only to his jurisdiction but also to himself as he recovers from his grief over his wife Emma's death. Leaphorn's movement from despondent apathy to a reawakened curiosity and an appetite for life forms part of a pattern that includes his own healing and acceptance of Emma's death and the reaffirmation of his self-identity and Navajo roots. The ethnographic material that gives the novel its rich density of texture and emotional power is revealed through characterization, and Leaphorn emerges as a complex, fully developed, and heroic person.

Jim Chee is effectively juxtaposed to Leaphorn. A younger, more traditional Navajo (he is a *hatathali*, a singer of the Blessed Way), Chee initially does not particularly like the legendary Leaphorn, but he respects him, wants his approval, and finds himself quoting Leaphorn. Leaphorn regards Chee as smart and alert, but "bent," a romantic and a dreamer, yet he comes to admire Chee's detective skills and spiritual calling. Thus the two complement each other well; Chee is an intuitive, somewhat impulsive foil to Leaphorn's rational distrust of hunches and coincidences. Chee's adherence to traditional values serves to emphasize Leaphorn's skepticism. For example, when Chee discovers two murdered pot hunters, one a Navajo, he is deeply affected by his belief in *chindi*, the ghost representing all that was evil in the dead Navajo's being, and Chee must restore inner harmony through the cleansing ritual of a sweat bath. With the help of Janet Pete, his lawyer friend who is also recovering from a romantic entanglement with a white, Chee comes to terms with his loss of Mary Langdon, a white woman for whom he had once contemplated forsaking his Navajo culture. Chee's Navajo beliefs permeate his thoughts and actions, allowing Hillerman subtly to introduce tribal lore and anthropological material through characterization rather than through authorial comment.

Themes and Meanings

An absorbing and entertaining mystery story suffused with Navajo culture, the novel becomes a telling social commentary on the consequences of crosscultural relationships. Leaphorn and Chee, members of a racial minority whose self-identities are perpetually at risk in their exposure to the dominant white culture, dramatize in their thoughts, actions, and quest for harmony the importance of sustaining cultural tradition with cohesive meaning. Of the two, Leaphorn more easily compromises with the hard, practical reality of modern life, regarding Chee as a romantic trying to live by the Old Way in a competitive world. The novel's subtext is Leaphorn's need to reaffirm traditional values. This is conveyed in the pervasive symbolism of the fertility god Kokopelli, the flute-playing, humpbacked bearer of seeds. When Leaphorn paddles down the San Juan River in search of Friedman-Bernal, he is identified with Kokopelli, and his quest becomes an affirmation of life and the continual renewal of the present by the past.

The crosscultural theme is mainly objectified in the tension between the organic, interrelated beauty and harmony of the Navajo way, with its emphasis on family relationships, balance, and sense of the spiritual infusing all of life, in contrast to the moral expediency of a materialistic white culture based on competition, professional rivalry, and greed for prestige and fortune. The beliefs, taboos, rituals, and intricacies of clan structure provide Chee and Leaphorn with interior rules by which to live. In contrast, deracinated Navajos who are indifferent to taboos vandalize graves, and Randall Elliot, thwarted by the tangled bureaucratic laws and regulations protecting unexplored sites, resorts to violent crime. According to Leaphorn's moral code, justice is a higher principle than bureaucratic law enforcement. He has no compunction about letting Brigham Houk disappear after the deranged man kills Elliot, for Houk's action illustrates the Navajo wisdom that things even up: Those who practice evil are self- destructive.

Those characters responsible for crime and "evil" are not judged but are understood as reflecting the distortion of cultural values. Indeed, the white lust for riches and reputation is the moral equivalent of the origin of evil in Navajo myth. Thus Randall Elliot is as much a victim of his wealthy background and professional aspirations as he is a murderous villain. Even the tragedy that befalls the Houk family illustrates the consequences of the acquisitive life, which can lead to derangement and death. Deracinated Navajos such as Slick Nakai and Jimmy Etcitty, who forsake their heritage to embrace the "Jesus Way," are portrayed with sympathy. Their surrender to the temptation to trade the precious Indian artifacts of the past for material gain is only a symptom of the disorder that attends the crosscultural loss of identity and the failure to see the life-affirming value of the past for the present.

Critical Context

A Thief of Time, the eighth novel in Hillerman's series of eleven mysteries set on the vast Navajo Reservation, represents a significant artistic achievement in the depth and complexity of the author's portrayal of Navajo culture. Always a masterful storyteller, Hillerman has uniquely infused the classic novel of detection, which emphasizes the linear thrust of action, with the psychological and spiritual complexity of holistic Navajo beliefs, creating through the consciousnesses of Leaphorn and Chee a rich texture of interlinking details and events. The structure becomes almost nonlinear (like the Native American oral tale), as apparently disparate threads from past and present and from remote distances are woven together into a single, unified pattern of meaning, discoverable only through the Navajo perspective of Leaphorn and Chee.

The first three of Hillerman's mysteries, *The Blessing Way* (1970), *Dance Hall of the Dead* (1973), and *Listening Woman* (1978), feature Leaphorn, the modern, older, cynical detective. Jim Chee, a younger, more traditional detective who reconciles his vocation as a tribal policeman with his avocation as a *yataali*, a Navajo singer, is the main character of the next three novels, *The People of Darkness* (1980), *The Dark Wind* (1982), and *The Ghostway* (1984). Leaphorn and Chee are finally brought together in *Skinwalkers* (1986) and are reunited in *A Thief of Time* (1988). Hillerman continued to pair the two in *Talking God* (1989), *Coyote Waits* (1990), and *Sacred Clowns* (1993), but it is in *A Thief of Time* that he most effectively provides a balanced portrayal of characters whose own personal growth and interaction are central to the conflict and its resolution.

Although Hillerman disclaims writing "mainstream" novels and calls his work "category fiction," he successfully engages the reader in a compelling anthropological mystery with social and moral significance. It is a tribute to Hillerman's mastery of his craft that the reader never bumps into the author with his arms full of ethnographic materials; Hillerman's substantial anthropological knowledge is conveyed artfully through the interaction of setting, plot, and characterization.

Bibliography
Bakerman, Jane S. "Tony Hillerman's Joe Leaphorn and Jim Chee." In *Cops and Constables: American and British Fictional Policemen*, edited by Earl F. Bargainnier and George N. Dove. Bowling Green, Ohio: Bowling Green State University Popular Press, 1986. Shows how Hillerman's novels address the realistic complications peculiar to fictional law-enforcement officers in a vast setting where jurisdictions overlap. Considers how Leaphorn and Chee maintain independence, resourcefulness, and a sense of justice in a cynical milieu of crime and violence. Focuses on the way ethnicity informs characterization.

Engel, Leonard. "Landscape and Place in Tony Hillerman's Mysteries." *Western American Literature* 28 (Summer, 1993): 111-122. Insightful analysis of Leaphorn's search for pattern in crime as a way of reestablishing his relationship to the Earth. Landscape imagery and sense of place are seen as at the core of Hillerman's narrative method.

Erisman, Fred. *Tony Hillerman*. Boise, Idaho: Boise State University, 1989. Extensive treatment of Hillerman's work. Useful consideration of the theme of time— personal, professional, and cultural—in *A Thief of Time*, the "most regionally and humanly evocative of all the Navajo police stories."

Roush, Jan. "The Developing Art of Tony Hillerman." *Western American Literature* 28 (Summer, 1993): 99-110. Argues convincingly that Hillerman has created a new genre; the anthropological mystery. Shows how Hillerman's fiction has shifted from romance to the novel.

Schneider, Jack W. "Crime and Navajo Punishment: Tony Hillerman's Novels of Detection." *Southwest Review* 67 (Spring, 1982): 151-160. An analysis of how Hillerman adapts the classical detective novel to the vast Southwestern landscape.

Schneider sees the books' setting as not a passive background but as playing "an active role in the novels."

Clifford Edwards

A THOUSAND ACRES

Author: Jane Smiley (1949-   )
Type of plot: Family
Time of plot: 1979 through the early 1980's
Locale: Iowa
First published: 1991

> *Principal characters:*
> VIRGINIA (GINNY) COOK SMITH, the daughter and wife of farmers, the
> novel's narrator
> ROSE COOK LEWIS, Ginny's sister and the mother of two daughters
> CAROLINE COOK, Ginny and Rose's younger sister, an attorney
> LAURENCE (LARRY) COOK, the sisters' father, a strong-willed, domineer-
> ing man
> TY SMITH, Ginny's husband
> PETE LEWIS, Rose's husband
> HAROLD CLARK, Cook's friend and the owner of a neighboring farm
> JESS CLARK, Harold's long-absent son, who becomes both Ginny and
> Rose's lover upon his return
> LOREN CLARK, Jess's brother, who has remained on the family farm with
> his father

The Novel

Set on a farm in Iowa, *A Thousand Acres* draws on William Shakespeare's *King Lear* (c.1605) in its story of an aging farmer who decides to divide his land among his three daughters. His decision alters the family's life forever and forces his oldest daughter, Ginny, the book's narrator, to confront her past.

The story opens in 1979 in Zebulon County, Iowa, as Larry Cook announces his decision to split his land among his children. Cook's married daughters and their husbands agree to the plan, but his youngest daughter, Caroline, who has left the farm and is now an attorney, voices her disapproval and is cut out of the arrangement by her father. The plan unfolds quickly, and though Ginny herself has misgivings about it, Cook is a domineering man whose family rarely challenges him.

For Ginny's husband, Ty Smith, a hardworking man who has treated his father-in-law with respect and patience, the agreement offers a chance to undertake a hog-farming project of which he has long dreamed. Ginny and Ty have been unable to have children—Ginny has suffered five miscarriages, only three of which she has revealed to her husband—yet their marriage is placid, steady, and comfortable. Rose and Pete's relation is less successful—he drinks and is sometimes abusive—but they have two daughters, Pammy and Linda.

Larry Cook's decision coincides with the return of Jess Clark, the son of Cook's neighbor and friend, Harold Clark. Jess has not been home since he fled to Canada during the Vietnam War, and his return is an event in the small community. His brother, Loren, has remained at home with his father on the family farm. Ginny is immediately drawn to Jess, who has lived the unsettled life of a drifter and returned with unfamiliar habits and ideas. The two eventually become lovers, as Ginny begins to grow dissatisfied with Ty.

Soon after his land has been divided between Ginny and Rose, Larry's actions become increasingly erratic and give rise to considerable tension within the family. The two sisters decide to be firm with their father and set rules for his behavior, which leads him to seek out Caroline and repair his rift with her. During a violent thunderstorm, Larry refuses to come indoors and later tells Harold Clark that his daughters turned him out of the house. As the storm rages, Rose confronts Ginny with the truth about their childhood, truth that Ginny has long since repressed; following their mother's death when they were teenagers, their father had sexually abused both girls.

At a church dinner, Harold Clark denounces Ginny and Rose and what he perceives as their mistreatment of their father, who is now living with the Clarks. He also turns on Jess, whom he had seemed to favor over Loren, claiming that Jess is plotting to gain control of the farm. Several days later, Harold is blinded while treating his fields with anhydrous ammonia. Ginny and Rose also learn that Caroline is suing them on behalf of their father in an attempt to regain control of the farm, and Ginny discovers that Ty has provided Caroline with information about the night of the storm. Ty also learns the truth about Ginny's miscarriages, and the gulf between them widens.

Following a drunken quarrel with Harold, Rose's husband Pete drowns in the local quarry, a possible suicide, and Rose confesses to Ginny that she, too, is having an affair with Jess. When Ginny learns that it is Rose whom Jess loves and that her sister knows of their affair, she conceives a plan to poison Rose with a jar of homemade sausages, which Rose puts aside and never eats. The lawsuit brought by Caroline is settled in favor of Ginny and Rose, and Ginny takes a thousand dollars from Ty and leaves the farm.

She settles in St. Paul, where she finds work as a waitress. When she at last contacts Rose several months later, she learns that their father died of a heart attack shortly after the lawsuit was concluded. Several years pass before Ty appears suddenly one day with the news that his portion of the farm has failed; he announces that he is moving to Texas and would like a divorce. The following spring, Rose, who has since broken up with Jess, suffers a recurrence of breast cancer, from which she will not recover, and she asks Ginny to take her daughters. While sorting through items in the farmhouse with Caroline before it is auctioned off, Ginny considers confronting her sister with their father's sexual abuse, but ultimately says nothing. She returns to St. Paul and builds a life with her nieces.

The Characters

Ginny, the book's narrator, is also its central figure. A quiet farmwife who dislikes confrontations and remains emotionally dominated by her father, she is living with repressed memories of abuse and incest that have unknowingly shaped her adult life.

Although she is outwardly content in her marriage, she longs for children and has spent most of her life accommodating herself to other people's wishes. When memories of her father's abuse resurface, her emotional world is shattered. The situation is exacerbated by her pain over the outcome of her affair with Jess. Her attempt to poison her sister is an outgrowth of her despair and long-suppressed anger; afterward, she is able to regain her emotional balance and begin a new life.

Rose has not repressed her memories of incest, and she is filled with rage and hatred for her father. Her own marriage is often unhappy and sometimes abusive, yet she is in many ways freer that Ginny. Rose is able to express herself openly and is unafraid of her own feelings. Yet, she too remains under her father's thumb, spending her life as a farmer's wife and giving in to Larry Cook's demanding, domineering ways. Her determination to safeguard her own daughters gives a focus to Rose's life, and she faces her death with courage, tying up loose ends and arranging for her children's care.

Larry Cook remains largely an enigma as seen through the eyes of the daughters he has abused and molested. A hard, powerful, often deliberately cruel man, he appears throughout the novel to be suffering from the onset of senility. His erratic behavior is at first suspected by Ginny and Rose to be a ploy, but it eventually becomes clear that he is not acting. He has trouble distinguishing between his daugters, and he comes to believe that Caroline is dead. His decision to divide his land is perhaps a result of his weakening mental powers, although his behavior remains as consistently difficult and selfish in his decline as it has been throughout his life.

Jess Clark, lover to both Ginny and Rose, is ultimately selfish as well. A tantalizingly foreign presence in the community, he arrives at a moment when upheaval within the Cook family leaves both women vulnerable to his charms. A vegetarian with an interest in Eastern philosophy and organic farming, he believes he is rebuilding his relationship with his father, and he is stunned when Harold denounces him. Unable to sustain a serious commitment, he leaves Rose and returns to the West Coast.

Ty Smith, Ginny's husband, is a decent, hardworking man whose dreams extend only as far as expanding the farm's hog-raising capabilities. Following the division of Larry's land, however, Ginny's perception of Ty undergoes a shift. She begins to see that his amiable, placating manner, while genuine, also makes it possible for him to manipulate those around him. Unaware of his wife's history of incest, he is unable to understand the feelings that color her relationship with her father.

Caroline Cook, like her father, remains largely a mystery to her two sisters. Although they have reared her and have attempted to shield her from the behavior they received from their father, their efforts are misunderstood by Caroline, who sees them as cold and manipulative. Caroline is also not unmotivated by self-interest, exulting in her position as her father's favorite.

Themes and Meanings

A Thousand Acres is not only a modern-day retelling of the *King Lear* story, it is a rethinking of the story as well. Each of the major characters in the novel corresponds to a character from the play, often sharing the same first letter of their names:

Ginny/Goneril, Rose/Regan, Larry/Lear, Caroline/Cordelia. Jane Smiley's purpose, however, is to reexamine the dynamics of the play's relationships and work against the reader's expectations in her portrayal of the novel's characters.

In its portrait of an aging king who decides to divide his kingdom among his three daughters and soon finds himself displaced and ill-treated by the elder two after he has cast out their sister for her honesty, *King Lear* demonstrates clearly that its sympathies lie with Lear and his youngest daughter, Cordelia. Smiley, however, refuses to accept the play at face value. She has remarked, "I never bought the conventional interpretation that Goneril and Regan were completely evil," adding that Shakespeare's version "is not the whole story." In her retelling of the story, Larry Cook has been as ruthless and controlling in his treatment of his daughters as he is in his acquisition of land; in his eyes, both are his property.

In the case of Ginny and Rose, this extends to incest, an act that has more to do with power than with sexual desire. Its effect on the two sisters has shaped their adult lives and is the underlying factor in their uneasy relationship with their father. Caroline remains unaware of her father's abusive behavior, having been protected throughout her childhood by Ginny and Rose, and she is now unable to understand her sister's anger and fear. The division of Larry Cook's farm raises powerful emotional issues for everyone involved, eventually shattering the family completely.

The parallels to *King Lear* also extend to the neighboring Clark family. Like Lear's friend and adviser the Duke of Gloucester, Harold Clark has two very different sons and is blinded during the course of the story. Unlike Gloucester, however, who is tricked and betrayed by one of his sons, Harold plays his sons against each other, letting them believe that he may alter his will in favor of Jess. The principal factor influencing relationships within both families is the father's manipulative and controlling behavior.

Indeed, the central theme of *A Thousand Acres* is the layers of complex emotional issues that inform the lives of all families. Actions by grown children that, taken out of context, may seem heartless or ungrateful are often the result of behavior years earlier on the part of their parents, whose respected positions within their community serve as a shield for their true natures. When the truth is finally acknowledged, the structure of the family crumbles, revealing a foundation built on deception and cruelty rather than love.

In keeping with its theme of hidden causes, the book also features a secondary storyline involving the damage done by unseen chemicals that have drained from the fields into the family's drinking water. Rose has developed cancer, and Ginny has suffered five miscarriages; although no conclusive link is ever proven, the implications are clear. For the Cooks, a family history filled with hidden dangers—both physical and psychological—has resulted in a legacy of irreparable harm.

Critical Context

The complexities of human relationships are at the heart of the Jane Smiley's work, and intimate portraits of families make up the majority of her novels, novellas, and short stories. Even her historical saga *The Greenlanders* (1988), an epic novel set in the fourteenth century, focuses on families and relationships that help bring the era she has re-created to life.

Most of Smiley's work involves portraits of contemporary life, as is the case with her short-story collection *The Age of Grief* (1987), which was nominated for the National Book Critics Circle Award. The book's title story is told from the point of view of a man whose marriage is failing; her 1989 novellas *Ordinary Love and Good Will* published together, also feature strong narrative voices from characters whose family lives have taken unexpected and unhappy turnings. This narrative device is one that Smiley uses to extraordinary effect in *A Thousand Acres*, as the reader experiences the unfolding events from Ginny's point of view. Like Smiley's earlier work, the novel places families and their interactions at the heart of its story and uses them as a means of exploring the universal aspects of the human experience.

A Thousand Acres is Smiley's best known and most acclaimed novel, although she has been the subject of much critical praise throughout her career. In addition to its favorable critical reception, the book received both the National Book Critics Circle Award and the Pulitzer Prize.

Bibliography
Carlson, Ron. "King Lear in Zebulon County." *The New York Times Book Review* 96 (November 3, 1991): 12. Carlson offers a thoughtful critical look at the novel and Smiley's use of the *King Lear* story within it.
Duffy, Martha. "The Case for Goneril and Regan." *Time* 138 (November 11, 1991): 92. Offers comments from Smiley on her work as well as background on her life.
Fisher, Ann H. Review of *A Thousand Acres*, by Jane Smiley. *Library Journal* 116 (October 1, 1991): 142. Brief but very favorable review.
Publishers Weekly. Review of *A Thousand Acres*, by Jane Smiley. 238 (August 23, 1991): 44. Offers both a brief synopsis and a critical appraisal of the book. Praises the novel as Smiley's "best yet."
Shapiro, Laura. *Newsweek* 118 (November 18, 1991): 82. Shapiro provides both a positive critical view and background on Smiley.

Janet Lorenz

THROUGH THE IVORY GATE

Author: Rita Dove (1952-   )
Type of plot: Bildungsroman
Time of plot: The 1950's through the early 1970's
Locale: Ohio, Wisconsin, and Arizona
First published: 1992

Principal characters:

VIRGINIA KING, a puppeteer and an aspiring actress
BELLE EVANS, her mother, withdrawn and genteel
ERNIE EVANS, her father, who opened vistas to her
ERNIE EVANS, JR., her brother
CLAUDIA EVANS, her rebellious younger sister
GRANDMA EVANS, her grandmother
AUNT CARRIE, her father's sister
CLAYTON EVERETT, Virginia's first and most intense love
TERRY MURRAY, a single father who falls in love with Virginia
RENEE BUTLER, a student who admires Virginia
GINA, a puppet created by Virginia, her mask or other self

The Novel

Rita Dove's *Through the Ivory Gate* is a tale of a young African American woman's growing up, learning to use her varied artistic abilities despite obstacles, and beginning her career.

The frame action is set in Akron, Ohio, at the end of the Vietnam War era, with flashbacks to the 1950's and early 1960's and to events that took place in Wisconsin and Arizona. The third-person limited-omniscient narrative provides a full portrait of the main character, Virginia King, and an insight into what the coming of age must have been like for a talented African American woman of her era.

The "Prelude" to the story catches a glimpse of the child Virginia rejecting a black doll for a white one, then neglecting dolls, and finally finding the white doll not only outgrown but also ruined and decayed. The grownup Virginia has substituted puppets for dolls. The first chapter begins the present action, which takes Virginia back to her hometown of Akron, where she will begin a season as an artist-in-residence, teaching puppetry in a public grade school.

The time is the unsettled 1970's, and Virginia's life is at a standstill. In college, she has trained to be an actress, but at this time there are few calls for African American actresses. The question she must answer for herself is this: What can she and should she do with her abilities, which include mime, music, and puppetry as well as straightforward acting?   The artist-in-residence program provides her with some breathing space, but she will shortly need to make irrevocable decisions. Defining her goals is difficult because her sense of self is uncertain, partly owing to the prejudices she has encountered in growing up in the 1950's, but also because of her family life. She has never understood why her family suddenly moved from Ohio to Arizona and why they seemed personally changed after this move; her young adulthood has been obscured by this mystery. She believes that her return to her former home will help her to solve it, and she thinks that learning more about her family will make her better able to plan her future.

Upon her return to Akron, Virginia learns to be more self-possessed when dealing with groups, and her expertise impresses many. Children with psychic wounds and their equally hurting parents reach out to the artist for healing. The puppets help the children to explain their problems, and this is the first step toward regaining health.

Virginia begins a love affair with the father of one of her students, and speaking more frankly through Gina, the puppet she has created, she makes strides in self-expression. Yet the direction of her life is still undecided. Skillful use of flashbacks show what factors led to her lack of decision: her pleasant childhood's interruption by the unexplained move, her first real love affair with a fellow musician (who finally left her for a man) and her satisfying experiences with Puppets and People, a talented troupe that went bankrupt. Her life has also been punctuated by indications that African Americans are not encouraged to pursue her kind of goals—especially that of being an actress.

Amid her teaching experiences, she visits her father's mother, now in a rest home, and her aunt, and she finally learns the family secret from Aunt Carrie. In adolescence, her father had had an incestuous relationship with his sister. When her mother learned about this, long afterward, she made the family move away from Akron to Arizona, although she never got used to the hot, arid climate and always hated Arizona. The father, however, soon made the desert his home, and he taught his children its wonders and dangers. With the gaps in the family history filled in and the success of her assignment in the grade school, Virginia is ready to move on to her next assignment when she receives a cali from Nigel, an old colleague who is now a play director. He is now an off-Broadway director, and he has a part for Virginia if she can drop what she is doing (after her next brief assignment) and go to New York. She is now mature enough to take this gamble.

There are some subplots as well: Virginia is so involved in all of her activities that she does not notice the intensity of one hurting child, Renee, who then injures herself in an attempt to win Virginia's attention; this incident teaches Virginia humility. How she deals with the challenges of getting ordinary, non-intellectual people interested in art is another slight diversion. A third is the preparation for and final presentation of the children's puppet play. At the end of the story, Virginia is ready to leave Akron, having swept away the shadows from her life and having been reconciled with both hcr grandmothcr, who had known the story, and her aunt. Her coming of age completed, she is ready to face the challenges of the uncertain life of the stage.

The Characters

Virginia's development and point of view are at the center of the novel. She believably changes from a tentative although enthusiastic young puppeteer to a woman in control of her life. Her discovery of the family secret really plays a minor part in her development, which comes mostly from her practice of her art and the observation of the effect of her art on others. She comes across as a sympathetic young artist who must deal with racial prejudice as well as the general indifference to art and culture that was part of the era.

Belle, her mother, flees from life, and it seems to Virginia that her childhood has been punctuated by her mother's inexplicable warnings. These make more sense after Virginia discovers the family secret. Belle's sense of personal outrage has prevented her from full participation in her family and has created barriers between herself and her children. She is hyper-respectable, perhaps partly in reaction to the shock of her husband's adolescent incestuous relationship. Although she loves her children, she seems to be constantly warning them not to expose themselves to any risks—in effect, not to live.

Ernie King has always made his children's education his prime interest. He has done most of the parenting, especially after the move, and has instilled in his children a love for history and culture. He carries a mysterious sense of sadness, which is accounted for by Aunt Carrie's revelation. He has been partly responsible for his daughter's artistic and cultural interests.

Aunt Carrie is in many ways the opposite of Belle. A woman who has had a hard life with much hard work and pain, she is accepting of the grittier side of human experience, and her openness is helpful to Virginia. Virginia finds that she has an element of Aunt Carrie in her.

Grandma Evans has been part of the family mystery. It always seemed to the child Virginia that the well-loved grandmother had suddenly withdrawn from the family, to appear again only when the youngest child, Claudia, was born. When Virginia learns that knowledge of the incest story and its repercussions had caused her grandmother's behavior, she feels close to her grandmother again.

Besides Virginia, perhaps the most fully developed character is Clayton, who is drawn into a love affair with Virginia by their mutual love of music. His homosexuality proves to be stronger than his love for her, however, and he finally leaves her. His defection is a blow to her developing self-esteem and makes her doubt the possibility of a lasting love relationship. When she compares her present feelings for Terry Murray with her past feelings for Everett, however, she concludes that she is not really in love with Terry.

Terry himself is a straightforward, quintessentially normal middle-class African American whose love and concern help Virginia grow. Her attachment to him, though, will clearly not be sufficient to keep her from pursuing her career as a dramatic artist.

Themes and Meanings

One major theme of the novel is that disguises and masks may facilitate truth and healing. Another is that growing up is difficult, especially for an African American girl born in the 1950's , particularly if she wishes to be an artist.

The title of this novel comes from Homer's *Odyssey* (c. 800 B.C.). Homer's epic contains a passage that describes two gates from which dreams issue, the gate of horn and the gate of ivory. Those dreams that come through the gate of ivory are deceptive, but those that issue from the gate of horn are truthful. It is Virginia's job to distinguish truth from falsehood in understanding her family's past. On the other hand, she is also a puppeteer, a dealer in illusion, but this kind of illusion is a healing fiction that helps those who become involved in it to learn to accept themselves and others. Memories as well as dreams are deceptive in this narrative, which interweaves imagination and reality, illusion and truth, to create a fable of healing through art.

The puppets themselves are a strong presence in the story. Through their apparent artificiality and their pose as amusement, they allow their creators to speak otherwise hidden truths. Virginia speaks through Gina, and the children speak through the characters they have created. Through these masks, they arrive at genuine communication. Masks, puppets, acting, and other ways in which meaning is communicated indirectly play a major part in the novel; the scenes that describe puppet shows and puppet play suggest the magic of the art. Not only do the puppets and other disguises of art help individuals to face their problems, but they also help to facilitate understanding among people of different backgrounds and races. At the end of the novel, it is Halloween, and masks, laughter, and a sense of general good feeling dominate the scene.

The book is also a women's coming-of-age novel that shows both the typical problems of an adolescent and also the special difficulties of African Americans. The adolescent's ordinary conflicts—the desire to excel versus the desire to be accepted, the need to resist parental pressure—are portrayed in vivid detail. The problems caused by being the only African American in various groups are described with humor, and yet the reader still gets a sense of the kind of isolation such a situation would produce. The precise and evocative details in the flashbacks give a strong impression of the 1950's and early 1960's, with that era's narrowness and its innocence. The limited options of that time for women are realistically presented. So is the heroine's rejection of these limitations as she enters the more promising 1970's with understanding and courage. As a coming-of-age novel, *Through the Ivory Gate* is an unusually friendly and upbeat book.

Critical Context

Rita Dove is better known as a poet than as a novelist. Her third poetry collection, *Thomas and Beulah* (1986), received a Pulitzer Prize, and she has been named poet laureate of the United States. *Through the Ivory Gate* is clearly a poet's novel—it is lyrical, it contains patches of near-poetry, and its plot, despite the suspense, is secondary to its other elements. Passages of the novel would be well suited to oral presentation, as it is clear that attention has been paid to sound as well as to meaning.

The book may be read for the sheer lyricism of it, for its description and demonstration of the healing power of art. It also provides a good example of a relaxed and relaxing coming-of-age novel, or *Bildungsroman*. Virginia King is an appealing protagonist whose experiences may be matched or approximated by readers of varied ages and races. The novel also provides a strong sense of the time periods it represents; the subtle changes in background provide a sense of the differences between these time periods, especially as these differences relate to race relations. The book is also a *Kunstlerroman*, or novel about the development of an artist, and those factors that directed the heroine toward her art are painstakingly detailed.

Bibliography

Brody, Jennifer. "Genre Fixing: An Interview with Rita Dove." *Poetry Flash* 238 (January, 1993): 1, 9-11, 22-23. Dove discusses how writing her novel was different from writing poems. She also discusses factors that influenced her work.

Callaloo 14 (Spring, 1991). This special issue contains several articles on Rita Dove's poetry and an interview with her. Articles by Bonnie Costello, Ekaterini Georgoudaki, and Mohammed-B Teleb-Khyer help to place Dove's poetry in context with that of other African American women writers. These articles also define themes and concerns that are present also in her novel.

Georgoudaki, Ekaterini. *Race, Gender, and Class Perspectives in the Works of Maya Angelou, Gwendolyn Brooks, Rita Dove, Nikki Giovanni, and Audre Lorde*. Thessaloniki, Greece: Aristotle University of Thessaloniki, 1991. Although this book considers poetry, its reflections on Dove's poetry may be applied to her novel. The book provides a solid background for studying current African American women's poetry. Its analysis of the societal elements in these women's work is clear and direct.

Schneider, Steven. "Coming Home: An Interview with Rita Dove." *The Iowa Review* 19 (Fall, 1989): 112-123. This extended interview gives a sense of the writer's personality and commitment to her craft. Dove's comments show how much she is concerned with language as an arrangement of sounds. Although the novel had not yet been written at the time of the interview, the information she gives here about herself gives insight into the sources of Virginia.

Seaman, Donna. Review of *Through the Ivory Gate*, by Rita Dove. *Booklist*, September 15, 1992, 122. This review concentrates on plot, but it gives some sense of the writer's style, calling Dove "a melodious and meticulous writer."

Janet McCann

TRACKS

Author: Louise Erdrich (1954-   )
Type of plot: Family
Time of plot: Winter, 1912-Spring, 1924
Locale: Matchimanito, a fictional reservation in North Dakota
First published: 1988

> *Principal characters:*
> NANAPUSH, an Anishinabe elder who tells Fleur's story of survival to
>   Lulu, his adopted granddaughter
> PAULINE PUYAT, the other narrator, a fanatical nun
> FLEUR PILLAGER, a survivor of epidemics and deprivations thought to
>   possess supernatural powers

The Novel

Tracks deals with the devastation of the Anishinabe (also known as Chippewa or Objiway) people between the winter of 1912 and the spring of 1924 in Matchimanito, North Dakota. The novel focuses on the life of Fleur Pillager and those with whom she comes into contact, dramatizing their struggle for survival as well as their many-faceted conflicts. In alternating chapters, the story is narrated by Nanapush, a tribal elder, and Pauline Puyat, a fanatic nun of mixed heritage. The two narrators complement but at times also contradict and undermine each other.

At the age of seventeen, Fleur is rescued by Nanapush during a severe winter when inhabitants of Matchimanito are found dead from consumption and starvation. After recovery, she goes to Argus to work at a butcher shop. There, she meets a younger girl, Pauline, who has known her as a survivor of two drownings and hence is convinced that Fleur is the chosen one of Misshepeshu, the lake monster. Pauline reports how Fleur, having aroused the desires of three male workers and beaten them at the card table, is sexually assaulted. Russell, Pauline's nephew, tries to stop it but to no avail. Later, a tornado strikes the town, and the three men take refuge inside a meat locker, refusing to let Pauline and Russell in. Russell shuts them in from the outside, freezing two of them to death. After the incident, Pauline returns to the reservation, where she learns that Fleur is pregnant. It is uncertain how Fleur becomes pregnant, but according to Nanapush, through personal insights and love medicines, he has helped Eli Kashpaw, a hunter, win her passionate love. Fleur's childbirth proves to be so difficult that she almost dies. The baby, given the name of Lulu Nanapush, is in fact the person Nanapush addresses throughout his narrative.

Meanwhile, Pauline becomes a helper in Argus at a farm belonging to Bernadette Morrisey. Awakening to her sexuality, Pauline experiments with Napoleon, Bernadette's brother, but finds herself attracted to Eli instead. Spurned by him, she retaliates with the love potions, thus causing Eli to have sex with Sophie, Bernadette's daughter. Sophie is punished by her mother, who sends her away. She goes to Fleur's cabin and kneels in her yard for days on end, jeopardizing the relationship between

Fleur and Eli. To avenge Sophie, Clarence, Bernadette's son, attacks Margaret, Eli's mother, by tying her up and shaving her bald. The insult leads Margaret, Nanapush, and Fleur to retaliate.

The sexual relationship between Pauline and Napoleon has led to her pregnancy. After giving birth to Marie, whom she turns over to Bernadette, Pauline joins Sister Anne's convent, where she sees visions of Christ. Determined to remove the devil from Indian country, she returns to the reservation. Fleur, who is again pregnant, gives birth prematurely one day when Pauline comes to visit. Pauline is too clumsy to help Fleur stop the bleeding. Fleur loses consciousness, and the baby dies.

The winter begins to get harsh again, and food is running out. Furthermore, Father Damien, the Catholic priest, brings news that the land allotted to the Pillager, Kashpaw, and Nanapush families would be foreclosed unless they pay their taxes. Faced with the crisis, Fleur is affected by a mysterious illness. She undertakes a healing ceremony,· which Pauline disrupts ruthlessly. Eventually, the Kashpaws, Nanapush, and Fleur manage to pool their resources to pay the taxes. Nector Kashpaw (Eli's brother), entrusted to take the money to pay the taxes, betrays Nanapush and Fleur by making the payment toward Kashpaw land. The betrayal agonizes Fleur, alienates her from Eli, and causes her to attempt suicide by drowning.

Pauline, increasingly determined to become a martyr of her new faith, attempts to confront the lake monster—her idea of Satan. In her delusion, she runs into Napoleon and strangles him instead. Afterward, she takes her vow and becomes Sister Leopolda.

The lumber company has started cutting down the trees near Fleur's cabin. Desperate, Fleur sends Lulu to the government school for the sake of safety and plots her revenge. Secretly, she has sawed the trees around her cabin at the base, so that they remain lightly held. When the lumber company's men come to move her by force, the trees tumble down, crushing men and wagons beneath them. Finally, Fleur leaves her home ground. Having witnessed the way influence is exercised by bureaucratic means, Nanapush runs for tribal chairmanship in order to help the Indians. He is elected and, after many attempts, manages to retrieve Lulu from the government school.

The Characters

Although Fleur is the central figure of the novel, the reader's understanding of her character is mediated by Nanapush and Pauline, who also serve as the narrators of the novel.

From the perspective of Nanapush, Fleur is a real victim, like many others including himself, of harsh winters, diseases, starvation, government policies, and the scheming of outsiders such as lumber companies and even mixed-blood Indians. A bond exists between Nanapush and Fleur, who warmly calls him "uncle" and treats him as such. For Nanapush, however, Fleur is not only human and daughterly, but also symbolic of the historical predicament of the Anishinabe. As a young woman, Fleur has won his recognition by holding on to the traditional way of life, thus making her an ideal companion for a young man like Eli, who also lives by traditional ways. Thanks to her spiritual and moral strength, which surpasses her passion for Eli, she has turned into a woman warrior in the end, though paying the high price of losing her daughter and husband for her refusal to compromise.

The charming and eerie qualities of Fleur as a character are largely derived from Pauline's narration, unreliable as it is because of Pauline's delusions. From her perspective, Fleur is both a peer and a legend. As a peer, she is a model and a rival for Pauline, who is fascinated and overshadowed by her magnetic attraction, especially her sexuality, which Pauline tries to emulate, or else jeopardize. As a legend in the eyes of Pauline, Fleur is not only a miraculous survivor of drownings and hardships, but also a powerful sorceress endowed by the lake monster with the ability to wreak havoc. Yet as Pauline's religious fanaticism increases, for her Fleur begins to lose her individuality; instead, she has come to stand for the kind of Satanic paganism that Pauline must deter and oppose. Willfully, Pauline has turned Fleur into a flat character by obliterating the latter's genuine personality, an important part of which is Fleur's humane treatment of her and her nephew.

Because of her delusions, Pauline is an eccentric character. She is given more character development and psychological depth than the others, and her own experiences are rather extraordinary. Not unlike Fleur, she is a victim of the times; being a mixed-blood, however, allows her to imagine and to test the possibility of being non-Indian. Her confusions about herself as a woman and as an Indian have led to blunders of calamitous proportions, as for example her sexual liaison with Napoleon and her scheme on Sophie and Eli. Overcompensating for her guilt as well as her sense of insecurity, Pauline becomes a devious megalomaniac who, in the name of white religion, sanctifies herself and demonizes the others, in effect becoming an instrument of oppression with a martyr complex. From a literary point of view, however, Pauline's psychological problem is also the source of the many magically dramatic episodes in the novel.

By contrast, in the case of Nanapush, the cultural model for his character is not Christian saints but the Native American trickster. Not only is his name reminiscent of the trickster figure Naanabozho, his wit, resourcefulness, and trickery in both speech and action also qualify him as a trickster. More important, just as the trickster can be a cultural hero, Nanapush has indeed become a hero of his tribe in his struggle, as an elder and later on as the tribal chairman, to regain control of the tribe's destiny. Being the foster parent of Lulu, whom he teaches to respect her mother and appreciate her origin, Nanapush embodies the vitality and resilience of the native culture.

Intricately related to one another in life but diametrically opposed in their perspectives, Nanapush and Pauline together provide a fantastic and yet realistic portrayal of Fleur as a stubborn survivor of her clan. In the process of their narration, they also characterize themselves and each other as representatives of two ways of life emanating from a single tragedy.

Themes and Meanings

The struggle for survival is one of the most obvious themes in *Tracks*. All the major characters in the novel are survivors of not only the environment, famines, and epidemics, but also the historical reality of genocide, dispossession, and deprivation. Despite the sense of doom overshadowing the entire Matchimanito reservation upon the encroachment of outside interests, however, upholders of the tribe's cultural tradition have fought in the best way they can: Fleur by crushing the lumber crew and Nanapush by campaigning for the position of tribal chairman.

The struggle for survival, which reaches tragic proportions, is closely related to the theme of cultural conflict. Ostensibly, the Christianity of Pauline, though half-baked, is pitted against the traditional wisdom of Nanapush, who is nevertheless conversant with white culture. The native way of life, together with its tribal kinship system and symbiotic relationship with the environment, is challenged by the white way of life, including its nuclear family, exploitation of natural resources, greed for land, and oppression by legal codes. The mixed-bloods, caught between the two ways of life, lean toward one pole or the other, but while adapting to the cultural change, they also exhibit symptoms of dysfunctionality and confusion. Their predicament, which is epitomized by the conversion of Pauline, pervasive alcoholism, incestuous marriages aimed at amassing land, the subsequent loss of land due to swindling, the disintegration of family ties, and so forth, is also a kind of tragedy bordering on pathos.

Out of the entropic and fragmentary chaos created by cultural conflict, however, in *Tracks* there are also prospects of a cultural synthesis, which conceivably could begin from the mutual "contamination" of the white and the native cultural conditions. Pauline's Christianity, for example, is rife with indigenous beliefs and visions, whereas Nanapush, despite his traditionalism, is conditionally receptive to the white practices that hold promises for the revival of the tribe. These mutual "contaminations' suggest the possibility of certain cultural exchanges that might lead to a new consciousness for the community.

The drive toward a new consciousness is in fact the motivating force behind the seemingly dichotomized perspectives of Nanapush and Pauline, whose narratives are dialogic rather than mutually exclusive, though in the competition for credibility and authority it is Nanapush's narrative that succeeds in reestablishing a sense of order. Significantly, the implied audience of Nanapush, Lulu, can be regarded as the receptacle of the new consciousness. Growing up in the middle of her mother's struggles but educated at the government school, where she is segregated from her traditional heritage, Lulu is not unlike the mixed-bloods trapped between two worlds. Nanapush exhorts her to seek out Fleur, and despite her resistance to his narrative (she stops her ears), she is inevitably reintroduced to her roots and the destiny of her people. Although the formation of the new consciousness hinges on Lulu's willingness and ability to integrate the two cultures in her future life, Nanapush has left enough tracks for the pursuit through his artful storytelling.

Critical Context

Tracks (1988) is designed, chronologically, as the first in a tetralogy about the lives of a group of Anishinabe originating from Matchimanito, a fictional locale based on the White Earth Reservation in North Dakota. The action started in *Tracks* is extended and expanded in *The Beet Queen* (1986) and *Love Medicine* (1984). Because the characters in the novels are intricately related through marriages and liaisons, they constitute a huge, extended family; as such, the cycle can be seen broadly as a family saga. Since the novels share in common the technique of multiple narrators who have stories of their own to tell, the polyphonic saga as a whole is an archive of a cross-section of Native Americans whose destinies intersect and diverge.

The creation of Matchimanito as a world populated by characters steeped in the myths and legends of the Anishinabe is by no means just an aesthetic diversion. Rivaling William Faulkner's Yoknapatawpha County, Mississippi, in the magnitude of social significance, the world of Matchimanito is also a space for history to be rediscovered, imagined, explored, clarified, and interpreted.

Tracks is a literary text charged with such a historical mission, the focal concern of which is the dispossession of native land and its aftermath. As Louise Erdrich and Michael Dorris explained in a 1988 article, "Who Owns the Land?," by that time only 53,100 out of 830,000 acres originally promised to the Anishinabe remained in the tribe's possession. The grim conditions on the White Earth Reservation, on which Matchimanito is based, epitomize the historical injustices imposed upon the Anishinabe and exemplify the intercultural and internal conflicts as well as the social problems created by the legal instruments of the United States government. Although Erdrich as an artist has always resisted moralizations, the collective memory by which her novel is informed leaves conspicuous tracks to be traced.

Bibliography
Erdrich, Louise, and Michael Dorris. "Who Owns the Land?" *The New York Times Magazine* 137 (September 4, 1988): 32-35. Published about the same time as *Tracks*, this feature article about the White Earth Reservation clarifies many of the historical issues and social concerns related to the setting and the characters in the novel.
Larson, Sidner. "The Fragmentation of a Tribal People in Louise Erdrich's *Tracks*." *American Indian Culture and Research Journal* 17 (Spring, 1993): 1-13. A review of the novel, with special focus on the impact of the General Allotment Act of 1887, which was to divide tribally allotted lands among individual Native Americans.
Rainwater, Catherine. "Reading Between Worlds: Narrativity in the Fiction of Louise Erdrich." *American Literature* 62 (September, 1990): 405-422. A semiotic reading of *Tracks*, focusing on narrative codes that contribute to its thematization of liminality, fragmentation, and cultural conflict.
Sergi, Jennifer. "Storytelling: Tradition and Preservation in Louise Erdrich's *Tracks*." *World Literature Today* 66 (Spring, 1992): 279-283. Discusses *Tracks* in the light of tribal tradition, mythic condition, and storytelling.
Towery, Margie. "Continuity and Connection: Characters in Louise Erdrich's fiction." *American Indian Culture and Research Journal* 16 (Fall, 1992): 99-122. An overview article that maps out the intricate—fragmented but connected—relationships

among the characters in *Tracks*, *The Beet Queen*, *Love Medicine*, and episodes possibly intended for the fourth volume of the family saga.

Balance Chow

TRIPMASTER MONKEY
His Fake Book

Author: Maxine Hong Kingston (1940-   )
Type of plot: Bildungsroman
Time of plot: The 1960's
Locale: San Francisco and Sacramento, California
First published: 1989

Principal characters:
> WITTMAN AH SING, a Chinese American antiwar activist
> NANCI LEE, the most beautiful Chinese American girl of Wittman's college days, an aspiring actress
> TAÑA DE WEESE, an insurance adjuster who marries Wittman

The Novel

Tripmaster Monkey is Maxine Hong Kingston's portrait of the artist as a Chinese American who attempts to assert his identity by blending together the two sides of his heritage. Using the Vietnam War as the backdrop, Kingston has also captured the exuberant antiestablishment sensibility of the Bay Area, immortalizing the flower-power counterculture of the psychedelic 1960's. Whereas the "tripmaster monkey" in the title alludes to the hero of a Chinese folktale and the hippies of American subculture, the "fake book" refers to the novel's similarity to "music fake books," which, according to Kingston, may contain many basic melodies or plots other people can develop.

The action begins with the depression of Wittman, a fifth-generation native Californian who is contemplating suicide everyday after graduating with a bachelor's degree in English from the University of California at Berkeley. Working part-time as a toys salesman at a department store in San Francisco, Wittman, who aspires to be a writer, often feels alienated much the same way as the young poet in Rainer Maria Rilke's *The Notebooks of Malte Laurids Brigge* (1910), passages of which he recites as he goes about his daily business. Conscious of his Chineseness as well as his Americanness and conceited about his intellectual prowess, he looks for others of his kind. His first candidate is Nanci Lee, who aspires to be an actress. He dates her, shows her his trunk of poems, and declares his intention to write a play for her. Offended by her lack of sensitivity to his talents and identity crisis, however, he scares her away by acting crudely.

As the action progresses, Wittman encounters, in his workplace, a "stocking guy," a beatnik-hermit who happens to have been published as a Yale Younger Poet. Though encouraged by him, Wittman finds his own job frustrating; after making clockwork toy monkeys perform simulated copulation on Barbie dolls in front of his customers, he fires himself. Unemployed, he goes to the wedding party of Lance Kamiyama, a Japanese American friend and rival with a successful career. On the way, he runs into

Judy Louis, a Chinese American who so bores him to death with her nosiness and snobbishness that he pretends to be Japanese in order to evade her stereotyping. At the party, he engages in round after round of verbal combat and intellectual wrestling, abusing and abused by his friends, with whom he has developed a love-hate relationship. Among the group is Yoshi Ogasawara, a smart pretty woman whom he takes as a nemesis because of her tireless discourse, replete with demonstrations, on the "epicanthic fold" typical of the eyelids of many Asians. Later on at the party, after anecdotal and satirical conversations about films, race, lifestyle, Nazism, nuclear war, and other topics of interest to him, Wittman discover Taña De Weese, a beautiful blonde who descends upon him like an angel. She gets along with him so well that the next morning they start having a serious but unromantic sexual relationship, which shortly afterward leads to their being declared husband and wife by a conscientious objector who claims to be a priest of the Universal Life Church.

Having found the personal and intellectual companionship of Taña, Wittman begins to act purposefully. He takes Taña to Sacramento to visit his mother, Ruby Long Legs (formerly an opera star), and his father, Zeppelin Ah Sing (a retiree who publishes a newsletter advocating the art of living on minimal means). Taña is also introduced to more than a dozen former "Flora Dora girls" who contributed to China's and America's cause during World War II. Their presence inspires Wittman to involve them in his forthcoming play.

During the visit, Wittman learns that his parents have taken PoPo (his grandmother of uncertain origins) out to the Sierra Mountains and abandoned her there. Horrified, he and Taña try to find her but to no avail (as Wittman discovers later, she has gone to San Francisco with a man, Lincoln Fong, her newfound hero and love). Going back to San Francisco, Wittman files for unemployment benefits, lives like a pig with Taña, and concentrates on the writing of his play, which is a formidable melange of folktales derived from classical Chinese novels, with the Monkey King as the main character. With the help of friends, relatives, and the residents of Chinatown, the play is launched in due course at a community center and proves to be a phenomenal success. Upon the triumphant close of the play, the action of which takes several days to complete, Wittman improvises a one-man show. Interacting with the audience, he gives a lengthy but critical monologue about cultural identity, war, love, and lifestyle. The completion of Wittman's apprenticeship as an artist is signaled by the audience's enthusiasm and approval.

The Characters

Although the novel contains several delightful characters, it is Wittman who is the focus throughout; all the others are seen through his eyes. Hence, the entire novel can be regarded as an extended character study of Wittman, with the other characters shedding light on his life and illustrating his philosophy. In characterizing Wittman, Kingston not only captures Wittman in action, but also relies heavily on the prolific verbalization of his inner consciousness.

On the social level, Wittman is characterized as both a misfit and a gadfly with a cause. Unlike his fellow Asian Americans such as Lance, Nanci Lee, and Judy Louis, he is ill prepared, both intellectually and academically, for a stereotypical career (such as engineering) that would readily earn him success and recognition from his peers, parents, relatives, and the mainstream society. This apparent failure is partly responsible for his inferiority complex (and megalomania), which he often exploits by adopting a hostile stance toward the people he comes across, including the new Chinese immigrants in the streets, the customers at the department store, and even his friends at Lance's party. Yet although his life is a shambles, like many other Americans of his generation who defy the draft in order not to fight an unacceptable war in Vietnam, Wittman also stands on a moral high ground, which makes his cynicism an act of courageous rebellion. While his witty diatribes against the stereotyping of Chinese Americans at times sound vindictive and self-contradictory, his outbursts against wars, atomic bombs, Nazism, and modern life bespeak the pacifism of his generation. His concluding monologue is a culmination of this sensibility.

On the cultural level, Wittman is portrayed as a juggler of cultures who, caught between two heritages that he both claims and disclaims, attempts to arrive at a synthesis. On the one hand, as a fifth-generation native Californian, he asserts his American identity by distancing himself from the "F.O.B.'s" (Chinese immigrants "fresh off the boats"). On the other hand, aware of the racial prejudices leveled against Chinese Americans, he also defends the Chineseness of his heritage and berates the insensitivity of those who either subscribe to stereotypes or refuse to recognize Chinese Americans as Americans. On balance, although Wittman is equally obsessed with certain aspects of both cultures (such as films and Cantonese operas), for him, Chineseness—in the way he defines it—weighs a little more than Americanness, because it is by Chineseness that he hopes to redefine his American identity. This is best symbolized by his relationships with two young women. He loses Nanci Lee, a Chinese American, but wins Taña, a Caucasian, essentially for the same reason: his insistence on being an American of Chinese descent, warts and all. His success as an artist would not have been possible without such a commitment.

Themes and Meanings

The themes and meanings of *Tripmaster Monkey* are derived from the character of Wittman as an artist and a Chinese American. As an apprentice to the art of writing, Wittman is sufficiently prepared—even tediously erudite—for his calling, but he has yet to find a voice to win recognition. Kingston's constant reference to *The Notebooks of Malte Laurids Brigge* is a reminder of this lonely struggle. This struggle is set back, early in the novel, by Wittman's failure to impress Nanci Lee with his poetry and by the realization that even a published Yale Younger Poet is going nowhere and has abandoned poetry altogether. With his sense of alienation compounded by such loneliness, his identity crisis as a writer intensifies. Fortunately, however, Wittman's artistic career is saved by his own cultural heritage and family upbringing, the common denominator of which is the folk tradition. The Cantonese opera, the cultural fabric that sustained generations of Chinese Americans (who in turn have helped to shape America into the country it is), contains materials from Chinese novels that can somehow be used to address the issues of the times; the form, however, has fallen into oblivion. Wittman's genius lies in the realization that he is the artist who could rebuild the Pear Garden (the Chinese theater) in the West and give a new life to this theater. Creating order out of the chaos of his life and his world, he has launched a communal play with a pacifist vision, winning instant approval and blessing from the community. In this sense, the one-man show in the last chapter is not a manic monologue but rather a celebration of his newfound voice as an artist who has come of age.

Closely connected with Wittman's struggle as an artist and a draft-dodging hippie is his campaign against the notion that the Chinese people are inscrutable and cannot be American. Wittman is exasperated by the fact that, wherever he turns—in films, readings, and daily life—Chinese Americans have been mistreated, misunderstood, misrepresented, and above all excluded from the definition of "American" despite the fact that they have created part of America. Because the American self as he knows it is defined by ethnicity, he is provoked into obnoxious harangues whenever people fail to acknowledge the validity of this uncompromisable definition. Even Chinese Americans are legitimate targets of his attacks when they subscribe to Caucasian views. This theme of Wittman's self-definition is recapitulated throughout the novel. Invariably angry whenever he thinks about it, Wittman cannot resist sarcastic tirades that seem never to end—hence the Rabelaisian verbosity of the novel. Concomitant with the theme of self-definition are Wittman's efforts to rediscover, reclaim, and celebrate his Chinese heritage and share it with his community, by preaching if necessary. Such an affirmation of his Chineseness does not contradict his position that he is an American, but it does complicate his self-definition somewhat; his challenge hence hinges on how he can grapple with both his American and Chinese identities at the same time without compromising either one. Ultimately, it is both heritages on which he wishes to lay his hands as a "Chinese no hyphen American."

Critical Context

Tripmaster Monkey is Kingston's answer to critics who, unable to decide whether her earlier book-length narratives (*The Woman Warrior: Memoirs of a Girlhood Among Ghosts*, 1976 and *China Men*, 1980) are factual or fictional, hesitate to give full credit for her work. Kingston writes *Tripmaster Monkey* as a testimony of her abilities and as a proof of her belief that fiction is by no means more difficult to write than memoirs and family histories. More important, having told the story of her parents' generation in two separate narratives, Kingston finds it appropriate to shift attention to her own generation, who have come of age as biculturals with problems, solutions, imaginations, and visions of their own. *Tripmaster Monkey* is only the beginning of an ongoing statement about such a generation, with Wittman as its impressive spokesman.

What Wittman has achieved in the novel has great symbolic significance for many Chinese Americans. Combining two kinds of wisdoms culled from two cultures, Wittman has put the history of America into the perspective of the Cantonese operas that once sustained the communities of Chinese pioneers who helped to develop the frontiers of the United States. By involving the community in reviving the Chinese theater, Wittman has fulfilled his personal quest as well as given a new life to an old tradition. Above all, through Wittman, Kingston has added an indelible historical dimension to the myth of the American Dream.

Wittman also addresses issues that concern the United States as a whole. As Kingston suggests, nothing in modern life is immune to Wittman's cornucopian if cynical commentaries. Impulsive as he is, Wittman is actually quite systematic in his protest against the dehumanizing condition of modern society, which at its worst moments has given rise to the Holocaust, nuclear weapons, and the Vietnam War. Through his cross-cultural and trans-temporal play, Wittman is stating that war and its propaganda ought to stop, that history has proven how even the best of warriors with the best tactics and the best weapons have invariably lost, and that peace, not war, is the real revolution of the modern world.

Bibliography
Banez, Lourdes G. "The Talk Story: Maxine Hong Kingston's Narrative Technique in *The Tripmaster Monkey*." *Likha* 11, no. 2 (1989-1990): 17-24. Discusses the "talk story" approach used in the writing of the book.

Chin, Marilyn. "A MELUS Interview: Maxine Hong Kingston." *MELUS* 16 (Winter, 1989): 57-74. An insightful conversation between Chin and Kingston on the topics of *The Woman Warrior, China Men, Tripmaster Monkey*, writing, and Chinese Americans.

Ling, Amy. *Between Worlds: Women Writers of Chinese Ancestry*. New York: Pergamon Press, 1990. Contains an informative section on *Tripmaster Monkey*. The book is also an excellent introduction to the tradition behind Kingston.

Loke, Margarett. "The Tao Is Up." *The New York Times Magazine*, April 30, 1989, 28-34. A portrait of Maxine Hong Kingston showing her at home. Includes discussion of how she synthesizes Asia and America in her works.

Balance Chow

TRUE GRIT

Author: Charles Portis (1933-   )
Type of plot: Western
Time of plot: 1878-1903 (narrated in the 1920's)
Locale: Arkansas and Choctaw Nation territory in Oklahoma
First published: 1968

> *Principal characters:*
> MATTIE ROSS, the fourteen-year-old daughter of Frank Ross, whose murder by Tom Chaney she sets out to avenge
> REUBEN J. "ROOSTER" COGBURN, a deputy U.S. marshall who, both in his official capacity and in Mattie's pay, assists her in the pursuit of Chaney
> SERGEANT LABOEUF, a Texas Ranger who, in pursuit of Chaney for the murder of a Texas state senator, accompanies Cogburn and Mattie
> TOM CHANEY, alias CHAMBERS, a robber and murderer whose real name is Theron Chelmsford
> LUCKY NED PEPPER, the leader of the robber gang that Chaney joins
> YARNELL POINDEXTER, a freeborn black man hired by Frank Ross and devoted to the Ross family
> COLONEL G. STONEHILL, an auctioneer
> J. NOBLE DAGGETT, Mattie's lawyer
> MRS. FLOYD, a boardinghouse landlady from whom Mattie rents a room

The Novel

True Grit is a study of the indomitable spirit of three representative Americans: a hard-living, heavy-drinking lawman, Rooster Cogburn; young Mattie Ross, who hires Cogburn because of his reputation for grit and who proves herself to possess the same quality; and Sergeant LaBoeuf, a disciplined, clean-living lawman who is mercenary enough to contemplate maximum reward money. In varying degrees, all the characters in the novel, including the outlaws, either have "true grit" or show respect for it.

In seven unnumbered chapters, this short novel re-creates the idiom, melodrama, and morality of nineteenth century adventure fiction, particularly the dime-novel Western adventure stories. The events are related by Mattie Ross, who, in her late fifties or early sixties, looks back from her current situation as an unmarried, one-armed banker caring for her invalid mother, to the second year of the Rutherford B. Hayes Administration. Back then, her father, Frank Ross, had ridden from his home near Dardanelle in Yell County, Arkansas, to Fort Smith to purchase horses and had been shot to death and robbed by his companion, Tom Chaney. She recalls the details of her determined and ultimately successful mission, as a fourteen-year-old, to make Chaney pay for his crime.

She is first accompanied, traveling from her home to Fort Smith, by Yarnell Poindexter, a freeborn black man from Illinois, whom her father had hired to look after the Ross family and farm until his return from Fort Smith. Mattie shows her spunk early by winning a battle of wills with Colonel Stonehill, the fort's auctioneer: He is intimidated by her threat of legal action and repurchases horses he had sold to her father. As she sets out in pursuit of Chaney, her companions are the fortyish Cogburn, for whose services she has agreed to pay one hundred dollars, and a thirtyish Texas Ranger sergeant with the gender-bent name of LaBoeuf who, intent upon both justice and a large reward, is pursuing Chaney for a murder that Chaney had committed in Texas.

Cogburn and LaBoeuf constitute an odd couple. Although they are separated in age by only a decade, LaBoeuf is of a new order and Cogburn is of the old. LaBoeuf is well-groomed, wears large shining spurs, goes by the book, and has acquired skills and judgment from training and discipline. Cogburn, resembling President Grover Cleveland in mien, girth, and moustache, is something of an outlaw turned lawman. He has only one eye, is slovenly in dress, drinks self-indulgently, and makes more errors in judgment than he cares to acknowledge.

Much of the narrative develops the respect that each of the three pursuers comes to have for the other two. Mattie holds her own in the rigors of outdoor living and keeps up with the two seasoned lawmen; Cogburn and LaBoeuf grow to respect and, often grudgingly, to rely upon each other.

There is mutual respect also between the lawmen and their outlaw quarry. Lucky Ned Pepper is admired for his leadership quality and his fortuitous elusiveness, his cohorts for their unwillingness to betray their kind, and even Chaney for the consistency and durability of his deceitfulness. The lawmen and outlaws address one another sometimes as equals to whom matters of law are divisive incidentals, but more often as competitors in a contest that provides life with meaning.

The climactic showdown is filled with rough-riding, exchanges of pistol and rifle fire, wounds, fatalities, falls, snakebites, and the triumph of justice. Lucky Ned Pepper and Tom Chaney are killed by, respectively, LaBoeuf and Cogburn. Mattie falls into a cavern pit and breaks her left arm, which is then bitten by a rattlesnake. The wounded Cogburn descends into the pit to rescue her, and both must be extricated by LaBoeuf, who engineers the feat by tying the rescue rope to Mattie's indomitably spirited pony, Blackie. Blackie will be ridden to death, carrying both Mattie and Cogburn at an unrelentingly furious gallop toward medical aid. Mattie's life is saved, but her arm must be amputated just above the elbow.

In the epilogue to the revenge story, LaBoeuf, who carried the corpse of Theron Chelmsford, alias Tom Chaney, back to Texas in fulfillment of his mission, is not heard from again. Cogburn reverts to activities that will cost him his marshalship and will lead him, as part of the evidentiary legend of the Old West, into "Wild West" shows, where he appears on exhibit with Frank James and Cole Younger. After Cogburn's death in 1903, Mattie transfers his remains to her family burial plot. Mattie herself permits her younger siblings, Victoria and Little Frank, to live their lives away from home while she commits herself to the care of their mother and to spinsterhood. She brings her proven ability in money matters into a successful banking career.

Although they enter into no formal marriage, Mattie and Cogburn become married in spirit, that indomitable spirit that is true grit. Mattie makes no effort to maintain contact with LaBoeuf after his return to Texas, but she diligently follows the subsequent doings, both actual and legendary, of Rooster Cogburn. Little Frank will often tease his sister Mattie about Cogburn's being her "secret sweetheart;" and Mattie's satisfaction in living with the memory and near the remains of her hired protector bear out the substance of the epithet.

The Characters

Mattie Ross is a devout Presbyterian who supports her sincere beliefs and principles with pertinent references to the New Testament. She is honest and will not persist in a falsehood even in an effort to deceive the murderer Tom Chaney. She is as forthright with outlaws as she is with law-abiding citizens. Her strength is shown in her ability both to get men to act in accordance with her wishes and to resist the commands of men. Her political persuasion is that of postbellum Southerners: She is a confirmed Democrat. She is outspoken and does not mince or waste words. Her narration shows that she clearly adheres in later life to the principles and values that she presents herself as having adhered to during her fourteenth year.

Rooster Cogburn is an embodiment of the Old West, with its code of personal, as opposed to legislative, justice. When he is enlisted by Mattie at the age of forty-three, his way of life is already on the way out. He participates in the advent of legal justice by becoming a marshal, after the manner of Wyatt Earp, and he does his best to help the new order, embodied in LaBoeuf, to displace his own. As a Southerner, he had seen his civilization collapse in the Civil War, during which he had served not in the regulation Confederate Army but with William Quantrill and his outlaw raiders. The end of his age is commemorated by his becoming a living exhibition piece.

Sergeant LaBoeuf is duty bound and dedicated to his job as a Texas Ranger. Some of his orthodox methods of police work test the patience of Cogburn and strike the reader as verging on the comic; in almost every instance, however, they happen to be more effective than the old ways of enforcing the law. Well-trained, trim, and with a youthful cowlick, he is in dramatic contrast to the overweight, heavy-drinking Cogburn, who once falls off his horse in drunkenness and at another time is pinned under his horse; he is then spared death at the hands of Lucky Ned only by the crack shooting of LaBoeuf.

As a freeborn black man, Yarnell Poindexter is also representative of a new order. The status of blacks had changed with the defeat of the Confederacy, but the contempt that many whites had for them would linger. Yarnell, dignified and intelligent in his services as Mattie's protector, must on one occasion settle for Mattie's scolding of a train conductor she calls "nigger."

Lucky Ned Pepper is a small, agile, and opportunistic outlaw. Cogburn not quite grudgingly admires his talents in crime and his practicality, which in one incident strikes Mattie as cruel and incomprehensible; Ned deserts a dying young gang member who has saved his life. The understanding and respect that Cogburn and

Lucky Ned have for each other lends dimension to the novel.

Tom Chaney, also known as Chambers, born Theron Chelmsford, is the closest of the characters to pure villainy. Despite his lack of talents and dignity, however, he is, in his self-pitying whining and his clumsy criminality, not inhuman and not incomprehensible to the reader. As LaBoeuf is Cogburn's antithesis, so Chaney is Ned Pepper's.

Themes and Meanings

Employing humor and impeccably crisp and credible dialogue to preclude any trace of sentimentality, Portis celebrates in his setting and characters his native Arkansas and the values and virtues of an America resilient enough to continue to live by the mythic dream of integrity and independence from which it is constantly awakened. Portis affirms a noble and heroic America even as he exposes the base accoutrements of nobility and heroism. The noble LaBoeuf is merely an efficient and somewhat narrow-minded policeman. The heroic Cogburn is something of a stubborn vigilante. Nevertheless, LaBoeuf's noble actions save Cogburn's life and complement Cogburn's heroic actions in saving Mattie's.

Nobility and heroism are tested in a crucible of transition during the two decades that follow the Civil War, and Portis shows them to undergo change without suffering annihilation. The old century moves toward the new century, and Mattie, as an encapsulation of pragmatic and God-fearing America, is as much at home in the new as she had been in the old. The Old South and the Old West, which meet in Arkansas, refashion their ways of living but not their indomitable spirit. Reconstruction will end in 1877 by order of the narrowly elected Republican president Rutherford B. Hayes, in keeping his pledge to the insistent South; the mission of strong-willed and self-confident Mattie begins in the wake of this event.

Moreover, Mattie, with her resoluteness and her facility for moving men into her field of purpose, anticipates the women's suffrage movement that will culminate in the Nineteenth Amendment to the Constitution in 1920, well within her own lifetime. Yarnell Poindexter, standing firm in his freedom and in his work, likewise anticipates the Civil Rights movement, which will begin in the 1940's and will progress in tandem with a new feminist movement in the 1960's.

As a celebration of America, with all of its faults and all of its promise, *True Grit* offers a tentative corrective to Herman Melville's brilliantly cynical *The Confidence Man: His Masquerade* (1857). The book also provides a contrast to negativistic countercultural movements of the 1960's that often sought to disparage the American archetypes that *True Grit* embraces.

Critical Context

That *True Grit* is Portis' masterpiece is the result at least in part of its celebratory scope and its thematic depth. It surpassed his exceptionally well-received first novel, *Norwood* (1966), in critical praise, which continues to identify it as a classic. None of his later novels—*The Dog of the South* (1979), *Masters of Atlantis* (1985), and

Gringos (1991)—matched his second novel in reception and acclaim. Initial comparisons of Mattie Ross to Huckleberry Finn came to be recognized as superficial and strained. What invites *True Grit* into the company of American regionalist classics is not coincidental and partial resemblances, but the genuine regionalist's deeply subjective identification of self with his or her regional roots in a stylistic objectification of that identity.

The style of Portis, a career journalist, is understandably journalistic, but only in that it effects a translation of the merits of good journalism—brevity, concision, lucid exposition, and rapid pace—into fictional narrative. The journalistic element does not account for Portis' humor, which informs each of his novels from *Norwood* through *Gringos* and which neither veers toward the bitter or the sardonic, as Mark Twain's can, nor intimates social protest, as Erskine Caldwell's often does. Portis' humor is usually an appeal, not against injustice, but in favor of the good sense and pragmatic morality that promote justice.

Bibliography

Garfield, Brian. "Song and Swagger of the Old West." *Saturday Review* 51 (June 29, 1968): 25-26. Garfield differentiates the quality and scholarly accuracy of *True Grit* from those of hackwork Western novels. He sees Portis' novel as one that raises the standards of the Western genre and as one that is imbued with truth instead of being rife with cliché and half-truth. He neglects, however, to mention the element of Southern honor that complements the integrity of the Old West.

Shuman, R. Baird. "Portis' *True Grit*: Adventure Story or *Entwicklungsroman*" *English Journal* 59 (March, 1970): 367-370. Shuman argues that *True Grit* is a "developmental novel" that traces the coming of age and psychological maturation of Mattie Ross and that its Western trappings are merely its format. Shuman insists that the most moving and important passage in the novel is not the achievement of revenge with the death of Chaney, but the description of Mattie's falling into the "cave" and being rescued therefrom. With going so far as to see in this a version of the classical journey to the underworld, symbolic of conversion or rebirth to maturity, Shuman classifies it as an event of initiation.

Wolfe, Tom. "The Feature Game." In *The New Journalism*. New York: Harper & Row, 1973: This chapter concludes with reference to Portis as a feature writer who realized the dream of achieving literary status. Wolfe surmises that the success of journalists as novelists may presage novelistic journalism's superseding the novel as literature's "main event."

Roy Arthur Swanson

TYPICAL AMERICAN

Author: Gish Jen (1956-   )
Type of plot: Social realism
Time of plot: The 1940's to the 1980's
Locale: China and New York City
First published: 1991

> *Principal characters:*
> RALPH CHANG, a Chinese American mechanical engineer
> THERESA CHANG, Ralph's older sister, a Chinese American doctor
> HELEN CHANG,, Theresa's best friend from China, Ralph's wife
> OLD CHAO, Ralph's superior at the university, a friend of the Changs
> GROVER DING, a third-generation Chinese American businessman and
> entrepreneur

The Novel

Typical American is a novel about three Chinese immigrants and how they are inspired, seduced, and betrayed by the promise of the American Dream. The book is divided into five parts: "Sweet Rebellion," "The House Holds," "This New Life," "Structural Weakening," and "A Man to Sit at Supper and Never Eat." The titles roughly sketch the protagonists' journey through the novel, from rebellion to prosperity to deterioration and alienation. The parts are further divided into short chapters with cleverly appropriate titles such as "A Boy with His Hands Over His Ears," "Love Animates," and "A Brand of Alchemy, Indeed."

In "Sweet Rebellion," Jen follows Yifeng Chang from his native village in China to the United States, detailing his immigration difficulties, his choice of the American name Ralph, and his entry into American academia as a mechanical engineer. Ralph struggles to learn the nuances of English and has his first brushes with romance. His newly arrived sister, now called Theresa, joins him in New York, and Ralph marries her best friend, Helen, another Chinese immigrant

In "The House Holds," the three set up house together. Ralph continues to ascend the academic ladder, under the tutelage of a fellow immigrant nicknamed Old Chao, and Helen begins her medical studies. Relations in the little family shift under the strains of life in America, but advances are made: Theresa becomes a doctor, Ralph completes his Ph.D., and Helen gives birth to two daughters. Meanwhile, Ralph begins reading and dreaming about wealth and success. One night, while dining at Old Chao's, the Changs meet Grover Ding, a self-made American businessman of Chinese descent who captures Ralph's imagination.

"This New Life" brings more changes. Ralph, after much worry, receives tenure at the university, and with that security the family buys a suburban home. Theresa, devoted to her work and essentially quite lonely, starts having an affair with Old Chao. When Ralph and Helen find out about Theresa's affair, their censure creates unbearable tension in the little family.

In "Structural Weakening," the tension breaks the family apart, as Theresa moves into an apartment of her own. Meanwhile, Ralph's aspirations lead him to seek out Grover Ding, and he impulsively accepts an opportunity from Grover, giving up his university position to invest in a fast-food chicken restaurant. At first, all goes well, but eventually structural weaknesses in the building show it to be much less of a bargain than it seemed. In an emotional parallel to the business developments, Grover and Helen have a passionate affair, protected by Ralph's single-minded focus on the business. Grover soon disappears, however, and the Changs realize that they have been victims of shady dealing. As the restaurant deteriorates into uselessness, the Changs face economic and emotional disaster.

The novel's last part, "A Man to Sit at Supper and Never Eat," fulfills the dire promise in a surprising climactic sequence of events. The house is offered for sale, even as Theresa rejoins the troubled family. Ralph learns of Helen's infidelity, and the tension between them reaches violent proportions. Ralph's blind fury eventually leads to a bizarre accident that leaves Theresa in a coma, and the family is battered with grief. In the end, the Changs move into an apartment in the city, Theresa emerges from her coma, and the family begins to rebuild.

The novel is told in a third-person voice that establishes a swift, playful rapport with the reader. Jen moves freely among the characters' viewpoints and shifts tempos and time frames to fill in necessary details, only loosely anchoring the story in a specific geographic or temporal context. The narrative is full of references to Chinese culture and history; italics indicate the Chang's bilingual domestic life, and Chinese phrases are transliterated and explained. The breezy, almost cartoonish style of the earlier parts gradually gives way to a brooding, dramatic sobriety as the story winds toward its conclusion.

The Characters

Ralph is the first protagonist Jen introduces. He is a likeable, innocent young man who, in striving for success and an American identity, becomes ambitious, irresponsible, moody, and insensitive. He is a dreamer whose imagination often runs unfettered, but he lacks the circumspection and caution that will keep him and his family out of trouble. It is his fascination with success formulas and his adulation of Grover that wreak havoc on the family.

Theresa is a foil to Ralph, a large, straitlaced woman who survives on reserve and caution. Her story "curls from this sad truth: that as much as Ralph, growing up, should have been her, she should have been him." Innately a leader, she is relegated to third-wheel status in the family. She represents the traditional Chinese value of family devotion, a value that she abandons but to which she ultimately returns. At the same time, she is American, and her puzzled and illicit love for Old Chao is a source of liberation and identity.

Helen, conversely, is a slight, delicate woman with a surprising resourcefulness and knack for adaptation. At first, she is the grounded force that anchors Ralph's moods

and dreams. Yet if she begins her life in American with images from fashion magazines and dreams of suburbia, she ends with an alienation and hopelessness that lead
to her corruption. For Helen, marrying Ralph meant "officially accepting what
seemed already true—that she had indeed crossed a violent, black ocean; and that it
was time to make herself as at home in her exile as she could." The task turns out to
be more difficult than imagined.

Old Chao is portrayed as a generous and well-meaning friend to the family whose
involvement in their troubles comes from very human, if not wholly honorable,
impulses. Grover Ding, on the other hand, is never fully revealed, to either the Changs
or the reader, beyond the fact that he is the charming "imagineer" he appears to be.
The other characters, such as Chao's long-suffering wife Janis, are treated with respect
and distance, and the Changs' daughters Callie and Mona are ever-present reminders
of the innocence that their parents are slowly, unwittingly losing.

Themes and Meanings

Typical American is a novel about migration: across the globe, across four decades,
and across an expansive moral and emotional landscape. Unlike many earlier European immigrants to the United States who came fleeing poverty or hunger, Chinese
American immigrants such as Ralph come in search of educational opportunities in
advanced scientific fields. Ralph would have been a member of the elite in China, and
in the beginning of the novel, he and other such immigrants become small pawns in
the ideological battles of the Cold War.

The first adaptation to life in America is the choice of a name, which comes in
Ralph's case rather haphazardly, and the mastery of the English language, the source
of many comic moments. In a delightful twist of language, the Changs adopt a family
nickname—the Chinese Yankees, or "Chang-Kees" for short. The term encapsulates
their struggle: They are Americanized but are still inwardly Chinese. Ralph, Theresa,
and Helen strive for assimilation, wearing American clothes, speaking American
slang, and living in an American home. Jen writes, "In China, one lived in one's
family's house. In America, one could always name whose house one was in; and to
live in a house not one's own was to be less than a man."

Family is a theme that permeates the novel. It is the link that connects Ralph and
Theresa and Helen, more even than romantic love. For Ralph and Helen, marrying is
the right thing to do, a choice their Chinese parents would applaud. Similarly, Ralph's
later rejection of Theresa, her shamed exile from the home, and her return in time of
duress, are all rooted in family cohesion. Yet the traditional Chinese dedication to
family is pitted against, and eventually lost to, the classical American devotion to
independence and individualism, and the confrontation results in contradictions:
Ralph has no difficulty underreporting his income, a "typically" American practice
embodied in the ringing of the cash register, but he nevertheless cannot adopt the
equally Western and modern attitude that would tolerate his sister's affair.

The structure of the family and the role of women are transformed as tradition
confronts liberal attitudes in contemporary America. The family focuses on Ralph's

career even as Theresa struggles as arduously to become a doctor. Theresa's independence and Helen's resourcefulness, and later their courage to have extramarital affairs, go beyond the traditional and accepted female roles. Such disruptive departures from tradition result from the positive yearnings for assimilation and belonging: Indeed, if Ralph had not accepted Grover as a role model for success, Grover never would have seduced Helen.

Love is not absent from the novel, but it is only rarely seen in a pure or innocent form. The romantic and sexual relationships are all imperfect, volatile, and dependent on dishonesty and accommodation. Impure love ultimately leads to alienation and the loss of all feeling, the insensate state made manifest in Theresa's comatose condition.

Partly to blame for the failure is the difficulty of translation, of learning to communicate in a new language. In moving from one world to another, the Changs have to learn not only what the new words mean but also what the new concepts and practices signify. Ralph fails miserably at truly understanding Grover Ding's counsels. Early in their relationship, Grover advises Ralph to "know who you're dealing with," and Ralph affirms, imperfectly, "Know who I'm deal with." The tragedy, of course, is that he cannot even begin to recognize the base nature of the man whose advice he so eagerly accepts.

Communication and understanding are key, and one of the lessons that Helen teaches Callie and Mona about talking is the importance, sometimes, of "not continuing." The American way of talking, it seems, is continuous and inexhaustible, whereas members of the Chang family, especially the women, often let the silence make their points. Implicit in this view of communication is a metaphor for the dangers of ambition and materialism. The Changs become assimilated in their focus on external status symbols: Their lives revolve around their job titles, their house, their car, their future opportunities for wealth and power. They begin to take what they have for granted, and look instead beyond it into the far realms of their imaginations. Rather than depend on the knowable, Ralph begins to believe in some mystical American deity composed of sheer arrogance and willpower. "Risk was the key to success. Clothes made the man." He covers his office walls with capitalistic catchphrases and fully believes them. Like talk that continues beyond the point when silence would serve better, so can aspiration overshoot reality. Playing with business terms and concepts, Jen makes the point clearly: Rather than keep his overhead to a minimum, Ralph decides to build a second floor to his restaurant, but the added weight creates too heavy a burden for the weak foundation, and eventually the whole building comes crashing down.

Early in the novel, in commenting ruefully on the foibles of the strange society that surrounds them, the Changs develop the habit of calling things "typical American": "typical American don't-know-how-to-get-along" and "typical American just-want-to-be-the-center-of-things." The phrase becomes a refrain in their lives as they grow to recognize and identify prevailing values. Yet the Changs eventually become blind to "typical American" qualities, and ultimately, in spite of themselves, end up embodying them.

Critical Context

Jen is an American-born writer of Chinese descent who traveled to China to explore her cultural heritage. A graduate of Harvard University, she attended business school briefly but soon turned to creative writing. Her reading of the immigration experience as portrayed by Jewish American writers is one of the major influences in her work. For her writing, Jen has received fellowships from the National Endowment for the Arts and the Bunting Institute at Radcliffe College.

Typical American is Jen's debut novel, preceded only by the publication of several short stories in *The New Yorker* and *The Atlantic*. Upon its appearance in 1991, *Typical American* was immediately acclaimed for its original voice and viewpoint, its use of humor and pathos, its insights into the Chinese American immigrant experience, and its deep indictment of typically American values.

With *Typical American*, Jen has been heralded as a member of a new generation of Chinese American writers. Modern Chinese American writing began to emerge in 1950 with the publication of Jade Snow Wong's *Fifth Chinese Daughter*, an autobiographical novel about assimilation into American culture. Other books that built the tradition include Maxine Hong Kingston's *The Woman Warrior: Memoirs of a Girlhood Among Ghosts* (1976), a collection of autobiographical stories and traditional tales; Bette Bao Lord's *Eighth Moon: The Story of a Young Girl's Life in Communist China* (1964); and Wong's autobiographical novel *The Immigrant Experience* (1971). Among Jen's contemporaries in the 1980's and 1990's are Amy Tan, known for her novels *The Joy Luck Club* (1989) and *The Kitchen God's Wife* (1991), and Playwright David Henry Hwang, whose *M. Butterfly* (1988) earned him Tony and Drama Desk Awards.

Bibliography

Mojtabai, A. G. "The Complete Other Side of the World." *The New York Times Book Review*, March 31, 1991, 9-10. Mojtabai examines *Typical American* in terms of the themes of migration and mutation, the intelligence of Jen's prose, and the questions posed by the book. The favorable review is accompanied by an interview with Jen by Laurel Graeber.

Simpson, Janice C. "Fresh Voices Above the Noisy Din." *Time* 137 (June 3, 1991): 66-67. An article profiling four Chinese American novelists that places Jen alongside Amy Tan, David Wong Louie, and Gus Lee. Simpson briefly discusses each novel, quotes the authors, and attempts to link them to one another and to the context of Chinese American writing.

Snell, Marilyn Berlin. "The Intimate Outsider." *New Perspectives Quarterly* 8 (Summer, 1991): 56-60. A thoughtful and extensive interview with Jen exploring the sociopolitical implications of *Typical American*. Jen discusses American values, the tradition of American literature, and her role as an immigrant writer.

Storace, Patricia. "Seeing Double." *The New York Review of Books* 38 (August 15, 1991): 9. A review of *Typical American* focusing on the novel's theme of duality. Includes a synopsis and an exploration of duality in both the joining of opposites and the coexistence of parallels.

Zia, Helen. "A Chinese Banquet of Secrets." *Ms.* 12 (November-December 1991): 76-77. A review of nine novels by Chinese American women writers, with major focus on Jen, Amy Tan, Sky Lee, and Carol Tsukiyama. In discussing *Typical American*, Zia looks primarily at Theresa and Helen. The article effectively places Jen's women beside other comparable female protagonists.

Barry Mann

THE VALLEY

Author: Rolando Hinojosa (1929-   )
Type of plot: Social realism
Time of plot: The 1920's to the 1970's
Locale: The Texas-Mexico border
First published: The Valley (1983; revised from *Estampas del valle y otras obras/Sketches of the Valley and Other Works*, 1973)

> *Principal characters:*
> RAFA BUENROSTRO, the autobiographical protagonist of many of the sketches
> DON MANUEL GUZMÁN, a former revolutionary modeled after Hinojosa's father
> JEHÚ MALACRA, the son of Tere Noriega and Roque Malacra, orphaned at an early age
> AUNT CHEDES BRIONES, Jehú Malacra's aunt, who helps to rear the orphaned boy
> DON VÍCTOR, a former revolutionary connected with the circus
> GILBERTO CASTAÑEDA, the husband of Marta Cordero, whose brother, Baldemar, he sees murder Ernesto Tamez
> BALDEMAR CORDERO, Gilberto's friend and brother-in-law
> ERNESTO TAMEZ, a man stabbed to death by Baldemar Cordero

The Novel

This collection of sketches about Rolando Hinojosa's fictional Belken County, situated just north of the Mexican border in Texas, was Hinojosa's first major publication. Originally, it was rendered in Spanish with English translations by Gustávo Valadéz and José Reyna under the title *Estampas del valle y otras obras/Sketches of the Valley and Other Works.* Hinojosa himself translated it under the present title in 1983, adding some material and a set of photographs from his family album. The collection constitutes a novel by some definitions of the term, but it also is the first major segment of Hinojosa's evolving multivolume "Klail City Death Trip" series. Hinojosa focuses on the area around his birthplace, Mercedes, Texas (Klail City in his series). In these sketches, he attempts to capture the ambience of the area and its people.

The Valley lacks the real plot, the dramatic climax, the carefully planned denouement, and the clearly identifiable protagonist found in conventional novels. Nevertheless, it contains pervasive characters, including the frequent narrator, Rafa Buenrostro, the biographical details of whose life closely approximate Hinojosa's. It also presents Jehú Malacara, seen through many eyes at various stages of his development. The last pages of the book, "A Life of Rafa Buenrostro," focus on Rafa.

Three early sketches—a total of twenty-three printed lines—focus on Rafa's early school experience and evoke the sense of separation Mexican American children feel from their Anglo classmates and teachers. The three paragraphs that constitute these sketches are not directly related to one another. Rather, each provides a snapshot of something connected with that early school experience: the teacher, Miss Moy, is described in five lines; a Hispanic girl lies about what she had for breakfast to make herself seem more like her Anglo classmates (eight lines); Rafa punches Hilario Berrago in the mouth during recess (ten lines).

From these school sketches, Hinojosa moves directly to a short vignette about a man from the water company coming to shut off the Ponce family's water supply because they have not paid their bill. The next sketch moves to a neighboring town, Flora, and has no direct connection with what has preceded it.

A six-line sketch follows telling about how in Edgerton the narrator's father had once fired three shots at a man who was trying to knife him. As these sketches unfold, readers, probably at first bewildered at encountering unfamiliar characters in unfamiliar towns, begin to develop a sense of the region about which Hinojosa is writing. The individual sketches may lack plot, yet from them emerge details useful elsewhere throughout this book and the others of the "Klail City Death Trip" series.

One sustained narrative among the sketches focuses on Baldemar (Balde) Cordero's fatal stabbing of Ernesto Tamez in a barroom brawl. Balde's friend, Gilberto (Beto) Castañeda, is married to Balde's sister, Marta. They all live together in Klail City. Beto, witness to the stabbing, gives a deposition recounting what happened. Through it, readers learn the backgrounds of Balde and Beto and of other characters they have previously encountered in the book. A sketch of Beto Castañeda follows.

Some characters in this collection emerge more fully developed in subsequent volumes of the series. Jehú Malacra is a typical example. In this book, readers first meet Jehú's grandfather, an unnamed narrator, and his long-dead great-grandfather, Braulio Tapia. Jehú's father, Roque Malacra, visits the narrator, a widower, requesting his daughter Tere Noriega's hand in marriage.

In fewer than twenty lines, the narrator consents to this request and reflects upon his having visited Braulio Tapia many years before seeking permission to marry Braulio's daughter Matilde, Tere's mother. He also recalls that Braulio's wife, doña Sóstenes, was dead when he approached his prospective father-in-law, as the narrator's wife is dead when Roque approaches him.

In these parallel circumstances, one senses the recurrence of human events that is part of continuance in a county such as Belken. Hinojosa's family lived in the South Texas area from the 1740's and became "accidental" American citizens in 1845, when the boundary between Mexico and the United States was redrawn a few miles south of where they had previously lived as Mexicans. *The Valley* and subsequent volumes follow Jehú Malacra from his birth through his childhood, his war experiences, and his rise as an officer in the local bank and second husband of Becky Escobar, to whom Hinojosa later devotes a full volume, *Becky and Her Friends* (1990).

The Characters

Rafa Buenrostro, the autobiographical narrator of many of the sketches, is a splendid observer. Secure in his identity, he understands the people around him in Hinojosa's Belken County. He also is ambitious and knows something of the world outside Belken's circumscribed boundaries. He has served in the Korean War and is planning to attend the University of Texas at Austin; he also benefits from his position as the youngest son in a family of five. Rafa does more reporting than judging. He appreciates the circumstances of Belken County's Mexican American citizens and understands the lapses and missteps they make.

Jehú Malacra is depicted from birth to young manhood. Losing his parents early, he is reared partly by Aunt Chedes Briones and grows up with his three cousins, Édu, Pepe, and Vicky. Vicky Briones distresses her mother by joining the circus, but her doing so enables Jehú to work with don Víctor in transporting circus props from town to town. Jehú becomes a solid citizen in Hinojosa's later volumes and also develops into a person of some integrity who challenges his boss at the bank. In this volume, readers see Jehú as a circus roustabout and message carrier as he wrestles with the dilemmas people face reaching adulthood.

Emilio Tamez is presented in a brief sketch as someone to whom bad things happen. He lost his right ear in a barroom brawl, but before that, at age eleven, he slipped as he was jumping from wagon to wagon, injuring himself badly enough that he still limps. He can read and write in both Spanish and English, but, according to Hinojosa, he is stupid. He receives considerable abuse.

Ernesto Tamez's relationship to Emilio is unclear. Balde Cordero kills Ernesto in a bar in Klail City. It is evident, however, that Ernesto is related to Emilio, and one character states that Ernesto's family is "an odd bunch."

Balde Cordero stabs Ernesto, but because he is drunk at the time, he does not remember doing so. The implication is that Balde, who is sentenced to fifteen years in prison for murder, is as much a victim as Ernesto.

One sketch entitled "Don Manuel Guzmán" is about Hinojosa's father, who appears in other sketches throughout the book. The father owned three cleaning establishments and part of a bakery. Loyal to the Mexican government, he finally became a policeman in the Mexican district of Klail City and is presented as an ex-revolutionary who matures into a solid citizen. Don Manuel represents a man poised between two cultures, but he is clearly a genuine part of only one of them: He is Mexican to the core.

Braulio Tapia, mentioned briefly in an early sketch bearing his name but relating the story of his son and granddaughter, is presented more fully in a later historical sketch, one of the few that delves into Belken County's history as a part of Mexico. Hinojosa depicts don Braulio, born in 1883, as a revolutionary of the same ilk as don Manuel, who knew Pancho Villa and Álvaro Obregon personally.

Don Víctor is part of the revolution, a Mexican lieutenant colonel married to a Mexican Jew. After she, their son, and their unborn child die of Spanish influenza in 1920, however, the grief-stricken don Víctor ends up in Belken County with the circus. In don Víctor, as in most of his other characters, Hinojosa, providing minimal information, demonstrates how people evolve into what they are.

Themes and Meanings

Hinojosa's main thrust in this first volume of the "Klail City Death Trip" series has to do with establishing the sense of recurrence and continuity that characterizes his fictional (and actual) county in South Texas. The boundary changed in 1845, but the drawing of a line on a map cannot change the hearts, souls, or heritage of a citizenry.

Hinojosa's sketches, if viewed in the light of the full series, also have to do with how people mature into what they eventually become. If his characters are inconsistent, Hinojosa makes no apology, saying merely that people are not consistent as they go through life. Some things about them remain the same, some change. In Hinojosa's eyes, consistency of character is not a valid human trait.

In this volume, as in the others in the series, there is really no dominant character; even in *Becky and Her Friends*, Becky Escobar cannot be called a dominant character in the usual sense. Rather than writing about one or more protagonists, Hinojosa writes about a community of people. Readers meet most of them without being given much background: They just appear on the page engaged in living some small part of their lives.

Some critics disdain this approach, yet it replicates the way people come to know and understand society in real life. People happen upon scenes and draw from them what they can with the information available to them.

Those who judge Hinojosa negatively should remember that when Gertrude Stein replicated actual speech patterns with great accuracy in *Three Lives* (1909), readers accustomed to having authors run interference for them between actual speech and the dialogue of most novels were appalled. Yet in that experimental novel, Stein broke new stylistic ground that led many subsequent authors to reconsider how they would present dialogue in their fiction.

Hinojosa has reassessed the ways human beings derive information from actual occurrences in their lives. In the volumes in his series, he has no misgivings about plunging directly into ongoing action. If one suddenly is plunged into a scene that depicts an event in Flora, Hinojosa does not pause to tell his readers where Flora is or what kind of town it is. He does that elsewhere in the book, but he does not interrupt the ongoing action of his story to provide details without which his readers can still perceive the action.

One cannot deny that an initial reading of a book such as *The Valley* bewilders and confuses readers. Hinojosa, who holds a doctorate in Spanish literature from the University of Illinois and is well schooled in literature, is bent on achieving a depiction that mirrors actual reality. Upon completing this book, readers have a sense of community that few more conventional novels impart.

Critical Context

The 1960's were crucial to Rolando Hinojosa's development as a writer. He completed a five-year stint as a high school teacher and factory laborer in Brownsville, Texas, and in 1962 began graduate studies at New Mexico Highlands University, receiving the master's degree in 1963. He then moved to the University of Illinois at Urbana for doctoral work.

Hinojosa and his wife arrived in Illinois just before the strident racial uprisings of the 1960's, a period that focused attention upon the problems of blacks. Out of this period grew a hospitable atmosphere for black protest literature and, subsequently, for black literature that had been produced earlier. In this climate, all minority literatures began to be encouraged and reevaluated.

Just before completing the doctorate, Hinojosa took a teaching job at San Antonio's Trinity University, where, fortunately, he came under the influence of Tomás Rivera. Rivera encouraged Hinojosa's writing, urging him to submit a manuscript to the Quinto Sol competition, which Rivera had won in 1970. Hinojosa submitted the original version of *The Valley*, which took the prize in 1972 and resulted in the book's publication the following year.

Bibliography

Hinojosa, Rolando. "Chicano Literature: An American Literature in Transition." In *The Identification and Analysis of Chicano Literature*, edited by Francisco Jiménez. New York: Bilingual Press, 1979. Hinojosa contrasts the interest in black writing to that in Hispanic writing. He foresees a developing interest in Chicano literature. His predictions have proved accurate.

_____ . "This Writer's Sense of Place." In *The Texas Literary Tradition: Fiction, Folklore, History*, edited by Don Graham, James W. Lee, and William T. Pilkington. Austin: University of Texas Press, 1983. Hinojosa discusses how he transformed the area where he grew up into his fictional county. One senses here the dichotomy he felt as a part of two cultures. Schooled to value his heritage, he could not, however escape Hispanic-Anglo tensions.

Leal, Luis. "History and Memory in *Estampas del valle*." In *The Rolando Hinojosa Reader: Essays Historical and Critical*, edited by José David Saldívar. Houston: Arté Publico Press, 1985. Deals with how Hinojosa structured his memories of childhood to formulate his novel. Also shows how local history infuses Hinojosa's writing.

Saldívar, José David. "Our Southwest: An Interview with Rolando Hinojosa." In *The Rolando Hinojosa Reader: Essays Critical and Historical*, edited by José David Saldívar. Houston: Arté Publico Press, 1985. In this interview, Hinojosa talks about the evolution of his work. He acknowledges his debt to Tomás Rivera, who encouraged him to offer his work for publication. The piece is valuable in that it traces the progression of Hinojosa's writing.

_____ . "Rolando Hinojosa's *Klail City Death Trip*: A Critical Introduction." In *The Rolando Hinojosa Reader: Essays Historical and Critical*, edited by José David Saldívar. Houston: Arté Publico Press, 1985. This essay provides an overall assessment of the "Klail City Death Trip" series and illustrates how Hinojosa conceives of his work. Useful for Hinojosa's comments on local color.

R. Baird Shuman

VINELAND

Author: Thomas Pynchon (1937-   )
Type of plot: Social realism
Time of plot: The late 1980's
Locale: Northern California
First published: 1990

Principal characters:

ZOYD WHEELER, a former hippie, a government pensioner and handyman
PRAIRIE, Zoyd's daughter, who is questing for information about her mother
FRENESI GATES, Prairie's mother and Zoyd's former wife, a onetime radical who is now an undercover government agent
BROCK VOND, a government prosecutor who was once Frenesi's lover and is now her controller
DL CHASTAIN, a onetime friend of Frenesi, Prairie's guide in her quest
HUB and SASHA GATES, Frenesi's radical parents, who are involved in the film industry
HECTOR ZUÑIGA, a television-mad drug agent

The Novel

Zoyd Wheeler has been living a quiet life in Vineland, a fictitious town in Northern California, with his daughter Prairie. Zoyd does odd jobs for neighbors, grows marijuana, and collects a government pension for committing a crazy act every year: specifically, for throwing himself through a plate-glass window in a local restaurant in front of television cameras. Prairie works in a local health-food pizza parlor and hangs out with a rock band, Billy Barf and the Vomitones.

Things are changing at the novel's beginning. The site of Zoyd's annual fling is shifted without explanation, and there are rumors of a major government antidrug operation in the area. Various kinds of police and federal troops are seen in Vineland. Hector Zuñiga warns Zoyd that Prairie is in danger, probably from Brock Vond. There are rumors that Vond has lost track of Frenesi, an agent whom he controls, and that he will try to find her by using Prairie. Prairie, on her own, is anxious for more information about her mother; Zoyd and Sasha Gates, Prairie's grandmother, have told her only that Frenesi is underground, hiding from government agents because of her activities in the 1960's.

Prairie, warned by her father that she should leave the area, goes with the band to Southern California, where they are scheduled to play at a Mafia wedding while pretending to be an Italian band. In the powder room, Prairie accidentally draws the attention of DL Chastain, a martial-arts expert who had been close to Frenesi in the turmoil of the 1960's. DL introduces Prairie to the Sisterhood of Kunoichi Attentives, whose files reveal to the young woman the activities in which her mother had been involved as a member of a radical film collective.

DL's life is presented in considerable detail. Daughter of a career Army enlisted man, she had become a student of martial arts with a renowned teacher while her father was stationed in Japan. Her skills, far beyond normal, were sometimes made use of by others in ways she could not always control; at one point, she was programmed to kill Brock Vond but failed. She has taken control of her own life and is now a partner of another master of the martial arts, Takeshi Fumimota, who has his own unusual history.

From the archives at the retreat and from DL, Prairie learns that Frenesi had participated in the rebellion at a small California college, had encountered and been fascinated by Brock Vond, had been seduced by him, and had served as his agent in the murder of a popular professor named Weed. The murder, along with the imminent occupation of the campus of the college by police and federal troops, had brought the rebellion to an end. Frenesi had been spirited away by Vond and sequestered in a secret government camp. Rescued by DL, she had eventually married Zoyd and given birth to Prairie before returning to Vond and becoming an underground government agent.

In the meantime, Frenesi has become wedded to her new life. She has married again to another undercover agent, Flash, and has another child, a son named Justin. She and Flash have been moved from town to town, wherever their services were needed. At the time when Prairie begins her search, however, Frenesi's world is coming apart. The Ronald Reagan Administration has cut off funding for Brock Vond's operation, and Frenesi sets out with Flash and Justin for Vineland.

Prairie also returns to Vineland with DL and Takeshi Fumimota in time for the periodic reunion of Sasha Gates' family; the community feeling of the family helps to dissipate the threat of government intervention. Prairie finally meets her mother, and there is something close to a reconciliation between them. In the end, Brock Vond attempts to kidnap Prairie, who he claims is his daughter; the attempt is frustrated, and he is condemned by higher forces in the government. The raid is called off, the troops and police withdraw from the area, and there is a happy ending, at least temporarily, for Prairie, her friends, and her relatives.

The Characters

Frenesi Gates is among the most fully developed and interesting characters in all of Pynchon's work. She is seen from the point of view of the third-person narrator and also from the perspectives of her mother, Zoyd, Prairie, and DL as well as the Senior Attentive of the Sisterhood. Totally committed to the feminist film collective with which she is associated, daughter of her radical parents in her devotion to social causes, Frenesi is nevertheless fascinated, attracted, and repelled by Brock Vond and by the kind of authoritarian power he represents. At first, she tries to play games with Vond, then she falls in love with him; finally, she is made to face the extent of her own degradation. Over her protests, Vond gets her to transport the gun that will kill Weed, the professor who is at the heart of the student uprising. Once she has done this, she can place no limit on what she will do, and her life working as an agent for Vond is an inevitable next step. Still, as she is seen with Flash and Justin, she has not become a woman without conscience. She misses Prairie and regrets having left her, although she could see no alternative at the time. When the funds dry up and she is cast out of her work by a change in government policy, she instinctively returns to the reunion of her mother's clan. There, she discovers something like mercy and some sort of peace.

The other characters are less original and less developed. Prairie is presented as a typical teenaged daughter of hippies, hip herself but self-sufficient and imaginative. When DL takes her to the feminist institute, Prairie takes over a disorganized kitchen and becomes the much-admired chef for the whole organization. When the place is raided, she leaves with DL and Takeshi Fumimota without losing her cool. She wants to find her mother and is shocked by what she learns about Frenesi, but in the end, she neither sentimentalizes nor rejects her mother.

DL Chastain is a superwoman, not only strong physically but also a sensitive guide for Prairie's search. Zoyd is a typical hippie grown older and wiser, caring for Prairie but willing to let her find her own way. Hector Zuñiga is a parody of a drug-enforcement agent, himself helplessly addicted not to drugs but to television. Sasha Gates is a warm woman, politically dedicated to radical causes, caring enough about Prairie to work out an accommodation with Zoyd for the girl's care despite her scorn for Zoyd. Hub Gates is a fine technician, somewhat less political than his wife.

Brock Vond is clearly the villain of the novel. He has used his authority as a kind of roving prosecutor to harass anyone with whom he disagrees, and he deliberately corrupts Frenesi. In the later stages of the action, he is willing to bring all the forces of a repressive government to bear on the entire Vineland community in order to bring Frenesi to heel and to secure Prairie, whom he believes to be his daughter. His failure and destruction at the end are nearly melodramatic, as if, despite all the power it is shown to have in the novel, evil cannot finally win.

Themes and Meanings

Thomas Pynchon's continuing concern with the restrictions placed on the individual by society provides the main intention of *Vineland*: to show the dangers of excessive government control of individual lives and, specifically, to criticize the measures taken during the Reagan years to inhibit independent political activities and the use of drugs such as marijuana, which Pynchon presents as relatively harmless. The police and other enforcement agencies in the novel use powers given to them by recent laws to seize the homes of people suspected of marijuana trafficking: they disrupt lives and ruthlessly invade the privacy of innocents.

Brock Vond is used to give a face and specific qualities to these dangers. His relationship with Frenesi Gates is intended to make clear the extent to which individuals can be corrupted and seduced by uncontrolled power. The fact that Vond is a prosecutor indicates that the law, which ought to be a shield for individuals, is instead being used to intimidate and corrupt them, for no purpose other than to exert control. Vond also makes use of detention camps constructed to house suspect persons in case of a national emergency; for Pynchon, these are no more or less than potential concentration camps.

Nevertheless, *Vineland* is less bleak than Pynchon's other fictions in the suggestions it carries about the possibility of meaningful lives for its characters. Zoyd and Prairie do survive, Frenesi is given a kind of peace, though not necessarily redemption, and the villain is disposed of before he can corrupt Prairie. America toward the end of the century is far from ideal, but it is not entirely a wasteland.

Critical Context

Vineland is the most overtly political of Thomas Pynchon's novels. Themes and ideas from the earlier books are given more direct expression, as if Pynchon had decided that readers and critics were not understanding his principal ideas. The book contains clear-cut distinctions between good and bad characters, and it is the only one of Pynchon's novels to comment directly on the domestic political scene.

At the same time, *Vineland* is, like the earlier novels, varied in its prose styles, making use of wild and sometimes profane humor, original song lyrics, and caustic addresses from the narrator to the characters, among other devices. While it is the first of Pynchon's novels to deal explicitly with supernatural events—including a class of beings called Thanatoids, the shades of people who are dead but not quite gone, and the fact that DL Chastain is invested with superhuman powers—the supernatural has never been entirely excluded from Pynchon's fictional world. If it is less encyclopedic than Pynchon's most famous novel, *Gravity's Rainbow* (1973), *Vineland* is also more accessible.

Bibliography

Callens, Johan. "Tubed Out and Movie Shot in Pynchon's *Vineland*." *Pynchon Notes* no. 28/29 (Spring, 1991): 115-141. Pynchon's interest in films, demonstrated especially in *Gravity's Rainbow*, is seen as even more essential in *Vineland*. Not only are major characters, including Frenesi and DL Chastain, involved in film-making, but the novel also details Hector Zúñiga's obsession with television, which is more real to him than life, and the necessity for Vond's men to destroy the archives of the film collective, as if this action would erase the past.

Hite, Molly. *Ideas of Order in the Novels of Thomas Pynchon*. Columbus: Ohio State University Press, 1983. Although too early to include a discussion of *Vineland*, this excellent study of Pynchon's work provides essential information about the author's interest in various kinds of order (social, political, and philosophical). Useful for understanding Pynchon's method in opposing excessive political order to more personal kinds of order (such as martial art and music) in *Vineland*.

Keesey, Douglas. "*Vineland* in the Mainstream Press: A Reception Study" *Pynchon Notes* no. 26/27 (Spring, 1990): 107-113. This study summarizes and comments on the important reviews of *Vineland*, pointing out that most reviewers focused their attention on the political elements in the novel and that few reviewers made any attempt to deal with the relationship between Pynchon's ideas and his art.

Rafferty, Terrence. "Long Lost." *The New Yorker* 66 (February 19, 1990): 108-112. One of the few reviews to argue that Pynchon's artistic achievement in *Vineland* is in large measure the result of the overt political element. Rafferty asserts that the novel gains, rather than loses, because Pynchon is trying to make specific points about political conditions in the United States. Unlike many reviewers, Rafferty sees *Vineland* as a major step forward in Pynchon's career.

Rushdie, Salman. "Still Crazy After All These Years." *The New York Times Book Review* 95 (January 14, 1990): 1, 36-37. The noted novelist praises Pynchon's novel highly, calling attention to its political message and also emphasizing the author's choice of anonymity. Rushdie is most interested in Pynchon's condemnation of political and social conformity and the ways in which governments and other organizations attempt to enforce their views.

John Muste

A VISITATION OF SPIRITS

Author: Randall Kenan (1963-   )
Type of plot: Social realism
Time of plot: 1984 and 1985
Locale: Tims Creek, North Carolina
First published: 1989

> *Principal characters:*
> HORACE CROSS, a sixteen-year-old high school student who is struggling against his homosexuality
> JAMES MALACHAI GREENE (JIMMY), the principal of Tims Creek Elementary School and minister of the First Baptist Church of Tims Creek
> EZEKIEL CROSS (ZEKE), the grandfather of Horace, who represents family and the tradition against which Horace struggles
> RUTH DAVIS CROSS, the great-aunt of Horace, a ninety-two-year-old woman whose feud with the world starts within the Cross family and extends into elevators and restaurants
> GIDEON STONE, a classmate of Horace and his first lover, a young man who has accepted his own homosexuality

The Novel

Alternating between April, 1984, narratives of Horace's experience with magic and December, 1985, narratives of a family visit to a dying cousin, *A Visitation of Spirits* tells the story of a sixteen-year-old African American boy who cannot transform himself away from homosexuality and so cannot continue to face his family and his community.

A Visitation of Spirits is divided into five major sections, each including April, 1984, and December, 1985, narratives. The story is told predominantly from a limited-omniscient perspective; the center of consciousness shifts within these sections among Horace, Jimmy, Zeke, and Ruth. Three segments entitled "Confession" (two from Jimmy, one from Horace) break the pattern of alternation, with each of the confessions showing the two figures wrestling with their own memories.

The 1985 narratives center on Jimmy, Aunt Ruth, and Uncle Zeke driving to see their cousin Asa, seriously ill in the hospital. These scenes reveal the family at work. Aunt Ruth and Uncle Zeke argue and accuse each other, with Jimmy trying to act the peacemaker; he is playing the role of clergyman rather awkwardly because he is first and foremost a nephew. Their journey takes them to a hospital; once there, Ruth cannot abide the falseness of those who would pray for Asa to live. Their journey home from the hospital finds them in a restaurant, where a white waitress and Ruth argue. The struggle between generations as well as between black and white energizes the scene. No peace within the family results from the meal they share, but a truce of sorts is implicitly declared after their car has broken down and then been fixed.

During the hospital visit, in a scene between Ruth and a young girl who invites her to play video games, the family finds rest and communion. After Ruth plays her first game, her expression is "like a revelation." She and Zeke, who have been arguing relentlessly all day, share a moment of conciliation "as pure and honest as the rain." Jimmy is relieved to have them acting as family.

The other central thread of the novel takes place on the night of April 29 and the morning of April 30, 1984, and is told from Horace's consciousness. Kenan begins with midday on April 29 as Horace cuts a class to sit in the library. There he chooses the exact animal into which he will ritually transform himself that night. The next section shifts to the morning of April 30; Horace is holding a gun on Jimmy at the elementary school grounds. A reader then follows the narrative to fill in the night of April 29 with Horace, a night in which the young man calls forth the demons that possess him and makes a ritual journey to the church, the high school, the theater, and finally the elementary school.

At the church, Horace is baptized into demonology in a sanctuary filled with the spirits he has called forth, some recognizable as townspeople and some misshapen and nightmarish. Horace wants not to be alone as he moves through his night; he continually looks for the demon to shield him and to become him. He always hears the demon's taunting but does as the demon bids. At the high school, he once again sees what appear to be familiar townspeople and misshapen spirits, a mix that figuratively represents Horace's straits: He is one of the inhabitants of Tims Creek, yet he is "misshapen" in his sexual desires and so cannot remain in the world of the townspeople. Making his way from the theater and to the elementary school, Horace (less and less recognizably himself throughout the night) becomes completely spirit as he holds a shotgun on Jimmy and forces him to walk into the woods. Horace's hope that witchcraft would transform him is realized for that brief moment of Otherness, when the demon speaks for Horace to Jimmy. Kenan ends the narration of the morning of April 30 with an intense physical description of Horace's body after he has committed suicide, an unforgettable transformation from life to death. Horace had journeyed to the places in which he sought community and acceptance, in the process finally becoming the demon he judged himself to be.

The Characters

Horace reveals the state of the spurned in the United States. His struggle against himself and his struggle to be accepted result not in acceptance but rather in insanity and death. Horace perceives in his grandfather and great-aunt "an armor one wore to beat the consequences, invisible, but powerful and evident." Horace is, throughout the novel, unable to clothe himself in this armor and so cannot endure. Horace attempts to belong, to join a community, throughout his brief life. As a grade school boy, his friend John Anthony had been his partner in science projects, field trips, sack races, and a love of books, "always books." John Anthony, however, became a sports hero and an auto mechanics student. He becomes popular with the girls, and he grows distant from Horace—the good student—who tries to replace John Anthony with an amorphous academia.

Horace's academic ambitions place him within reach of Gideon Stone, with whom he is assigned to complete a science project, the ultimate result of which is Horace's first homosexual encounter. Unable to accept his own sexual urges, Horace fights against his feelings by joining the track team and beginning to socialize with a group of "white boys" at the high school, boys who have moved to Tims Creek recently. His friendship with those other outcasts from the school is forbidden by his grandfather when Horace comes to the Thanksgiving dinner table with an earring in his newly pierced ear. Horace, no longer the determined student, must watch as Gideon steps into the group and earns a college scholarship. Horace never finds that armor "in the edge of his grandfather's voice, in the stoop of his great-aunt's walk. . . . Integrity. Dignity. Pride." His night of visitation with spirits he spends naked and vulnerable.

James Malachai Greene occupies an uneasy space: He is the religious and intellectual grandson and the redeemer of his mother Rose's sins against the family. Yet his inability to comfort Horace contributes significantly to Horace's suicide. Horace had, at considerable cost to himself, asked the minister if attraction toward men could be all right. The Reverend Jimmy Greene responded that Horace was experiencing adolescent confusion and would change. Horace asked what would happen if he could not change, to which the minister responded that he should pray about it and he would change. After Horace's suicide, the Reverend Greene is left to remember the earlier question and the death scene itself, feeling his failure to help Horace. Continually struggling between others' expectations of him and his own desires, he is, finally, the one called by Horace to be his witness.

Ruth Davis Cross, determined to be self-reliant and resentful of the Cross family wealth and pride, realizes her own culpability in her husband Jethro's alcoholism and flight from responsibility. Ruth outwardly accepted Jethro, playing the role of the good wife. Ruth illustrates further division within the family, feeling the weight of her in-laws' condescension. Her attraction to her husband's cousin Asa makes Ruth feel unworthy, a feeling over which she triumphs as she plays the video game with the child and then declares that snow is coming. Ruth has endured, reared her children, and ultimately accepted her own shortcomings.

Ezekiel Cross tried to rear Horace correctly. Zeke, ironically enough, counseled Horace away from judgment and prejudice against Gideon Stone. Horace had hoped that his grandfather would not allow him to work with a boy from such a disreputable family. Zeke unwittingly placed Horace in irresistible partnership with Gideon, a partnership that Horace cannot continue because of his family and his religious training. Then, when Horace had become friends with several white boys who had recently moved to Tims Creek, Zeke forbade Horace to see the boys, effectively driving him away from his last group of friends. Ezekiel at the close of the narrative remains unaware of Horace's need for acceptance as the key to his suicide. Zeke believes that his own mistake was in not making Horace work in the fields and keep busy.

Gideon Stone is a high school student who stands in contrast to the tormented

Horace in accepting and openly admitting his homosexuality. Gideon's family is also the opposite of the Cross family: The Stones make and sell bootleg whiskey, they are not churchgoers, and their home is cluttered and badly needs repair. This "disreputable" family nevertheless values Gideon and supports him. Gideon's speech is consistently clever, demonstrating his ability to deflect the criticisms of other teenagers, again a clear difference from Horace's response to criticism.

Themes and Meanings

The book's central themes are memory and communion. These themes merge in the novel's accounts of hog butchering and tobacco curing, accounts that remind readers of the roots of this novel in people's rituals of survival and community. These rituals are told in the second person, insistent on remembrance and common ritual: "You've seen this [hog killing], haven't you?" "You're familiar with this [tobacco curing], aren't you?" The hog-killing description is entitled "Advent." The parallel between the hog butchered and Horace dead suggests the community's role in Horace's death. Horace as the Christ sacrificed is also suggested in both the title "Advent" and in numerous references to the crucifixion. In a less violent ritual, tobacco curing again draws attention to remembrance: "[I]t is good to remember that people were bound by this strange activity . . . bound by the necessity, the responsibility, the humanity." The repetition and hard work apparent in the task parallel the life of Jimmy Greene as he lives in 1985, rising at five every morning to work on his sermon, always arriving at the elementary school by seven, and leaving school late in the evening. Jimmy Greene and Horace Cross live the rhythms of their respective rituals, yearning for true community and belonging.

Another theme evident in the story of Horace Cross is the powerful need for transformation. Horace seeks through magic to change himself into a hawk with all of its freedom and power, but the magic succeeds only in making him hear and see the spirits and demons that accompany him on his final night. His minister's earlier assurance that he would change is ironically true: Horace has prayed to demons and has changed from a troubled young man to a psychotic young man. His visions lead him to see his own *Doppelgänger* three times, the third time culminating in Horace's shooting his own spirit and seeing the blood flow from the vision of himself. From that moment, Horace as the reader recognizes him is gone, replaced by the one who follows the voice of the demon—a voice that next tells him to shoot himself.

Underlying Kenan's story of Horace Cross and Jimmy Greene is the constant of community. The narrative time sequence itself reinforces the continuity of the family and community, despite Horace's suicide. More than a year and a half after the suicide, the family that mourns Horace continues to visit the sick, cook meals, clean house, and go to work. Jimmy could have followed his own brother's advice and left Tims Creek after his wife died, but he stays within the community, his days following a pattern dictated by his work. Although Kenan leads the reader to feel the loss of Horace intensely, the novel ultimately proves the power of community.

Critical Context

A Visitation of Spirits was published toward the beginning of a period in the late 1980's and early 1990's which saw a substantial number of books by gay writers and about gay life. Publishers by the end of the 1980's had recognized the intense public interest in the gay community as well as the gay community's book-buying habits. At one level, the novel was guaranteed an audience because of its powerful treatment of a young man's homosexual experience. Once published, the novel earned consistently good reviews, not only for its innovatively structured accounts but also for its strong portrayal of character and rural life.

The novel explores the landscape of Randall Kenan's own childhood in eastern North Carolina, fleshing out the history of a community whose characters he continued to explore in his collection of short stories, *Let the Dead Bury Their Dead* (1992). In the title story, Kenan tells the history of Tims Creek, founded by runaway and freed slaves, some of whom had been called from their graves by a necromancer who had murdered the oldest son of a white master. Black magic, botany, and homosexuality (all strongly present in the novel) also recur in the collected stories. As compellingly magical as many of Zora Neale Hurston's accounts of Florida, Kenan's works operate within the tradition of African American authors, recalling a slave past and incorporating magic that enables black people to transcend their boundaries, whether those boundaries are imposed by slave owners or by loving grandfathers.

Bibliography

Brophy, Beth. "Books by and About Gays Find a Niche in Big-Time Publishing." *U.S. News and World Report*, April 16, 1990, 42-43. Brophy notes the willingness of publishers to support, even seek, works by homosexuals. The subjects of gay fiction are, she notes, universal themes. Brophy's concise article provides a good start for an examination of publishing and fiction by gays.

Essence. Review of *A Visitation of Spirits*, by Randall Kenan. 20 (September, 1989): 28. A laudatory review that notes main characters, setting, and the tension that moves the plot along.

Nixon, Will. "Better Times for Black Writers." *Publishers Weekly*, February 17, 1989, 35-40. Nixon compiles the divergent views of a number of black writers, Kenan included, who discuss the African American writer's road to publication. Having presented the argument that black women writers have a readier ear at most publishers, Nixon quotes Kenan: "Men don't have Zora Neale Hurston as a buzz word." Nixon briefly chronicles the rise of a black publishing industry, noting the importance of the Harlem Writers Guild.

Publishers Weekly. Review of *A Visitation of Spirits*, by Randall Kenan. May 12, 1989, 283. Discusses briefly the "powerful strain of mysticism" in the novel. The review also notes Kenan's "rare gift for naturalism, capturing the texture of farm life in vivid detail." The one criticism of the novel comments on the "jarring" shifts in time and tone.

Virginia Quarterly Review. Review of *A Visitation of Spirits*, by Randall Kenan. 66

(Winter, 1990): 22. Places Kenan in the company of Trey Ellis, Percival Everett, Don Belton, and Yolanda Barnes as writers depicting the black experience. The review points out that Kenan's novel is one in which "the only bigotry is demonstrated by older blacks." The tightly structured, daring form of the novel earns praise.

Janet Taylor Palmer

WAITING TO EXHALE

Author: Terry McMillan (1951-   )
Type of plot: Social realism
Time of plot: The 1990's
Locale: Denver, Colorado, and Phoenix, Arizona
First published: 1992

> *Principal characters:*
> SAVANNAH JACKSON, a thirty-six-year-old African American woman who moves from Denver to Phoenix
> BERNADINE HARRIS, Savannah's former college roommate, whose husband has left her for a younger white woman
> ROBIN STOKES, an underwriter for an insurance company
> GLORIA MATTHEWS, a single parent who owns her own hair salon
> TARIC, Gloria's son, who is just discovering sex

The Novel

In *Waiting to Exhale*, the four central female characters are members of an organization called Black Women on the Move (BWOM). The problem is that these bright, attractive, and loving women have themselves been on the move too long. They see themselves coming near to middle age fearing that they will not be able to find or sustain a sexual relationship with a black man whom they consider to be eligible. Savannah, with her mind set on a career and upward mobility, has been in three live-in relationships over a period of nine years, and she is holding her breath (waiting to exhale) until the time when she can locate someone whose interests are reasonably close to hers who is faithful, attractive, knowledgeable, and a good lover, attributes evidently extremely scarce among men.

As the novel opens, Savannah is planning a move from Denver, where she holds a well-paying but dead-end job, to Phoenix, where she has accepted a less well-paying job but one that fulfills her creative needs and one that she thinks promises more upward mobility. While in Phoenix, Savannah stays with her college roommate, Bernadine, whose "successful" marriage has just collapsed, her husband having left her for a younger white woman. Bernadine is left to cope with two children, a large house, and considerable stress over money at a time when she should be receiving benefits from her husband's prosperous career. Not only does he leave her, but he carefully hides all of his assets so as to try to make a very small settlement and small alimony payments.

Robin, described as flashy and a bit vulgar, has had a series of lovers, all undependable, although she wants to marry and have children. She enmeshes herself in relationships with men who take advantage of her. In her latest such relationship, she foolishly thinks that if she is good enough to her lover, he will eventually propose. Propose he does, but to another woman, with whom he has been having a simultaneous affair.

Gloria, friend to all the women, has a beauty salon and is hairdresser for them all as well. She is successful enough to employ four operators. Gloria's major concern is her son, Taric, who was the result of an indiscretion when she was a senior in college. Her former husband declared himself homosexual and left her and Taric, but he visits every two years, playing an unimportant role in Gloria's life as well as in Taric's.

Through the course of the novel, each woman experiences a kind of coming of age. Gloria finally has a heart attack, brought on by the stress of being without sufficient help at her shop (one of the operators has AIDS), the business of rearing Taric, and overeating. She recovers quickly, however, and finds Martin, a new neighbor, by her bedside, along with Taric and her "sisters," Savannah, Bernadine, and Robin. Martin looks as if he will replace her absent husband and be a father to her son. Bernadine works hard with her lawyer to uncover her former husband's assets and is rewarded by a settlement. She also receives a telephone call from a man she had once dated and whom she thought she would never see again, and with his promised visit she enters a new world. Savannah comes to an acceptance of her circumstances and is comforted by the rewards of her job. In addition, she is able to begin the process of breaking her smoking habit. Robin is pregnant by the man she has been unable to order away, and although she will not have a husband, she will have a child.

The Characters

The events of *Waiting to Exhale* are told in the first person through Savannah and Robin, and in the third person from the viewpoints of Bernadine and Gloria. The shifts in point of view help the reader to discern one character from another, since there is little difference in voice. This technique also serves to separate each woman from the group as a whole. Following each woman in alternating chapters serves to make each one the protagonist of her own subplot and to give the reader a sense of four different stories. Nevertheless, there is sufficient interaction among the four women when they meet and sufficient emotion displayed to consider them as a composite protagonist in a larger whole.

Gloria and Bernadine are the better rounded of the characters, largely because the third-person point of view allows for a wider scope. The two women also experience the most pain and come closest to a happy ending. Through many years of single parenthood, Gloria nurses, sustains, and teaches her son proper behavior, and in the end she is rewarded. Taric, in spite of bad influences all around him, chooses an honorable and reasonable path to a future life, and Gloria's helping hand and friendly demeanor to a neighbor quickly win his support and love. Bernadine reaches the point of near collapse, but through her own determination and hard work, she propels herself to a happy ending.

Savannah and Robin have problems with their parents, and their love and concern for them add dimension to their characters. For the most part, however, the two women suffer as a result of their inability to perceive the worth of people they meet and their willingness to seek sex where they find it. Three times in the novel McMillan reveals the dangers associated with promiscuity, including pregnancy out of wedlock, herpes, and AIDS. Robin's pregnancy at the end of the novel seems more positive than negative, since a child even without a live-in father is a positive value for Robin.

Themes and Meanings

Toward the end of *Waiting to Exhale*, during a celebration of Gloria's birthday, Savannah asks: "Whatever happened to the good old days?" Gloria demands to know what good old days she is talking about, but the question is well put and the answer clear. Men of the "buppie" generation apparently feel no need to court women in the old-fashioned way—no need to commit or to be faithful during a relationship. Women, apparently as open in their sexual needs as men and as willing to participate in sex before commitments are made, are readily available. The problem appears to be that women still seem to need commitment; they still seem to be looking for the good old-fashioned man. Gloria finds such a man in Martin; kindness and admiration lead to love before sex in their relationship. Bernadine too is lucky to find such a man.

It would be a mistake, however, to define Savannah and Robin, and to a lesser extent Bernadine and Gloria, solely in terms of their need for a relationship with a man. They have overcome odds and are doing better than their parents did. They are competing in the real world and making their way themselves. They participate in worthwhile projects and support them with both time and money. They are caring and questioning in a world where human values are not as clearly defined as they once were. Ultimately, *Waiting to Exhale* is an examination of what women of the baby-boom generation—particularly African American women—experience as they carve out new roles and lives for themselves.

Critical Context

Waiting to Exhale is McMillan's third published novel. *Mama*, her first, was published in 1987, and *Disappearing Acts*, her second, was published in 1989. Unlike other black women writers whose works are often lyrical and densely symbolic, McMillan works mainly on the level of social realism, relying on a linear plot line and irony to shape the novels and provide both themes and structure. The novels are set in urban locations, and the female protagonists are lusty, frank, and often profane. They are sometimes married and sometimes have children; the men in their lives are usually violent, alcoholic, or so frustrated by social conditions that they cannot function normally as the women desire. Consequently, the women are left with, for example, the five children that Mildred Peacock has in *Mama* and the need somehow to support them by any means possible. Mildred finds work wherever she can and sex when it offers itself. In *Disappearing Acts* , McMillan deals with another strong black woman, Zora Banks. Banks is a musician who is making her living as a teacher in a junior high school. She has moved from Ohio to New York in an attempt to further her ambitions to be a songwriter and recording artist. Problems arise when she meets Franklin, a high-school dropout and intermittent construction worker. Their love for each other is continually threatened by differences in education, ambition, and job security. Frank-lin is given to blaming the whole white world for his plight, and, as might be expected, is finally moved to extreme violence against Zora Banks.

Issues raised in *Mama* and *Disappearing Acts* reappear in *Waiting to Exhale*. These continuing concerns include unstable marital relationships, problems of rearing children in hostile environments, inequities in class and education between black men and women, and questions of where, when, and how satisfactory sexual relationships can take place in a time of changing morés and cultural values.

Bibliography

Isaacs, Susan. "Chilling Out in Phoenix." *The New York Times Book Review* 97 (May 31, 1992): 12. Isaacs makes the point that the book is enjoyable to read but breaks no new literary ground. Rather, the novel is part of a subgenre that focuses on friendship among women. Isaacs praises the novel for its "wicked wit," "breezy humor," and effective treatment of a group of women who remain friends in good times as well as bad.

Publishers Weekly. Review of *Waiting to Exhale*, by Terry McMillan. 239 (March 23, 1992): 58. Praises the novel for its portrayal of four women bound together in "warm, supportive friendship," for its authenticity in characterization, and its broad appeal to a mainstream reading public. Like many of the novel's reviews, this one comments on the profusion of profanities used by the women, which some readers may find disconcerting.

Sellers, Frances Stead. Review of *Waiting to Exhale*, by Terry McMillan. *The Washington Post Book World* 22 (May 24, 1992): 11. Sellers comments on the astonishing success of a novel written for and about educated black women, not yuppies but "buppies," who represent a new black middle class, a subject and a commercial market only recently being explored. Generalized "male-bashing" and the characters' preoccupation with artifacts and morés of the pop culture, Sellers says, grow wearisome.

Smith, Wendy. "Terry McMillan." *Publishers Weekly* 239 (May 11, 1992): 50-51. A thoughtful overview of McMillan's career up to the publication of *Waiting to Exhale*. Based largely on an interview with the author, who energetically defends her depictions of African American men.

Time. Review of *Waiting to Exhale*, by Terry McMillan. 140 (July 20, 1992): 87. Brief review comments that the novel is "high class" soap opera and that the "soap is ivory," the black women being the "whitest black people" seen since television's *The Cosby Show*. Characterizes the novel as a battle between the sexes.

Mary Rohrberger

THE WEDDING

Author: Mary Helen Ponce (1938-   )
Type of plot: Comic realism
Time of plot: The 1950's
Locale: Taconos, a fictional town in Southern California
First published: 1989

> *Principal characters:*
> BLANCA MUÑOZ, a young Mexican American woman who marries
>   Sammy-the-Cricket Lopez
> SAMMY-THE-CRICKET LOPEZ, leader of the Tacones gang
> LUCY MATACOCHIS, Blanca's best friend, a bossy authority on the ways
>   of the characters' world
> TUDI, a Tacones gang member who wishes for a peaceful life
> SALLY, a friend of Blanca who likes Tudi
> FATHER RANGER, the unconsciously hypocritical parish priest

The Novel

    The Wedding fictionally re-creates a small-town barrio (neighborhood) near Los Angeles in the 1950's and traces events surrounding the wedding of Blanca Muñoz and Sammy-the-Cricket Lopez. Ironically contrasting a young woman's romantic dreams with her world's reality, the novel portrays working-class Mexican Americans' ability to live spirited lives on the fringes of society.

    The Wedding's two parts, told by an omniscient narrator, focus mainly on Blanca. The first part ranges from the characters' childhood to just before the wedding. The second part narrates the traditional events of the barrio wedding day.

    The novel begins when the eighteen-year-old Blanca and the twenty-two-year-old Cricket start dating. Both are junior-high-school dropouts with menial jobs; Blanca plucks turkeys, and Cricket collects garbage. Blanca, living at home, helps her mother with expenses. She and her girlfriends fantasize about romance and excitement—specifically, an ideal man with a steady job and a "cool" car. Unglamorous and inexperienced, Blanca lacks criteria for judging men. She finds Sammy-the-Cricket impressive because in fights he knocks his opponents senseless. Cricket is a *pachuco*, one of the 1950's Mexican American youth who wore tailored, baggy "zoot suits" and often were involved in street gangs. Leader of Los Tacones, the neighborhood gang, Cricket had earned his nickname by stomping a member of the rival Planchados gang after beating him up.

    On their first date, Blanca and Cricket see *Gone with the Wind*, a film Blanca has seen ten times, at the drive-in with their friends Tudi and Sally. Tudi, driving his own car, refuses Cricket's urging to ram a car of Planchados who are peacefully leaving the drive-in. During the courtship, Cricket gets Blanca pregnant. Her condition apparently prompts Cricket's offhand suggestion that they marry; however, since the narrative does not mention the couple's intimacies, Blanca's pregnancy becomes obvious only at the wedding dance.

As Blanca plans the wedding, her life's reality intrudes upon her romantic hopes. Blanca wants to be the first in her family to marry ceremonially and thus make her family respectable. Blanca also confronts Cricket's silent, obsessive will to dominate. Cricket sees a wedding as a means of increasing his own social status. Realizing he will not contribute toward expenses, even an overnight honeymoon, Blanca works overtime at turkey-plucking to earn extra money. Traveling by bus to Los Angeles, she buys her wedding dress at a bridal store that sells refurbished factory seconds to Mexican American brides. She selects a *Gone with the Wind*-style gown that allows her to see herself as a real bride and trendsetter, the first bride in Taconos to wear a "colonial" wedding dress. The marked-down veil, adorned with *azares* (wax orange blossoms traditionally worn by Mexican American brides), symbolizes Blanca's yearnings for the wedding and her future.

The wedding day occurs against Blanca's ambivalence: excitement at the day's events; irritation with her expanding body; regret at surrendering her independence and her future paychecks to Cricket; anticipation of her wifely status. During the morning wedding mass, said by Father Ranger, misfortunes undercut romance. Cricket, hung over from partying with his friends, wears his "boppers" (dark glasses), and Blanca must hold him upright. The junior bridesmaid throws up on the hand-embroidered kneeling cushions. Neither bride nor groom receives the sacrament of communion because Cricket, in a screaming fit, had refused to prepare by going to confession.

After the mass, the high-spirited events proceed ceremonially. The wedding party cruises the streets in the Tacones' cars festooned with paper flowers. After the wedding breakfast at maid-of-honor Lucy's, the cars parade into Los Angeles to have the wedding pictures taken. The afternoon reception features a meal provided with dignity by Blanca's mother and the neighborhood women. The Tacones speculate about the possibility that the Planchados might crash the evening's dance. The prevailing opinion among the young people is that only dances with fights are any good.

The wedding dance presents a panorama of guests and wedding participants who are hoping that something will happen. Blanca, recognizing Cricket's ugly egotism, feels unwell but eager for the splendid occasion. She revels in dancing, especially fast numbers. Cricket, threatened by Blanca's skill, sulks because his inept dancing endangers his reputation. As the celebration heightens, Blanca starts to miscarry. When the Planchados arrive, a melee of fighting and dancing ensues. Two ambulances are required: one for the groom and the Planchados leader, and one for the miscarrying bride, who insists that Cricket will change and is worth keeping. Blanca enters the hospital emergency room talking about her beautiful wedding.

The Characters

Blanca Muñoz, the main character, engages the reader's affection despite her narrow vision. Developed through narrative rather than omniscient analysis, she is portrayed as young and fun-loving. She is typical of her poor Mexican American community in that she does not really look ahead to her lack of expectations or her bleak future. She yearns for the good life of love, excitement, and possessions, as these values filter into her lower-class Mexican American town through films, music, and merchandising. In the passivity and remoteness that her man, Cricket, expects of her and in the wifely role she expects to assume, she further typifies difficulties confronting Mexican American women of the 1950's. Blanca plans her wedding to give her life excitement and meaning.

Sammy-the-Cricket Lopez, Blanca's boyfriend and leader of the Tacones gang, provides a vivid example of misplaced values among Taconos' blue-collar males and of the dead-end status that mainstream society assigns uneducated Mexican American men. A *pachuco*, he spends weekends on streetcorners dressed in his zoot suit, preoccupied with egotistical *machismo* (exaggerated masculinity) and waiting for something to happen. With fine irony, his clothes function as the chief image of his leadership. Instead of financially helping his indulgent mother, he works only to buy his tailor-made wardrobe, a habit that does not augur well for Blanca's future paychecks. Though his viciousness as a fighter redeems him in the eyes of some of Taconos' young people, his leadership is negative and local. His failure at transactions with Blanca and with the larger community reveals him as a marginalized personality who can deal with life only through the gestures of frustration.

Father Ranger, the parish priest, quickly loses the reader's respect. He regards his assignment to the Taconos church as an opportunity to indulge his own interests. He recognizes the community's problems and the irrelevance of some of the church's teaching. His apathy makes him emblematic of an institution that could empower its members but instead is part of the problem.

Lucy Matacochis, Blanca's best friend, serves as a tough, quick-witted, abrasive foil to Blanca. Giving the reader a clear-eyed view, she sees Cricket's meanness and advises Blanca not to stay with him. Though she leads a self-involved, rough young life and works in her aunt's bar, she knows how to look out for herself. She presents a flawed but positive image of a Mexican American woman trying to protect her body and her future.

Tudi, Cricket's driver and errand-runner, serves as a foil to Cricket. Recognizing that the rival gangs work amicably side by side during the week, he wishes for peace in the young people's lives. Though decent, Tudi is both literally and metaphorically toothless. Dominated by Cricket and turning to him for guidance in crises, Tudi helps to cause trouble.

Sally, who is sketchily developed as one of Blanca's numerous girlfriends, provides an example of the unselfish values inherent in the community. Gentle and giving, she appreciates Tudi's decency and dislikes Cricket's bullying egotism.

The women of "los turkeys," Blanca's coworkers, serve as a chorus. Advising Blanca and celebrating her mating, they exemplify a vigorous life force.

Themes and Meanings

With humor and sympathy, *The Wedding* treats themes important to Latinos, women, and a multicultural society. The novel is a coming-of-age story that tells of a teenage girl's maturing as a woman. Developing this universal theme, the novel strikingly dramatizes adolescent girls' preoccupations with their physical appearance, their future as women, and men. Since Blanca succeeds within her frame of reference, the novel also dramatizes the reality that many women face quite limited possibilities.

Ponce establishes the themes of *The Wedding* mainly through the Mexican American cultural context. One way she establishes background is through names, the meanings of which may be ironic—"Blanca" and "Taconos," for example. Ponce also ironically develops the novel's cultural themes. She celebrates Blanca's great event while depicting the flaws of Blanca's and the community's frame of reference. In the larger arena, the straightforward narrative reveals the real poverty of the Taconos community. The characters have no myths, superstitions, or dreams to guide them. On the outskirts of "Los," as the young people call Los Angeles, they are cut off from the imaginative past of their Latino heritage. The young men have only posturing *machismo*; the women, scraps of stories and current misinformation about contraception and abortion.

The narrative implies a related social and historical theme: that mainstream institutions have stunted Mexican American minorities by colonizing (isolating and dominating) them to keep them out of the way. The setting of the 1950's, a period of relative complacence and prosperity for American society, creates a backdrop for this concept. Ponce exemplifies the young people's wish to join the mainstream in the fact that they speak their own barrio English rather than Spanish. The schools should provide linguistic and cultural transitions to the larger society; however, they include Blanca and the other Mexican Americans only halfheartedly, with the result that all the young people drop out by the eighth grade. The church, which could provide continuity with a spiritual past and strength to reestablish cultural identity, continues its rituals without seriously engaging the lives of the people in its charge. Blamed for not having skills, the characters have access only to dangerous or physically unpleasant jobs. The novel suggests that though the young people are fascinated by Los Angeles, they have learned to be wary of contact with the larger world and prefer to stay in their neighborhood.

Ponce proposes that, lacking expectations, deprived communities find ways to keep themselves alive. Taconos creates a high-spirited life in events themselves, in spectacle, not in the meaning behind events. Weddings, fights, whatever happens is important. The gangs, which trade insults and punches rather than bullets or knifings, tangle more from boredom and the wish to create action than from hostility. Each event of the wedding day—the mass, the breakfast, the parading cars, the reception, the dance—is as important to the participants as ritual, though none is endowed with overarching meaning. Dramatizing the reasons for the physical and inner poverty of the barrio and its women, Ponce respectfully acknowledges their vitality. Capturing the details of the characters' lives, Ponce's humor affirms serious issues.

Critical Context

Focusing on Mexican American women, *The Wedding* enlarges the themes of Ponce's volume of short stories *Taking Control* (1987). Ironic narratives of sometimes unrecognized failure, these stories depict women attempting to live out their own standards in relation to their Latino culture. Ponce participates in the vigor of Latina fiction writing in the late 1980's, years when Latina writers reflected on their identity in relation to the United States' literary mainstream, to mainstream feminism, and to their own heritage.

Ponce's straightforward narrative, focusing on the characters' actions and conscious lives, distinguishes her method from the dream-sequence and stream-of-consciousness techniques of Latina authors writing in English such as Lucha Corpi in *Delia's Song* (1989) and Cristina Garcia in *Dreaming in Cuban* (1992). Like a number of Latina writers, Ponce takes risks with the English language. Using Spanish phonetic spellings for words in conversations, Ponce veils meaning momentarily and thus reveals the characters' cultural difference. Though she narrates with sometimes broad comicality in *The Wedding*, Ponce's use of humor links her with an aspect of Latina writing that is beginning to receive critical attention.

The Wedding treats the special bicultural reality of Latina women at the same time that it connects with the feminist mainstream. An obvious but important focus of the novel is female subjectivity (woman as the subject of events and of her own life).

The novel also expresses the feminist interest in perceptions of the female body. Constantly evoking the body, its dampness, its smells, and its visceral reactions, Ponce "writes the body." The young women's inscribing their faces and nails with vivid 1950's cosmetics proclaims their sexuality, the color they wish their lives to have, and their outsider status. In her 1990 essay "The Color Red," Ponce observed that in the 1950's, lower-class Mexican Americans wore bright colors that Mexican Americans wanting an "American" look regarded as too vivid.

Through constant references to Blanca's uncomfortable flesh, the novel emphasizes the basic physical level of reality that women in the community occupy. In its silences, the novel also encompasses the concept of women's secret knowledge—about Blanca's intimacy with Cricket, her pregnancy, and her most private emotions.

Bibliography

Hernández, Guillermo. "Satire: An Introduction." In *Chicano Satire: A Study in Literary Culture*. Austin: University of Texas Press, 1991. Hernández examines *pachucos* as historical and literary figures. Originally often seen as comical, this urban counterculture gradually became seen as threatening. Hernández discusses the *pachucos'* trademark "zoot suit" as a distortion of mainstream culture's business suit.

Magnarelli, Sharon. "Taking Control." *Hispania* 71 (December, 1988): 844-845. A review of Ponce's 1987 volume of short stories. Magnarelli focuses on the characters' ironic inability to "take control," a theme Ponce reinforces in *The Wedding*. Magnarelli discusses the characters' "paradoxical combination of insight and blindness," a paradox underlying Blanca's character.

Rebolledo, Tey Diana. "Walking the Thin Line: Humor in Chicana Literature." In *Beyond Stereotypes*, edited by María Herrera-Sobek. Binghamton, N.Y.: Bilingual Press, 1985. This article provides background for Ponce's narrative and linguistic techniques. Rebolledo finds humor used creatively in Chicana writing to deal with anger and to struggle against stereotypes. She lists seven functions of humor in Chicana writing.

Vallejos, Tomás. "Social Insights." *American Book Review* 11 (January, 1990): 13. Vallejos explores sexism in Chicano culture and associates the structure of Ponce's novel—thirteen chapters in part 1 and nine in part 2—with an Aztec prophecy of thirteen time periods of heaven followed by nine periods of hell. He notes that the novel sets the "heavenly" illustrations of the traditional Chicano wedding against the "hellish" reality of the Chicano working class.

Vásquez, Mary S. Review of *The Wedding*, by Mary Helen Ponce. *Hispania* 73 (December, 1990): 1005-1007. Vásquez focuses on Ponce's skill with dialect and on the wedding, which as spectacle fulfills Blanca's dreams. She comments that the "poignant tension between too much and too little" informs the second half of the novel.

Barbara G. Bartholomew

WHEAT THAT SPRINGETH GREEN

Author: J. F. Powers (1917-   )
Type of plot: Philosophical realism
Time of plot: The 1940's to the 1980's
Locale: The American Midwest
First published: 1988

> *Principal characters:*
>
> FATHER JOE HACKETT, a Roman Catholic priest who struggles to find a spiritual life within the confines of the church
>
> FATHER WILLIAM STOCK, a money-oriented priest who is pastor of St. Francis and Clare's, the church that the young Joe Hackett attends
>
> FATHER BILL SCHMIDT, a curate at Joe Hackett's church who moderates his early radicalism and becomes a hardworking parish priest
>
> FATHER LEFTY BEEMAN, a priest who has trouble attending to the business and pastoral affairs of a parish
>
> MONSIGNOR TOOHEY, a brusque administrator of the archdiocese who is the boyhood and clerical enemy of Joe Hackett

The Novel

Wheat That Springeth Green traces the spiritual development of a Roman Catholic priest, Father Joe Hackett, from an adolescent display of the outward manifestations of saintliness at the seminary, through a middle period in which he sinks deeper into the ways of the world, to a final and sudden transformation in which he achieves a true and unassuming spirituality.

The novel is divided into three sections. The first section covers the main character's youth, his time in the seminary, and his early years as a curate in a parish. The early years of Joe Hackett are ordinary, with little to suggest any deep yearning for a religious life. He says that he plans to be either "a businessman or a priest." He is the only child of parents who own a local coal company, so business is a natural career for him. He also seems to be attracted to the life of a priest, however, since it appeals to his idealism and desire to help the poor. His youthful days end with a similar division in his career choices; he experiences a sexual initiation but then confesses that sin. Joe will not overcome this division between the body and the soul until the end of the novel.

At the seminary, Joe has a yearning for a fuller spiritual life, in contrast to both the majority of students and the faculty. This desire, however, is more a matter of pride than holiness. Joe seems to equate spirituality with wearing a hair shirt; he wears the hair shirt even after the rector has asked him not to. As a result, he becomes isolated and is in conflict with nearly everyone in the seminary. Ironically, when Joe becomes a priest in a parish, he finds that the pastor, Father Van Slagg, spends all of his time in the church pursuing the spiritual life that Joe has desired so fervently. As a result, Joe is forced to deal with the everyday events of the parish; he has no time for prayer or contemplation. He then spends five years at Archdiocesan Charities working as an administrator. He has more time for prayer but little desire to engage in contemplation. He moves further from a spiritual life with each office he holds.

In the next section, Joe is a pastor of his boyhood parish, St. Francis and Clare's, and he has abandoned all desires for a fuller spiritual life. He drinks and eats too much. He is portrayed as watching baseball on television with a drink in his hand, and he is never seen praying in the church. He is, instead, engaged in parish projects such as building a rectory or searching for the proper bed to purchase for his new assistant priest. When that assistant, Bill Schmidt, takes up his position, he is contrasted with Joe Hackett; Bill has some of the same spiritual pretensions that Joe had in his younger days. When the young curate and his friends discuss problems in the church, Joe takes the conservative position he scorned at the seminary. Bill and his friends make Joe uncomfortable; this helps to prod him out of the passivity and comfort into which he has fallen. There are other assaults on his role as a priest; he gets telephone calls from an unidentified parishioner calling his saintliness into question. This unidentified voice is providential, since it challenges Joe to alter his worldly life and stirs him from his spiritual sloth.

A deeper conflict develops in Joe's parish when the archbishop of the diocese sends out a high monetary assessment to all parishes. Joe has prided himself on not turning the pulpit into a money-making operation as his former pastor, Father Stock, did. He decides not to appeal to his parishioners but to badger delinquent parishioners to pay their share. The search for the necessary funds exhausts both Joe and Bill, but his conflict is providentially resolved when Father Stock dies and leaves Joe a legacy of ten thousand dollars. Joe uses the legacy to meet the assessment of the archbishop. It also enables him to spare his parishioners. Joe's determination not to turn the church into an institution that is more concerned with money that the Gospel suggests that Joe still has a desire for a fuller spiritual life. The title of the novel is from a song that describes the emergence of green wheat after it has been buried for many days in the dark earth; Joe Hackett is about to emerge from his spiritual slumber.

A change in Joe comes about in the last section of the book. He takes a vacation and visits a religious house of the Blue Friars, where he refuses both food and liquor, a clear indication that he is changing his life. He spends the rest of his vacation working at a Catholic Worker house for derelicts in Montreal, a pastoral activity that Joe never considered in his role as a parish priest and pastor. In the last episode of the book, there is a surprise party for Joe, and it is revealed that he is leaving the parish to become a Catholic Worker. He is abandoning his life of ease and his obsession with material things. He discovers a true spiritual life as he ends his life of ease and accepts the "cross" that is the lot of those who follow Christ.

The Characters

Joe Hackett is the protagonist of the novel; the point of view is limited omniscient, and everything is filtered through his consciousness. He is a man and a priest with many faults. His early attempts at spirituality come more from pride than love of God. He wears a hair shirt to show his saintliness, but it is merely an outward sign. He is closer to the Pharisees of the New Testament than to Christ. He soon discovers that he has no time to develop his spiritual side; he must spend all of his time attending to the business of the parish. When he becomes a pastor, all spiritual thoughts seem to vanish. His life as a pastor is marked by visits to the liquor store and by watching television with a drink, and his pride has been replaced by an acceptance of worldly things. His one heroic moment is ironically linked to the world; he prevents a robbery at his local liquor store. There is, however, a yearning in Joe for a fuller and truly spiritual life, which he finds at the end of the novel.

Bill Schmidt is Joe's curate, and he begins as a typical young priest who wishes to overturn all the rules and practices of the church. His rebellion is a mirror image of the earlier stance of Joe, and he helps Joe to see himself more fully. In addition, Bill acts as a goad to challenge Joe's life of ease. Bill's friendship with a drop-out from the seminary creates conflict between him and Joe, but Bill gradually changes as he sees the irresponsibility of his earlier views, and he begins to work selflessly in the parish. In a sense, he is acting like the true pastor of the church, as the unidentified caller keeps reminding Joe.

Father Felix is a monk who comes to St. Francis and Clare's every Sunday to say Mass. He loves the life of the monastery. In contrast to Joe, he has little need for material things. He also is not as conservative as Joe is in church matters, as he displays some sympathy for Bill and his friends, especially their anger at the stress the church places on money and business matters. He is used as an ironic foil to Joe, although he is comically represented in the abstruse sermons he delivers, which are filled with allusions to the medieval world and seem to produce unexpected results.

Father Lefty Beeman is another comic character. He is an incompetent priest who has twice been appointed as a pastor and has twice failed. He is interested in the politics of the church, although he always seems to be wrong about new developments and appointments. He is, perhaps, Joe's closest friend, and he repeatedly joins him for drinks. At the end of the novel, he is given another chance at becoming a pastor as he takes over St. Francis and Clare's.

Father William Stock is the antagonist in the novel. He spends all of his time raising funds for the church. Every sermon is a demand for money, and he is called "Dollar Bill" by his exasperated parishioners. He changes at the end of his life, however, sending Joe a note admitting his guilt and giving him a legacy to right the wrong.

Monsignor Toohey is an amusing character who manages to enrage everyone in the novel with his irritating style as a diocesan administrator. He is a boyhood enemy of Joe Hackett who continues to plague him in the priesthood.

Themes and Meanings

Wheat That Springeth Green has many themes. The first deals with the dual roles of a Catholic priest. A priest is supposed to spend his life in prayer and contemplation in order to be brought closer to God. Yet he also has to involve himself in fund-raising, building, supervising a school, and seeing to the administration of a parish if the church is to be sustained. Paradoxically, it is harder for a man who has supposedly dedicated his life to God to find time to speak with God; a priest has to serve both God and Mammon. Neither Father Van Slagg's life of prayer nor Father Stock's worldliness resolves the dilemma. Joe Hackett does not seem able to find a way out of this dilemma, and his interaction with people inside and outside the church is deficient in spirituality. It is only when Joe truly gives himself to others by working at a Catholic Workers home for derelicts that he discovers a spiritual role within the world. He is then called on to make sacrifices and give up his ease and desire for the things of the world.

Powers also examines the contrast between true and false spirituality. False spirituality is portrayed as relying on outward signs such as the hair shirt. It calls attention to the person performing self-conscious rites and isolates a person from others. Powers shows these practices as pretentious and unfulfilling. True spirituality consists of unassuming deeds rather than public displays of sanctity. When Joe accepts the "cross" at the end of the novel, he does so in a quiet and selfless manner. A true spiritual life seems to be defined as not merely removing oneself from the world but in giving oneself to those in need within the world. When Joe is ministering to derelicts in Montreal, he is on the true path. He is told to "keep it up," a sure indication that he has finally found his true vocation.

Finally, Powers explores the Roman Catholic church as a historical institution. He shows the problems and difficulties the church has in adapting to challenges by young priests for changes and the continuing need for expanding facilities in the burgeoning suburbs. Powers documents the problems some priests have with alcohol in this novel and in his earlier fiction. Joe Hackett makes so many visits to the liquor store that it becomes an ironic motif in itself. The structure of the novel suggests that there is a built-in division that all parish priests must face. As secular priests, their mission is to be among the people they serve. Yet how can they be within the world and not surrender to it? *Wheat That Springeth Green* acknowledges this problem and suggests that it cannot be successfully resolved by abandoning parish work. Priests must live a life dedicated to helping those in need and rejecting the comforts and snares of the world. That life of caring necessarily involves living simply as a priest instead of as a businessman or administrator.

Critical Context

Wheat That Springeth Green is J. F. Powers' second novel, and it continues his investigation of the life of the American priest. The earlier collections of short stories, *Prince of Darkness and Other Stories* (1947) and *The Presence of Grace* (1956), dealt with the problems of the Catholic priesthood. In stories such as "The Valiant Woman," Powers suggests that salvation is an outgrowth of daily annoyances and problems. A life of calm and ease is not, to Powers, a Christian life; the worldly priest at the end of "The Prince of Darkness" is given a letter informing him that Christ gives people "not peace but a sword." For Powers, the enemy is not Satan but the spiritual sloth that a life of ease creates. The fuller portrait of an American priest in *Morte d'Urban* (1962) is very similar to that in *Wheat That Springeth Green*. Both characters are captured by the wiles of the world but reverse their course suddenly at the end of the novel. Father Urban becomes the saintly leader of his community of priests, and Joe Hackett joins the Catholic Workers. Powers' vision is essentially comic both in its representation of the absurdities that come with the priestly life and with his optimistic resolution of the spiritual struggle of those priests. Divine providence is still there to redirect his wayward priests who have lost their way on the path to Christ.

Bibliography

The Atlantic. Review of *Wheat That Springeth Green*, by J. F. Powers. 262 (January, 1988): 15. A brief, unsigned review of the novel that stresses Powers' elegant writing and humor.

Clark, Walter H., Jr. "A Richter Scale Can Be Handy." *Commonweal* 115 (November 4, 1988): 592-594. Includes a discussion of the theological implications of the novel. Clark sees the spiritual change within Joe, and he credits Bill Schmidt with helping to bring about that change.

Hagopian, John V. *J. F. Powers*. New York: Twayne, 1968. This first full-length study of Powers was published twenty years before *Wheat That Springeth Green*, but it remains a useful introduction to Powers' life and works. Hagopian discusses Powers' important stories, and there is an extensive analysis of *Morte d'Urban*.

Iannone, Carol. "The Second Coming of J. F. Powers." *Commentary* 87, no. 1 (1989): 62-64. This essay presents a brief overview of Powers' work and a fuller discussion of *Wheat That Springeth Green*. Iannone criticizes what she sees as the sudden and unconvincing ending of the novel.

Moynihan, Julian. "Waiting for God in Inglenook." *The New York Review of Books* (December 8, 1988) 51-52. Moynihan stresses the balance of joy and sorrow in the novel, and he points out the effectiveness of the comic scenes.

James Sullivan

WHITE BUTTERFLY

Author: Walter Mosley (1952-   )
Type of plot: Detective and mystery
Time of plot: 1956
Locale: Los Angeles, California
First published: 1992

Principal characters:

EZEKIEL "EASY" RAWLINS, a clandestine property owner and part-time detective

REGINA RAWLINS, Easy's wife, a nurse who is troubled by Easy's apparently ill-gotten wealth

EDNA, the Rawlins' infant daughter

JESUS, Easy's adopted son, a Mexican American rescued by Easy in an earlier novel

RAYMOND "MOUSE" ALEXANDER, Easy's best but most dangerous friend

QUINTEN NAYLOR, the black policeman who originally tries to get Easy involved with the investigation

MOFASS, the front man for Easy's business operations

ROBIN GARNETT, the first white victim in the series of murders Easy is asked to investigate

The Novel

White Butterfly takes place in 1956. Ezekiel "Easy" Rawlins, the hero of Walter Mosley's previous two detective novels, is now married to a beautiful black nurse named Regina. Easy and Regina are rearing two children, their infant daughter, Edna, and Jesus, a young Mexican American boy rescued by Easy in an earlier adventure. This life is not idyllic, however. Easy has not told Regina about his secret business holdings or the detective work he does on the side for friends and the police. There are also other instances of miscommunication between the two that cloud the future of their marriage.

The situation worsens when Easy is approached first by black policeman Quinten Naylor and then by a slew of high city officials for help in tracing a serial murderer loose in Watts. This final burst of attention is brought about by the first white victim, Robin Garnett. Up until this time, the victims had been black prostitutes and exotic dancers. The white victim, however, was a college student from a respectable family. Like the other victims, her body was partly burned and mutilated. Easy resents the sudden concern of the white officials, apathetic when the victims were black. He is nevertheless coerced into helping when the police threaten to pin the crimes on Easy's best friend, Mouse.

Easy goes to work, frequenting bars and asking questions that lead him to a suspect and to a disturbing revelation. The white coed led a double life, coming down to Watts to work as a stripper/prostitute known as "the White Butterfly." When Easy reports this to the police, he is told to abandon this line of inquiry, partly because the girl's father is a former district attorney. Curiosity gets the better of Easy, and he goes to speak to the girl's mother, who is understandably upset. The police chastise Easy and penalize him by arresting Mouse. Easy talks the police into releasing Mouse, and the two of them track the suspect, a black man, to San Francisco. They locate him just in time to witness his death in a bar fight, one set up by the local police. They also learn that San Francisco has had a chain of similar serial murders about which the black population was never informed. The suspect's death becomes the final step in a scandalous coverup.

Frustrated, Easy returns to Los Angeles, where he learns that Robin Garnett supposedly had a baby. When he attempts to put the girl's parents in touch with the woman keeping the baby, he is arrested for extortion. Easy reveals that Robin was killed by her father, Vernor Garnett, in order to avoid embarrassment over his daughter's conduct. Garnett's connections to law enforcement officials had given him knowledge of the serial murders, and he had tried to pass his daughter's murder off as another in the series.

Amid all this, Easy decides to be more open with Regina, but it is too late. Regina has run off with another man, taking Edna with her. Easy is left heartbroken, turning to the bottle until Mouse and Jesus bring him back from the brink of self-destruction.

A side plot involves Mofass, the man who manages Easy's business holdings. Mofass gets himself into trouble with white developers from whom he received a bribe. Although Easy will not bail Mofass out of trouble, the two work together to get the upper hand over the white businessmen. Although Easy's marriage fails, he is able to solidify his finances and, therefore, his independence.

The Characters

Easy Rawlins is in many ways the typical private investigator of hard-boiled detective fiction. He works essentially for his own ends and is a free agent. He has a strong desire to uncover truth, even if he is the only one who ever possesses it, and to bring about justice, even when it is inconsistent with the law. A healthy dose of compassion, as exhibited by his love for his adopted son, Jesus, makes Easy a particularly well-drawn model of the hard-boiled detective as pioneered by major figures such as Dashiell Hammett's Sam Spade, Raymond Chandler's Phillip Marlowe, and Ross MacDonald's Lew Archer. In short, Easy is a crusader for justice and truth in an unjust and illusory world.

Easy is not flawless. He drinks too much and is susceptible to certain male impulses. Easy is also complex. His character combines cynicism, based on his knowledge of the ways of the world, with idealism, based on his belief in a better world with which his conduct is in accord. Easy's racial identity is also crucial to understanding his character. Whereas other private eyes are alienated philosophically from an unjust world, Easy himself is a member of an oppressed race. Part of the challenge he faces involves dealing with white powerholders from a position of socially imposed inferiority. Easy manages to triumph despite this obstacle, solving mysteries and keeping the authorities off his back. He also struggles to keep an even keel in his personal life.

Mouse represents a different model of accommodation to American racism. Put simply, Mouse is a killer. Easy, too, could kill when he served in the armed forces during World War II, but he has scruples and hesitates to use violence. Mouse has a hair-trigger personality, particularly when he perceives a threat to his manhood. As such, he is adept at dealing with the heavy-handed white developers in *White Butterfly*. In the two previous Easy Rawlins novels, it was Mouse who killed the primary villain, in the nick of time to save Easy. This suggests a complementary relationship between Easy and Mouse. Without Easy, Mouse's violence would be random and ultimately self-destructive; without Mouse, Easy would have been dead well before the events in *White Butterfly* ever took place.

Quinten Naylor represents a third model of accommodation to racial inequality and injustice. Educated and decidedly "East Coast" in his demeanor, Naylor deals with the racial obstacles facing him by achieving a position of authority. Unlike Easy, Naylor has to stay within the law, even when the law is unjust. On the other hand, Naylor is treated as an equal by most of his fellow police detectives and, within certain narrow limits, is able to reduce the severity of police brutality and other injustices suffered disproportionately by African Americans. Naylor works from within the system to make small but significant dents in American racism.

Mofass, Easy's front man, is consumed by greed. His response to racial subordination is to use his wits to accumulate wealth through any means available. Unfortunately, Mofass somehow always manages to outsmart himself, suggesting that greed is ultimately self-destructive.

Regina, Easy's wife, plays a small but important role in the novel. Because of the inner turmoil experienced by Easy as he deals with racial oppression, he finds it difficult to open up to Regina. They miscommunicate in tragic ways and ultimately break up. Although the theme is not overtly elaborated, Easy's marriage to Regina is a hidden casualty of racism, as is the general relationship between black men and women in American literature and life.

Robin and Vernor Garnett are also, in a manner of speaking, victims of racism. Robin is drawn to Watts by the forbidden fruit of black sexuality. Vernor Garnett is driven to murder by the disgrace of interracial relationships even as recently as the 1950's.

Themes and Meanings

White Butterfly is a hard-boiled detective novel that explores important racial themes. The hard-boiled genre features a lean style of language, suspense, fast-paced action, and psychological as well as social realism. As Raymond Chandler pointed out in his essay "The Simple Art of Murder," hard-boiled detective literature differs from the more "civilized" British detective story in its focus on the "mean streets" of America's cities and real motives behind human behavior. Rather than unraveling puzzling crimes (for example, locked door mysteries), hard-boiled writers explore the puzzle of the human heart.

The detective in hard-boiled literature is usually a lonely "knight," full of human flaws yet somehow devoted to truth and justice, so devoted that he or she is willing to risk life and limb for a small payment or no payment at all. Unlike police officers, hard-boiled detectives are not limited by their bureaucratic position or by the law; they do face other limits. They usually end up coping with the world's injustices rather than bringing about complete reform.

Easy Rawlins is just such a loner. Despite his personal flaws, he takes risks and bends rules to make the world a little better. He also has a hunger to know the truth, though he is willing to lie if it serves his purposes. What distinguishes Mosley's work is that the social realism he deals with involves the issue of race. The theme of color in Mosley's title is notable and alludes to Duke Ellington's song "Black Butterfly."

Following such prominent authors as Richard Wright, Ralph Ellison, and Chester Himes, Mosley explores the problems of black identity in a hostile homeland, police brutality (as well as more subtle forms of discrimination), and the depth of black alienation. Perhaps most poignant is his treatment of violence as a theme. Mosley's Easy Rawlins hesitates to use violence except in self-defense. On the other hand, Easy is aided by his friend Mouse's willingness, even eagerness, to use violence. This collaboration between Easy and Mouse speaks directly to the dilemma faced by black Americans as they struggle for the appropriate means to obtain justice.

Mosley's examination of race in America also has a historical dimension. Mosley's first three novels are part of a projected eight-book series chronicling the history of Watts (and the United States) from 1948 to the early 1990's.

Critical Context

White Butterfly is Walter Mosley's third novel, following *Devil in a Blue Dress* (1990) and *A Red Death* (1991). All three books feature Easy Rawlins and Mouse, and all three have been commercially and critically successful. Part of Mosley's success can be attributed to the existence of a ready market for variations within the hard-boiled detective genre.

This genre is associated most often with early pioneers Dashiell Hammett, Raymond Chandler, and Ross MacDonald, but by the time Mosley started writing there were dozens of successful authors working within the genre. In addition, the previously white, male realm of the private investigator had given way to a diverse group, including a number of female detectives as well as an occasional African American, such as Jackson F. Burke's Sam Kelly, Ken Davis' Carver Bascombe, and Ed Lacy's Toussaint Moore.

Mosley has established himself as something more than a detective writer, however. He has used the form of the traditional hard-boiled detective story to explore important racial themes. Mosley has notable predecessors in this respect. Hammett explored the issue of race briefly in his short story "Nightshade" (anthologized in 1944), and Harry Whittingham's 1961 novel *Journey into Violence* explores southern racism in a political context. Mosley's closest precursor is Chester Himes. Himes's first novel, *If He Hollers, Let Him Go*, takes place in Los Angeles and uses a hard-boiled prose style to explore the issues of racial justice and black alienation. Himes's novel ends with the main character, Bob Jones, about to enter the Army in 1943; Mosley's Easy Rawlins starts his tales just after serving in the war.

Bibliography

Baker, Robert A., and Michael T. Nietzel. *Private Eyes: One Hundred and One Knights, a Survey of American Detective Fiction, 1922-1984*. Bowling Green, Ohio: Bowling Green State University Popular Press, 1985. Provides a lively introduction to the range of variations on the hard-boiled detective theme. Illustrates Easy Rawlins' precursors as well as his uniqueness.

Chandler, Raymond. *The Simple Art of Murder*. New York: Pocket Books, 1953. Chandler's essay that gives the book its title distinguishes the hard-boiled detective genre from the less realistic "British" mystery genre, exemplified by the work of Agatha Christie.

Geherin, David. *The American Private Eye: The Image in Fiction*. New York: Frederick Ungar, 1985. Geherin examines some of the more prominent fictional private eyes, discussing development and common attributes. Features a chapter on the "compassionate" private eyes, among whom Easy Rawlins would certainly be numbered.

Hitchens, Christopher. "The Tribes of Walter Mosley." *Vanity Fair* 56 (February, 1993): 46-50. Using the favorable comments of newly elected president Bill Clinton as a springboard, this interview features Mosley's assessment of his mixed (black and Jewish) cultural roots.

Hughes, Carl Milton. *The Negro Novelist: A Discussion of the Writings of American Negro Novelists, 1940-1950*. Freeport, N.Y.: Books for Libraries Press, 1967. Looking at authors such as Ralph Ellison, Chester Himes, and Richard Wright, this book reveals deep-seated themes explored by an earlier generation of pioneering black writers. Despite his identity as a detective novelist, Mosley's work clearly harks back to these themes.

Lomax, Sara M. "Double Agent Easy Rawlins: The Development of a Cultural Detective." *American Visions* 7 (April/May, 1992): 32-34. Provides some details on Mosley's life and career. Also makes a preliminary attempt to fit his work into the tradition of black literature.

Mason, Theodore O., Jr. "Walter Mosley's Easy Rawlins: The Detective and Afro-American Fiction." *Kenyon Review* 14 (Fall, 1992): 173-183. Discusses Mosley's first novel, *Devil in a Blue Dress*, in the light of the African American novelistic tradition. Cites several modern critics as providing a solid foundation for reading Mosley's and other African American detective fiction.

Mosley, Walter. "A Message Louder than a Billion Pleas." *Los Angeles Times*, May 5, 1992, p. B7. In this brief commentary article, Mosley discusses the Rodney King episode and subsequent uprising in Watts. Mosley asks readers to consider the videotape excerpts of King's beating by police in the light of the oral history of black Americans. Mosley's projected series of novels will look specifically at the Watts riots of the 1960's and 1990's.

Ira Smolensky

WHITE NOISE

Author: Don DeLillo (1936-   )
Type of plot: Philosophical realism
Time of plot: The 1980's
Locale: Blacksmith, a fictional college town in the United States
First published: 1985

> *Principal characters:*
> JACK GLADNEY, a college professor specializing in studies of Adolf Hitler
> BABETTE GLADNEY, Jack's neurotic wife
> STEFFIE GLADNEY, their nine-year-old daughter, obsessed with health
> HEINRICH GLADNEY, Jack's son by a previous marriage, whom Babette
>   fears will become a mass murderer
> MURRAY JAY SISKIND, Jack's friend, an Elvis Presley specialist
> ALPHONSE STOMPANATO, the head of the popular culture department
> WILLIE MINK, Babette's drug supplier and seducer

The Novel

At once hilarious and horrifying, Don DeLillo's *White Noise* dramatizes a contemporary American family's attempt to deal with the mundane conflicts of day-to-day life while grappling with the larger philosophical issues of love, death, and the possibility of happiness in an uncertain world. The novel is divided into three sections. All incidents, images, and exchanges among characters in the first section, "Waves and Radiation," culminate thematically in the second section, "The Airborne Toxic Event." The third section, "Dylarama," chronicles not only the direct effects of the "event" but also the indirect but even more profound changes in the way the characters subsequently see themselves and their world.

The novel's first-person narrator is Jack Gladney, a college professor specializing in studies of Adolf Hitler. Many of the other characters are also in some sense observers of contemporary culture: Murray Jay Siskind, an Elvis Presley specialist; Jack's other colleagues in the popular culture department; his son Heinrich, who translates technical information to his father and the reader; and his daughter Steffie, whose obsession with health has made her into an expert in drugs and medical matters. The bulk of the novel is less a sequence of important events than a series of dialogues concerning various interests and obsessions.

Immediately after the opening chapter, with its description of incoming college students—luggage, stereos, tennis rackets, and other equipment in tow—Jack goes home and discusses with his wife Babette what he has just witnessed. In the middle of the discussion, Babette remarks that she can hardly imagine people with such material wealth being concerned with death. The comment seems irrelevant to the subject at hand, and neither she nor Jack pursues it. DeLillo has subtly introduced a theme that will grow larger over the course of the novel, that of death, and how one can live in full knowledge of its inevitability.

The remainder of part 1 follows much the same pattern, with Jack and someone else discussing a phenomenon that at first may seem only mildly interesting (the ominously beautiful sunsets, some strange pills of Babette's that Jack discovers) but that involve associations that acquire greater power through repetition (the environment, conspiracies of one kind or another, and, always, death).

The action begins to accelerate in part 2, in which a train derailment unleashes a noxious drifting cloud. The fact that no one knows much with certainty about the cloud—or if "they" know, they are not telling—adds to Jack and his family's anxiety. Eventually, they leave their home and join a caravan of refugees fleeing the toxic event zone. Jack is briefly exposed to the cloud. The family finally is quarantined alongside hundreds of others in a large barracks. Nine days later they are allowed to return home.

In part 3, Jack and his family must deal with the physical and emotional effects of the toxic event. For Jack, the most tangible effect is a "nebulous mass" discovered during an X-ray examination. The mass may mean nothing or it may mean, eventually, death. Jack is equally worried about Babette after he finds a cache of Dylar tablets. He learns that the drug is designed to treat a peculiar neurosis, the excessive fear of death. After confronting Babette, Jack also finds that she has been "purchasing" the experimental drug by having sex with the sleazy Willie Mink. Jack confronts Willie, then shoots him, but not fatally.

The novel ends, appropriately, with very little resolved. Mink is in the hospital but apparently thinks he has shot himself. Babette still fears death, as does Jack, and the sunsets are still ominously glorious.

The Characters

One of the principal philosophical conclusions of *White Noise* is that people act less than they are acted upon, as victims of forces beyond their control or knowing. Appropriately, Jack, the central character, does very little in the novel. His one dramatic action is to shoot Willie Mink, but this has no more practical effect on the direction of the novel than the tossing of a pebble has on the course of a river. Jack sees, listens, thinks, and comments, but there is little that he can do. Mostly, he thinks about death and chaos in reference to himself, his family, and ultimately American society.

Babette broadens and intensifies the emotional impact of themes that Jack, early in the novel, considers mostly in the abstract. When it is discovered that the apparently normal Babette has been taking drugs (at the expense of giving herself to the contemptible Willie Mink), for example, Jack realizes that her fears are symptomatic of life in modern America.

Similarly, their nine-year-old daughter Steffie's precocious knowledge of pharmaceuticals and health matters indicates her to be a budding Babette. At some point in the future she will become obsessed with death, if she is not already.

Her half-brother Heinrich serves a similar, although more complex, function. Like

Steffie, he is precociously aware of the intricacies of modern technological society, his field of expertise being science and the media. Whereas Steffie is vigilant in protecting herself and her parents against potential harm, Heinrich is fascinated with and more a product of his culture. In one funny and disturbing scene, Heinrich and his father argue for three pages whether it is raining. Heinrich refuses to acknowledge what his senses clearly tell him because the radio weather report said that it would not rain until later in the day.

Murray Jay Siskind is involved in none of the major scenes in the novel, but he provides the reader, through his conversations with Jack, with insights into popular American culture. The scene in which Jack and Murray simultaneously lecture to a class on the lives of Hitler and Elvis, for example, is a comic and thought-provoking masterpiece.

Lecherous, amoral, rodent-like Willie Mink is modern society sunk to its sleazy, wretched low. He serves as a marker of the depths of American culture and morals.

Because contemporary culture is so vividly and convincingly rendered, DeLillo's characters impress the reader with their individual realities. Their most important function, however, is to represent certain thematic positions or reactions to various aspects of modern society. They are less actors than voices in a symposium on life and death in America.

Themes and Meanings

In *White Noise*, the characters themselves announce the themes—death, the nature of reality, government conspiracies, the possibility of happiness in contemporary America—and then analyze them through their thoughts and especially through their conversations throughout the novel. *White Noise* is, therefore, as much a symposium or colloquy as it is a traditional realistic novel.

The various themes and conflicts in the novel can be summed up in one question: Why are modern people so unhappy? No character in the novel suffers from hunger or poverty. The novel begins and ends, in fact, in a context of material comfort and plenitude. The opening scene of parents helping their sons and daughters unload their belongings in preparation for the first days of college makes Jack uneasy and leads Babette to think of death. The last scene takes place in a supermarket with shelves laden with items that the characters certainly have the wherewithal to purchase; because the shelves have recently been rearranged, however, the shoppers are unsettled to the point of neurosis and desperation.

One problem with American life may be that people mistakenly believe that their problems are idiosyncratically modern and American. They try to invent new remedies, such as psychoanalysis, space-age drugs, and self-indulgent material goods, for afflictions that are not new at all. *White Noise* is replete with imagery connecting the present and the past. The black cloud issuing from the train derailment, for example, reminds Jack of a Norwegian death ship. Jack, his family, and the others fleeing the cloud are not, he realizes, much different from refugees of ages past. Jack is not the only one to make such a connection. His son Heinrich laments or enthuses (it is not always possible to tell with Heinrich) that they seem to have been plunged back into the Stone Age. Later, a fellow refugee complains that they have all been quarantined like lepers in the Middle Ages.

Jack and the others concern themselves with death, love, infidelity, the fear of the unknown, and the question of what is knowable. These are problems and issues that have plagued humanity since Adam met Eve. If the problems seem worse today, it is not because the issues have changed—death is death, after all—but because people seem to have convinced themselves that the afflictions of the human heart, body, and spirit can be addressed and assuaged by modern technology.

The characters in *White Noise* are surrounded by things that consume their time, energy, and hope but ultimately do no good. Television and radio bombard them with information that is of no real value. The computers that supposedly have transformed the world cannot save it from regressing to the Stone Age. Babette's Dylar may be a wonder drug, but it does not save her from fear of death. If modern people are more unhappy than their predecessors, it is because disillusionment—with themselves and with the sparkling edifice of modernity—has been added to the age-old infirmities of humanity.

Critical Context

Although once almost a cult figure in contemporary American fiction, by the 1980's Don DeLillo had carved out that most desirable of literary niches for himself, as both a best-selling novelist and an award-winning darling of critics. This position was cemented in 1985 with the publication of *White Noise*, a best-seller and winner of the American Book Award.

DeLillo has built his reputation on a series of novels remarkable for their variety of subject matter within a consistency of theme. *Ratner's Star* (1976) is a science-fiction novel; *The Names* (1982) is a novel of political intrigue; and *Libra* (1988) is a historical novel dramatizing and offering a theory of the assassination of John F. Kennedy. Not all are as funny as *White Noise* often is, but in all of them DeLillo shows himself to be a witty writer who can vividly invoke a cast of colorful characters beset by paranoia and the catastrophes of modern life.

DeLillo's style is distinctive and his themes are consistent, so that one can identify a DeLillo novel after reading only a few paragraphs, despite the variety of subject matter. DeLillo nevertheless does not work apart from and outside literary tradition. His like-minded contemporaries and literary antecedents are more obvious than obscure.

The contemporary writer with whom DeLillo is most obviously aligned is Thomas Pynchon, who, in novels such as *Gravity's Rainbow* (1973), dramatizes humanity's precarious existence in a technological nightmare-world where conspiracy abounds.

Both DeLillo and Pynchon are inheritors of two recent literary movements, the Beat school and the "black humor" movement. The Beat writers—Jack Kerouac and Williams S. Burroughs prominent among the novelists and Allen Ginsberg most famous among the poets—lent their manic voices in the 1950's and 1960's to an outcry against a materialistic, soulless American plutocracy. DeLillo's Jack Gladney would surely share their sentiments. The black humor or absurdist writers—among them Joseph Heller and Eugène Ionesco—offered less a specifically political and American agenda than a philosophical stance toward humanity and its condition: Life is absurd, and in the face of it all one can do, most often, is to laugh hysterically. All of these writers belong to the rich tradition of satirists who look unflinchingly at people and their pretentions, communicating their horror and humor to the reader.

Bibliography
Aaron, Daniel. "How to Read Don DeLillo." *South Atlantic Quarterly* 89 (Spring, 1990): 305-319. Aaron provides a general survey of the salient elements in De-Lillo's fiction. He addresses various themes and concerns under such headings as "catastrophe" and "conspiracy." *White Noise* figures prominently in his examples.
DeCurtis, Anthony. " 'An Outsider in This Society': An Interview with Don DeLillo." *South Atlantic Quarterly* 89 (Spring 1990): 281-304. Especially important and interesting because DeLillo is generally so reluctant to speak or write about himself. Most of the interview focuses on *Libra*, then recently published. The last several pages, however, largely concern *White Noise*.
Goodheart, Eugene. "Some Speculations on Don DeLillo and the Cinematic Real." *South Atlantic Quarterly* 89 (Spring, 1990): 355-368. Goodheart notes that DeLillo characteristically puts the "existence of the self into question." This old theme is made fresh by the use of cinematic techniques that make the characters, even in their own eyes, two-dimensional. *White Noise* is discussed at length.
King, Noel. "Reading *White Noise*: Floating Remarks." *The Critical Quarterly* 33 (Autumn, 1991): 66-83. King begins with a theoretical discussion of the term "postmodern." He concludes that *White Noise* is at once a "quite traditional novel" and a meditation of the postmodern. The novel shows modern times as an age of "distorted communication and information."
McClure, John A. "Postmodern Romance: Don DeLillo and the Age of Conspiracy." *South Atlantic Quarterly* 89 (Spring, 1990): 337-353. McClure addresses the concept of the conspiracy, prevalent in DeLillo's fiction. Historical currents are the stuff of romance; DeLillo's modern heroes locate romance in espionage and conspiracy. McClure discusses DeLillo in a context of such writers as Joseph Conrad, E. M. Forster, and Graham Greene.

Dennis Vannatta

WIND FROM AN ENEMY SKY

Author: D'Arcy McNickle (1904-1977)
Type of plot: Historical realism
Time of plot: The first half of the twentieth century
Locale: Western Montana, in the area near Flathead Lake and St. Ignatius
First published: 1978

Principal characters:

BULL, the leader of the Little Elk Indian tribe
HENRY JIM, Bull's elder brother, who adopts the ways of whites
ANTOINE, Bull's grandson, recently returned from a government school
  in Oregon
TWO SLEEPS, a holy man, a seer adopted by the tribe
POCK FACE, Bull's nephew, who kills a white man
LOUIS, Pock Face's father
THEOBALD, Pock Face's mild-mannered cousin, son of Basil
TOBY RAFFERTY, the superintendent of the government agency that over-
  sees the Little Elk Indians
DOC EDWARDS, a government physician
JIM COOKE, Adam Pell's nephew, who is murdered by Pock Face
ADAM PELL, the builder of a dam on Little Elk land
THE BOY, a Native American intermediary

The Novel

In *Wind from an Enemy Sky*, D'Arcy McNickle, a member of the Confederated Salish and Kutenai tribes of the Flathead Indian Reservation, born and educated in Montana, writes of the difficult period in American history during which the United States government attempted to subdue Native Americans peacefully. McNickle, a government employee for most of his life, presents a balanced view of what occurred during this period in one small Native American enclave in the Flathead Lake-St. Ignatius area of Montana.

On the surface, McNickle presents the story of a Native American extended family that includes Pock Face, who, carrying his grandfather's rifle, steals furtively into a canyon where white developers have built a dam on tribal land. The Little Elk Indians equate the damming of their river with its murder. The dam has an immediate negative impact upon fishing and farming on their tribal lands.

As Pock Face and Theobald, his cousin, approach the dam, they spy a white man walking across its surface. Pock Face fires one shot. Jim Cooke, ironically on his last day of work before going east to marry, dies instantly.

The remainder of the story revolves around the government's efforts to mete out justice to the murderer. This surface story, however, provides the justification for a compelling subtext that illustrates the difficulties involved when one well-established culture attempts to impose itself upon another. *Wind from an Enemy Sky*, maintaining throughout an objective view of two disparate cultures, proffers a poignant political and social statement about culture and values in multi-ethnic settings.

Readers will feel empathy for members of the two major societies depicted in the novel, even though these societies remain at loggerheads and are divided within themselves. Toby Rafferty, the government agent in charge of the Little Elk Reservation, and Doc Edwards, the agency physician, have compassion for the Native Americans with whom they work.

Rafferty, for example, demonstrates trust and sensitivity toward Bull and his followers, releasing them from custody on their own recognizance after the murder to attend the final hours of Henry Jim's life. Doc Edwards, who treats Henry Jim as death nears, employs the tactics and technology of white medicine, yet he never loses sight of the faith and reliance that Henry Jim and his kinspeople repose in tribal ways of treating illness.

Despite this, the crucial and undeniable fact is that the whites who represent the dominant culture are unabashedly out to annihilate the Native American culture. The whites deal as kindly as they can with their Native American charges, but they shamelessly try to homogenize them into mainstream American life.

The whites' most effective tactic is forcibly to wrest Native American children from their families, shipping them to government schools. There, officials take the children's native clothes and burn them, then cut their hair and delouse them—all great affronts to Indian culture. The younger the children, the better their chance of acculturation.

Bull's grandson is snatched from his family while Bull is hunting one day. The boy is sent to a government school in Oregon, some thousand miles from his home, there to be stripped of his identity. He is assigned the new name of Antoine Brown; he learns how to pray and eat and be civil. He is told to forget his home and his people. Meanwhile, his mother, Celeste, devastated at being robbed of her only child, becomes a raving lunatic and soon dies. Only then is the boy permitted to return to Montana and his family.

McNickle never suggests that whites are motivated by evil intentions, yet their intentions are so greatly in conflict with Native American custom that they pose an insuperable barrier between the cultures. The dam that the white power structure has imposed upon the Indians symbolizes the incursions the dominant society makes upon tribal lands and traditions, much as the dam does in Thomas King's *Green Grass, Running Water* (1993).

Whites such as Adam Pell and Toby Rafferty champion Native Americans, but in doing so, they alienate the very people they champion. Whites, for example, become restive when Indians sing at crucial times when the whites need to talk with them. They cannot understand why Indians frequently answer questions allegorically, through tale-telling rather than directly.

On the other hand, both Rafferty and Doc Edwards know that when they enter an Indian abode, they should not initiate the conversation. They are on someone else's turf, and, following Native American tradition, they allow their host to speak before they attempt utterance, no matter how pressing their business.

McNickle depicts Native Americans as passive, unfailingly loyal, intelligent, and, to whites, enigmatic. They handle problems in their own ways. They consider whites noisy and aggressive, often commenting that agitated whites shout. The Indians counter with neither loudness nor aggression.

The Characters

Bull, the son of Enemy Horse, is the patriarch of his tribe. He is used to represent stalwart Native Americans who dare to resist acculturation and maintain traditional values. He lives in a changing world, but he clings tenaciously to his heritage. Although he seeks accord with the whites officially representing the dominant culture, he refuses to knuckle under to them. He is a thorn in the flesh of those who think that a good Native American is one who forsakes tribal traditions and enters the mainstream of American life.

Henry Jim, Bull's elder brother, has joined the white world. He cooperates with government officials. He has built a wooden house in which his daughter-in-law, a member of a tribe to the south, has gone so far as to cover the floors and windows with cloth—much to the dismay of his Native American relatives, most of whom will not enter his house, preferring to stay outside on their horses when they need to see him. Henry Jim has fenced his land as the whites do. He cannot, however, shake his Native American roots. As death approaches, he moves from his house into a tepee outside it, reverting to his tribal customs as his life runs out.

Two Sleeps, not originally a member of the tribe, appeared in the tribal village one day, beaten, exhausted, and hungry. The elders were about to expel him when he collapsed. Of necessity, they ministered to him. He then shared with them a vision that he had about a herd of buffalo he sensed was grazing nearby. When this vision proved to have substance and the Indians had killed enough buffalo to feed themselves for the foreseeable future, they accepted Two Sleeps as their holy man, their seer. They took him into their community and venerated him, by that act reflecting their mystical orientation.

Antoine represents the Native American who, although snatched from his culture, refuses to forget it and ultimately returns to it. He is, basically, a moderate young man in whom one sees some of the charisma that characterizes Bull, his grandfather, whom he might one day succeed.

Pock Face, on the other hand, is an angry youth who has bolted from the government school. He is outraged that the dominant society is robbing his people of the very resources they need to survive. The symbol of this theft is the dam Adam Pell has built on tribal land to collect the river water that Pock Face's tribe, living downstream from the dam, requires for its sustenance. Pock Face, in his own view, commits a moral act of vengeance by randomly killing Jim Cooke.

Toby Rafferty wants genuinely to help the Native Americans whose welfare and control are his official responsibility. He represents the well-meaning "new-settlement-house humanist," as McNickle calls him. His intentions are indisputably excellent, but they are building blocks that pave the road to hell.

Doc Edwards, Rafferty's close friend, is the official physician of the Little Elk Agency and has refused advantageous transfers because he believes in what he is doing. He is sensitive to his Native American charges but is never able to surmount the barriers that separate the two cultures.

Adam Pell, the builder of the dam, considers himself a true champion of Native Americans, both in the United States and in Peru. He has a utopian vision of what technological progress can mean to the Little Elk, but he cannot communicate this vision to them, nor has he sought their counsel in developing it.

Themes and Meanings

Wind from an Enemy Sky is concerned largely with the inability of the Native American and dominant societies in the United States to communicate productively with each other. As McNickle presents it, Native American society is deeply suspicious of the dominant society that has, through the years, oppressed it. Promises made have seldom been promises kept. The suspicions that keep Indians from interacting productively with government agencies are spawned not by paranoia but rather by extensive bitter experience.

The dam the government built has diverted a river on which the Indians depend. The waters that the dam captures will nourish the fields of white homesteaders, to whom the government has sold Indian lands at $1.25 an acre. The Native Americans look upon these land sales as forms of robbery. Added to this justifiable charge is the charge that white officials have kidnapped Indian children and sent them to distant government schools against their will.

Among the most pervasive and impressive symbols in this novel is that of the Feather Boy medicine bundle. This sacred artifact is taken by a reservation clergyman, Stephen Welles, and given to Adam Pell's museum in exchange for a stipend the museum bestows upon Welles's church. Welles mendaciously assures Pell that the medicine bundle was given to the museum with the full knowledge and consent of the tribe.

As Henry Jim lies dying, he calls for the return of the medicine bundle, which is thought to possess spiritual properties. Toby Rafferty writes to Adam Pell asking for its return and explaining its importance to the Little Elk. Pell and his staff search the museum's storerooms for this contribution, carefully cataloged, then placed in long-term storage.

To Pell's distress, the medicine bundle, when found, has irreparably deteriorated. Pell decides to visit the reservation and to make amends to the tribe by parting with a solid-gold Inca statue he had obtained with great difficulty and at considerable expense after years of searching. His motives are perfectly acceptable by the standards of his society, but his reparations are incredibly insulting to the Native Americans with whom he is trying to reach an accord. They view his demeanor and his proposal, quite correctly, as outrageously condescending.

To make matters worse, the Indians, ever modest, are to be given a statue of a nude figure. Pell's gesture is insensitive in the extreme, but not intentionally so. Rafferty, better attuned to Native American sensitivities than Pell, attempts to dissuade him from telling the Indians that their sacred medicine bundle has been lost. Yet Pell, honest and forthright, tells the Indians of the loss and of the generous indemnity he proposes making to compensate them, simultaneously robbing them unwittingly of their hope and demeaning their heritage.

Pell's disclosure leads an outraged Louis, in a tribal meeting with government officials, to grab Bull's rifle. Bull leaps up, wrests the rifle from Louis, and shoots Pell dead. He then fires the rifle at Rafferty and kills him. At this point, The Boy, a Native American intermediary between his people and government officials, does what he has to do: He aims his pistol at Bull and shoots him dead.

Thematically, McNickle suggests by these acts the inevitability of tragedy in dealings between Native Americans and representatives of the dominant society. He also demonstrates how some Native Americans—Henry Jim and The Boy, for example—move into the white world or attempt to straddle the two worlds, placing them in impossible positions. For Henry Jim, it is impossible to shake the Native American heritage, which the dying man finally embraces again.

Critical Context

D'Arcy McNickle's novel was produced at a time when ethnic sensitivity and multiculturalism were gaining considerable prominence in literature. As part of Harper and Row's Native American Publishing Program, *Wind from an Enemy Sky* was published along with books by such other Native American writers as Heyemeyohsts Storm, James Welch, Adolf Hungry Wolf, Duane Niatum, Simon Ortiz, and Nas' Naga.

Other Native American novelists were also making headway in the 1970's. N. Scott Momaday's *The Way to Rainy Mountain* (1976) appeared two years before McNickle's novel. In 1978, the same year the *Wind from an Enemy Sky* was issued, the University of Minnesota Press published one of Gerald Vizenor's earliest books, *Indians and Whites in the New Fur Trade*. As early as 1936, McNickle himself had published *The Surrounded*, which was widely considered the finest Native American novel prior to World War II. McNickle's *Runner in the Sun: A Story of Indian Maize* appeared in 1954, followed in 1973 by *Native American Tribalism*, published by the Oxford University Press.

A decade before *Wind from an Enemy Sky*, a flood of African American writing spawned a renewed interest in minority literatures. Native American, Chicano, feminist, and gay and lesbian literature began to share with African American literature the prominence that the social upheavals of the 1960's had generated. The trend would continue in succeeding years, as the works of minority writers became accepted parts of the academic canon. As an early pioneer of the Native American novel, D'Arcy McNickle has benefited from this reappraisal, receiving belated recognition as an important voice in American fiction.

Bibliography

Larson, Charles R. "Books in English in the Third World." *World Literature Today* 53 (Spring, 1979): 247. Larson calls *The Surrounded* "the most significant novel by an American Indian written before World War II." He then discusses the forty-year lapse between that book and *Wind from an Enemy Sky*, which he sees as concerning "conflicting loyalties *within* the Indian community."

Owens, Louis, "The 'Map of the Mind': D'Arcy McNickle and the American Indian Novel." *Western American Literature* 19 (Winter, 1985): 275-283. Owens discusses *The Surrounded* and *Wind from an Enemy Sky*, focusing on the problems of communication between the white and Indian worlds.

Parker, Dorothy. *Singing an Indian Song: A Biography of D'Arcy McNickle*. Lincoln: University of Nebraska Press, 1992. Details McNickle's early years at a boarding school and his lengthy career as an agent for the Bureau of Indian Affairs. Provides information crucial to the interpretation of his fiction.

Purdy, John Lloyd. *Word Ways: The Novels of D'Arcy McNickle*. Tucson: University of Arizona Press, 1990. A thorough critical discussion of McNickle's fiction. Purdy focuses on McNickle's use of Native American oral tradition to enhance the written conventions of the novel.

Ruppert, James. *D'Arcy McNickle*. Boise, Idaho: Boise State University, 1988. An entry in the Western Writers Series that gives a good overview of McNickle's life and work.

Vest, Jay Hansford C. "Feather Boy's Promise: Sacred Geography and Environmental Ethics in D'Arcy McNickle's *Wind from an Enemy Sky*." *American Indian Quarterly* 17 (Winter, 1993): 45-68. Focuses on the Little Elk tribe's medicine bundle and its relationship to the Native American environmental ethic. Sees *Wind from an Enemy Sky* as a trickster narrative.

R. Baird Shuman

WINTER IN THE BLOOD

Author: James Welch (1940-　　)
Type of plot: Psychological realism
Time of plot: The early 1970's
Locale: Northern Montana
First published: 1974

> *Principal characters:*
> THE NARRATOR, a young Blackfeet man struggling to put the deaths of his father and brother behind him
> TERESA, the narrator's mother, a practical, hardened woman, a survivor
> THE OLD WOMAN, Teresa's mother, one of the few remaining links to the narrator's ancestry
> YELLOW CALF, a blind elder, either mystical or insane
> FIRST RAISE, the narrator's father, who, like his son, was a wanderer
> MOSE, the narrator's brother

The Novel

Winter in the Blood intertwines the narrator's tale of passage from a boy to a man with the mysterious story of his grandmother's role in the Blackfeet tribe's tragic past. The book consists of four sections of varied lengths and a brief epilogue.

Winter in the Blood begins as the narrator returns home from a drunken escapade to find that Agnes, the woman with whom he has been living, is gone and has stolen his gun and electric razor. Attempting to forget about the woman and his things, the narrator helps his mother and Lame Bull with the ranch chores. Lame Bull marries Teresa, making him an owner of the ranch, a role into which he throws himself with relish.

Teresa's marriage triggers the narrator's memory of his father and brother's deaths. He talks with Teresa about First Raise and is disturbed by the fact that she remembers their life together much differently than he does. Teresa further uproots her son by telling him that there is no work for him on the ranch now that Lame Bull is in charge. When Agnes is spotted in Malta, the narrator decides to go after her. As his thoughts return to Agnes, he makes the reader aware of his grandmother's reasons for hating the young woman. Once the youngest wife of a Blackfeet chief, the grandmother hates Crees for what she believes to be their treachery. Crees had scouted for the cavalry, the Long Knives, who chased the Blackfeet from their home at the base of the mountains. The narrator repeats his grandmother's story of a winter of starvation and the death of her husband. She was cast out by the tribe in mourning for their chief. The narrator believes his grandmother when she says that the women of the tribe envied her beauty. He also believes the rumor that a half-breed drifter with whom his grandmother settled down wasn't his real grandfather.

The narrator temporarily sets aside his grandmother's story and catches a ride to

Dodson, a nearby town with a bus stop. The narrator travels on to Malta, where he is quickly caught up in a series of bewildering events. He Helps Agnes' brother roll a drunken white, meets an Easterner running from a mysterious past, and falls into bed with a barmaid.

Back home briefly at the beginning of part 2, the narrator visits Yellow Calf and is drawn to the blind old man who claims to understand the calls of animals. On the road again, checking out a report of Agnes in Havre, the narrator runs into the Easterner, who is running from the Federal Bureau of Investigation (FBI), and agrees to drive him across the Canadian border. Before the two can set out, the narrator's companion is apprehended, and the narrator is punched in a bar by Agnes' brother. Tired "of town, of walking home hung over, beaten up, or both," he hitches a ride back to the ranch in part 3. His grandmother has died. The narrator and Lame Bull dig the woman's grave. He is reminded of hacking First Raise's grave out of the frozen earth and remembers the time he and his brother ran their father's cattle, the day Mose was struck on the highway and killed.

In part 4, the narrator returns to Yellow Calf's shack. Yellow Calf knows the truth about the narrator's grandmother. The Blackfeet thought that the woman, the newest member of the tribe, had brought them "bad medicine," that she had been responsible for their devastation. The narrator wonders how his grandmother avoided starvation in the abandoned tepees on the edge of camp. Yellow Calf does not say so, but the narrator is convinced that the old man hunted to feed his grandmother, kept her alive, and had a child with her. Yellow Calf is his real grandfather.

On the way home from Yellow Calf's shack, the narrator discovers a cow stuck up to her chest in mud. It is the same wild-eyed animal that started the panic of his father's cattle on the day that Mose was killed trying to stop the herd from running across the highway. Roping the cow to his saddle horn, the narrator mounts his horse, Bird, and attempts to pull the beast out of the muck. When Bird loses his footing and falls, throwing the narrator to his back, the cow slips down the bank of the slough in which she had been stuck. Lying unable to move, listening to the two animals' final cries, the narrator experiences a feeling of pleasant calm as he is soaked by a summer rain.

The old woman's lonely burial is related in the epilogue. Teresa moans as Lame Bull utters a vague memorial. The book concludes with the image of the narrator throwing his grandmother's tobacco pouch into her grave.

The Characters

The narrator seems hopeless. The reader must decide whether it is bad luck or bad judgment that plagues him. A recurring symbol of his frustration is his belief that the river has no fish in it, a conviction he holds in spite of the many locals and tourists who insist that they catch fish in the river all the time.

That the narrator continues both to fish and to believe that the river is barren is a paradox that perfectly combines the senses of perseverance and of doom that charac- terize him. The combination is useful, however, in the pursuit of his grandmother's tragic story. For uncovering the act of kindness Yellow Calf had performed, the narrator is rewarded with the truth about his heritage.

Teresa is both a caring and a callous mother. She killed Amos, the duck who won the family's heart by surviving a grisly accident, but served him for a special Christmas dinner. She reinforces the notion that even sources of nurturing, such as the land and one's precious memories, can be brutal. Her marriage contributes to a feeling evoked throughout the book that the glory of the past can never be fully recovered. In place of the dramatic and powerful First Raise, Teresa has the unremarkable Lame Bull. The union of Teresa and Lame Bull, however, shows the narrator that personal tragedy can be overcome, that life goes on.

The old woman, like her grandson, is never called by name. This shared emptiness links the narrator and his grandmother. The old woman's incessant rocking is echoed by the narrator's wanderings to and from town and back and forth between the past and the present. Instead of contributing to the erosion of the narrator's identity, the old woman's death enriches her grandson's understanding of family history. His grief takes the form of curiosity strong enough to uncover a truth that restores his pride. The tobacco pouch in the narrator's hands as he stands over his grandmother's grave is a sign of the increased compassion for and understanding of the old woman.

Yellow Calf draws from the narrator an optimism, a faith, that the young man rarely exhibits. The narrator is skeptical concerning the elder man's professed ability to understand the calls of wild animals, but he is tender in Yellow Calf's presence. When the narrator understands that the old man is his grandfather, he speaks with more pride than at any other time in the novel, and he is never more at ease with the memory of his father than when recalling that First Raise had brought him to Yellow Calf as a boy. Yellow Calf's goodness partially redeems the narrator's own sense of worth.

First Raise and Mose represent a time when the narrator felt less alone in the world. His memories of a breakfast cooked by First Raise and a trail ride with Mose are richly detailed, suggesting the reverence with which the narrator preserves them. First Raise and Mose also illustrate the difficult relationship to whites that has influenced the narrator's coming of age. First Raise played the clown for white people in the bars in Dodson; Mose and the narrator grew up idolizing the white cowboy in Western films. Through these associations, the book reminds the reader that the politics of race are at work.

Themes and Meanings

Winter in the Blood is a psychological self-portrait, the record of its first-person narrator's attempts to comprehend and endure tragic loss. The other characters who populate the world of the novel become foils for the exploration of one individual's mental life and the cultural legacy this existence reflects.

Several times the narrator speaks of creating distance between himself and his psychological demons. He is aware that he must heal himself, but he almost always undertakes disastrously wrong courses of treatment. He attempts to stem the grief that has flooded through him since the deaths of his father and brother by escaping his boyhood home for towns and bars. His appetites are dangerous tools. Drinking leads inevitably to fighting or to debilitating sexual encounters, or both, and leaves the narrator in the bruised, defeated state in which the reader first encounters him. His self-destructive personal life does not keep him from thinking of his dead father and brother. As the young Blackfeet man begins to tell his tragic stories, the reader has the sense that the narrator's excursions into memory are as unstoppable as his forays into town.

Further complicating the situation is the issue of the narrator's faulty memory. Teresa remembers events differently from her son, and her versions make it hard for the narrator to revere First Raise, to think of his father as a hero. He has known his grandmother's story for so long that he does not realize that he is not sure how it ends. The narrator's memory, like a historical record, is always under construction and subject to change. His search for the very tales he is telling emerges as a major theme of the book.

The mental act of storytelling comes to depend on the physical activity by which the details of the stories are accumulated, as if the narrator's restless wandering literally shakes loose the memories of First Raise and Mose. The culmination of this idea is the narrator's incredible attempt to pull the wild-eyed cow from the mud, much as he has succeeded in pulling his grandmother's secret from Yellow Calf. That his final test is physical, a question of his strength alone against the elements, is a poignant reminder that, despite making nourishing connections with his past, the narrator will never permanently shake the sense of isolation that plagues him.

In addition to the theme of personal loss and recovery, the novel discusses the idea of cultural dislocation. The impact of Western expansion on the Blackfeet tribe is represented by the grandmother's story of the winter of starvation. The same forced relocation that separated the tribe from its traditional home separated the narrator from his cultural roots. Through Yellow Calf, the narrator is able to reconnect with his tribe, and the novel is able to join the personal and cultural narratives. Yellow Calf emerges both as a Native American hero and as the narrator's real grandfather. Yellow Calf lends a proud aspect to a past that the narrator had formerly viewed only as a source of shame.

Critical Context

In *Winter in the Blood,* James Welch introduces the themes and techniques he would continue to develop in later works. The novel begins the project of establishing through literary means the identity of the Native American. Welch was born in Browning, Montana, a small town that serves as the headquarters of the Blackfeet reservation. He attended high schools on both the Blackfeet and Fort Belknap reservations in Montana. He is the author of a book of poems, *Riding the Earthboy Forty* (1971), that evokes life on the reservation, and he was at one time a professor of Indian studies at the University of Washington; his efforts toward cultural preservation have thus been varied and significant. The themes and techniques of his first novel reflect this concern. The narrator is able to understand that his true pursuit is not of his appetites but his heritage. His boyhood heroes had been the white cowboy actors who rode and roped on the big screen. This ironic confession demonstrates the scarcity in Western arts of representations of Native Americans, a lack that Welch himself seeks to fill.

The first-person narrative of self-discovery and the elaborate time sequence of the novel are techniques that illuminate the theme of cultural reconstruction. The plot switches between three time frames: the present, the narrator's youth, and the youth of his grandmother. As the narrator reexamines his own past, he realizes that the history of his people is a forgotten but nevertheless important part of his consciousness. Welch's later works *The Death of Jim Loney* (1979), *Fools Crow* (1986), and *The Indian Lawyer* (1990) are perhaps more ambitious in scope, but the impetus for these works is located in the pathos, comedy, and celebration that has attracted the attention of scores of critics to *Winter in the Blood.*

Bibliography

Davis, Jack L. "Restoration of Indian Identity in *Winter in the Blood.*" In *James Welch*, edited by Ron McFarland. Lewiston, Idaho: Confluence Press, 1986. Davis sets Welch's tale of a rediscovered Native American identity against the historical backdrop of "the military conquest of American Indians." The critic argues that, as a work of imagination, the novel challenges and expands the historical and anthropological assumptions by which the Native American condition is generally understood.

Gish, Robert. "Mystery and Mock Intrigue in James Welch's *Winter in the Blood.*" In *James Welch*, edited by Ron McFarland. Lewiston, Idaho: Confluence Press, 1986. Gish is concerned with the technical achievements of the novel. He articulates the relationship between content and form, focusing on the combined presence of tragedy and comedy.

Ruoff, A. LaVonne. "Alienation and the Female Principle in *Winter in the Blood.*" In *James Welch*, edited by Ron McFarland. Lewiston, Idaho: Confluence Press, 1986. Ruoff examines all aspects of femininity in the novel, even the relationship between the wild-eyed cow and her calf. She supplements her discussion with fascinating research into Cree, Gros Ventres, and Blackfeet tribal customs.

Sands, Kathleen M. "Alienation and Broken Narrative in *Winter in the Blood.*" *American Indian Quarterly* 4 (May, 1978): 97-105. Sands is a prominent critic of Welch and other Native American writers. She discusses the relationship between theme and structure in the novel, arguing that the concept of alienation is underscored by the narrator's attempt to locate himself within the novel's several time frames.

Tatum, Stephen. "Distance, Desire, and the Ideological Matrix of *Winter in the Blood.*" *Arizona Quarterly* 46 (Summer, 1990): 73-100. This essay focuses on the theme of desire. Tatum places the narrator's pursuit of women and feelings of alienation in the context of Native American culture.

Nick David Smart

THE WITCHES OF EASTWICK

Author: John Updike (1932-   )
Type of plot: Philosophical
Time of plot: The late 1960's
Locale: Eastwick, Rhode Island
First published: 1984

> *Principal characters:*
> ALEXANDRA SPOFFORD, a sculptress who controls storms
> JANE SMART, a cellist who sometimes flies
> SUKIE ROUGEMONT, a reporter who casts love spells
> DARRYL VAN HORNE, a crass yet charismatic inventor and newest Eastwick resident
> CLYDE GABRIEL, the boozy editor of the *Eastwick Word*
> FELICIA GABRIEL, a self-righteous crusader for decency
> JENNY GABRIEL, Clyde and Felicia's daughter, who returns to Eastwick
> CHRIS GABRIEL, Jenny's dull brother

The Novel

Set in a typical small New England town, *The Witches of Eastwick* offers a witty, irreverent, and pointed glimpse of small-town people and values, but with a twist. The three main characters are witches, and amid local gossip, scandal, and sorcery, they seek the perfect relationship by any means.

The Witches of Eastwick is divided into three chapters. These sections ("The Coven," "Malefica," and "Guilt") respectively introduce the players and the situation, resolve the various conflicts that arise, and detail the aftermath. The story is related by an unseen, omniscient narrator who is a town resident.

The story begins as the three principal characters, Alexandra Spofford, Jane Smart, and Sukie Rougemont—all divorced, and whose former husbands are literally gathering dust on shelves in their homes—prepare to meet at Sukie's for one of their weekly "Thursdays." At such rendezvous, the three relax with a few drinks, gossip about the latest affairs they are having with various tired Eastwick husbands, and practice witchcraft.

During the first section of the novel, the narrator details the minutiae of life in Eastwick; however, the focus remains largely on the three witches, the various tricks and pranks they play (at times outright nasty), and their own boredom-generated affairs. The reader becomes acquainted with Alexandra's deep, earthy rootedness and power; with Jane's cranky, precise nature and passion for music; and with Sukie's good-natured, inquisitive sensuality.

Darryl Van Horne makes his appearance at a community concert. Ostensibly, he has come to Eastwick to further his aim of inventing a solar-energy-collecting paint, but little is actually known of Darryl. The town is enthusiastic about his plans to renovate an old property that has been a tax drain on the community for some time. His near-grotesque appearance and "New York vulgar" manner repulse some, including the more sensitive Alexandra, but his brash and outspoken coarseness charms others, especially Jane. Immediately, it is clear that Darryl is interested in the three witches, and shortly, through appeals to each of their secret desires, he has managed to coax all of them into visiting the old Lenox mansion, which he is lavishly remodelling to suit his hedonistic purposes.

Soon, Darryl and the three witches are frequent companions at his home. There, sometimes on his dome tennis court (where tennis balls undergo startling transformations), but especially within the environs of his decadently lavish "playroom," which includes a mammoth teakwood Jacuzzi, the four cavort sensuously, waited upon by Darryl's servant, Fidel.

Meanwhile, changes are taking place within the community. Ed Parsley, the young, militant Unitarian minister, lately Sukie's lover, runs off to join the peace movement. (He is later killed while making a bomb.) Prim Brenda Parsley, Ed's wife, finding a hidden assertiveness within herself, takes over the church's ministry. Felicia Gabriel, the shrewish moral crusader, begins to find an odd assortment of feathers, thumbtacks, and insects issuing from her mouth unexplainedly. Clyde Gabriel, Sukie's boss and the editor of the *Eastwick Word*, consumed by alcohol-induced guilt and in constant misery brought on by his wife's nagging, kills her with a fireplace poker, then hangs himself. This event brings Clyde and Felicia's children, Jenny and Chris, back to Eastwick. Soon, the two youths begin to take part in the regular festivities at the old mansion.

Things begin to sour among the Eastwick fivesome of Darryl, Alexandra, Jane, Sukie, and Jenny as jealousies start to surface. Alexandra, Jane, and Sukie all nurture fantasies concerning an eventual life together with Darryl, but he surprises and ultimately alienates the three by his announcement of marriage to the young Jenny. Stung by this seeming rejection, the witches conjure a spell aimed at avenging themselves upon Darryl and his smug new bride. Jenny becomes increasingly ill, and though Sukie and, especially, Alexandra have remorseful thoughts about their deed, they do nothing about it.

At the story's end, power begins slowly to shift among the female residents of Eastwick. In the aftermath of Jenny's long sickness and eventual death, Alexandra, Jane, and Sukie drift apart as a new coven forms from newer residents. The narrator reveals how the three eventually go on to form new lives away from Eastwick, but the memory of their presence seems to linger ethereally among the quaint byways of the small community.

The Characters

It is clear from the detailed opening that Alexandra, in her late thirties, is the driving force behind the small coven and the focus for the author's principal characterization. She seems to derive her power from the earthly elements, and her command of elemental forces is demonstrated by her control of a summer storm and by her "bubbies": small clay statuettes that she sells at local boutiques. Yet Alexandra can also be moody and vain. As well as storms, her momentary whims can cause death. She alternately engages the reader's empathy and awe with her earth-mother characteristics and engenders fear when, for example she impulsively wills the death of a squirrel marauding in her garden. Through her own self-doubts, Alexandra demonstrates the shifting concerns of power, love, and sexuality being examined in the story.

Jane Smart, also in her late thirties, is a cellist, and that facet becomes the primary focus for her characterization. Jane is willful, hostile, and gifted; she is impatient with much save the passion for her music. Wildly decadent given the proper motivation, Jane demonstrates the self-indulgent ego that cares for little except personal gratification. It is through Jane that the reader begins to understand how power corrupts.

Sukie Rougemont, in her early thirties, is a reporter for the *Eastwick Word*. The reader cannot help but see Sukie in a favorable light. Alexandra's constant comments about Sukie's "monkeyish" curiosity and energetic, girlish demeanor add to this impression. Sukie is shown to be sympathetic and caring, but her outward manner of exuberance and sympathy may mask a certain cunning and calculation that can be chilling. Her seeming good nature may belie a sense of powerlessness and guilt that fuel a jealousy that ultimately becomes destructive.

Darryl Van Horne, though not specifically referred to as such, is a demonic manifestation. From his arrival out of nowhere to his orgies at the Lenox mansion, Darryl epitomizes those things the reader will consider crude, obnoxious, and vulgar; however, Darryl is also strongly charismatic. His tastes are eclectic. The furnishings of his home reflect a desire to acquire objects of art but also reveal an insensitive nature that disregards enduring artistic merit. He furnishes his home opulently only in relation to his own need for gratification. Therefore, his playroom, the scene of wild bacchanals, is minutely appointed to service every physical pleasure or desire, while the rest of his house is a scattering of furniture and uncrated objects.

Jenny Gabriel returns to Eastwick lost and unsure of herself. Confronted with the gruesome deaths of her parents, she and her ineffectual brother Chris are befriended by Darryl and the three witches. Soon, Jenny's seemingly shy nature is conquered, and she joins in the frequent debauches. Finally, she consents to Darryl's marriage proposal. Yet Jenny may not be the total innocent she at first seems. She is quick to recognize the essential power struggle between herself and the witches, and she seeks to consolidate her own position by becoming Darryl's wife. Her effort proves her undoing, however, for the witches perceive a threat and act to preserve their own sense of family, which Jenny has usurped.

Themes and Meanings

As with many stories, this novel can be read from different perspectives. On one level, it posits the possibility of instant wish gratification and questions the moral implications of such a proposition: Would such power corrupt? and to what degree? What is the nature of such corruption? How much pleasure is too much? On another level, the novel is a somewhat bawdy romp filled with satiric pokes and jabs at small-town Americana.

It is through the everyday lives of the principal characters that these themes are explored, as well as others concerning religion, gender, and morality. The narrator guides the reader through Alexandra's middle-aged doubts about herself and her consequent use of witchcraft to prop up her unexciting life. Chiefly through Alexandra, readers come to know how daily annoyances can be taken care of with a murmured spell, or a thought. Readers also see, however, the darker side to such power, as when Alexandra's petulance causes the elderly Mrs. Lovecraft to break her hip. In the same way, Jane's passion for the cello becomes an obsession under the tutelage of the devilish Darryl. In the end, her instrument lies in splinters, testament and analogy to her own shattered ambitions. Sukie's caring, free-spirited innocence also undergoes a transformation, and she changes from the buoyant confidante of Alexandra into a vengeful witch.

Darryl might be thought of as both focus and source for the witches' powers, yet he never demonstrates any supernatural abilities himself, nor is he suggested to be otherworldly in any but superficial ways. He seems wholly unsurprised and comfortable with whatever the three women do. Darryl seems to feed the witches' needs while at the same time feeding upon their lavish attentions. He is largely seen as a passive receptor, and Updike may thus be suggesting that evil and corruption are fed more by human needs than from outside sources.

The story examines the consequences of unchecked power and may be asking the reader to consider the issue of moral behavior. What if, with a nod of the head, one could bypass the normal social checks and balances and, for example, get rid of the neighbor's annoying dog? Could anyone be counted upon to exercise control with such power? In *The Witches of Eastwick*, the three witches constantly circumvent such controls. Besides being alternately amusing, thrilling, and lascivious, the novel gently brings such considerations to the reader's attention.

Critical Context

The Witches of Eastwick can be seen as something of a departure for John Updike, yet the book is also a continuation of themes expressed in his earlier fiction. The work's mythological nature does have at least one precedent in Updike's third novel, *The Centaur* (1963), but aside from that, the novel reveals Updike's continuing regard for detailing the smallest aspects of daily life with meticulous care. His preoccupation with what goes on behind closed doors and his penchant for scrutinizing dreary existence have struck some critics as obsessive; still, Updike's skill at portrayal cannot be denied, even by his harshest detractors.

To many critics, the writing in *The Witches of Eastwick* is generally thought to be as good as that in some of Updike's best efforts, including *The Poorhouse Fair* (1959), *Of the Farm* (1965), *Couples* (1968), and the Pulitzer Prize-winning *Rabbit Is Rich* (1981), which immediately preceded *The Witches of Eastwick*. Yet some critics have also blasted Updike's novel for being pretentious, mean-spirited, and overly indulgent. As well, *The Witches of Eastwick* has been thought by some to demonstrate an essential dislike for women.

Since the period of his earliest works, critical focus has shifted from a concern with Updike's lush, detailed style to a consideration of his themes, which, some say, he treats in a shallow and inconsequential manner. Much of the severest criticism might be summed up by the charge that Updike writes very well about nothing much. Updike has countered by claiming that such critics are looking only for ever-increasing thrills. He suggests that the normal and the real are profound in their own respects.

Bibliography

Bloom, Harold, ed. *John Updike*. New York: Chelsea House, 1987. In his introduction, Bloom commends the artful style of *The Witches of Eastwick*, focusing especially on the characterizations of the three witches. To Bloom, this is more than a satiric novel; it reaches into horror for its powerful effect. Though Bloom praises the novel's concluding passages, he suggests a stylistic flaw in them as well.

Campbell, Jeff H. *Updike's Novels: Thorns Spell a Word*. Wichita Falls, Tex.: Midwestern State University Press, 1987. Chapter 5 contrasts Updike's *Marry Me: A Romance* (1976), *Couples*, and *The Witches of Eastwick*. Campbell focuses first on the sociological aspects of these novels, and especially on the deterioration of marriage. With regard to *The Witches of Eastwick*, Campbell discusses themes of feminism, the demythologizing of Satan, and the balancing of self between the internal and external worlds.

Newman, Judie. *John Updike*. New York: St. Martin's Press, 1988. Newman suggests that *The Witches of Eastwick* questions the relationship between imaginative power and political power. Her analysis thoroughly investigates the story's major characters, and she concludes by demonstrating how the novel might be read as commentary on the Vietnam War.

Verduin, Kathleen. "Sex, Nature, and Dualism in *The Witches of Eastwick*." *Modern Language Quarterly* 46 (September, 1985): 293-315. Verduin considers the heated controversy Updike's work generated among feminists and demonstrates how the author highlights the complicity between women and nature in the novel, especially through the vehicle of witchcraft. A scholarly treatment of women's shifting roles in society as revealed by Updike's various characterizations of women.

Welsh, J. M. "Bewitched and Bewildered Over 'Eastwick,'" *Literature and Film Quarterly* 15, no. 3 (1987): 152-154. Contrasts Updike's novel with the 1987 film version. Though Welsh regards the novel as superior, he sees the ending as weak. He concludes that the film has plenty of popular appeal but little connection with the apparent concerns of the novel's author.

George Thomas Novotny

THE WOMAN WHO OWNED THE SHADOWS

Author: Paula Gunn Allen (1939-   )
Type of plot: Psychological realism
Time of plot: The 1970's
Locale: Albuquerque, New Mexico; San Francisco, California; and Oregon
First published: 1983

>   *Principal characters:*
>   EPHANIE ATENCIO, a half-breed Pueblo Indian from Guadalupe
>   ELENA, a childhood friend of Ephanie
>   STEPHEN, a cousin and lifelong friend of Ephanie
>   TERESA, a white friend of Ephanie who calls herself a witch
>   THOMAS YOSHURI, a Nisei man whom Ephanie marries
>   AGNES ATENCIO, Ephanie's daughter
>   BEN ATENCIO, Ephanie's son

The Novel

   In her novel *The Woman Who Owned the Shadows*, Paula Gunn Allen employs Laguna women's traditions to trace one woman's search for psychic balance. The novel is divided into four parts, each preceded by a prologue. These prologues tell the traditionally oral stories of Thinking Woman, also known as Spider Woman or the Grandmother, and of her two sister goddesses whom she sang into being, Uretsete and Naotsete. The bodies of the four parts are sectioned into short vignettes that follow middle-aged protagonist Ephanie Atencio as she struggles to gain a sense of self and purpose. Allen parallels Ephanie's own experiences to the goddess stories and in doing so establishes the acceptance of traditional woman lore as the key to a woman's individual spiritual harmony.

   Told in stream-of-consciousness style, the novel begins with Ephanie, recently abandoned by her husband, in a state of mental turmoil. She vaguely hears Stephen's attempts to aid her in grasping reality, yet she feels suffocated by him and longs for him to understand her and to let her be herself. With Elena, Ephanie had been who she wanted to be; as children, the two seemingly had complete understanding of each other, seeing themselves as Snow White and Rose Red, as two halves of a whole. Ephanie recounts their separation and the final words of betrayal spoken by Elena that separated them forever. Ephanie connects this memory to her present need for a friend, someone who will accept her as Stephen does not. After Stephen makes love to her, she realizes that something is "out of time, off-pace." She flees Albuquerque, leaving her children with her mother.

   Settling in San Francisco, Ephanie sends for her children. The three experience city life and attend the local powwows, looking for acceptance into that community as something connected to and yet different from their home. Ephanie is discontented, however. Going to the Indian Center less and less, she rationalizes her withdrawal by claiming a desire to see "how the other half lives." She spends more time with the non-Indian friends she has made at her group therapy session, particularly Teresa. Ephanie and Teresa grow close, though Ephanie is always troubled by feelings of disconnectedness and isolation. She meets Thomas Yoshuri, who claims to "need" Ephanie. In desperation, hoping to find care for her children and a reason for her own existence, Ephanie agrees to marry Thomas despite Teresa's warnings and her own misgivings.

The marriage predictably fails, and Ephanie, now pregnant, runs off to Oregon, where she gives birth to twin boys. Thomas joins her for the birth and stays with her until, not long afterward, Tommy dies of crib death. Part 2 ends with their final separation and divorce.

In part 3, again alone and now also experiencing guilt about her young child's death, Ephanie yearns even more desperately to be understood. She recalls the stories of disrespect shown toward Iyatiku and searches for the meaning in her dreams of the strange *katsina*, messenger between the spirits and the people. She visits Guadalupe with Teresa, but this trip only stirs up the mysterious disquiet within her. During their return to California, Ephanie and Teresa stay in Colorado with some friends of Teresa who are full of statistics about the injustices wielded against indigenous people. Ephanie resents her people being seen as romanticized victims by those who blame anyone but themselves. She retraces the shunning of her family by her own community because of her grandmother's marriage to a white man. Connecting all of this, Ephanie is again overwhelmed and angered by lack of understanding. Possessed with the desire to do something, to take power in any way possible, Ephanie hangs herself, instantaneously regrets her action, and cuts herself free with the knife propitiously stuck in her pocket.

In the final section of the novel, Ephanie madly searches, though for what she is not sure, through books and her own writing. Eventually she discovers the key to her own enlightenment. More stories of the goddesses come to her; through these and stories of her family's life, she begins to see pain. Ephanie's struggles, her stories, and her writings intertwine, forming circles that she prays will lead her to understanding. She is certain that if she could understand, people, beasts, and the earth would be healed.

Finally, she unleashes the memory of her childhood fall from an apple tree and how, overpowered by the anger and guilt of her fall, she stifled the energy and freedom of her spirit. A spirit woman comes to her and tells her the stories of the goddesses of her people. Through this oral telling, Ephanie understands the combinations and recombinations that form the whole of reality. She puts the fragments of herself back together and sings with the surrounding shadows that have taken the shapes of women, women singing and stepping in balance and harmony.

The Characters

The characters in *The Woman Who Owned the Shadows* serve largely as focal points for Ephanie as she examines her own pain and strives to take control of her life. The members of Ephanie's family, namely her mother and grandmother and her children, are not developed characters. The short explanations of the love Ephanie's grand-mother held for her tribal ways, despite being shunned, in addition to her mother's own feelings of isolation, provide the necessary background for Allen's development of Ephanie as a woman divided both from mortal women and the goddess women in her life. Similarly, Elena's character is not developed to any significant degree, but instead the childhood friend's apparent betrayal of Ephanie confirms Ephanie's blame of external forces and people for her own internal isolation.

In the same manner, the two men in Ephanie's life provide stimulus for further examination of her internal dilemmas. Stephen is presented as a ghostly character. He is introduced during Ephanie's initial mental desperation, the most disorienting and fragmented passage in the novel. That he is continually rejected by Ephanie, though he seems to be a consistently loyal friend, hints at the (eventually revealed) underlying mystery in Ephanie's unhappiness.

Thomas, too, is only sketchily drawn. He is rejected by society because of his Japanese heritage, yet he is also deprived by that same society of his Japanese culture. His unhappiness parallels Ephanie's isolation. Neither can separate from his or her respective heritage and join white American society; neither can experience the life that ancestral culture offers. Thomas shows no interest in attending to Ephanie's needs in any way, remains selfconsumed and unconnected to his short-term wife, and thus leaves Ephanie still searching for understanding.

Teresa is both generous and good-hearted, though Ephanie is repeatedly disheart-ened by her impression that Teresa, too, fails to understand her. Teresa's virtues, patience and tolerance, are exhibited by her efforts to convince Ephanie to accept the Colorado women, despite their insulting presumptions, based on their good intentions and their attempts to understand unfamiliar cultures. The rift that comes between the two women is temporary. Teresa will benefit from Ephanie's final awakening—the spirit woman who comes to Ephanie tells her that she must now "Give it [her newfound knowledge] to your sister, Teresa. The one who waits. She is ready to know."

Ephanie's gradual awakening to and synthesis of the traditional stories, her family stories, and her own experiences is the heart of the novel. Allen fastidiously renders Ephanie's initial depth of confusion and distress, attributing it to her divided and warring sense of self. The novel commences with Ephanie's utter lack of comprehen-sion of the time or place in which she exists. She looks inside herself, but she is bewildered by her external and internal senses. She is unaware of her inner division even though she expresses it from the very start, referring to her name as "half of this and half of that." Allen sets up Ephanie's fragmentation of self and then moves her continually toward a realization of that disunity and the ultimate "re membering" of the parts.

Themes and Meanings

The discovery of self through the acceptance of tribal traditions is a central theme of Allen's novel. The frequency of tribal stories appearing in the main text increases from the beginning of the novel to the end, just as Ephanie's comprehension of the connections between her life and the stories of the goddess women of her Guadalupe people increases. Her path toward self-discovery is established once she performs her own rite of exorcism and begins sweeping away the alien gods in her life, namely Thomas at this point. Spider, the goddess Grandmother, becomes increasingly more powerful in her consciousness. Ephanie attempts suicide only to discover in herself a fierce will to live; her life-affirming self wins over her destructive self. Her understanding deepens. She sees the blooming apple tree of light as the tree in her own childhood, and she sees Sky Woman, who in her "arrogance and brightness" had taken a fall, as herself, who had experienced her own childhood fall. She discovers that the stories exist to fit into life, that all along the stories were tied to the suppressed stories of her own existence.

Although at the beginning of the novel she was disoriented, by the end of the novel Ephanie unifies herself and realizes the tribal notion of time as inner harmony. She understands the combinations and recombinations that had so puzzled her. The visualization of reality as a coherent whole—a web of interwoven events, humans, and spirits—connects Ephanie to her people, tribal reality, and ritual ways.

The last prologue tells of how Spider will seduce the uninitiated into her cave and never free them if they do not have "the special protection that only knowledge can give." Ephanie reaches understanding and learns the knowledge that is necessary for the "initiated." She overcomes the absence of ritual teaching in her childhood and discovers, through the tribal narratives she integrates with her own life, the element of ritual tradition within herself. The experiences and stories of the past become a timeless part of the current moment, in which ritual past is the nurturing life force of the present.

Critical Context

Allen, who describes herself as of mixed Laguna Pueblo, Sioux, and Lebanese American heritage, is a scholar, a professor, and a poet. *The Woman Who Owned the Shadows*, her first novel, was published by the feminist press Spinsters/Aunt Lute and is Allen's testament to the empowerment and direction that tradition offers to the individual. In the work, she examines how Native Americans can incorporate their tribal beliefs into twentieth century America. The layering of tribal stories within the main plot, as well as fundamental reliance on a tribal notion belief of the interconnectedness of reality, firmly establishes *The Woman Who Owned the Shadows* in the genre of tribal literature. She follows in a tradition of Native American writers who operate on tribal sensibilities, such as N. Scott Momaday and Leslie Marmon Silko. The novel, additionally, makes a zealous feminist statement emphasizing the matriarchal line of power through knowledge and female spirits.

In 1986, Allen's feminist critical study on woman lore in Native American traditions, entitled *The Sacred Hoop: Recovering the Feminine in American Indian Traditions*, was published. In that work, she discusses both the feminine and feminist aspects of tribal traditions and history as well as current Native American literature and critical studies. Within the book, she critiques her own novel and the works of a number of well-established Native American writers. Her discussion of tribal literature skillfully illuminates the complexities inherent in describing an art form rooted in a particular culture. Allen explores the assumptions underlying literary criticism and the writing of literature, examining concepts such as ceremonial time as compared to Western industrial time and the use of myth and dream vision in Native American literature.

Allen has written two major volumes of poetry, *Shadow Country* (1982) and *Wyrds* (1987), in addition to many chapbooks of poetry. She edited a collection of critical essays entitled *Studies in American Indian Literature* (1983) and a collection of Native American women's myths entitled *Grandmothers of the Light* (1991). Additionally, a portion of Allen's work entitled *Raven's Road* appeared in a 1986 collection of works in progress by Native American writers.

Bibliography

Allen, Paula Gunn. "Who Is Your Mother? Red Roots of White Feminism." *Sinister Wisdom* 25 (1984): 34-36. This article, in which Allen discusses what she calls "gynarchial societies," illuminates Allen's vision of a holistic female-centered society. She explains the similarities between Native American female-centered traditions and the peace-seeking radical movements of the West. Allen suggests that it is vital for feminists and society in general to turn toward this tradition to heal a warring existence.

─────────── . "Whose Dream Is This Anyway? Paula Gunn Allen: Generation, Regeneration, and Continuance." In *The Sacred Hoop: Recovering the Feminine in American Indian Traditions*. Boston: Beacon Press, 1986. Allen describes the Keres supreme being Grandmother Spider and shows how her novel reflects the relationship between woman lore and the events in an individual's life. She also discusses time and structure, suggesting that the four geographic locations in the novel parallel the four female life phases in Keres cosmology. Finally, in this short but useful discussion, Allen explains her attempt to emulate the oral tradition and her belief that traditional rituals are life-affirming in whatever form they are presented.

Lang, Nancy Helene. "Through Landscape Toward Story/Through Story Toward Landscape: A Study of Four Native American Women Poets." *Dissertation Abstracts International* 52 (September, 1991): 918A. Although Lang does not discuss *The Woman Who Owned the Shadows*, she does examine Allen's poetry in regard to its emphasis on land and the significance land holds in tribal tradition. Intended for academic readers.

Sevillano, Mando. "Interpreting Native American Literature: An Archetypal Approach." *American Indian Culture and Research Journal* 10, no. 1 (1986): 1-12. Sevillano does not discuss *The Woman Who Owned the Shadows* but discusses *The Sacred Hoop* as well as Allen's work in general. Examining archetypes, Sevillano classifies Native American stories under folk narrative.

Van Dyke, Annete. "The Journey Back to Female Roots: A Laguna Pueblo Model."

In *Lesbian Texts and Contexts*, edited by Karla Jay and Joanne Glasgow. New York: New York University Press, 1990. Van Dyke discusses the basic Pueblo belief system, establishing an understanding of this culture as vital to the understanding of Allen's novel. The chapter is easily accessible to most readers and thoroughly explores *The Woman Who Owned the Shadows* as a "ritual handbook" that reclaims "woman-ness" and the importance of female self-affirmation. Van Dyke additionally analyzes how Allen leads the reader through the same healing process as experienced by her protagonist, Ephanie.

Tiffany Elizabeth Thraves

A YELLOW RAFT IN BLUE WATER

Author: Michael Dorris (1945-   )
Type of plot: Family
Time of plot: The 1960's to the 1980's
Locale: Montana and Washington
First published: 1987

> *Principal characters:*
> RAYONA, the fifteen-year-old daughter of a Native American mother and
>   a black father
> CHRISTINE, Rayona's mother, a woman in her forties, who must come to
>   some accommodation with her impending death and her often chaotic
>   life
> AUNT IDA, the supposed mother of Christine and of Lee
> DAYTON NICKLES, Lee's closest friend
> EVELYN and SKY, a married couple who befriend Rayona
> FATHER HURLBURT, a Catholic missionary
> FATHER TOM NOVAK, Father Hurlburt's assistant
> ELGIN, Rayona's father

The Novel

A Yellow Raft in Blue Water explores relationships among four generations of a Native American family. The novel is organized into three sections, each narrated by a woman of the family: the first section by Rayona, a girl of fifteen; the second, by Christine, her mother; and the third by Aunt Ida, generally supposed to be Christine's mother. Moving backward through the three generations, the book gradually illuminates the origins of the tensions still poignantly felt by the characters.

Structurally, and perhaps thematically, Christine is at the center. She is terminally ill, but neither Elgin, the estranged husband with whom she still shares occasional brief reconciliations, nor Rayona, their daughter, is willing to acknowledge this truth. After all, Rayona tells herself, her mother has been a regular customer of the Indian Health Service in Seattle. And Elgin has other things on his mind: He has decided to put his relationship with another woman on a permanent footing. Leaving the hospital, Christine, accompanied by Rayona, points her battered car toward the Native American reservation in Montana where she grew up and which she left more than twenty years before.

As Rayona sees it, when they arrive at the reservation, Christine dumps her daughter on the doorstep of the woman who has always insisted on being called Aunt Ida, even by her daughter Christine. Where Christine has gone, Rayona does not know, but life with Aunt Ida is intolerable. When Father Tom suggests that Rayona accompany him to a "Teens for Christ" convention, Rayona is unenthusiastic, but at least it might make a change. Along the way, some abortive sexual fumbling occurs, and the embarrassed Father Tom, who was the instigator, is relieved when Rayona decides she will go back to Seattle rather than return to the reservation.

Rayona never makes it to Seattle. She finds work at Bearpaw Lake State Park and enjoys something that vaguely resembles a family life with Evelyn, a superficially hard-bitten but fundamentally generous woman, and Sky, her faded hippie husband. Attending a rodeo with Evelyn and Sky, Rayona enjoys a surprising triumph. Riding in place of her cousin Foxy Cree, who is too drunk to perform, Rayona wins an award and discovers a talent. The horse, it turns out, belongs to Dayton Nickles, an old friend of Christine's brother Lee, who was a great rider. Dayton brings Rayona back to the reservation and to Christine.

In Christine's view, she has not abandoned Rayona. Accepting the inevitability of her death, Christine hoped to place Rayona under the care of Aunt Ida, who is, after all, the girl's grandmother. In the face of Aunt Ida's cold greeting, Christine fled because she no longer had the strength to fight, and because she did not want Rayona to see her mother brought low.

Christine explains none of this to Rayona; she has never been one to explain herself. Yet it is part of her narrative, as is the story of her relationship with her brother Lee. The relationship was intense enough to make Christine jealous of Dayton, Lee's best friend. Spurred by this jealousy, she goads Lee, whom the reservation regards as symbolizing the hope of the future, into enlisting in the military, thus pointing him in the direction of his death. Christine left the reservation even before Lee did, and it was on the day that Dayton's letter informed her of her brother's death that she met Elgin.

It is, ironically, to Dayton that a dying Christine turns for support after leaving Rayona at Aunt Ida's. Dayton left the reservation himself, but he has returned after serving time in jail on a charge of having sexually molested a teenaged boy. Dayton makes Christine welcome, and it is he who reunites Christine and Rayona.

Aunt Ida's narrative brings the novel to its conclusion. If Ida has always insisted that Christine call her Aunt Ida, that is because she is not Christine's mother. Christine's biological mother is Clara, the sister of Aunt Ida's mother; Christine's father is Lecon, Aunt Ida's father. The relationship had developed when Clara had come to nurse her ailing sister. Scandal was avoided by a ruse that created the impression that the child's mother was the fifteen-year-old Ida, while the father was unknown.

Ida reared Christine, but always in the fear that Clara might reclaim her daughter at any time. This fear, in turn, created in Ida a fear of the pain that might arise for both Ida and Christine should Christine come to depend on Ida's love.

It was different with Lee. Lee was truly Ida's. His father was Willard Pretty Dog, a disfigured veteran of World War II, but not even Willard knows this. No one can take Lee away; Ida can love him openly. This, and not the preference for the male child that Christine had supposed, explains the difference in Ida's treatment of the two.

Only Father Hurlburt, the priest who becomes Ida's most trusted friend, knows the truth in all this. He is with Ida as the novel ends. It is the day on which Christine, still an adolescent, loses her faith, a faith she will recover as she approaches death. In the dark, Father Hurlburt cannot see what Ida is doing. He is a loyal friend and a good man, but, as a man with cut hair, he does not recognize the rhythm of braiding.

The Characters

Three powerful women, each representing a different generation, dominate the novel. Each of these women—Rayona, the fifteen-year-old girl; Christine, her mother; and Aunt Ida, supposedly Christine's mother—also functions as the narrator of one of the novel's three parts. It is, then, above all through their own voices and through the thoughts, feelings, and perceptions expressed in those voices that readers come to know the characters. In Rayona, readers recognize the adolescent's uncertainties about her own identity and her place in the world. For Rayona, these anxieties are intensified by her mixed racial heritage and by the instabilities of her family life. It is no wonder that she is tempted to borrow an identity when she reads the letter the solid, middle-class De Marcos have written to their daughter Ellen. Yet it is no surprise that Rayona is able to leave this bourgeois fantasy behind, as her experience at the rodeo and her reconciliation with the mother whose illness Rayona can now accept allow her to come to terms with who she herself is.

Christine speaks on the run. Staying in one place, physically or emotionally, has never been her strongest trait. She went through a series of boys and men on the reservation, which she left years ago. She has never settled in a single place. She thought that in her relationship with Elgin she was settling on a single man, but when Elgin began to wander, it was not in Christine's nature to stand still. Now she is in a hurry. She has, she knows, only a short time to live, and she must get her life into whatever kind of shape it can now assume. Her return to the reservation allows her to reestablish some degree of continuity with her past. She faces the destructive consequence of her past jealousy and, in doing so, becomes open to friendship with Dayton. Yet she is still concerned for the future: What will become of Rayona?

The third member of this trio is Ida. Like Rayona and Christine, Ida faced a crisis in her midteens, and the consequences of that crisis are felt by the two younger women. The obligation of caring for Christine and the fear of losing her have to a considerable degree determined the face Ida presents to the world, even to those closest to her. Fear kept Ida from identifying the father of Lee, her natural son; what if the father one day decided to claim the son? When, in the first two parts of the novel, readers see Ida through the eyes of Rayona and Christine, she seems distant, forbidding, and unwelcoming. It is only when she is finally allowed to speak for herself that she is revealed as a woman of powerful feelings, capable of moral heroism.

Each woman tells in her narrative more than she will ever tell either of the others. Christine will die in the belief that Aunt Ida is her mother and that Ida has never allowed her daughter to call her by her proper name, Mama.

Themes and Meanings

A Yellow Raft in Blue Water might be read as a meditation on family, on the mysteries of self and community, on the search for identity as individual and as member of the larger group, and on the pursuit of independence in the light of the reality of interdependence.

The main characters of the novel, Rayona, Christine, and Ida, while deeply involved with one another, remain in important ways isolated. They touch one another at a multitude of levels, but they communicate with one another only indirectly and, it sometimes seems, haphazardly. Family relationships have been distorted by the family secret that Ida carries, but family remains at the heart of the story.

The characters derive some of their identity from their complex relationship to the Native American community, but after Lee's death, the interaction of Ida and of Christine, who has moved off the reservation, with the community at large becomes limited. Moreover, Christine has married a black man, and Rayona, of mixed racial heritage, fantasizes an identity on the basis of a letter sent to someone else, a daughter of the white middle class.

As Catholics, the three women are also members of a faith community. Dorris hardly offers an idealized portrait of the Church (the priests, for example, are depicted as vessels of clay), and the book implies no necessary affirmation on the author's part of religion in general or of Catholicism in particular. Yet two of the novel's three parts close with Christine's spiritual crisis, her loss of faith, suggesting that the character's Catholic identity, however complicated and ambiguous, is not to be taken lightly.

What complicates the characters' relation to the community as much as anything is the pursuit of independence. Both Christine and Rayona set out on their own; each is motivated, at least in part, by a desire to reject the mother who has, it seems, rejected her. Yet each character will learn the truth of interdependence, and if this is a novel of setting out, it is even more strongly a novel of return. Rayona returns to Christine. Christine returns to the reservation, to the Church, to Ida. Dayton Nickles is a pivotal figure. He is instrumental in Rayona's return, and he gives Christine the shelter and support she needs; yet the women also bring the gift of warmth and caring to a lonely man. It is perhaps as a gesture toward the theme of interdependence, with its suggestions of interaction and interweaving, that Dorris ends the novel with the image of two friends, Ida and Father Hurlburt, the Catholic priest who is also part Indian, sharing a concern for Christine, while Ida braids her hair, twisting, tying, blending.

Critical Context

An anthropologist by profession, Michael Dorris made his debut as a novelist with *A Yellow Raft in Blue Water*. Dorris' wife, Louise Erdrich, is also a novelist; her *The Beet Queen* had been published in 1986 to critical acclaim. The two commonly work in close collaboration; a later novel, *The Crown of Columbus*, was in fact signed by both. Their normal procedure, however, is to attribute authorship to whoever writes the first draft. The other partner then functions as an editor, offering comments and suggesting revisions. The book may go through several drafts and is not finished until both partners agree on every word. Although the arrangement is unusual, the result has been an impressive body of work.

Both husband and wife are part Indian, and as *A Yellow Raft in Blue Water* illustrates, the Native American experience has been for them an important subject. The characters in their works are a long way from the stereotypical Indian—howling, breech-clouted savage or faithful Tonto—of American popular culture, and certainly a novel such as *A Yellow Raft in Blue Water* serves an important corrective function. Yet if Dorris rejects the old stereotypes, it seems far from his intention to substitute for them the puppets of any ideology. Rather, he lets readers see his characters in all of their troubled humanity, and he shows their world in all of its everyday reality.

Bibliography
Broyard, Anatole. "Eccentricity Was All They Could Afford." *The New York Times Book Review*, June 7, 1987, 7. Broyard observes that in *A Yellow Raft in Blue Water* Dorris describes a dying culture. The reviewer also notes that there is not much conventional plot but that the book's women are beautifully realized, and that the real movement of the novel lies in the way the three versions of their story comment on and harmonize with one another.

Chavkin, Allan, and Nancy Feyl Chavkin. *Conversations with Louise Erdrich and Michael Dorris*. Jackson: University Press of Mississippi, 1994. A gathering of interviews with Dorris and his wife that have appeared in various sources since the late 1980's. The interviews also cast light on the values—literary, ethical, spiritual—that inform the couple's work. Indispensable to any serious study of either writer.

Kakutani, Michiko. "Multiple Perspectives." *The New York Times*, May 9, 1987, p. B13. Kakutani notes the similarity in narrative method between this novel and *The Beet Queen* and comments that a strength of Dorris' novel is its depiction of elusive states of mind through tiny details. Kakutani's observation that the men in the novel are either sex objects or cads seems surprisingly off the mark.

Lesser, Wendy. "Braided Lives Under Big Sky." *The Washington Post Book Week*, May 31, 1987, 5. Dorris' style is seen as a matter of pressing down on the prosaic until it yields its own poetry in a sharp observation of reality. The mundane, through cumulative effect, becomes the marvelous. Dorris, Lesser comments, also creates a number of good minor characters.

MacCurtain, Austin. "In Free Fall." *The Times Literary Supplement*, March 11, 1988, 276. MacCurtain observes that the device of multiple narrators gives density and richness of texture to the story. Its themes emerge without an omniscient authorial voice. Yet the high literary polish of the narratives may distort the terms in which such people see themselves and tell their stories.

W. P. Kenney

YOU MUST REMEMBER THIS

Author: Joyce Carol Oates (1938-)
Type of plot: Family
Time of plot: 1946-1956
Locale: Port Oriskany, New York, a fictitious city
First published: 1987

>   *Principal characters:*
>   ENID MARIA STEVICK, a delicate and scholarly adolescent girl who has an obsessive affair with her half-uncle Felix
>   FELIX STEVICK, a former prizefighter, now trading in real estate, whose passionate affair with his young niece is the central action of the novel
>   WARREN STEVICK, Enid's brother, a Korean War veteran, now a peace activist
>   LYLE STEVICK, the bookish, anxious father of Enid and Warren, half-brother of Felix

The Novel

You Must Remember This is a chronicle of the Stevick family from 1946 to 1956. The primary movement in the novel involves the love affair between Enid Maria Stevick and her half-uncle Felix. The novel also deals with many other love relationships of Stevick family members.

The novel begins with a shocking description of Enid's attempt to commit suicide by ingesting an overdose of aspirin. The story then moves back to an earlier time in the family history, the time that led to the suicide attempt. Enid's preoccupation with death as a child is clear as she looks at a picture of a boy who tried to escape from a Nazi death camp. Oates describes the poverty of the Stevick family and the neighborhood in which they live, an area in which the air is polluted by chemicals from nearby factories. There is an emphasis on sex and violence in their lives.

The first and only time that Enid sees her Uncle Felix box occurs when Lyle Stevick takes his children to a boxing match. Enid is the youngest child of the Stevick family in attendance. Although she is shocked and almost overwhelmed by the blood and violence of what she sees and wonders why people would want to hurt each other like that, she is impressed at seeing her uncle in a new way. Felix seems a person that Enid does not know, and she wonders if he would know her.

One senses the sexual undercurrent between Enid and Felix from the beginning. On the beach near the summer cottage of Geraldine and Neal O'Banan, the sister and brother-in-law of Enid, Felix offers to give fourteen-year-old Enid a boxing lesson. The "boxing lesson" becomes more sexual in nature as it continues. Felix is snake-quick in his movements, which leave Enid frustrated because she cannot return his blows. After a while, Enid springs at her uncle in a frenzy, and Felix sees that he has gone too far. Love and hate are often closely connected in the relationship of Felix and Enid.

The day after the boxing lesson, Felix offers to take Enid for a drive. They visit the vast old Hotel Rideau, which Felix has purchased. Felix and Enid begin to play a game of hide and seek, which ends with the drunken Felix attacking his niece.

Felix apologizes the next day, but his attack awakens in Enid her latent adolescent passion for her uncle. Felix realizes immediately that he has made a terrible mistake. Since Enid is the daughter of his half-brother Lyle, the attraction is even incestuous. Felix pleads with Enid to keep silent and to forget his attack on her. Enid's passion has been aroused, however, and she will not end her affair with her uncle. When Felix tries to end their relationship, Enid, in a romantic gesture, attempts suicide by carefully ingesting forty-seven aspirin tablets. Partly from guilt and fear and partly because Enid's strong will to die attracts him, Felix recommences their surreptitious love affair after Enid leaves the hospital. The intense feelings of the lovers contrast sharply with the drab, conventional world of the other Stevick family members.

The furtive romance of Enid and Felix goes on, in motels far enough from Port Oriskany that no one will identify them. Felix gives drinks of vodka and wine to his niece to "loosen her up." Their clandestine affair continues, with Felix at first being careful not to make any mistakes during their encounters. Oates details the blood, pain, violence, and anger that accompany Enid's loss of virginity in this love-hate relationship.

Felix is out of town often, involved in real-estate transactions. Enid continues attending high school, developing a circle of friends. Felix sees Enid occasionally, but a traumatic experience for him occurs when he glimpses Enid outside her school at lunch time with a circle of friends, male as well as female. Possessively, jealously, he carries her away from her school, and they make love in his car. In his jealousy and passion, Felix fails to take precautions, and Enid finds herself pregnant. Felix arranges for her to have an abortion. The blood, pain, resentment, and guilt that Catholic Enid feels at her abortion are convincingly described.

Felix loses his youth in the course of the novel as Enid loses her attraction for death. The novel ends as the former lovers go their separate ways. Felix is hospitalized after being severely beaten by the father of Jo-Jo Pearl, the young man, now deceased, for whom Felix was a mentor in boxing. After Felix recovers, he telephones Enid to say that he is going to be married and will move away from Port Oriskany. Enid also will leave Port Oriskany, to study music at the Wescott School in Rochester,

The Characters

Enid Stevick, the central character in *You Must Remember This*, is another of Oates's intelligent, talented young scholar heroines. Enid is by turns cold and fragile; like Connie in the story "Where Are You Going, Where Have You Been?", Enid has two sides to her personality. There is Enid Stevick, shy, intelligent, Roman Catholic, a model student, always receiving high grades. The other side of Enid is "Angel-face," the daring, conniving, sensual side. "Angel-face," with the encouragement of some older girls, is a shoplifter, and, repeating "Why not?" about the affair, propels Enid into the passionate but destructive relationship with her handsome young Uncle Felix.

Felix Stevick is the most vibrant character in the novel. He is an extremely attractive former prizefighter. Felix is an outsider, troubled by his illegitimate birth and the suicide of his father. Felix exercises an instinct for self-destructive violence. This impulse to self-destructive behavior in Felix is what attracts him to Enid after her attempted suicide and leads him to continue their obsessive, incestuous affair. Felix is attractive but lonely and alienated, seeing himself an outsider except in the prizefight ring or in his lover's arms.

Warren Stevick is the brother of Enid, the only male in a family of three sisters. He served in the Korean War and was seriously wounded. During his struggle to survive, Warren had an epiphany. Always helpful and considerate of others, he realized that his mission in the future must be to help others. In his idealistic political journey, he becomes a pacifist, then serves on an unsuccessful Adlai Stevenson presidential campaign, and finally works for Children's Aid in a Philadelphia slum neighborhood. In his contacts with his favorite sister, Enid, he makes perceptive statements applying to the central themes of the book.

Lyle Stevick is the bookish head of the Stevick family, father to Enid, Warren, and their two sisters. Lyle has a dead-end job as the owner of a second-hand furniture store. He worries about government corruption and fears enemy bombs; his main obsession is building a backyard bombshelter. His worries typify, although in a ludicrous fashion, the worries of many people in the late 1940's and early 1950's.

Themes and Meanings

The main focus of this work is on love in its many forms. In addition to the love affair that gives momentum to the action, many other sorts of love are depicted in this novel, especially familial love and romantic love. The author's main point is that love does not carry with it any particular knowledge. As Warren Stevick writes to his sister Enid, "The people I have loved most in my lifetime (including you) I haven't known at all." It is only when Oates's characters are away from family and lovers, with people who do not know them or have not known them for very long, that they find themselves.

The primary impetus for the author was the recollection of the decade 1946 to 1956; she focuses on selected areas of American life during that decade. The novel is suffused with the romance, nostalgia, and, to the author, innocence of that epoch. Oates gives the reader a sense of the era by mentioning well-known film stars, politicians, popular singers, and television personalities. Arthur Godfrey, Jack Benny, Marilyn Monroe, and Dinah Shore are all named to give a sense of the times, as are major political events: nationwide, the Joseph McCarthy hearings and the Stevenson campaign; worldwide, the Korean War and the fear-inducing spread of Communism.

This novel, Oates's seventeenth, centers on the passionate love-hate relationship between Enid and Felix. Here love resembles lust in its purely physical, unthinking nature. The lovers do not know each other completely. Enid does not know much about the career of Felix as a boxer, about his mother, about his relationship to his father (who had committed suicide), or about the source of the money that Felix seems to have in abundance. Felix is similar to Jay Gatsby in that mysteries surround him. He is often restless and becomes angry if Enid questions him too much about his life.

Felix thinks he knows his teenage niece well, especially after they commence their affair, but he learns that there is an element of calculation as well as sensuality in her nature. The half-joking "boxing lesson" that Felix offers Enid turns serious as Enid springs at him in an erotic fury. The next day, the drunken Felix attacks Enid. He apologizes for his behavior and pleads with Enid to keep silent, by this time realizing that he had been manipulated into consummating a drunken pass he regretted immediately. The romantic gesture of Enid's attempted suicide is another conniving attempt on her part to continue their mutually destructive, incestuous relationship. Felix recognizes and is attracted to a will power as strong as his own. The violent nature of their hopeless, destructive love is best symbolized by the shocking and detailed description of the abortion Enid has to undergo toward the end of the novel.

Love relationships unaccompanied by knowledge are evident in two other cases in the novel. Both love affairs involve men of the Stevick family, whose thoughts Oates paints convincingly. One sees romantic love in the story of Warren and Hannah, and one sees the return of familial love after the mysterious incident between Lyle Stevick and Elvira French. In each case, the mysterious nature of love, particularly the extent to which people may be lovers physically and still not know each other, is affirmed.

Critical Context

You Must Remember This preserves lower-class American life as it existed in the United States in the 1950's. Oates describes vividly and in detail the New York State setting of her childhood. The author writes that, in her mind, she traverses Port Oriskany's streets and ponders its buildings, houses, vacant lots, and, most of all, the canal that runs through it as it did through her birthplace, Lockport, New York. The canal, in Enid's fevered imagination, as in Oates's own, seems an object of utter beauty.

The novel is perhaps the most personal of the author's novels. Oates once wrote that the contours of Enid Stevick's soul very much resemble her own. The novel is also the history of an era the author loved. It focuses on certain selected aspects of American life, most notably politics (the antipodes of the Red Scare and the early pioneering antinuclear arms movement represented by Warren Stevick). In addition to politics, Oates evokes remembrances of popular culture in the 1950's, primarily music and Hollywood films. She includes the names of popular songs with suggestive and evocative titles such as "Stormy Weather" and "These Foolish Things." She mentions the names of film and television stars. She identifies the cars people drove (Felix is always driving a shiny new car) and remembers the professional prizefighting that vast numbers of Americans watched weekly on television and the great champions who were in their prime in that era. Oates knows much about boxing; in 1987, she published a nonfiction book, *On Boxing*, which showed her expertise in that area.

Enid is of a background similar to that of the author. Oates was a teenager in the

1950's, as Enid is. Even in stature, the slim frame of Enid resembles the build of the author. Yet except in its setting and in a few of its specific incidents, the novel is not autobiographical. The setting, the fictitious city of Port Oriskany, New York, is an amalgam of two cities: Buffalo, the first large city in the experience of the author, and Lockport, the city of her birth and the home of her paternal grandmother. Oates attended sixth grade and all of junior high school in Lockport, and the city conse-quently is suffused with the extravagant dreams of early adolescence, such as the dreams of Enid Stevick. Adolescent dreams tie in with the working title of the novel, "The Green Island." The greenness suffusing the novel is the greenness of nostalgia, of romance, of innocence.

In this novel, Oates turned back to the realistic novel after a quartet of experimental novels, including mystery, a romance, and a tale of Gothic horror. One sees the influence of Emily Dickinson in Enid's preoccupation with death and of D. H. Lawrence in the description of the passionate love between Felix and Enid. The irrational nature of intense feeling is beautifully depicted here. As Warren Stevick tells Enid near the end of the novel, love carries with it no knowledge.

Bibliography

Bloom, Harold, ed. *Joyce Carol Oates*. New York: Chelsea House, 1987. A scholarly collection of criticism devoted to the works of Oates. Although without specific reference to *You Must Remember This*, the work offers insights into the behavior of females similar to those in this novel. "The Terrified Women of Joyce Carol Oates," by Mary Allen, is especially good. The volume contains a perceptive introduction and a useful bibliography.

Milazzo, Lee, ed. *Conversations with Joyce Carol Oates*. Jackson: University Press of Mississippi, 1989. Part of the Literary Conversation series, this volume has seventeen pages containing references to *You Must Remember This*. The author also responds to the frequent criticism of the violence in her writing. Essential for a student of Oates, especially of *You Must Remember This*, the book contains an introduction, bibliography, chronology, and index.

Oates, Joyce Carol. *On Boxing*. Garden City, N. Y.: Dolphin/Doubleday, 1987. This eloquent study shows the thorough knowledge of the sport of boxing possessed by Oates, who discusses boxing from every aspect, including its history; famous boxers, past and present; boxing as a drama in American tragic theater; and boxing from a feminist point of view, as the most masculine and violent of contact sports. She then moves her discussion of boxing into a metaphysical meditation on time and death. Includes boxing photographs by John Ranard.

_____ . *(Woman) Writer: Occasions and Opportunities*. New York: E. P. Dutton, 1988. This collection of thirty-five essays includes the preface to *You Must Remember This* as well as essays on boxing and on Mike Tyson which will aid in understanding the boxing scenes in this novel. There are also essays on literary theory, the writer, and the woman writer in particular. Showing Oates's extraor-dinary breadth of interests, it is of great assistance in understanding *You Must*

Remember This as well as other Oates works.
Updike, John. "What You Deserve Is What You Get." *The New Yorker* 63 (December 28, 1987): 119-123. This thoughtful, insightful essay by one of Oates's most well-respected contemporaries offers perceptive comments, both positive and otherwise, about the novel, which he calls "exceedingly fine."

Linda Silverstein Gordon

YOUR BLUES AIN'T LIKE MINE

Author: Bebe Moore Campbell (1950-   )
Type of plot: Historical realism
Time of plot: The 1950's to the 1980's
Locale: Hopewell, Mississippi
First published: 1992

>   *Principal characters:*
>   FLOYD COX, a bigoted, poor white man convicted of killing Armstrong
>   Todd
>   LILY COX, Floyd's wife
>   LESTER COX, Floyd's father
>   JOHN EARL COX, Floyd's brother
>   ARMSTRONG TODD, a fifteen-year-old black man killed for speaking to
>   Lily Cox
>   IDA LONG, a mixed-race woman who knows Lily
>   ODESSA DANIELS, Armstrong's grandmother
>   DELOTHA TODD, Armstrong's mother
>   WYDELL TODD, Armstrong's father
>   CLAYTON PINOCHET, a white newspaper editor
>   STONEWALL PINOCHET, Clayton's father, a pillar of Hopewell

The Novel

Set in the town of Hopewell in the Mississippi Delta, *Your Blues Ain't Like Mine* is the story of the lynching of a black man by a family of whites. The novel traces the story of the lynching and the subsequent effect on different members of both the town and Armstrong Todd's family.

Your Blues Ain't Like Mine is divided into fifty-one chapters. The story is told by an omniscient narrator, but from several different points of view: those of the Cox family, the family of Armstrong Todd, and the Pinochet family.

The novel opens in the home of Lily and Floyd Cox, poor whites in the segregated town of Hopewell. Floyd owns a pool hall and juke joint frequented by blacks. While at the pool hall, Armstrong Todd, a black teenager from Chicago who has been sent to live with his grandmother Odessa, speaks French to Lily. This seemingly minor incident causes a violent reaction on the part of Floyd's family, who encourage him to teach Armstrong a lesson about how he should behave in the presence of his supposed betters. The anger accelerates to the point that Floyd, Lester, and John Earl drive to the Quarters, the black neighborhood, and murder Armstrong in his grand-mother's backyard.

Lily is not at all comfortable with the murder that has taken place, but she is bullied into not protesting by her abusive husband and his domineering family, which is governed by the bigotry of their past as poor whites in the Deep South. The family decides to lie if they are confronted about the murder. They reason that the death of a "nigger" will not make any difference to the local authorities. The move for desegregation is taking hold, however, as is the Civil Rights movement. The local authorities believe that they must at least have some pretense of a trial if they are going to avoid more bloodshed.

Caught in the middle of the racial tension is Clayton Pinochet, the editor of the *Hopewell Telegram* and member of one of the most prominent families in Hopewell. It is expected that he will adhere to the old Southern values. Clayton, however, is part of the generation that begins to question the separation between blacks and whites. He had employed Armstrong at the newspaper and found him to be a bright young man with whom he enjoyed talking. In addition, Clayton has for many years had a black mistress, Marguerite. His father, Stonewall Pinochet, cannot understand his son's seeming affection for blacks and constantly admonishes him for not conforming to the bigoted ways of the old guard.

Delotha Todd, Armstrong's mother, comes to Hopewell from Chicago when Armstrong is murdered; she too struggles with Southern ways. When she goes to the train station to arrange for her son's body to be taken to Chicago, she finds that, since he is black, his coffin will have to go in the livestock car. In addition, the white town leaders want to prevent Armstrong's body from leaving Hopewell, because they fear that the newspapers in Chicago might print stories that would cause bad publicity. Delotha must sneak the body out of town in a truck in the middle of the night.

As the novel progresses, the lives of all those involved in Armstrong's murder change. Lily and Floyd find that, because of the changing attitudes toward blacks, they are ostracized by the rest of the town. Their attitudes, as well as those of the upper-class whites, have started to become old-fashioned, if not obsolete.

Delotha and Wydell, estranged before Armstrong's murder, are drawn back together. They open a combination barbershop and women's hairdressing salon in Chicago and become successful. They also have three more children, two daughters and a son to whom Delotha is obsessively attached; she often calls him by his dead brother's name. Yet their grief for Armstrong does not leave them. Wydell returns to drinking, and Delotha becomes more and more depressed. Finally, they lose their business. In addition, Wydell, Jr., gets in trouble at school, causes problems at home, and finally ends up in a gang. He is saved in the end by his father, who has enough gumption to know that only he can save his son.

In Hopewell, the town grows and changes as the story progresses from the early days of the Civil Rights movement to the mid-1980's. Clayton Pinochet decides that he must follow his conscience, and he begins tutorial classes for blacks. His resolution is tested fully, however, when he learns that Ida Long, a black woman who has been his friend and whose son he has tutored, is actually his half-sister. Ida must also come to terms with being the daughter of Stonewall Pinochet. She comes into her own when she tells Clayton that she wants her share of the estate and that she wants everyone to know the identity of her father. Clayton is caught between the old and new worlds. When he is asked to take his father's place among the Honorable Men of Hopewell, he decides that he is not, in his father's eyes, an honorable man. In order to be honorable in his own eyes, he leaves his past behind and tells Ida that they will work out a settlement. The novel ends with Wydell and his son returning to Hopewell in search of the peace that they both desire.

The Characters

Armstrong Todd, a fifteen-year-old African American from Chicago, is portrayed as someone caught in the wrong place at the wrong time. He is accustomed to the more accepting North and tests the limits of acceptance in the South when he speaks French to Lily Cox. Tragically, he finds that the South is not ready to accept a black man who is educated and has the presumption to show that he is educated. Armstrong is portrayed as an intelligent young man with a promising future; however, there is a daring streak in him which is anxious to challenge the established order. It is this streak that causes him to offend Floyd Cox and that eventually causes his death.

Floyd Cox, an uneducated white man, is painted as an almost stereotypical bigoted white Southern male. He and his family are poor, and Floyd and his wife Lily are the poorest of the entire family. He and Lily both dream of a better life, but Floyd is caught by both economic conditions and his own attitude. Like his peers, he believes that if it were not for blacks, he would be better off economically. When Armstrong speaks French to his wife, the act is all the provocation Floyd needs. His manhood has been threatened, and he reports the incident to his father and brother. They goad him into teaching Armstrong a lesson. Floyd really does not want to provoke a fight; he is content to exaggerate his previous confrontation. Yet he goes along with Lester and John Earl, showing his basic inability to make major decisions for himself. The need to fit in and go along with the established order is too strong for him.

Lily Cox, Floyd's wife, does not agree with Floyd's actions. In fact, Lily really does not understand segregation, partially because she has a secret friend. She and Ida Long share an affection for watching the trains at the station. They enjoy each other's company, and Lily is at a loss to understand why they should not be friends.

Clayton Pinochet is the editor of the *Hopewell Telegram*. He is ashamed of his father's bigotry; in fact, Clayton actually prefers the company of blacks to that of whites, a fact that disturbs Stonewall Pinochet. Throughout the novel, Clayton must battle his internal conflict and his domineering father.

Wydell Todd, Armstrong's father, had left Delotha and become a drunk. He finds out that his son has been murdered and returns to Delotha. They find that they now have common ground and decide to try to make their lives work. Ironically, Wydell is originally seen as an alcoholic who is unable to do anything for himself. After his son's death, he becomes the strong member of the marriage. He gets his barber's license, and it is he who encourages Delotha to try to leave the past behind. Ultimately, it is also Wydell who must try to save their son, Wydell, Jr., from gangs and street life.

Delotha Todd, Armstrong's mother, sent Armstrong to be with Odessa, her mother. She thought he would be better off in Hopewell than in Chicago. Although she and Wydell do become financially successful, she is never able to put her grief over Armstrong in perspective.

Ida Long, a light-skinned black woman, is Lily's friend at the train station. Ida has had to live with the fact that she does not know who her father is and has always been told by her peers that she does not have a father. After her stepfather dies, she goes through his papers and finds that she is the daughter of Stonewall Pinochet, one of the most blatant bigots in Hopewell. Ironically, she and Clayton are good friends, and she must decide what to do. She emerges as a strong, determined woman when she tells Clayton that she wants not only a share of the estate but also recognition that she does have a father.

Themes and Meanings

The major issue confronted in the novel is change and its effects. Some of the changes are brought about by the shock that the murder of Armstrong Todd causes. Other changes are brought about by the shifting views of society. All the changes are painful for the people involved. Armstrong Todd's family must somehow manage the grief that is brought about not only by his death but also by the way he died. The Cox family must somehow try to justify their decision to commit murder and must realize that society's shifting values make their act no longer acceptable. Stonewall Pinochet and his contemporaries must watch their world, which is based on the idea that whites are better than blacks, start to crumble. Clayton Pinochet, caught in the middle of the changes, must somehow try to make sense of the fact that, even though he is from one of the aristocratic families, he really does prefer the company of blacks.

Campbell's main point is that any change is difficult. A person's social standing does not matter; when the values of a society start to change, all people find that their place in society shifts, and this shift can cause friction.

The murder of Armstrong Todd was based on the 1955 murder of Emmett Till, a fourteen-year-old who was lynched for speaking to a white woman in a Mississippi town. Campbell fictionalizes the incident and then carries the story past the bare details by examining the effects this event would have on three distinct groups of people.

Campbell presents the themes to the reader by telling the stories of three very different groups of people—the Todds, the Pinochets, and the Coxes. Each group must learn to manage the changes that occur. It is interesting to see how the lives of the characters overlap and, as the novel progresses and the times change, begin to merge.

Critical Context

Your Blues Ain't Like Mine is Bebe Moore Campbell's first novel; she had previously written short stories and two nonfiction books. Her first nonfiction work, *Successful Women, Angry Men,* was published in 1986. She published her memoir, *Sweet Summer: Growing Up With and Without My Dad,* in 1989.

Campbell, a longtime journalist, has contributed to *Savvy, Essence, Lear's* and many other publications; the bulk of her work is concerned with social issues. In 1980, she received a literary grant from the National Endowment for the Arts. She has also been a regular contributor to National Public Radio broadcasts.

Bibliography

Campbell, Bebe Moore. "Growing Up Black." *Seventeen* 49 (December, 1990): 102-105. In this article, Campbell interweaves interviews with three young black women with information about what it is like to grow up black in the United States in the 1990's. She discusses societal stereotypes and bigotry. The article is an illuminating look at how young black women see themselves within society.

_____. Interview by Sybil Steinberg. *Publishers Weekly* 235 (June 30, 1989): 82-83. Campbell discusses her nonfiction books, her own history, and how it has contributed to her writing. Gives valuable background information on the author's writing career.

Essence. "Graceful Passages." 21 (May, 1990): 130-136. In this article, several authors discuss the changes in their lives and the world in the past twenty years; Campbell discusses the influence of the blues on her life. She also talks about the importance of inspiration to her writing.

Langstaff, Peggy. "Getting to the Novel: How and Why Some Experienced Nonfiction Writers Made the Transition to Storytelling." *Publishers Weekly* 239 (November 16, 1992): 35-37. Campbell discusses her previous attempts at writing fiction and outlines her nonfiction publishing career.

U.S. News and World Report. "Working Wives, Threatened Husbands." 102 (February 23, 1987): 46. Contains valuable information on Campbell's views concerning the dynamics of two-career marriages. Provides the reader with some understanding of the relationships of the characters in *Your Blues Ain't Like Mine*.

Victoria E. McLure

CUMULATIVE TITLE INDEX

XIII

CUMULATIVE TITLE INDEX

CUMULATIVE TITLE INDEX

CUMULATIVE AUTHOR INDEX

CUMULATIVE AUTHOR INDEX

CUMULATIVE AUTHOR INDEX